Horror Literature

H. G. Wells

Horror Literature

A Core Collection
and Reference Guide

Edited by

Marshall B. Tymn

R. R. Bowker Company
New York & London, 1981

Published by R. R. Bowker Company
1180 Avenue of the Americas, New York, N. Y. 10036
Copyright © 1981 by Xerox Corporation
All rights reserved
Printed and bound in the United States of America

Library of Congress Cataloging in Publication Data
Main entry under title:

Horror literature.

  Includes indexes.
    1. Horror tales, English—Bibliography.
  2. Horror tales, American—Bibliography.
  3. Gothic revival (Literature)—Bibliography.
  4. Supernatural in literature—Bibliography.
  5. Supernatural—Poetry—Bibliography.
I. Tymn, Marshall B., 1937–
Z2014.H67H67   [PR830.T3] 016.823′0872 81-6176
ISBN 0-8352-1341-2
ISBN 0-8352-1405-2 pbk   AACR2

Contents

Foreword

The horror story has long been regarded in the critical eye as the rather inferior relation of the ghost story. On reflection, this opinion can actually be seen as self-inflicted, for the genre of the terror tale—the story that depends on the development of menace in the plot and a mounting sense of unease in the reader to achieve its effect—has been lavishly supplied with works of unashamed sensationalism that now enjoy lasting notoriety in the public mind. Such works range all the way from Matthew Lewis's pioneer Gothic novel, *The Monk*—that "gruesome, unclean romance" first published in 1795—to the modern flood of paperback books with such lurid titles as *Squirm, Slither,* and so on.

The ghost story, by contrast, has been more restrained in even its most colorful examples, always remaining *definable* as a tale of the normally unseen—the supernatural—world. And therein lies a major problem for the critic; just what is the *horror story*? There have, of course, been innumerable studies of the ghost story, but few, indeed, specifically devoted to the tale of horror. It is, therefore, something of a pleasure to be able to say that with the publication of this book, an important step has been taken toward overcoming this regrettable situation. By carefully studying and surveying the development of horror literature in its widest terms, we can begin to get a picture of what its component parts are.

It is convenient and justifiable to start the book with the Gothic romance, and although it is true to say that this played a major part in formulating the horror story as we have come to know it today, the recounting of tales of fear had been going on long before this literary "happening." The inspiration for these Gothic tales of haunted castles, tortured heroes, and stricken maidens is clearly the old myths and folktales evolved in the mists of time, as well as the fables of daring deeds against the spirits of darkness. For in their infancy on this planet, humans soon came to appreciate that the dark spawned much they did not understand and much they had reason to fear. From this it was but the smallest step to populating the shadows with the wildest flights of their imaginings. Indeed, there are many elements that we recognize in the modern horror story that are to be found in those early legends and fables: the battle of good and evil, the many and varied creatures of darkness and death, and, perhaps most important of all, man's conquest of his own inherent fear.

Such grim stories, which are common to all peoples and which defy accurate dating for their origins beyond the fact that they come from the "earliest times," are, for me, the roots of the horror story, the striplings of our awakening knowledge and intelligence gestating among our fears and traumas about life and environment—little though we may have understood them. Haven't we all inherited our ancestors' primitive fear of the dark? Don't we still see a menacing shape at the head of the stairs just as they saw something untoward in the shadow of the cave or forest dwelling? Time has done nothing to change this instinct; and one of its effects has been our taste for and the evolvement of the horror story as we find it today in any bookstore or on any library shelf. It is the story form that *this* reference book sets out to chart.

My own work in the horror story genre has involved the surveying of these stories from their most obvious point of emergence, the Gothic romance, through to the present day, but with the addition of suitable examples by the most important practitioners of the art. My published collections include the mammoth *Gothic Tales of Terror* (1972), a title that speaks for itself, by way of *The Shilling Shockers* (1978), a study of the Gothic "bluebooks" or chapbooks, which pirated the often enormously long Gothic novels and reprinted the most exciting episodes. They cover the Victorian era of *The Penny Dreadful* (1975) with its breathtaking serials, the peculiarly interwar American phenomena of the lurid *Fantastic Pulps* (1975), and in most recent times the continuing series of *Unknown Tales of Horror* (1976), which have resurrected work by established masters of the genre and presented them along with contributions by new writers seeking to emulate them. In all these books, I have tried to demonstrate what I firmly believe to be the most important quality any horror story must possess along with its ability to chill the reader: the quality of entertainment.

As I have said, the horror story genre as a whole has condemned itself in the eyes of many people by its excesses. Indeed, recently we have seen the development of what can most easily be called "butcher shop horror"—stories in which brutality, violence, and general nastiness are introduced far more for their own sake than for any specific requirements of the plot. These elements, in fact, have often been considered more important by the writer than the need to entertain readers. "Revolt them," "sicken them," the writer seems to be saying, *that's* what they want from a horror story. In my opinion, we are so constantly being appalled by much that we see and hear in real life that we have no need of it in our favorite literary form as well. That such "butcher shop horror" seems to be successful with certain sections of the public I cannot deny, but I condemn it for failing to satisfy that vital requirement of entertainment, if for no other. This viewpoint is one I know to be shared by others—readers, students, and critics alike—and this book also reflects a similar outlook in seeking to identify and examine the best qualities of the horror story.

Another important aspect of this reference book, *Horror Literature,* is the study of the men and women who have written horror fiction over the years—fascinating, inquiring, dedicated people, too often typified as being in the same tormented mold as Edgar Allan Poe, yet in actuality skilled writers, many of whom would surely rank with other renowned literary figures were it not for the unfortunate reputation of their type of story. To the enthusiast they are well-known, highly regarded, and some even cult figures—however, a work such as this can provide the reasoned study and analysis that will allow these writers to begin to be seen in their true light and to have the worth of their contributions properly evaluated.

An additional feature of this volume that I must commend is its list of books that form a core collection of horror literature (see Core Collection Checklist). This is a brave undertaking because opinions vary so considerably as to the respective merits of many works (H. P. Lovecraft, for instance, has his idolizers as well as those who find his stories verbose hackwork), and the stature of certain authors can and does alter with changing fashions. In this respect, I profoundly hope that horror fiction will not be subjected to the excesses of debate and theorizing that currently blights science fiction, and in which some people are busy attributing, on the one hand, the most profound and, on the other hand, the most mistaken meanings to stories, far beyond the conception and intentions of the author. Beware the critic who would obscure the writer's plan to entertain, say I!

Yet guidance of the kind offered here is a very good thing, because as many of the most universally acclaimed horror novels and short stories become increasingly difficult to obtain in the face of publishers' reluctance to reprint them—not to mention the skyrocketing prices secondhand copies often fetch—newcomers will find much information to help them develop their overview of the genre while awaiting the reading or actual acquisition of certain titles. Collecting works of this kind becomes fascinating and addictive, but reading about them and their creators can be equally enjoyable. I am sure enthusiasts both old and new will find enjoyment in the company of the various well-informed contributors to this guide.

By way of conclusion, I should like to add that despite the view sometimes expressed that horror literature is a rather narrow and limited field, over the years it has explored many areas of interest from the depths of the unconscious mind to those primitive, but still potent, fears of the dark. For the best supernatural horror stories, those that have stood the test of time, are neither so presumptuous as to claim to be able to explain the human psyche, nor too naive to expect unquestioning belief on the part of the reader. They demand our attention, certainly, and to a degree a suspension of certain parts of the armory of so-called sophistication into which modern society has strait-jacketed us. We may be nervous about what paths the horror story can lead us along, but we should never be afraid of the genre itself. At its best, as this timely and welcome volume sets out to show, it provides a form of entertainment, mental stimulation, and excitement few other forms of literature can match.

Peter Haining
Boxford, Suffolk, England

Preface

The decade of the 1970s saw a great rise of interest in horror literature. The growing popularity of horror fiction is evident in the increase in the number of new and reprint titles published each year, and in the appearance of critical studies devoted exclusively to horror fiction. Along with this proliferation of titles, both primary and secondary, has arisen the need for bibliographic control of the literature. It was primarily this need that brought about the present volume.

Horror Literature is the first reference book compiled for horror fiction, poetry, and the pulp magazines. It is intended to serve a wide audience as an acquisitions tool for building core collections in libraries; as a guide to the literature for teachers and students; as a reference handbook for scholars and researchers; and as a comprehensive introduction to horror literature and its related activities for interested readers who wish to acquaint themselves with the major works in the field.

The historical essays that introduce each chapter outline the growth of horror literature in England and America from its origins in the Gothic romance to its manifestations in contemporary literature. As such they serve to define not only the parameters of the genre, but the genre itself. By its very nature, much of horror literature contains elements of the supernatural—demons, apparitions, vampires, the undead; yet, it need not always contain these supernatural elements. The essence of horror fiction is fear and terror—manifested in the dread of unknown forces. One type of horror, the psychological, makes use of implied situations, in which the fear is totally in the mind (the terms *weird* and *macabre* are sometimes used to describe this type). In physical horror, the threat of bodily harm or the menace of death causes a terror that often paralyzes the intended victim. In the broadest sense, these two types represent the major branches of horror fiction. But the literature does not always conform to preconceived models or notions of plot structure. Howard Phillips Lovecraft, in his *Supernatural Horror in Literature,* reminds us that "the final criterion of authenticity [in the horror tale] is not the dovetailing of a plot but the creation of a given sensation . . . whether or not there be excited in the reader a profound sense of dread, and of contact with unknown spheres and powers; a subtle attitude of awed listening, as if for the beating of black wings or the scratching of outside shapes and entities on the known universe's utmost rim." Lovecraft has, better than most, outlined the aesthetics that underly the choice of works for inclusion here.

In several important respects, *Horror Literature* is a unique reference tool. The annotated bibliographies of novels and anthologies that comprise Chapters 1 through 4 contain almost 1,100 key works set in a historical framework. Chapter 5 furnishes valuable commentary on the specialty horror pulps, an important outlet for writers in this field during the 1930s and 1940s. Chapter 6 surveys the field of supernatural verse, making an important contribution to research in this neglected area of the literature. Chapters 7 through 12 provide comprehensive coverage of the various scholarly works and fan activities within the field, and include material that has never before been systematically listed. The whole volume provides access to more than 1,300 titles, many of which were difficult to locate but are included here in the hope that the increasing interest in horror literature will encourage publishers to make long out-of-print works more readily available. The effort has been to provide the most complete survey of horror literature yet published.

The bibliographic citation for each title specifies author or editor, title, publisher, year of first English-language edition, and publisher and year of current reprint edition if available. Books are listed under the most commonly used name of the author. Nationality of the author or editor is given if other than American. A few foreign-language editions are included in Chapter 1 in an attempt to more completely define the scope of this formative period. Sources used to verify first edition and reprint titles were *American Book Publishing Record, Books in Print, British Books in Print, British Museum General Catalogue, Cumulative Book Index, National Union Catalogue, Paperbound Books in Print,* and *Whitaker's Cumulative Book Index.* A number of specialized checklists and indexes were also consulted.

Annotations for works in Parts I and II provide succinct plot summaries, noting principal themes and comparable works. In some cases, critical judgments have been made about a particular work. Notable stories in collections and anthologies are mentioned.

Each annotated title is preceded by an entry number, such as 1–75, 4–103, which is used for cross-reference whenever the title is mentioned elsewhere in the volume. The entry numbers also allow easy reference to any title in the book. Core collection titles have been marked with an asterisk. These were chosen on the basis of one or more of the following criteria: the influence of the work in the field or on other writers; critical and/or popular acceptance; importance of the work in the author's canon; and historical importance, especially for older works. The remaining titles are relatively less important than the core collection itself, but should nonetheless be included by those libraries and individuals systematically acquiring the major works in the field. All titles reflect the personal judgment of the individual contributors, each of whom had primary responsibility for the selection of works in his respective period.

I would like to express my deepest gratitude to the contributors, whose expert knowledge of the field and whose painstaking efforts in researching and compiling their respective chapters have made this a meaningful contribution to scholarship in this field. I would also like to extend my appreciation to Peter Haining, the most prolific anthologist of horror fiction in the world, for his commentary. A special thanks goes to Nancy Volkman, Senior Editor, and R. R. Bowker for their help. Finally, I would particularly like to thank my wife, Darlene, who offered invaluable advice and editorial assistance throughout the preparation of this manuscript.

Marshall B. Tymn

Contributors

Marshall B. Tymn (editor). Marshall B. Tymn, Associate Professor of English at Eastern Michigan University, Ypsilanti, is director of the national Workshop on Teaching Science Fiction and the author of numerous reference works and articles on science fiction and fantasy literature. His publications include *A Research Guide to Science Fiction Studies* (co-compiler); *Index to Stories in Thematic Anthologies of Science Fiction* (co-compiler); *American Fantasy and Science Fiction: Toward a Bibliography of Works Published in the United States, 1948–1973; The Year's Scholarship in Science Fiction and Fantasy: 1972–1975* (co-compiler); *Fantasy Literature: A Core Collection and Reference Guide* (co-compiler); and *The Science Fiction Reference Book.* His articles have appeared in *Extrapolation, Choice, CEA Critic, English Journal, Mosaic, Media & Methods, English Language Arts Bulletin, Analytical and Enumerative Bibliography,* and other journals. He is editor of the largest critical series in the field, *Contributions to the Study of Science Fiction and Fantasy* (in preparation, Greenwood). He is also advisory acquisitions editor for G. K. Hall's *Masters of Science Fiction and Fantasy* bibliographic series; and bibliographer for *Writers of the 21st Century Series* (Taplinger). Tymn is a former officer of the Science Fiction Research Association, a member of Science Fiction Writers of America, and president of Instructors of Science Fiction in Higher Education. He holds a Ph.D. in American Culture from the University of Michigan. His continuing interest in American literature of the romantic period is reflected in his *Thomas Cole's Poetry* (1972) and *Thomas Cole: The Collected Essays and Prose Sketches* (1980).

Peter Haining (Foreword). Ranking as the most prolific anthologist of horror fiction in the world, Peter Haining has edited scores of books since the 1970s. For his anthologies Haining strives to select lesser-known items, grouping them logically into cohesive themes. They are supported by comprehensive notes that add depth to the fiction. His most important anthologies are: *The Craft of Terror* (1966), *The Gentlewomen of Evil* (1967), *The Evil People* (1968), *The Midnight People* (1968), *The Unspeakable People* (1969), *The Hollywood Nightmare* (1970), *The Wild Night Company* (1970), *Clans of Darkness* (1971), *The Necromancers* (1971), *The Ghouls* (1971), *The Magicians* (1972), *The Lucifer Society* (1972), *Great British Tales of Terror* and *Great Tales of Terror from Europe and America* (1972), *The Nightmare Reader* (1973), *The Magic Valley Trav-*

ellers (1974), *The Ghost's Companion* (1975), *The Penny Dreadful* (1975), *The Fantastic Pulps* (1975), *The 1st Book of Unknown Tales of Horror* (1976), *Weird Tales* (1976), *The Ancient Mysteries Reader* (1976), *The Black Magic Omnibus* (1976), and *The Shilling Shockers* (1978). Haining has also compiled *The Sherlock Holmes Scrapbook* (1974), *The Dracula Scrapbook* (1976), *The H. G. Wells Scrapbook* (1978), and *The Jules Verne Companion* (1978). *Terror!* (1976) is a collection of horror artwork from books and magazines, followed by a similar compilation, *Mystery!* (1977). Haining's other books are chiefly nonfiction and cover a host of topics from the Channel Tunnel to graveyard wit.

Frederick S. Frank (Chapter 1). An Associate Professor at Allegheny College, Meadville, PA, since 1970, Frederick Frank has maintained a long-standing interest in British and American Gothicism both as a bibliographer of the form and as a critical interpreter of the Gothic novel's place in the romantic movement. His articles on Gothicism and its connections with romantic literature have appeared in such journals as *Revue de Littérature Comparée, American Transcendental Quarterly, Bulletin of Bibliography, Revue des Langues Vivantes, The Sphinx, Orbis Litterarum,* and *Extrapolation.* Dr. Frank has edited and written the scholarly introduction to Shelley's two Gothic novels, *St. Irvyne* and *Zastrozzi* (both Arno), and is currently a member of the editorial board of the journal, *Gothic: The Review of Supernatural Horror Fiction.* He is also assembling materials for a book on Poe's use of the European Gothic tradition, to be entitled *Plutonian Shores: The Meta-Gothic Achievement of E. A. Poe.*

Benjamin Franklin Fisher IV (Chapter 2). Benjamin Fisher is a member of the English Department at the University of Mississippi and editor of *University of Mississippi Studies in English.* His primary interests include Poe, mystery-horror literature of the Victorian-Edwardian periods, and detective fiction. His books and articles on these subjects include: *The Very Spirit of Cordiality: The Literary Uses of Alcohol and Alcoholism in the Tales of Edgar Allan Poe, Poe at Work: Seven Textual Studies,* and "Sensation Fiction in a Minor Key: The Ordeal of Richard Feverel" (*Nineteenth-Century Literary Perspectives: Essays in Honor of Lionel Stevenson*). He is currently researching the works of Wilkie Collins, William Mudford, Rhoda Broughton, Mrs. J. H. Riddell, John Dickson Carr, Frederick Irving Anderson, and Edgar Allan Poe. Dr. Fisher is a member of the editorial board of *Gothic: The Review of Supernatural Horror Fiction* and a contributor to its annual bibliography; compiler of "Fugitive Poe References: A Bibliography" in *Poe Studies;* and a member of a team compilation, "Current Poe Bibliography," in the same journal. He has in progress a manuscript of bibliographical materials about Gothicism. He is president of the Poe Studies Association and a member of the board of directors of the Edgar Allan Poe Society.

Jack Sullivan (Chapter 3). Jack Sullivan is a member of the faculty of the New School for Social Research, New York University. He is a regular reviewer for the *New York Times Book Review*, the *Saturday Review*, and the *Washington Post;* the author of *Elegant Nightmares: The English Ghost Story from Le Fanu to Blackwood;* and editor of *Lost Souls: A Collection of English Ghost Stories*. Sullivan has published articles in *Harper's*, *New Republic*, and other magazines, and is co-editor of "The Reader's Almanac," an author interview show on public radio.

Gary William Crawford (Chapter 4). Gary Crawford holds an M.A. in English from Mississippi State University and has been active in the field of horror literature for several years. He is publisher and editor of *Gothic: The Review of Supernatural Horror Fiction*, and has published book reviews in *College Literature* and *University of Mississippi Studies in English*. Crawford is a writer of supernatural horror fiction, his latest work appearing in *Fantasy Tales* magazine.

Robert Weinberg (Chapter 5). Accepted as one of the leading authorities on the American pulp fiction field, Robert Weinberg has edited and published a variety of material on the subject including a series of pulp magazine reprints under the general titles *Pulp Classics* and *Famous Fantastic Classics*, and a horror anthology, *Far Below and Other Horrors*. He is co-compiler of *The Hero Pulp Index* and *Reader's Guide to the Cthulhu Mythos* and compiler of *The Annotated Guide to Robert E. Howard's Sword & Sorcery*. He has also edited *Lester Dent: The Man Behind Doc Savage* and *WT50* (later revised as *The Weird Tales Story*). Weinberg is the author of several hundred articles about the pulp fiction field, has edited nearly 20 collections of stories from the magazines, and has served as editorial advisor to several publishers for their various reprint programs. He holds the World Fantasy Award (1978) for his contributions to the field of fantastic fiction scholarship. Weinberg is co-owner of Pulp Press, dedicated to preserving the best of the pulps in hardcover. He lives in Oak Forest, IL, where he and his wife operate a mail-order book business specializing in fantastic literature.

Steve Eng (Chapter 6). Steve Eng is associate editor for two magazines concerned with horror fiction, *The Romantist* and *Gothic: The Review of Supernatural Horror Fiction*. He has published over 400 poems in numerous periodicals, from *The Arkham Collector*, *Nyctalops* and *The Lyric*, to *The Anthology of Magazine Verse*, and has edited *Elusive Butterfly and Other Lyrics*. In 1979 he received a Science-Fiction Poetry Association "Rhysling Award" and in 1980 was the recipient of the fantasy Small Press Writers and Artists Organization "Best Poet" award. A resident of Nashville, Eng is a Syndic of the F. Marion Crawford Memorial Society.

Mike Ashley (Chapters 7–12). Mike Ashley, who lives in England, is a researcher in the related fields of science fiction, fantasy, horror, and historical fiction. He has edited several anthologies, including *The History of the Science Fiction Magazine* (4 volumes), *Souls in Metal, Weird Legacies,* and *The Best of British SF*. His reference publications include *Who's Who in Horror and Fantasy Fiction* and *Fantasy Readers Guide*. He has contributed bibliographical articles to *Science Fiction Monthly* and other journals and is now working on several projects in the science fiction and fantasy fields, as well as a number of novels.

Horror Literature

Part I
Fiction

1
The Gothic Romance
1762–1820

Frederick S. Frank

To assemble a meaningful bibliography of the eighteenth-century Gothic novel during its major phase is a risky expedition in literary archeology. Most of the horror titles that were once low priced, popular, or widely available through numerous circulating libraries have now become rare books or obscure milestones in literary history. Scores of Gothic novels were originally made and marketed for a mass audience addicted to the amusements of horror, and it is ironic that they should currently be the object of scholars seeking to define the darker side of romanticism or the quarry of collectors striving to possess rare editions—such as the lurid masterpiece *Horrid Mysteries,* by the Marquis von Grosse, printed for William Lane in 1796 by the largest Gothic manufacturer and distributor of that age, the Minerva-Press. The priceless relics of the Gothic school are not such widely known books as *The Castle of Otranto, The Mysteries of Udolpho, The Monk, Melmoth the Wanderer,* and *Frankenstein,* which have resisted the tides of taste and maintained their status as landmarks of the form. To grasp the authentic dimensions of the Gothic surge—which dominated the experimental field of novel writing for more than 40 years, between 1770 and 1810—the collector and literary his-

3

torian must devote him- or herself to the detection of more transient titles, such as *The Mysterious Bride; or, The Statue Spectre* (1800) and *The Phantoms of the Cloister; or, The Mysterious Manuscript* (1795). Such works more accurately reflect Gothicism's long reign of terror over readers and writers during the closing decades of the eighteenth century.

To recover the many lost or forgotten Gothics from the forbidden chambers of the vast castle of English and continental literature is the primary goal of the present bibliographical search. The leading Gothophile of the twentieth century, Michael Sadleir, recognized the need for such a bibliographical project while amassing his incomparable private collection of scarce or out-of-print Gothics during the 1920s. Robert K. Black, the later owner and executor of the Sadleir Gothics, wrote:

> In addition to its historical significance, such a group collection provides the specialized student with an accessibility of material under one roof unobtainable elsewhere in the country. Only the major Gothics have ever been reprinted; the vast majority must be had in first edition or not at all. Such authors as Regina Roche, Mrs. Meeke, Louisa Sidney Stanhope, Elizabeth Helme, Francis Lathom, Clara Reeve, the Porter Sisters, Charlotte Smith, George Walker, and Mary Robinson are virtually forgotten now, but in their own day they held enthralled a nationwide reading public.[1]

Since Black noted the necessity for collecting and cataloguing Gothic rarities, Gothic bibliography has not kept pace with the extensive attention given by scholars to the analysis and revaluation of the form.[2] Stimulated by Dorothy Scarborough's *The Supernatural in Modern English Fiction* (1917) and Edith Birkhead's *The Tale of Terror: A Study of the Gothic Romance* (1921), the history of the Gothic novel and its place in the rise of romanticism and a depth psychology have been meticulously traced by such literary investigators as Montague Summers, J. M. S. Tompkins, Eino Railo, Robert D. Mayo, and more recently by Devendra P. Varma, Maurice Lévy, Coral Ann Howells, and Elizabeth MacAndrew. Equally, the plethora of scholarship on the Gothic novel in monographic and article form has received due bibliographical attention.[3] But within the ranks of these Gothic specialists will be found the name of only one bibliographer committed to the documentation of the primary source itself, that is, the works of the greater and lesser Gothic novelists. Only the indefatigable Montague Summers, in his *Gothic Bibliography* (1941), dared to undertake a systematic arrangement of the peculiar and elusive titles that were mass-produced during the Gothic period.

Because of Summers's eccentric erudition and passion for completeness, his primary bibliography is marred by its very thoroughness and minuteness. Summers included many titles that are distinctly un-Gothic and anti-Gothic, and he imposed almost no discernible bibliographic limits on his inventory of the period. Thus, his Gothic bibliography is a detailed picture of the reading habits and publishers' practices of that age, but it is not directive and definitive with respect to the essential literature of Gothicism, as the present bibliography aims to be. Furthermore, prospective bibliographers of the Gothic novel appear to have heeded too earnestly the warning that Summers gave to future researchers in his exhaustive history of the Gothic novel, *The Gothic Quest* (1938):

> So vast are their numbers, so rare have the romances themselves become, that a Bibliography of the Gothic Novel must be an undertaking of extraordinary difficulty and perplexity. Dilemmas and problems confront one at every step. The question continually arises whether such and such a novel is sufficiently Gothic to be included, or whether it is to be regarded as a social or domestic novel. One is bound to be elastic in every direction. At what date may the Gothic novel be said to have begun? At what date did the Gothic novel finally lose itself, submerged in other forms and appearing under another guise? . . . There must be some lines of demarcation; some rules and method must be observed; that is to say, unless without any disposition or rationale lists are to be set down upon paper, to look after and arrange themselves as best they can.[4]

The bibliography of the Gothic novel eventually compiled by Summers is a massive tabulation of fiction of all varieties, with many terrific or horrific titles buried in his large lists of individual authors' whole output. Summers did not segregate the Gothic work of many authors from the sentimental, didactic, or domestic fiction of the same writers, and he chose to annotate items only at random. In contrast, by seeking to avoid the error of elasticity "in every direction," the present bibliography strives to be a focal sampling of that fiction of the period which is undeniably Gothic by way of setting, character, incident, or style. To qualify for inclusion, a work need not contain every piece of equipment associated with the original infernal machine of Walpole's *Castle of Otranto,* but it must exhibit at least one or two salient Gothic features, locales, or tendencies as are found universally in the two schools of horror and terror—the authentic supernatural and the artificial supernatural—that flourished during the period.

Building on the foundation left by Summers, the present bibliography offers a representative selection of specimens, major and minor, of every artifact of Gothic literary activity in England, Germany, France, and the United States between 1762 and 1820. Although arbitrary, these dates have their significance in the rise and fall of the Gothic novel. In 1762 appeared Thomas Leland's *Longsword, Earl of Salisbury,* an elaborately plotted romance of chivalry complete with grandly gloomy architecture, extravagant sufferings and wanderings, and an enthusiastic picture of an imaginary Middle Ages. Although Leland subtitled his novel *An Historical Romance,* the book was not a straightforward chronicle, but the writer's fantastic reconstruction of an invented "Gothic" past. Because it is marginally Gothic, except for the absence of a pronounced element of the supernatural, Leland's *Longsword* becomes a logical starting point for a bibliography of Gothicism. The second date, 1820, saw the publication of Charles Robert Maturin's *Melmoth the Wanderer*, often acknowledged by literary historians as the culminating masterpiece of the Gothic movement. It is evident, however, in its more profound tones that Maturin really wanted to write epic tragedy, but was shackled to the stylistic corpse of a moribund Gothic tradition. In Maturin's work we may sense both the triumph and the disintegration of the Gothic genre; hence, the date 1820 presents itself as a proper moment to exit from the haunted castle whose labyrinth we entered some 58 years earlier.

Holding strictly to these historical boundaries, the design of the bibliography contains many titles that can no longer be found in print and isolates a number of important Gothic efforts that had only a single edition. Indisputably, the Gothic era was an age of literary quantity more than artistic quality, of imitation more than originality. Gothic novel writing was a very competitive and overcrowded field, and it appears that mediocre and inept Gothics had as much chance for survival with publishers and readers as skillfully crafted and well-sustained shockers. Paradoxically, tawdry work frequently forced well-wrought Gothics out of the marketplace, and any bibliography of the period that claims to be comprehensive must accept the whimsical commercial atmosphere in which these hundreds of Gothic novels were rapidly written and cheaply published. Thus, a promising and ingeniously executed Gothic novel such as Joseph Fox's *Santa Maria; or, The Mysterious Pregnancy* (1797), which successfully blended the very different Gothic procedures of Mrs. Radcliffe and Matthew (Monk) Lewis, vanishes after one printing, whereas *Barozzi; or, The Venetian Sorceress* (1815), a somewhat lethargic and confused double-decker Gothic, enjoyed several editions in Victorian times and is currently one of the revived Gothics in the Arno Press series.[5]

Comprehensive but not exhaustive, the bibliography's coverage of the varieties of Gothic experience presents annotated examples of the four principal types of Gothic romance that evolved from Walpole's prototype (first published in 1765): historical Gothic; natural or explained Gothic; supernatural or inscrutable Gothic; and equivocal or ambiguous Gothic. Although these categories often overlap to yield hybrid types, and although the masterworks of Gothicism transcend the conventions of the categories to which they belong, the four classifications have proved useful since they were proposed by Montague Summers and later refined by G. R. Thompson. Within the broad categories, some bizarre subspecies of Gothic romance multiplied. They were usually composed around one object, character, place, or effect singled out from Walpole's thesaurus of terror. Thus, under the general headings we discover such restrictive forms as cavern or grotto Gothic, tower or turret Gothic, crypt or vault Gothic, and the romance of the ruin. In a Gothic novel where the victory of evil is a distinct possibility, the novel is often villain-centered; conversely, where goodness and order win out at last, the novel is often maiden-centered.

The historical Gothic, which always contains some royal or aristocratic personages who actually lived, operates out of a fabricated past or remote "Gothic" era abounding in violent values and savage superstitions. This branch of the Gothic may or may not include apparitions and other supernatural hardware, but typically most historical Gothics do find room for a castle specter or a haunted vault. Outstanding historical Gothics like Sophia Lee's *The Recess: A Tale of Other Times* (1785) and Ann Ker's *Edric the Forester; or, The Mysteries of the Haunted Chamber* (1817) introduce the supernatural to intensify an awe for a sublimely Gothic past.

Natural or explained Gothic, which quite commonly intersects with historical Gothic, startles the reader by its initial suggestion of genuinely supernatural figures or occurrences, but undermines its own power by belated natural or scientific explanations for occult horrors and terrors. The mode was perfected by Ann Radcliffe and expertly duplicated by Radcliffean disciples such as America's Charles Brockden Brown, who used the technique of explained Gothic to underscore the fallibility of the human mind. The bibliography displays many examples of the suspended and then relieved terrors of this form.

Supernatural or inscrutable Gothic assaults and demolishes the reader's belief in self-control and a rationally ruled universe. Its phantoms are genuine and cannot be driven off by the skeptical eye; its threatening architectural sites are truly alive with a biology and a will independently their own; its monsters, ogres, demons, and ghastly villains can actually slay with the eye or converse with Satan. Animated skeletons, walking statues, and vocal corpses move about as easily as the hero-villain and persecuted maiden in the pages of the supernatural thriller. The terminal unreason of supernatural Gothic attains its most outrageous degree in the German *Schauer-romane* of the late 1790s. The supernatural Gothic at its hideous extreme can be described as "high Gothic," an unrelieved and unexplained mood of horror where there is "no insinuated mystery or gradual acclimatization of the soul to dread; the authors work by sudden shocks, and, when they deal with the supernatural, their favorite effect is to wrench a mind suddenly from scepticism to horror-struck belief." [6]

Equivocal or ambiguous Gothic, a later development of the form, concentrates on the defective sensibilities of a narrator, who may or may not accurately interpret the related Gothic experiences. Equivocal Gothic exposes the vulnerable psychology of the mind under stress; it refuses to resolve the question of whether the supernatural is an objective reality or the subjective projection of an unbalanced intellect. The majority of the Gothics catalogued in this bibliography lack the psychological and moral subtleties required by ambiguous Gothic, but in those cases where the reliability or the sanity of the narrator is an issue in question—as in Charles Brockden Brown's *Edgar Huntly; or, The Memoirs of a Sleepwalker* (1799) or certain "night pieces" by E. T. A. Hoffmann—the interpretive implications of the equivocal Gothic mode become a vital consideration.

Within the confines dictated by the four prevalent kinds of Gothic, this bibliography takes into account every identifiable mutation of Gothic fiction that was active in the period. Six criteria have been applied in selecting what might be called "necessary Gothics" for establishing a foundation collection. Without emphasizing one at the expense of any other, the bibliography contains examples of:

1. Pure or high Gothic—novels, tales, dramas, dramatic adaptations from Gothic novels, and unfinished fragments, whose principal literary goal is to terrify, horrify, startle, or thrill the audience and whose apparatus and atmosphere derive from the working model for all Gothic novels, Horace Walpole's *Castle of Otranto*. To be classified by the bibliographer as "pure" Gothic or "high" Gothic, a work must aim to electrify and not to edify its readership. Thus, T. J. Horsley Curties's *The Monk of Udolpho* (1807), a Gothic novel whose sole aim is to shock the reader, is rated as "pure" Gothic; Charlotte Dacre's *Zofloya; or, The Moor* (1806), which displays a moral appendage, falls slightly short of "high" Gothic even though its content is highly Gothic.

2. *Schauer-romane, romans noirs,* or *Ritter- und Räuber-romane.* A sufficient number, but not a compendious census, of German *Schauer-romane* (shudder novels) and French *romans noirs* (dark novels), whose grotesque power and nightmarish techniques of evoking horror strongly influenced the direction of English Gothicism in the 1790s. The scholar Eino Railo labeled such Teutonic terror *Burgverliess* Gothic, a term that implies no exit for the reader from the unremitting horrors of the Germanic version of the haunted castle. *Burgverliess* and *Schauer-romantik* Gothic is often anonymous or spurious in authorship, as in the baleful title, *Die blutende Gestalt mit Dolch und Lampe; oder, Die Beschwöhrung im Schlosse Stern bei Prag* (1799), translated as *The Bleeding Shape with Dagger and Lantern; or, The Oath at Stern Castle near Prague,* an unsigned Gothic shocker that proves to be a hasty plagiarism of von Oertel's first German translation of M. G. Lewis's *The Monk* (1797).

3. Didactic or philosophical Gothic. Illustrations of didactic, polemical, or doctrinary Gothicism, in which the customary contraptions and conditions of Walpole's castle are used to symbolize various political or religious concepts; the aim is to revolutionize or radicalize the thinking of the reader. Such enlightened or "impure" Gothic is an obvious debasement of the original objectives of the Gothic writer. At the same time, the practice of fusing the Gothic with the ideological cannot be overlooked, since such a tendency suggests the link between the Gothic novel and the later Victorian novel of conscience and social purpose. The philosophically and psychologically attuned novels of William Godwin and Robert Bage reveal this tendency to exploit the Gothic for propagandistic motives.

4. Fringe Gothic or Gothic parody. Various works of the period whose plots and themes exhibit intermittent Gothic traits and whose settings and characters are occasionally, but not consistently, Gothic in description and behavior. This category of selection also allows for some extraordinary versions of the haunted castle or menacing mansion. Books and writers placed

here can be called "fringe" Gothic, since the requisite moods of terror and horror are not predominant, but alternate with sentimental, primitivistic, melancholic, exotic, and other nonsensational effects. With its totally Gothic title and partially Gothic action, Charlotte Smith's *Old Manor House* (1793) demonstrates the mixed qualities of "fringe" Gothic. Burlesques and parodies of the Gothic novel such as Eaton Stannard Barrett's *The Heroine; or, The Adventures of a Fair Romance Reader* (1813) and the rare French lampoon, Bellin de la Liborlière's *La Nuit Anglaise; ou, les aventures jadis un peu extraordinaires* (1799) (the work signed by R. P. Spectroruini)—which Maurice Lévy calls "the best *pastiche* of the Gothic genre ever written" [7]—also find their place in the bibliography in a separate category beyond the fringe.

5. Chapbook, bluebook, or pulp Gothic. A limited listing of pulp Gothics or shilling shockers, ancestors of the dime novel and the Victorian penny dreadful, extrapolated from the excess of throwaway Gothics that were mass-produced by publishers eager to profit from the Gothic craze. A separate bibliography of this recycled or "junk" Gothic would be a voluminous effort by itself.[8] Many of these garishly illustrated and shoddily made chapbooks and bluebooks turn out to be clumsy piracies or plagiarized abridgements of legitimate and popular Gothics. Almost worthless in their own day, the shilling shockers are extremely scarce today and regarded by collectors as premium items. Hence, the acquisition of such dubious literary treasures ought to be a final, rather than a first, step in the building of a basic Gothic collection. Usually designated as a chapbook or bluebook in the annotation, the title of the typical pulp Gothic crudely thrusts itself upon the reader and loudly announces the macabre particulars of its plot, as in *The Midnight Groan; or, The Spectre of the Chapel, Involving an Exposure of the Horrible Secrets of the Nocturnal Assembly: A Gothic Romance*, an anonymous chapbook appearing in 1800.

6. Translation or sham translation. A digest of translations of English and American Gothic productions into French and German and a reciprocal register of *Schauer-romane, romans noirs,* and *Ritter- und Räuber-romane* (knight and robber novels) rendered into English. Imported English Gothic titles seem to have held a special attraction for the French, whose national imagination had been conditioned for the horrors of the high Gothic by the bloody excesses of the Revolution. While French novelists and playwrights furnished the revolutionary public with their share of *romans noirs,* the mainstream of Gallic Gothicism may be seen in the torrent of translations that flowed from the pens of both aristocrats and ordinary citizens. The first French translation of Radcliffe's *Mysteries of Udolpho* (1794) is by the highborn Comtesse Louise Marie Victorine Chastenay de Lanty. The average citizen-translator was more drawn to the virulent anti-Catholic themes of the monastic shocker. Hence, we find a committee of four, the citizens Deschamps, L. B. D. Desprès, Benoist, and De Lamare, turning *The Monk* into French in the fifth year of the revolutionary calendar, 1797. Many of these translations

were so creative, innovative, and free that the original English Gothic source remained visible only in outline. By the turn of the century, the Germans were exporting almost as many of these titles as they were importing. The translating of *Schauer-romane* and *Ritter- und Räuber-romane* in vast quantities by the English insured the continuing cross-fertilization of the two Gothic schools during the first decade of the nineteenth century. Like the French translators, the English took extravagantly creative liberties with their German material. When M. G. Lewis translated Johannes Zschokke's robber-romance, *Abällino, der Grosse Bandit* (1794) as *The Bravo of Venice* (1804), he practically rewrote the story, beginning with the unrecognizable title. Offering no eclectic survey of Gothic translations, the bibliography nevertheless takes note of the international cross-currents of Gothic imports and exports.

The single number from (1) to (6), which appears in parentheses at the end of the bibliographical data preceding each annotation in this chapter, refers to one of the six selection criteria just described and enables the user to place the work in one of the six divisions: (1) pure or high Gothic, (2) *Schauer-roman, roman noir,* or *Ritter- und Räuber-roman,* (3) didactic or philosophical Gothic, (4) fringe Gothic or Gothic parody, (5) chapbook, bluebook, or pulp Gothic, and (6) translation or sham translation.

Throughout the bibliography, an asterisk (*) preceding an entry number designates that title as indispensable to even the most rudimentary Gothic collection. It also indicates that the particular work was historically influential and artistically respectable and that it remained popular long after the Gothic tidal wave had subsided. The test of such popularity arises from the fact the work enjoyed at least a second printing or that it was periodically revived by Victorian publishers or that it was reissued in such argosies as *The Romanticist and Novelist's Library* (1839), edited by William Hazlitt, or *Ballantyne's Novelist's Library* (1821), under the supervision of Sir Walter Scott. Both these series, incidentally, are invaluable storehouses of the curios of Gothic literature. An asterisk also denotes that a Gothic book or play retained its following beyond the terminal date of 1820 even though it might have been omitted from the revivals of Hazlitt and Scott. A number of such rediscovered Gothic classics have been reissued by the Arno Press Gothic series, under editor Devendra P. Varma.

Nonstarred titles throughout the bibliography mark the many Gothic works that are relatively scarce or difficult to obtain today. The absence of the asterisk also indicates a Gothic that imitates some well-established form or that derives its content from a collective or group style, such as sham translations from the German, which prevailed in the late 1790s. Titles without asterisks may be taken to have secondary historical importance for the development of the Gothic genre, although they are not necessarily artistically inferior to starred titles of a similar classification. Usually, a nonstarred title has been through only one or two editions; frequently this means that the sample is so rare that it is out of reach even for connoisseurs and collectors of ample means and must, therefore, be obtained in facsimile from one of the large libraries with extensive and expensive Gothic holdings. The peerless source for the location of these rare Gothics is the Sadleir-Black Gothic Collection housed in the Alderman Library at the University of Virginia. A similarly excellent collection of Gothic plays is the Larpent Collection of Gothic Drama in the Huntington Library.[9] The abbreviation SB appearing in an entry indicates that it can be found in Sadleir-Black.

Titles in French and German have also been assigned starred designations where appropriate and the proper (1) to (6) division indicator. Foreign titles are translated in the annotations; where a translation of the whole work into English can be determined, such information is also furnished. The country of origin for all authors is the United Kingdom (U.K.) unless otherwise specified.

Before turning to the bibliography itself, let us briefly examine the Gothic novel's inception, ascendancy, remarkable proliferation, and swift disintegration after 1820. The connotations of the term *Gothic,* as well as the emergence of a Gothic aesthetic—which found pleasure or saw a peculiar beauty in spectacles of pain, violence, supernatural fear, and grotesque architectural fantasy—are important considerations in plotting the trajectory of the Gothic novel on the graph of literary history.

Gothic feelings existed in English literature for several decades prior to Walpole's formalization of these responses into a first Gothic novel (1765). The English Gothic novel burst upon the scene with a malign vigor that would change the tone and direction of the novel; yet Walpole's creation was simply an enlargement of the revolt against reason in art that had already begun with the graveyard poets during the previous generation. Fatigued by the restraints imposed upon the imaginative life by the rules of neoclassicism, the graveyard poets had decorated their lines with Gothic feeling. Their morbid enthusiasm aptly illustrates what Walpole observed in the preface to the second edition of *The Castle of Otranto,* that "the great resources of fancy have been dammed up by a strict adherence to the common life." [10] Here is one of the graveyard poets, Thomas Warton the Younger, in a poem entitled "The Pleasures of Melancholy," published 20 years before *Otranto,* in 1745. Standing in ecstatic anxiety upon the threshold of the Gothic world, he sounds precisely like a Gothic victim on the verge of an abbey confinement.

> As on I tread, religious horror wraps
> My soul in dread repose. But when the world
> Is clad in Midnight's raven-colored robe,
> In hollow charnel let me watch the flame
> Of taper dim, while airy voices talk
> Along the glimmering walls, or ghostly shape
> At distance seen, invites with beckoning hand
> My lonesome steps, through the far-winding vaults.[11]

What we hear in the moods of the graveyard poets and subsequently in the work of the Gothic novelists is a set of hopes and fears somewhat akin to religious awe. A Gothic confrontation has in it that aspect of religious experience which involves a surrender of the self to something larger and rationally incomprehensible. When Warton's lonely wanderer strays into the Gothic world, he rediscovers the power of darkness in pleasing the imagination. At the same time, he experiences the sublime fright of finding himself in a dimension beyond the rational. Here is a depraved, unstable, decaying environment that is reminiscent of hell and whose very appeal seems to be an extension of its terrifying and godless qualities.

The essence of a Gothic work is this crossover from a safe and orderly deistic universe into a strange and fearful region presided over by demons and circumscribed by twisting passageways and "far-winding vaults." That such a journey was a sublime experience would shortly be explained by Edmund Burke, who recognized the inevitability of a Gothic upheaval. In the important treatise *A Philosophical Inquiry into the Origin of Our Ideas of the Sublime and Beautiful* (1757), Burke identified the psychological connections between horror and terror and the expansion of the soul or awakening of the dormant imagination. For Burke, a Gothic event or character could have all the sublime intensity of a religious or numinous experience, with overwhelming agony and dread taking the place of traditional grace, divine insight, or transfiguration. Burke's analysis of the all-consuming horror that encourages Gothic readers to admire evil, worship decay, and abandon themselves to darkness can be instantly understood as the premise upon which high Gothic or pure Gothic rests. Here is Burke's rationale for the Gothic aesthetic, a theory of pleasure in fear that would soon lead to horror for horror's sake.

> Astonishment is that state of the soul in which all its motions are suspended with some degree of horror. In this case the mind is so entirely filled with its object that it cannot entertain any other, nor by consequence reason on that object which employs it. Hence arises the great power of the sublime, that, far from being produced by them, it anticipates our reasonings and hurries us on by an irresistible force. . . . No passion so effectually robs the mind of all its powers of acting and reasoning as fear. For fear being an apprehension of pain or death, it operates in a manner that resembles actual pain. Whatever therefore is terrible with regard to sight, is sublime too, whether this cause of terror be endured with greatness of dimensions or not.[12]

Burke's exposition of the psychology of the Gothic points backward to the delicious shudder of Warton's nocturnal wanderer as well as forward to the maiden entrapped within the "long labyrinth of darkness" underlying Walpole's first Gothic castle. If we rely on Burke, it becomes clear that the Gothic originates in a desire to displace reason and to surrender one's rational will to moments of sublime dread that are nearly equivalent to religious possession or mystic illumination. It remained only for Walpole and his successors to invent those objects and situations whose awesome mystery could effectively displace reason and elevate the imagination to a peak of pleasure arising out of its contact with the ineffably gruesome. Burke had not predicted, he had simply described, the climate of emotionalism out of which the Gothic novel was to grow.

Burke did not use the adjective *Gothic,* although his reference to the great power that "hurries us on by an irresistible force" anticipates the breathless pattern of action of the most successful Gothic novels. Yet the term *Gothic* had a wide currency in Burke's day and was available to him as an abusive epithet, had he chosen to particularize the varieties of sublime terror in which the graveyard poets indulged. For the Augustan writers such as Pope, Addison, Fielding, and Gay, the term *Gothic* had only negative or pejorative value. When they applied it, they did so contemptuously, to signify inferior taste in architecture, painting, or writing. Until the term was neutralized in the mideighteenth century and then sensationalized in the titles of countless novels, it meant "uncouth," "barbaric," "uncivilized," "boorish," and from the standpoint of the neoclassical artist, "undisciplined or formless."

Historically, Gothic was identified with the wild tribes who had extinguished the light of Roman civilization by sacking the eternal city under the leadership of the Gothic chieftain Alaric in 410 A.D. Architecturally, Gothic signified a style of cathedral building that was considered more pagan than Christian, less sanctified than savage, and offensive in all ways to the Palladian ideals of symmetry, balance, and grace of line. When the Gothic novelists transformed the cathedral or medieval abbey into a ruin—that is to say, when dilapidation was added to the decadence and barbaric obscenity already associated with these monstrous monuments of the dark ages—the Gothic novel acquired its central metaphor and most durable prop. When the walls burst and the turrets crumble at the climax of *The Castle of Otranto,* the first Gothic novelist has created the first haunted ruin, a perennial feature of the Gothic's landscape of dreams, a symbolic prison for the romantic spirit, and a deserted token of a fallen world. Speaking of the power of the ruin over the Gothic imagination of the 1760s, Michael Sadleir has acutely applied Burke's general arguments about the sublime to the mouldering castle:

> To the Gothistic eye . . . a ruin was itself a thing of loveliness—and for interesting reasons. A mouldering building is a parable of the victory of nature over man's handiwork. The grass growing rankly in a once stately courtyard; the ivy creeping over the broken tracery of a once sumptuous window; the glimpse of sky through the fallen roof of a once proud banqueting hall—all of these moved to melancholy pleasure minds which dwelt gladly on the impermanence of human life and effort, which sought on every hand symbols of a pantheist philosophy. Then again, a ruin expresses the triumph of chaos over order, and the Gothistic movement was, in origin at least, a movement toward freedom and away from the controls of discipline. [13]

Ardently participating in the vanguard of the medieval revival that swept through the arts in the 1750s, and sensing a change in attitude toward things Gothic, Horace Walpole cloistered himself in the elegant British country house he had purchased at Strawberry Hill and eagerly began to construct a medieval shell around its Georgian frame. It was within this self-indulgent setting so conducive to nightmare that the first Gothic novel was written. While casting about for a provocative subtitle for the second edition of *The Castle of Otranto,* Walpole no doubt caught a "glimpse of sky through the fallen roof" of his fake fortress or felt the dark energy flowing from the phony battlements and plaster towers of Strawberry Hill and quickly scribbled "A Gothic Story" after the castellated main title. Although many later critics and general readers have denounced the term as absurd or unmanageable, Walpole's labeling of his novel as Gothic accurately caught the quintessence of the form in a single word. If persistent usage by all kinds of readers and writers over the years is any test of value, Walpole made both a correct and a brilliant choice. From *Otranto* to the modern Gothic, we find frantic characters in claustrophobic predicaments; they are Gothically contained by some version of a mighty and mysterious building whose terrible potency seems out of all proportion to its feeble, crazed, or helpless human owners. In fact, from the very first stage of Gothic, the building possesses the occupants or holds them in bondage.

Walpole thought of his toy as Gothic in two distinct ways. Temporally, he returned the reader to a pretended past full of the sinister thrills and supernatural excitements of medieval life. In such an atmosphere, Walpole declared in the preface to the second edition, the reader might expect to see the characters occupying "extraordinary positions," [14] but he cleverly did not specify that the initial "extraordinary position" would reveal a sickly young man crushed beneath a gigantic flying helmet, which had descended upon him like a lunar module making a carefully calculated landing. Spatially, he placed all his characters—including the hero-villain, Manfred—at the mercy of a sentient piece of Gothic architecture, whose substructure becomes the fiendish floor plan for scores of Gothic novels to come. Beginning with *The Castle of Otranto* and perhaps achieving its highest plane of horror in Poe's "House of Usher," Gothic architecture is imbued with the character and will of its former owners. Place becomes personality, as every corner and dark recess of the Gothic castle exudes a remorseless aliveness and often a vile intelligence. Frequently, it is this total and unnatural biology of walls, staircases, galleries above, and oubliettes below that keeps the characters "in a constant vicissitude of interesting passions," [15] as the maiden flees through dark vaults from the erotic urges of the villain and the villain in turn struggles against his own repulsive desires.

The blueprint of Gothic terror can be traced directly back in the history of the Gothic novel to Walpole's underground. The dynamics of the Gothic reach downward toward absolute darkness and perpetual enclosure within the hell of the castle. "The lower part of the castle was hollowed into several intricate cloisters; and it was not easy for one under so much anxiety to find the door that opened into the cavern. An awful silence reigned throughout those subterraneous regions, except now and then some blasts of wind that shook the doors she had passed, and which grating on the rusty hinges were re-echoed through that long labyrinth of darkness." [16] Here we have the fundamental imagery of Gothic crisis—a hysterical subterranean wayfarer (typically a trembling maiden) depicted in the act of frightened flight through an atmosphere that Milton might have described as "darkness visible." [17] Lost in the maze of intertwining passageways, the Gothic character also takes a secret delight in being victimized by the architectural organism of the castle itself and by such suborganisms as trapdoors, lightless niches, and slimy narrowing tunnels leading inward and downward to the odious and unexplored depths of the castle. It can be claimed that this "long labyrinth of darkness" winds its way for some 50 years through the tradition of the English novel and that the Castle of Otranto's basement is Walpole's lasting contribution to the form.

Since the first architect of the novel of terror named his book *Gothic,* there have been many attempts to define the Gothic novel. Generally, there are two ways of defining Gothicism. The older way is to explicate the Gothic in terms of its standard devices, beginning with the haunted castle. By this method, the definition reverts to the elaborate technology of terror found in *The Castle of Otranto* and points out similar paraphernalia that then establishes a given work as Gothic. Clearly, according to this definition by content or formal characteristics, a work cannot be called Gothic unless it displays some of Walpole's machinery in some form. Such formulaic superscriptions are offered by Thrall, Hibbard, and Holman in *A Handbook to Literature,* where they define the Gothic novel by content rather than intent: "a form of novel in which magic, mystery and chivalry are the chief characteristics. Horrors abound; one may expect a suit of armor suddenly to come to life, while ghosts, clanking chains, and charnel houses impart an uncanny atmosphere of terror." [18]

Definition by content, which uses Walpole's parts-list, will suffice for a superficial identification of Gothicism, but it carries the implication that Gothic literature is merely superficial fiction without any deeper thrust. However, the Gothic is now being reread and redefined by contemporary critics with regard to its psychodynamics and its conscious or unconscious effects upon the audience. If the Gothic does have artistic and psychological depth as well as sensational breadth—and certainly in its American strain it does—then, the newer approach to the Gothic, which defines the form in terms of its effect, ought to supplement the enumeration of parts.

The history of the Gothic novel and its impact on modern literature suggest that Gothicism cannot be conclusively defined simply by studying the rewiring of Walpole's dynamo. A more satisfying definition was proposed by

Howard Phillips Lovecraft in his appreciative miniature history of the Gothic, *Supernatural Horror in Literature* (1927). Lovecraft was among the first to be interested in what a Gothic novel does to or for its readers. Hence, his definition of the Gothic takes into account the psychodynamics of the Gothic response. Gothic literature, Lovecraft maintains, is "a literature of cosmic fear." Its potency lies in the creation of "a certain atmosphere of breathless and unexplainable dread of outer, unknown forces." The Gothic achieves its maximum effect when there is "a hint expressed with a seriousness and portentousness becoming its subject, of that most terrible conception of the human brain—a malign and particular suspension or defeat of those fixed laws of Nature which are our only safeguard against the assaults of chaos and the daemons of unplumbed space." [19]

Working from Lovecraft's proposition of "cosmic dread," G. R. Thompson brings the Gothic into alignment with Burke, who analyzed sublime horror as a category of the religious or mystical experience that overwhelms the egotistical security of the reader. Says Thompson:

> Gothic dread is of body, of mind, and of spirit. The high Gothic romance seeks to create an atmosphere of dread by combining terror and horror with the element of inscrutable mystery. Terror suggests the frenzy of physical and mental fear of pain and death threatened from without. Horror suggests the sense from within of something incredibly evil or morally repellent. Mystery suggests something beyond these—something productive of a nameless apprehension that may be called religious dread in the face of the wholly *other*. [20]

Is not such religious dread exactly what Thomas Warton's trembling pilgrim felt as he approached the Gothic shrine?

For the bibliographer, the definitions offered by Lovecraft and Thompson ask us to take the Gothic seriously as an enduring form by exposing the primal emotional foundations upon which the Gothic novel stakes its existence. Its power finally depends not on a literal interpretation of the devices themselves, but on the reader's conversion of these devices into private symbols, which represent his or her own sense of the supremely unholy, the supremely diabolic, the supremely dreadful. To read the high Gothic, then, is to feel cosmic dread or to catch a glimpse of one of those "daemons of unplumbed space" capable of throwing open the hell-gates within ourselves. The greatest Gothic writers always succeed in putting us into hideous contact with our own murky depths of being, where Lovecraft's "outer unknown forces" are matched by inner unknown forces hidden in the darkest core of the self. Generalizing from the functional definitions of Lovecraft and Thompson, we can define the Gothic novel, tale, and drama as a violently destructive or sadomasochistic fantasy of the multiple self, in which various hypothetical personalities or repressed and unwanted identities are released into an architectural dream collage in which anything *can* happen and usually *does*.

Under these conditions, the force of evil is both exceptional and occasionally heroic; the satanic heroes of the Gothic, whether they be mad monks or devil-driven women, strike the reader as particularly fascinating, since such fallen beings obviously possess the capacity for great virtue—which sometimes brings the Gothic within range of the tragic. Such characters also represent rejected zones of our inner selves. Their brutal or uncontrollable behavior and malicious energy evoke that terror without pity that accompanies the recognition of the supremely unholy forces at the core of self. One common theme in the Gothic is the re-education or initiation of a rational skeptic into the mysterious ways of the castle. The character's entrance into the castle can be understood as a repenetration of the inner self, or a dangerous journey inward into areas of the unconscious mind long abandoned to the reasonable life, a voyage backward into one's brutish origins. Defining the Gothic in terms of its psychodynamic appeal is also a way of saying that the Gothic novel from its beginnings and throughout its flowering can and should be regarded not simply as escapist and popular art but also as cathartic fiction. For both Gothic readers and writers of the late eighteenth century, Newton's safe universe was temporarily annulled by the refreshing anarchy allowed by the form.

Both the forbidden passions and the figure of the satanic hero—the man who risks all for evil—were vigorously present in the new tradition of the novel in the work of Walpole's predecessor and emotional mentor, Samuel Richardson. If Walpole obtained his Gothic scenery and supernatural appliances from the graveyard poets and the Gothic building craze, he based his techniques of characterization upon the sexological melodrama found in Richardson's first novel, *Pamela; or, Virtue Rewarded* (1740) and his masterpiece, *Clarissa; or, The History of a Young Lady* (1749). These two sentimental novels of male pursuit and female distress offered the sensation-starved public two tearful sagas ending in a victory of virtue over vice—but not before each of the heroines suffers an almost unbearable quota of physical and psychological persecution at the hands of a strong-willed seducer. While virtue is rewarded in both novels (as vice will be triumphant or evil will enjoy its victory in some phases of the high Gothic), the Gothic overtones of Richardson's work are unmistakable.

Reading Richardson with the Gothic of Walpole in view, we recognize him at once as the progenitor of the maiden-villain collision in the underground, which launches the chase through darkness in *The Castle of Otranto*. Taking the psychologies of Richardson's characters—the seducer-villain, Robert Lovelace, and the saintly maiden, Clarissa Harlowe—Walpole cleverly medievalized and supernaturalized various Richardsonian events and arenas of action to place the theme of virtue in distress in a Gothic context. Confessing her terror at the threat of being impounded within an awful and lonesome dwelling (in this case, her Uncle Antony's remote château), Clarissa speaks the language of the Gothic novel's incarcerated maiden:

"But if this, neither, is to be granted, it is my humble request that I may be sent to my Uncle Harlowe's, instead of my Uncle Antony's. I mean not by this any disrespect to my Uncle Antony: but his moat, with his bridge threatened to be drawn up, and perhaps the chapel terrify me beyond expression, notwithstanding your witty ridicule upon me for that apprehension." [21]

Her pursuer, Robert Lovelace, delights in the destruction of virtue itself as personified by Clarissa, and brags of his cruelty in the familiar idiom of the Gothic hero-villain. Responding to Clarissa's obsessive dream of live burial, Lovelace reverses his victim's masochistic death wish, turning it in his imagination into an expression of sadistic lust. Here in its earliest form in Richardson we find the unspeakable crime or the dark act of evil passion and erotic atrocity that occupies a central place in the structure of the later Gothic novel and drives the hero-villain toward his spectacular doom. Clarissa has had a Gothic dream in which Lovelace "carries her into a churchyard; and there, notwithstanding all her prayers and tears, and protestations of innocence, stabs her to the heart, and then tumbles her into a deep grave ready dug, among two or three half-dissolved carcasses." [22] As he muses upon his strategy for abducting and raping Clarissa, he speaks the cruel rhetoric of the villain of the high Gothic contemplating his victim:

"Here have I been at work, dig, dig, dig, like a cunning miner, at one time, and spreading my snares like an artful fowler, at another, and exulting in my contrivances to get this inimitable creature absolutely into my power. . . . Night, *midnight, is* necessary. Surprise, terror, *must* be necessary to the ultimate trial of this charming creature." [23]

These threats are against virginity, not against life; in Gothic novels such as *The Monk* and *The Italian; or, The Confessional of the Black Penitents,* the female prisoners are threatened with an unnamed something that is far worse than rape, as seduction gives way to destruction in the dramatic interplay between maiden and villain. In Lovelace, Walpole and later Gothics discovered the forerunner for their majestically evil hero-villains, men or supermen of strong but divided passions whose erotically disturbed selves could not resist succumbing to criminal tendencies unrestrained by conscience and reason. With Richardson's polarization of character into masculine evil and feminine innocence, the foundations for Gothic conflict were established. The two opponents in the sexual contest come to stand for the basest and noblest drives within the self as the self seems to split in half. Lover and beloved are exaggerated into victimizer and victim, pursuer and pursued, precisely the relation of the villain to the maiden in the typical Gothic novel of amatory or bestial lust among the ruins.

In this duel to the death between two ontological opposites in Richardson's work, many Gothic elements are present before the fact: we have a perverted, although remorseful, villain, who is a ruthless erotic criminal and who perpetrates a central brutal event. Lovelace is the first of a line of tor-

mented tormentors or Gothic men of feeling who substitute terror for tears
in their treatment of women. Richardson's Gothicizing also introduces the
archetypal heroine of so many Gothic novels, the woman of feeling, who is
by temperament something of a hedonist-hysteric, addicted to nightmarish
fantasies of carnal anguish and cravings for sexual martyrdom in some remote subterranean setting, and who secretly desires to be brutalized rather
than loved by a mysterious and abnormal male. The Richardsonian villain
is motivated by desires that he knows to be evil but cannot control; the Richardsonian maiden is similarly compelled to replace normal love with a set of
gruesome or Gothic experiences, which include premature burial and necrophiliac rape. With the Gothic partnership of hero-villain and persecuted
maiden already prepared by Richardson, it remained only for the first
Gothic novelist, Horace Walpole, and his brood of followers to perfect the
Gothic: this they achieved by removing the tedious, didactic promise of "virtue rewarded," by recostuming Richardson's Lovelace and Clarissa in ecclesiastical or baronial garb, and by moving the action from Richardson's bou-
doirs to the tenebrous underground of a medieval edifice. In Gothifying
Richardson, the Gothic novelists seized upon the emotional inhibitions of
the weeping readers of sentimental fiction, then proceeded to dry their eyes
with hell-fire.

The rapid rise of the Gothic after Walpole's *Castle of Otranto* witnessed the
division of Gothic fiction into two more or less antithetical factions. A domesticated or moderate Gothic—such as that in Clara Reeve's *Old English
Baron: A Gothic Story* (published in 1777 under the non-Gothic title, *The Champion of Virtue*)—attempted to correct Walpole's headlong plunge into the un-
mitigated supernatural; it offered the new Gothic audience a rational compromise to offset the outrageous implausibilities of Walpole's Gothic.
Reeve's novel contains one phantom—the ghost of a slain relative—who appears in a forbidden apartment of Lovel Castle, where the disinherited
young hero, Edmund Twyford, must spend three uneasy evenings; but *The
Old English Baron* is never truly terrifying. Only a single section of Reeve's
castle is haunted, and her specter is far more didactic than horrific, moving
with the dignity and elegance of an Augustan gentleman; it is he who holds
the key to the castle's proper ownership. Reeve's installation of a forbidden
chamber (the eastern apartment) is an inventive stroke, which was to add a
permanent fixture to the interior of the haunted castle in novels of the genre.
Every later ordeal involving a corpse vigil or immurement in a chamber of
horrors owes its origin to the inner sanctum of *The Old English Baron*.

Aside from the eerie medievalism of its haunted wing, Clara Reeve's historical saga is a regression to the muted Gothicism of Leland's *Longsword*.
Her candid purpose was to edify, not electrify, the reader, and her inclusion
of a solitary ghost and a single Gothic episode was from her conservative
point of view "a sufficient degree of the marvelous to excite the attention." [24]
Reeve's Gothicism is not insipid or incompetent, but it is clearly a secondary

effect in her work and never achieves anything close to thematic status as it does in the high Gothic.

If the timid Gothicism of *The Old English Baron* is a delicate half-turn of the screw in the development of the Gothic novel, William Beckford's *Vathek: An Arabian Tale, from an Unpublished Manuscript* (1786) is a quantum leap, for Beckford's vision of the Gothic is as radical and exotic as Reeve's Gothic usages are conservative and domestic. Beckford was a sensualist, a hedonist, an archdiabolic romantic, a connoisseur of ancient ruins, an accomplished orientalist, and a compulsive and lifelong builder of towers. His passion for the supreme climb, or its reverse, the ultimate descent, was so overriding that he may be described as a "toweromaniac" or a "grottophiliac." As a Gothic writer, he had the pernicious gift of perpendicular imagination so necessary for realizing the upper and lower limits of Gothic fantasy. Beckford constructed an enormous Saracenic-Gothic abbey at Fonthill in Wiltshire to enclose his sadistic dreams; the building remains one of the boldest expressions of the Gothic revival impulse, which also led Walpole to convert his ordinary villa into an extraordinary pre-Otranto castle at Strawberry Hill.

Like Walpole, Beckford found in the Gothic a means of self-dramatization, but unlike Walpole he sent his characters off on a perverse downward quest for damnation itself—and he ended *Vathek* by bringing them within sight of Satan (or Eblis, as he is called in the Muhammadan tradition) and to the hell of their own desires. Demonic in design, preposterous in tone, and surrealistically arabesque in decor, *Vathek* is as revolutionary and as controversial as its strange creator. The weird catalogue of Beckford's Gothicism is executed with all the clarity of an opium sleep. *Vathek* demonstrates just how far back into the caverns of the irrational the Gothic spirit was willing to venture, once the Gothic artist had made the decision to demolish the old categories of reality and replace them with fanciful realities of his own making. Beckford's legacy to the development of the Gothic tradition lay in his attitude that an inverted moral framework could release the imagination and convey it beyond the conventional boundaries of good and evil as demarcated by the neoclassic value system. Thus the devil, not God, is the highest authority and prime mover of Vathek's universe; the unspeakably repulsive becomes the attractive; hell, not heaven, becomes the spiritual goal of the wandering protagonist; and damnation supplants salvation as the soul's sharpest desire. With *Vathek,* the satanic hero who consciously chooses evil and then makes a kind of religious quest out of this choice creates a climate of reverse morality in which such satanic Gothics as Lewis's *Monk* could take root.

Two images of power or perverted aspiration give *Vathek* its model Gothic structure. The action of the novel takes place along a vertical axis of exquisite villainy and "blue fire" horror; it offers stairways to damnation, Gothic pits containing comic monster ghouls who must be fed on children, and a Technicolor underground where Vathek's sorceress mother, Carathis, conducts her obscene rites amid ornate, charnel decor and the shrieks of one-eyed Negresses. Following the axis in the opposite direction reveals Vathek's retirement to a tower, a gesture of supreme isolation and transcendence of human limits. Throughout the novel, the dissatisfied hero seems to be constantly either climbing toward the absolutes of light, solitude, and eternal life or descending to darkness, anguish, and opulent damnation. Atop one of his flaming towers, Vathek the caliph entertains himself with the mass strangulation of his subjects; in the depths of the earth and within the Palace of Subterranean Fire Vathek embraces the sacrament of evil and joins the immense throng of the damned when he finds his heart ringed by a demonic halo of hell fire.

The Beckfordian landscape is perfectly suited to the limitless "algolagnic" fantasies that Beckford brought to the irrational pleasures of his Gothic novel. Making the pilgrimage toward damnation takes Vathek through a Gothic geography that brings the Gothic novel to the limits of perversity and splendid irrationality. Across plains of black sand, through swarms of wormwood-colored flies, past a corps of cripples and cubit-high dwarfs, and into blizzards of fiery snowflakes, Beckford's Islamic Faust makes the Gothic's first voyage of no return in his search for an infernal Xanadu. The European Faust desired power and pleasure, but Beckford's over-reacher already possesses these, "for of all men, he was the most curious" and "wished to know everything; even sciences that did not exist." [25] In Vathek's abhorrence of limits, we have an "extraordinary position" of mind or imagination, which will be encountered again in the towering physiognomies of the Gothic villains of the 1790s. The inexplicable evil of Radcliffe's Montoni and Schedoni, the diabolic stature of Lewis's Ambrosio (a Faust of sex), and the cosmic defiance of Maturin's Melmoth the Wanderer spring from Beckford's archetype of perversity.

The disgust of each of these characters for mortal and rational limits is symbolically expressed in their lethal eyes. As an image of power, the eye that slays or paralyzes resembles the all-seeing eye of God, except that its gaze is malignant and not benign. The eye of the hero-villain, a weapon first beheld in the features of Vathek, indicates the character's desire for a visionary penetration that is beyond normal notions of good and evil. Although the face of Walpole's Manfred is never described, the second great hero-villain of Gothic literature has the mighty eye that is the focal point for the destructive energies of so many later Gothic tormentors. Vathek's "figure was pleasing and majestic; but when he was angry, one of his eyes became so terrible, that no person could bear to behold it; and the wretch upon whom it was fixed instantly fell backward, and sometimes expired." [26] What is sublime in the makeup of the Gothic hero-villain is also at the same time injurious or deadly. Thus, Burke's idea of horrid beauty is concentrated in the awesome eye of Vathek, whose mysterious potential and supernatural faculties cannot be understood or even tolerated by merely human glances.

At a midpoint between the wild, progressive Gothicism of Beckford's *Vathek* and the tame, regressive Gothicism of Clara Reeve's *Old English Baron* falls the talented shadow of Ann Radcliffe. Copied, parodied, and finally overthrown by the bloodstained pens of the writers of *Schauer-romantik* Gothic, the five novels published by Radcliffe between 1789 and 1797 determined the course of the Gothic movement during its mature phase. While her Italianate villains remain terrible and terrifying figures, she relegates them to the penumbra of the plot, choosing to let the spotlight of fear fall upon the anxieties of the heroine, whose phobic imagination and neurotic self-victimization become the central concerns of the reader. The frightened orphan of *The Mysteries of Udolpho* (1794), Emily St. Aubert, and the hypersensitive victim of monastic imprisonment in *The Italian* (1797), Ellena di Rosalba, are Gothic literature's first unreliable observers, a concept of characterization that is fundamental to the power of Radcliffean Gothic. Each maiden is a psychologized extension of the pursued Isabella, whose primary function in the labyrinth of Otranto had been to scream as she groped her way out of the haunted castle and into the rescuing arms of young Theodore. On the conscious level, Radcliffe's heroines desire the same safety and freedom from the supernatural snares of the castle as Isabella, but on the imaginative and unconscious levels her entrapped virgins welcome the opportunity to embrace the terror that surrounds them. The type of neurotic intelligence that eagerly converts natural phenomena into supernatural Gothic stimuli was Mrs. Radcliffe's special achievement in the Gothic field. Using Walpole's Isabella as a physical model and Richardson's Clarissa as a psychological model, she donated to the adulthood of the Gothic novel in the 1790s one of its most permanent, stock figures: the quaking silhouette of the perturbed maiden subjecting herself to those very same dismal journeys and appalling incarcerations from which she shrinks in dread.

Much of the atmospheric power of *The Mysteries of Udolpho* is the result of what Emily St. Aubert's haunted mind does with the morbid data placed at its disposal. In her vicarious involvement with the dark, irrational Gothic world, Emily imagines suffering at the hands of the villain, Montoni, at his foreboding castle in the distant Appenines, and faints dead away when faced by the horror of the black veil in one of Udolpho's dimly illuminated chambers. Her hyperemotional responses illustrate perfectly the methods of Radcliffean novel making. This is gradual Gothic. It uses an illusory supernatural to provoke suspense and terror and to heighten the peculiar pleasure or overpowering awe that is felt in the presence of the unknown or unknowable. Of authentic aggression, there is very little in the leisurely plots of Radcliffe, although the crepuscular monk, Schedoni, in *The Italian* comes very close to killing Ellena di Rosalba until she is revealed to be his niece; of unsolved mystery there is nothing at the end of each story as Mrs. Radcliffe devised a technique of prolonging maidenly terror through the mistaken apprehension of a nervous observer who, in the words of Emily's dying father, "is continually extracting the excess of misery or delight from every surrounding circumstance." [27]

The central method of Radcliffean Gothic is to coax the reader with supernatural events, which produce fainting, weeping, or panic in the hedonist-hysteric heroine; many pages after the events, the author then reduces the causes of terror to the natural, the normal, and the probable. In a modern edition of *The Mysteries of Udolpho*, Emily St. Aubert peers behind the black veil on page 248 and promptly falls into a prostrate stupor, but what she sees is not disclosed until page 662. The unspeakably hideous is finally unveiled as a false appearance, but only after 414 pages of intervening suspense for both heroine and reader. This procedure of "explained Gothic" remained an attractive formula for those Gothic novelists who were repelled by the loathsome supernatural of Beckfordian and *Schauer-romantik* schools and who wished to emphasize the psychology of terror rather than the physiology of horror. Late in her career and after Gothicism had ebbed, Radcliffe differentiated between the words *terror* and *horror,* terms that are sometimes used synonymously but should not be. "Terror and horror," she asserted in an essay published posthumously in 1826, "are so far opposite, that the first expands the soul, and awakens the faculties to a high degree of life; the other contracts, freezes, and nearly annihilates them. . . . And where lies the great difference between horror and terror, but in uncertainty and obscurity, that accompany the first, respecting the dreader evil?" [28]

The hedonist-hysteric heroine believes in the religious possibilities of terror. Her perturbed intellect or unregulated imagination is nourished by neurosis and anticipates with pleasure the very worst of fates for itself behind the massive walls of a gloomy fortress. Emily St. Aubert approaches Montoni's Castle di Udolpho in a state of mind that is very near to that of religious reverie before the portals of a temple or shrine. For the many followers and imitators of the Radcliffean Gothic novel, such a contemplative or poetic trance before the facade of the haunted castle is a mandatory moment of high terror and soul expansion:

> Emily gazed with melancholy awe upon the castle, which she understood to be Montoni's; for, though it was now lighted up by the setting sun, the gothic greatness of its features, and its mouldering walls of dark grey stone, rendered it a gloomy and sublime object. . . . Silent, lonely, and sublime, it seemed to stand the sovereign of the scene, and to frown defiance on all, who dared to invade its solitary reign. As the twilight deepened, its features became more awful in obscurity, and Emily continued to gaze, till its clustering towers were alone seen, rising over the tops of the woods, beneath whose thick shade the carriages soon after began to ascend. [29]

The emotional tension between the terrible and the tantalizing is the pervasive method of Radcliffean Gothic. The original haunted castle of Walpole has been expanded by Radcliffe into an object so stupendous, so picturesque, so awesome, so poetic, and so sentient that it now overshadows all the human characters of the book. The castle prospect, which becomes a scenic test of the Gothic novelist's skill at gripping the audience through the romance of the ruin, is less a dramatic description than an elegy to the fearful delights that await the supplicant upon entrance into the Gothic world. Radcliffe did not add characters or apparatus to the developing Gothic novel, but she did magnify the landscape of the soul through her eerie topographies and dark skylines of castellated nightmare.

Because of their lingering devotion to lyric moments of sublime terror, Radcliffean Gothics appear almost static when compared with the dramatic velocity and overt horror of Matthew Lewis's *The Monk* (1796), the *ne plus ultra* Gothic novel of the eighteenth century. Its turbulent abominations and notorious pursuit of some ideal of the hideous place the work at the very center of the *Schauer-romantik* Gothic. Bleeding nuns, decaying infants, violent matricide, subterranean fornication, nauseous vaults, sepulchral rape, inquisitorial torture, a satanic femme fatale, and the spectacular immolation of the Monk himself highlight the novel's drastic inventory of relentless horror. In a repudiation of the gentler Gothic of Radcliffe, *The Monk* has no mysteries, no nerve-wracking suspense, no pretended supernatural, and no pity for its sufferers and sinners. By ignoring all the subtler ways of terror, Lewis altered the course of the Gothic novel and completed the transition to the demonic-irrational begun by Beckford. In shifting the emphasis from terror to horror in the mid-1790s, Lewis packed into his book all the lethal luggage that previous Gothic novels had contained, while inserting some unique diablerie of his own concoction; he thereby transformed the English Gothic novel into something very close to the violent *Sturm und Drang* (or storm and stress) romanticism of the German romancers he had encountered while residing at Weimar in 1792. To the Beckfordian elements of soul-selling and devil worship, Lewis added a Wandering Jew episode; an atmosphere of explicit eroticism in which Satan's envoy, the wicked Matilda, is consistently presented as a demon of carnal desire; and the annihilation of a convent by an enraged mob in a scene suggestive of the politics of the revolutionary era.

The revolutionary fury of the masses is an energy no less brutal than the despotic force of church and state. What officially disturbed but secretly delighted *The Monk*'s international audience was the novel's cataclysmic portrayal of both the old order and the new. Neither tragic action nor a positive sense of self were possible in the chaotic gap between the two zeitgeists; only the extreme Gothicism of the *Schauer-romantik* could express such captivity of individual spirit. In Ambrosio, the monk, Lewis gave his readers a Gothic hero-villain; the character represents frustration of body and soul in the face of a universe where God has failed and Satan has become equally unacceptable as a surrogate divinity.

Anticlericalism—or more precisely, an indictment of the Catholic Church—had scarcely been visible in the English Gothic novel before

Lewis's work. Maidens had usually been locked away in haunted castles, not in cathedral catacombs. With *The Monk*, the dehumanizing influence of monastic office, the harsh training of Catholic clergy, the dark power of an exclusive social institution, and the warping of the personality by the misdirection of the passions all enter the bloodstream of the Gothic novel as Lewis skillfully manipulates the ecclesiastical environment into a general metaphor of repression. The rapid growth of evil in the protagonist is a direct consequence of the blockading of Ambrosio's natural self by the institution to which he is chained. Between the "exterior sanctity" [30] of his saintly but hypocritical public self and the "culpable emotions" [31] of his innermost being there is no moderating personality that can manage the contradictory drives of his lacerated nature. Yet Ambrosio is not evil incarnate, but rather goodness aborted and greatness twisted. Where the insular motivations of Beckford's Vathek are hardly depicted at all and where Radcliffe's Gothic hero-villains are distanced and obscured, Lewis advanced the psychological excitement inherent in Gothic villainy and exposed the reader to the torn mind and soul of this strange and terrible creature.

In short, *The Monk* is not merely the first significant monastic shocker on the English Gothic scene; it is also a narrative in which metaphysical horror shares a place beside physical shock and disgust. This is achieved by its element of psychomachia, or battle within the soul of the Gothic hero, which has a horrific effect upon the reader almost as powerful as the novel's repulsive situations and supernatural haberdashery. According to Lewis's behavioral theory, Ambrosio's internal conflict involves a "contest for superiority between his real and acquired character." On this Gothic battleground, "the different sentiments with which education and nature had inspired him, were combating in his bosom: it remained for his passions, which as yet no opportunity had called into play, to decide the victory." [32] In the hands of Matthew Lewis, the Gothic proved that it could accommodate the psychological depth later to be seen in the mature Gothic of Maturin and the Shelleys in England and Poe and Hawthorne in America.

Lewis's ugly eroticism, his sadistic picture of society, and his allegiance to supernatural horror became the accepted conventions of Gothic fiction after the publication of *The Monk* in 1796. The theme of evil is tied in to a crisis within the self that Lewis chose to portray in terms of an eruptive sexuality in the main character, which could end only in homicide or suicide or both. Ambrosio's denied self begins to stir early in the novel with his lecherous contemplation of the Madonna after whom he lusts. It is clear even before the Monk has committed any of his gruesome crimes against women that he is victimized by his own unconscious appetites. For the religious ideal of devotion to spirit, Lewis substitutes adulation of flesh; at the same time he places Ambrosio in an "extraordinary position" of mind, against which the artificial morality of the Monk's upbringing is no defense.

In stark contrast to the eerie underground settings of the terror-Gothic as practiced by Radcliffe and her followers, *The Monk*'s subterranean milieu conducts the reader to the horror of horrors, which Radcliffe had been reluctant to expose. Both the sepulchral rape of Antonia and the ghastly incarceration of the pregnant nun, Agnes, are reported in sickening detail and with a sort of putrid precision, which has moved a modern critic to conclude that Lewis's implicit aim must have been "some ideal of absolute atrocity." [33] The vague thrills of Radcliffean darkness give way to the slimy stench of premature burial in the vaults of the convent. Here Ambrosio violates and murders his own sister upon a mattress of cadavers and here Agnes—like Poe's anonymous victim of the Inquisition in "The Pit and the Pendulum"—lies "sick sick unto the death" [34] amid the corpses of previous victims. Crudely, audaciously, Lewis puts the reader into contact with the *Schauer-romantik* ideal at its point of maximum disgust and horrid shock; we seem finally to touch the extreme limit of the physical Gothic in the ordeal of Agnes in an underground of no return:

> Four low narrow walls confined me. The top was also covered, and in it was fitted a small grated door, through which was admitted the little air that circulated in this miserable place. A faint glimmering of light, which streamed through the bars, permitted me to distinguish the surrounding horrors. I was oppressed by a noisome suffocating smell; and perceiving that the grated door was unfastened, I thought that I might possibly effect my escape. As I raised myself with this design, my hand rested upon something soft: I grasped it, and advanced it toward the light. Almighty God! What was my disgust! my consternation! In spite of its putridity, and the worms which preyed upon it, I perceived a corrupted human head, and recognized the features of a nun who had died some months before. I threw it from me, and sank almost lifeless upon my bier. [35]

At its nihilistic extreme, this is no-exit or *Burgverliess* Gothic, in which the fine sensibilities of the innocent maidens, Agnes and Antonia, cannot save them from the worst of deaths in the Gothic depths. Equally shocking and equally alluring as a Gothic death to the makers of the *Schauer-roman* is the destruction of Ambrosio. To counterbalance the sensational agonies of the two innocents who meet Gothic death in the depths, Lewis moves imaginatively to the opposite extreme of the axis of horror—toward an apex of supernatural anguish that gave to the horror-Gothic a new horizon of ruthlessness. Ambrosio's punishment and execution take place on an Olympian scale; Lewis gives his novel a mythic climax in the sky and a celestial fall of the Gothic hero that brings the Gothic novel to a new peak of horror. Originally, it had been Satan who was expelled from heaven by God; in Lewis's Gothic version of the myth of damnation, it is Satan himself who casts the Gothic Everyman from the sky. It is the best Gothic finale thus far in the history of the form, a summit of supernatural horror often imitated but never duplicated by the fiend-mongers of the *Schauer-romantik* school.

The Monk's spectacular *Götterdämmerung* offered future Gothicists the epit-

ome of "extraordinary positions." From a precipice on a remote mountain-
top in the Sierra Morena, Lucifer "darts his talons into the monk's shaven
crown," soars heavenward with his screaming prey, and at the pinnacle of
pain, releases his sinful cargo to finish the saga of self-eradication on the
pointed rocks below. There is a larger-than-life quality in the Promethean
position that Lewis's virile rebel assumes at the novel's quasi-epic ending,
here quoted in part:

> Headlong fell the monk through the airy waste; the sharp point of a rock received
> him; and he rolled from precipice to precipice, till, bruised and mangled, he rest-
> ed on the river's banks. . . . The sun now rose above the horizon; its scorching
> beams darted full upon the head of the expiring sinner. Myriads of insects were
> called forth by the warmth; they drank the blood which trickled from Ambrosio's
> wounds; he had no power to drive them from him, and they fastened upon his
> sores, darted their stings into his body, covered him with their multitudes, and in-
> flicted on him tortures the most exquisite and insupportable. The eagles of the
> rock tore his flesh piecemeal, and dug out his eyeballs with their crooked beaks. A
> burning thirst tormented him; he heard the river's murmur as it rolled beside
> him, but strove in vain to drag himself toward the sound. For six miserable days
> did the villain languish. On the seventh a violent storm arose; the winds in fury
> rent up rocks and forests; the sky was now black with clouds, now sheeted with
> fire; the rain fell in torrents; it swelled the stream; the waves overflowed their
> banks; they reached the spot where Ambrosio lay, and, when they abated, carried
> with them into the river the corpse of the despairing Monk. [36]

In the wake of the shock waves generated by the outrageous horror of *The
Monk,* the Gothic novel discarded its sophisticated veneer, severed most of its
relations with the gentler novels of sensibility, and "dared to be popular" [37]
at the expense of high seriousness and artistic respectability.

The Monk was pirated, parodied, and appropriated by the shilling-shocker
industry, whose tawdry imitations glutted the bookstalls as the century drew
to a close. [38] *Almagro and Claude; or, Monastic Murder Exemplified in the Dreadful
Doom of an Unfortunate Nun* (1803) and *Don Sancho; or, The Monk of Hennares: A
Spanish Romance* (1803) are typical anonymous bluebook annexations of portions of Lewis's thunderous plot. *Almagro and Claude* reduces the entire novel
to 40 blunt pages; the chapbook brings Ambrosio from false holiness to true
damnation in a four-page epilogue after sketching the miseries of Agnes under the altered name of Almagro in its main section. Women readers with an
appetite for female diabolism, like Jane Austen's Catherine Morland in
Northanger Abbey, could revel in such titles as *Rosario; or, The Female Monk,* an
adaptation that tells the story of Ambrosio's damnation from the wicked
woman's point of view. By 1798, a brutal and expert burlesque entitled *The
New Monk: A Romance,* by R. S. (possibly the Gothic novelist, Richard Sickelmore), cleared the way for future Gothic parodies. *The New Monk* is a precise,
paragraph-by-paragraph, satiric dismantling of Lewis's Gothic novel, but
like Jane Austen's spoof on the excesses of the Radcliffean heroine in *North-*

anger Abbey (written in 1798 at the height of the Gothic mania, but not published until after her death in 1818), R. S.'s lampoon honors what it mocks by containing several scenes of genuinely Gothic force, rather than the Gothic farce it might appear to be if read out of context.

The shilling-shocker dilutions of *The Monk* cheapened the reputation of the Gothic novel, making it a candidate for *fin de siècle* extinction. But contrary to their anticipated decline, the rival Gothics of Lewis and Mrs. Radcliffe persisted and kept the Gothic flame burning high throughout the opening decade of the nineteenth century. In his study, "How Long Was Gothic Fiction in Vogue?" Robert D. Mayo tells us that both brands of Gothicism "enjoyed popularity and fully maintained, if [they] did not increase, [their] audience for about a decade after Mrs. Radcliffe's last novel. [Mayo refers here to *The Italian* (1797).] When the vogue did show signs of abatement in 1807, it was yet half a dozen years before interest may be said to have generally lapsed." [39] Thus, 35 years after Walpole had opened the portals of the haunted castle, Gothic readers and writers were still eagerly crowding through its ponderous jaws.

As the century changed, Gothic fiction obstinately refused to give way to more temperate expressions of romanticism. Too many readers had grown accustomed to the Gothic formula to return to the meeker delights of sentimental fiction. Instead they almost seemed to demand repeated doses of the elixirs of terror and horror in spite of the fact that invention or any kind of technical orginality became practically impossible after the achievements of Ann Radcliffe and Monk Lewis. But originality was apparently the last quality that the Gothic readership desired or expected; for the first time in literary history, a reader-cartel had come to dictate both the quantity and the quality of its reading fare and insisted that the product be manufactured with a cloying sameness. Shelley was well aware of the rigidities of taste that still prevailed among the Gothic readership when he wrote to the publisher, Stockdale, of his own Gothic effort, *St. Irvyne; or, The Rosicrucian* (1811), stating that his book was "a thing which almost *mechanically* sells to circulating libraries." [40]

The rampant commercialization of Gothicism after 1800 did not prevent a few Gothic authors from attaining dignity of form and originality of style if not of theme in their Gothic experiments. Along with Shelley's remarkable pair of inspired Gothics, *Zastrozzi* (1810) and *St. Irvyne*, Mary Shelley's *Frankenstein; or, The Modern Prometheus* (1818) and Maturin's *Melmoth the Wanderer* (1820) both transcend the lax and shoddy standards imposed upon Gothic writers by Gothic readers during the decadent phase of Gothicism. The Gothic work of the Shelleys and Maturin's epic Gothic, however, were not typical. As the Gothic novel deteriorated from triple-decked or multi-volumed romance bound between expensive and occasionally elegant boards into flimsy novelettes on graying paper and in gaudy wrappings, it was evident that the Gothic novel's clientele would accept almost anything under the stereotyped rubrics of terror or horror, especially if priced below a single shilling.

As artistic standards declined and public taste refused to grow jaded, raucous Gothic titles spread like flowers of evil planted by rapacious publishers across the literary landscape. The harvest of horror was bountiful, as shown in such English bluebooks as *The Bloody Hand; or, the Fatal Cup: A Tale of Horror* (circa 1800) and *The Wandering Spirit; or, The Memoirs of the House of Morno* (1802). Not to be outdone, the German Goths specialized in ghastly and terrific titles that held forth the ultimate Gothic gratification. Two lurid examples are worth citing for their Teutonic ingenuity: *Die Totenfackel; oder, Die Höhle der Siebenschläfer (The Torch of Death; or, The Cave of The Seven Sleepers)* (1798) and *Udo der Stählerne; oder, Die Ruinen von Drudenstein (Udo, the Man of Steel; or, The Ruins of Drudenstein)* (1799). Given the excessive availability of such Gothic delicacies, it hardly seems necessary for Jane Austen's Catherine Morland to ask, as she does of the Gothic reading list presented to her by Isabella Thorpe, "But are they all horrid? Are you sure they are all horrid?" [41]

The uncritical addiction of such readers as the palpitating Catherine Morland to anything Gothic explains why the Gothic industry was always busy and why supply could never seem to keep up with demand. But in spite of its profitable popularity, the Gothic novel after 1800 contained the seeds of its own demise. The fact that the trends in literature seemed to be "all horrid" was a source of irritation to the more serious romantics, who were trying to recruit and re-educate the neoclassic audience at the end of the eighteenth century and found themselves losing the contest for attention to the absurdities and banalities of the Gothic novelists. In his preface to the second edition of *The Lyrical Ballads* (1800), Wordsworth interrupted his discourse on the aims of poetry to level a complaint against the hordes of "frantic novels" that pandered to the "degrading thirst after outrageous stimulation." [42] What Wordsworth did not realize in his romantic manifesto was that the despised Gothic novels were simply another manifestation of "the spontaneous overflow of powerful feelings," Wordsworth's famous definition of poetry. [43] No doubt, the Gothic phenomenon should be viewed as an exceptional but valid case of such overflow, since its powerful feelings were often sexual or psychopathic, but rarely, if ever, "recollected in tranquility." [44] Other romantics sounded the death knell of the Gothic as an independent form. In a lighter vein, Lord Byron undermined the haunted castle with this neat excoriation of his friend, Monk Lewis, in *English Bards and Scotch Reviewers* (1809):

> Oh! wonder-working Lewis! monk, or bard,
> Who fain wouldst make Parnassus a churchyard!
> Lo! wreaths of yew, not laurel, bind thy brow,
> Thy muse a sprite, Apollo's sexton thou!

Whether on ancient tombs thou tak'st thy stand,
By gibb'ring spectres hail'd, thy kindred band;
Or tracest chaste descriptions on thy page,
To please the females of our modest age;
All hail, M.P.! from whose infernal brain
Thin-sheeted phantoms glide, a grisly train; . . .
Again all hail! if tales like thine may please,
St. Luke alone can vanquish the disease;
Even Satan's self with thee might dread to dwell,
And in thy skull discern a deeper hell. [45]

Neither Wordsworth's mordant complaints nor Byron's stinging jollity could by themselves "vanquish the disease" of Gothicism. It continued to thrive like a stubborn literary fungus in the forest of romanticism for at least another decade. Yet dissenting attitudes like these were beginning to force a shift away from the dissipated diversions fostered by horror for horror's sake.

Despite their official enmity, the major romantic poets recognized in the Gothic novel a powerful imaginative tool; Byron, Coleridge, Shelley, Southey, and even Wordsworth found themselves exploring the forbidden energies of this supposedly obsolete form. Obsessed with the disharmonious grandeur of the Gothic universe, Byron himself borrowed the name of the first hero-villain of the first Gothic novel when he entitled his Faustian drama *Manfred* (1816). The first scene of the first act is placed in "a Gothic gallery" where Manfred broods upon "The burning wreck of a demolish'd world,/A wandering hell in the eternal space." [46] Such heroic pessimism clearly owes both its imagery and its philosophy to the dark and fragmented outlook of the Gothic novelists. Others followed Byron's lead and plundered the haunted castle for ideas, language, characters, and settings. In *The Bride of Lammermoor* (1819), Sir Walter Scott christens his gloomy hero Ravenswood, attaches him physically and psychologically to a decaying tower named Wolf's Crag, and has Ravenswood gallop to his death in the quicksand. In *Kenilworth* (1821), also by Scott, the beautiful Amy Robsart is shut away from the world's eyes in the medieval manor house of Cumnor Hall, where she is vigorously persecuted by Sir Richard Varney and driven to a violent death. Scott's reproductions of Gothic stage business and character psychology argue strongly that the English Gothic novel never did experience a final spasm and death, but continued to develop; it submerged itself first in the visions of the romantics and then in the austere social realism of the Victorian poets and novelists, where it continued to surface with its customary sinister energy as both symbol and fact of the dark enigmas of existence.

In the 60 prolific years between Leland's *Longsword* and Maturin's *Melmoth the Wanderer* the Gothic novel had gone from ingenious prototype to lethargic stereotype, a pattern of growth and deterioration similar to many other literary movements. Yet, in the historical respect, the Gothic novel had a luckier aftermath than many other genres, for it never has known obsolescence and never will go out of fashion. The bones of the Gothic novel may lie securely in the graveyard of literary history in one thousand unmarked caskets, but the Gothic spirit continues to range freely beyond its literary grave to invade and reshape our brightest literary dreams. To the opening of these unmarked caskets, the bibliography now devotes itself.

A Postscript (but Not an Epitaph)

Thus the Gothic novel lingered on, like some aged saurian that had managed to survive the heyday of the giant reptiles, while all around it the climate was slowly changing. A new spirit of Cockney realism had begun to illuminate the English novel, and as it gained brilliance, the specters of Gothic fancy flickered and paled and dissolved, at last, into broad Victorian daylight. [47]

Notes

1. Robert K. Black, "The Sadleir-Black Gothic Collection: An Address before the Bibliographical Society of the University of Virginia on May 12, 1949," printed as a pamphlet by the Alderman Library of the University of Virginia, Charlottesville, Va., 1949, p. 14. Black purchased the Sadleir Gothics in 1937 and in 1942 donated the collection to the University of Virginia, where it has continued to grow.

2. There have been three noteworthy attempts in the twentieth century to produce a primary bibliography of the Gothic novel. These are: Jakob Brauchli, *Der Englische Schauer-roman um 1800, Unter Berücksichtigung der unbekannten Bücher: Ein Beitrag zur Geschichte der Volksliteratur* (Weida: Thomas & Hubert, 1928) *[The English Schauer-roman around 1800, Together with a Consideration of the Unknown Books; A Contribution to the History of Popular Literature]*; Montague Summers, *A Gothic Bibliography* (London: Fortune, 1941; rpt. New York: Russell & Russell, 1964); and Maurice Lévy's excellent "Bibliographie chronologique du roman 'gothique' 1764–1824" ["Chronological Bibliography of the Gothic Novel"] appearing as an appendix in his *Le Roman "gothique" anglais 1764–1824 [The English Gothic Novel 1764–1824]* (Toulouse: Association des Publications de la Faculté des Lettres et Sciences Humaines de Toulouse, 1968), pp. 684–708. It is an irony of bibliographical endeavor that the modern Gothic now has a full and annotated bibliography of its own while the eighteenth-century Gothic novel has not received annotated attention until the present bibliography. See Elsa J. Radcliffe, *Gothic Novels of the Twentieth Century: An Annotated Bibliography* (Metuchen, N.J.: Scarecrow, 1979).

3. The full-length histories of the Gothic novel are: Dorothy Scarborough, *The Supernatural in Modern English Fiction* (New York: Putnam, 1917; rpt. New York: Octagon, 1967); Edith Birkhead, *The Tale of Terror: A Study of the Gothic Romance* (London: Constable, 1921; rpt. New York: Russell & Russell, 1963); Eino Railo, *The Haunted Castle: A Study of the Elements of English Romanticism* (London: Routledge & Kegan Paul, 1927; rpt. New York: Humanities Press, 1964); Montague Summers, *The Gothic Quest: A History of the Gothic Novel* (London: Fortune,1938; rpt. New York: Russell & Russell, 1964); Devendra P. Varma, *The Gothic Flame,*

Being a History of the Gothic Novel in England: Its Origins, Efflorescence, Disintegration, and Residuary Influences (London: A. Barker, 1957; rpt. New York: Russell & Russell, 1966); Robert D. Mayo, *The English Novel in the Magazines, 1740–1815, with a Catalogue of 1375 Magazine Novels and Novelettes* (Evanston, Ill.: Northwestern Univ. Press, 1962); Maurice Lévy, *Le Roman "gothique" anglais, 1764–1824* (Toulouse: Association des Publications de la Faculté des Lettres et Sciences Humaines de Toulouse, 1968); Coral Ann Howells, *Love, Mystery, and Misery: Feeling in Gothic Fiction* (New York: Humanities Press, 1979); Elizabeth MacAndrew, *The Gothic Tradition in Fiction* (New York: Columbia Univ. Press, 1979).

Secondary bibliographies of scholarship on the Gothic novel excel in thoroughness and number the work done on primary Gothic sources. The major bibliographies of Gothic criticism are: Richard P. Benton, "The Problems of Literary Gothicism," *Emerson Society Quarterly* 17 (1972), 5–9; Frederick S. Frank, "The Gothic Novel: A Checklist of Modern Criticism," *Bulletin of Bibliography* 30 (1973), 45–54; Dan J. McNutt, *The Eighteenth-Century Gothic Novel: An Annotated Bibliography of Criticism and Important Texts* (New York: Garland, 1974); Benjamin Franklin Fisher IV, "Ancilla to the Gothic Tradition: A Supplementary Bibliography," *American Transcendental Quarterly* 30 (1976), 22–36; Frederick S. Frank, "The Gothic Novel: A Second Bibliography of Criticism," *Bulletin of Bibliography* 35 (1978), 1–14, 52; Kay J. Mussell, "Gothic Novels," in *Handbook of American Popular Culture,* ed. by M. Thomas Inge (Westport, Conn.: Greenwood, 1978), pp. 151–169.

4. Summers, *Gothic Quest,* pp. 239–240.

5. The Arno Press Gothic novel series contains 30 titles representing the entire spectrum of Gothicism from Leland's *Longsword, Earl of Salisbury* (1762) to William Child Green's *The Abbot of Montserrat; or, The Pool of Blood* (1826). All Arno reissues are marked with asterisks in the annotations.

6. J. M. S. Tompkins, *The Popular Novel in England, 1770–1800* (London: Constable, 1932; rpt. London: Methuen, 1969), p. 245.

7. Maurice Lévy, "English Gothic and the French Imagination: A Calendar of Translations," in *The Gothic Imagination: Essays In Dark Romanticism,* ed. by G. R. Thompson (Pullman, Wash.: Washington State Univ. Press, 1974), p. 154.

8. For a representative collection, see Peter Haining, ed., *The Shilling Shockers: Stories of Terror from the Gothic Bluebooks* (New York: St. Martin's, 1979).

9. For a comprehensive survey of Gothicism on the stage, see Bertrand Evans, *Gothic Drama from Walpole to Shelley* (Los Angeles: Univ. of California Press, 1947).

10. Horace Walpole, *The Castle of Otranto,* in *Three Gothic Novels,* ed. by Mario Praz (Harmondsworth, England: Penguin, 1973), p. 43.

11. Thomas Warton the Younger, "The Pleasures of Melancholy," in *Eighteenth Century Poetry and Prose,* ed. by Louis I. Bredvold, Alan D. McKillop, and Lois Whitney (New York: Ronald, 1956), pp. 565–566.

12. Edmund Burke, *A Philosophical Inquiry into the Origin of Our Ideas of the Sublime and Beautiful,* in *Eighteenth Century Poetry and Prose,* p. 1165.

13. Michael Sadleir, *The Northanger Novels: A Footnote to Jane Austen,* English Association Pamphlet Number 68, November 1927, p. 7.

14. Walpole, *Castle of Otranto,* p. 44.

15. Ibid., p. 40.

16. Ibid., p. 61.

17. John Milton, *Paradise Lost,* Book I, line 63.

18. William Flint Thrall, Addison Hibbard, and C. Hugh Holman, *A Handbook to Literature* (New York: Odyssey, 1960), p. 215.
19. Howard Phillips Lovecraft, *Supernatural Horror in Literature* (New York: Ben Abramson, 1945; rpt. New York: Dover, 1973), p. 15. In its original form, Lovecraft's long monograph appeared in *The Recluse*, a very short-lived periodical, in 1927.
20. G. Richard Thompson, *Romantic Gothic Tales, 1790–1840* (New York: Harper & Row, 1979), pp. 6–7.
21. Samuel Richardson, *Clarissa; or, The History of a Young Lady* in *The Works of Samuel Richardson*, ed. by Sir Leslie Stephen (London: Henry Sotheran, 1884), IV, 337.
22. Ibid., V, 72.
23. Ibid., V, 400.
24. Clara Reeve, *The Old English Baron: A Gothic Story*, in *Seven Masterpieces of Gothic Horror*, ed. by Robert D. Spector (New York: Bantam, 1963), p. 106.
25. William Beckford, *Vathek*, in *Three Gothic Novels* (Harmondsworth, England: Penguin, 1973), pp. 152–153.
26. Ibid., p. 151.
27. Mrs. Ann Radcliffe, *The Mysteries of Udolpho: A Romance, Interspersed with Some Pieces of Poetry*, ed. by Frederick Garber (New York: Oxford Univ. Press, 1970), pp. 79–80.
28. Mrs. Ann Radcliffe, "On the Supernatural in Poetry," *New Monthly Magazine* 7 (1826), 147.
29. Radcliffe, *Udolpho*, pp. 226–227.
30. Matthew Gregory Lewis, *The Monk* (New York: Grove Press, 1952), p. 229.
31. Ibid., p. 88.
32. Ibid., p. 239.
33. Leslie Fiedler, *Love and Death in the American Novel* (New York: Criterion, 1960), p. 115.
34. Edgar Allan Poe, "The Pit and the Pendulum," in *Edgar Allan Poe: Selected Writings*, ed. by David Galloway (Harmondsworth, England: Penguin, 1975), p. 261.
35. Lewis, *Monk*, p. 385.
36. Ibid., pp. 419–420.
37. John Garrett, "The Eternal Appeal of the Gothic," *Sphinx: A Magazine of Literature and Society* 2 (1977), 5.
38. See the brief, witty study of the Gothic bluebook trade by William Whyte Watt, *Shilling Shockers of the Gothic School: A Study of Chapbook Gothic Romances* (Cambridge, Mass.: Harvard Univ. Press, 1932; rpt. New York: Russell & Russell, 1967).
39. Robert D. Mayo, "How Long Was Gothic Fiction in Vogue?" *Modern Language Notes* 58 (1943), 62.
40. Percy B. Shelley, Letter to the publisher J. J. Stockdale, August 1, 1811.
41. Jane Austen, *Northanger Abbey*, ed. by Ann Ehrenpreis (Harmondsworth, England: Penguin, 1978), p. 61. The novels of the Northanger Gothic septet are: *The Castle of Wolfenbach* (1793) by Eliza Parsons; *Clermont* (1798) by Regina Maria Roche; *The Mysterious Warning* (1796) by Eliza Parsons; *The Necromancer; or, The Tale of the Black Forest* (1794) by Peter Teuthold as translated from the German of Lawrence Flammenberg; *The Midnight Bell* (1798) by Francis Lathom; *The Orphan of the Rhine* (1798) by Eleanor Sleath; and *Horrid Mysteries* (1796) by Peter Will as translated from the German of the Marquis of Grosse.
42. William Wordsworth, "Preface to the Second Edition of the *Lyrical Ballads*," in

The Complete Poetical Works of William Wordsworth (Boston: Houghton Mifflin, 1911), X, 11.

43. Ibid., X, 9.
44. Ibid., X, 31.
45. George Gordon, Lord Byron, *English Bards and Scotch Reviewers,* in *The Poetical Works of Lord Byron* (New York: Oxford Univ. Press, 1957), p. 117.
46. Byron, *Manfred: A Dramatic Poem,* in *Poetical Works of Byron,* p. 390.
47. Peter Quennell, "The Moon Stood Still on Strawberry Hill," *Horizon Magazine* 11 (1969), 117.

Bibliography

Note: To allow the reader a better understanding of the evolvement of the eighteenth-century Gothic novel, the entries in this bibliography are arranged in alphabetical order by author and then in chronological order of titles under the author.

1-1. Acton, Eugenia de. **The Nuns of the Desert; or, The Woodland Witches.** Minerva-Press, 1805. (4)
The novel's confused plot marks an inferior attempt at scientifically explained Gothic. Eugenia de Acton's proper literary calling was the novel of manners, not Gothic fiction. Her attempt to "blend a short but consistent system of morality with probable story" proves more facetious than frightening; she includes among her bizarre cast an ape named Hindo and an articulate dog named Brimo. Following Brockden Brown's ventriloquist explanation of Carwin's powers of voice in *Wieland* [1–46], Acton tries to append similar scientific justification for her beasts' weird vocal gifts, but fails to convince. The persecutions and wanderings of the nuns have the status of slight subplot. After Mrs. Radcliffe's "Highlandization" of the Gothic in her *Castles of Athlin and Dunbayne* [1–313], a Macbethian staff of weird sisters frequently joined the religious sisters in Gothic casts. But like many domestic authors of the period who flirted with the Gothic, Eugenia de Acton lacked the serious commitment to the demonic required to make the absurd both believable and terrifying.

1-2. Albrecht, Johann Friedrich Ernst (Germany). **Dolko der Bandit, Zeitgenosse Rinaldo Rinaldinis (Dolko the Brigand, Rinaldo Rinaldini's Contemporary).** Gottfried Vollmer, 1801. (2) (SB)
The author of several anti-Catholic pamphlets, Albrecht (1752–1814) had also explored Gothic themes in *Skissen aus dem Klosterleben* (1786) *(Sketches of Monastic Life)*. *Dolko* is a robber romance that closely imitates and purports

to be a sequel to C. A. Vulpius's highly successful *Rinaldo Rinaldini, der Räu-berhauptmann* [1–390].

1–3. Alexena; or, The Castle of Santa Marco. Minerva-Press, 1817. (1) (SB)
This anonymous but technically competent Gothic joins the exciting horrors of the monastic shocker with the dark machinations of the Inquisition. The Radcliffean format of the curious maiden's perpetual distress is expanded to include three suffering heroines, Ellena, Evelene, and Alexena, who take their separate turns at sharing the predicaments and ordeals that lurk within the walls and numerous crypts of Santa Marco. The novel also offers an exquisite torture chamber, which can be reached only "through innumerable windings, and dreary passages, the floors of which were covered with sawdust, while clammy sweats covered the cold, damp walls." The usual castle tyrant and master erotic criminal, Count Baretto, is equally memorable as a villain "on whose brow every vice that disgraces man appears to have been written in legible characters."

1–4. Allard, Mary Gay (France). **Eléonore de Rosalba; ou, Le Confessional des penitents noirs (Eléonora de Rosalba; or, The Confessional of the Black Penitents).** J. J. Paschoud, 1797. (6)
The English Gothic novel was translated with incredible rapidity by French translators, who sometimes condensed their English sources. Such is the case with this hasty translation of Mrs. Ann Radcliffe's *The Italian; or, The Confessional of the Black Penitents* [1–317]. The vulture-eyed monk, Schedoni, with the death's head upon his sleeve, as well as Ellena di Rosalba's enforced sojourn with the convent, had a strong appeal for the French Gothic audience.

1–5. Almagro and Claude; or, Monastic Murder, Exemplified in the Dreadful Doom of an Unfortunate Nun. Dean & Munday, 1803. (5)
A short and shocking pulp Gothic, this is a typical anonymous abridgement in bluebook form of Lewis's *The Monk* [1–218]. The original lovers and victims of monkish intrigue, Raymond and Agnes, have been altered to Almagro and Claude while the Ambrosio story of sexual temptation, soul-selling, and aerial damnation is detached and featured in a brusque four-page epilogue to bring the bluebook up to the publisher's required quota of 40 pages.

1–6. Andrews, Charles. **The Spectre.** John Stockdale, 1789. (4)
An epistolary Gothic consisting of 52 letters, *The Spectre* is a gentle love story in Gothic guise. The spectre that appears to young Hilmot throughout the romance is an amorous and lovesick, rather than avenging, spirit. In a belated and well-timed revelation scene, the pursuing specter reveals itself to be a young woman who is bent upon proving her devotion to young Hilmot by adapting her ingenious Gothic disguise to advance her love. There are sa-

tiric elements here as well as a delicate handling of the standard blood-curdling encounter with the female demon.

1-7. Andrews, Miles Peter. **The Mysteries of the Castle: A Dramatic Tale in Three Acts.** T. N. Longman, 1795. (1) (SB)

A copy of this operatic dramatization of Mrs. Ann Radcliffe's *The Mysteries of Udolpho* [1–316] is to be found in the Larpent Collection of Gothic drama in the Henry Huntington Library. First acted at Covent Garden in January 1795, the Gothic opera shows Andrews's irrepressible wit in its odd mixture of terror and buffoonery. As in Gilbert and Sullivan's *Ruddigore,* Andrews mocks the absurd devices of Gothic melodrama, but from the point of view of the insider. While the gloomy Count Montoni survives intact from the Radcliffean source, Andrews's addition of the characters Hilario and Julia and his location of some of the action in Calabria indicate how fast and loose was the dramatist's resetting of *Udolpho.* Andrews had already shown his talent for Gothic burlesque in his absurd musicale of 1781, *The Baron of Kinkvervankotsdorsprakingatchdern.*

1-8. The Animated Skeleton. Minerva-Press, 1798. (1)

An above-average specimen of explained supernatural, *The Animated Skeleton* quickly attracted an illustrated French translation by André Cantwell. Count Albert, who believes that he has assassinated his rival, Count Richard, is disturbed by strange noises that emanate from certain remote chambers in an abandoned wing of his château. Determined to discover the cause of these sounds, he explores the sealed wing somewhat in the manner of the curious maiden in her explorations of the castle interior. Perceiving a reddish fire from a charcoal furnace, he probes the burning mystery, only to find himself gripped by the bony hand of a skeleton. Later, the artificial "ghost" of Count Richard appears to explain this gory event. He had only pretended to swallow the poisoned cup. The ambulant skeleton was the body of his valet mechanically rigged to terrify Count Albert into confession and repentance. Cantwell's translation [1–54] improves the Gothic effects by compressing the story.

1-9. The Apparition. Hookham, 1788. (1)

A heritage of horror stalks an ancient family in this early Gothic novel, which seems to derive its formula of the avenging ghost of the castle from Clara Reeve's *The Old English Baron* [1–322].

1-10. Arnold, Samuel James, Jr. **The Creole; or, The Haunted Island.** C. Law, Hookham & Bell, 1796. (4)

Arnold was primarily a playwright who specialized in sentimental melodrama. His single attempt at Gothic fiction is an interesting experiment at generating Gothic moods in a tropical Caribbean setting. Believing that he has found an island paradise, the English explorer quickly learns that he has strayed into the Gothic world instead. The forbidding gloom and exotically

eerie landscapes of the faraway and menacing beauty of the island anticipate the Gothicism of Conrad in the twentieth century.

*1-11. Austen, Jane. **Northanger Abbey.** John Murray, 1818; Penguin,
1978. (4)
Northanger Abbey is a superb spoof and posthumous lampoon (published the
year after Jane Austen's death) of the manufactured hysterias of a would-be
Radcliffean heroine. The satire is aimed more at the naïveté of novel readers
than at the writers of the Radcliffean school of the 1790s. Various passages
even suggest that Jane Austen might have written an excellent Gothic novel
herself had she been so inclined. Her heroine, Catherine Morland, becomes
enamored of the Gothic romance while on holiday in Bath when she is given
a beginner's reading list of up-to-date Gothics by Isabella Thorpe. Immediately infatuated by the ordeals of the distressed maidens in *Udolpho* [1–316],
The Orphan of the Rhine [1–358], *Clermont* [1–325], and others, Catherine proceeds to formulate her life as if she were a persecuted maiden in the pages of
a Gothic romance. She accompanies the Tilneys (General Tilney nearly becomes Montoni's double in her imaginative eye) to Northanger Abbey,
where she insists upon behaving like a frightened female prisoner within a
haunted castle even though the Abbey is modern, elegant, and well lighted.
By dead of night she discovers a mysterious manuscript; by light of day she
gazes not upon a bloodstained parchment but upon someone's overlooked
laundry list. Finally de-Gothified and punished for her Radcliffean imaginings, Catherine completes her self-education by renouncing the Gothic view
of life and turning from sensibility to good sense. Jane Austen's expert de-
bunking of the Gothic is never vitriolic and shows a close knowledge of the
prevalent Gothic styles of the 1790s.

**1-12. The Avenger; or, The Sicilian Vespers: A Romance of the
Thirteenth Century.** J. J. Stockdale, 1810. (5) (SB)
The unknown author of *The Avenger* was aggressively honest in his preface in
asserting his money-making motives. "Latterly," wrote the Gothic profiteer,
"the demand in the market for ghosts, necromancy, and murders, has so
much increased, that the romance has become by far the most profitable line
of business, and enables me to maintain myself, my wife, and four children,
two of them nearly grown up, in all the comforts of life, with imaginary
wretchedness." The novel itself is a routine Gothic as well as a potpourri of
"ghosts, necromancy, and murders"; it makes no effort to hide its direct borrowings from Edward Montague's 1807 thriller, *The Demon of Sicily* [1–264],
and Isaac Crookenden's *Horrible Revenge; or, The Monster of Italy!!* [1–79].

1-13. Baculard d'Arnaud, François de (France). **Euphémie; ou, Le Tri-
omphe de la réligion (Euphémie; or, The Triumph of Religion).** Lejay,
1768. (3)

Montague Summers tells us that the novels and dramas of Baculard d'Arnaud (1716–1805) "had a great influence on the development of Gothic romance. His tone is often more than a little morbid, and he reflects Young's *Night Thoughts,* Hervey's *Meditations Among the Tombs,* and the sensibility of Richardson." His horrific drama, *Les Amants malheureux; ou, le Comte de Comminge* (1764) *(The Unfortunate Lovers; or, The Count of Comminge),* served as a Gothic prelude for *Euphémie,* with its cryptic scenery and interred Trappist monks. Both *Euphémie* and *Les Amants* are dramatic pageants of dungeon atrocities and medieval Catholic intrigue and are filled with the fiendish apparatus of the monastic shockers. Plot is quite secondary to the elaborate Gothic decor and sentimental situation in *Les Amants,* in which the Count's unfeeling father imprisons him within the fetid cells of the Abbey de la Trappe. Four years later, *Euphémie* extends and heightens this familiar strain of anticlerical horror. The theatricality of the Gothic's charnel settings along with the dramatic introduction of Catholic horrors were Baculard d'Arnaud's primary contributions to the emergent Gothicism of the English.

1–14. Bage, Robert. Man as He Is. Minerva-Press, 1792. (3)
While Bage's polemical novels are only marginally Gothic in their occasional violent effects, he remains the most important and certainly the most serious novelist to be associated with Minerva-Press during the Gothic apogee of the 1790s. Written somewhat in the manner of the Victorian novel of ideas, *Man as He Is* presents a graphic picture of the profligacy of high society in London and Paris. The epistolary structure of the novel permits the interplay of radical ideas and allows Bage to air various theories of social behavior for the young man as he encounters various temptations to decency. Sir George Payne, the young initiate, has recently attained his majority and come into a large fortune. To gratify his curiosity and to test the power of his inheritance, he embarks upon a career of pleasure and dissipation. Falling in love with the high-minded Miss Coleraine, he finds both his rakish values and his selfish intentions severely tested by her forthright rejection of his suit. To win her, he must first conquer his own baser self. The Gothicism of Bage's work is chiefly a background effect and is to be detected in the dark world of metropolitan debauchery that undermines the inherent nobility of young Payne.

1–15. Bage, Robert. Hermsprong; or, Man as He Is Not. Minerva-Press, 1796; Turnstile Press, 1951. (3)
Less psychological than Godwin's *Caleb Williams* [1–128], *Hermsprong* resembles the propagandistic mode in its frontal assault on outmoded institutions and degenerate traditions. The story traces the development of an English aristocrat raised by the savages of North America. Away from the corruptive centers of civilization, he learns the lessons of sincerity and simplicity through the natural life. The artificial and superficial patterns of unnatural living receive Hermsprong's passionate criticism when he returns to his Eng-

lish homeland. Purchasing an estate in Cornwall, he finds that there can be no return to nature inside the haunted castle of the English social system. Lord Grondale, Hermsprong's avaricious neighbor, represents all that is wrong with the life of empty privilege. The ensuing rivalry between the naturally good squire and the socially depraved squire might have resulted in a series of Gothic deeds, but Bage never carries his social conflict to these limits. Grondale's daughter loves Hermsprong but also feels a loyalty to her father. Here again we find Gothic possibilities left undeveloped by Bage, whose characters stand for competing ideas rather than for competing emotions, the more usual case with the Gothic cast.

1-16. Ball, Edward. **The Black Robber: A Romance.** A. K. Newman, 1819. (2)
Also using the surname "Fitzball," Ball (1792-1873) was a notable writer of melodramas. The present title is an anglicized version of the German robber romances of Vulpius and Schiller. Ball's robber chieftain, who has been driven to a career of crime by the unjust attitude of society toward his dispossessed family, is very much in the tradition of the Byronic brigand. In fact, Byron's Conrad in his tale *The Corsair* (1814) was probably the direct model for Ball's black-clad brigand who is also a man of "one virtue and a thousand crimes."

1-17. Ballin, Rossetta. **The Statue Room: An Historical Romance.** H. D. Symonds, 1790. (4)
This historical Gothic is a weak imitation of Lee's highly successful *The Recess* [1-214]. The promising Gothic suggestion of the title is never adequately fulfilled in the narrative, since the enormous statues that fill one great chamber of Shrewsbury Castle never come alive in the prescribed Walpolesque manner, as does the colossus of Alfonso the Good in *The Castle of Otranto* [1-398]. The historical plot concerns the pathetic adventures of Adelfrida, the fictitious daughter of Henry VIII and Catherine of Aragon, who is the usual Gothic child of mischance and vengeful parents. Spurned, harassed, and eventually poisoned by the power-mad Queen Elizabeth, Adelfrida gives birth to Romelia, who inherits her mother's dark legacy. The pathetic figure of the persecuted royal exile in Gothic novels had become a prerequisite of the cast after the success of *The Recess.* Typically, the unwanted royal waif is castellated, cursed, and finally removed. Scott gives us a refreshingly moving portrayal of this well-worn situation in the imprisonment and death through a trap-door of Amy Robsart in *Kenilworth* (1821).

*1-18. Barbauld, Anne Letitia Aikin. **"Sir Bertrand"** in *Gothic Stories.* G. Nicholson, 1797; in *Gothic Tales of Terror,* ed. by Peter Haining, Taplinger, 1972. (1)
First published in 1773 and preceded by an important essay entitled "On the Pleasure Derived from Objects of Terror," the "Sir Bertrand" fragment

has sometimes been erroneously ascribed to Barbauld's husband, the Reverend Rochemont Barbauld. The greatness of the Gothic fragment lies in its attempt to generate pure terror without an over-reliance upon Walpole's machinery. And in her medieval preternaturalism, Barbauld is at least Walpole's equal if not his superior. In the fragment, a grim bell is heard by a wandering knight who turns aside to investigate "an antique mansion." Upon entering the dark building he is confronted by such Gothic experiences as the touch of a cadaverous hand and the horrid manifestation of a corpselike knight "thrusting forward the bloody stump of an arm." Finally, he gains entrance to a remote chamber where a shrouded lady, clearly an early version of a Gothic sleeping beauty, stirs in her coffin at his approach. With a kiss upon her hideously cold lips, the knight releases her from death and the scene instantly shifts to a gay feast. Here, the Gothic fragment aborts. Nevertheless, the initiation of the quester into the marvelous horrors of the strange castle culminating with his nocturnal visit to the chamber of lovely death places Barbauld's fragment squarely at the head of the tradition of feudalized Gothic.

1-19. Barnby, Mrs. **Kerwald Castle; or, The Memoirs of the Marquis des Solanges.** Maidstone, 1803. (4)
The English translation of J. A. Jullien des Boulmiers's sentimental novel of 1766, *Mémoires du Marquis des Solanges,* is an example of how a translation could sometimes Gothify a non-Gothic source. To the French plot of pleasant and idyllic country living Mrs. Barnby appended a castle, a curse, and an unspeakable family secret.

1-20. Barrett, C. F. **Douglas Castle; or, The Cell of Mystery: A Scottish Tale.** A. Neil, 1803. (5) (SB)
Of bluebook quality, this crude and confused shilling shocker appears to be a hasty blend of such Gothic ingredients as Reeve's haunted suite in *The Old English Baron* [1-322], here renamed the "Cell of Mystery," and Radcliffe's introduction of Highland materials into the Gothic marketplace in her *The Castles of Athlin and Dunbayne* [1-313]. Barrett's castle tyrant is a Gothicist's cheap copy of Macbeth; his plot is a hodgepodge of a dozen Gothic happenings. William Watt has the last word on cheap imitations such as *Douglas Castle* when he observes: "No Gothic castle was complete without its 'deserted wing.' . . . After reading a dozen shockers, we begin to realize that deserted wings are reserved for the explorations of curious heroines or rightful heirs, like Reeve's, bent on solving the mystery of a murder perpetrated by the ancestors of the current usurper."

1-21. Barrett, C. F. **The Round Tower; or, The Mysterious Witness: An Irish Legendary Tale of the Sixth Century.** Tegg & Castleman, 1803. (5) (SB)

A second Gothic bluebook by the industrious Barrett. The occurrence of the word "tower" in a title indicated the theme of the romance. In this case, we have a muddled plagiarism of Palmer's well-written and widely read tower Gothic, *The Mystery of the Black Tower* [1–288]. Like many of its garish companions, *The Round Tower* pilfers both story and characterization from a successful Gothic novel and is one of a horde of Gothic counterfeits that flooded the market during the first decade of the nineteenth century.

*1–22. Barrett, Eaton Stannard. **The Heroine; or, The Adventures of a Fair Romance Reader.** Henry Colburn, 1813; Mathews & Marrot, 1927. (4)
In contrast to Austen's gentle mockery of Gothic attitudes and readers' tastes in *Northanger Abbey* [1–11], Barrett's Gothic satire is brutal and destructive as it shows the disgust of an intelligent reader over the prolonged Gothic craze. His scatterbrained heroine, Cherry Wilkinson, who changes her name to Cherubina de Willoughby after an infectious reading of several of the right Gothic romances, has all the uncontrolled passions of Catherine Morland without any of Jane Austen's heroine's mind or wit. Not content with undercutting the absurd style and preposterous plotting of Gothic romance, Barrett took *The Heroine* almost to the limits of parody in his extended sneer at triple-decker Gothics. The plot is a crazy conglomeration of stock Gothic events and frantic phrases. Cherubina studies every male face she encounters, anxiously looking for the proper "Schedoniac contour" [1–317]. She misconstrues Covent Garden Theatre for a haunted castle and is indulged by Lady Gwyn, who willingly poses as her wicked aunt. The Gothic novel's mandatory inset story is burlesqued by the insertion of the grim memoirs of Lady Hysterica Belamour under the suitably gruesome Italianate rubric, *Il Castello di Grimgothico*. Taking up residence in Monckton Castle, which she supposes to be an abandoned chateau troubled by strange sounds and gory apparitions, Cherubina then surrounds herself with eerie tapestry and threatening architecture. Such disgust for Gothic excesses as is evident in the corrosive skill of *The Heroine* accelerated the shift in readers' attitudes back toward a fiction of normality and social usefulness.

1–23. Beauclerc, Amelia. **Eva of Cambria; or, The Fugitive Daughter.** Minerva-Press, 1810. (4)
Wrongly attributed to Emma De Lisle, *Eva of Cambria* places its action in Wales in the thirteenth century. The theme of the persecuted daughter is so heavily sentimentalized as to make the romance less Gothic than lachrymose in the manner of Mackenzie's *Julia de Rubigné* [1–235].

1–24. Beauclerc, Amelia. **The Castle of Tariffa; or, The Self-Banished Man.** B. Crosby, 1812. (4)
Like Lucas's *The Castle of Saint Donats* [1–227], Beauclerc's *The Castle of Tariffa* is a novel of domestic manners falsely advertised as a genuine Gothic by virtue of its apparently horrific title. Such sham Gothics misrepresenting their

true content were part of the stock in trade of all circulating libraries. As late as 1812, the placement of the Gothic noun "Castle" within a novel's title was a common device for catching the attention of the readership.

*1–25. Beckford, William. **Vathek: An Arabian Tale, from an Unpublished Manuscript.** J. Johnson, 1786; Penguin, 1973. (1)
With its majestically sadistic hero-villain, comic monster ghouls, doorways to damnation, Technicolor terrors, hilarious horrors, and memorable climax in the Halls of Eblis (or the Muhammadan hell), Beckford's oriental Gothic fantasy attains all the summits of absurdity, irrationality, and pleasurable anguish as encouraged by the spirit of Gothic release. Nothing short of damnation itself can satisfy the Caliph Vathek, grandson of Haroun-al-Raschid. In a perverse thrust toward heaven he builds a private tower whose chambered pinnacle is reached by 1,500 steps. He and his court delight in kicking a rolling Indian who has transformed himself into a spheroid for their sadistic amusement. At the bidding of his sorceress mother, Carathis, Vathek renounces Mohammed and immerses himself in occult pursuits. From a pit-guarding Giaour who demands an entrance fee of fifty children, Vathek discovers a portal to the subterranean palace of eternal flame, where he might behold the pre-Adamite sultans and meet Eblis himself. Obeying his megalomaniac desires, Vathek deserts his capital city of Sammarah to make his perverse pilgrimage to hell. En route to his rendezvous with the lord of the lower world, he falls in love with Nouronihar and beholds all the bizarre wonders of an unmatched Gothic underworld. These include a pyramid of skulls, reptiles with human faces, and eventually the fiery throne of Eblis. One of the prime scenes in Gothic literature occurs in the subterranean palace of fire when Vathek's breast becomes transparent and his heart is suddenly haloed with hell fire. He now faces the prospect of wandering forever with heart ablaze through the endless hallways of his own unanswered desires. Such a victory of evil over good bedazzled Gothic readers and became an important breakthrough for the form.

1–26. Beckford, William. **The Episodes of Vathek.** Swift, 1912. Tr. by Sir Frank T. Marzials. (1)
The *Episodes* are a triad of tales under the titles "The Story of Prince Alasi and the Princess Firouz-kah," "The Story of Prince Barkiarokh," and "The Story of Princess Zulkais and the Prince Kalilah." The three tales were intended as a sequel to *Vathek* [1–25] but were not translated from the French until long after Beckford's death. The sly oriental Gothicism of each tale reflects the same sort of perversity and grotesque wit to be found in Vathek's infernal pilgrimage. In its French form, the first episode had an undisguised homosexual theme—it was referred to as the *Histoire des Deux Princes* or *History of the Two Princes,* but Beckford later feminized one prince's name into Firouz-kah. Love in the tale proves fatal and corrupt as Firouz-kah, acting as a Gothic succubus, persuades Prince Alasi to renounce Mohammed and

seek damnation instead. The prospect of eternal fire, which drew the Caliph Vathek downward to Eblis, is the chief allurement for the two lovers, who choose Gothic agony over heavenly ecstasy in their Plutonian quest. The criminal temptress who lures her lover on to his damnation has ties with the wicked women of Gothic fiction, such as Matilda in *The Monk* [1–218], whose love is an invitation to perdition. The second and third episodes continue the theme of warped love that terminates in hellish urges. "Barkiarokh" is particularly pertinent for certain categories of the Gothic because of its necrophiliac content. Gazahidé, a woman abused by the degenerate Prince Barkiarokh, is sexually assaulted while in a deathlike trance. In the unfinished third episode, Princess Zulkais, who has conceived an incestuous attraction for her twin brother, Kalilah, descends into hell to consummate her desire.

1–27. Bennett, Agnes Maria. **Ellen, Countess of Castle Howel.** Minerva-Press, 1794. (4)
Published during the same year as the famous *Mysteries of Udolpho*, Bennett's work is another instance of a domestic novel hiding behind what could be a Gothic title. To survive with both publishers and readers, the domestic novelists of the 1790s in the camp of Jane Austen and Fanny Burney often found it necessary to embellish their ordinary family sagas with extraordinary Gothic titles. This was usually accomplished by brandishing the word "Castle." Ellen's history of struggle and matrimonial woes is taken directly from Chaucer's Griselda story of the patient and enduring wife whose quiet fortitude finally overcomes a callous husband.

1–28. Bennett, Agnes Maria. **Vicissitudes Abroad; or, The Ghost of My Father.** Minerva-Press, 1806. (3) (SB)
Consisting of six volumes, Bennett's novel is a kind of moral treatise in Gothic dress. An orphaned lady is assisted in her ordeal of growing up by the benign specter of her father, who creates crises for his daughter, then appears opportunely to extricate her from all adversity. Edification of youthful readers and not terror or Gothic titillation is the novelist's aim, although she does not hesitate to bring in Gothic props where these can be used to gain the reader's attention.

1–29. Bertin, L. F. (France). **La Caverne de la mort (The Cavern of Death).** H. Nicolle, 1799. (6)
A French translation of the anonymous and powerful shocker of 1794, *The Cavern of Death* [1–59], published by J. Bell. Bell would also be the publisher of *The Monk* [1–218] two years later.

1–30. Bertin, T. P. (France). **Edgar; ou, Le Pouvoir du remords (Edgar; or, The Power of Remorse).** Delalain, 1799. (6)
A satisfactory French translation of Sickelmore's popular Gothic romance, *Edgar; or, The Phantom of the Castle* [1–352]. As the didactic subtitle suggests,

the French translations frequently sentimentalized the original hard Gothicism of their English sources.

1-31. Der Bezauberte Helm; oder, Der Ritter vom Riesensäbel (The Enchanted Helmet; or, The Knight of the Giant Sabre) (Germany). Altona, 1797. (2) (SB)
This rare title is a fine specimen of the German *Ritter-roman*. The motif of enormous weaponry, in the huge saber borne by one hundred knights in *The Castle of Otranto*, was not original with Walpole. Its presence in this untranslated German work suggests that the author had read Walpole's Gothic romance and quickly adapted the great helmet and huge sword to his tale of magic and gigantism. Many such German romances of Gothic chivalry await revivals and competent translations, and no full-length scholarly study of the late eighteenth-century *Schauer-roman* and *Ritter-roman* exists in English. Some descriptive summaries of this strange and rare breed of German Gothicism may be found in Ernst Margraf, *Der Einfluss der Deutschen Literatur auf den Englischen Schauer-roman (The Influence of German Literature on the English Shudder-novel)*, Schmidt, 1901.

1-32. Bird, John. The Castle of Hardayne. Kearsley, 1795. (1)
Bird's work is a stereotypical romance of ruins. Hardayne Castle is completely staffed with a spectral inhabitant to freeze the blood and raise the Gothic expectations of the pining maiden, who diligently pursues her thrills behind Hardayne's ominous walls. The always-gripping nightmare of the specter at the bedside is brought off with some skill by Bird, whose ease of Gothic rhetoric shows more than usual technical control over a jaded style of novel writing. His capability is especially evident in the creepy descriptions of Hardayne's dilapidated exterior. The Castle of Hardayne pleases what Michael Sadleir has called the "Gothistic eye" with its "shattered walls stained with a variety of beautiful mosses, or shadowed with the broad masses of ivy, through which the grey tint of Gothick ornaments would sometimes peep, and give a pleasing relief to the deep green shades. The court was very extensive, but almost entirely overgrown with weeds and brambles." As usual in a Radcliffean perspective, the castle itself is featured as the chief character in the story.

1-33. The Black Convent; or, A Tale of Feudal Times. Minerva-Press, 1819. (1)
The horrors of the Inquisition and the terrors of priestcraft threaten the confined heroine of this late monastic shocker. The example of the convent confinement of Radcliffe's Ellena di Rosalba in *The Italian; or, The Confessional of the Black Penitents* [1-317] continued to exert a strong influence on the makers of the novel of religious persecution. "Feudal Times" in this rare title is a loose historical label, since the heroine (Elvira) undergoes her convent ordeal in the Renaissance atmosphere of the fifteenth century. The monastic

shocker almost never locates itself in England; *The Black Convent* departs from this pattern by using the border country as its milieu.

1–34. The Black Valley; or, The Castle of Rosenberg. Ann Lemoine, 1803. (5)
This Gothic bluebook is a copied, condensed, and crude reproduction of Veit Weber's shocking and sensational tale, *Der Schwarze Tal (The Black Valley)* [1–393]. In typical fashion, the bluebook is adorned with garish illustrations and is a blend of the atrocious sexual motifs of *The Monk* [1–218] and the ugly supernaturalism of the German *Schauer-romantik* school.

1–35. The Bloody Hand; or, The Fatal Cup: A Tale of Horror! Stevens Circulating Library, n.d. (5)
A typical Gothic delicacy from the crowded shelves of a typical circulating library of the period, *The Bloody Hand* is a pirated collocation of several successful Gothic titles. The screaming titles of such penny dreadfuls always promised much more to the reader than the shabbily plagiarized text delivered. Montague Summers comments, "It was the aim of the writer of the bluebook to give his narrative as exciting a title as possible; secondly, to cram into his limited space as many shocking, mysterious, and horrid incidents as possible." The 72 pages of *The Bloody Hand* do exactly this by plundering every character and incident from the Gothic stockpile of the 1790s. Such titles were priced at sixpence for 36 pages and a single shilling for a full cup of horror.

1–36. Die Blutende Gestalt mit Dolch und Lampe; oder, Die Beschwöhrung im Schlosse Stern bei Prag (The Bleeding Shape with Dagger and Lamp; or, The Oath at Castle Stern near Prague) (Germany). Prague, 1797. (2)
This anonymous *Schauer-roman* proves to be an abridged piracy of Von Oertel's 1797 German translation of Lewis's *The Monk*. The unknown Teutonic Gothifier followed the formula of his English bluebook brethren by altering a few names to give his stolen Gothic an air of originality. Thus, the persecuted nun, Agnes, becomes Berta in this version. Of special interest to the historian of *The Monk*'s illegitimate literary offspring is the German Gothicist's appropriation of one lurid episode from Lewis's romance—the appearance of the Bleeding Nun at Raymond's bedside in the Castle of Lindenberg—to endow his plundered work with a gory title.

1–37. Boaden, James. Fountainville Forest: A Play in Five Acts. Hookham & Carpenter, 1794. (1) (SB)
Conceived of as a dramatic condensation of Radcliffe's *The Romance of the Forest* [1–315], Boaden's *Fountainville Forest* reduces the lengthy topographical rhapsodies in the novel to succinct dramatic flourishes. The fugitive La Motte, the anxious Adeline, and the odious Marquis of Montalt are transferred intact from novel to drama. Boaden generally follows his revisionary

attitude toward Radcliffe's technique of the explained supernatural and accelerates the somewhat sluggish pace of plot in the Radcliffean source. When we hear Boaden's Adeline declaim, "A powerful impulse drives me onwards and my soul rises to the coming horror," we know that Boaden's maiden knows what Gothic is all about. In his promotion of a true Gothic aesthetic of the authentic supernatural, Boaden sought to bring a new sublimity to Gothic theater. His energetic ghosts, while less articulate than old Hamlet perhaps, were more perambulatory and bloodcurdling.

1-38. Boaden, James. **The Italian Monk: A Play in Three Acts.** G. G. & J. Robinson, 1797. (1) (SB)
First acted at the Haymarket Theatre in August 1797, this Gothic drama is also available to the researcher as a prompter's copy in the Larpent Collection of Gothic plays at the Henry E. Huntington Library. An ingenious Gothic playwright, Boaden converted several Gothic novels to the demands of the stage. His dramatic imagination was fed by the visual thrills that abounded in the *Schauer-romantik* tradition; in particular, he liked to display the robed judges of the sinister *Vehmgericht* or secret fehmic court. Germanic gloom is prominent in *The Italian Monk* as Radcliffe's indirect suspense gives way to Boaden's onstage horrors in his dramatization of *The Italian* [1-317]. In his expert account of Gothic novels on stage, *Gothic Drama from Walpole to Shelley* (1949), Bertrand Evans says of Boaden's work: "His decision, therefore, was to omit not Mrs. Radcliffe's excesses, but her natural explanations of the supernatural. For the first time, a playwright undertook to out-Gothicize a novelist."

1-39. Bonhote, Elizabeth. **Bungay Castle: A Novel.** Minerva-Press, 1796. (1) (SB)
Like Parsons's *The Mysterious Warning* [1-291], *Bungay Castle* is a Gothic's Gothic. The novel uses a mysterious ventriloquist's death-dealing voice as its central Gothic effect. The heroine, Roseline, and the voice-throwing hero, Albert, are standard Gothic people, while the storms, ruins, and subterranean surprises as well as the Baron's terrible compartments within Bungay Castle's honeycombed interior are familiar enough to Gothic devotees. Making the usual escape through the mouldering maze beneath the castle, Roseline has experiences that are pure Gothic: "Here they met with many difficulties: in some places huge stones had fallen from the walls,—in others the archway was so low they were almost obliged to crawl,—while toads, snakes, and various kinds of reptiles impeded their progress." Not only is Bonhote well versed in the furnishings of the Gothic underground, she may also be regarded as the mistress of a special effect known as the subterranean squeeze. The claustrophobic narrowing of tunnels around her heroine's beautiful frame is one of her great trademarks. Nor does she ever compromise her unadulterated Gothic with the fiction of ideas. As she declares

in the Preface to *Bungay Castle,* "A novel was never intended as a vehicle for politics."

1-40. Bornschein, Johann Ernst Daniel (Germany). **Friedrich Graf von Struensee; oder, Das Dänische Blutgerüst (Count Friedrich Von Struensee; or, The Danish Execution Scaffold).** Flensburg & Altona, 1793. (2) (SB)
As a writer of *Räuber-romane* and *Schauer-romane,* Bornschein specialized in gruesomely sanguinary scenes. Mysterious executioners, undefined crimes, and the agony of the scaffold itself are part of the gruesome scenery of this forgotten and untranslated farrago of anguish and despair.

1-41. Bounden, Joseph. **The Murderer; or, The Fall of Lecas.** Minerva-Press, 1808. (4)
A novel of mystery and natural terror as well as a primitive detective story, *The Murderer* traces the career of a congenital criminal from his youthful sadism to his grim demise. The novelist avoids the temptation to moralize and concentrates instead upon the exquisite cruelties of the criminal, whose desire to enjoy pain at any price bears some resemblance to John Moore's repulsive Zeluco [1-268].

1-42. Boutet de Monvel, Jacques-Marie (France). **Les Victimes clôitrées (The Victims of the Cloister).** Lepetit, 1792. (3)
This sensational and morbid play is a first-rate dramatic example of the virulent anticlerical fashions in stage literature during the revolutionary period. The victimization of the characters has obvious links with the entrapment of Diderot's unwilling novice in *La Réligieuse* [1-95]. The drama's principal plot is luridly Gothic. The libidinous priest, Père Laurent, employs the convent as a jail to lock up and torment his sexual prize, the innocent and lovely Eugénie. In Père Laurent we have a lecherous predecessor to Lewis's Ambrosio, Radcliffe's Schedoni, and later, Victor Hugo's Claude Frollo. The figure of the priest as monster is not unique to Gothic literature, but the amorous ambitions and tendencies toward torture in the personality of Père Laurent render him a paradigm of the Gothic novel's murderous monk.

1-43. Breton, J. B. J. (France). **La Visite nocturne (The Nocturnal Visit).** Gueffier, 1801. (6)
A French translation of Roche's complicated and slow-moving Gothic novel of 1800, *The Nocturnal Visit* [1-326].

1-44. Brewer, James Norris. **The Witch of Ravensworth.** Corri & Colburn, 1808. (1)
In this Macbethian Gothic and sadistic extravaganza, the reader encounters the colossal seven-and-one-half-foot frame of the Baron de la Braunch, whose progressive involvement with the dark powers of evil lead him to awful crimes. This variety of sorcerer/sorceress Gothic is a busy branch of the novel of horror; many Gothic novels appear to originate on Macbeth's

blasted heath or atop the battlements of Elsinore Castle. In *The Witch of Ravensworth,* incantations, bloody rituals, and midnight covens designed to arouse the "black and deep desires" of the huge Baron are standard fare.

1-45. Bromley, Elizabeth Nugent. **The Cave of Cosenza: A Romance of the Eighteenth Century.** G. & J. Robinson, 1803. (5) (SB)

Cavern or grotto Gothic clearly approaches the limits of the ludicrous in this perplexing romance. Various royal personages, counts, countesses, and even a chancellor of the exchequer with his ledgers intact form a Gothic congregation taking refuge from some obscure and vague peril within the Cave of Cosenza. Even the most uncritical Gothic addict of that era must have been put off by this unintelligibly plotted book. Far-fetched situations can be both tolerated and enjoyed when they are consistently related to the general fabric of Gothic fantasy, as they are in Beckford's *Vathek* [1-25]. But in the case of *The Cave of Cosenza,* the silly simply remains the silly, while any thrill and shock disappear in the face of the author's ineptitude.

*1-46. Brown, Charles Brockden (U.S.). **Wieland; or, The Transformation.** H. Caritat, 1798; Kent State Univ. Press, 1977. (3)

Brown redesigned the Radcliffean species of Gothic romance to the American setting and founded an American school of Gothicism. Its serious intellectual and psychological intensity may be followed from its beginnings in Brown through Hawthorne, Poe, and James in the nineteenth century to the works of Faulkner, Flannery O'Connor, and Joyce Carol Oates in the twentieth century. *Wieland* is a dark and violent fable of mental horror and moral terror told retrospectively by Clara Wieland, whose powers of character show that she is no mere duplication of the swooning Radcliffean maiden. The family malady of the Wielands is an odd form of religious mania. Early in the novel, the father of the house perishes by spontaneous combustion in his private temple on the banks of the Schuylkill River. The son of the house, Clara's brother Theodore, believes he hears the voice of God and takes the lives of his wife and children in obedience to divine command. Into this web of pedocide and theological psychosis slinks the enigmatic figure of Carwin (Cain plus two letters), the first and one of the finest of American Gothic villains. Carwin has the features of Radcliffe's Montoni and Schedoni, but instead of the eye that maims or slays, he possesses a Gothic supervoice. Carwin is a biloquist or ventriloquist and he uses his preternatural talent ambivalently for good and evil ends, telling Clara at one point, "My only crime was curiosity." Just as Clara is about to be murdered by her own brother, Carwin intercedes with his ventriloquial power to order young Wieland to "Hold!" Theodore takes his own life and Carwin moves on into the unplumbed forests of Pennsylvania. Clara Wieland's impassioned reconstruction of her Gothic past is cathartic as she comes to terms with her own potential for self-destruction. Brown's American Gothic novel replaces natural explanations with scientific causation and sets a sophisticated example for serious American Gothicists like Nathaniel Hawthorne.

*1–47. Brown, Charles Brockden (U.S.). **Arthur Mervyn; or, The Memoirs of the Year 1793.** H. Maxwell, 1799; Holt, 1962. (3)
Brown's second novel is a primitive yet refined specimen of urban Gothic. The city of Philadelphia under an epidemic of yellow fever substitutes for the horrors of the traditional haunted castle. While the mechanics of the plot are more complex than *Wieland*'s, the basic story still involves a young person learning to recognize and reckon with the Gothic aspects of his own deeper self. Young Arthur Mervyn, the somewhat untrustworthy narrator of the memoirs, is a version of the Yankee simpleton whose moral education takes place in a city of dreadful night. Driven from his father's household, he takes employment with the degenerate Welbeck, a forger, swindler, and master criminal who lives in society only in order to live off it. Welbeck is an up-to-date portrait of a Gothic egotist whose schemes for controlling others both fascinate and repel Mervyn. Welbeck becomes a kind of corrupt father figure to the young man. When Mervyn himself contracts yellow fever, we understand Brown to be symbolizing his sickness of conscience. Adventures among the plague victims in darkened streets, the macabre motions of the public burial teams, and Welbeck's network of evil give the novel a solidly Gothic fabric and foreshadow the American mode of horror. Out of the restructured perplex of *Arthur Mervyn,* Hawthorne would derive the idea for his much-admired story, "My Kinsman, Major Molineux."

*1–48. Brown, Charles Brockden (U.S.). **Ormond; or, The Secret Witness.** H. Caritat, 1799; Hafner, 1962. (3)
Using a fusion of Richardsonian and Gothic materials and crises, *Ormond* is Brown's second novel of the city under plague. Against a background of yellow fever in Philadelphia moves the strange and blighted villain, Ormond. The woman in distress and Ormond's worthy victim is the beautiful Constantia Dudley, whose blind and bankrupt father, Stephen Dudley, is brutally murdered by Ormond's repulsive accomplice, Craig. The final chapters of the novel are thoroughly Gothic in pace and tone as Ormond holds Constantia prisoner in a "solitary and darksome abode," terrifies her with the corpse of the murdered Craig, and threatens her with necrophiliac rape unless she submits to his advances while she is still alive. The vocabulary of Radcliffean emergency is clear enough in Constantia's predicament: "The mansion was desolate and lonely. It was night. She was immersed in darkness. She had not the means, and was unaccustomed to the office of repelling personal injuries. What injuries she had reason to dread, who was the agent and what were his motives, were subjects of vague and incoherent meditation." Eventually, Constantia turns upon her tormentor and in a gesture of independence for all harassed Gothic virgins stabs Ormond and frees herself from his rule. Brown's *Ormond* was widely read by the English intelligentsia.

The Shelleys were much impressed by Brown's moral erudition and by his new Gothic heroine whose actions had countered the villain's perverted theories of power.

*1–49. Brown, Charles Brockden (U.S.). Edgar Huntly; or, The Memoirs of a Sleep-Walker. H. Maxwell, 1799; College & University Press Services, 1974. (3)

Haunted castle becomes haunted forest complete with hideous pit and ghostly Indians in one of the best early examples of naturalized American Gothic fiction. The ambiguous and contortive narrative is cast in the form of letters from Edgar Huntly to Mary Waldegrave, with the sanity of both the narrator and the characters of his strange dream life constantly held in abeyance. Much of the novel's twilight action is a probing of the irrational world of sleep; Brown is here able to convey the image of life as uncontrollable and unintelligible nightmare. The opening of the novel is one of the most effective night scenes in Gothic literature as young Edgar Huntly, spying upon the somnambulistic behavior of Clithero Edny, observes him in the act of digging a pit at the base of a tree deep in the forest and sobbing as he does so. The belated scientific explanation of this bizarre incident is that Clithero is a sleepwalker. Gradually, Huntly himself loses a rational grip on his own life to become a sleepwalker too; Brown presents the phenomenon of somnambulism as a psychological metaphor for the darkest recesses of the unconscious mind. Such is his new version of the Gothic castle that lies within ourselves. One evening, completely without warning, Huntly awakens to find himself stranded at the bottom of what seems a frightful pit and is unable to explain how he got there or how to work his way back to the surface. His ordeal in the pit probably gave Poe several ideas for his supreme exercise in underground anguish, "The Pit and the Pendulum." With the realization by Edgar that he himself is a sleepwalker, Brown fixes the new Gothic proposition of how fragile and vulnerable the rational self always is.

1–50. Brown, Elizabeth Cullen. The Sisters of Saint Gothard. Minerva-Press, 1819. (3) (SB)

Something of a defense of the now much-maligned monastic life and Catholic clergy, Brown's novel is sentimentalized Gothic. Convent life and training are still depicted as a warping experience for the human spirit, but no wicked prioress appears in her pages. While the atmosphere is one of cloistered gloom and while the reader feels that strange and terrible events are going on in the hidden cells of Saint Gothard, nothing startling ever takes place directly. In her useful study, *Catholicism and Gothic Fiction* (1946), Sister Mary Muriel Tarr sums up the appeal of such mildly lugubrious books as *The Sisters of Saint Gothard:* "Neither Catholic dogma nor the religious life is thought to be worthy of the intellectual assent of reasonable beings. Yet, Catholic dogma in practice can provide situations highly pleasurable to the emotions, and the appurtenances of religious life have qualities extremely satisfying to the lover of the picturesque. Catholicism in Gothic fiction, therefore, presents ample materials for the exercise of both sense and sensibility. Sense rejects the dogma; sensibility revels in the decorations."

1–51. Buchholz, Carl August (Germany). **Lutardo; oder, Die Banditenhauptmann (Lutardo; or, The Bandit Chieftain).** J. F. Unger, 1804. (2) Buchholz's *Räuber-roman* was inspired by, and is a close imitation of, Zschokke's *Abällino* [1–422]. All benevolent outlaws such as Lutardo and Abällino trace their romantic lineage back to Schiller's Karl Moor in *Die Räuber* (*The Robbers*) [1–337].

1–52. Bürger, Gottfried August (Germany). "Lenore" in **Göttinger Musenalmanach,** J. C. Dieterich, 1773. (2)
This famous Gothic ballad features the spectral character of the skeleton horseman and cadaverous lover. Lady Lenore's lover has died in the Thirty Years War. As she grieves, the slain Wilhelm appears on horseback beneath her window and carries her off on a wild night gallop. When Wilhelm unveils his gaunt, skeletal countenance, Lenore joins him in death. The numerous variations of this chilling reunion include the Scottish "Sweet William's Ghost" as well as Lewis's "Alonzo the Brave and Fair Imogine" in Chapter 9 of *The Monk* [1–218].

1–53. Burke, Mrs. **The Secret of the Cavern.** Minerva-Press, 1805. (1)
Apparently, there is only one surviving copy of this grotto Gothic, in the Bodleian Library.

1–54. Cantwell, André Samuel Michel (France). **L'Château d'Albert; ou, Le Squelette ambulant (Albert Castle; or, The Animated Skeleton).** Ancelle, 1799. (6)
This shortened French translation of the anonymous shocker, *The Animated Skeleton* [1–8], has some crudely powerful woodcuts.

1–55. Carey, David. **The Secrets of the Castle.** B. Crosby, 1806. (5)
Of crude bluebook quality, this confused Gothic uses such Walpolesque mechanisms as the ancestral curse and the paternal apparition to bring a hysterical young heiress face to face with her fated family. As is normal with bluebook productions, neither invention nor imagination play any part in the rapid production of this less-than-shocking second-hand Gothic.

1–56. Carr, George Charles. **The Towers of Urbandine.** York & Hull, 1805. (1)
An exciting compendium of Gothic gadgetry, events, and characterization, *The Towers of Urbandine* is a Gothic drama that towers above all its dramatic rivals. Carr provides four separate persecutors and six interlocking victimization plots set in a devastated abbey, a haunted castle, a menacing convent, a slimy cavern, and a "bosky" forest. The play begins with a kind of sinister prelude, which finds Rosaline and her father visited by a mysterious

stranger at their abbey hideaway. For undisclosed reasons, Rosaline is commanded by the stranger to proceed to the Castle of Urbandine, where she is promptly assaulted by Gondemar, hideous son of Baron Otho. Baron Otho, whose lecherous wishes exceed his son's, enters into Gondemar's sadistic sports. Constantine, Gondemar's decent brother and the champion of Rosaline, comes to save her from cavern rape but is done in by Gondemar, leaving Rosaline again helpless. Complicated escapes and elaborate emergencies follow in hair's-breadth sequence as Rosaline wriggles her way out of the castle only to find herself the prisoner of vicious banditti. The bandit captain, when unmasked, proves to be none other than Gondemar, now become a creature torn by fratricidal remorse. As per Gothic schedule, Constantine reappears (his fatal wound being not so fatal) and his followers lay siege to the robbers' cave. Rosaline is again rescued as the good brother confronts his nefarious counterpart. Gondemar's suicide brings down the curtain on this paramount Gothic melodrama. All the histrionic tendencies and techniques of the varying Gothics of Walpole, Radcliffe, and Lewis are tied into one bloody knot by Carr's stupendous melodrama.

1–57. Carver, Mrs. **The Horrors of Oakendale Abbey.** Minerva-Press, 1797. (1)

This novel was unsigned at publication, but later attributed to Carver in Minerva Library Catalogue 128 issued in 1814. The work is a reasonably satisfying imitation of Radcliffe's maiden-centered Gothic. In addition, this Gothic romance takes advantage of the sanguinary atmosphere of the French Revolution "when Paris was deluged with human gore." The *émigré* heroine, Laura du Frene, manages to reach England just as the terror is igniting, but is soon parted from her mother and finds herself pursued by Lord Oakendale. Her incarceration in Oakendale Abbey, a menacing fortress in Cumberland, follows shortly. Here, she undergoes the ordinary Udolphoesque alarums and excursions, all belatedly explained. The dead bodies seen hanging about the abbey, for example, are the residue of obscene experiments in dissection. Adhering to the customary genealogical twist, Laura turns out to be the lost niece of Lord Oakendale while Laura's lover, the inept palladin, Eugene, is revealed to be the son of Lady Oakendale by a previous lover. Despite its cumbrous genealogical denouement, *The Horrors of Oakendale Abbey* is an effective remodeling of Radcliffean Gothic romance to accommodate the all-too-real horrors of Citizen Robespierre and the Terror.

1–58. The Castle of Udolpho: An Operatic Drama in Five Acts. T. & E. Hughes, 1808. (1) (SB)

An example of one of several musical versions of Radcliffe's best-known novel, *The Mysteries of Udolpho* [1–316]. Operatic transpositions of Gothic novels enjoyed marked popularity on both the English and French stage. The Gothic extravagances found in such musicales were recalled by Gilbert and Sullivan in their melodramatic masterpiece, *Ruddigore; or, The Witch's Curse* (1887); in mockery of Gothic stagecraft, the figures in several portraits descend from their frames at the beginning of the second act.

1–59. The Cavern of Death. J. Bell, 1794. (1)

The fatal rivalry between the castle usurper, the Baron of Dornheim, and the noble Sir Albert marks this high-grade facsimile of Walpole's *The Castle of Otranto* [1–398]. Dornheim's personality is much like that of Walpole's Manfred, whose "virtues were always ready to operate when his passion did not obscure his reason." Although the novel bore the subtitle *A Moral Tale,* the work itself can only be called fake or mock didactic in its emphasis upon supernatural thrill and the sulphurous lights that glow in the cavern of death's tenebrous recesses.

1–60. The Cavern of Horrors; or, The Miseries of Miranda: A Neapolitan Tale. Hurst, 1802. (5) (SB)

William W. Watt, in his *Shilling Shockers of the Gothic School: A Study of Chapbook Gothic Romances* (1932), informs us that two editions of this lurid work appeared in 1802, followed by a truncated version in 1815, all by different publishers. The copy contained in Sadleir-Black was published by Dean & Munday, a notorious purveyor of pirated bluebooks. The record for Gothic faints is surely owned by the miserable Miranda, who loses consciousness no less than 11 times in 59 pages. Miranda magnifies the fragile sensibilities of the Radcliffean heroine; conversely, the long and richly descriptive passages from Radcliffean sources are so severely trimmed as to provide the eager reader with nothing but climaxes without proper lyric suspense or sinister preparation. Like the cheaply derivative *Almagro and Claude* [1–5], *The Cavern of Horrors* is a pulp Gothic put together by greedy publishers who made no attempt to conceal their Gothic larcenies.

1–61. Cazotte, Jacques (France). **Le Diable Amoureux (The Amorous Devil).** Lejay, 1772. (4)

This lighthearted story of an amiable and fun-loving succubus was translated into English in 1810 under the title *Biondetta; or, The Enamoured Spirit* for the publisher John Miller. The unknown translator Gothified the English version and dedicated his work to M. G. Lewis. The amorous devil, Biondetta, is conjured up by Don Alvaro Maravillas amid the Gothic ruins of Portici; she appears first as a camel and then as a dog. After many exotic and passionate adventures with his succubus, Don Alvaro renounces the lovely demon just in time to be saved from plunging over a precipice. Montague Summers revokes the claim made by Mario Praz in *The Romantic Agony* (1933) that Biondetta was the source for Lewis's Matilda, the devil lady in *The Monk*.

1–62. Charlton, Mary. **Phedora; or, The Forest of Minski.** Minerva-Press, 1798. (1) (SB)
Despite its enormous length (1,459 pages in the four-volume first edition), the novel's orthodox Gothic plotting and characterization are quite simply followed. Little fatherless Phedora, soon to be motherless as well, lives in bucolic seclusion with the widow Eudocia Rubenski in a Livonian village in late seventeenth-century Poland. Livonia is ravaged by war and pillaged by marauders from Russia, Sweden, and Prussia, who roam the forest of Minski. With her sweet grace and admirable, if quite passive, valor Phedora emerges as the allegorized spirit of indestructible Polish liberty. As a version of the persecuted maiden, she also has ties with the virtuous sisterhood of de Sade's Justine [1–331] and Dickens's holy child, Little Nell, of *The Old Curiosity Shop* (1841). Phedora's favorite cedar tree is brutally cut down, her virtue is under constant threat from the dreadful landholder, Ulric Stenau, and she becomes the abused prisoner of the Cossacks where the Russian monster, Captain Matheowitz of the "mutilated paw," plans sadistic deeds against her. When Phedora comes across a wild boy, Alexy, in the Forest of Minski, her natural benevolence instantly tames him. Following her forest wanderings and exiles, we finally understand that Phedora is not a human being at all, but the indomitable spirit of Poland herself. When she emerges from her gruesome imprisonment in the fortress of Konigstein as the new Countess of Czerkowi, the spirit of Polish freedom is understood to have reasserted itself.

1–63. Charlton, Mary. **The Homicide.** Minerva-Press, 1805. (1) (SB)
Less political in its implications than *Phedora* [1–62], *The Homicide* is a lengthy and murky chronicle of a long series of murders. Unlike the lucid plotting of *Phedora,* the action of this novel as well as the obscure motivation of the principal character, Markov, is almost impossible to decipher. As a Gothic writer, Charlton was far better at depicting female suffering than masculine villainy.

1–64. Chateaubriand, François-René de (France). **Atala; ou, Les Amours de deux sauvages (Atala; or, The Love of Two Savages).** Chez Migneret, 1801; New American Library, 1961. (4)
Chateaubriand spent his childhood in the desolate castle of Combourg in Brittany. His exotic romance, *Atala,* takes place in the remote American wilderness, which Chateaubriand fills with grand passions and magnificently tropical landscapes. Atala is an Indian maiden whose fatal love for the Natchez warrior, Chactas, is told to the Frenchman, René, by Chactas in his old age. Swearing to remain a virgin, Atala has fallen in love with Chactas and helped him to escape burning at the stake by her own tribe. Wandering the Louisiana forests, they take refuge with the kind hermit priest, Father Aubry. Torn by her virginal promise and her unconquerable passion for Chactas, Atala poisons herself. The romance shows much of the sensibility of Gothic characters and contains descriptions of storms and redolently sinister

landscapes, as well as the fatal passions associated with the star-crossed lovers of the typical Gothic novel. In "The Tale of the Indians" in Maturin's *Melmoth the Wanderer* [1–244], we find a tropical idyll right in the midst of his Gothic romance, which derives its eerie beauties from Maturin's appreciation of Chateaubriand's *Atala*.

1–65. Chateaubriand, François-René de (France). **René; ou, Les Effets des passions (René; or, The Effects of Passion).** Chez Migneret, 1802; New American Library, 1961. (2)
A second romance of the unexplored American wilderness and a sequel to *Atala* [1–64], *René* exhibits a similar mixture of Rousseauistic passions and Gothic landscaping. The story takes the form of a brief monologue by René to old Chactas and the French missionary, Father Souël. After many wanderings, which have made him jaded with civilization, René has sought the solitude of the American wilderness. Plagued by suicidal thoughts, he is prevented from taking his own life by his sister, Amélie, who has loyally followed her brother to bring him comfort. When Amélie discovers her own incestuous and unnatural desires for her brother, she retreats to a convent, leaving René alone and melancholy once more. Like impassioned Gothic heroes such as Lewis's Ambrosio and gloomy wanderers such as Melmoth, René can find happiness nowhere in this world and is victimized by his own passions. The isolated hero set against forceful and violent natural scenery was a romantic condition often copied by the Gothic novelists. Like the Gothic writers, Chateaubriand gives his readers the distinctly terrifying sensation that there is no way back to normality for the sick and alienated young wanderer, who must either take his own life or transform his own disappointment over his morose existence into a life of crime.

1–66. Chilcot, Harriet. **Moreton Abbey; or, The Fatal Mystery.** Publisher unknown, 1786. (1)
Chilcot (afterwards Mrs. Meziere) had authored a Gothic narrative poem entitled *Elmar and Ethelinda: A Legendary Tale* (1783) and was apparently an enthusiastic follower of Walpole's Gothicism in *The Castle of Otranto*. The obscure Gothic novel *Moreton Abbey* is cited by Montague Summers in his *Gothic Bibliography* by title and date only with no further data given. It is given an entry in the present bibliography as an example of a "lost Gothic," although it can be assumed that the work is in the tradition of *Otranto*, since the author was known to be an admirer of Walpole's supernatural medievalism.

*1–67. Choderlos de Laclos, Pierre-Ambroise-François (France). **Les Liaisons dangereuses; ou, Lettres recueillies dans une société et publiées pour l'instruction de quelques autres (Dangerous Connections; or, Miscellaneous Letters about a Society Published for the Instruction of a Few Others).** Durand, 1782; New American Library, 1962. (3)

A pair of masterfully evil characters dominate this epistolary novel of seduction, libertine conspiracy, and the craft of corruption. Valmont and Madame de Merteuil form a confederacy of crime and set out to enjoy seduction for seduction's sake merely to feed their ruinous appetite for pleasure. The victims of this ruthless pair are Madame de Tourvel and the devout young Cécile. Eventually, like Richardson's satanic rake, Lovelace, Valmont dies in a duel at the hands of Darceny while Madame de Merteuil pays for her iniquities by being disfigured by the pox. The letters have all the familiar Gothic passions: love of evil for its own sake and malicious pursuit of supremely sadistic pleasures; cold, unnatural and pitiless desire to ruin innocence; a demonic pact between two remorseless egotists who believe only in the law of self-serving lust. The Gothic novel's synthesis of wicked female and emancipated woman is reflected in the warped soul of Madame de Merteuil, who secretly works her revenge against her partner in sadism, Valmont, even as she seems to assist his seductive schemes. *Les Liaisons dangereuses* may be said to form the link between the French appreciation of Richardson's novels of feminine distress and the Gothicism that characterized the age of revolution.

1–68. Clifford, Francis. **The Ruins of Tivoli: A Romance.** J. F. Hughes, 1804. (5)
Much longer than the standard 72 pages of the shilling shocker, this work nevertheless shows all the other characteristics of the bluebook trade. *Ruins* is a fusion of the mouldering architectural sites to be found in Rochean romances such as *Clermont* [1–325] and Italianate villainy such as that of Radcliffe's *A Sicilian Romance* [1–314]. The presence of the word *ruin* in a Gothic title did not necessarily insure its presence in the bluebook's text; but in the case of *The Ruins of Tivoli,* the hectic action does focus upon the toppled pillars and overgrown walls of a vaguely Roman site where the young heroine, Belmora, comes nightly to seek the mystery of her mother's death and her own destiny.

1–69. **La Cloche de minuit (The Midnight Bell)** (France). Nicolle, 1798. (6)
The anonymous French translation remains faithful to the original in this rendering of Francis Lathom's *Midnight Bell* [1–206].

1–70. Cobb, James. **The Haunted Tower.** MS. in the Larpent Collection, 1789. (4)
Cobb's play follows in the burlesque spirit of O'Keefe's dramatic lampoon of Gothic drama, *The Banditti; or, Love in a Labyrinth* [1–282]. The mock Gothic elements include Reeve's addition to the haunted castle, the ghostly suite, along with that proven Gothic device, the dark tower that contains an even darker secret. The proprietor of Cobb's haunted tower is the Baron of Oakland, a half-witted peasant who has stumbled somehow into the baronetcy. The awful secret of the tower involves the fact that its hidden panels connect

with the Baron's wine cellar—his wild and wayward servants are using the tower for their nocturnal drinking sprees. Thus, the strange lights and noises coming from the tower are explained away as rowdy servants in their cups. In a stroke of comic undercutting of the usual Gothic crisis of the tower mystery, the bumbling Baron surprises the revellers at their wine and pandemonium ensues.

1–71. Constant, Samuel (France). **Caleb Williams; ou, Les Choses comme elles sont (Caleb Williams; or, Things as They Are).** Genève, 1795. (6)
This French translation of Godwin's important political version of the Gothic novel, *Caleb Williams* [1–128], preserves all the Gothic trappings.

1–72. The Convent Spectre; or, Unfortunate Daughter. T. & R. Hughes, 1808. (1) (SB)
Slightly superior in quality to the tawdry bluebooks of the Gothic period, *The Convent Spectre* is a satisfactory Radcliffean amalgam of Gothic shrieks, cavern freaks, and astounding supernatural appearances and occurrences. Elements of the monastic shocker in the form of the ghost of a murdered nun also enter the romance. Fear of the unknown is suggested by the movement of the specter along the chapel aisles, although nothing very startling actually occurs in this muted Gothic.

1–73. Correlia; or, The Mystic Tomb. Minerva-Press, 1802. (1) (SB)
One of the best of the many unsigned Gothic novels, *Correlia*'s artful terrors contrast with the ineptitude of such anonymous fiascos as *Montrose; or, The Gothic Ruin* [1–266]. The novel opens in somber cadences: "The clock from the elevated turret of Wheinhausen Castle had with slow, majestic stroke tolled the hour of ten, and was followed by the deep and no less solemn bell of the chapel." In this castle on the banks of the Danube, Madame Martili is guardian to a beautiful child, niece of Lady Frederica, the lady of the castle. Frederica's sister, Correlia, died under strange circumstances at eighteen and is prominently interred in the chapel. As Lady Frederica is about to pronounce her marriage vows with Baron Heildestheim, a man who was once a Protestant and is now a Catholic, the lights in the chapel are extinguished and a horrid shriek comes from the mysterious tomb of Correlia. When Madame Martili's ward (also named Correlia) grows up, she becomes morbidly fond of the tomb and its "creaking noises," since it seems to hold some dark secret regarding her birth. Does the first Correlia actually lie within? What guilty part did Aunt Frederica play in her death? Such Radcliffean questions produce the usual Gothic swoon in the heroine as "her eyes with sacred horror pervaded the solemn darkness that every minute deepened and heated her fancy." After the narrative is interrupted by several lengthy inset tales, the lugubrious details of Lady Frederica's conspiracy against her sister are clarified, but the supernatural moanings from the tomb are not. After some vile experiences with her aunt's agent, the uncouth Benvilini, Correlia

the second is restored to ownership of the castle. The modified Radcliffeanism of *Correlia* makes the work important in the shift toward unexplained horror endorsed by the *Schauer-romantik* school.

1-74. Count Roderic's Castle; or, Gothic Times. Thomas Bradford, 1795. (1) (SB)

The author of this Otrantoesque romance was very possibly an American, since the work was published in Philadelphia. The historical plot, brimming with Walpolesque trappings and standard members of the Gothic cast, brings together the various threads of treachery, loyalty, royal murder, and rightful possession of the castle in the restoration of Emanuel to the throne of Lombardy. What is missing is the author's willingness to introduce supernatural elements; his sense of the Gothic is limited to the conflict between medieval savagery and the emergent chivalry of the late Middle Ages. The scene is eleventh-century Lombardy. Roderic the hardy, a venerable warrior, prepares for old age by seeking "a castle of his own near the frontiers of a lately conquered province—a retreat, in which the bolts of Astopho's wrath were but little likely to reach him." His son Rhinaldo, along with the fascinating but absent Isabel, the hermit Father Anthony, the noble prisoner Count Tancred, the servants Ruggiero and Fabian, and the cruel and ferocious Count de St. Armand suggest that the anonymous writer had done his Gothic reading widely. Both the castle and the adjacent convent of St. Julian ("its Gothic spires hung over the brow of the rock with an awful eminence") contain their quota of cadaverous surprises and architectural alarms. Tracking down the murderer of Count Roderic and finally recovering the long-missing Isabel are tasks familiar to any young Gothic hero. Without resorting to the supernatural, *Count Roderic's Castle* has every other piece of Gothic gadgetry associated with historical Gothicism.

1-75. Cramer, Karl Gottlob (Germany). Haspar à Spada: Eine Sage aus dem dreizehnte Jahrhundert (Haspar à Spada: A Saga of the Thirteenth Century). J. B. G. Fleischer, 1794. (2)

Cramer (1758–1817) was the writer of several *Ritter-romane* and *Schauer-romane,* among which *Haspar* is the most important for its influence upon terrifying medievalism in the English novel of horror. The knight, Haspar, is a fleeing victim of feudal tyranny. Catholic treachery also enters the saga in the person of Père Luprian, upon whose portrait Radcliffe might have been relying in her drawing of Schedoni in *The Italian* [1-317].

1-76. Crandolph, Augustus Jacob. The Mysterious Hand; or, Subterranean Horrours! Minerva-Press, 1811. (1)

The exquisite Gothic title of this forgotten shocker is far more titillating than the actual pace of the plot, which is sluggish and uncertain. After the success of Mary-Anne Radcliffe's *Manfroné; or, The One-Handed Monk* [1-318] in 1809, several untalented Gothic scribblers attempted to exploit her achievement.

In Crandolph's long and obscure Gothic, the terrible hand reaches after many maidens in the dark but never quite seizes. The hand belongs to a defrocked Capuchin who hides in a cavern near his former monastery. Into this unlikely abyss comes a series of Gothic maidens looking for exactly the sort of adventure in the dark that the mysterious hand extends. All of Crandolph's gropings are quite inferior to the use of the hand in *Manfroné*.

1-77. Croffts, Mrs. **Ankerwick Castle: A Novel.** Minerva-Press, 1800. (4)
A well-made historical novel with Gothic overtones, *Ankerwick Castle* is didactic fiction with a point to make about the virtues of persistence. The structure is epistolary, depicting through letters the separation of the beautiful Countess of Middleton from the worthy Beaumont during the reign of Henry VII. The date of the novel again demonstrates how imperative the word *castle* had become in a novel's title even if the book itself was a throwback to sentimental and didactic fiction.

1-78. Crookenden, Isaac. **The Skeleton; or, Mysterious Discovery.** A. Neil, 1805. (5) (SB)
Probably the most notorious counterfeiter of legitimate Gothic novels, Crookenden specialized in stealing Gothic plots and converting his "borrowed" materials into bluebooks with screaming titles. Thus, *The Skeleton* proves to be a refabrication of the anonymous *Animated Skeleton* [1-8] of 1798 together with bits and pieces of the author's extensive Gothic gleanings.

1-79. Crookenden, Isaac. **Horrible Revenge; or, The Monster of Italy!!** R. Harrild, 1808. (5)
Another shilling shocker based loosely upon Montague's popular and sensational *The Demon of Sicily* [1-264] of 1807. Crookenden's Italian monster also derives from Schedoni and Ambrosio and has the blood of Dacre's *Zofloya* [1-90] in his veins.

1-80. Crookenden, Isaac. **The Spectre of the Turret; or, Guolto Castle.** R. Harrild, n.d. (5)
A half-dozen tower Gothics are mixed together and condensed into this garish bluebook. Crookenden's multiple plagiarisms from successful tower Gothics are not without a certain genius as well as an eye for the captivating Gothic title. The most horrific event of this pulp Gothic, a headless apparition peering down from the turret at the distracted heroine, is accompanied and underscored by several crude drawings.

1-81. Cullen, Stephen. **The Haunted Priory; or, The Fortunes of the House of Rayo.** J. Bell, 1794. (1) (SB)
Although its critical reception was hostile, *The Haunted Priory* is a well-executed specimen of pure Gothic that brings a lyric energy to its supernatural scenes. The story takes the form of a Gothic journey or perverse quest, thus placing the book in a category of Gothic recently called "demonic quest ro-

mance." Like a knight errant in a medieval saga, the young son of the House of Rayo goes on a journey to avenge his father's death. Guided across the Sierra Morena by a titanic, mysterious figure, the young man comes upon a strange chapel on Christmas Eve. As he enters the priory, the ghostly voices chanting the mass sink into dark silence in the deserted church. Exhausted, the voyager slumbers and suddenly receives a dream visit from an armored figure who holds forth a key. Thus far, not a single sinister happening has been explained. The suspenseful mood resembles that of the medieval romance, *Sir Gawain and the Green Knight,* or the poetic gloom of Keats's "Eve of St. Agnes." The young wanderer awakens to find the priory in ruins. Assisted by an old baron, the father of the murdered Rayo, the two pry open a crypt to discover the skull of the missing relative. The business of revenge is subdued or even forgotten in the horror of this moment. Cullen's Gothic has an explicit dream quality about it, which gives to his presentation of the supernatural a surreal and eerie power.

1-82. Cullen, Stephen. **The Castle of Inchvally: A Tale Alas! Too True.** J. Bell, 1796. (1)
A monastic shocker appearing during the year of *The Monk* [1-218], *The Castle of Inchvally* exploits the terrors of Catholicism. The castle is the dreadful lair of a band of lecherous monks who, led by their lustful abbot, smear themselves with phosphorescent paints and bloody garb to conduct their obscene ceremonies. Within the castle they startle their female victims into submission. An important Gothic acoustic, the demonic snicker or ghostly chuckle, often echoes through the corridors of Inchvally Castle as the depraved rituals proceed. The tortured laughter of Maturin's Melmoth [1-244] when in the presence of helpless suffering may owe its origins to Cullen's manipulation and development of this sound effect. Gloating over one shackled and flagellated victim, one of Cullen's blood-smeared monks emits "a long, loud laugh, such as a giant in malignant mirth might be supposed to utter."

1-83. Curties, T. J. Horsley. **Ancient Records; or, The Abbey of Saint Oswythe.** Minerva-Press, 1801. (1) (SB)
With its fallen Gothic magnificence, lurking brigands, and cursed tradition, the Abbey of Saint Oswythe is an ideal place of confinement for the lovely Rosaline, a close cousin of all Radcliffe's quaking heroines but particularly near in nervousness to Adeline in *The Romance of the Forest* [1-315]. In his preface to this reproduction of Radcliffean Gothicism, Curties paid enthusiastic homage to Radcliffe: "Its mysteries, terrific illusions, its very errors must be attributed to a love of romance, caught from an enthusiastic admiration of *Udolpho*'s unrivalled Foundress." Whereas most of the male Gothic novelists were drawn to the degenerate horrors of the *Schauer-roman* and the flashy atrocities of Monk Lewis, Curties preferred the sublime terrors of the *roman noir* legacy left by Mrs. Radcliffe. Eventually, all the mysteries that beset Sir Alfred St. Oswythe and his beautiful ward, Rosaline, are given natu-

ral explanations, but not before Rosaline has had her chance at Gothic enjoyments within the dark abbey. These frightful pleasures include a variation of the black veil episode in *Udolpho* [1–316], in which Rosaline is tempted to tilt back the lid of a mysterious casket and peer at its putrid contents. Her words on the verge of this horrid investigation crystallize the Radcliffean spirit of Gothic ecstasy: "Dare I raise the mysterious lid of that horrific coffin?—Dare to do so?" And with this half-turned screw of terror the scene grows shadowy and the reader waits—and waits.

1–84. Curties, T. J. Horsley. **Saint Botolph's Priory; or, The Sable Mask.** J. F. Hughes, 1806. (1) (SB)
The mask that conceals a royal visage would be used frequently by later writers of historical romance. This novel is placed in the troubled reign of Charles I and makes some use of Cromwellian politics; yet the names of the characters sound less like English aristocrats than like the cast of an Elizabethan revenge drama. Odovico St. Aubespine has retreated to Saint Botolph's Priory on the Isle of Wight with his fair daughter, Roselma. The story opens amid a Gothic tempest as Odovico mumbles over some secret concerning the death of Count Val de Blandemonde. As the storm rages, a stranger appears seeking shelter at the priory. De Rochemonde (actually Adolpho de Blandemonde) is one of Cromwell's henchmen. The ugly de Rochemonde takes his revenge upon the father by possessing and tormenting his daughter and threatening her with wedlock. Adhering to the common Gothic pattern, it develops that Odovico is not Roselma's true father. She is the child of a "terrific unknown" whose face is hidden behind the sable mask. At the unveiling, rather like the lifting of the black veil that hangs over the portrait in *Udolpho* [1–316], Gondolpho de Blandemonde, whom Odovico had not murdered as was previously thought, is revealed. The righteous brother restores justice and love and all Gothic dangers promptly evaporate. Less coherent than his other Gothic work, Curties's romance contains some fine descriptions of storms; this aspect of the narrative may have influenced the opening of Percy Bysshe Shelley's *Saint Irvyne* [1–350].

*1–85. Curties, T. J. Horsley. **The Monk of Udolpho.** J. F. Hughes, 1807; Arno, 1977. (1) (SB)
Regarded by Gothic scholars as Curties's masterpiece, the book shows his debt to Mrs. Radcliffe's *Italian* (1–317) as well as her *Mysteries of Udolpho* (1–316). The father of the lovely Hersilia of Placenza has gambled away his dukedom, leaving her only the Castello di Alberi. Before he can take his own life, Father Udolpho, a superb ecclesiatical villain, murders the duke. The young and perfect courtier, Val Ambrosio, consoles Hersilia and declares his love, but Father Udolpho plots against her happiness. He directs the attentions of the repulsive Sanguedoni upon Hersilia, who finds herself forcefully conveyed to Castello di Alberi, making the traditional Gothic journey through desolate and infernal terrain. After her incarceration, Father

Udolpho discloses himself to be none other than Sanguedoni, a creature "bold in guilt, triumphant in the success of his dark projects, cruel, bloodthirsty, insidious, remorseless and deceitful, formed to delude, and self-trained from boyhood to manhood in every vice." Finally cornered and ensnared in his fortress lair by the officers of the Inquisition, Sanguedoni commits suicide. By exaggerating the Italianate terrors, Curties moved beyond the milder Gothicism of *Ancient Records* [1–83] and approached the horrid candor of *The Monk* [1–218].

1–86. Curtis, Julia Ann Kemble (used pseud. Ann of Swansea). **Sicilian Mysteries; or, The Fortress Del Vechii.** Henry Colburn, 1812. (1) (SB)
An acquaintance of the great actor Edmund Kean, Ann of Swansea also wrote under the name Julia Hatton. Although *Sicilian Mysteries* is primarily a Radcliffean Gothic based on the moods of Radcliffe's *Sicilian Romance* [1–314], the novel also contains some of the paraphernalia of horror so characteristic of the *Schauer-roman*. The miserable Rosalie's first view of the castle where she is to be immured is a kind of type-scene in maiden-centered Gothic fiction. Like Emily St. Albert before the battlements of Udolpho Castle, Rosalie has similar emotions before the walls of the Fortress del Vechii. She "gazed on its mouldering walls and nodding watch-towers with sensations of horror. Its dilapidated state, struck the dreadful suspicion on her heart, *that she was brought there to suffer*." Readers also must have been reminded of both the black veil and the horrors of the Inquisition when "a heavy bell tolled and a black curtain being drawn aside, discovered a machine thickly studded with small spikes, which had a number of wheels and chains annexed to it." The sadistic habits of Lewis's Ambrosio must also have been recalled when the monk, Elzili, drugs and ravishes the innocent Viletta in a violent and voluptuous climax in the underground cells of del Vechii. The sexual crimes depicted in this Gothic novel suggest that the influence of Sade and his followers was becoming strong even among female Goths, who might have been expected to conform to the delicate standards of Radcliffe when treating themes of sexual peril.

1–87. Curtis, Julia Ann Kemble (used pseud. Ann of Swansea). **The Secret Avengers: or, The Rock of Glotzden.** Minerva-Press, 1815. (1)
A weak revival of the themes and situations used in *Sicilian Mysteries* (1–86), this novel simply transports the Fortress del Vechii and its palpitating heroine to a Scandinavian seacoast.

1–88. Cuvelier de Trie, Jean Guillaume-Antoine (France). **Le Bandit sans le vouloir et sans le savoir (The Bandit without Will and Desire).** Barba, 1809. (2)
While the *Räuber-roman* was principally the literary property of Germany, a few French versions do exist, as in this paraphrase of *Rinaldo Rinaldini* [1–390].

*1-89. Dacre, Charlotte (used pseud. Rosa Matilda). **Confessions of the Nun of Saint Omer.** J. F. Hughes, 1805; Arno, 1972. (3) (SB)
Not without lurid and melodramatic violence, the work is as much philosophic as Gothic in its commentary upon repressive modes of living. Significantly, the terrors and secret passions of closed convent life are held up to criticism in a manner reminiscent of Diderot's exposé in *La Réligieuse* [1-95].

*1-90. Dacre, Charlotte (used pseud. Rosa Matilda). **Zofloya; or, The Moor: A Romance of the Fifteenth Century.** Longman, Hurst, Rees & Orme, 1806; Arno, 1974. (4) (SB)
Rosa Matilda's magnum opus is an outstanding and influential example of the novel of sheer horror, in which the satanic figure functions as a moral agent of deserved retribution. The novel centers on the lurid criminal career of Victoria de Loredani, a feminized and secularized version of Lewis's soul-selling monk, Ambrosio. Tormented by Count Ardolph and carried off to the terrible Il Bosco, Victoria escapes and embarks upon a career of passionate villainy herself. Visited by the strange presence of the Moor, Zofloya, in a dream, Victoria forms a diabolic partnership with this son of Satan, who then assists her in removing her husband, Berenza, who stands in the way of Victoria's concupiscent plans for herself. Desiring Henriquez, Berenza's brother, she solicits the aid of Zofloya in gaining his bed. To avoid the judgment of the Inquisition, she pledges her soul to Zofloya. In a scene that parallels the power of the destruction of Ambrosio in *The Monk* [1-218], the devilish Moor claims his prize. He "grasped more firmly the neck of the wretched Victoria—with one push he whirled her headlong down the fearful abyss."

*1-91. Dacre, Charlotte (used pseud. Rosa Matilda). **The Libertine: A Novel.** Cadell, 1807; Arno, 1974. (3) (SB)
Something of a throwback to the sorts of psychological persecutions and conflict between lust and honor to be found in the works of Richardson, *The Libertine* has less overt sadism and shocking diablerie than *Zofloya*. The heroine must resist the unconscious forces of lust within herself as well as the advances of the determined and resourceful libertine, a direct descendant of Richardson's Lovelace.

*1-92. Dacre, Charlotte (used pseud. Rosa Matilda). **The Passions.** Cadell, 1811; Arno, 1974. (3) (SB)
The epistolary structure and austere moral tone of Dacre's final novel suggests that at the end of her literary career she turned from the disgusting thrills of the physical Gothic to the novel as a vehicle for psychological and ethical ideas. *The Passions* bears an interesting correspondence with Brockden Brown's deep and abiding concern with the darker areas of the human mind. Higher and more sophisticated types of Gothicism are anticipated in this last work.

1–93. De la Mark and Constantia; or, Ancient Heroism: A Gothick Tale.
Tegg & Castleman, 1803. (5)
A chapbook Gothic Romeo and Juliet, the hero and heroine hold to the
"mark" and are ever "constant" throughout their separations and adversities. Literally every incident and locale in this shilling shocker is lifted directly from this or that successful Gothic novel. Even the dialogue is an obvious appropriation of the stilted exchanges of love and loyalty between such
pairs as Theodore and Isabella in the depths of Otranto.

1–94. Deschamps, J. M.; J. B. D. Deprès; P. V. Benoist; and P. B. de Lamare (France). **Le Moine (The Monk).** Maradan, 1797. (6)
A first French translation of Lewis's notorious Gothic classic, *The Monk* [1–
218], this committee project also has a remarkable illustration of the novel's
ghastly aerial climax. We should note again how rapidly an English Gothic
best-seller reached the French Gothic consumer. J. Bell had published the
original novel in 1796.

*1–95. Diderot, Denis (France). **La Réligieuse (The Nun).** Buisson, 1796.
First English trans., G. G. Robinson and J. Robinson, 1797; Penguin, 1977.
(3)
Begun as a literary hoax and joke upon the Marquis of Croismare, *La Réligieuse* is a fast-paced, first-person narrative in which a young woman describes in detail a series of barbaric convent confinements and punitive ordeals, clearly a Gothic motif. Through its title and in its episodes of
persecution within the religious community, Diderot's work has some strong
ties with the misfortunes of Agnes in Lewis's *The Monk* [1–218]. The in-
voluntary novice who tells the story is Suzanne Simonin, an illegitimate
child who is condemned to a life of servitude in various nunneries by her un-
loving parents. Sentenced to three convents, she undergoes physical and psychological tortures and sexual perils worthy of the most tormented of Gothic
heroines. Diderot's gloomy chapels and lugubrious penitential cells add a
strong note of Gothic atmosphere to the morbid interiors of various mother
houses. For her recalcitrance, Suzanne is confined to a punishment chamber
(*in pace requiescat* in the parlance of the nuns), and because of her innocent
beauty she becomes the target of the lust of a lesbian mother superior. Like
many Gothic novels, *La Réligieuse* uses the restrictive environment of the religious life as a situational metaphor for repression and as a symbol for the unnatural warping of the passions by outmoded and exclusive institutions.

1–96. Doherty, Ann. **The Castles of Wolfnorth and Monteagle.** Hookham,
1812. (4)
A Highland Gothic in the Radcliffean mode, Doherty's work appears to be a
reproduction in kind of Radcliffe's first attempt at Gothic fiction, *The Castles
of Athlin and Dunbayne* [1–313]. Rival earls clash and bring death and despair
to their children in this historical Gothic.

1-97. Don Algonah; or, The Sorceress of Montillo. T. Hurst, 1802. (5) (SB)
This shilling shocker features an obsessed young hero, who, like the wounded
castle guest of Poe's "Oval Portrait," is infatuated with the miniature of a
beautiful young woman discovered in a strange and ruined castle. Motivated by a passion to know firsthand the deadly figure depicted in the miniature, the hero devotes his life to the quest for the dream lady. Such irrational pursuit of forbidden beauty leads the hero on a course of various Gothic
alarums and excursions. He encounters Baron Ardulph and the nefarious
Don Algonah, both of whom are satisfactory abbreviations of the regulation
Gothic villain. Characteristic of the bluebook industry, the romance's title
has little relevance to the events and characters contained within.

1-98. Don Sancho; or, The Monk of Hennares; A Spanish Romance. J. F.
Hughes, 1803. (5) (SB)
Another pulp reduction of the most sensational incidents of *The Monk*, the
bluebook concentrates its action on Ambrosio's assaults on his mother and
sister, Raymond's liaison with the bleeding nun, and the obscene sufferings
of Agnes in the slimy cellars of St. Clare. This plagiarized condensation of
The Monk should be compared with *Almagro and Claude* [1–5].

1-99. Drake, Nathan. "The Abbey of Clunedale" in *Literary Hours.* J.
Mitchell, 1804; in *Gothic Tales of Terror,* ed. by Peter Haining. Taplinger,
1972. (1)
Drake's *Literary Hours* was an ongoing collection of essays and stories published between 1798 and 1804. To *Montmorenci, A Fragment,* Drake appended
an important essay on Gothic theory entitled "On Objects of Terror." Other
Gothic pieces in *Literary Hours* that merit bibliographical mention are *Henry
Fitzowen: A Gothic Tale* and *Sir Egbert.* Literary hour number 20 is "The Abbey of Clunedale," a Radcliffean set piece whose "considerable power of
narrative" much impressed Montague Summers, although Edith Birkhead
in *The Tale of Terror* found it a feeble replica of Radcliffe's method of the "explained supernatural." In the story, a murderer named Clifford visits the
crumbling ruins of the abbey by night to do penance at the tomb of his wife
for slaying her brother. As he humbles himself, he is taken for a phantom.
The strong feature of the story is not its human characters, but the abbey
itself, which is splendidly done in the high Gothic manner and proves to be
an excellent illustration of what Drake's essay meant by the power of an
"object of terror."

**1-100. Ducray-Duminil, François Guillaume (France). Alexis; ou, La
Maisonette dans les bois (Alexis; or, The Little House in the Forest).** Mara-
dan, 1789. (2)
In spite of its pastoral title, Ducray-Duminil's early *roman noir* displays nearly
every element of the Radcliffean terror novel. As demonstrated by Robert
D. Mayo, the book is also the probable source of Radcliffe's *The Romance of*

the Forest [1–315]. Deep within the bandit-infested forest of Chamboran stands the *maisonette* or hermitage of the innocent Clairette, her guilt-ridden father, Candor, and their servant, Germain. Candor has retired from society, having been tricked into murdering his own wife and child. Directly beneath the idyllic cottage lie a subterranean sepulchre and a network of passageways containing the remains of the murdered pair. Eventually, the exploratory and curious Clairette will find a secret staircase and embark upon the tenebrous journey through the catacombs in quest of the dark truth about herself and about the mysterious young wanderer, Alexis, who takes refuge with Candor during a storm. Complicated adventures in the underground ensue with the usual Gothic outcome as the relationship between Alexis and his sylvan hosts is revealed.

1–101. Ducray-Duminil, François Guillaume (France). **Victor; ou, L'Enfant de la forêt (Victor; or, The Child of the Forest).** LePrieur, 1796. (2)
An English translation in four volumes of this popular *roman noir* was done by Minerva-Press in 1802. As a Gothic child of dark destiny, Victor is simply a reincarnation of *Alexis*'s offspring.

1–102. Ducray-Duminil, François Guillaume (France). **Coelina; ou, L'Enfant du mystère (Coelina; or, The Child of Mystery).** LePrieur, 1798. (2)
An English translation of this *roman noir*, which applies the same formula as *Alexis* [1–100] and *Victor* [1–101], was made by the successful Gothic novelist Mary Meeke and published in 1803 by Minerva-Press. For synoptic data, see Pixérécourt's dramatic adaptation of the novel [1–302].

1–103. Ducray-Duminil, François Guillaume (France). **Paul; ou, La Ferme abandonée (Paul; or, The Abandoned Farmhouse).** LePrieur, 1799. (4)
A solitary hero with a sensitive and poetic soul, rural solitude and Gothic melancholy, and a search for missing parents characterize the work. Ducray-Duminil may have been influenced in his picture of the melancholy of rural life by Helme's widely read *The Farmer of Inglewood Forest* [1–157], a sentimental Gothic appearing in 1796.

1–104. Dufrenoy, Madame (France). **Santa Maria; ou, Les Grossesse Mysterieuse (Santa Maria; or, The Mysterious Pregnancy).** Vignon, 1800. (6)
An aristocratic translation of Joseph Fox's complicated but interesting Gothic of 1797, *Santa Maria; or, The Mysterious Pregnancy* [1–119].

1–105. Dufrenoy, Madame (France). **Le Jeune héritier; ou, Les Appartements défendus (The Young Heiress; or, The Forbidden Apartments).** Vignon, 1801. (6)
A modified French translation of Linley's historical Gothic of 1800, *Forbidden Apartments* [1–224]. Clara Reeve's remarkably portable Gothic device of the closed wing or sealed room of the castle remained attractive throughout the

Gothic period. The room, which contains the secret of the hero's or heroine's noble identity, never ceased to please the Gothic appetite.

1–106. Dunlap, William (U.S.). **Fountainville Abbey.** David Longworth at the Dramatic Repository, Shakespeare-Gallery, 1807. (1)
First performed in 1795, the melodrama is founded on Radcliffe's *The Romance of the Forest* [1–315].

1–107. Durdent, R. J. (France). **La Main mysterieuse; ou, Les Horreurs souterraines! (The Mysterious Hand; or, Subterranean Horrours!).** Dentu, 1819. (6)
A lengthened French version of the Gothic shocker of 1811, Crandolph's *The Mysterious Hand; or, Subterranean Horrours!* [1–76].

1–108. Durston Castle; or, The Ghost of Eleonora: A Gothic Story. Publisher unknown, 1804. (5)
Durston Castle is a bibliographical example of the subliterary dregs of the Gothic movement. Although Montague Summers identified the title in *The Gothic Quest,* the work itself, like so many Gothic chapbooks, "was literally read to pieces." If the Gothic novel soared to genius in Radcliffe, Lewis, and Maturin, it more frequently sank to obscure rubbish in the swarm of bluebooks that marked the period. While *Durston Castle* is a lost Gothic, it is not difficult to speculate about the plundered and crude nature of its content.

1–109. Duval, Alexandre Vincent Pineux (France). **Montoni; ou, Le Château d'Udolphe (Montoni; or, The Castle of Udolpho).** Migneret, 1797. (6)
A melodrama adapted from Radcliffe's *The Mysteries of Udolpho* [1–316], Duval's elaborately plotted play enjoyed huge success. Duval rearranged the story to bring *Udolpho*'s shadowy villain into the spotlight; at the same time, he did not forget the theatrical value of a Gothic prima donna, and he therefore kept Emily St. Aubert's castle sufferings before the spectator. Because Radcliffean Gothic is far more lyric than dramatic, Duval's problem of staging involved transforming the static moments into audiovisually exciting episodes. To accomplish this, he brought Montoni's machinations to center stage while adorning the castle of Emily's imprisonment with dozens of pleasing Gothic contraptions to augment the veiled portrait.

1–110. Eidous, Marc Antoine (France). **Le Château d'Otrante: Histoire Gothique (The Castle of Otranto: Gothic History).** Prault, 1767. (6)
A first French translation of the first English Gothic novel, *The Castle of Otranto* [1–398], taken from the text of the second edition of Walpole's manual to Gothicism. A copy of the translation was presented to Horace Walpole during a Paris visit.

1–111. Elson, Jane. **The Romance of the Castle.** Minerva-Press, 1800. (1)
In this acceptable derivation from Radcliffean Gothic, the lonesome and or-

phaned Rosalind is carried off to the remote Castle of Llangwellein in the Welsh countryside. Among other nocturnal adventures, Rosalind's candle is extinguished by a sudden gust of wind as she explores the castle vaults, seemingly with a copy of *The Mysteries of Udolpho* as her guidebook. In her devotion to a non-Gothic public, Elson soberly announced that her purpose in these night adventures was instructive as well as suspenseful, but it is difficult to find anything enlightening in Rosalind's Gothic prowlings. Like other overeager heroines in the Radcliffean camp, Rosalind slowly learns to distinguish Gothic illusions from waking realities. In her dedication, Elson wrote this somewhat misleading statement about her work: "Though it may not display a superior brilliancy of genius, nor abound in strokes of wit and humour, the excellence of the moral may atone for other deficiencies." But the novel's Gothic deficiencies remain more entertaining than its obtuse morality.

1–112. English, John. The Grey Friar and the Black Spirit of the Wye. Minerva-Press, 1810. (3)
Possibly written with Charles Brockden Brown's eerie ventriloquist, Carwin [1–46], in view, the novel features a ventriloquist brigand and uses the delayed scientific explanation to account for his peculiar vocal powers and deceptions. English's point verges on Brown's didactic manipulations of the Gothic; what seems mysterious or beyond comprehension is always explicable to those beings who are wise in the ways of higher scientific reasoning. The hero-villain, who uses his biloquial powers ambiguously, asserts the message of the novel when he orates: "The principles of natural philosophy are known but to very few; the phenomena of nature are, therefore, often reckoned miraculous, because they are not understood." Even the style of this plea for enlightenment has the intellectual tone of Brown's characters.

1–113. Erwina; oder, Zauber, Minne und Mutterliebe (Erwina; or, Magic, Love and Mother Love) (Germany). C. Haas'schen, 1819. (2)
An anonymous and late *Ritter-roman* that may be by several hands, the work appears to be an amalgam of *Rinaldo Rinaldini* [1–390], *Aböllino* [1–422], and such works as *Der Bezauberte Helm* [1–31].

1–114. Der Felsenbewohner: Scenen des Schreckens und der Freude (The Cliffdweller: Scenes of Terror and Joy) (Germany). Reichs-Commissions-und-Industrie Bureau, n.d. (5) (SB)
This rare work is one of the few surviving editions of a Germanized shilling shocker or bluebook. The compiler appears to have plundered freely from the English bluebook traffic while adding ingredients from his own native *Schauer-romane* where needed. There is little joy and much terror in his Gothic meanderings as we are shown a parade of lurking monsters, odd beasts, and mad idealists who have taken to living at the edge. No single plot is discernible in the romancer's Gothic tangle.

1-115. Fenwick, Eliza. **Secresy; or, The Ruin on the Rock.** Knight, 1795. (1) (SB)

The mighty and dark castle, the trembling maiden, and a dark ganglion of family guilts and secrets suggest the formulaic nature of this Gothic romance. Castles along the Rhine became standard sites for English Gothicists.

1-116. **Die Folgen; oder, Begebenheiten in dem Schlosse Raxall (The Succession; or, Events at Castle Raxall)** (Germany). Johann Christian Sinner, 1799. (1) (SB)

Weird events and strange sounds have filled Raxall Castle since the usurpation of the old Baron Raxall and his death at the hands of his ambitious brother. *Die Folgen* is a *Schauer-romantik* transcription of the Gothic formula of *The Castle of Otranto;* like Walpole's architectural dénouement, which ends Manfred's control over the castle, the German version terminates in a restoration of the good with the return of family power to the best of the line.

1-117. Fontallard, J. F. (France). **L'Abbaye de Netley: Histoire du moyen age (Netley Abbey: A Story of the Middle Ages).** Ledoux, 1801. (6)

A French translation of Warner's elaborate Gothic romance of 1795, *Netley Abbey: A Gothic Story* [1-401].

1-118. **La Forêt; ou, L'Abbaye de Saint-Clair (The Forest; or, The Abbey of Saint Clair)** (France). Denné, 1794. (6)

A free-ranging, anonymous translation of Radcliffe's popular and widely influential Gothic novel of 1791, *The Romance of the Forest* [1-315].

1-119. Fox, Joseph, Jr. **Santa Maria; or, The Mysterious Pregnancy.** G. Kearsley, 1797. (1) (SB)

Complex Gothic gears and a provocative title insured the wide acceptance of Fox's romance in all Gothic circles. For purposes of sadistic action, Fox transcribes Shakespeare's Friar Lawrence into the remarkable priest-predator, Father Conrad. His extremely busy Gothic novel is a bizarre fusion of monastic treachery and ecclesiastical lust as copied from Monk Lewis and Walpolesque Gothic's enigmas of genealogy. Santa Maria, daughter of Count Rodolph, is found on her wedding morn "in the icy arms of death." In a cadaverous revival that looks ahead to Poe's "Ligeia," the expired heroine instantly revives after last rites and discloses her "mysterious pregnancy" before the young Rinaldo can consummate the nuptials. Santa Maria then flees from her enraged father, who dispatches Bernadini and Goddard to Martarono Castle to assassinate Rinaldo for compromising his daughter's virginity. At this point, the malicious Carthusian, Father Conrad, enters the story. By means of a sleeping potion, Father Conrad had engineered the unconscious violation of Santa Maria by Count Philip Contarini, who "fully and grossly satisfied his impious lusts." For once in a Gothic novel, this tangle of sexual crimes is punished without the intervention of the Inquisition. By mixing themes and materials from the monastic shocker and castle thriller, Fox concocted a sadist's delight to compete with the tamer sexual innuendoes of Radcliffe.

1–120. Frances, Sophia L. **The Nun of Misericordia; or, The Eve of All Saints.** Minerva-Press, 1807. (1) (SB)
The horrors of the convent include both natural and supernatural problems for Adelaide. Her ordeal in the catacombs and sanguinary trials suggest strongly that the author had found a means to synthesize the monstrosities of the cloister depicted in Diderot's *La Réligieuse* [1–95] with the depraved doings in the dungeon of the abbey of St. Clare in *The Monk* [1–218]. Blood gushes freely from the descriptions of maidenly torture as in the following passage: "Streams of blood still seemed to flow from her bosom, and stain her long white garments, and her cheeks were deadly pale, her eyes fixed, and her whole lovely face marked with death." The fierce anti-Catholicism of *The Nun of Misericordia* quite naturally stimulated a French translation by Madame Viterne in 1809.

1–121. Freneau, Philip (U.S.). **The House of Night.** Francis Bailey, 1788; in *Poems of Freneau,* ed. by Harry Hayden Clark. Hafner, 1960. (3)
A confluence of splendid Gothic imagery and scenery from the graveyard poets dominates this dream excursion of 136 quatrains. The nocturnal traveler, like Warton's melancholy Gothic wanderer, visits the interior of the House of Night and beholds all the majestic horrors of the Gothic world. He enters into a dialogue with death himself, who lies dying in his own dark palace. Composing an epitaph for death, the wanderer ends his quest for dark truth by moralizing upon the certainties of the grave and the vanity of human wishes. The picture of death upon his own deathbed is memorably Gothic and suggests that Freneau had studied various Gothic novels for inspiration: "Turning to view the object whence it came, / My frighted eyes a horrid form survey'd; / Fancy, I own thy power—Death on the couch, / With fleshless limbs, at rueful length, was laid. / Around his bed, by dull flambeaux' glare, / I saw pale phantoms—Rage to madness vext, / Wan, wasting grief, and ever musing care, / Distressful pain, and poverty perplext. / Sad was his countenance, where only bones were seen / And eyes sunk in their sockets, dark and low, / And teeth, that only show'd themselves to grin."

1–122. Fuller, Ann. **Alan Fitz-Osborne: An Historical Tale.** Robinson, 1786. (1)
Although the title seems more historical than horrific, Fuller's work remains an important step in the evolution of genuine horror-Gothic. According to Montague Summers, "The tale is extremely Gothic and shows very clearly the influence of *Otranto,* but it is not clearly very historical, although the period is the reign of Henry III, and the hero, Alan, takes part in the Barons'

Wars." The plot joins the customary genealogical mysteries with several purely *Schauer-romantik* elements. Alan's wife, Matilda, is slain by her lecherous brother-in-law, Walter Fitz-Osborne, who is subsequently bedeviled in the form of nightly visitations by the blood-gouted figure of the murdered lady. The gory shape at the bedside becomes a kind of type scene in Gothic romance and has a value for the Gothicist nearly equivalent to Reeve's haunted chamber. The authentic specter at the bedside of her assassin shows that some women writers of Gothic fiction were quite prepared to follow a different route of terror than that of the explained Gothic shortly to be charted by Radcliffe.

1–123. Garnier, Germain (France). **Caleb Williams; ou, Les Choses comme elles sont (Caleb Williams; or, Things as They Are).** H. Agasse, 1796. (6)
The French translation of Godwin's philosophical novel of 1794, *Things as They Are; or, The Adventures of Caleb Williams* [1–128].

1–124. Genlis, Felicité de Saint-Aubin (France). **Adèle et Théodore; ou, Lettres sur l'éducation (Adèle and Théodore; or, Letters on Education).** M. Lambert et F.-J. Baudouin, 1782. (3)
An important influence on Radcliffe, Genlis's moral tale contains the Gothic situation of a wife held prisoner in a subterranean cell by a jealous and sadistic husband. The hidden wife is a familiar pathetic fixture of the Gothic plot, from her appearance in Radcliffe's *Sicilian Romance* [1–314] to Grace Poole's mad ward of Thornfield Hall in Charlotte Brontë's *Jane Eyre*. A voluminous writer of popular and sentimental romances, many of which are interlaced with Gothic equipage, Genlis believed in the novel as an instrument of edification and used Gothic devices and materials to enhance her didactic aims. A later work, *Les Veillées du château (Tales of the Castle)* (1784) furnished the Radcliffean school with numerous ideas and scenic inventions.

1–125. Das Gespenst in der Abtei Balderoni (The Phantom of Balderoni Abbey) (Germany). Schimmelpfennig, 1802. (2) (SB)
This obscure and never-translated German Gothic appears to be an imitation of such popular English abbey shockers as the unsigned *Phantoms of the Cloister* [1–176] and *The Spectre Mother* [1–368].

1–126. Gleich, Joseph Alois (Germany) (used pseuds. Dellarosa and H. Walden). **Die Totenfackel; oder, Die Höhle der Siebenschläfer (The Torch of Death; or, The Cave of the Seven Sleepers).** Haas, 1798. (2)
A prolific producer of *Schauer-roman*, Gleich wrote several dozen ultra-Gothic titles during his lifetime (1772–1841). None of his work seems to have been translated, and it is all very scarce today. The Sadleir-Black Gothic Collection contains three of Gleich's shudder novels, whose titles alone convey the extreme Gothicism of their content. Thus, we have *Wallrab von Schreckenhorn; oder, Das Todtenmahl um Mitternacht (Wallrab von Schreckenhorn; or, The Meal of Death at Midnight)* and several other equally horrendous titles. Emphasis on

ugliness and a candid and excessive presentation of the disgusting supernatural characterize *Die Totenfackel* as well as Gleich's other work. The shrill
craft of the *Schauer-roman* perhaps reaches its apogee with Gleich's undeniable talent for bold atrocities.

1-127. Gleich, Joseph Alois (Germany). **Udo der Stählerne; oder, Die Ruinen von Drudenstein (Udo the Man of Steel; or, the Ruins of Drudenstein).** Haas, 1799. (2)
The *Schauer-roman* is interesting for its use of the figure of the enormous man,
the haunter of the dilapidated castle. Walpole's Alfonso resided within the
walls of Otranto while he grew to an enormous size. Udo's stature and power
rival the virtuous Alfonso and anticipate the most famous brooding brute
among Gothic writers, the monster in Mary Shelley's *Frankenstein* [1–348].
Since the Shelleys read German and since P. B. Shelley was fond of wild
German romances, it is possible that Gleich's *Udo* was known to the Shelleys
and exerted some influence on the making of *Frankenstein*.

*1-128. Godwin, William. **Things as They Are; or, The Adventures of Caleb Williams.** B. Crosby, 1794; Norton, 1977. (3) (SB).
A critique of class structure, unjust social and legal privilege, and the cor-
ruptibility of the human spirit, Godwin's novel of ideas intersperses Gothic
equipment, characters, and locales with radical social commentary to ignite
the passions of the audience for revolutionary change. In the Gothic novels
of the 1790s, haunted castles often signified a decayed social structure; in
Godwin's work, society itself takes the role of the haunted castle, as a prison
of legalized violence and institutionalized cruelty. *Caleb Williams* is also a
psychological tale of criminal detection in which the aristocratic murderer,
Falkland, pursues and persecutes the proletarian detective, his servant and
secretary, young Caleb Williams. Falkland has killed the dissolute squire,
Barnabas Tyrrel, but conceals his crime, allowing one Hawkins to be accused, convicted, and executed. The suspicious Caleb constantly watches his
master, whose once-noble character has grown gloomy and mean-spirited as
a result of his hidden transgression. The psychological changes in Falkland
caused by unexpressed guilt foreshadow a mentalized Gothic theme that
Hawthorne would use repeatedly. Caleb discovers the dark truth, but Falkland has the law on his side. Like a tormented maiden in a Gothic novel, Caleb is relentlessly pursued and abused by his depraved master. The dungeon
scenes, the secret held in the mysterious box in Falkland's chamber, and the
ambidextrous agent of terror, Gines, are among the many prominent Gothic
properties borrowed by Godwin from the Gothic kit. In using the Gothic as a
vehicle for social horrors and the twistings of a tormented mind, Godwin
gave impetus and example to the higher Gothic of the Americans, particularly his contemporary, Charles Brockden Brown. Brown's novel of the
night, *Edgar Huntly*, is in the Godwinian tradition [1–49].

*1-129. Godwin, William. Saint Leon: A Tale of the Sixteenth Century.
G. G. and J. Robinson, 1799; Arno Press, 1972. (3)
Written in a stilted and somewhat obtuse style, *Saint Leon* is inferior in both
ideology and Gothicism to *Caleb Williams* [1-128]. The novel exploits the interest of the Gothic novelists in the philosopher's stone, alchemy, and the
quest for the elixir vitae. Its finest Gothic character is not the dissipated
wandering knight, Saint Leon, but the Hungarian giant, Bethlem Gabor,
who has the sinister fascination of Radcliffe's titanic monk, Schedoni, in *The
Italian* [1-317]. Saint Leon is a noble member of the court of Francis I. He is
distinguished for his soldierly qualities, but notorious for his gambling and
dissipation. Taking his wife, Marguerite, he retires to the pure living of a
Swiss canton to recover from his misfortunes. Poverty and misery are the lot
of Saint Leon until he is visited by a mysterious old man who is fleeing from
the Inquisition. Saint Leon conceals and befriends Zampieri, the Wandering
Jew figure, who bestows the secret of immortality upon Saint Leon in return.
But possessing the philosopher's stone only isolates Saint Leon from human
fellowship and love. He is arrested by the Inquisition on suspicion of sorcery,
escapes, makes his way to Hungary, and encounters Bethlem Gabor, in
whom he finds a kind of spiritual twin in the "sublime desolation of a
mighty soul." In an attempt to gain the secret of immortality, Gabor imprisons Saint Leon in a subterranean vault from which he is rescued by his son,
Charles, leading a siege. The Gothicism of the novel is visible in its dungeon
sequences, in the graphic description of the brutal death of Hector, a black
servant, and in the gruesomely real pictures of the *auto de fé* of the Inquisition. Nevertheless, the Gothic remains a vehicle rather than an end in
itself for Godwin, whose central purpose is not to alarm but to edify the
reader by revealing the disastrous consequences of wealth and power. The
best modern assessment of Godwin's marginal Gothicism is by Wallace A.
Flanders, "Godwin and Gothicism: St. Leon," *Texas Studies in Language and
Literature* 8 (1967): 533–545.

**1-130. Goethe, Johann Wolfgang von (Germany). Götz von Berlichingen
mit der Eisernen Hand (Götz von Berlichingen with the Iron Hand).** B. L.
Walthard, 1776. (2)
Printed privately in 1773 at Frankfurt am Main, *Götz* is a loosely constructed
and panoramic drama in 58 historical scenes. The *Ritterspiel* or drama of
chivalry presents a robber-knight who takes upon himself the defense of the
weak in the face of the selfish princes and nobles. Götz is a sixteenth-century
nobleman who is forced into outlawry by social conditions that his conscience cannot tolerate. Goethe's dramatic art combines the *Ritter* with the
Räuber-roman traditions, thus bringing together the two major German influences on the English Gothic novel in its first phase. The plot concerns a feud
between Götz and the imperious Bishop of Bamberg. Adalbert von Weisslin-
gen, the bishop's crone, is held prisoner in Götz's castle; while incarcerated

he is smitten with Götz's sister, Maria, and shifts his allegiance to the fugitive knight. Liberated from the castle of Götz, he forgets Maria and transfers his affections to Adelheid von Walldorf, a favorite of the bishop's court. From mixed motives, which include both the desire for power and the desire for social justice, Götz leads a revolt of the peasants, which fails; Götz finds himself a prisoner of Adalbert, the man he once had imprisoned. Bitter and alienated, yet still able to fight against the meanness of the times, Götz finally dies a warrior's death on the field of battle. In Götz's variant character may be seen that palimpsest of good and bad passions that often drives the Gothic hero-villain to his spectacular and sometimes glorious doom.

1-131. Goethe, Johann Wolfgang von (Germany). Die Braut von Korinth (The Bride of Korinth). Musen Almanach, 1798. (2)
In his letters, Goethe described this Gothic ballad as "das vampyrische Gedicht," the vampire poem. A sexual union with a woman who is later discovered to have died prior to the young man's encounter with her is the gruesome situation of Goethe's contribution to the literature of necrophilia. The psychopathic motif of uninhibited corpse gratification enhances the vampire theme. An eerie love affair between a mortal and an undead creature of the night had folklore origins and was often seized upon by Gothic balladeers and novelists. Goethe's cadaverous beloved will be found again in the vaults of E. A. Poe, while a similar union between the living and the dead had appeared in Bürger's "Lenore" [1–52].

1-132. Gothic Stories: "The Enchanted Castle: A Fragment"; "Ethelbert; or, The Phantom of the Castle"; "The Mysterious Vision; or, Perfidy Punished." S. Bailey, n.d. (5)
A cheaply manufactured bluebook anthology that contains plagiarized miniaturizations of several legitimate Gothics, this collection of terrific titles exemplifies the downward path into pulp and puerility followed by the commercial fiend-mongers. "Ethelbert," for example, seems to be a badly mutilated condensation of Cullen's *The Haunted Priory* [1–81].

1-133. The Gothic Story of Courville Castle; or, The Illegitimate Son, A Victim of Prejudice and Passion. S. Fisher, 1804. (5) (SB)
This curious bluebook is a reduction of the Edmund Twyford story from Reeve's *The Old English Baron* [1–322]. Displaced heirs who have their noble heritage revealed to them during an evening of terror within the castle's forbidden chamber always seem to bear the name Edmund in Gothic fiction. The entire title of the bluebook is a summary of the novelette itself and reads: *Owing to the Early Impressions Inculcated with Unremitting Assiduity by an Implacable Mother, Whose Resentment to Her Husband Excited Her Son to Envy, Usurpation and Murder: But Retributive Justice at Length Restores the Right Heir to His Lawful Possessions. To Which Is Added the English Earl; or, The History of Robert Fitzwalter.*

1-134. Gouges, Olympe de (France). **Le Couvent; ou, Les Voeux forcés (The Convent; or, The Constrained Vows).** Duchesne, 1792. (4)
First performed in October 1790, this anticlerical melodrama resembles Boutet de Monvel's *Les Victimes cloîtrées* [1–42] in its lurid depiction of the enforced religious life. Both Montague Summers and Maurice Lévy draw the parallel between the victims of clerical crime and repression and the wretched situation of the pregnant nun, Agnes, in *The Monk*. While in Paris in the summer of 1791, Lewis saw performances of *Les Victimes cloîtrées* as well as Marsollier's *Camille; ou, Le Souterrain* [1–237]; both plays, like *Le Couvent*, have elaborate underground scenery, suffering nuns and persecuting abbesses, and a potent revolutionary message.

1-135. Green, Sarah. **The Carthusian Friar; or, The Mysteries of Montanville.** Sherwood, Neely, Jones, 1814. (1) (SB)
Tempests, ruins, a wicked and scheming abbess, and a reincarnation of Radcliffe's colossal monk, Schedoni, are integrated with some skill in this four-volume revival of Radcliffean Gothic. At Montanville Priory, the heroine is confronted by a monastic ogre almost as abominable as Radcliffe's skeletal father confessor, for there amid the abbey gloom she faces "a dark figure taller by three times than any man. It lifted up a face as white as ashes and extended a long, withered hand, all bones, with which it seemed to beckon." Green's mastery of Gothic mechanics was as sound as her control of the Radcliffean formula of the maiden's belated delivery from the supernatural world.

*1-136. Green, William Child. **The Abbot of Montserrat; or, The Pool of Blood.** A. K. Newman, 1826; Arno, 1977. (1)
This late and thundering Gothic is written in the horrific tradition of Monk Lewis with additional stylistic debts to Maturin's *Melmoth the Wanderer* [1–244]. The relentless supernaturalism of the story is real, with the disappointing exception of the bloody pool, which is belatedly explained away as a chemical trick. The hero-villain of the tale is the power-crazed monk, Obando, whose pact with the demonic Zatanai and whose celebration of infernal rites must have reminded all Gothic readers of similar diabolic agreements in *The Monk* [1–218]. Assisted by the Mephistophelian Zatanai, the Faustian Obando strangles Abbot Ambrose and arranges for the murder of his brother, Roldan, a brigand figure on loan from the still influential tradition of the *Räuber-roman*. Accused of having traffic with the powers of darkness by the always handy Inquisition, the new Abbot of Montserrat bargains away his soul to Zatanai to escape torture. Obando is hurled from an enormous height to a Gothic death much like Ambrosio's in *The Monk;* but unlike Lewis's defiant sinner, Obando has renounced his allegiance to evil in an ending that weakens Green's otherwise potent Gothic. The urbane fiend, Zatanai, is an exceptionally good revival of another snatcher of overreaching mortals, Dacre's *Zofloya* [1–90].

1-137. Grosett, Emilia. **The Spirit of the Grotto; or, The Castle of Saint George.** Mason, 1799. (1)

The situation is typical of numerous grotto Gothics; a remote underground cell of the otherwise comfortable Castle of Saint George is said to be haunted by a pathetic phantom, who resembles the person of the heroine's murdered father. The Hamletism of this standard sort of Gothic plot is evident.

1-138. Grosette, Henry William. **Raymond and Agnes; or, The Bleeding Nun of Lindenberg.** Larpent Collection MS., 1797. (1)

A hell-fire dramatic adaptation of one segment of the triple plot of *The Monk* [1-218], Grosette's melodrama can be regarded as a type of dramatic bluebook. The two sensational acts follow Don Raymond's pursuit of the Bleeding Nun of Lindenberg Castle, whom he supposes to be his beloved Agnes in apparitional disguise. Exquisite arrays of trapdoors and a fiery ascent to heaven by the nun at the climax altered Lewis but pleased the eyes of the Gothic audience. As is so often the case with Gothic drama, flashy spectacle and elaborately contrived supernatural stagecraft took precedence over story or development of character. Yet the drama is no crude farrago of monkish parts, like so many of the pirated bluebooks copied from Lewis's Gothic masterwork.

*1-139. Grosse, Karl (Germany). **Horrid Mysteries.** Trans. by Peter Will. Minerva-Press, 1796; Folio, 1968. (1)

Michael Sadleir regarded *Horrid Mysteries* as the best of the seven Northanger novels, the septet of horrid titles recommended to Catherine Morland for her Gothic edification in *Northanger Abbey* [1-11]. The novel itself illustrates a branch of Gothic fiction that deserves to be recognized as a separate school in its presentation of the terrors of the secret societies of the Continent. Taking its cue from Naubert's *Hermann von Unna* [1-279] and other novels dealing with the *Vehmgericht* (or secret Fehmic Tribunal), the action of *Horrid Mysteries* concerns the savage and cabalistic activities of the Illuminati brotherhood and various freemason sects, whose intrigues and skulduggery were aimed at world revolution. The highborn hero, the Marquis of G., falls under the spell of the secret fraternity, swears the vile oath of blood, and finds himself committed to a life of anarchist crimes against his own social class. Desperately involved with the evil tribunal, he travels the courts and countries of Europe trying to raise a movement against the schemes and intrigues of the Illuminati. Apocalyptic events, assassinations, sudden disappearances, and a variety of Gothic entrapments stalk the hero's quest. Yet in spite of its length and intricacy of plot, the story of the persecuted Marquis is easily followed; it is consistent at all points with the narrative laws of flight and pursuit through a larger labyrinth—the novel's movement is from country to country rather than from corridor to corridor within a haunted castle. The style of the translation occasionally exhibits magnificent gloom, as in the description of the "cracking of half-decayed crosses on the graves." Sadleir estimated that "*Horrid Mysteries* is surely the most potent *Schauer-roman* of them all; certainly in its English version it is the most defiantly fantastic of any novel of the period."

1–140. Guénard, Elisabeth Baronne de Méré (France). **Lise et Valcour; ou, Le Bénédictin (Lisa and Valcour; or, The Benedictine).** Pigoreau, 1799. (2)
The prolific Baronne de Méré Guénard (1751–1829) turned out *romans noirs* as well as many other varieties of fiction with mechanical speed and regularity. The tenderness of love is pitted against the harshness of the monastic life with all its attendant Gothic cruelties. This sentimental romance owes much to Saint-Pierre's *Paul et Virginie* [1–333] as well as to the older pathetic story of Eloise and Abélard.

1–141. Guénard, Elisabeth Baronne de Méré (France). **Les Forges mystérieuses; ou, L'Amour alchimiste (The Mysterious Smithies; or, The Alchemist of Love).** Privately printed by the author, 1800. (2)
A *roman noir* that mixes magic potions and fatal passions in subterranean settings, *Les Forges* tells the story of a deadly elixir and an equally deadly desire to possess eternal love by bartering away the soul.

1–142. Guénard, Elisabeth Baronne de Méré (France). **Les Capucins; ou, Le Secret du Cabinet noir (The Capuchins; or, The Secret of the Black Cabinet).** Marchand, 1801. (2)
A genuine and powerful *roman noir* that strongly imitates the suspenseful procedures surrounding the mysterious black veil of *Udolpho, Les Capuchins* is an outstanding example of the Radcliffean strain in French Gothic fiction.

1–143. Guénard, Elisabeth Baronne de Méré (France). **Les Trois Moines (The Three Monks).** Chez Marchand, 1802. (4)
H. J. Sarratt's English translation (published by B. Crosby) of this comic Gothic in 1803 attests to the popularity of the anticlerical theme with English Gothic audiences. Much of the novel can be described as monastic picaresque accompanied by Gothic overtones and jokes on the form. The three monks—Dominico del Frazo, Silvino Fezzali, and Anselme Georgani—get into all kinds of amorous mischief and compromising sexual situations because of their irrepressible urges for rascality. Eventually, Silvino will become a Franciscan, Anselme will become a Benedictine, and Domenico will become a Cistercian, although the taking of holy orders does little to curb their fleshly appetites. Here, the restriction of the natural passions by the artificial piety of the cloistered life is treated comically rather than with the usual melodramatic and heavy horror of the monastic shocker. Yet the rowdy sadism of many of the three monks' exploits, the psychological sufferings of souls chained to an institution that denied the passions their natural outlets, and the death of Silvino by poison are distinct Gothic elements; they indicate that much of the novel's content was consciously designed to satisfy

the expectations of those Gothic readers who had found delight in the works of Monk Lewis and the infamous Marquis de Sade.

1-144. Guénard, Elisabeth Baronne de Méré (France). **Le Château de Vauvert; ou, Le Chariot de feu de la rue d'enfer (The Castle of Vauvert; or, The Chariot of Fire on the Street of Hell).** Lerouge, 1812. (2)
A rare example of *roman noir* that introduces *Schauer-romantik* materials to heighten its unrelieved atmosphere of supernatural shock. To find an equivalent in psychopathic fantasy and irrational release, one must look to Beckford's *Vathek* [1–25] for an adequate comparison. The interior of Vauvert Castle has flaming chambers, ectoplasmic tapestries, and a staff of ghoulish caretakers who transact their business of licentious persecution with Gothic gusto.

1-145. Hamilton, Ann Mary. **The Forest of Saint Bernardo.** J. F. Hughes, 1806. (1)
Also appearing in 1806 was Liss Hamilton's *The Forest of Montalbano.* Both works were published by J. F. Hughes and both novels were rather unimaginative transcriptions of Radcliffe's forest Gothic, *The Romance of the Forest* [1–315]. One work is a plagiarism of its Gothic predecessor, but it is impossible to determine who stole from whom. Both forest Gothics from Hughes feed shamelessly off the literary remains of Radcliffe.

1-146. Hans von Bleyleben; oder, Der irrende Geist bei Toplitz (Hans von Bleyleben; or, The Wandering Spirit of Toplitz) (Germany). Karl Barth, 1797. (2) (SB)
Advertised brashly on the frontispiece as "Eine Geistergeschichte" (a ghost story), *Hans* is a technically solid *Schauer-roman.* The spirit of a murdered relative hangs about the family estate at Toplitz and demands attention by ringing bells and setting off strange lights at midnight.

1-147. Hanway, Mary Ann. **Falconbridge Abbey: A Devonshire Story.** Minerva-Press, 1809. (4)
An inconsequential attempt to mix the Gothic with sentimental pictures of feudal history, *Falconbridge Abbey* evokes little fright and even less nostalgia for the Middle Ages in its confused picture of the reign of Henry II. A missing heir with a curious birthmark and a tyrannical uncle are stock figures in the second-hand plot. This novel could have gained Gothic respectability by admitting a phantom or two, but the abbey is spookless.

1-148. Hardenbrass and Harverill; or, The Secret of the Castle. Sherwood, Neely & Jones, 1817. (1) (SB)
A violent fraternal rivalry, a walking and talkative portrait of a murdered patriarch, and many more Gothic implements from Walpole's ever-useful warehouse of Otranto are to be found in this stereotypical romance of the late Gothic period. A dull and virtuous brother (Haverill) dedicated to find-

ing his father's murderer and a fascinating and nefarious brother (Hardenbrass) equally dedicated to Gothic chicanery and interesting vices is a modular Gothic plot. Despite its overuse, the readership still craved such well-worn formulae as late as 1817.

1–149. Harley, Mrs. **Saint Bernard's Priory: An Old English Tale.** Privately printed and sold at Swift's Circulating Library, 1786. (1)
Designated by Montague Summers as a "distinctly amateurish" duplication of Lee's *The Recess* [1–214], the novel strives to be Gothic by inserting the Walpolesque tool of the animated statue to provide a supernatural overlay missing from its parent historical romance. The priory stands astride an extensive underground where Elgiva and her two daughters, Maud and Laura, have been forced to reside for many years. Before he can see to their deliverance, the gallant Lord Raby must pass through a chamber where he is confronted by his father in colossal form. Here, in one of the better Gothic moments in the tale, Lord Raby gazes in awe "upon a high pedestal where arrayed in armour, a waving plume of feathers on his casque, and in his hand a pointed spear, stood the image of Lord Raby's father." In a departure from the architectural climax of *The Castle of Otranto* [1–398], there is no mighty explosion of the walls by the giant figure at the weak ending of Harley's derivative Gothic.

1–150. Harley, Mrs. **The Castle of Mowbray: An English Romance.** Stalker & H. Setchell, 1788. (1) (SB)
Like its predecessor, *Saint Bernard's Priory* [1–149], *The Castle of Mowbray* is a somewhat insipid effort to Gothify the format of historical romance by blending Walpolesque trappings with pseudohistory. The period of the action is the monarchy of Edward I, although the royal character is relegated to the background, a practice that Scott would later adopt. Elwina, a model Gothic ingenue, is hounded by the profligate, Edric, a silken son of pleasure who descends from the seducer-heroes of Richardson. The Gothic novelist again shows her predilection for walking statues; danger is deterred when the stone figure of Elwina's father, the Earl of Mowbray, abandons its pedestal to rescue his daughter from the wiles and guiles of Edric. While the supernatural effect is slightly mismanaged, the novelist shows a better technical command of Walpole's mechanisms than in *Saint Bernard's Priory*. Such paraphernalia maintained their appeal for the Gothic novelist set upon showing the victory of virtue over vice at a timely moment. Harley was by no means alone in using the living statue of the protective father as a Gothic *deus ex machina*.

1–151. Harvey, Jane. **Minerva Castle.** Minerva-Press, 1802. (4)
A sentimental romance masquerading under a Gothic title. The castle lacks ghosts but does contain a pining orphan who is seeking her parentage.

1-152. Harwood, Caroline. **The Castle of Vivaldi; or, The Mysterious Injunction.** Minerva-Press, 1810. (1)
Reissued by the publisher Davis in 1840 under the revised title *The Castle of Vivaldi; or, The Mysterious Casket,* this four-volume Gothic continued to attract readers well into the post-Gothic period. In Radcliffe's *The Italian* [1–317], Vincentio de Vivaldi was cast in the role of romantic rescuer of the suffering maiden, Ellena di Rosalba. Caroline Harwood keeps the name but converts the personality into the castle villain of the piece while furnishing his castle with every known Gothic prop. The 1840 title more accurately reflects the central Gothic device and situation, since the forbidden chamber of Vivaldi Castle holds an iron chest that is never to be opened and from which strange noises constantly emanate.

1-153. Hasworth, H. H. **The Lady of the Cave; or, The Mysteries of the Fourteenth Century.** Minerva-Press, 1802. (4)
The royal child concealed in a cavern and watched over by maternal or paternal specters was a commonplace of the historical romance. Hasworth's imitation of a well-worn Gothic predicament also appears to be the basis for the anonymous bluebook of the same year, *The Cavern of Horrors; or, The Miseries of Miranda* [1–60].

1-154. Haynes, Miss C. D. **Augustus and Adelina; or, The Monk of Saint Barnadine.** Minerva-Press, 1819. (4)
True and virtuous love threatened by enforced separation and convent confinement link the work with the anticlericalism of many previous Gothics. The monk of Saint Barnadine himself is ineffectual as a monastic villain, for he is less pernicious than simply meddlesome in keeping the lovers apart in their cruel religious communities. Haynes was trying to domesticate the monastic shocker in her three-volume work and succeeded all too tediously in accomplishing just that.

1-155. Haynes, Miss C. D. **Eleanor; or, The Spectre of Saint Michaels.** A. K. Newman, 1821. (1)
A conventional revival of the Radcliffean Gothic, the novel mechanically and automatically brings the maiden to the castle, which contains the secret of her destiny, and turns her loose to explore. Her encounter with the chapel ghost who is well-versed in the enigmas of her genealogy is both inevitable and laborious. By the third decade of the nineteenth century, the Gothic novel had lost its grip on the reading public and had become a twitching corpse. Haynes shows a complete technical mastery of the Radcliffean keyboard; but the melody of true terror is gone.

1-156. Haynes, D. F. **Pierre and Adeline; or, The Romance of the Castle.** B. Crosby, 1814. (4)
The father of C. D. Haynes, D. F. Haynes specialized in sentimental and pastoral effects rather than Gothic terrors. Orphaned children who display

unmistakable signs of noble lineage, living in a cottage on the edge of the shadow cast by the gloomy castle, is again a stereotypical Gothic plot. The adjacency of forest and castle, of children and local tyrant, always implied a clash of values and usually terminated in the formulaic restoration of the children to proper ownership and rightful title. Elements of Ducray-Duminil's romance of the displaced child, *Alexis; ou, La Maisonette dans les bois* [1–100], left an imprint upon Haynes's storytelling. *Pierre and Adeline* was reprinted for Hazlitt's *Romanticist and Novelist's Library* in 1841.

1–157. Helme, Elizabeth. **The Farmer of Inglewood Forest.** Minerva-Press, 1796. (4)
Marginally Gothic and more like a rhapsodic recollection of the morbid moods of the graveyard poets, *The Farmer of Inglewood Forest* is now a forgotten favorite, though it remained in print throughout the nineteenth century. Tearful visits to churchyards and the melancholy charms of rural solitude dominate this sentimental Gothic. Godwin, the Farmer of Inglewood Forest, struggles to achieve a pastoral existence amid marital crises, domestic disappointments, and recurrent deaths. In its lachrymose moods, the novel looks backward to the fatal sensitivity toward life to be found in Mackenzie's famous *The Man of Feeling* [1–234] as well as ahead to the rural realism and pastoral security of George Eliot's *Adam Bede* (1859). The Gothic characteristics of the book may be best observed in the graveyard meditations of characters such as young Edwin, who broods upon the burial site of Agnes Bernard, a young lady who "went mad for love and died." Gray, Akenside, Blair, the Wartons, and the other graveyard poets would have applauded a muted Gothic that might be called a romance of the tombstones.

*1–158. Helme, Elizabeth. **Saint Margaret's Cave; or, The Nun's Story: An Ancient Legend.** Earle & Hemet, 1801; Arno, 1977. (1)
The novel is a synthesis of cavern Gothic in the Radcliffean mode and the more lurid procedures of the monastic shocker. The oppressed heroine finds a troglodytic refuge, a secret-revealing hermit, and a variety of Gothic thrills in her cavernous retreat from enslavement in the convent. In such details, the novel is a far purer Gothic achievement than *The Farmer of Inglewood Forest* [1–157]. The novel also uses the common frame device of the recovered ancient manuscript to give the events a properly antique distancing. A boarder in a religious house is given a packet of aged documents for safekeeping by the abbess; one of these fading papers proves to be the "nun's story." By 1800, it would seem that no Gothic novel could be published without some variation of the lost manuscript come at last to light. Even the greatest of the Goths, C. R. Maturin, turned to the device to decorate and advance the narrative in "The Tale of the Indians" in *Melmoth the Wanderer*. [1–244].

1-159. Henry, P. F. (France). **Le Château mystérieux; ou, L'Héritier orphelin (The Mysterious Castle; or, The Orphan Heir).** Denné, 1798. (6)
An anonymous English novel entitled *The Mystic Castle; or, Orphan Heir* (1796) produced this French translation of a run-of-the-mill Gothic.

1-160. Hernon, G. D. **Louisa; or, The Black Tower.** W. Gordon, 1805. (1) (SB)
Inspired by such commercially successful tower Gothics as John Palmer's *The Mystery of the Black Tower* [1-288], Hernon's Gothic romance caters to the continuing taste for the terror associated with ancient turrets and Druidic landmarks. Gerrard and his lovely daughter are voluntary tower dwellers living in seclusion in an otherwise deserted black tower in Lancashire. A robber gang under the virtuous leadership of the exotic brigand, Captain Rifle, seizes Louisa, but returns her unharmed to tower and father. Young Sir Frederick Orien, who has been attacked and left for dead by Rifle's outlaws, is taken to the black tower; Louisa restores him to health. Meanwhile, a ghostly woman in white prowls the region. She turns out to be Captain Rifle's estranged wife, who is intent on doing harm to all who come into her orbit. Amplifying these Gothic peregrinations are Louisa's father's clandestine excursions to the forbidden chamber of the black tower. It is finally revealed that the secret room contains the preserved cadaver of his wife, and his retirements are all reunions with the dead beloved. The important Gothic motif of the hidden corpse of a lover, husband, or wife is to be noted later in Gothic tales by Hawthorne ("The White Old Maid") and Faulkner ("A Rose for Emily").

1-161. Hiffernan, Paul. **The Heroine of the Cave.** Larpent Collection MS., 1775. (1)
This early Gothic drama can be classified as *comédie larmoyante,* a tearful mixture of humor and terror. The dank cavern became the ghastly abode of legions of Gothic heroines in the 1790s, but the date of Hiffernan's play indicates just how early the cavernous scenario entered the bloodstream of the Gothic imagination.

1-162. Hitchener, William Henry. **The Towers of Ravenswold; or, The Days of Ironside.** Chapple, 1814. (4)
The actor W. H. Hitchener put his skills in melodrama to the writing of a historical Gothic that is placed in Norman times. The book appeared in the year of Scott's *Waverley; or, 'Tis Sixty Years Since,* a first historical novel that signaled the breakup or submergence of Gothicism as the dominant literary form.

*1-163. Hoffmann, Ernst Theodor Amadeus (Germany). **Die Elixiere des Teufels: Nachgelassene Papiere des Bruders Medardus (The Devil's Elixir: Posthumous Papers of Brother Medardus).** Duncker & Humblot, 1815. (2)

Inspired by *The Monk* and owing much to various legends of Faustian alchemy and overreaching, *Die Elixiere des Teufels* perhaps marks the artistic zenith of the *Schauer-roman* in German Gothicism. Hoffmann's story centers on the criminal career of the Capuchin monk Medardus, whose powerful gifts of oratory and passionate nature make him a close Gothic relative of Lewis's Ambrosio. Losing his eloquent vocal powers, he is tempted to imbibe the devil's elixir and subsequently finds himself entrapped in a cycle of terrible transgressions. He causes the death of his half-brother, Count Victorin, and his uncontrollable lust drives him to assault Aurelie, a penitent entrusted to his pious care. After the murder of Hermogen, Medardus finds himself haunted and bedeviled by a strange double figure or *Doppelgänger*. His twin stands in for him after he is arrested for murder. Taking refuge in a monastery, Medardus discovers his evil heritage amid some ancient papers, which detail the ominous history of his fated family. He is descended from an ancestor who became Satan's slave by tasting the forbidden elixir, and he is marked for additional monstrous deeds. When Aurelie returns to the monastery as a nun, Medardus's lust is renewed, but the pathetic girl is stabbed to death in the chapel by Medardus's sinister twin before he can consummate his desires. In a sort of Radcliffean *coup de gothique,* the double is revealed as the supposedly slain Count Victorin. Hoffmann's work relates to the sexual atrocities and frenzied demonism of *The Monk* [1–218], but more significantly, the novel anticipates the use of the double figure as an emblem of conscience and retribution—the angelic half of the base self.

1–164. Hoffmann, Ernst Theodor Amadeus (Germany). **"Phantasiestücke"** and **"Kunstmärchen"** in *Nachtstücke (Night Pieces).* Realschulbuchhandlung, 1817; in *The Best Tales of E. T. A. Hoffmann,* ed. by E. F. Bleiler. Dover, 1967. (1)

Much of Hoffmann's output in the field of short fiction may be considered Gothic with definite tendencies toward the *Schauer-romantik* modes. But Hoffmann's manipulation of the Gothic is often subjective or ambiguous; the reader can never declare with certainty whether the demonic beings and horrific events exist outside the vision of the narrator or whether they are mental projections and traumas of disturbed characters. According to G. R. Thompson, the tales of Hoffmann function "on the supernatural level and the psychological level simultaneously." The ambiguities of Hoffmannesque Gothic are best depicted in the following cluster of tales: "Der Sandmann" ("The Sandman"); "Das Majorat" ("The Entail" or "The Inheritance"); "Der Unheimliche Gast" ("The Weird Guest"); "Die Bergwerke zu Falun" ("The Mines of Falun"); "Die Automata" ("The Automaton" or "The Robot"); "Das Fräulein von Scuderi" ("Mademoiselle de Scudéri"). In "Der Sandmann," the demon of Nathanael's childhood, the repulsive Coppelius, stalks him through life in quest of Nathanael's eyes. The story also contains the robot theme of "Die Automata" in the form of the mechanical doll,

Olimpia. "Das Majorat" is a long story that bears comparison with Poe's "The Fall of the House of Usher." "Die Bergwerke zu Falun," first published in 1819 in *Die Serapionsbrüder (The Serapion Brethren),* uses the Gothic motif of a perfectly preserved body in a Swedish mine. The story has further interesting connections with Mackenzie's Gothic novel of 1801, *Swedish Mysteries; or, The Hero of the Mines of Delecarlia* [1–233]. A decade before Poe, Hoffmann had offered a prototype for the modern detective story in "Das Fräulein von Scuderi," a story about a Parisian crime wave and its solution during the age of Louis XIV. These tales along with many others by Hoffmann insure his Gothic reputation as a pioneer in grotesque fantasy.

*1–165. Hogg, James. **The Private Memoirs and Confessions of a Justified Sinner.** Longman, Hurst, Rees, Orme, Brown & Green, 1824; Grove Press, 1959. (3)
Hogg's powerful novel of the double life studies the depraved effects of religious fanaticism (in this case, Scottish Presbyterianism) on the possessed sinner, Robert Wringham. The novel is structured as a complicated and intertwining series of narratives and has a complexity that is somewhat like the concentric construction of Maturin's *Melmoth the Wanderer* [1–244]. Hogg's eccentric structure reflects the schizophrenic condition of the main character, who is driven by an all-consuming desire to kill his twin brother. To extend the identity crisis ever further, a mysterious third twin enters Wringham's life after the tennis court murder of the brother. The third twin begins to assume the slain twin's features and accuses Wringham of violent misdeeds, which he cannot remember. He finally makes a suicidal agreement with the new double and completes his own damnation. Clearly, a new and deeper vein of Gothic had been unearthed by Hogg—a Gothic in which the primal monster is "the self behind the self concealed." The sinner knows this when he confesses: "I not only looked around me with terror at everyone that approached, but I was become a terror to myself; or, rather, my body and soul were become terrors to each other; and, had it been possible, I felt as if they would have gone to war. I dared not look at my face in a glass, for I shuddered at my own image and likeness." Hogg's theme of the disintegration of the self paved the way for the mature Gothics of Poe and Hawthorne in the 1830s.

1–166. Holcroft, Thomas. **The Inquisitor.** Larpent Collection MS., 1798. (1)
A Gothic play purporting to expose the dank horrors and secret doings of the Inquisition. The solemn and sinister figure of the Inquisitor, a master of torture, intrigue, and perverted power, was a natural outgrowth of the ecclesiastical monsters and madmen of the monastic shocker. Inquisition Gothic had established itself as a distinct vogue following Naubert's *Hermann von Unna* [1–279], although Holcroft's drama was more directly influenced by Radcliffe's *The Italian* [1–317] of the previous year.

1-167. Holcroft, Thomas. **A Tale of Mystery.** Larpent Collection MS., 1802; in *The Hour of One: Six Gothic Melodramas,* ed. by Stephen Wischhusen. Fraser, 1975. (1)

First performed at Covent Garden on November 13, 1802, Holcroft's blaring melodrama was based directly on two contemporary French sources: the dramatist Pixérécourt's *Coelina; ou, L'Enfant du mystère* [1-302], which was it-self a derivation of Ducray-Duminil's romantic novel [1-102] of the same name. Holcroft preserved both the melodramatic extravagance and the mu-sical accompaniment that Pixérécourt had appended to Ducray-Duminil's story of the unfortunate child.

1-168. Holstein, Anthony Frederick. **Love, Mystery, and Misery!** Minerva-Press, 1810. (1) (SB)

Between 1809 and 1815, William Lane's Minerva-Press published a dozen titles by the pseudonymous Gothic prodigy, Anthony Frederick Holstein, whose real identity remains unknown. Each of the novels displays a thor-ough command of various Gothics and each shows the author's technical fa-miliarity with the rival methods of Lewisite horror and Radcliffean terror. *Love, Mystery, and Misery!* is an expert title that incorporates in proper se-quence the major business of the Radcliffean myth of the young woman re-moved from her family, castellated, menaced, made miserable by malicious events from which no egress seems possible, and finally improbably rescued from the depths. Holstein's novel follows the misadventures of Madame de Saussure and her delectable daughter as they are subjected to the usual Gothic dangers behind a forest of crumbling battlements. The modern Gothic critic Coral Ann Howells chose to apply the combination of passions in Holstein's title to her recent study of Gothicism's development, *Love, Mys-tery, and Misery: Feeling in Gothic Fiction* (1979).

1-169. Holstein, Anthony Frederick. **The Assassin of Saint Glenroy; or, The Axis of Life.** Minerva-Press, 1810. (1)

The novel exhibits the three primary elements of a successful Gothic—love, mystery, and misery—as set forth by the prolific Holstein. To these is added the theme of the inconvenient corpse, a major Gothic innovation in this ro-mance. Percy Lennox, a master of infinite disguises, is discovered by his be-loved, Lady Augusta Cameron, bending over a mutilated body. Spurning her lover as a murderer and calling him the assassin of Glenroy, she breaks off the engagement and drifts inexplicably into a life of dissipation. Amid a context of tangled events and Gothic intrigues, Percy gradually exonerates his noble name. Although a happy ending and a reconciliation seem called for, Holstein betrays the expectations of the reader by bringing Percy to sui-cide and Augusta to deeper degradation. The violent events of the novel coupled with its sordidly pessimistic outcome make it an unusual Gothic en-trée on the crowded Minerva-Press menu. Here, terror and tragedy are not assuaged or averted by virtue and common sense, as in the ordinary Radcliffean thriller. Whoever Holstein was, he (or perhaps she) was praised by the *Critical Review,* which frequently passed harsh judgments upon the Gothic glut. The reviewer said: "We know of no horror-monger of the present age like Mr. Anthony Frederick Holstein; he has the faculty of whisking us from a murder to a ball, from a gloomy dingle haunted by a frightful nun to a concert room, and this with so much agreeable facility that we hardly know where we are. In fact he carries off the palm for murderous writing from all his brother quill-drivers of the day."

1-170. The Horrors of the Secluded Castle; or, Virtue Triumphant. T. Hughes and R. Hughes, 1807. (5) (SB)
The single worthwhile aspect of this subliterary and subliterate shilling shocker is its enticing title. How will horror engender virtue? The bluebook never explains the relationship. Ernestine, for reasons also never given, is locked away in a frowning fortress, endures it all, and emerges with her virtue both intact and presumably triumphant. But triumphant over what and how? The shocker never specifies. Why such a laborious formula for terrifying should continue to enthrall all classes of readers remains a cultural puzzle. But enthrall it did as the duration of the shilling shocker industry shows.

1-171. Houghton, Mary. The Mysteries of the Forest. Minerva-Press, 1810. (1)
A rewriting of Radcliffe's popular *The Romance of the Forest* [1-315], the novel has the requisite Gothic length, but is pallid and mechanical beside the artistry of Radcliffe. In Houghton's version, Adeline becomes Adele, and La Motte's career as a bandit is converted into a complicated and totally detached inset story. Forest Gothic was a difficult key in which to compose; Houghton's narrative dissonance is one of many samples of failures to reproduce the eerie music of Radcliffe.

1-172. Huish, Robert. The Mysteries of Ferney Castle: A Romance of the Seventeenth Century. Henry Colburn, 1810. (1) (SB)
Although attributed by Montague Summers in his *Gothic Bibliography* to Robert Huish, this Gothic romance is actually by George Lambe and is signed by G. Lambe, Esq., in the Sadleir-Black copy. The novel itself is an utterly conventional Gothic. Its characters and settings have a vague, false feudalism about them that belies the seventeenth-century period expressed in the subtitle. The site of Ferney Castle is the Cornish coast, an English Gothic locale that rivals the banks of the Rhine for the proliferation of ruined castles.

1-173. Huish, Robert. The Brothers; or, The Castle of Niolo. William Emans, 1820. (1)
The origin of the erroneous attribution of *Ferney Castle* [1-172] to Huish is explained by a glance at its frontispiece, which lists Lambe's novel with

Huish's work. A fraternal contest for ownership of the castle done against a vague but violent medieval backdrop gives Huish's romance its outstanding Gothic qualities and insured its sales even as Gothicism was fading out. The clash of power for proprietorship of the castle offers at least one terrific or horrific spectacle per chapter for the Germanic cast. The governess, Mademoiselle Schlaffenhausen, the attacking and foraging brother, Rosenheim, and the foolish seneschal, Old Rupert, suggest a romance of chivalry and villainy as well as magic and the grotesque, which goes back to Malory's *Morte d'Arthur* for its temper.

1-174. Hunt, J. P. **The Iron Mask; or, The Adventures of a Father and Son.** Minerva-Press, 1809. (4)
A bulky and clumsy historical romance, *The Iron Mask* presents the visored figure in various dangerous situations as a mysterious protector of the young hero. When the visor is finally raised at the end of several volumes, the father is at last revealed. Suspense over identity of a parent is ineptly managed here.

1-175. Hunter, Rachel. **Letitia; or, The Castle without a Spectre.** W. Robberds, 1801. (4) (SB)
This long but very gentle Radcliffean parody laughs understandingly at the absurd efforts of Letitia to provide her imagination with a constant supply of Gothic shudders and titters. Like other mock Gothics in the vein of *Northanger Abbey* [1-11], the novel is not without its genuinely forceful Gothic moments, as when the heroine peers down a dark shaft and sees the glare of one monstrous eye. The four volumes of lighthearted undercutting of Gothic crises also suggest that Hunter was satirizing the length and ponderous bulk of the typical maiden-centered Gothic of the 1790s.

1-176. I. H. **Phantoms of the Cloister; or, The Mysterious Manuscript.** Minerva-Press, 1795. (1) (SB)
Another enormous triple-decker Gothic in the Radcliffean mold, the novel bears the curious signature of I. H. It contains some better-than-average maternal nastiness toward the heroine, Henrietta, and stages its action within the walls of a cloister-crammed castle on the River Tyne during the reign of Henry V. The opening sentence thrusts the reader headlong into the Gothic world: "In a part of Northumberland still remain the mouldering ruins of a castle, standing on the summit of a precipice, and commanding a beautiful prospect of the adjacent country." At the moment of death, Lord Somerville charges his daughter to beware of Tancred's heirs and to marry no man but Ulster. Then, devouring a strange piece of parchment, he dies. While awaiting the funeral, Henrietta "discovered the headless trunk of her father, mangled in a shocking manner." In the true Radcliffean spirit, nothing is explained and the narrative shifts illogically to the woes of a second heroine, Eliza, and her sufferings at the hands of a depraved steward, Oswald, who

seems somehow to be connected with Henrietta. Raped by Oswald in a robbers' den, Eliza learns from Oswald what she must do to gain her birthright: "Search for the skeleton which terrified you and learn the mysteries of the tower of Harcourt. These only can explain the Phantoms of the Cloister." Near the end of volume three, we discover that the phantoms of Maitland Cloister are actually robbers in ghostly disguise. Clearly, I. H. was something of a Gothic amateur and his attempt to duplicate Radcliffean methods was not proficient.

*1-177. Ireland, William Henry. **The Abbess: A Romance.** Earle & Hemet, 1799. Edited by Benjamin Franklin Fisher IV. Arno, 1974. (1)
Cruel and lurid Catholicism and the agonies of the Inquisition mark this inspired imitation of *The Monk* [1-218]. In addition, the violent content of *The Abbess* establishes the attraction of sadistic themes and extraordinarily voluptuous characters for the Gothic audience of the late 1790s. The Florentine atmosphere is heavy with the ominous portents of ecclesiastical cruelty and religious terror. Count Marcello Porta desires Maddelena Rosa, who is held within the convent of Santa Maria del Nova. Penetrating the cloisters with the aid of the monk Ubaldo, the count makes his way to an inner cell inhabited by a promiscuous beauty whom he takes to be his desired Maddelena. In a scene whose sexual candor is designed to compete with Ambrosio's erotic furies in *The Monk,* Porta consummates his lusts with the monastic temptress, only to find out after the fact that she is not Maddelena but Mother Victoria Bracciano, head of the community and seducer-superior. The amours between the abbess and the count intensify in a licentious pattern of self-gratification that recalls Ambrosio's involvement with Matilda; and, as in *The Monk,* the crimes of love eventually attract the attention of the Inquisition. The novel's spectacular *auto da fé* or ceremony of heretic extermination is truly one of the most abominable scenes in all Gothic literature. In a more direct fashion than Monk Lewis, Ireland explicitly related the oppressive conditions of the religious life with eruptions of destructive sexuality.

1-178. Ireland, William Henry. **Rimualdo; or, The Castle of Badajos.** T. N. Longman & O. Rees, 1800. (1) (SB)
Less expressive in its romantic sadism than *The Abbess* [1-177] and less potent in its drastic Gothic effects than Ireland's later masterpiece, *Gondez the Monk* [1-180], *Rimualdo* must be regarded as a routine and carefully formulated Gothic by an extraordinary Gothic writer. The castellated characters adhere to all the rules of Gothic behavior. On duty in the Gothic novel are the adequately nefarious Marquis de Badajos; his incredibly virtuous son, the Count Rimualdo, whose filial loyalty to an evil father passes all comprehension; and the fair and constant Constanza, a fainting victim for all seasons. The castle and its resident specter are the real Gothic attractions of the

book. Like Hamlet, the young count collides with the ghost of a slain relative; like the regulation Gothic maiden, he swoons when he visits a ruined chapel in the depths of the forest and confronts some gaunt being while the Gothic tempest comes crashing down on schedule. Ireland's Gothic rhetoric has in it those bombastic qualities that made him one of literary history's most successful Shakespearean forgers. Ireland's "so potent art" also had its stylistic impact on the grandiose passages in Maturin's *Melmoth the Wanderer*.

1-179. Ireland, William Henry. **Bruno; or, The Sepulchral Summons.** Hemet & Earle, 1804. (1)
The Gothic figure of the walking and stalking brute who lurks about graveyards renders *Bruno* a superior contribution to the emergent genre of the monster novel, later, of course, to be refined and perfected by Mary Shelley in *Frankenstein* [1-348]. The figure of the murderous ogre had also turned up in the pages of the *Schauer-roman* as evidenced by Gleich's *Udo der Stählerne* [1-127].

1-180. Ireland, William Henry. **Gondez the Monk: A Romance of the Thirteenth Century.** Earle & Hucklebridge, 1805. (1) (SB)
Ireland's masterpiece and a historical Gothic novel deluxe, *Gondez* begins its action at the Battle of Methven on June 19, 1306. Following a bloody defeat, King Robert de Bruce and a mysterious youth, Huberto Avinzo, escape the field and take refuge in the Gothic monastery of St. Columba on the Isle of Oronzo. Much of the story is concerned with the adventures of Huberto and his quest to learn his true name and parentage, a familiar Gothic pattern. The Abbot of St. Columba is the frightful Gondez, certainly the supreme monastic monster in the pages of the Gothic novel, for "his features were strikingly prominent and marked with every line that pourtrays internal craft, malice, cruelty, and revenge." This beast of the cloisters is indeed a study in high Gothic portraiture, for his maliciousness is enhanced by "the cadaverous complexion of his countenance and the falling in of his cheeks, added to which, his mouth was hideously wide, round the falling extremities of which forever seemed to play the smile of mingled deceit and ineffable contempt." The monastery contains an unusually disgusting version of the resident specter in the personage of the "Little Red Woman," who lurks in niches and eventually assists the Inquisition in bringing the villainous Gondez to justice. Put to the rack, Gondez reveals his true identity to be Giovanni Maldichini, whose machinations have deprived Huberto of his birthright. The device of the fugitive nobleman masquerading as a priest was previously used by Radcliffe and many others, but Ireland brings to his treatment of this tedious charade a Gothic energy rarely felt. Huberto's name restored, his persistence also wins him the precious Ronilda, while Gondez pays for his crimes by "a slow fire."

*1–181. Irving, Washington (U.S.) (used pseud. Geoffrey Crayon). **"The Spectre Bridegroom"** in *The Sketch Book*. C. S. Van Winkle, 1820; in *Romantic Gothic Tales,* ed. by G. Richard Thompson. Harper & Row, 1979. (4)

Irving's sportive or risible Gothic is to be seen in many of his tales. Mockery of the genre is highly evident in "The Spectre Bridegroom" when the bemused narrator remarks, "It is well known that the forests of Germany have always been as much infested with robbers as its castles by spectres." The names of the principals in the story, Baron Katzenellenbogen (cat's elbow) and Herman von Starkenfaust suggest Irving's satiric purposes in this droll presentation of the goblin horseman who abducts the Baron's daughter. The ghastly midnight rider is no specter after all, but young Herman who has engaged in a supernatural charade to woo the Baron's daughter. Irving's wit was also stimulated by his reading of Bürger's Gothic ballad, "Lenore" [1–52].

1–182. Irving, Washington (U.S.) (used pseud. Geoffrey Crayon). **"Adventure of the German Student"** in *Tales of a Traveller*. Carey & Lea, 1824; in *The American Tradition in Literature,* ed. by Bradley, Beatty, and Long. Norton, 1967. (1)

The story is a pure or high Gothic tale with nothing of Irving's customary comic twist in it. The lonely student Gottfried Wolfgang resides in a chamber in Paris just as the Reign of Terror is reaching its full fury. As he broods and dreams, he becomes transfixed by the lovely face of a beautiful dark lady. Wandering near the scaffold of the guillotine on the Place de Grève, he suddenly beholds the haunting creature of his dreams clad in black on the steps of the "horrible engine." They retire to Wolfgang's chamber, where she gives herself to him. On the following morning, Wolfgang leaves her side "to seek more spacious apartments suitable to the change in his situation." Upon returning he finds the lady dead in the bed; a policeman enters and unfastens a black collar around her neck, and her head promptly rolls on the floor. Wolfgang's lady love had been beheaded on the previous day. Knowledge of his necrophiliac evening of love proves unbearable for Wolfgang, who is carried screaming to the madhouse. The tale's Gothic acoustics and characterization show Irving's professional acquaintance with various branches of the Gothic tradition, along with his wish to psychologize the crude materials of the European horror tradition. Irving's donations to the development of the Gothic in America have been defined by John Clendenning in "Irving and the Gothic Tradition," *Bucknell Review* 12 (1964), 90–98, and Donald A. Ringe in "Irving's Use of the Gothic Mode," *Studies in the Literary Imagination* 7 (1974), 51–65.

1–183. Isaacs, Mrs. **Glenmore Abbey; or, The Lady of the Rock.** Minerva-Press, 1805. (1) (SB)

The work might be classified as automatic or secondhand Gothic, since Isaacs simply takes the Radcliffean equipment and doubles it to secure her effects. To the threatening abbey of Glenmore is added the equally pernicious castle of Macruther. The novel also offers two maiden-hysterics, Ellen and Adeline, thus doubling the role played by Emily St. Aubert in *The Mysteries of Udolpho* [1-316]. The opulent topographies are also taken from Radcliffe's pictures of castle terrain. As the maiden pair contemplate the abbey, their emotions are wholly Radcliffean: "Such was the external appearance of the whole edifice, that Ellen contemplated it with a degree of awe which she could not repress; and Adeline seemed to shrink with horror from the view it presented." The precarious Highland fortress of Macruther is perched upon a "prospect of immense rocks, piled above one another to a height equal to the castle itself."

1-184. Jephson, Robert. **The Count of Narbonne.** Larpent Collection MS., 1781. (1)
First performed at Covent Garden in November 1781, Jephson's dramatization of the first Gothic novel, Walpole's *The Castle of Otranto* [1-398], omits both the first and final Gothic catastrophes of the falling helmet and the falling castle, but invents some substitute stagecraft to accommodate the Gothic absurdities of Walpole's original castle. In Jephson's version, the Italianate place names and characters are wholly Frenchified. The usurping Manfred becomes Raymond of Narbonne, a gloomy, guilt-ridden tyrant who possesses his castle through a legacy of evil. Hippolyta is transformed into Hortensia while Isabella and Theodore survive intact. Jephson's melodrama takes advantage of the theatricality and operatic dialogue of Walpole's first Gothic and also drops some of the gadgetry to emphasize the guilty anguish of Manfred in the Count of Narbonne's apostrophes to his conscience.

1-185. Jones, Henry. **The Heroine of the Cave.** T. Evans, 1775. (3) (SB)
A sentimentalized and maudlin picture of the Isabella figure in *Otranto*, this early Gothic drama has the heroine, who has been driven from the castle, take refuge with an erudite hermit. Apparently, the Sadleir-Black collection has the only surviving copy of Jones's obscure play.

*1-186. Kahlert, Karl Friedrich (Germany) (used pseud. Lawrence Flammenberg). **Der Geisterbanner: Eine Wundergeschichte aus mündlichen und schriftlichen Traditionen gesammelt (The Spectral Flag: A Wondrous Tale Collected from Oral and Written Traditions.** Trans. by Peter Teuthold as *The Necromancer; or, The Tale of the Black Forest*). Minerva-Press, 1794; Folio Press, 1968. (2)
Possibly the weakest and certainly the most obscure and incoherent of the seven Northanger novels in terms of its dense plot, *The Necromancer* nevertheless achieves some stunning Gothic effects. The translator informs all credulous Gothic readers in his preface that "the strange and mysterious events which occur in this little performance are founded on facts, the authenticity

of which can be warranted by the translator who has lived many years not far from the principal place of action." The principal place of action is Germany's Black Forest, which teems with haunted castles and warlocks' dens. But reaching the main story of the necromancer Volkert, buried within the interior of the novel's multiplotted and oblique narrative, is itself an ordeal for the reader, whose abilities to follow the labyrinthine infrastructure are severely tested. The legend of Volkert is placed within the frame story of the two friends Hermann and Hellfried, whose nocturnal peregrinations bring them to "the Gothic remains of a half-decayed castle" where the tomb of Godrey Haussinger (A.D. 1603) is discovered. Volkert's story, which exists in the traditional Gothic form of the mysterious manuscript dictated by the necromancer as he awaits execution, deals with his morally repellent career of necromancy, or the raising of the dead. The Gothic imagery in Volkert's portion of the narrative has its own vivid power: "A flash of lightning hissed suddenly through the dreary vault, licking the damp walls and a hollow clap of thunder roared through the subterraneous abode of chilly horror." Volkert is a strange and magnetic figure who is half good and half evil, or half demonic wizard and half benign man of feeling, whose self-ambiguities anticipate Shelley's Ginotti in *Saint Irvyne* [1–350] as well as the alluring Gothic villain Carwin in Charles Brockden Brown's *Wieland* [1–46].

1-187. Kelly, Isabella. **Madeline; or, The Castle of Montgomery.** Minerva-Press, 1794. (1)

A first Gothic novel in which the author apprentices herself to the trade of castle terror, *Madeline* owes most of its material to Radcliffe's pre-*Udolpho* romances. The soon-fatherless Madeline is the pining prisoner of Castle Montgomery. Like all properly trained Radcliffean heroines, she is more alarmed over what might happen to her than what actually does happen to her. A bad uncle and an even worse aunt have conspired to chivvy Madeline out of her inheritance by frightening her to death. Their phony supernatural illusions at Castle Montgomery work on Madeline only because she palpitates in every situation where a simple investigation would expose the trickery. The novel's mechanics suggest that Isabella Kelly was teaching herself how to concoct a good Gothic in this early book.

*1-188. Kelly, Isabella. **The Abbey of Saint Asaph.** Minerva-Press, 1795; Arno, 1977. (1)

Although this passable Radcliffean imitation has a huge number of characters, its inner cast consists of the usual Gothic family and the usual hereditary travails. Kelly's dexterity in applying the technique of the explained supernatural equals, if it does not actually surpass, the craftsmanship of her mistress in this respect, Ann Radcliffe. The heroine, whose name is Jennet, is diligently victimized by the exciting seducer Lord Belmont, an intelligent reincarnation of the Richardsonian roué, Lovelace, in Gothic costume. His prurient tactics have a kind of pungent melodrama about them, as when the narrative heats up to the following description: "He clasped her to his tumultuous bosom, while his hand, with indecent freedom, wandered over her lovely bosom." Lord Belmont reserves the ruins of the Abbey of Saint Asaph specifically for the terrorizing of Jennet. It is here that a phosphorescent apparition and a peripatetic skeleton plague the maiden until natural order is restored by the disclosure that the burning ghost is a trick done with phosphorus and the animated bones are accomplished by the scramblings of a rat. Readers who delighted in the kind of suspense and artificial horror generated by *Udolpho*'s black veil were very easily won over by Kelly's turnings of the screw.

1–189. Kelly, Isabella. **The Ruins of Avondale Priory.** Minerva-Press, 1796. (1)

Storms, ruins, prophetic dreams of doom, and the orphaned maiden imprisoned within the picturesque Gothic obscurity of a haunted priory characterize this excellent facsimile of Radcliffe's fictional formula. The fainting spells and poetic panics of the hysterical Ethelinde within the dark precincts of Avondale Priory constitute one prolonged shudder before she is safely released from her imaginative entombment in the false dreamworld of the Gothic. One typical Gothic panic can be cited to define the tone of the entire novel: "Motionless with horror, a moment she stood aghast, when gathering a degree of frantic courage from desperation, she rushed forward, but her strength failing, she grasped a hanging bell, and sunk lifeless on the floor." To read the Gothic novels of Kelly is to understand very quickly what Michael Sadleir meant when he declared that Gothics were written according to a "group style."

1–190. Kelly, Isabella. **Tales of the Abbey, Founded on Historical Facts.** Symonds, 1800. (4)

An anthology of Gothic legends apparently culled from the various historical Gothics that had flooded the market at the turn of the century.

1–191. Kelly, Isabella. **The Baron's Daughter: A Gothic Romance.** J. Bell, 1802. (1)

Having paid her homage to Radcliffe and the school of terror in her previous work, Kelly turned her attention to the craft of *Burgverliess* (or no-exit) Gothic in *The Baron's Daughter.* Befriended and sponsored by Monk Lewis, who provided her with plot materials from his own fertile Gothic brain, Kelly produced a highly respectable counterfeit of *The Monk* in this novel, which is significantly subtitled *A Gothic Romance.* By "Gothic" Mrs. Kelly meant sanguinary, supernatural, and sickening, rather than simply medieval or uncivilized. Lewis was also instrumental in getting Bell to publish her work. The romance itself lacks the libidinous indelicacies of *The Monk,* but is still a very acceptable effort in the art of sadistic horrorification. The deceased baron's daughter, Magalena, is vigorously persecuted by agents of both church and state; after much anguish she at last realizes that her persecutors are her own scheming relatives.

1-192. Kendall, A. The Castle on the Rock; or, Memoirs of the Elderland Family. H. D. Symonds, 1798. (4)
The novel is a somewhat trite imitation of the historical Gothic mode of *The Recess* [1-214]. As the family falls into decline their castle crumbles and creaks, thus becoming the visible symbol of advancing decadence.

1-193. Ker, Ann. The Heiress of Montalde; or, The Castle of Bezanto. Kerby, 1799. (1)
An extremely scarce Gothic romance, Ker's work contains the expected elements of castle mystery. The castle is held by a wrongful possessor; supernatural events expose and punish the usurper; after many trials, the heiress recovers her heritage and her name. The single surviving edition of the romance is in the British Museum.

1-194. Ker, Ann. Adeline Saint Julian; or, The Midnight Hour. J. & E. Kerby, 1800. (1) (SB)
The period of this very slow developing Gothic is the France of Louis XIII and Cardinal Richelieu. Action begins near the town of St. Amans in Languedoc in 1632, as the Baron de Semonville and his son, Alfonso, are beset while returning from Paris by some eerie music from a forest grove and turn aside to investigate. There have been rumors of a mysterious lady of St. Amans who haunts the glades. The lady is the lovely Adeline, a seamstress who spends part of her time with her guitar in the woods. As an infant, she was consigned to the care of Madame de Belmont by her mother, Eloize de Beauclair St. Julian, who had been hounded into her grave by Count Victor St. Julian. A Gothic mystery naturally surrounds Adeline's destiny, and Alfonso's involvement with Adeline naturally leads to separation and persecution at the hands of the outwardly ascetic and inwardly lecherous inquisitor, Dampiere. Adeline is detained, then Gothically entertained, in Count St. Julian's castle of St. Clair in Roussillon. Adeline's mother had undergone a similar detention and had been visited at midnight by a frightful apparition bent upon compelling the countess to renounce her noble title. In clumsy fashion, the business of birthright is rectified, the count is punished for driving his wife to her doom, and Adeline emerges from the midnight trials of terror to the bright dawn of matrimony with Alfonso. The pattern of poetic justice so common to maiden-centered Gothic is laboriously executed in this entangled Gothic. Ker apparently believed that each page of her Gothic required its own complex and intertwined plot.

1-195. Ker, Ann. Edric the Forester; or, The Mysteries of the Haunted Chamber. J. F. Hughes, 1817. (1)
Despite its stylistic crudities and some residual cumbrousness, this historical Gothic shows that Ker's proficiencies as a Gothic novelist had developed af-

ter the farrago of *Adeline Saint Julian* [1–194]. Her subtitle carries reminders of the orthodox Gothic ordeal of the evening inside the awful room, a situation that goes back to Edmund Twyford's experience in Reeve's *The Old English Baron* [1–322]. In its historical placement, *Edric* is also Gothic in the formal sense, since the historical epoch is the Norman Conquest. Edric, like Theodore in *Otranto*, is an insipid hero and absent from the story at long intervals in order to permit the three Gothic women to despair, suffer, and faint at center stage. Ellen and Elgiva, somewhat in the manner of the royal twins confined in Sophia Lee's *The Recess* [1–214], are locked away in a medieval dungeon whose details are curiously like one of the towers of London. Their release is effected by the courageous Lady Jane, who uses a Gothic ruse that has worked before. She stations herself within a supposedly haunted room and plays with professional precision the role of the avenging ghost. As late as 1817, the explained Gothic methods of Radcliffe could still be joined with pseudohistorical material to achieve instantaneous Gothic success.

1–196. Kerndöffer, Heinrich August (Germany). **Die Ruinen der Geisterburg; oder, Die warnende Stimme um Mitternacht (The Ruins of Castle Spectre; or, The Warning Voice at Midnight).** Friedrich Schödel, 1805. (2)
This *Schauer-roman* is an ingenious synthesis of two successes of the English Gothic school: Lewis's 1798 drama, *The Castle Spectre* [1–219] and Parsons's *The Mysterious Warning: A German Tale* [1–291]. Kerndöffer (1769–1846) had also written an ambitious corollary to Vulpius's *Rinaldo Rinaldini* [1–390], a *Räuber-roman* entitled *Karlo Orsino: Räuber und Zeitgenosse des Rinaldo Rinaldini (Karlo Orsino: Robber and Contemporary of Rinaldo Rinaldini)* (1803).

1–197. Kotzebue, August von (Germany). **Menschenhass und Reue (Misanthropy and Remorse).** Deutsche Schaubühne, 1788. (2)
No German dramatist of Gothic tendencies was more popular on the English stage during the period than August Friedrich Ferdinand von Kotzebue (1761–1819). In *The Haunted Castle*, Eino Railo lists 17 plays by Kotzebue that were translated and performed in England during the heyday of the Gothic novel. *Der Opfertod (The Sacrificial Death)* and *Der Graf von Burgund (The Count of Burgundy)* had a special sensational appeal for audiences attuned to Gothic pathos. *Menschenhass und Reue* was translated as *The Stranger* (1796) by Benjamin Thompson and produced by Sheridan in the Drury Lane repertoire for 1798. The sentimentalized plot has an errant wife and a tyrannical, misanthropical husband whose cruelties are nearly psychopathic. Kotzebue's dramas emphasized the sorts of passions found in the Gothic.

1–198. Laboissière, M. F. (France). **Le Château du Comte Roderic; ou, Les Temps gothique (Count Roderic's Castle; or, Gothic Times).** Collin, 1807. (6)
A French translation of the 1795 anonymous Gothic published in Philadelphia, *Count Roderic's Castle; or, Gothic Times* [1–74].

*1–199. Lamb, Caroline. **Glenarvon.** Henry Colburn, 1816; republished by Colburn in 1865 as *The Fatal Passion;* Curtis Books, 1973. (1)

Done with some narrative skill in the Radcliffean manner and mold, *Glenarvon* is a fictionalized and Gothicized remembrance of Lady Caroline Lamb's stormy and unhappy love affair with Lord Byron. She had described the notorious Byron like a Gothic heroine gazing upon a Gothic villain as "mad, bad, and dangerous to know." Her autobiographical heroine is the enrapturing Calantha Deleval, who returns with her doting and gentle husband, Lord Avondale, to the romantic site of her girlhood, an ancient castle on the Irish coast. The idyllic marriage and the couple's strong loyalty seem stout enough to deter the recrudescence of the curse of the castle. In a Gothic novel, however, evil must be stronger than good and fear greater than joy, even if temporarily. During an evening of bad weather, an evening meteorologically suited to the entrance of a Gothic villain, a stranger bearing a single enigmatic name appears and becomes their uninvited guest. He has all the morose and proud Byronic assets capable of drawing the purest woman to the darkest damnation. Here we have the authentic model for Heathcliff in Emily Brontë's *Wuthering Heights* and Rochester in Charlotte Brontë's *Jane Eyre.* Byron declared that his Gothified portrait was a poor likeness, since he had not sat still long enough for an accurate picture of the detested master. *Glenarvon* remains a minor chapter in the Byron saga of ruined lives as well as an important link between the old maiden-centered Gothic of Radcliffe and the neo-Gothic experiments of all three Brontë sisters.

1–200. Lambe, George. **The Mysteries of Ferney Castle: A Romance of the Seventeenth Century.** Henry Colburn, 1810. (1) (SB)

Bibliographical confusion gave the authorship of this Gothic romance to Robert Huish [1–172], but the copy in the Sadleir-Black Gothic collection is signed by "G. Lambe, Esq."

1–201. Lancaster, Agnes. **The Abbess of Valtiera; or, The Sorrows of a Falsehood.** Minerva-Press, 1816. (1)

The novel extends and varies the sensational theme of the amorous abbess as taken from Ireland's *The Abbess* [1–177]. Where Ireland had followed the example of Lewis in his portrayal of sexual violence, Lancaster's abbess inspires very little wonder and less terror in her sexual indiscretions. The novel is inferior in every way except length to Ireland's exciting Catholic horrors.

1–202. Lansdell, Sarah. **Manfredi, Baron Saint Osmund: An Old English Romance.** Minerva-Press, 1796. (1)

Manfredi is a well-made Gothic novel whose characters and situations are often genuinely supernatural. As the name of the baron suggests, Lansdell used Walpole's *Castle of Otranto* [1–398] as a working model. Minerva-Press Gothics seldom offered illustrations; *Manfredi*, however, has a frontispiece that depicts the reclusive heroine in a dungeon cell. Summers reproduced this fine illustration in *The Gothic Quest,* accompanied by the following quotation from the novel's text: "The appearance of the ruins was extremely grand ... and the sculptured arches closely entwined by mantling ivy seemed to say that magnificence had once there held its lofty reign." A valuable source of illustrators' practices and an article accompanied by plates is Montague Summers's "The Illustrations of the Gothick Novels," *Connoisseur* 98 (1936), 266–271.

1–203. Lansdell, Sarah. **The Tower; or, The Romance of Ruthyne.** Harry Smith, 1798. (1) (SB)
This tower Gothic is a kind of monastic shocker in the vertical; all the usual appliances of terror normally distributed throughout the castle or abbey are collected in one turret. As the heroine, Matilda, pries open a door that opens upon a deserted chamber of the tower, she stands on a threshold occupied by legions of hysterical castle explorers and peers into "a room hung on all sides with black, lighted by one high narrow window, and in the middle, a coffin, covered with a black pall." Obeying Radcliffe's first law of Gothic motion, the heroine faints and the reader waits while the story winds its complicated way through a second and third volume to ascertain the mystery of the weird chamber and awful casket.

1–204. Lanty, Comtesse Louise Marie Victorine Chastenay de (France). **Les Mystères d'Udolphe (The Mysteries of Udolpho).** Maradan, 1797. (6)
The earliest French translation of Radcliffe's famous Gothic novel of 1794, *The Mysteries of Udolpho* [1–316]. Although England and France were at war for much of the decade of the 1790s, Gothic literary relations remained cordial. French writers supplemented their output of *romans noirs* and fiction *frénétique* by translating practically every English Gothic title of any notoriety. The French translators often changed episodes and added characters in moving from castle to *château,* but in the case of the Lanty *Udolpho* we have a strictly purist translation, which takes no such creative liberties.

1–205. Lathom, Francis. **The Castle of Ollada.** Minerva-Press, 1795. (1)
The prolific Lathom was an active maker of Gothic novels for nearly 40 years, from his first novel, *The Castle of Ollada,* to the final flickering of his Gothic flame in 1830, *Mystic Events; or, The Vision of the Tapestry.* Lathom was a man of the theater; perhaps his Gothic genius for "his swift piling of horror upon horror," as Peter Haining describes it, may be traced to his theatrical roots as both actor and playwright. This first Gothic novel by the young actor-author might be called a Castilian Gothic, for its Spanish cast and locale seem planned to attract readers of every exotic taste. *Ollada* is also, in all respects, a novel made to order for the busy circulating libraries of the period. Placed in late medieval Spain, the novel is a maiden-centered Gothic; it tells the story of the beautiful and destitute Eliza, whose desires for a full life are thwarted by the cold ambitions of her father. To please his readers accord-

ing to the contemporary formula, Lathom worked the haunted castle of Ollada into the tapestry of the maiden's ordeals. By *Ollada*, Lathom established
himself as an adept penny-a-line Gothicist.

*1-206. Lathom, Francis. **Midnight Bell: A German Story Founded on Incidents in Real Life.** H. D. Symonds, 1798; Folio, 1968. (1)
The acoustical title of the novel suggests an instance of how one Walpolesque or Radcliffean sound effect could become the foundation for the entire Gothic romance. However, the Gothic promise of the title is not quite
fulfilled in the narrative. The solemn bell summons a band of renegade
monks to dark meetings in a ruined fortress. But its toll is not especially au-
dible until very late in the novel; the story itself concentrates on the misadventures of Alphonsus, a German émigré, who joins a host of other Gothic
heroes in pursuing his birthright amid dungeon and catacomb. The Germanic realism proclaimed in the subtitle is a phony allurement to catch the
eye (and purse) of the *Schauer*-romantically inclined reader who had come to
adore sham translations from nonexistent German sources. An interesting
fillip of *The Midnight Bell* was Lathom's exploitation of the reign of terror; he
cleverly contemporized the terrors of the Gothic by showing the imprisonment of Alphonsus in the Bastille. Jane Austen thought enough of the novel
as a Gothic stereotype to place it on Catherine Morland's reading list of
seven great Gothics in *Northanger Abbey* [1-11].

1-207. Lathom, Francis. **The Fatal Vow; or, Saint Michael's Monastery.** B.
Crosby, 1807. (1)
Lathom's chronicle is a compact historical Gothic with some attention given
to historical verisimilitude. The events take place in the environs of St. Michael's Monastery in Cornwall late in the reign of Henry II. Here, the handsome knight, Reginald de Bruce, is enamoured of Christabelle, whose
mother's family name is concealed from her by her father, Glencowell. After
a mandatory abbey confinement, Christabelle is freed and taken to court by
Reginald, now disclosed to be Coeur de Lion. While Richard is at the
French wars, Christabelle aids Queen Eleanor in a scheme of revenge
against Rosamund de Clifford, Henry's mistress. At the Palace of Wood-
stock, Christabelle discovers the resemblance between Rosamund's face and
a miniature shown to her by her father of her missing mother. Having been
sworn by her father never to reveal her identity to the woman depicted in
the miniature, Christabelle now finds herself a participant in her father's
matricidal scheme as a consequence of her fatal vow. Retiring to the convent
of St. Ursula, she emerges briefly to extricate Richard from his Austrian detention and soon perishes in his arms. Lathom's historical extravaganza and
his Gothification of history had its impact on Scott and may be observed
particularly in such novels as Scott's *The Monastery* [1-342].

1-208. Lathom, Francis. **The Unknown; or, The Northern Gallery.** Minerva-Press, 1808. (1)

The murky ecclesiastical politics of the reign of Mary Tudor form the background of this slick historical Gothic. Part of the tale deals with Henry Fitzroy of Framingham Castle in Suffolk, purported to be the illegitimate son of Henry VIII by Lady Elizabeth Talboyse. Another spliced segment of the tale follows the last days of the martyred bishop, Hugh Latimer, and his daughter, Eleonora. In his preface, Lathom asserts his intention of Gothifying history: "The tales which are at the present day the most in request, are undoubtedly those which unite with a considerable degree of the marvellous, some portion of history." Thus, the portraits taken from real life of the crafty Bishop Gardiner and Sir Percival Godolphin alternate with an imagined Gothic cast, including a female hermit, Agatha, an obnoxious villain, Sir Hildebrand, and his noble brother, Valentine, who will come forth at last as Latimer's lost son. The Northern Gallery is a suite of sealed apartments in the Castle of Worcester where the usual Gothic taboo of no admittance applies. When Latimer takes refuge in the castle, "every key was put into his possession save that which opened the first door of the northern gallery." As it turns out, the gallery is a hideout for the renegade nobleman, Godolphin, who has murdered his confederate, Baron Branville, within its precincts. The gallery also contains the secret of Valentine's relationship to Latimer. Lathom ends the novel with a burst of historical veracity by having Latimer conveyed to the Tower and eventually burned. While his control of the historical Gothic mode is not perfect, the novel is a fairly consistent fusion of history, pseudohistory, and horror. The craft of complex subplotting, the downfall of many inferior Gothic writers, is well managed by Lathom, whose ability to tell several stories simultaneously was rarely surpassed by his fellow Goths.

1-209. Lathom, Francis. **Italian Mysteries; or, More Secrets Than One.** Minerva-Press, 1820. (1) (SB)

Concerning Lathom's steady Gothic output and his willingness to experiment with the various species of Gothic on hand in the period, Montague Summers wrote: "Lathom is an extremely representative figure among the novelists of the last decade of the eighteenth, and the first thirty years of the nineteenth century." The late Gothic *Italian Mysteries* shows the versatility of Lathom's Gothic imagination, for the novel is almost a total break with his predilection for historical Gothic forms. Monkish villainy, monastic incarceration, and medieval gloom are familiar Gothic conditions in this tale of the young woman consigned against her will to the convent where she must patiently await her deliverance. *Italian Mysteries* appears to be Lathom's single effort to cash in on a revival of the monastic shocker of the previous decade.

1-210. Lathy, Thomas Pike. **The Invisible Enemy; or, The Mines of Wie-litska: A Polish Legendary Romance.** Minerva-Press, 1806. (1) (SB)
If the Poland of Charlton in *Phedora; or, The Forest of Minski* [1-62] is sinister and suspenseful in the Radcliffean mode, Lathy's later and cruder Slavonic Gothic takes the *Schauer-romantik* approach to Polish terrain. As indicated in the subtitle, much of the action is subterranean; Lathy indulges in the ugly supernatural in his scenes of blood-coated scaffolds and animated skulls. The sanguinary spirit of Monk Lewis is very much on the loose in Lathy's idea of the Gothic as a nauseous medium. The characters seem to exist solely for the sake of the creation of horrendous incident and have little of that power of evoking sympathy found in milder forms of the Gothic. The lovers Rhodiska and Theresia are amply persecuted by the wicked Gramani, their invisible foe. Like so many high Gothics belonging to the first decade of the nineteenth century, Lathy's book is more remarkable for its Gothic effects than for its handling of character or ingenuity, but his subject matter here has a curious similarity to E. T. A. Hoffmann's story "Die Bergwerke zu Falun" [1-164]. A later Gothic novel by Lathy, *Love, Hatred, and Revenge: A Swiss Romance* (1809), offers a title that can stand as a summary of his extreme Gothic imagination.

1-211. Lawler, Dennis. **The Earls of Hammersmith; or, The Cellar Spectre.** Larpent Collection MS., 1814. (4)
An incisively clever burlesque of all the ludicrous excesses of Gothic staging and acting, Lawler's lampoon must be regarded as the dramatic counterpart to Barrett's biting parody of all Gothicism, *The Heroine; or, The Adventures of a Fair Romance Reader.* Cobb's *The Haunted Tower* [1-70] had also pointed the way for future mockers of the rampant Gothic tradition on the stage. Lawler's hilarious plot reduces the seriousness of Gothic melodrama to outlandish cartooning and frantic conduct that is nevertheless accurately Gothic. The Manfred/Montoni figure becomes Lord Bluster; the dull virtues of the Theodore/Vivaldi figure are consolidated in Sir Walter Wisehead, who volunteers to spend a night in a Gothic chamber to prove his worthiness to Lady Margaret Marrowbones. While he is keeping his horrid vigil, the phantom of a footman materializes to present him with a dreadful warning from the ghost of the Dowager Countess of Hammersmith: "Wed not Lady Margaret Marrowbones! She is your grandmother!" A postscript warning informs Sir Walter, "Your father is imprisoned in the castle: yon secret door leads to his dungeon." With the aid of Lady Simple, Walter finds his lost father, whose appearance causes her great shock because he needs a shave. Having neatly ridiculed all the ghastly business of the *Schauer-roman*, Lawler caps his lampoon with a mockery of the *Räuber-roman*. To defeat the coldblooded Lord Bluster, Sir Walter enlists in a robber band and quickly masters the rhetoric of the noble outlaw. Lawler's accomplished parody should have been the coup de grace for Gothic melodrama, but Gothic theatrics persisted upon

the English stage for at least another ten years after Bluster's bluster and Wisehead's stupidities.

1–212. Layton, Mrs. Frederick. **Hulme Abbey.** William Fearman, 1820. (4) Layton also wrote under the name of Jemima Plumptree. This very late attempt at reviving Clara Reeve's domesticated Gothic proves to be quite mechanical. The abbey is a place of monastic gloom and superstition, but fails to engender much actual terror.

1–213. Lee, Harriet, and Sophia Lee. **The Canterbury Tales.** G. G. & J. Robinson, 1797–1805. (4) (SB) Issued in five volumes, the collaborative effort of the Lee sisters borrows the Chaucerian format. Seven snowbound travelers staying at an inn in Canterbury relate "the most remarkable story he or she ever knew or heard of!" Montague Summers observes that *The Canterbury Tales* "are highly romantic rather than Gothic, although here and there we have touches of the terror-novel." *Kruitzner,* a tale of hereditary evil, is said to have influenced the invention of Byron's tragedy, *Werner; or, The Inheritance,* while the young lady's tale, *The Two Emilys,* has the Gothic sensibility.

*1–214. Lee, Sophia. **The Recess: A Tale of Other Times.** T. Cadell, 1783–1785; Arno, 1972. (1) The novel is the prototype for all later historical Gothics. In its union of fictionalized royal history and Gothic scenery, *The Recess* was the natural aftermath of Reeve's *The Old English Baron* [1–322], and it no doubt helped to launch Radcliffe into her first novel, a Highland Gothic entitled *The Castles of Athlin and Dunbayne* [1–313]. "The Recess" refers to a clandestine underground suite beneath the grand abbey of St. Vincent, a building that still shows all the scars of Henry VIII's devastation of the monasteries. Hidden away from all royal eyes within the recess are the twins, Matilda and Ellinor, secret daughters of Mary Queen of Scots by the Duke of Norfolk. Both are doomed to lives of perpetual disaster "at the savage hand of Elizabeth." Ellinor goes insane after following her beloved Essex to Ireland and dies mad, but not before she has paid a phantasmic call on Elizabeth in her bedchamber. The wailing figure of the gruesome lady at the bedside becomes almost a mandatory scene in historical Gothic romance. *The Recess* suggested patterns of suspense to Scott, who converted the persecuted twins into the single inmate, Amy Robsart in *Kenilworth,* also a victim of the vindictive Elizabeth. Similarly, the device of a hidden room containing an unwanted or an unhinged relative or some terrible family secret continued to impress Gothic writers and readers alike. The numerous Gothic progeny of Sophia Lee's important historical Gothic are noted throughout this bibliography.

1–215. Legge, F. **The Spectre Chief; or, The Bloodstained Banner: An Ancient Romance.** Bailey, 1800. (5)

A rapidly and crudely made bluebook that gathers most of its material from various *Räuber-roman* in circulation at the end of the century. The lurid frontispiece shows the silhouette of a creature of the night bending with poised dagger over a well-illuminated female bosom.

*1-216. Leland, Thomas. **Longsword, Earl of Salisbury: An Historical Romance.** W. Johnston, 1762; Arno, 1974. (4)

Often regarded as English literature's first historical novel, *Longsword* combines the chivalric atmosphere of the times of Henry III with the soon-to-be-popular Gothic properties of the wicked monk and ancient abbey. J. M. S. Tompkins sums up the novel's proto-Gothicism: "*Longsword*, which professes to be based on 'ancient English historians,' does indeed make occasional use of the data of history; its main attractions, however, are monkish villainy and wifely truth, war, imprisonment and flight, together with a well-wrought scene of suspense and terror, which anticipates the methods of the Gothic Romance." The character of the hero is based on the crusader William de Longspée, third Earl of Salisbury. When Longsword faints with exhaustion before the portals of an ancient abbey, he is given hospitality and rest. Soon victimized by Count Mal-leon, he escapes his clutches and makes his way to the shrine at Canterbury, only to find that the treacherous Raymond has usurped his castle while he has been away from England. Raymond's accomplice, the ambidextrous and crafty monk Reginald, is the sire of an unholy brood of hypocritical monastic villains who stalk through the pages of the Gothic. Enduring many complex dangers, wanderings, and poisonous plots against his life, Longsword finally regains authority over his castle, which has been suffering under the control of Lord Raymond and his odious creature, Grey. *Longsword* is crowded with complicated action and morally ambiguous characterization. Moreover, it presents several characters later considered essential for the historical Gothic and the monastic shocker: the retired crusader and the fiendish priest. Lacking only in the bizarre and the supernatural, the novel seems to be poised on the threshold of unadulterated Gothicism.

1-217. Levesque, Charles P. (France). **Rosalia; ou, Les Mystères du Château de Glawerka (Rosalie; or, The Mysteries of the Castle of Glawerka).** No publisher, 1799. (6)

The English text for this French translation remains unidentified, but the title of this lost Gothic suggests a novel in the Radcliffean tradition. No French publisher is named.

*1-218. Lewis, Matthew G. **The Monk: A Romance.** J. Bell, 1796; Oxford Univ. Press, 1973. (1)

The arch-Gothic novel of the eighteenth century, *The Monk* deeply shocked and simultaneously delighted all devotees of the Gothic muse. With its potent mixture of satanism, supernaturalism, and erotic sadism, the book quickly established itself as the *locus classicus* of the novel of horror. In its infamous indecency and putrid detailing of horrors, *The Monk* was also a conscious rebuttal to the nonviolent values of Radcliffean Gothic romance. Lewis spliced two lurid plots, introducing elements of monastic fiendishness and ecclesiastical torture into each. The monk's own story is the sordid and sensational biography of Ambrosio, an abbot of Capuchins in Madrid, and a 33-year-old man of apparent integrity and sanctity. But beneath this saintly exterior, Ambrosio's soul is aflame with lechery and pride. A minion of the devil, one Matilda de Villanegas, infiltrates Ambrosio's cloister disguised as the novice Rosario, and cunningly tempts Ambrosio to a sexual fall. Once aroused, Ambrosio's libidinous depravity knows no limits. He kills his own mother and rapes his own sister on a mattress of rotting cadavers in the vaults of the monastery. Condemned to death by the Inquisition, he bargains away his soul to Satan with Matilda's suave encouragement. In a memorable climax that many Gothic writers would imitate but never duplicate, Lucifer himself sinks his claws into Ambrosio's skull and bears him high into the sky before releasing the monk to impalement and lingering death on the rocks below. The second plot contains the story of Don Raymond and his fated love for the unwilling nun Agnes, who has been driven into the convent by her brutal baroness aunt and later censured by Ambrosio for breaking her vows in her love for Raymond. The subplot permitted Lewis to insert the famous episode of the bleeding nun, who appears in Raymond's bedchamber at the Castle of Lindenberg. Also encountered in the subplot is the figure of the Wandering Jew, a character deriving from medieval legendry and eagerly seized upon by the Gothic novelists. Finally, the disgusting sequence of Agnes's childbirth in the slimy dungeons of the Abbey of St. Clare is also reserved for the subplot. As if the Gothic menu were still not bloated enough, Lewis decorated the text with ten slabs of verse of varying quality. The Gothic ballad "Alonzo the Brave and Fair Imogine" echoes the theme of Bürger's "Lenore" [1–52] and remains justly famous. The extravagant Gothicism of *The Monk* made the book an immediate center of controversy; its literary merits are still being debated. But the book's effect on the direction of the Gothic novel can hardly be overstated. In a recent revaluation of the Gothic novel's importance in literary history, the critic R. D. Hume evaluates the achievement of Lewis and his followers in this way: "Horror-Gothic assumes that if events have psychological consistency, even within repulsive situations, the reader will find himself involved beyond recall."

*1–219. Lewis, Matthew G. **The Castle Spectre.** J. Bell, 1798; in *The Hour of One: Six Gothic Melodramas,* ed. by Stephen Wischhusen. Fraser, 1975. (1) Lewis's powerful Gothic melodrama contains a supply of Gothic gadgetry pleasing to the gory needs of *The Monk*'s clientele. The play was often revived after its premier performance on December 14, 1797. In fact, Montague

Summers records a performance at the Gaiety Theatre in May 1880. The scene is Conway Castle, which is under the domination of the usurper and fratricidal tyrant, Earl Osmond. Kenric, Osmond's seneschal, has helped Earl Reginald to escape his brother's murderous intentions by seeing to his concealment in one of the castle's numerous *oubliettes*. The lovely Angela, the castle's proper heir, is also safely hidden from Osmond's bloody plans in a peasant's nearby cottage. Here, she is courted by the courtly rustic, Edwy, who later proves to be Percy, Earl of Northumberland, an adequate foil to Osmond's tyranny. Angela finds herself the prisoner of the Cedar Room in Conway Castle, but is guided to freedom and a reunion with her father, Reginald, by Father Philip. Osmond appears, then Percy appears, and then the castle specter appears to intervene between the rivals. As Osmond stands in trepidation before the ghostly vindicator, the wronged Angela stabs him. This operatic plot shows a blend of Otrantoesque props and people. And true to his supernatural standards, there is no belated explanation of the *coup de gothique* that brings the castle specter onstage. The technology of the play demanded some ingenious stagecraft on the part of the set builders, who were required to arrange for a wall to crash in at one point.

1–220. Lewis, Matthew G. **Adelmorn the Outlaw.** Not published, 1801. (1)
With its standard Gothic machinery and its unwieldy amalgam of the lurid and the ludicrous, *Adelmorn* is a mediocre redoing of the more successful *Castle Spectre* [1–219]. The plotting is thoroughly mechanical and banal, as the avenging phantom enters right on cue to see to the dénouement. The scheming and devious Count Ulric, perhaps a slightly more than ordinary Gothic scoundrel, has secured for himself the wrongful ownership of the castle by murdering the former count and placing the guilt upon Adelmorn with such a deft hand that even Adelmorn believes himself to be the killer. The noble young man is forced into a life of outlawry and is soon joined in his forest hideaway by Princess Imogen, also the victim of a nasty relative. Heeding a supernatural voice that urges him to return to seek justice against the usurping Count of Bergen, Adelmorn makes his way back to Saxony, where he is promptly captured and dungeoned by the tyrant. A timely bolt of lightning demolishes the wall of Adelmorn's prison, revealing Father Cyprian, the former accomplice of Count Ulric in the murder of Count Roderic and exile of Adelmorn. As Adelmorn is about to be put to death, Cyprian exposes Count Ulric; in rapid Gothic fashion the ghost of Count Roderic rises from the grave while brandishing a fiery dagger and demanding Ulric's full confession. The play is something of a Gothic set piece that offers an inventory of poorly integrated castle props, but lacks the straightforward power of *The Castle Spectre.*

1–221. Lewis, Matthew G. **Tales of Wonder.** Bulmer, 1801. (1)
For a synoptic description and analysis of this work as well as an explanation of the bibliographical confusion with *Tales of Terror,* which is not by Lewis,

see Eng's entry [6-32] in the section on Supernatural Verse. According to Summers, "The *Tales of Wonder* have seventeen poems by Lewis; five poems by Scott; a poem apiece by H. Bunbury, J. Leyden, and (burlesque) George Colman, jun., as well as seven anonymous poems. Of the latter, one is a translation of Bürger's *Lenore;* and another, 'The Bleeding Nun,' is founded on the fourth chapter of *The Monk.*"

1-222. Lewis, Matthew G. **The Wood Daemon; or, The Clock Has Struck.** Larpent Collection MS., 1807. (1)
Frequently performed throughout the nineteenth century, *The Wood Daemon* has flashes of Gothic brilliance and clearly deserves a permanent place in the annals of Gothic theatre. The plot has the gruesome characteristics of the German *Märchen,* a kind of fairytale in the wider sense in that it has supernatural elements but need not necessarily introduce fairies. The hideous peasant Hardyknute strikes a bargain with the wood daemon to gain handsomeness and military invincibility, in return for which he must pay the daemon a human sacrifice on the seventh of August at one o'clock. Installed in the castle of Holstein, Hardyknute is visited by a mysterious child bearing the symbol of the bloody arrow on his arm. Hardyknute's betrothed, Una, recognizes the marked Leolyn as the castle's true owner. As Leolyn is prepared for sacrifice by Hardyknute in a subterranean cell, Una works his rescue. As one o'clock strikes, Hardyknute is seized by furies for failure to pay the wood daemon his debt of flesh. All the baleful paraphernalia of the Gothic are here: winding staircases descending to impenetrable darkness; a remorseful tyrant and overreacher; fiendish justice; an atmosphere of sinister enchantment. The Spenserian tonalities are also notable along with the demonic bargain, which must finally call the hero-villain to dreadful account.

1-223. Liborlière, Bellin de la (France). **La Nuit anglaise (The English Night).** Edition in the Bibliothèque Municipale de Grenoble, 1799. (4)
Disinterred by the leading bibliographic scholar of French Gothicism, Maurice Lévy, Liborlière's eclectic satire of Gothic conventions relates with great gusto the inane adventures of Monsieur Dabaud (a possible wordplay on Mr. Indeed-an-ass) in the overheated literary world of the Gothic novel in the late 1790s. Here we have the French equivalent of Austen's first-line dismantling of the Gothic in *Northanger Abbey* [1-11] coupled with the expert disgust of Barrett's *The Heroine* [1-22]. The novel's inflated subtitle is surely a last word in inspired buffoonery, as the pretentiousness of the Gothic is here hoisted by its own petard. The subtitle reads: *ou, Les Aventures jadis un peu extraordinaires, mais aujourd'hui toutes simples et tres communes, de M. Dabaud, Marchand de la Rue Saint-Honoré à Paris; roman comme il y en a trop, traduit de l'Arabe en Iroquois, de l'Iroquois en Samoyède, du Samoyède en Hottentot, du Hottentot en Lapon et du Lapon en Français. Par le R. P. SPECTRORUINI, Moine Italien, 2 vols., se trouve dans les ruines de Paluzzi, de Tivoli; dans les Caveaux de Ste Claire; dans les châteaux d'Udolphe, de Mortymore, de Montnoir, de Lindenberg, en un mot dans tous les endroits où il y a des Revenans, des Moines . . . des Bandits, des Souterrains et*

une TOUR DE L'OUEST. As a punishment exercise of sorts, the bibliographer consigns the translation of this amazing subtitle to the reader.

1-224. Linley, William. **Forbidden Apartments.** Minerva-Press, 1800. (1)
An imitative historical Gothic written in the tradition of Reeve's *The Old English Baron* [1–322] and anticipating Lathom's *The Unknown; or, The Northern Gallery* [1–208]. The disinherited young hero must spend the required evening in a long-sealed cell block of chambers in order to qualify as proper heir of the castle.

1-225. Llewelyn, Mrs. **Read, and Give It a Name.** Minerva-Press, 1813. (1)
The brusque vulgarity of the title says it all. Minerva-Press Gothics were generally somewhat above the tawdry level of the bluebooks, but a new low was reached in this four-volume blot on literary history; namelessness is quite a proper fate for it.

1-226. Lovel Castle; or, The Rightful Heir Restored: A Gothic Tale. Dean & Munday, 1818. (5)
In this typical shilling shocker the anonymous Gothicist has appropriated and abbreviated the plot of Reeve's *The Old English Baron* [1–322]. The frontispiece shows a black-and-white illustration of the visored ghost appearing to Edmund Twyford in the haunted wing of Lovel Castle. As is true of so many Gothic bluebooks, the entire plot of the shocker is solemnly recited in condensed terms in the serpentine subtitle. The subtitle proclaims that *Lovel Castle* is a "Gothic Tale" *Narrating How a Young Man, the Supposed Son of a Peasant, by a Train of Unparalleled Circumstances, Not Only Discovers Who Were His Real Parents, But That They Came to Untimely Deaths; With His Adventures in the Haunted Apartment, Discovery of the Fatal Closet, and Appearance of the Ghost of His Murdered Father; Relating, Also, How the Murderer Was Brought to Justice, With His Confession, and the Restoration of the Injured Orphan to His Title and Estates.*

1-227. Lucas, Charles. **The Castle of Saint Donats; or, The History of Jack Smith.** Minerva-Press, 1978. (4) (SB)
Somewhat satiric in tone, *The Castle of Saint Donats* is a sentimental picaresque with Gothic overtones. The nocturnal interview between the disinherited wanderer, Jack Smith, and his supposedly dead father, the Duke de Merité, seems to be standard Gothic fare, but this supernatural episode and others are undercut by the raillery of Lucas's preface, in which he writes "A castle without a ghost is fit for nothing but—to live in; and, were it generally the case, the poor novelist might starve and the book-seller publish sermons. Had not my castle been luckily honoured by a visitor of this kind, I had never ventured to transmit these authentic memoirs to the eyes of the public, nor had I contaminated their genuineness by the introduction of a fictitious being." The novel again illustrates how the presence of the word "castle" in a title could sometimes be deceiving, since Saint Donats is neither truly haunted nor in a crumbling condition. And Jack's struggle to regain

his heritage following his return from Italy is more domestic than Gothic. By 1798, all prospective authors knew that the word "castle" was practically mandatory at the Minerva-Press and elsewhere for a novel to be accepted for publication.

1–228. Lucas, Charles. **The Infernal Quixote: A Tale of the Day.** Minerva-Press, 1801. (3) (SB)

A Gothic political fantasy as well as a dark, bitter, and amusing social warning against revolutionary ideas in the hands of unscrupulous writers and thinkers, *The Infernal Quixote* is a fictional response to the radical philosophies of William Godwin and a conservative answer to the dangerous Jacobean notions of Bage [1–15] and Holcroft. In fact, the savage wit of Lucas's novel makes it a first-rate Swiftian satire on that vogue of half-philosophic, half-Gothic fiction activated by Godwin and Bage in the 1790s. Lucas set out to ridicule various revolutionary premises including the alleged superiority of the individual to the state. His antihero and infernal Quixote, Lord James Marauder, is no harmless eccentric tilting against windmills like his Spanish namesake, but a truly dangerous and downright diabolic incendiary, a picaresque anarchist who exploits revolutionary ideas and slogans to satisfy his lust for power. Marauder's intrigues help to foment the Irish uprising of 1798 and the consequent fictional collapse of the British government and social order. Conservative Christianity and a solid sense of social order are represented in the novel by the character of Wilson, an intellectual counterweight to Marauder's perversions and hypocrisies. Since Marauder is a truly satanic personality and is devoted to making evil his good, he has some obvious links with the brotherhood of Gothic villains who often live in a society as social or sexual parasites. There are Gothic touches in *The Infernal Quixote*, but like America's Charles Brockden Brown in *Ormond* [1–48], Lucas was more interested in educating his audience about the perils of revolutionary ideology in the wrong hands.

1–229. Lusignan; or, The Abbaye of La Trappe. Minerva-Press, 1801. (1) (SB)

The novel is based on the 1765 drama by Baculard d'Arnaud, *Les Amants malheureux; ou, Le Comte de Comminge* (*The Unfortunate Lovers; or, The Count of Comminge*). The anonymous English work presents a version of the Radcliffean love triangle, love among the ruins as it might be called. The Marquis de Lusignan is the victim of the cunning and degenerate Abbé la Haye. On the eve of his marriage with Emily, the Marquis finds himself removed to a dungeon while the Abbé exults in his wicked success. Making his escape after the usual elaborate suffering in subterranean darkness, Lusignan is conducted to Emily's sepulcher in the Chapel of St. Jago. Distressed with life, he renounces the world and enters the Abbaye of La Trappe in Normandy to seek spiritual peace, only to find there in the cloister his beloved Emily not dead after all but disguised as the brother Ambrose. With an undeniable talent for the morbid and mortuarial, the anonymous author turns the novel into a kind of Gothic *Romeo and Juliet* as Lusignan perishes on his beloved's body. The ecclesiastical villainy and the pronounced element of morbid eroticism unite to make the novel seem a synthesis of the sensibilities of Richardson, Radcliffe, and Diderot. Tortured lives coming to an agonizing focus lend *Lusignan* a fatal beauty played off against the moral ugliness of an overinstitutionalized world. The perverse priest, the Abbé la Haye, is presented as a product of this world.

1–230. Lyttleton, Mr. **The German Sorceress.** Minerva-Press, 1803. (1)
A weak and confused wizard-Gothic that purports to be a translation from a "lost" German legend, *The German Sorceress* compares unfavorably with better witchcraft Gothics such as Catherine Smith's *Barozzi; or, The Venetian Sorceress* [1–361].

1–231. Mackenzie, Anna Maria. **Mysteries Elucidated.** Minerva-Press, 1795. (1)
A follower of the methods of the historical Gothic, Mackenzie united suspenseful terror with semifictional royal history in *Mysteries Elucidated.* Like Lee in *The Recess* [1–214], she favors the naturally pathetic situation of the youthful royal prisoner hidden away and menaced within a remote Gothic building. With admirable Radcliffean procrastinations, all the mysterious confinements and ghostly charades are "elucidated." The novel's invented history deals with a fictive heir to the throne during the troubled reign of the weak king, Edward II. Mortimer's conspiracy and the emergence of the strong ruler, Edward III (1327–1377), add some historical authenticity to the Gothic fabric.

1–232. Mackenzie, Anna Maria. **Dusseldorf; or, The Fratricide.** Minerva-Press, 1798. (1) (SB)
With its psychological interplay between malicious or criminal master and an upright but powerless servant, this huge Gothic (691 pages) is a type of Godwinian psychodrama reminiscent of *Caleb Williams* [1–128]. The Germanic naming and locales also indicate the strong Teutonic coloration, which began to invade English Gothicism following Teuthold's translation of *The Necromancer; or, the Tale of the Black Forest* [1–186] and Peter Will's translation of the Marquis von Grosse's *Horrid Mysteries* [1–139]. Godfried Haustein, former chaplain to Count Dusseldorf of Brandenburg and Countess Alexovina, receives a letter threatening his death. Like Caleb Williams, Godfried apparently possesses an incriminating secret that "something had been done in this house that nobody knows." Hounded by the vindictive Osmond Count Dusseldorf, Godfried flees with his daughter, Sophia, to Norway. The pattern of flight and pursuit, frequently restricted to the castle underground, is now enlarged to an international scale as the fratricidal

count uses his power to separate Godfried and Sophia and to punish Godfried for his possession of the family secret. Seizures by mysterious horsemen, captivity within lonesome dwellings, and chaotic melodrama fill every page of the narrative as the invisible hand of injustice drives Godfried from country to country. There are so many climaxes, alarms, and dire emergencies that all Gothic suspense is soon lost. The mystery of who is the brother-killer is never very mysterious, as it properly should be in a well-conceived Gothic novel that centers its terrors upon a horrible family secret. Michael Sadleir's own book plate and a few of his marginalia appear in the first edition, contained in the Sadleir-Black collection.

1–233. Mackenzie, Anna Maria. **Swedish Mysteries; or, The Hero of the Mines of Delecarlia.** Minerva-Press, 1801. (1)
Although most bogus Gothic translations were from fabricated French or German sources, this particular work bore the claim that it was "translated from a Swedish manuscript by Johanson Kidderslaw." The novel was not attributed to Anna Maria Mackenzie until the title was offered for sale in the Minerva-Press Catalogue of 1814. Hence, we have a spurious Gothic translation probably by an unknown author. The work itself can be described as a subterranean *Räuber-roman*.

*1–234. Mackenzie, Henry. **The Man of Feeling.** Cadell, 1771; Norton, 1958. (4)
One of the most tearful of the sentimental novels of the eighteenth century, *The Man of Feeling* has some clear affinities with Gothic characterization, moods, and settings. The novel's ultravirtuous and lachrymose hero, Harley, is as excessive in his uncontrollable benevolence as the Gothic protagonist is extreme in his passionate evil. Confronted by injustice, universal distress, unrequited love, and a society without feeling, Harley eventually dies of joy after a career of ineffectual altruism accompanied by repeated fits of weeping. When this kind of character can no longer cry he becomes a Gothic man of feeling whose benevolence turns to malignancy. Using the device of the lost manuscript, Mackenzie's novel commences with chapter 11 and is cast in the form of a fragmented posthumous biography of the man of feeling's futile search for love and justice in a callous world. The object of Harley's affection, the tender, beautiful, and sensitive Miss Walton, is a socialized version of the maidens of Radcliffe and her followers. The short novel abounds in vignettes of suffering, which move the man of feeling to tears no less than 47 times. Harley visits Bedlam madhouse, reunites a prostitute with her father, but is too shy to translate his passions into a declaration of love for Miss Walton. If we invert the extravagant goodness and self-isolation of Mackenzie's odd hero, we get a Gothic villain on a par with Ambrosio in *The Monk* [1–218].

1–235. Mackenzie, Henry. **Julia de Rubigné.** W. Strahan, 1777. (4)
Again using the frame device of the lost manuscript, the novel takes the form
of epistolary fragments and juxtaposes three pairs of correspondents. Unlike
The Man of Feeling [1–234], Mackenzie provides a mysterious but clearly delin-
eated villain, Montauban, whose activities and residences are nothing if not
Gothic. The sentimental love story is carried by the letters flowing between
Julia and Maria; they tell of her absent admirer, Savillon, whose life in Mar-
tinique enables him to inveigh against the slave trade and other barbarities.
The Gothic love story is advanced by the exchange between Montauban
and his Spanish cohort, Segarva. There is an inset story of a melancholy
Englishman, Martin, whose guilt over the drowning of his wife finds a sympathetic soul in Savillon. Believing Savillon to be dead, Julia marries the
corrupt and egotistical Montauban and soon is forced to assume that routine
Gothic position of confinement in the menacing mansion of her cruel and
enigmatic husband. Julia's architectural apprehensions on the threshold of
Montauban's estate are much like the emotions of the Gothic maiden as she
approaches the dismal castle at sunset. With true Gothic savoir-faire, Montauban persecutes and then poisons Julia from motives that remain obscure.
But Julia recovers from all to return to her writing desk and communicate
her education in evil to Maria. Mackenzie's Montauban may be the missing
link between Richardson's seducer-hero and the psychopathic baronial or
ecclesiastic tormentors of the Gothic novels that followed.

1–236. Manners, Mrs. **Castle Nouvier; or, Henry and Adelaide.** B. Crosby,
1806. (1)
A routine two-volume historical Gothic that contains the usual characters in
their usual predicaments. Manners's castle is stocked with a resident specter
of a slain relative; a fearsome feudal tyrant who manages to keep Henry and
Adelaide locked away from each other for much of the narrative; and a floor
plan of trap-doors and escape hatches, which eventually lead the lovers to
release and enlightenment. Manners (or Lady Stepney) had taken all the
prosaic instrumentalities of Gothic fiction and created an utterly formulaic
product in adherence to the Gothic group style.

1–237. Marsollier des Vivetières, Benoit-Joseph (France). **Camille; ou, Le
Souterrain (Camille; or, The Underground).** Brunet, 1791. (3)
This three-act anticlerical comedy was seen by Monk Lewis during his Parisian sojourn of 1791. The play is also related to the pre-Gothic themes of
Monvel's *Les Victimes Clôitrées* [1–42]. In a letter, Lewis comments on the
drama as follows: "There is an opera called Le Souterrein [*sic*] where a
Woman is hid in a cavern in her jealous husband's house and afterwards by
accident her Child is shut up there also without food and are not released till
they are perishing with hunger."

1-238. Matthews, Charlotte. **Griffith Abbey; or, The Memoirs of Eugenia.** Oddy & Godwin, 1807. (4)

A domestic novel with an abbey title, *Griffith Abbey* belongs to the category of historical fiction. Eugenia is troubled by a single report of a family ghost, but her more besetting problems involve the selection of a proper husband. The phenomenon of the novel of manners masquerading behind a Gothic title is again in evidence.

*1-239. Maturin, Charles Robert (used pseud. Dennis Jasper Murphy). **The Fatal Revenge; or, The Family of Montorio.** Longman, Hurst, Rees & Orme, 1807; Arno, 1974. (1)

From his beginnings as a Gothic novelist, Maturin was addicted to ultra-complicated plots whose dramatic commotion rivals the tangled tragedies of blood of the Elizabethan playwrights, and Jacobean melodramatists—Marlowe, Tourneur, Webster, and Chapman. The infinitely elaborate trappings of the Elizabethan revenge play seem to serve Maturin as a model in *Montorio*. The year is 1670. Count Orazio is married to Erminia di Vivaldi, who detests Orazio as much as he adores her. Orazio's brother plots to gain Erminia's love and arranges to use the young officer, Verdoni, to inflame Orazio's jealousy. Enraged, Orazio kills Verdoni, which also causes the demise of Erminia, since she had been secretly in love with Verdoni before marrying Orazio. Now demented, Orazio secludes himself on a desert island and swears vengeance on his brother when his sanity returns. So far, the plot sounds more like a Shakespearean tragicomedy than a Gothic novel with its echoes of the Othello-Cassio-Iago triangle and Prospero's island exile in *The Tempest*. Disguising himself as the monk Schemoli (a close counterfeit of Radcliffe's Schedoni in *The Italian* [1-317]), Orazio returns to engineer his fatal revenge. Working by insinuation and indirection as a good Gothic villain should, Schemoli intimidates his brother's two sons, Annibal and Ippolito, into a parricidal scheme against his brother. By the usual perverse genealogical twist, Schemoli learns that the two assassin sons are his own and that he has turned his progeny into murderers. Mortified by this trick of fate, Schemoli poisons himself. To supplement the revenge plot, there is also plenty of monastic and inquisitional atrocity and a shrill style of poetic horror that will later become central in *Melmoth the Wanderer* [1-244].

1-240. Maturin, Charles Robert. **The Wild Irish Boy.** Longman, Hurst, Rees & Orme, 1808; Arno, 1977. (3) (SB)

More patriotic than Gothic (but with certain touches of terror), *The Wild Irish Boy* was Maturin's political answer to Lady Morgan's *Wild Irish Girl* [1-285] of 1806. Maturin's Protestant sympathies did not prevent him from opposing the Act of Union and from using this novel as a platform for nationalistic propaganda.

1–241. Maturin, Charles Robert. **The Milesian Chief.** Henry Colburn, 1812. (1) (SB)

The novel is a curious amalgam of Gothic places and effects with Maturin's militant Irish nationalism and animosity toward the Act of Union with England. The background for the tale is the Irish uprising of 1798. There is a strong Celtic-Gothic quality in the tower retreat of the ruined Milesian chief O'Morven, who has sequestered himself within a grim turret in a last act of Irish defiance. His son, the gallant Connal, opposes the repressions of the degenerate English officer Wandesford, and competes against Wandesford for the love of Armida Montclare, who has married Wandesford out of boredom and has now become a virtual prisoner in Lord Montclare's castle in Connaught on the seacoast. Young Connal is taken prisoner in battle fighting for Irish liberty and is shot; Armida takes her own life on Connal's bullet-riddled body. These melodramatic events are described in the idiom of the Gothic romance, as are the wild scenes of Ireland ablaze with English hatred. *The Milesian Chief* was much admired by Sir Walter Scott, who took from it both inspiration and material for the most thoroughly Gothic of his own novels, *The Bride of Lammermoor* [1–341].

*1–242. Maturin, Charles Robert. **Bertram; or, The Castle of Saint Aldobrand.** John Murray, 1816; Corti, 1956. (1)

A popular and frequently revived Gothic drama, Bertram was first given at Drury Lane on May 9, 1816, with the renowned Edmund Kean as Bertram. Justly praised by Scott and Byron, Maturin's play consolidated Byronic hero and Gothic villain into a single character. Among the Gothic dramas of the period, many of them mediocre, *Bertram* deserves to remain the preeminent Gothic stage spectacle. Descending directly from Schiller's noble brigand, Karl Moor, in *Die Räuber,* Bertram is perhaps the culmination of crime and virtue, tenderness and cruelty, and vulgarity and sophistication; his love for Imogine is laced through with the vile passions of the Byronic-Gothic abuser. Bertram's enemy is the calculating St. Aldobrand, Imogine's Machiavellian father, who has had Bertram banished before the outset of the play. Returning from exile to become the leader of a band of desperadoes, Bertram is shipwrecked near the Castle of St. Aldobrand. Attempting to renew his attachment to Imogine, he is furious to find that St. Aldobrand has married her off to another. Alternating between fits of kindness and spasms of brutality, Bertram pursues his doomed love even as St. Aldobrand plans to return to the castle with a royal commission to condemn him. Spurning escape, Bertram faces St. Aldobrand, slays him, and follows vengeance with suicide. Driven insane by these circumstances, Imogine wanders off to die. The Gothic gloom that engulfs the fated pair of lovers impressed Sir Walter Scott. Lucy Ashton and Ravenswood in *The Bride of Lammermoor* [1–341] descend in part from Maturin's characters.

1-243. Maturin, Charles Robert. **Women; or, Pour et Contre.** Longman, Hurst, Rees, Orme & Brown, 1818. (4) (SB)
Preceding *Melmoth the Wanderer* by two years, this political and social novel's Gothicism is slight. Maturin shows his interest again in the tumult of Anglo-Irish affairs and radical solutions to English tyranny.

*1-244. Maturin, Charles Robert. **Melmoth the Wanderer.** Hurst & Robinson, 1820; Nebraska Univ. Press, 1961. (1)
Maturin's monumental Gothic novel impressed and influenced Goethe, Byron, Pushkin, and Hawthorne in its own era as well as Balzac, Wilde, and Baudelaire later in the century. The novel is a convergence of all the components of the "Romantic Agony" and a truly epic Gothic in the high style. Its tragi-Gothic elements include Faustian loss of soul and self, the moral crisis of the satanic personality, the riddle of suffering, the dilemma of the overreacher in a limited universe, and the metaphysical problem of the never-ending life. Moods, material, and rhetoric all suggest that Maturin wanted to convert the nearly exhausted genre of the Gothic into a higher form. The eyes of Melmoth gleam with the diabolic radiance of perverted faith in evil. This grand, godless, godlike creature has mortgaged his soul to the devil and is condemned to wander through time in search for another sufferer or sinner in such agony that Melmoth will be able to trade destinies with him and obtain the rest of death. The narrative structure of this cosmic odyssey is complex, or more precisely concentric, as Maturin places tales within tales and narrators within narrators to yield a total of five interlocking Gothic stories in addition to the Wanderer's own biography. As Melmoth wanders, he encounters Stanton in the madhouse, Don Alonzo de Moncada in the terrible grip of the Inquisition, the lovely Immalee in a deserted tropical paradise, the starving Walberg family, and Elinor Mortimer. All these sufferers resist Melmoth's temptations to retain their painful humanity, and the Wanderer's sleepless expedition through the miseries of history brings him no rest. The monomaniac quest, like Captain Ahab's in *Moby Dick,* terminates destructively. All the rusty equipment of the Gothic romance is brought into play by Maturin in his effort to fuse the Gothic with the tragic. In fact, each of the five tales inside Melmoth's own story can be regarded as a type of Gothic novel in miniature; Moncada's story, "The Spaniard's Tale," is a monastic shocker that includes an episode of cannibalism; "Stanton's Tale" and the idyll of Immalee ("The Tale of the Indians") have Radcliffean overtones. His intellectual devotion to the psychology of despair and the torments of religious doubt secure for Maturin's *Melmoth the Wanderer* a special category of Gothic fiction.

*1-245. Maturin, Charles Robert. **The Albigenses: A Romance.** Hurst & Robinson, 1824; Arno, 1974. (4)
Maturin's final romance depicts with sadistic realism the persecution and eventual extermination of the Albigenses religious sect in 1209 by Pope In-

nocent III and the ever-ready Inquisition. The military end of the campaign was carried out with vigorous brutality by Simon de Montfort, who becomes the great villain of Maturin's historical novel. The Castle of Courtenaye and the young knight Sir Paladour seem closer to the chivalric spirit of Scott's medieval romances than to Radcliffe or Lewis. The Gothic scholar Maurice Lévy considers *The Albigenses* to be a hybrid work that integrates the supernatural cruelties of the Gothic with the emergent historical novel of chivalry and religious turmoil as written by Scott in such works as *The Monastery* [1–342].

1–246. McDonald, Andrew. **Vimonda.** Larpent Collection MS., 1787. (1)
An exquisite specimen of Gothic drama, the play has as its sole purpose to terrify, horrify, and mystify the audience; in meeting these goals, it succeeds admirably, for both the good characters and the bad bleed and expire before the curtain falls. Vimonda's father, Rothsay, has been murdered (or so it is thought) by the execrable Dundore and his henchman, Barnard. Unknown to all, however, Rothsay has recovered from his wounds and now lurks about a ruined pile adjacent to his usurped castle, his purpose being to spy upon his assassins by means of a spectral disguise. The ghostly hoax works and all parties believe him to be the apparition of Rothsay. Dundore meanwhile contrives to make Vimonda believe that her lover, Lord Melville, caused her father's death. Soon the "ghost" of Rothsay is also convinced of Melville's guilt. The general slaughter at the end of the play sees the good fall with the wicked in this unrelieved Gothic imbroglio when Dundore is killed by Lord Melville, Melville himself is poisoned, and Vimonda dies of shock. The actual identity of the specter of the ruins is artfully concealed in an approved Radcliffean manner until the end of the second act, when Rothsay reveals his living presence above his own tomb in one of the drama's better visual jolts.

1–247. Meeke, Mary (used pseud. Gabrielli). **The Abbey of Clugny.** Minerva-Press, 1795. (1)
A tireless writer of sentimental Gothic fiction, Meeke averaged better than a novel per year between 1795 and 1820. She also found time to translate Ducray-Duminil's *Coelina; ou, L'Enfant du mystère* [1–102] in 1798. Her first book is a trial Gothic containing elements of religious terror and the orthodox plight of the maiden sent into the convent to break her spirit. Other features of plot bear a strong resemblance to Isabella Kelly's *The Abbey of Saint Asaph* [1–188], a Gothic novel published by Minerva-Press in the same year.

*1–248. Meeke, Mary (used pseud. Gabrielli). **Count Saint Blancard; or, The Prejudiced Judge.** Minerva-Press, 1795; Arno, 1977. (1)
Well versed in the methods of Radcliffe and Reeve, Meeke attempted to combine terror and domesticity in this large Gothic romance. A trembling

maiden, an ambiguous villain, and a backdrop of priories, convents, and castles point to Meeke's mastery of the Gothic trends of the mid-1790s.

1-249. Meeke, Mary (used pseud. Gabrielli). **The Mysterious Wife.** Minerva-Press, 1797. (1)
Thomas Babington Macaulay, a Victorian devotee of this work by Meeke as well as others, summed up her Gothic formula for catching and keeping the reader's curiosity. Of her books, Macaulay wrote that every one is "just like another, turning on the fortunes of some young man in a very low rank of life who eventually proves to be the son of a duke." In the case of *The Mysterious Wife*, hereditary adversity is the lot of a young woman who eventually proves to be highborn.

1-250. Meeke, Mary (used pseud. Gabrielli). **The Sicilian.** Crosby & Letterman, 1798. (1)
Taking her cue from the success of Radcliffe's *The Italian* [1-317] of the year 1797, Meeke produced with her usual rapidity a fair version of the monastic Gothic complete with vague shadows, Catholic superstition, and even vaguer threats to the maiden's virtue.

1-251. Meeke, Mary (used pseud. Gabrielli). **The Mysterious Husband.** Minerva-Press, 1801. (1) (SB)
The novel is a masculinized sequel to the formula followed by Meeke in *The Mysterious Wife* [1-249].

1-252. Meeke, Mary (used pseud. Gabrielli). **Midnight Weddings.** Minerva-Press, 1802. (1) (SB)
This Minerva-Press best-seller again illustrates Meeke's absolute mastery of conventional Gothic surprises and jolting narrative tricks. This Gothic begins where most Radcliffean romances typically end—with the marriage of the hero and heroine—but not before the reader has been given almost in the graphic manner of Dickens the full biographical particulars of the young hero's life. Just as the nuptials are about to be solemnized in Chapter 5, the hero's identity is challenged and he is proved not to be Edmund Browning but a fellow of dubious lineage. Macaulay's [1-249] stock plot of the hero's efforts to win back his rightful name is then handled with considerable Gothic efficiency. After a plethora of adversities, Browning's origins prove to be not merely noble but royal; he turns out to be a displaced son of Louis XV. A second midnight wedding to the daughter of a French duke closes the circle of fortune and solves the marital predicament. Surely, Meeke's interrupted wedding is a melodramatic type-scene; its usefulness to later novelists may be witnessed in Charlotte Brontë's *Jane Eyre* with the revelation of Rochester's impending bigamy.

1-253. Meeke, Mary (used pseud. Gabrielli). **The Veiled Protectress; or, The Mysterious Mother.** Minerva-Press, 1819. (1) (SB)
Even as the Gothic novel was dying out, Meeke was still making money from the moribund form and still plotting her books around the figure of the lost heir. It required five volumes to unite mother and daughter in this sentimental Gothic.

1-254. Melville, Theodore. **The White Knight; or, The Monastery of the Morne.** Crosby & Letterman, 1802. (1)
The White Knight is an acceptable Gothic romance of the pseudofeudal type. Most of the traditional trappings as defined by Walpole in *The Castle of Otranto* [1-398] are preserved almost intact. The young, disinherited hero, Allan, is confronted at the outset by the verbose apparition of his revenge-demanding father. The heroine, Allida, constantly stumbles over protesting skeletons and brushes past amorous corpses as she investigates the clues to her identity amid the regulation subterranean hazards. The best character in Melville's Gothic is the tormented tormentor and keeper of the forbidden Monastery of the Morne, the white knight of death: "His aspect was severe and lowering; his mind, gloomy and suspicious; his person was the index of his mind; haughtiness and cruelty, were united to meanness and cowardice; and from an affectation of loftiness, though in reality from guilty fear, his person was as difficult of access as his dreary mansion."

1-255. Melville, Theodore. **The Benevolent Monk; or, The Castle of Olalla.** B. Crosby, 1807. (5)
The decent monk who honors his vows may have been an effort by Melville to counter the fiendish and lecherous image of the clergy so common to Gothic novels of the monastic shocker category. Yet the monk himself has almost no role to play and is something of a static character in the run-of-the-mill Gothic plot, which pits a bad brother against a good brother amid the prefabricated Gothic scenery of deserted castles and terrible underground torture chambers. The novel is an all-too-typical example of formulaic Gothic fiction manufactured to indulge an uncritical Gothic readership. In cultivating the work of Melville and other penny-a-liners, the publisher Crosby had apparently decided to challenge Minerva-Press's growing monopoly over Gothic goods and to lure away some of William Lane's loyal clientele.

1-256. The Midnight Groan; or, The Spectre of the Chapel, Involving an Exposure of the Horrible Secrets of the Nocturnal Assembly: A Gothic Romance. T. & R. Hughes, 1808. (5) (SB)
Packed audaciously into the bluebook's horrific title are all the mandatory mechanisms of the subterranean supernatural shocker. Faithful to the gross craft of the shilling shocker, *Midnight Groan* is a crude compilation of plagiarized Gothic scenes, events, and characters vastly curtailed and mawkishly

illustrated. The bluebooker seems to have done his principal plundering from the pages of Francis Lathom's *Midnight Bell* [1–206], although many other sources are visible. Secret tribunals meeting at midnight in a ruined abbey to conduct their obscene trials is a pilfering of the *Vehmgericht* theme of many German Gothics; specters who inhabit chapels are too numerous to mention, although the one in *Correlia; or, The Mystic Tomb* [1–73] may well have caught the bluebooker's eager eye. Taking whatever he wanted from wherever he wanted in the huge stockpile of legitimate Gothics, changing a name here and there, turning a French *château* into an Italian *castello,* and smearing over his thefts with a few original strokes of blood, the nameless bluebooker produced a classic of subliterature.

1–257. The Midnight Monitor; or, Solemn Warnings from the Invisible World. Champante & Whitrow, n.d. (5)
The anonymous bluebook is a condensation of various Gothic novels that used the supernatural voice of justice or doom as their central fixture of fear. Midnight monitors, solemn warnings, and hideous voices out of the night appear notably in Eliza Parsons's *The Mysterious Warning* [1–291], the major probable source for this shilling shocker.

1–258. Mitchell, Isaac (U.S.). **The Asylum; or, Alonzo and Melissa.** J. Nelson, 1811. (1)
The Asylum is a fascinating specimen of early American Gothic, in which the sublime woes of the Radcliffean heroine and the mouldering, feudal monuments of the English Gothic landscape have been exported intact across the Atlantic and reassembled in Charleston, South Carolina. For monkish superstition and dark intrigue, Mitchell substitutes the atmosphere of the American Revolution. Melissa, who has been promised to Beauman by her despotic father, elects to love and wed the noble but impoverished patriot Alonzo, and is immediately confined to a fully equipped and staffed haunted castle by her irate father. Alonzo translates his despair into revolutionary ardor and goes off to join the naval war against the British. Captured at sea, he is aided by Benjamin Franklin in making his way back to Charleston, where he casts himself upon Melissa's supposed grave. While there is much material that anticipates Fenimore Cooper's sea romances, the American castle and its terrors are genuinely Gothic in the Radcliffean fashion of explained supernatural. The phantoms who seem to torment Melissa are later revealed to be Tory smugglers in conspiracy with the British. Melissa, who is of course not actually dead, is eventually reunited with Alonzo after more international travails and castle ordeals. Mitchell's colonialized Gothic romance won a wide following and is an obvious transitional link between the primitive American Gothic of Charles Brockden Brown and the Gothic undertones of Cooper's romances of the forest and Melville's haunted forecastles.

1–259. The Monk of Hennares. J. F. Hughes, 1817. (5)
Like *Almagro and Claude* [1–5], *The Monk of Hennares* is a late imitation of *The Monk* [1–218]. Although much longer than the standard bluebook, the romance still belongs to the category of cheap, plagiarized shocker.

1–260. The Monk of the Grotto; or, Eugenio and Virginia. Minerva-Press, 1800. (6)
The work is a translation from the French of the sentimental romance of Charles-Antoine-Guillaume Pigault-Lebrun (1753–1835). The monastic disguise enables Eugenio to communicate his love to Virginia, and the grotto serves as secret meeting place. The settings and passions had a natural appeal for the English Gothic imagination.

1–261. Montagne, M. de la (France). **Ethelinde; ou, La Recluse du lac (Ethelinde; or, The Recluse of the Lake). Maradan, 1799. (6)**
A French translation of Charlotte Smith's sentimental and poetic Gothic of 1789 [1–363]. For a comprehensive bibliography of English novels translated into French during the period, the reader will wish to consult Harold Wade Streeter, *The Eighteenth Century English Novel in French Translation: A Bibliographical Study* (Benjamin Blom, 1970). Streeter's study was originally published in 1936 and reflects many English Gothic titles.

1–262. Montague, Edward. **The Castle of Berry Pomeroy. Minerva-Press, 1806. (1)**
Montague's first book is an orthodox Gothic romance in the tradition of Walpole's *Castle of Otranto*. An ancestral curse, eerie forebodings, secret chambers and lost manuscripts, Italianate villainy, and monkish mystery are blended into what can be regarded as workbook Gothic in which Montague tries out his powers as a Gothicist.

1–263. Montague, Edward. **Legends of a Nunnery: A Romantic Legend. J. F. Hughes, 1807. (1)**
The gloomy recesses of the cloister, the amorous Abbess, the naive novice, and the usual quota of Catholic terrors adorn this monastic shocker. The gruesomeness of several scenes in this work suggest Montague's desire to imitate or surpass the voluptuous sequences and brutal excitement of Ireland's *The Abbess* [1–177], to which *Legends of a Nunnery* seems to owe many of its best effects.

1–264. Montague, Edward. **The Demon of Sicily: A Romance. J. F. Hughes, 1807. (1)**
Consciously written as a close imitation of *The Monk* [1–218], Montague's erotic fantasy attempts to excel in lewdness and garish sexual atrocity the scenes of Lewis. Like Ambrosio, Father Bernardo lusts after the virgin herself and is led from crime to crime by his insatiable concupiscence. With the aid of a demon, he possesses the amorous nun, sister Agatha, who has already

given herself to Ferdinando de Montalino within the sanctum sanctorum. Father Bernardo then seizes the lovely maiden Angelina and descends into the dank vaults of the monastery with his screaming prize; here, he is just barely prevented by the abbot from engaging in the subterranean vice of cryptic copulation. As had Ambrosio and Matilda, Bernardo and Agatha must answer to the Holy Office for their crimes. To evade the stake, Bernardo bargains away his soul, while Agatha poisons herself. Interspersed with this raucous reworking of the Ambrosio story is a subplot concerning the evil Marchese de Carlentini, who has conveyed his wife, Theodora, to a tower for life. Montague does not interweave plot with subplot with anything approaching Lewis's skill, but his loathsome sadism is on a par with *The Monk*'s most brutal and cloacinal passages. Many Gothic novels turned out between 1800 and 1810 adapted a horror plot from Lewis and extracted a terror plot from Radcliffe. *The Demon of Sicily* can be considered a Gothic paradigm in this respect. Furthermore, the work quickly evoked another Italianate ogre, in Crookenden's *Horrible Revenge; or, The Monster of Italy!!* [1–79] in 1808.

1–265. Montford Castle; or, The Knight of the White Rose; An Historical Romance of the Eleventh Century. B. Crosby, 1796. (4)
In its exotic medievalism and atmosphere of Spenserian mystery, the novel resembles Leland's *Longsword* [1–216]. The mysterious figure of justice and perfect chivalry, who uses his magical talents to restore the Montford family to greatness, is authentically Gothic in the older sense of the term.

1–266. Montrose; or, The Gothic Ruin. R. Dutton, 1799. (1) (SB)
This muddled and murky Gothic is a prime example of the ineptitude of the field. Little can be said with confidence about the mazy motions of its narrative, since it consists of dozens of unfinished scenes and incoherent plots. The orthodox Gothic cast is present, but the players are unimaginatively handled and remain wooden. In the vicinity of Caernarvon, we meet the travelers— the Marquis of Clarendon, his son, Lord Norville, and his daughters, Caroline and Isabella. The subcast provides the talkative cottager Dame Morris, and the furiously eccentric Lady Malaga, who dresses only as the goddesses Venus or Diana. The hero-villain of this semihistorical Gothic is Colonel Montrose, who is struggling to preserve the dignity of a dying family name. "Only remember," exclaims Montrose's mad countess, for no particular reason, "you have a mother, reputed to be insane, and confined in a solitary apartment." In just this manner, the careless and confused Gothifier adds and subtracts characters without warning or purpose, while the secondhand rhetoric used to describe the ruin itself is poorly copied from Roche or Radcliffe: "The owl (whom the unusual light disturbed) screamed from the turrets; the terrified bats flitted across the chancel, and all was gloomy and re-

plete with dismay." *Montrose* is much more than the average Gothic fiasco; it may be cited as one of the novels of the period that defies all decipherment.

*1-267. Moore, George. **Grasville Abbey: A Romance.** G. G. & J. Robinson, 1797; Arno, 1974. (1)

In his modern edition of this Gothic, Mayo has pointed out that *Grasville Abbey* was the first full-length Gothic novel to begin as a serialized story in a ladies' magazine, a new trend of Gothic publishing that would shortly become a tide. The romance itself is a Radcliffean vehicle that competently duplicates the machinery of suspense found in *The Mysteries of Udolpho* [1-316] and *The Romance of the Forest* [1-315]. An advertisement for the novel from a circulating library catalogue condenses the plot into a few phrases and emphasizes the explanatory role filled by the monastic hermit in the work: "*Grasville Abbey*: A Romance Containing the Sufferings of the Maserini Family: by which the horrors of superstition are fully exposed, as was explained by Father Peter, the Hermit who was found concealed in a cell." For an extensive study of serialized Gothics, an area of Gothic production not covered in this bibliography, see the following two excellent studies by Mayo: "The Gothic Story in the Magazines," *Modern Language Review* 37 (1942), 448-454; "Gothic Romance in the Magazines," *Publications of the Modern Language Association* 65 (1950), 762-789.

1-268. Moore, John. **Zeluco: Various Views of Human Nature Taken from Life and Manners, Foreign and Domestic.** A. Strahan & T. Cadell, 1789. (4) (SB)

Although it lacks the morbid apparatus and eerie medievalism of the high Gothic novel, Moore's *Zeluco* has a protagonist so vicious that he would be at home in any castle or abbey as a sadist extraordinaire. The novel is a fictional life of a total degenerate, an ingenious bully, and a satanic malefactor who instigates suffering whenever and wherever he can. Yet the titanic cruelties of Zeluco are fascinating, and his unmotivated delight in pain engenders the same wonder over the enigma of evil found in the Gothic supermen. Born into a high Sicilian family, Zeluco inaugurates his brutal career by crushing a pet sparrow. From the ineffable pleasure that arises out of this deed there issues a disgusting series of detestable barbarities. Out of whimsical cruelty and at his command, a West Indian slave is flogged to death. In the manner of many Gothic monsters, he intrigues to possess a young woman; gaining her, he kills their offspring and drives her into madness. Only the stiletto of a rival rake can curb Zeluco's boundless ambition to harm or harass others. In the absence of supernatural gears, the novel studies the growth of evil in a strongly passionate nature that only half understands itself. Along with admirers among the ranks of the Gothic writers, Moore's *Zeluco* also earned Byron's praise in the preface to the first and second cantos of *Childe Harold,* where Byron describes his own strange hero as "a poetical Zeluco."

1-269. Morellet, André (France). **Les Enfants de l'abbaye (The Children of the Abbey).** Denné, 1797. (6)
A French translation of Roche's Minerva-Press Gothic of 1796, *The Children of the Abbey* [1-324].

1-270. Morellet, André (France). **Phoedora; ou, La Forêt de Minski (Phedora; or, The Forest of Minski).** Denné, 1799. (6)
A French translation of Charlton's well-received wilderness Gothic of 1798, *Phedora; or, The Forest of Minski* [1-62].

1-271. Morley, G. T. **Deeds of Darkness; or, The Unnatural Uncle.** Tipper & Richards, 1805. (1)
Walpole's infernal machine is in good working order in this satisfying Gothic, whose title alone is a magnificent eye-catcher. The two volumes trace the panics of the unhappy Josephina through a labyrinth of typical Gothic predicaments. For example, as the phobic Josephina stares nervously at a picture, "watching with straining eyes the painted canvass her fears were at last confirmed, and, dreadful to behold, it was slid back, and a man, masked and armed, stepped softly through the aperture, followed by three others!" Josephina is seized by the masked crew from the picture panel, but a Radcliffean delay ensues before the reader learns of their mission and her fate. Morley was able to maneuver this ordinary sort of Gothic disappearance into a long novel of genuine suspense and false alarms.

1-272. Mort Castle: A Gothic Story. J. Wallis, 1798. (1)
Dedicated to the Duchess of York, the anonymous *Mort Castle* (or castle of death) may have been a commissioned Gothic written to order for the duchess and her coterie of aristocratic Gothic readers. Maurice Lévy lists 26 noble subscribers to this Gothic gem, including the Duchess of Rutland the very honorable Lady Melbourne. The novel itself is scrupulously built on the *Otranto* plan, with the Gothic pair, Hubert and Amanda, subjected to the usual skeletal surprises and ghastly tests of courage within the castle of death.

1-273. Mortimore Castle: A Cambrian Tale. Minerva-Press, 1793. (1)
Bloody daggers, portentous manuscripts, and a Gothic reincarnation of the ghost of Hamlet's father all challenge the heroine, Anne, to seek her heritage in the dark chambers of Mortimore Castle in twelfth-century Wales. When the apparition of the slain father makes its entry, the pace of the passage suggests that the anonymous author kept act one of *Hamlet* open before him as he wrote, for we read a paraphrase of Horatio's words: "Forth issued from a side door, a tall figure, armed cap-a-pée; his vizer was up, his countenance was of a death-like hue, and his features were stern and menacing. He led by the hand a lady robed in white, with a black veil on her head and bearing a lighted torch." Gothic ghosts of this sort are the descendants of Shakespearean shades such as Banquo and Old Hamlet, but divested of all psychologi-

cal subtlety in order to perform their first and only function in the high Gothic—to terrify.

1-274. Musäus, Johann Karl August (Germany). **"Die Entführung" ("The Abduction")** in *Volksmärchen der Deutschen (Folktales of the Germans)*. C. W. Ettinger, 1787. (2)

Often mentioned by students of the Gothic as the source for the bleeding nun episode in *The Monk* [1–218], "The Abduction" relates the legend of the lovers' escape from a haunted castle on a special evening occurring once every five years, when, according to superstition, the sanguinary specter walks abroad. By custom, the castle portals are left unbarred to permit the exit of the bleeding shape. But Lewis's biographer, L. F. Peck, disputes this long-standing claim that the bleeding nun episode was taken from Musäus's Gothic story. See Louis F. Peck, *"The Monk and Musäus' Die Entführung,"* *Philological Quarterly* 32 (1953), 346–348, where he concludes that "while the two authors obviously used the same tradition, the episode in *The Monk* differs in so many ways from *Die Entführung* that it is by no means certain that Lewis was dependent upon Musäus."

1-275. Musgrave, Agnes. **Edmund of the Forest: An Historical Novel.** Minerva-Press, 1797. (4) (SB)

With its compassionate hermits, forbidding priories, and vague medievalism, the novel is an attempt to find a middle zone of Gothicism between Walpole's unrestrained supernatural and Reeve's careful control of incredible incidents within the historical context. Musgrave's romance brings the low-born young man from forest to castle to seek his destiny. Edmund's interview with the vocal portrait of his murdered ancestor gives the historical romance a mild Gothic overlay. Musgrave's extensions of Reeve's *The Old English Baron* [1–322] also furnished Ker with material for her forest-to-castle plot in *Edric the Forester; or, The Mysteries of the Haunted Chamber* [1–195].

1-276. The Mysterious Bride; or, The Statue Spectre. T. Hughes, 1800. (5) (SB)

Of bluebook quality, this not-too-shocking shocker mimics a number of Gothic works in which animated statues of supposedly deceased relatives claimed their places among the living. There are, of course, many pre-Gothic sources for organic statuary, as in the famous statue at the feast in the Don Juan legends and the bride of stone, Hermione, who comes to life in act five of Shakespeare's *Winter's Tale*. But the anonymous Goth's more immediate source here was Ballin's *The Statue Room: An Historical Romance* [1–17].

1-277. The Mysterious Penitent; or, The Norman Château. J. A. Robbins, 1800. (1)

In this elegant and comfortable Gothic, the heroine finds her husband and her destiny by undergoing the usual nocturnal adventures in the ancient building, which seems to be half castle and half monastery. The mysterious penitent is her husband-to-be in ecclesiastical disguise.

1–278. The Mystic Tower; or, Villainy Punished. Kaygill, n.d. (5) (SB)
An example of tower Gothic in cheapest bluebook form, this shilling shocker is hastily constructed with mechanical penny-a-line zeal. The plot itself appears to be taken almost literally from John Palmer's ingenious *Mystery of the Black Tower* [1–288]. For every artistically accomplished Gothic of any sort there were always dozens of eager Gothic parasites and profiteers ready to plunder and plagiarize.

1–279. Naubert, Christiane Benedicte Eugenie (Germany) (used pseuds. Professor Kramer, Johann Friedrich Wilhelm Müller, Professor Milbiller). **Hermann von Unna: Eine Geschichte aus den Zeiten der Vehmgerichte (Hermann of Unna: A Story of the Times of the Fehmic Tribunals).** Weygandschen, 1788; English trans., G. G. & J. Robinson, 1794. (2) (SB)
Besides *Hermann von Unna,* a lengthy and complex Inquisition-Gothic, Naubert (1756–1819) produced a shelf of romances and translations under various pseudonyms. The intricate plot of *Hermann von Unna* is ideally Gothic in its baroque designings and elaborate twists. The many intertwining stories render the narrative an astonishing polyphonic web done almost in the fashion of a medieval German romance of the stature of Wolfram von Eschenbach's *Parzifal.* The Westphalian youth Hermann, page to King Wenceslaus, falls in love with Ida Munster. The court of Wenceslaus is so unbearably dissipated as well as tainted with the dark deeds of the secret Fehmic tribunal that Hermann decides to seek the patronage of Sigismond of Hungary and takes his leave of Ida. Ida is accused of sorcery; through the chicanery of the wicked Princess of Ratisbon she is brought before the secret tribunal, which is masked in black and convenes in the dimmest of vaults. After acquittal, she is conveyed to the castle of her vain father, Count Wirtemberg. Because the houses of Wirtemberg and Unna are locked in a deadly feud, Ida's love for Hermann is forbidden. Meanwhile, Hermann's benefactor, King Sigismond, falls under the spell of Countess Barbe Cyly, a vicious nymphomaniac who uses sex to gain the Hungarian throne; spurned by Hermann, she confines him to a dungeon where he waits to face the dreaded *Vehmgericht* on a trumped-up charge of murder. In Prague, Ida has joined the reformist cause of John Hus and has been immured in the Convent of St. Anne by the anti-Hussites. Here, she is beset by a host of Gothic threats, including the possibility of being walled up alive. When all seems lost, her archbishop oppressor dies and Ida is restored to Hermann at long last. Although complicated, the romance moves at a brisk pace. In its English translations, *Hermann von Unna* became a veritable thesaurus of Gothic arcana for the makers of both the monastic shocker and the romance of the menaced maiden. In German, the work of Naubert no doubt influenced many of the *Schauer*-romanticists such as Grosse [1–139] and Gleich [1–126].

1-280. Nicholson, Mr. **The Solitary Castle: A Romance of the Eighteenth Century.** Minerva-Press, 1789. (4)

The strange, Beckfordian proprietor of the solitary castle has constructed an irrational dreamworld for himself and secluded himself there. His solitary castle contains a majestic hall "in which seven kings of England who reigned during the Heptarchy, frowned in marble: and to render the appearance of these statues perfectly terrible, the Captain had dressed them in suits of real and complete armour." Immersed in the "gloominess of the situation he had chosen," the isolated castle dweller is visited by a phantom suspended in a luminous sphere and invited to make an ascent by balloon to worlds unknown. Nicholson's fantasy has interesting connections with the dream excursions and imaginary voyages of science fiction; his hero, a man who retreats from the boredom of his own age, has interesting parallels in J. K. Huysmans's famous decadent novel, *A Rebours (Against the Grain)* (1884).

1-281. Nodier, Charles (France). **Smarra; ou, Les Démons de la Nuit (Smarra; or, The Demons of the Night).** Ponthieu, 1820. (2)

The weird and frenetic romanticism of Nodier (1780-1844), as well as his debt to the English Gothic novelists, is well demonstrated in this tale of the female demon or succubus. After a sinister banquet, the fiendish Smarra puts to death the lovers Polémon and Myrrhé, while implicating Lorenzo in this double murder. Outwitted by the succubus, Lorenzo is beheaded. Smarra is a demi-devil not unlike Matilda in *The Monk* [1-218] and also shares characteristics with the vampire in Goethe's *Die Braut von Korinth* [1-131]. Nodier also wrote an excellent French version of the *Räuber-roman, Jean Sbogar* (1818), whose hero-villain is a romantic criminal on a par with Zschokke's *Abällino* [1-422].

1-282. O'Keefe, John. **The Banditti; or, Love in a Labyrinth.** Larpent Collection MS., 1781. (4)

The comic opera first given at Covent Garden in November 1781 is an early theatrical parody of cavernous Gothic love affairs and wild trappings. For unclear reasons, the play's later title was changed to *The Castle of Andalusia*. *Banditti* can be described as a stage Gothification of the *Comedy of Errors*, in which the old ploy of master being mistaken for servant is put to use to mock Gothic themes of lost identity. The stage for his farcical contrivance is naturally a castle containing an "antique apartment" and the prerequisite sliding panels and secret portals for the timely entrances and exits of specters, lost uncles, and fierce bandits. O'Keefe also invented mock-Gothic names for his dramatis personae. Less successful than Lawler's later *The Earls of Hammersmith* [1-211], O'Keefe's parody was probably responsible for Cobb's dramatic satire on the histrionics of Gothic melodrama in *The Haunted Tower* [1-70].

1-283. Orlando. **The Chamber of Death; or, The Fate of Rosario; An Historical Romance of the Sixteenth Century.** Minerva-Press, 1809. (1)
Advertised by Minerva-Press as a two-volume sequel to *The Monk* [1-218] for the typical price of nine shillings, Orlando's work is a loosely rewoven tapestry of terror and horror made up mainly of strands of the Matilda-Ambrosio story stitched together with some threads of plot torn from Ireland's *Gondez the Monk* [1-180]. The narrative result is an excellent example of a pirated Gothic done in a secondhand style. In fact, the pseudonym may well be camouflage for several different hands, since the novel shows a sporadic construction.

1-284. **L'Orpheline du Château; ou, Emmeline (The Orphan of the Castle; or, Emmeline)** (France). Buisson, 1788. (6)
A rapidly manufactured French translation of Charlotte Smith's maiden-centered Gothic of 1788, *Emmeline: The Orphan of the Castle* [1-362].

1-285. Owenson, Sydney (Lady Morgan). **The Wild Irish Girl: A National Tale.** Richard Phillips, 1806. (4)
An inspiration for Maturin's *The Wild Irish Boy* [1-240] of the next year, Lady Morgan's antiquarian and nationalistic heroine, Glorvina, feeds her imagination on the splendid decomposition of ancient Irish culture. Her sublime tendencies cause her to revel Gothically in dreams of recovered Hibernian greatness. Glorvina is the last descendant of the nearly exhausted line of Connaught princes who takes upon herself the stewardship of a past now jeopardized by land-hungry English earls. Weak in plot, the novel abounds in romantic reminiscence and scenery and Gothic moods, which permits it to be categorized as Gaelic Gothic. It was an important topographical influence on Maturin's wild settings for his Irish historical sagas of independence.

1-286. Owenson, Sydney (Lady Morgan). **The Novice of Saint Dominick.** Richard Phillips, 1806. (4)
Priced at 18 shillings, this mild-mannered Gothic of the cloister is a delicate blend of Radcliffean anxiety, the novel of sensibility, and the comedy of manners. There is no wicked abbess here; the novice is protected and advised by the erudite grande dame Magdelaine de Montmorell. In her slight and reluctant Gothicism, Lady Morgan was catering to those readers for whom the bloody extremities of the *Schauer-roman* or bluebook Gothic seemed too prurient or absurd.

1-287. Palmer, John, Jr. **The Haunted Cavern: A Caledonian Tale.** B. Crosby, 1796. (1) (SB)
The censure of the *Critical Review* for December 1795 catches the weariness of the reviewers at the overabundance of grotto-Gothics in general: "The tale of shrieking spectres and bloody murder has been repeated until it palls upon the sense. It requires the genius of a Radcliffe to harrow up our souls with these visionary horrors." Deriving most of its shadowy Gothic situations

from the genius of Radcliffe, Palmer's Highland Gothic is one of the best survivals of the explained supernatural vogue. The time is the age of Henry VI; the place, a Gothic castle "in the wild and barren county of Aberdeenshire." The principals are the dissipated Sir James Wallace, his maltreated wife, Matilda of Glencairn, and their lovely daughter, Jane. When Matilda's decent brother, Lord Archibald, vanishes, Wallace brings his son, Eldred of Glencairn, to the castle where he can be watched. To cure him of his love for Jane, who has been given to the savage Highland chief Donald of the Isles, Eldred is confined to the haunted cavern. The tenebrous descriptions here are exquisitely loathsome in themselves and make the reader speculate that Maturin and Poe had perused Palmer's grotesque decor. Finally, liberation and reunion with Matilda come to the castle prisoner, while the supernatural events of his sojourn in the haunted cavern are accounted for. Palmer's work echoes and in some ways excels the Highland Gothic experiment of Radcliffe in her first novel, *The Castles of Athlin and Dunbayne* [1–313].

1–288. Palmer, John, Jr. **The Mystery of the Black Tower.** Minerva-Press, 1796. (1) (SB)
Rapidly composed to meet the new and spiraling demand for Gothics with towers or turrets in their titles, Palmer's second romance of 1796 has enough veracity in its historical substance to appeal to the followers of Lee and the taste for historical terror. The long reign of Edward III (1327–1377) forms the violent backdrop for the eventful career of Leonard, who has the task of finding his title and birthright in a maze of Gothic intrigues. The black tower, which is only one of an array of Gothic locations featured in the romance, is the special weapon of torment of the villain of the piece, Lord Edmund Fitzallan. This gloomy, runic relic of medieval cruelty contains the fair Emma, who has been roughly abducted by Lord Edmund. Extricating Emma is but one of the many Gothic tasks that adorn Palmer's brisk plot, which conducts the reader on a grand tour of Gothic castles and monasteries on the elusive trail of Leonard's heritage. With a skill that compensates for the plot's lack of originality, Palmer integrates the well-worn conventions of Gothic distress into what might be called a textbook tower-Gothic. Evidence of the book's impact may be detected in William Harrison Ainsworth's *Tower of London,* an early Victorian historical Gothic that owes much of its antiquarian spirit to Palmer's work.

1–289. Palmer, John, Jr. **The Mystic Sepulchre; or, Such Things Have Been: A Spanish Romance.** J. F. Hughes, 1807. (1)
Like the fine anonymous Gothic, *Correlia; or, The Mystic Tomb* [1–73], Palmer's romance builds its elongated suspense around the motifs of the empty sarcophagus and the sound from within a sealed tomb. In fact, the plotting is so similar to the story of *Correlia* that it is possible to guess that Palmer himself was the author of that anonymous Minerva-Press offering of 1802.

*1-290. Parsons, Eliza. **The Castle of Wolfenbach: A German Story.** Minerva-Press, 1793; Folio Press, 1968. (1) (SB)

Parsons's first Gothic novel is a complicated web of Germanic horrors and sentimental suspense. Jane Austen's decision to include it among the Northanger novels was probably dictated by the book's utter typicality as a Teutonic thriller. The heroine, Matilda Weimar, is doubly victimized by a lecherous uncle and the unnatural Count de Bouville, the frowning tyrant of Wolfenbach Castle. Befriended while on the run by the lady of the castle, Matilda barely has a chance to relate her sufferings before the bed of the mysterious benefactress is found empty. In exalted Gothic panic, Matilda cries out in the well-coached idiom of the Gothic maiden: "Good heavens! What scenes of murder and atrocious crimes must have been perpetrated in this castle; how great is my curiosity to know more of the unhappy Victoria so recently the cause of joy and sorrow and her unfortunate attendant, but their fate is enveloped in mystery and horror,—what mine may be heaven only knows." Add to this verbose hysteria a murdered Chevalier and the ordeal of Matilda's sister (Mrs. Courtney), locked in a windowless room with a hyperactive corpse, and we have all that could be wanted in the Germanization of the Radcliffean heroine's plights. At the end of Matilda's tempest-tossed adventures, Jane Austen's Catherine Morland must have breathed a sigh of relief over Parsons's reassuring final sentence after her heroine's deliverance from Wolfenbach: "Thus, after a variety of strange and melancholy incidents, Matilda received the reward of her steadiness, fortitude, and virtuous self-denial."

*1-291. Parsons, Eliza. **The Mysterious Warning: A German Tale.** Minerva-Press, 1796; Robert Holden, 1928. (1) (SB)

Plotted around the promising Gothic acoustic of the preternatural voice issuing from the night, *The Mysterious Warning* may well have furnished the American Gothic novelist Charles Brockden Brown with his ventriloquist theme in *Wieland* [1-46]. That this second German fakery also appears on Catherine Morland's reading list is further evidence of its popularity with those Gothic readers who craved sham translations. The story is more compact than the deviously told *Castle of Wolfenbach* [1-290]. Kneeling at the bedside of his dead father, Ferdinand perceives a mysterious voice instructing him in sepulchral tones to beware of his brother, Count Rhodophil. Throughout the remainder of the narrative, the admonishing voice denounces the past crimes of Rhodophil and exposes his planned nefariousness toward Ferdinand. Eventually, the old steward Ernest comes forward to explain that he had pretended to be the terrible voice and that he had felt morally bound to use his ventriloquial talents to divert Rhodophil's mischievous stratagems. From this clumsy Gothic implement of the protective voice, Brown was able to fashion the ambiguous verbal power of his half-evil man, Carwin, in *Wieland*.

1-292. Parsons, Eliza. **The Valley of Saint Gothard.** P. Norbury, 1799. (1)
(SB)
This monastic shocker is a transcription of the secular thrills and predicaments of Matilda Weimar inside the Castle of Wolfenbach [1–290] into ecclesiastical dangers and dreadful sites. The lonely abbey that awaits the
maiden in the valley of Saint Gothard is simply Wolfenbach Castle redeco-
rated and renamed. In *Catholicism in Gothic Fiction,* Sister Mary Muriel Tarr
comments on the sinister value of Catholic materials to works such as *The
Valley of Saint Gothard:* "Catholic materials serve the adventure-love-story elements in Gothic fiction, first of all, by providing a milieu for the action. Ecclesiastical ruins, passageways from castles to convents, chapels, monasteries,
convent cells, monastic prisons, chambers of the Inquisition, convent gardens, burial vaults in the crypts of chapels or abbey churches—these are
places for which characters in Gothic fiction have special predilection. . . . Allusions to things Catholic create illusions of times long past and
help to establish that peculiar spirit that passes in Gothic fiction for medievalism."

1-293. Patrick, F. C. **More Ghosts!** Minerva-Press, 1798. (4)
Patrick's spoofing novel is a spirited parody of various hair-raising situations
found throughout Radcliffe and her followers. Reeve's young heir, Edmund
Twyford, is also debunked in the figure of young Tom. Emily St. Aubert of
Udolpho is thoroughly lampooned in the swooning, easily terrified Miss
Bolton, a parson's daughter with pretensions toward Gothic heroineship.
The evil baron shows up as the obnoxious but innocuous Mr. Morney, proprietor of the local Gothic stockpile. Patrick forewarned her readers in her
preface that her book was "a burlesque upon the multitude of ghosts and
mysteries which have excited public curiosity in plays and novels for some
years past." However, her parody could be and apparently was marketable
as a genuine Gothic. The enterprising American publisher Caritat quickly
brought out an edition of *More Ghosts!* for Gothic customers in New York and
Philadelphia. Neither as amusing as Cobb's play, *The Haunted Tower* [1–70],
nor as corrosive in its burlesques as *The New Monk* [1–381], the novel was a
close enough approximation of serious Gothicism to be mistaken for the real
thing.

*1-294. Peacock, Thomas Love. **Headlong Hall.** T. Hookham, 1816; Dutton, 1961. (4)
Almost totally devoid of plot, this conversational novel takes place at the ancient and eccentric country seat of an equally eccentric host, Harry Headlong, Esq., during a Christmas holiday. Here are gathered Mr. Foster, the
perfectibilian; Mr. Escot, the deteriorationist; Mr. Jenkison, the status-quo-
ite; and the expert on the art of turkey-stuffing, Mr. Gaster. Later arrivals
include Mr. Cornelius Chromatic, Mr. Nightshade, Sir Patrick O'Prism,
Miss Philomela Poppyseed, and Mr. Panscope. The wild talk that flows is

more in the nature of mad monologue than conversation, with sundry bits of Gothic chatter rising intermittently from the general chaos of voices, as in Mr. Milestone's detached commentary on medieval building fads: "Mr. Milestone: Here is Littlebrain Castle, a Gothic, moss-grown structure, half bosomed in trees. Near a casement of that turret is an owl peeping from the ivy." Less directly a Gothic mockery than its companion books, *Nightmare Abbey* [1–295] and *Crotchet Castle*, *Headlong Hall*'s caricatures of talk nevertheless laugh with telling accuracy at the preposterous excesses of Gothic language and landscape.

*1–295. Peacock, Thomas Love. **Nightmare Abbey.** T. Hookham, Jr., and Baldwin, Cradock & Joy, 1818; Holt, Rinehart & Winston, 1971. (4) (SB)

With its mockery of shilling and shocking titles and its clever burlesques of the frantic conversation of certain leading romantic intellectuals, Peacock's novel assumes a place in the late literary history of the Gothic movement as an antidote against the runaway rhetoric of horror and the emotional absurdities of the high Gothic. In *Nightmare Abbey*, a garrulous group of eccentric romantics come together at the country house of Mr. Christopher Glowry and his Shelleyesque son, Scythrop, specifically for the purpose of out-talking each other. In a fatal thrust at all foolish readers of the *Schauer-roman* and tower-Gothics, Scythrop is depicted as retiring to "the southwestern tower, which was ruinous and full of owls," there to repose restlessly with a copy of "*Horrid Mysteries* under his pillow, and to dream of venerable eleutherarchs and ghastly confederates holding midnight conventions in subterranean caves." As is normal with Peacock, plot is secondary to the bizarre monologues of the characters, who often digress on Gothic subjects. Thus does Mr. Flosky, a metaphysical lunatic based on Coleridge, hold forth on apparitions as follows: "The door silently opened, and a ghastly figure, shrouded in white drapery, with the semblance of a bloody turban on its head, entered and stalked slowly up the apartment." Mr. Flosky's reading habits need no further description. For all their satiric expertise, Peacock's novels also had the serious aim of correcting false reading tastes and pointing out the foolishness of morbid romanticism.

1–296. Pickard, Mary. **The Castle of Roviego; or, Retribution.** J. Booth, 1805. (1) (SB)

Like the anonymous fiasco, *Montrose; or, The Gothic Ruin* [1–266], the four volumes of *The Casle of Roviego* only befuddle the reader. The plot is so obscure that it seems more designed to perplex than to mystify. The characters are equally derivative and unsatisfying, and the author has made no effort to conceal her plunderings from the more competent Gothics. Trite and cumbersome in style, mechanical in plot, and impossible to decipher, *The Castle of Roviego* represents the very lowest end of the Gothic literary spectrum.

1-297. Pigault-Maubaillarcq (France). **La Famille Wieland; ou, Les Prodiges (The Wieland Family; or, The Prodigies).** Moreaux, 1808. (6)
An extremely open translation of Charles Brockden Brown's American Gothic novel, *Wieland* [1-46]. The French translator refurbishes portions of the original plot to suit the tastes of readers of the *roman noir*.

1-298. Pilkington, Mary. **The Subterranean Cavern; or, The Memoirs of Antoinette de Montflorance.** Minerva-Press, 1798. (1) (SB)
Set in part in revolutionary France during the Reign of Terror, the romance exploits the violent atmosphere and secretive struggle for power of Robespierre's Paris. Antoinette's aristocratic father is menaced by the bloody hand of the ruthless Committee of Public Safety. Antoinette is a conventional Gothic heroine whose travails can be traced in part to her emotionally gullible nature. Warned by the dying nun Sister Angeline not to foresake "rational devotion," Antoinette tries to live by her emotions and pays the price in Gothic terror. To counterbalance her emotionalism, the novel offers a good portrait of the physiocratic freethinker La Favrière.

1-299. Pilkington, Mary. **The Accusing Spirit; or, De Courcy and Eglantine.** Minerva-Press, 1802. (1) (SB)
Shipwreck, religious terror, a wicked abbess, and the rascally monk Ignatius all block the way to happiness for De Courcy and Eglantine in this combined monastic shocker and historical romance of the fifteenth century.

1-300. Pilkington, Mary. **Ellen, Heiress of the Castle.** B. Crosby, 1810. (1)
A made-to-order Gothic romance that brings the trembling young heroine down various corridors of terror and mystery to her name and noble destiny. The Castle of Mordstein is well stocked with the usual horrific appliances and destiny-disclosing supernatural devices. Strange sounds, walking portraits, breathing tapestries, and a feudal despot with one terrible eye all suggest how strongly the inventions of Walpole contributed to the stagnation of any new Gothic development in the late stages of the form.

1-301. Pixérécourt, René-Charles-Guilbert (France). **Victor; ou, L'Enfant de la forêt (Victor; or, The Child of the Forest).** Barba, 1798. (2)
A dramatic adaptation of Ducray-Duminil's *roman noir* of 1796, *Victor; ou, L'Enfant de la forêt* [1-101].

1-302. Pixérécourt, René-Charles-Guilbert (France). **Coelina; ou, L'Enfant du mystère (Coelina; or, The Child of Mystery).** Se Vend au Théâtre, 1801. (2)
A dramatic adaptation of Ducray-Duminil's novel of 1798, *Coelina; ou, L'Enfant du mystère* [1-102]. Pixérécourt also wrote an important dramatic adaptation of *The Mysteries of Udolpho* [1-316] in 1799, entitled *Le Château des Appenins; ou, Le Fantome vivant (The Castle of the Appenines; or, The Living Phantom)*.

1–303. Place, M. de la (France). **Le Vieux baron anglois; ou, Les Revenants vengés (The Old English Baron; or, The Avenging Spirits).** Didot, 1787. (6)

A first French translation of Reeve's influential historical Gothic, *The Old English Baron* [1–322]; the subtitle is the translator's innovation.

*1–304. Polidori, John William. **The Vampyre.** Sherwood, 1819; Dover, 1966; Gubblecote Press, 1973. (1) (SB)

Generally recognized as the first vampire story in English literature, Polidori's novella is the forerunner of the sophisticated vampirism of Joseph Sheridan Le Fanu's *Carmilla,* Bram Stoker's *Dracula,* and in the twentieth century, Anne Rice's *Interview with the Vampire.* In German literature, the vampire theme had been given formal expression by Goethe in *Die Braut von Korinth* [1–131]. Polidori's animosity toward his erstwhile companion, Lord Byron, has overtones in *The Vampyre;* like Caroline Lamb's *Glenarvon* [1–199], the writing of the work was something of an act of literary revenge for Byron's coldness. Lord Ruthven, a handsome nobleman and lion of London society, is irresistibly charming except for "a dead grey eye," which marks him as aggressively sinister. Fascinated by Ruthven's magnetic personality, the youthful Aubrey accompanies the dissipated man to the Continent, but shortly has a falling-out with him. In Greece, Aubrey falls in love with Ianthe, but before they can marry she is assaulted by a vampire. Mysteriously, Lord Ruthven reenters Aubrey's life to assist him in recovering from despair. Traveling the Continent together once again, Ruthven is unexpectedly shot by brigands and makes Aubrey swear before dying that he will keep the secret of Ruthven's dissolute career unspoken for a year and a day. After exposure to moonlight and a seeming resuscitation, Ruthven's corpse unaccountably vanishes. Returning to London, Aubrey is shocked to find the dashing figure of Lord Ruthven again exerting its charm over high society. Driven nearly mad by this cadaverous resurrection, Aubrey rejoices briefly in the news of his sister's impending marriage. But the intended bridegroom is, of course, the vampire, Lord Ruthven, now devoted to feasting on Aubrey's sister. Bound by his rash oath, Aubrey must watch helplessly as Lord Ruthven works his will. While the attack on the fatality of the Byron friendship is clear enough, a more interesting feature of Polidori's *Vampyre* for the Gothicist is his presentation of the creature as a feeder on the wills and souls of his victims as well as their bodies. The motif of the foolish promise was also available to Polidori through Monk Lewis's Gothic melodrama, *The Wood Daemon; or, The Clock Has Struck* [1–222].

1–305. Porter, Jane. **Thaddeus of Warsaw.** Longman, 1802. (4)

Jane Porter's novel remained continuously in print throughout the nineteenth century. In the midst of the Gothic mania and a dozen years before Scott's first novel, *Waverley,* the historical novel was struggling to declare its literary independence from Gothic castles and monkish supermen. While still deeply entangled in the skeins of *Ritter-* and *Räuber-roman*, Jane Porter's *Thaddeus of Warsaw* indicates the rising tendency to make the Gothic function as a subsidiary effect or an aid to atmosphere rather than the whole subject of romance. The noble soldier, young Thaddeus, comes to terms with his English heritage after enduring a series of hardships and exiles. In the tradition of his famous ancestor, the Polish warrior-king John Sobieski, Thaddeus joins the forces of the Count Palatine and King Stanislaus to repel the Russian invader. Instead of liberty for Poland, Thaddeus witnesses crushing defeat, the destruction of Sobieski's castle, and deportation for himself. The young man's self-education etched against a background of violent nationalism and war remains rooted in Gothic styles and scenery. But Porter's work gave the historical branch of the Gothic novel the impetus needed to assert itself as an independent genre.

1-306. Porter, Jane. **The Scottish Chiefs.** Longman, 1810. (4)

Preceding Maturin's *Milesian Chief* [1-241] by two years, Porter's novel is a panoramic historical romance that uses the savage backdrop of medieval Scotland for Gothic pigmentation. The book chronicles the violent life and death of the chieftain, William Wallace, from the murder of his wife by the tyrannical English governor Heselrigge in 1296 to Wallace's own execution in the cause of Highland freedom. As in *Thaddeus of Warsaw* [1-305], we see the pure historical novel beginning to detach itself from cumbersome Gothic dependencies to become a form in its own right. In a stroke of national fervor appreciated by Scott, Porter concludes the novel non-Gothically by describing the great Scottish victory over the English at the Battle of Bannockburn in 1314. The work of Porter is the obvious transitional link between the historical Gothicism of Clara Reeve and Sophia Lee and the broader accomplishments of Sir Walter Scott.

1-307. Powell, James. **Wolf; or, The Tribunal of Blood.** Johnson, 1806. (2)

A free and highly innovative translation into English of Wächter's 1802 German romance of the secret Fehmic Court, *Die Rächenden; oder, Das Vehmgericht des achtzehn Jahrhundert (The Avengings; or, The Fehmic Tribunal of the Eighteenth Century)*. Unlike so many purported translations from the German, Powell's work is bona fide, if somewhat liberal. Wächter's story follows the model for the Fehmic theme set forth in Naubert's *Hermann von Unna* [1-279].

1-308. Powis Castle; or, Anecdotes of an Antient Family. Minerva-Press, 1788. (4) (SB)

If not quite a full-fledged satire in the Peacockian [1-294] vein, *Powis Castle* nevertheless aims some fine satiric shafts at the berserk characters and architectural quirks of the emergent Gothic craze. There are also strong reminders of Laurence Sterne's delightful lunacies of *Tristram Shandy* in the Gothic banter and behavior of the impoverished baronet Sir Walter Powis, whose father, Sir Godfrey, rode to hounds and wasted the family fortune. One of

Sir Walter's Shandyesque projects entails restoring Powis Castle to the dilapidated condition recognized as officially Gothic, for "now the castle, which by the best judges was esteemed the finest piece of Gothic architecture extant in England was gone terribly into decay." Meanwhile, the nearby "snug villa" of the modern upstart Mr. Fleming rivals Powis's faded Gothic grandeur. After some snickers over absurd Gothic building fashions and a lively Gothic cartoon of Sir Walter's uncle, Lord Wentworth ("He would wander for hours in the ivy-covered recesses which surrounded the castle, listening to the pensive note of a solitary owl"), the novel suddenly abandons its satiric tone and turns into a serious Gothic. The malicious Count Parmeni schemes to take Lady Julia away from Sir Walter and resorts to all the approved Gothic machinations to do so. When nothing works, he attacks Julia in the garden, but is driven off by the alert Sir Walter. Yet there persists some residue of Gothic satire in the anonymous author's triumphant dismissal of the wicked Parmeni: "The monster of iniquity, unable to stand the keen reproaches of the injured pair, slunk away like the guilty fiend from paradise." The mocking tone here suggests the artistic uncertainty of the writer over the direction of his novel on the verge of the ultra-Gothic 1790s.

1–309. Proby, W. C. **The Mysterious Seal.** Westley, 1799. (1)
This triple-decker Gothic is constructed around the device of the "door forever closed." Since the portal is forbidden, it is of course to this door that the curious maiden immediately proceeds once she is confined to the castle. Proby's manipulation of the Gothic gadget is not distinguished among the many Gothic writers who used it.

1–310. Proby, W. C. **The Spirit of the Castle.** Crosby & Letterman, 1800. (1)
Proby's second Gothic novel shows better control of the apparatus of terror. Conventional, but respectable, *The Spirit of the Castle* fuses the supernatural shock tactics of *The Castle of Otranto* [1–398] with the incarcerated inquisitiveness of the Radcliffean maiden. The hysterical heroine Cecilia is prone to fainting fits, but still eager to spend a stormy evening in the shadowy western apartment where the spirit of the castle is said by legend to reside. Among her other Gothic probings before her salvation from darkness by young Henri are an encounter with a picture come to life and the mandatory subterranean stroll through the castle crypts. Proby himself was an antiquarian scholar of some reputation who edited Pope's translation of *The Odyssey* (1725) and Dryden's translations of Virgil. His abilities as a classicist brought to his Gothifying a certain stylistic elegance not often found in the slapdash composition and wooden syntax of so many Gothic novels.

1–311. The Prophetic Warning; or, The Castle of Lindendorff. J. Ker, 1800. (5) (SB)
This mephitic bluebook tosses together parricide, nocturnal whispers, the return of cadaverous ancestors, and many other well-worn items of Walpo-

lesque furniture to entice the reader from climax to climax toward the stentorian doom of the villain and the reunion of the maiden with the denied heir of the castle. In its pungent prose and overt plagiarisms from the overstocked Gothic castles of legitimate Gothics, *The Prophetic Warning* is hardly literature, but it is an exemplary sample of the bluebook trade.

1-312. F. H. P. The Castle of Caithness: A Romance of the Thirteenth Century. Minerva-Press, 1802. (1)
With its open borrowings from the horrors of *Macbeth*, Caledonian or Highland Gothic emerged as a vigorous subform of the historical Gothic novel in such widely read works as Barrett's *Douglas Castle; or, The Cell of Mystery* [1-20] and Brewer's *The Witch of Ravensworth* [1-44]. The usurper of Caithness Castle is Macmillan, a ferocious Scottish cousin of Walpole's Manfred; his ambitions are closely akin to Macbeth's, since he is driven to crime by a blood lust and an almost heroic sense of evil. The romantic attractions of the novel's young champion, Edward, pale beside the dynamic vice of Macmillan, who dies "As one that had been studied in his death, to throw away the dearest thing he owed as 'twere a careless trifle."

*1-313. Radcliffe, Ann. **The Castles of Athlin and Dunbayne: A Highland Story.** T. Hookham, 1789; Arno, 1972. (1)
Radcliffe's self-apprenticeship to topographical and picturesque Gothic begins with her first novel, a dark tale of late medieval Scotland. The Gothic beauty that Radcliffe finds in the lochs and glens derives in part from her romantic reading in such sources as Collins's "Ode on Popular Superstitions of the Highlands" (1749). The story itself is a fable of intrigue, usurpation, and clan revenge between the two rival houses of Athlin and Dunbayne, whose feudal bastions give the novel its rather unusual double-castled title. The old earl of Athlin has been murdered by Malcolm, Baron of Dunbayne Castle. Malcolm is a regulation feudal tyrant and quickly fixes himself as the Gothic villain of the work. Earl Osbert of Dunbayne promises revenge and is aided in his design by the noble peasant Alleyn, who is much too chivalrous to be lowborn. An attack on Malcolm's stronghold fails, and Osbert and Alleyn find themselves in Malcolm's merciless grip. With cold satisfaction, Malcolm demands Osbert's sister, Mary, in exchange for his life. Amid much melodramatic commotion, Alleyn engineers Mary's freedom while Osbert discovers the imprisoned mother and daughter of the former Baron of Dunbayne. These complications only blur the original revenge plot, as Radcliffe fails to achieve any Gothic focus. Alleyn eventually kills Malcolm, who reveals Alleyn's noble birthright with a last gasp. Neither the heinous characters nor the virtuous achieve impressive stature in this early work. But the novel's sublime topographies and eerie castle interiors are workbook items that help Radcliffe to evolve her true Gothic *mise en scène*. Here she began to realize that the castle itself would become her most valuable Gothic character.

*1–314. Radcliffe, Ann. **A Sicilian Romance.** Hookham & Carpenter, 1790; Arno, 1972. (1)

Radcliffe's second novel introduces the stock Gothic situation of the nuptial prisoner later to be used by Charlotte Brontë in *Jane Eyre*, in which Rochester's mad wife is secretly locked away in Thornfield Hall. *The Sicilian Romance* is placed in 1580; the location is an isolated palazzo on the northern coast of Sicily where Ferdinand, fifth marquis of Mazzini, resides with his children and second wife, a dangerous and aggressive woman who is lovely and deadly. Wife number one still lives, but has been locked away in the deserted wing of the marquis's Gothic abode. The inquisitive son of the house notices odd lights flickering from the remote wing and sets out to investigate. In one of the finest scenes in Gothic literature, he makes a perilous descent down a rotting staircase, which seems to terminate in midair. Finally, all the supernatural occurrences are clarified by natural means and justice is dispensed, but not before many shudders and cold chills. The fundamental Radcliffean Gothic formula of terror slowly alleviated by the light of reason begins to develop here. The eerie magnificence of the facade of the Castle of Mazzini also shows Radcliffe's advancing awareness of the power of the castle as character in Gothic fiction. The critical opinion of J. M. S. Tompkins in *The Popular Novel in England, 1770–1800* will prove especially valid in the Gothics that follow *A Sicilian Romance:* "The *raison-d'être* of her books is not a story, nor a character, nor a moral truth, but a mood, the mood of a sensitive dreamer before Gothic buildings and picturesque scenery."

*1–315. Radcliffe, Ann. **The Romance of the Forest, Interspersed with Some Pieces of Poetry.** T. Hookham & J. Carpenter, 1791; Arno, 1974. (1)

Radcliffe's third novel opens dramatically in the middle of an emergency whose outcome is postponed for purposes of almost unbearable suspense, according to the Radcliffean formula of coaxing and then hoaxing the reader. The fugitive from justice, La Motte, hides in a strange and menacing mansion, but finds himself threatened by a tough figure who pushes a lovely girl into La Motte's arms, exclaiming, "If you wish to save your life, swear that you will convey this girl where I may never see her more. If you return within an hour you will die." The girl is Adeline, and she quickly stirs the jealousy of La Motte's wife when he installs his chance ward in a Gothic abbey. When the abbey is visited by the depraved Marquis Montalt, we discover through the usual series of complicated clues and interminable delays that La Motte is a highwayman who is using the abbey as his secret headquarters. The use of abbeys for this purpose would be repeated ad nauseam in the pages of Gothic fiction; in the anonymous *Phantoms of the Cloister; or, The Mysterious Manuscript* [1–176], Maitland Abbey is just such a robber den. Obeying the hints sent to her in a nightmare—a dream in which Adeline has beheld a darkly clad figure summoning her to a mysterious chamber—the heroine penetrates the tapestry of her own bedchamber to uncover a secret room and a mouldering manuscript. By a dim taper, she peruses the awful history of the father who has been driven to his death by Montalt. Out of this web of injustice and terror, Radcliffe gradually spins the retribution that exposes Montalt and the reformation that persuades La Motte to renounce his brigand's life and take up an idyllic residence in a Swiss chalet with Adeline. This overplotted novel became one of the immediate targets of Jane Austen's satire in *Northanger Abbey* [1–11]. On the positive side, Radcliffe was refining her craftsmanship of tension and terror in the interplay among villain, maiden, and castle.

*1–316. Radcliffe, Ann. **The Mysteries of Udolpho: A Romance Interspersed with Some Pieces of Poetry.** G. G. & J. Robinson, 1794; Oxford Univ. Press, 1970. (1) (SB)

The seminal terror Gothic romance and the premier maiden-centered Gothic of the eighteenth century, *Udolpho*'s vast influence in both its own time and ours can hardly be overestimated. The heroine, Emily St. Aubert, is the model hysteric for a legion of nervous and hypersensitive young ladies who spend the majority of their adolescence confined to massive, mouldering castles or abbeys. Taking their lyric inspiration from Emily's sublime traumas, these women secretly enjoy and even rhapsodize upon their Gothic fates. The impeccable and insipid young hero of *The Mysteries of Udolpho*, Valancourt, is swiftly shunted out of the main story to make ample room for the more interesting villainies of the ruthless Montoni. Montoni is an arch-villain and proprietor of Castle di Udolpho in the distant Apennines, whence Emily is conveyed from her pastoral home at La Vallée after being orphaned. "You speak like a heroine," Montoni sneers at her. "We will see if you can suffer like one." The transference of the anxious maiden from her safe world of parents and reason to an unsafe world of threatening males and Gothic passions donates a pattern of action to the Gothic novel that will become as important as the castle and its supernatural furnishings. Early in the story, Emily has observed her dying father weeping over the miniature of a beautiful lady. This is the initial mystery in a long chain of enigmas finally solved by the now-perfected technique of explained Gothic. The central mystery of all is the unnamed thing concealed behind the famous black veil in Udolpho's portrait chamber. Drawing aside the black curtain, Emily faints at the sight, but the reader does not share in what she saw until the novel is nearly over hundreds of pages later. Exploring other segments of the castle while she wonders what Montoni has in store for her, she finds actual blood on a stairway and ponders the fate of the Lady Laurentini, Udolpho's former mistress. A second castle ordeal takes Emily to Château Villefort, where she sinks into a Gothic panic over a pall-covered face in a forbidden chamber. At Villefort Emily finally learns the truth about Lady Laurentini's disappearance, as well as the identity of the beautiful lady in the cameo wept over by her father. These mysteries and others, including the long-awaited revelation of what lay behind the black veil, are cleared up by natural means. Montoni's evil schemes are neutralized, and Emily emerges from the Gothic world purged of the imaginative terrors induced by her unregulated sensibilities. And in finally possessing her father's secret she comes to know and to control herself in this Gothic *Bildungsroman*. The proliferation of Udolphoesque romance, which rapidly led to triteness and stereotyping of the form, does not minimize Radcliffe's achievement, for she steered the tradition, as Ellen Moers has remarked, "in one of the ways it would go ever after; a novel in which the central figure is a young woman who is simultaneously persecuted victim and courageous heroine."

*1-317. Radcliffe, Ann. **The Italian; or, The Confessional of the Black Penitents.** T. Cadell & W. Davies, 1797; Oxford Univ. Press, 1968. (1) (SB)
In contrast with the slow turning of the screw of suspense in *The Mysteries of Udolpho* [1–316], Radcliffe's final Gothic novel consciously competes with the horrific Gothic of Lewis and the villain-centered action of *The Monk* [1–218]. *The Italian* is dramatic rather than elegiac or lyric, with the heroine exposed to some authentic dangers. And the generically evil name of the villain (not just an Italian, but *the* Italian) now replaces the castle or forest titles that had characterized her four previous Gothics. Furthermore, the role of the hypersensitive maiden, Ellena di Rosalba, is contracted in order to emphasize the heroic evil of the death's-head monk, Father Schedoni, who dominates this novel's structure in a way that none of Radcliffe's shadowy males previously had. The figure of the young rescuer, Vincentio di Vivaldi, is also allowed to do much more inside the plot than was the case with Valancourt. Radcliffe was obviously revising her own previous methods for inspiring terror by indulging in horrific emergencies and by downplaying the lingering shadows of mystery. With his pallid, gigantic, and gaunt frame and vulture-like eye, Schedoni is an ideal Gothic advisor to Vivaldi's vindictive mother. Worming his way into her confidence by acting as her confessor, he schemes with the Marquesa to forestall the union of Vivaldi and Ellena and arranges a convent confinement for the hapless, hopeless, helpless maiden. In the convent she undergoes the regular persecutions of her breed when she is tormented by a coldhearted abbess and threatened with the taking of the veil. Meanwhile, a crepuscular monk (not Schedoni) has appeared almost ectoplasmically in a ruined archway and has warned Vivaldi that terrible consequences will follow unless he abandons Ellena. But Vivaldi persists, as the good Gothic hero should, and eventually frees her from her monastic jail. But their marriage ceremony is broken up by a gang of cutthroats under Schedoni's direction. Vivaldi is delivered over to the Inquisition. Ellena is faced once more with the basic Gothic problem of the menacing mansion when she is imprisoned within a lonely house on the shores of the Adriatic and placed under the cruel care of Schedoni's Gothic gremlin, Spalatro, a character who is almost a perfect replica of the superspy Daniel de Bosola in

Webster's blood tragedy, *The Duchess of Malfi* (1614). In one of the tensest scenes in Gothic fiction, Schedoni nearly murders the sleeping Ellena, but stays his poised dagger when he notices a locket containing his picture. Schedoni turns out to be both the monk of the archway after all and Ellena's uncle, the infamous Count di Marinella. In her movement from terror to horror fiction in *The Italian,* Radcliffe sounded a new octave on the Gothic scale. While many readers preferred the quieter terrors of *Udolpho, The Italian* may well rank as her masterpiece. This view is most recently reflected in Judith Wilt's *Ghosts of the Gothic: Austen, Eliot, and Lawrence* (Princeton Univ. Press, 1980): "First among those talents was Ann Radcliffe, in whose novel *The Italian* (1797) we find what I take to be the richest, clearest, most morally intense evocation of the classic Gothic universe. Here we find the subtlest working out of that doubly fathered father, the sinful monk, here a family full of evil spirits, here the most elegantly crafted atmosphere of Gothic time and space."

*1-318. Radcliffe, Mary-Anne. **Manfroné; or, The One-Handed Monk.** J. F. Hughes, 1809; Arno, 1972. (1) (SB)
Mary-Anne Radcliffe, the other Mrs. Radcliffe among the Gothics, was frequently confused with her namesake in Victorian reprintings of the perennially popular four-decker Gothic, *Manfroné.* The novel's grand assortment of Gothic scenery, alarms, and diversions shows that the second Mrs. Radcliffe knew what the Gothic was all about and knew equally well how to operate the complex machinery. The novel begins with a no-nonsense jolt to maidenly security. Rosalina di Rodolpho is sexually assaulted in her bedchamber by a grotesque, sable-mantled figure whose severed hand will shortly be found lying on the castle gallery floor. The identity of her maimed attacker remains Rosalina's obsession. Her remote and loveless father, Duca di Rodolpho, plays host to the dark-browed Prince di Manfroné at Castello di Coleredo. Manfroné has the classic Gothic physiognomy: "His brows protended over his scowling eyes, whose gaze were bent on the ground; his lips were of livid hue and closely pressed together." Setting out to destroy the happiness of his own child, the duke arranges to have the ferocious monk, Padre Grimaldi, take up residence in his castle in order to harry Rosalina. The cryptic Grimaldi, who dresses and moves like Schedoni [1–317], lurks about the dark corridors of the castle for the remainder of the romance. Accompanied by her maid, Carletta, on the usual exploratory adventure into forbidden sections of the castle, Rosalina finds the telltale sable mask in Grimaldi's apartments. Before she can flee, the powerful hand of the vile monk seizes her and conveys her across the lake of Abbruzzio to a secret hut. "What was her horror on perceiving he had but one hand!" Her assailant, of course, is the fearful prince masquerading as a churchman. But before the lecherous impostor can finish the rape that he began in volume one, the arm of justice gives him a death blow. "Here, the pen pauses," writes the second

Mrs. Radcliffe. Although the ending is spoiled, many parts of the novel can stand favorable comparison with *The Italian;* the severed hand lying on the castle pavement is an unforgettable effect.

1-319. Raspe, Rudolf Erich (Germany). **Koenigsmark der Räuber; oder, Der Schrecken aus Böhmen (Koenigsmark the Robber; or, The Terror of Bohemia).** Cassel, 1790. First English trans., J. Williams, 1801. (2)
Narrated by the famous and adept international liar, Heironymus Karl Friedrich Baron von Münchhausen, this widely admired and imitated *Räuber-roman* adds warlocks and werewolves to the normal company of brigands and romantic criminals. The events of the tale take place in the midseventeenth century when local robber chieftains held sway in their own districts with all the potency of potentates. So powerful is Koenigsmark and so brutal is his reputation that he is believed to be a special favorite of the archfiend himself, who has given the bandit the supernatural strength of a warlock. Two virtuous comrades-in-arms, Theodore and Herman, decide to track down Koenigsmark, who has murdered their fellow officer Adolphus Rosenberg, and rid the countryside of the bandit blight. Rosenberg's lovely wife, Adelaide, has become a special target of Koenigsmark's lust; her perils at the hands of the bandit beast conform to the orthodox distresses of the Gothic maiden. After an attack on a stronghold, Theodore is captured and thrown into the robbers' foul den, where he is befriended by the spirit of the slain Rosenberg, who assumes the familiar role of protective ghost. Finally brought to the bar of justice, Koenigsmark remains staunchly vicious to the last breath. As he is about to be racked, a muffled figure appears and stabs him to the heart. With unrelieved awe, all who witness the death of the bandit conclude that Rosenberg's ghost has had its revenge. The deluxe supernatural material of Raspe's romance is notably bold, as is his departure from the figure of the noble outlaw represented in Schiller's Karl Moor of *Die Räuber* [1-337]. At one point, an enormous spider bloating to a still-greater shape creeps across Raspe's Gothic stage. Yet behind all this audacious fantasy lurks the smirk of the professional prevaricator, Baron Münchhausen.

1-320. Ratcliffe, Eliza. **The Mysterious Baron.** Minerva-Press, 1808. (1)
A one-volume conventional Gothic identity fable, which sees the heroine discover the wickedness in her own father. This Gothic novelist sometimes spelled her name "Radcliffe" to identify herself with a famous personage and gain sales thereby.

1-321. The Recluse of the Woods; or, The Generous Warrior; A Gothic Romance. J. Roe & Ann Lemoine, 1809. (5) (SB)
Written with Charlotte Smith's *Ethelinde; or, The Recluse of the Lake* [1-363] in view, this gentle and genteel bluebook is not Gothic in the savagely supernatural sense but is Gothic as a fantasy of remote, medieval exoticism. The subtitle, *A Gothic Romance,* advertises horrible hardware, but in the bluebook

itself the benign figure of the chivalric stranger who issues from the forest glades in the manner of Gallahad supplants the menacing form of the mad monk or sinister baron. The work is definitely not a romance of the forest [1–315] in the startling Radcliffean sense, but a woodenly sentimental novel hiding beneath a Gothic label.

*1–322. Reeve, Clara. **The Old English Baron: A Gothic Story.** Edward & Charles Dilly, 1778. Alternate title: *The Champion of Virtue* (1777); in *Seven Masterpieces of Gothic Horror.* Ed. Robert D. Spector. Bantam Books, 1963; Oxford Univ. Press, 1967. (3) (SB)
The connecting corridor in the Gothic tradition between Walpole's *Otranto* and Radcliffe's *Udolpho* is Reeve's *Old English Baron* originally published under the didactic title *The Champion of Virtue.* Although Reeve asserted that her story was the "literary offspring" of *Otranto,* her novel bears little direct resemblance to Walpole's supernatural extravaganza. The book does appropriate Walpole's deception of the transcribed manuscript in returning the reader to the time of Henry VI's minority. Young Edmund Twyford, who seems to have humble origins, is patronized by Baron Fitzowen, an awkward cordiality that arouses the mean envy of Fitzowen's sons. To demonstrate his worthiness, Edmund consents to spend three nights of steadfast watchfulness in the haunted chamber or forbidden wing of Lovel Castle, an experience that will be repeated ad infinitum in later Gothic fiction. During this Gothic nightwatch, the work's only phantom enters briefly in full armor with visor down. In an additional Gothic touch that will prove useful to scores of later writers, Edmund conducts Fitzowen to a subterranean closet, which contains the bones of his slain father. Predictably, Edmund's mysterious heritage makes him the new master of Lovel Castle. Although the Gothic element is subsidiary to the settlement of the genealogical enigmas, Reeve gets credit for installing Gothic literature's first haunted chamber within the castle complex. Like Walpole's provocative devices, this necessary piece of Gothic furniture would shortly form the basis for mystery in Lee's historical Gothic, *The Recess* [1–214].

1–323. Ribie, César (France). **Le Moine (The Monk).** Gaité, 1797. (1)
A French dramatic version of *The Monk* with modifications taken from the French translation of the novel by the citizens Deschamps, Deprès, Benoist, and de Lamare [1–94].

*1–324. Roche, Regina Maria. **The Children of the Abbey.** Minerva-Press, 1796; Folio, 1968. (1) (SB)
A Northanger novel and one of the most emotionally delectable of the Minerva-Press Gothics, the book opens with the heroine's effulgent apostrophe to rural bliss, a mood of joy that cannot last for long in a Gothic novel: "Hail, sweet asylum of my infancy! Content and innocence reside beneath

your humble roof." Such pastoral ecstasy is brief for Amanda, who will shortly undergo a series of seductive crises and Gothic trials. Borrowing directly from the character of Madame Cheron, the wicked aunt figure in Radcliffe's *The Mysteries of Udolpho* [1–316], Roche disturbs Amanda's life with a bad fairy of her own and permits the wicked aunt to ruin her happiness and thwart her heritage for much of the book. Wandering the twisting corridors of the venerable abbey of Dunreath, Amanda supposes that she has received a ghostly visit from her mother, a sublime fright that must have touched a responsive chord in the soul of Jane Austen's Catherine Morland. The Gothic is less a form here than a vehicle for the release of the heroine's exquisite sensibilities. Long forgotten, *The Children of the Abbey*—along with Roche's other Gothic efforts—has become a part of the twentieth-century Gothic revival. See Natalie Schroeder, "Regina Maria Roche, Popular Novelist, 1789–1834," *Papers of the Bibliographical Society of America* 73 (1979), 462–468.

*1–325. Roche, Regina Maria. **Clermont: A Tale.** Minerva-Press, 1798; Folio, 1968. (1) (SB)

Clermont is among the seven horrid titles dispensed to Catherine Morland to complete her Gothic education in *Northanger Abbey* [1–11]. The book is a Radliffean Gothic with a distinct difference. Because of Roche's rapid handling of maidenly distress and ruinous pleasure, the horrific pace of the story is closer to the frenzied spirit of the *Schauer-roman* than to Radcliffe's sluggish plotting. *Clermont* also has what Michael Sadleir called the "Gothistic super-heroine" in the fragile doll, Madeline Clermont, a porcelain damsel with "eyes, large and of the darkest hazel, ever true to the varying emotions of her soul." Adjacent to Madeline's rustic cottage where she lives in blissful seclusion with her father is a spectacular ruin, which regularly emits "horrid noises and still more horrid sights." Poking about the crumbled battlements and moss-grown turrets of the place, Madeline meets the handsome and mysterious stranger, de Sevignie. Her life now sponsored by an equally mysterious countess, Madeline goes off with her to a remote château, where her apprenticeship to Gothic ruins prepares her for the business of terror now encountered. The countess expires after an attack by ruffians, leaving Madeline to the ugly designs of the countess's vile son-in-law. But she fortunately stumbles upon a secret passageway to freedom from the castle and makes her way to Paris. After enduring some foreign unpleasantries, she is reunited with de Sevignie, who has by this time discovered his noble roots. *Clermont* is an accelerated Radcliffean fiction that carries the reader through the nightmare landscape back into a vague and dateless past while satisfying the odd craving for pleasure in ruins and distress. Although the book is primarily a novel of suspense and terror, according to Natalie Schroeder, "Rochean Gothic is more akin to the *Schauer-roman* than to the filmy efforts of Radcliffean romance." See Natalie Schroeder, "*The Mysteries of Udolpho* and *Clermont:*

The Radcliffean Encroachment on the Art of Regina Maria Roche," *Studies in the Novel* 12 (1980), 131–143.

*1-326. Roche, Regina Maria. **The Nocturnal Visit: A Tale.** Minerva-Press, 1800; Arno, 1977. (1) (SB)

More turgid than turbulent, this complicated Gothic suggests a falling-off in Roche's powers as a storyteller. The first edition in the Sadleir-Black Collection exhibits the bookplate of Richard Brinsley Sheridan, thus indicating that Gothic novels were being purchased and read by men of taste and talent as well as young women conditioned only to tears and sighs. The Gothicism of this four-volume novel is lazy, leisurely. And very slow in developing, as if Roche had deliberately decided to reverse the speed she had shown in *Clermont* [1-325]. The heroine, Jacintha, is an unclaimed child of sorrow who lives with the curate Greville in rural seclusion in Wyefield near Holywell. The riddle of her true origins again forms the basis of the plot, but Roche is now too digressive and oblique to achieve any excitement with this standard Gothic mechanism. The virtuous champion Egbert Oswald is equally soporific. The reader must wait (if he or she has the patience) until page 230 of the third volume for a genuine Gothic experience. Here, Jacintha stands at last upon the sinister threshold of Dunsane Castle and voices the expected palpitations and enraptured horrors: "But if her imagination was here impressed with terror, her mind was not less affected with melancholy on beholding the mournful desolation of the building she was about to enter; for over the ruins of what was once a great and noble pile, the heart of sensibility involuntarily laments." Once incarcerated, Jacintha is forced to occupy a dim closet where a cold hand touches hers. This gruesome contact is the "nocturnal visit" that points the way to freedom and identity. After several more castles and a few more convents in volume four, the heroine is rewarded for her persistence by acquiring a surname and a father; the reader's persistence, however, has fewer compensations in this lethargic Gothic.

1-327. Roche, Regina Maria. **The Monastery of Saint Columb; or, The Atonement.** Minerva-Press, 1813. (1) (SB)

A dark journey through a heavily Catholic countryside, an abbey imprisonment, a malicious mother superior, and a hair's-breadth avoidance of the veil are the absolutely jaded and stereotyped components of this late monastic shocker.

1-328. **Rosenberg: A Legendary Tale.** Minerva-Press, 1789. (1)

Unsigned, but attributed to Mrs. Howell, the novel is an early example of Catholic terrors and the horrors of the religious life. Hermits, a Germanic setting, enforced flagellation, and monkish superstitions regarded as holy writ give the work a sinister overlay. An unfortunate nun's premature burial and a heretic's awful torture and death in the vaults of the monastery are events that point ahead to the charnel thrills of *The Monk* [1-218].

1-329. Rowson, Susanna Haswell. **The Inquisitor; or, Invisible Rambler.** Minerva-Press, 1788. (1)

Best remembered for her novel of domestic manners, *Charlotte Temple* (1791), Rowson also produced a sound and satisfying Inquisition-Gothic in *The Inquisitor*. The terrible priest Father Ignatius exploits his position with the Holy Office to work his selfish will for power over others.

1-330. G. R. **Castle Zittaw: A German Tale.** Minerva-Press, 1794. (1)

This obscure and rare Gothic novel is mentioned by Dorothy Blakey in her indispensable study, *The Minerva Press, 1790-1820* (The Bibliographical Society at the University Press, Oxford, 1939), but the sole surviving copy seems to be in the New York Society Library. The novel itself is a phony translation from the German and has some curious parallels with an authentic German translation published by Minerva during the same year, Kahlert's *The Necromancer; or, The Tale of the Black Forest* [1-186].

*1-331. Sade, Donatien-Alphonse-François Marquis de (France). **Justine; ou, Les Malheurs de la vertu (Justine; or, The Misfortunes of Virtue).** Girouard, 1791; Grove, 1965. (2)

Best described as the epitome of sexual Gothicism as well as a brutal, erotic parody of the moral life, *Justine* thrusts the Richardsonian-Gothic heroine into a spiked labyrinth of lust, cruelty, aberration, torture, and high-spirited depravity. Sade himself commented on the appropriateness of the Gothic impulse to an age of revolution, repression, and authorized cruelty; in an essay on the art of the novel, he mentions Monk Lewis and Radcliffe as writers fully attuned to the "age of iron." Justine herself is a caricature of naive virtue and a worthy Gothic victim. Pious, trusting, and convinced of the superiority of virtue in any situation, she is an expert burlesque of the invulnerable and saintly heroine—a comic compound of Voltaire's Candide and an all-purpose sexual tennis ball. Justine's life is an almost farcical series of atrocious victimizations, ogling assaults, flagellations, rackings, and torture-chamber sessions on a daily schedule. She falls prey to the sadistic free-thinker Count Bressac, who amuses himself by lashing her bleeding body with whips of all sizes as he lashes her mind with his progressive philosophy of the necessity for vice, the supremacy of depravity, the pleasure in giving and receiving pain, and nature's iron law of evil. She also attends the academy of the child-flogger Dr. Rodin, and is branded with hot irons for failing to adjust quickly enough to the curriculum. At a Benedictine convent, she becomes the sexual plaything of Dom Severino, a virile forerunner of Monk Lewis's Ambrosio. Stripped, beaten, phlebotomized, compelled to occupy a coffin, thrown into a dank pit, and forced to witness the mock crucifixion of a nude girl, Justine changes no attitudes and learns nothing from her travails. When she is at last exterminated by a highly cunning bolt of Gothic lightning, Sade evokes cheers rather than tears. The sanguinary inducements and nauseous horrors of *The Monk* [1-218] and *The Abbess* [1-177] seem already fully developed in the algolagnic vigor of *Justine*. What scene could be said to belong more centrally to the horror-Gothic mode than Justine being dragged to the edge of the pit? "He dragged her screaming to a huge cylindrical hole concealed in the far corner of the vault. He opened a lid and lowered a lamp into it so that she could better distinguish the host of dead bodies with which it was filled. Then, he lowered her slowly into the cadaverous abyss." Scholarship has unaccountably neglected Sade's strong connections with the Gothic genre. One of the few valuable analyses of Sade and Gothicism is Stephen Werner's, "Diderot, Sade, and the Gothic Novel," *Studies on Voltaire and the Eighteenth-Century* 114 (1973), 273–290.

1–332. Sade, Donatien-Alphonse-François Marquis de (France). **La Nouvelle Justine; ou, Les Malheurs de la vertu, suivie de l'histoire de Juliette, sa soeur; ou, Les Prospérités du vice (The Novel Justine; or, The Misfortunes of Virtue, Followed by the History of Juliette, Her Sister; or, The Fortunes of Vice).** Betrandet, 1797; in *Marquis de Sade: Selections from His Writings*, ed. by Simone de Beauvoir. Grove, 1953. (4)
A sequel to *Justine* [1–331], *Juliette* is the *Justine* fable of virtue punished in reverse. Juliette is Justine's worldly-wise, pragmatic sister, a kind of shrewd Moll Flanders figure who accepts Sade's natural laws of vice rewarded and a world governed by selfish appetites. Orphaned with Justine, she separates herself from her sister, begins her education in a brothel, then graduates to a career of crime and self-indulgence, which includes a husband-poisoning and the sins of the tavern. Prominent men are so fascinated by her wicked habits and ostentatious vices that her bad character brings her profit and fame. Sade's lesbian theme is quite pronounced; Juliette's sexual arrangements with men are callously commercial while her relationships with the old vixen Clairwil, with Princess Borghese, and with a strange clairvoyant named Madame Durand are deep and sincere. Although the narrative contains some Gothic attractions such as Juliette's encounter with the man-eating ogre Minski, the novel has fewer vicarious thrills for the masochistic reader than the odyssey of agony of her inanely virtuous sister in the companion piece. Essentially, this pair of sexual Gothics should be categorized as philosophical fiction in their attack on the benevolent doctrines of Rousseau and their pungent cartooning of the iron maiden of Richardson. Their influence upon the gory and sadistic aspects of Gothic fantasy, however, seems undeniable.

1–333. Saint-Pierre, Bernadin de (France). **Paul et Virginie (Paul and Virginia).** P. F. Didot Lejeune, 1787; in *Great European Short Novels*, ed. by Anthony Winner. Harper & Row, 1968. (4)
Combining exotic elements with Gothic passions, Saint-Pierre's famous novel depicts two Rousseauistic lovers going inevitably to their deaths. The sentimental tone of the love tragedy will be heard again in Chateaubriand's *René* [1–65] and *Atala* [1–64]. If not quite a Gothic Romeo and Juliet, Paul

and Virginie are hardly domestic sweethearts either. Growing up and falling in love amid the natural splendor of the Ile de France (Mauritius), they are torn from one another and from nature in adulthood and are given a barbaric introduction to the harsh institutions of civilization. Like the English Gothic heroine, Virginie is tormented by a wicked aunt and promptly cloistered when she proves recalcitrant to the ways of modern society. In a later scene, which blends Gothic horror and sentimental excess, she drowns before Paul's eyes. Rescue might have been hers, but modesty has prevented Virginie from shedding her nun's habit. Paul shortly follows her in death in this tearful piece of Rousseauistic propaganda. Like Henry Mackenzie's lachrymose, pre-Gothic novel, *The Man of Feeling* [1–234], *Paul et Virginie* illustrates French sentimental fiction at a point of no return and about to turn from tears to terror. In her 1979 study of the Gothic novel, *The Gothic Tradition in Fiction* (Columbia Univ. Press), Elizabeth MacAndrew regards *Paul et Virginie* as an important corollary to various Gothic moods and narrative premises.

1–334. Saint Victor, Helen. **The Ruins of Rigonda; or, The Homicidal Father.** Chapple, 1808. (5)
With its irresistible Gothic title, *The Ruins of Rigonda* centers upon the distressed maiden's secret emotional delight at the prospect of being confined eternally and violated nightly behind the devastated, but still impenetrable, walls of the frowning feudal fortress of Rigonda. As the prisoner of Rigonda contemplates the place of her impending incarceration, "the massy but almost crumbling gates closed behind her and she heaved a sigh and seemed as it were to have entered her tomb." Her keeper and her persecutor is, of course, her own father. The grim architecture throughout the work reinforces the Gothic idea or principle that mouldering masonry is always stronger and more self-containing than turrets and arches that have not fallen or crumbled.

1–335. Salardo der Schreckliche: Eine schauderhafte Erzählung aus Lorenzo's Papieren (Salardo the Terrible: A Horrifying Narrative from the Papers of Lorenzo). Schladebachschen, 1802. (2) (SB)
The diminutive *Schauer-roman* is an anonymous reduction of *The Monk* [1–218] that uses the device of the recovered lost manuscript to launch the story. Details of Lewis's plot share a place beside unauthorized borrowings from several contemporary *Räuber-roman*, with particular similarities between Salardo and Raspe's terrible bandit, Koenigsmark [1–319].

*1–336. Schiller, Johann Friedrich von (Germany). **Der Geisterseher: Eine Geschichte aus den Memoires des Graffen von O. (The Ghost Seer: A History from the Memoirs of the Count of O.)** G. J. Göschen, 1789; in *Gothic Tales of Terror: Classic Horror Stories from Great Britain, Europe, and the United States,* ed. by Peter Haining. Taplinger, 1972. (2)

A fragmentary novel, *Der Geisterseher* was serialized in Schiller's periodical, *Die Thalia*, from 1787 to 1789. Its spectacular supernatural content impressed both the English Gothic novelists and the major romantic poets, including Coleridge and Byron, who were greatly taken by the Armenian apparitionist's ability to call back spirits from the dead. A young prince residing in Venice is exploited by two strange adventurers, an Armenian and a Sicilian, whose accomplishments in the sinister art of necromancy link them with the fraudulent Sicilian alchemist and magician, the infamous Count Cagliostro (1743-1795). The prince's involvement with the ghost seer opens up themes of cabalism, alchemy, and cadaverous resurrection, materials that would later appear in many forms of English Gothic fiction. The influence of Schiller's bizarre memoir may also be seen in *The Necromancer; or, The Tale of the Black Forest,* a German Gothic import of 1794.

*1-337. Schiller, Johann Friedrich von (Germany). **Die Räuber (The Robbers).** I. B. Metzler, 1781; Penguin, 1980. (2)
First performed at Mannheim on January 13, 1782, Schiller's drama is the prototypical robber play. Its admirable bandit hero, Karl Moor, is a romantic criminal with a conscience—a true Promethean rebel with a cause. Through the machinations of his avaricious brother, Franz, Karl is disinherited and rejected by his father. Indignant at such fraternal villainy and paternal indifference, Karl turns against society's hollow values and allies himself with a robber band. The acts of violence perpetrated by the gang in the Bohemian forests set a tone for the banditti activity, which is a normal feature of the wilderness surrounding the haunted castle in Gothic fiction. Eventually, Karl's devotion to his cousin, Amalia, comes into conflict with his pledge of loyalty to his bandit brethren. Wracked by the emotional lacerations of *Sturm und Drang,* the beautiful soul of the hero-villain is nearly torn apart. In the melodramatics of the forest sequences and the pyrotechnics of the divided hero, *Die Räuber*'s pre-Gothic material was rapidly incorporated into the English Gothic bloodstream. The play also spawned numerous German *Räuber-roman,* among which the work of Raspe in *Koenigsmark* [1-319] and Vulpius in *Rinaldo Rinaldini* [1-390] are artistically outstanding.

1-338. Schreckenscenen aus den Ritterzeiten (Scenes of Terror from the Age of Chivalry) (Germany). Voss & Leo, 1792. (2) (SB)
A *Schauer-romantik* anthology of abridged Gothic pieces taken from many contemporary sources, including Schiller's *Geisterseher* [1-336]. One of the knightly tales of terror is a version of the popular fable of the demon or skeletal huntsman, *die Wilde Jäger,* a folklore specter on horseback who turns up frequently in English and American Gothic writings. Washington Irving certainly had such compilations as *Schreckenscenen* in mind in his jocular treatment of the Gothic in "The Spectre Bridegroom" [1-181].

1–339. Scott, Honoria. **The Castle of Strathmay: A Tale.** Tegg, 1814. (1)
A polite and tidy Gothic in the Radcliffean tradition. Strathmay Castle in thirteenth-century Cornwall holds the regular quota of genealogical mysteries and Gothic shocks for the venturesome maiden Valeria. As late as 1814, the year of Sir Walter Scott's *Waverley,* a walking portrait, a forbidden vault, or a vocal statue could still stimulate a sale.

1–340. Scott, Sir Walter. **The Black Dwarf.** Blackwood, 1816. (4)
Although the title has abundant Gothic promise, the novel itself is generally considered a failure because of Scott's uncertainties of narrative purpose. While his appearance is unquestionably monstrous, the hermit dwarf's deformity is outward only. Like Victor Frankenstein's odious creature, the black dwarf is a sensitive being full of natural kindness but cursed by nature with an unnatural shape. This figure of fairy-tale is called Elshender the Recluse or Elshie of Mucklestanes. Emerging from time to time from his lair of huge boulders, he devotes himself to performing kind deeds for the local residents, although he is detested for his intolerable ugliness. Without realizing or developing the theme's potential, Scott, like Mary Shelley, had hit upon the motif of the Gothic freak who longs only for love and acceptance in an unseeing world, which judges him only by outward standards. Dwarfism had appeared previously in the Gothic novel, notably in Beckford's *Vathek* [1–25], and would reappear in the work of the Victorian Gothicists. The comic evil of Daniel Quilp in Dickens's *Old Curiosity Shop* (1841), the gruesome justice of Poe's Hop-Frog, and the pathetic self-discovery of the dwarf in Wilde's "Birthday of the Infanta" all individualize the dwarf character in a direction that Scott had suggested in his portrayal of the pathetic grotesque in this interesting failure.

*1–341. Scott, Sir Walter. **The Bride of Lammermoor.** A. Constable, 1819; Dutton, 1973, ed. by W. M. Parker. (4)
Certainly the most Gothic of Scott's novels, *The Bride of Lammermoor* is also imbued with the somber sense of tragic fate of the sort heard in the Border Country ballads and later in the work of Thomas Hardy. The gloomy young hero, Ravenswood, seems taken directly from the Gothic tradition as he clings desperately to Wolf's Craig tower, the last architectural emblem of the once-proud and powerful lords of Ravenswood. By a chance meeting while hunting, Ravenswood saves the life of his family adversary, Sir William Ashton, and falls in love with the daughter of his enemy, Lucy Ashton. Their fated love forms the core of the tale. Lucy has many characteristics in common with the immured and abused maidens of Gothic fiction. Her romantic desires are frustrated by the cunning Lady Ashton, a close cousin of one of Radcliffe's vile aunts. Eventually, Lucy is driven mad by her own family and stabs the husband who is being forced upon her on the eve of her wedding day. In a Gothic climax that is also tinged with high tragedy, Ravenswood is swallowed up in the quicksand of Kelpie Flow as he gallops fu-

riously along the shore toward a showdown with Lucy's tormentors. Hence, the domestic bliss of the typical Radcliffean ending is shunned by Scott; his Gothic curtain descends on a debacle of madness and violent death. The forest scenes, the characters of Ravenswood and the Ashtons, and the gloomy descriptions of the environs of Wolf's Craig are firmly rooted in Scott's extensive knowledge of Gothic literature.

1–342. Scott, Sir Walter. **The Monastery.** A. Constable, 1820. (4)

Scott's extensive debt to the Gothic tradition is highly visible in *The Monastery*. While neither the monastic nor the baronial cast of the novel is sinister or lecherous, as would be the case in a true Gothic, both the settings and the interplay of character reflect Scott's willingness to refabricate the trite equipage of the Gothic. The monastery of the title is Kennaquhair and was inspired by Scott's tours of Melrose Abbey on the River Tweed. The time of the novel is midway through the reign of Elizabeth, with Catholic-Protestant troubles paralleling the border antagonisms between England and Scotland. England in the novel is represented by the arrogant Sir Piercie Shafton, who has been offered a refuge from his subversive activities by the abbot of Kennaquhair. The outline of the Gothic maiden survives in the high-spirited Mary Avenel, orphaned child of woe, but no collapsing hysteric like her chaste and chased predecessors among Gothic women of misfortune. The two sons of Simon Glendinning, caretaker of the monastery, vie for the affection of Mary. When the impetuous Halbert Glendinning wounds Sir Piercie in a duel, the phantasmagoric White Lady of Avenel intervenes to restore Sir Piercie to life and to work other supernatural miracles and marvels. This benign specter is instantly recognized as a lineal descendant of the apparition of the abbey, a stock Gothic character. The business of the white lady is no longer the simple Gothic function of haunting, appalling, or startling. She is a bringer of life and new values where all hope has vanished. Scott's relationship to Gothic fiction has never been adequately evaluated. For a general evaluation of Scott and the Gothic, consult Mody C. Boatright, "Scott's Theory and Practice Concerning the Use of the Supernatural in Prose Fiction in Relation to the Chronology of the Waverley Novels," *Publications of the Modern Language Association* 50 (1935), 235–261; and Walter Freye, *The Influence of "Gothic" Literature on Sir Walter Scott* (H. Winterberg, 1902).

1–343. Scott, Sir Walter. **The Abbot.** A. Constable, 1820. (4)

Written as a tag to *The Monastery* [1–342] of the same year, the novel follows the habit of Gothic titling, and by doing so must have created an instantaneous appeal to the eye trained in spotting the Gothic on booksellers' stalls. The exciting plot involves the escape of Mary Queen of Scots from her imprisonment in Lochleven Castle. By using an incident in the life of the royal fugitive, Scott's novel affiliated itself with Sophia Lee's historical Gothic, *The Recess* [1–214], which had also fictionalized the tragic events of the queen without a throne. Queen Mary is assisted in her escape by young Roland Graeme (actually the son of the House of Avenel), who has been delegated to spy upon her but whose chivalric instincts and Scottish loyalties motivate him to come to her aid. The romantic and parentless Roland would be quite at home in any Gothic novel where the theme of the mysterious birthright is in force; his Gothic ancestry extends back to the noble peasant Theodore in *The Castle of Otranto* [1–398]. The abbot of the title is no soul-selling monastic maniac, but the composed and intelligent Father Ambrose (formerly Edward Glendinning of *The Monastery*). Although the book retains the outlines of Gothic characterization as well as the locale of the monastic shocker, Scott dispenses with such artifices as the specter of the castle to achieve a distinct and distinguished historical romance in *The Abbot* and in *Kenilworth* in 1821.

1–344. The Secret Oath; or, Blood-Stained Dagger. Hurst, 1802. (5)
With its screaming, double-pronged title, this typical bluebook of the period harshly proclaims its Gothic wares. Often the main title of a bluebook and the subtitle have no connection with each other or no interrelationship within the narrative itself. The catch phrases merely serve as Gothic gimmicks and passwords to lure the shilling-shocker clientele back for another dose. The anonymous brewer of *The Secret Oath* follows the prescribed recipe for a marketable shilling shocker. The bluebook is a looseleaf collection of piracies from Lewis, Radcliffe, and even Grosse's *Horrid Mysteries* [1–139] in its use of the international conspiracy of freemasonry.

1–345. Selden, Catherine. **The English Nun.** Minerva-Press, 1797. (1) (SB)
Against the turgid background of Catholic superstition and authoritarianism, the English nun Louisa must choose between her faith and her passion for Edmund Lumley. While the novel is not without its Gothic moments, the love element and the sorrows of Louisa take precedence over shudder and shock.

1–346. Selden, Catherine. **The Count De Santerre: A Romance.** C. Dilly, 1797. (1)
Catherine Selden was also the author of *Villa Nova; or, The Ruined Castle,* an excellent romance of ruins. Monastic melancholy rather than monastic shock is the dominant mood of the romance. The ceremony of Olivia De Riviera's taking of the veil, however, is suitably grim, as are Elinor's emotions at the later interment of this nun. An almost poetic awe toward medieval Catholicism fills this book, whose style is very often a throwback to the morbid delights of the graveyard poets of the eighteenth century. Seen by moonlight, the fallen abbey of St. Austin makes a memorable Gothic picture, a graphic ruin that rivals any description of the forbidden Gothic world to be found in Radcliffe: The abbey of St. Austin "was entirely unroofed, and in many places of the mouldering walls wide chasms had already opened, and the mantling ivy alone prevented the tottering fabric

from yielding to the force of the blasts that descended from the mountains and waved the lonely heads of those plants that thrive in old buildings. That part of the fabric which bore the most striking traces of the desolating hand of time, was what once had been the cloisters and refectory: in these the owl and bat had long reigned unrivalled, except by the raven, that in the vaults beneath them, echoed in answer to his hoarse cries, and the melancholy hooting of the birds of night."

1-347. Sheil, R. L. **The Phantom; or, Montoni.** Larpent Collection MS., 1820. (1)

Sheil was a dramatizer of Gothic novels and C. R. Maturin's Irish contemporary. He was to Irish Gothic drama what Maturin was to the Irish novel of terror—its leading exponent. *The Phantom* is a freewheeling and highly sensationalized dramatic adaptation of Radcliffe's *Mysteries of Udolpho* [1-316]. Her shadowy villain, Montoni, who is more often heard about than heard or seen in the novel, is now spotlighted and given full supernatural status by Sheil. The function of Emily St. Aubert in Sheil's stage version is to suffer and to shriek, but not to emote sublimely as she does in the Radcliffean source.

*1-348. Shelley, Mary Wollstonecraft Godwin. **Frankenstein; or, The Modern Prometheus.** Lackington, Hughes, Harding, Mayor & Jones, 1818; Bobbs-Merrill, 1974. (3) (SB)

The most famous monster tale of the entire Gothic tradition, *Frankenstein* is as much a philosophical novel and a vehicle of humanitarian propaganda as it is a novel of terror. The character of the repulsive giant who is spurned by all other creatures is an archetype of loneliness and unmerited suffering. The scientist as overreacher is a new mutation of the Gothic villain, for the character had formerly been an abbot or a baron seeking only sexual or political power. Victor Frankenstein, pale student of the unhallowed arts, has Faustian dimensions and seeks power over nature itself. He probes deeply into the arcana of creation, discovers through Galvanic experiments the secret of imparting life to matter, and constructs a huge man who proves to be a disgusting parody of the human physique—a monster with greenish flesh, yellowish eyes, and misshapen limbs. As the ersatz God looks upon his ersatz Adam, he is so appalled and disgusted by his biological handiwork that he rejects the thing and then tries to resume a normal life of love, courtship, and marriage. Unloved, fatherless, lonely, and cast out, the artificial brute— whose soul is far nobler than any of the normal human souls in the novel— tries in various ways to establish ties of love with humankind, only to be taught that society is the true monster in its repudiation of this unwanted child of perverted science. Coming to loathe both its creator and creation, the creature kills Frankenstein's brother and also murders his fiancé, Elizabeth Lavenza, on the eve of their wedding day. After a cosmic dialogue with his monster, Victor Frankenstein begins to build a mate for the creature, but aborts the task out of fear of engendering a race of dangerous brutes. The novel climaxes with the familiar Gothic pattern of flight and pursuit done in reverse terms, as Victor tracks his creature into the arctic wastes only to die in this quest. The final image is that of the pitiable outcast; the monster is borne off into the darkness and the distance on a receding ice floe—only to reappear in Hollywood 115 years later. Mary Shelley was a Gothic revisionist; her aims in *Frankenstein* were clearly more mythic than horrific. Whether the novel can be denominated primitive science fiction is dubious, since there is no description of the process of making an artificial man and no laboratory melodrama. In addition, to call the novel high Gothic is also to misname it, since her work is a departure from the haunted castle and an approach to the tragedy of misspent intellect.

*1–349. Shelley, Percy Bysshe. **Zastrozzi: A Romance.** G. Wilkie & J. Robinson, 1810; Arno, 1977. (1) (SB)

The first of two *Schauer-roman* by Shelley, the precocious Gothicism of *Zastrozzi* gives signs of the great poet to come, since the book is also an allegory of the mind's self-destructive extremes. The common trappings of the novel of horror, such as nocturnal pursuit and incestuous nightmare, combine with Shelley's philosophical curiosity over a malign divinity as a substitute for belief in a benevolent creator. The hero-villain of the title, Zastrozzi, is a titanic creature excelling in stature Radcliffe's towering, scowling monk, Father Schedoni [1–317]. Percy's enormous man would spawn the theme of gigantism shortly thereafter in his wife's monstrous child in *Frankenstein* [1–348]. Zastrozzi plots against and persecutes his normal half-brother, Verezzi, using all manner of intrigue to drive him mad. Thus, Zastrozzi revenges himself upon the father for his wretched condition and illegitimacy. Like the somnambulating *Edgar Huntly* [1–49], Verezzi is subject to narcoleptic trances during which Zastrozzi also works his evil will upon him. Meanwhile the femme fatale of the novel, the wicked Matilda, competes against the virtuous Julia for Verezzi's love. In a rondo of stabbings, Verezzi stabs himself while Julia is stabbed by Matilda, who then falls into the clutches of the Inquisition—all of this carnage having been arranged by Zastrozzi. Having schemed the deaths of his father and brother, Zastrozzi can now exult in his freedom from human fraternity and paternity as he faces death. Having defied God and man, Zastrozzi dies in Promethean triumph on the rack of the Inquisition, an unrepentant Gothic hero to the end, like the miserable Ambrosio of *The Monk* [1–218]: "Even whilst writhing under the agony of almost insupportable torture his nerves were stretched, Zastrozzi's firmness failed him not; but, upon his soul-illumined countenance, played a smile of most disdainful scorn—and, with a wild, convulsive laugh of exulting revenge, he died." Here, in its Gothic form, is the Shelleyean-Promethean rebel of the later poetry.

*1–350. Shelley, Percy Bysshe. **Saint Irvyne; or, The Rosicrucian.** J. J. Stockdale, 1811; Arno, 1977. (1) (SB)

The young Shelley's second Gothic novel, the short and highly *Schauer-romantik* narrative, *Saint Irvyne,* is linked by tradition and theme to Godwin's Rosicrucian novel, *Saint Leon* [1–129] and to Maturin's later presentation of the Wandering Jew figure in *Melmoth the Wanderer* [1–244]. Like Zastrozzi, the mysterious and apparently ageless Ginotti (alias Nempere) is another amazing colossal man, whose Rosicrucian affiliations have brought him the secret of the elixir of life everlasting. But eternal life has not been accompanied by eternal bliss, as his desperate condition of mind and eye shows. The self-exiled and suicidal young hero of the piece is Wolfstein, a kind of Gothistic Werther, who screams his defiance at the universe and the god of chaos from atop alpine peaks during roaring tempests. The three women of the tale are the corruptible and corrupting Italian beauty Megalena de Metastasio, the supervirtuous Olympia, and Eloisa Saint Irvyne. Each female has sound Gothic credentials; each seems to have been a denizen of the dark castle before. The novel's major Gothic dilemma involves Ginotti's effort to escape from the curse of eternal life. He can achieve death only by passing on the secret of the elixir to another future superman ready to make evil his good. In this perverse quest, Wolfstein has been singled out by Ginotti as a likely victim for the ironic punishment of eternal life. The novel's Gothic climax is well-conceived and occurs in the subterranean passageways of the ruined château of Saint Irvyne; here, Shelley shows his technical skill at carrying out a Gothic death sentence in the high *Schauer-romantik* mode. When Wolfstein refuses to accept the secret of the elixir, Ginotti is suddenly incinerated by a beam of lightning in a *coup de gothique* of the sort used by de Sade to eradicate Justine [1–331]: "On a sudden Ginotti's frame mouldered to a gigantic skeleton, yet two pale and ghastly flames glared in its eyeless sockets." Still alive in death and now decarnalized or flayed of fleshly self, Ginotti must continue to wander down the corridors of time unable to break the curse of never-ending life. Shelley's kind of animated skeleton seems vastly more terrifying than the mechanized bones of a usual shocker such as *The Animated Skeleton* [1–8].

1–351. Shrewtzer Castle; or, The Perfidious Brother: A German Romance, Including the Pathetic Tale of Edmund's Ghost. A. Neil, 1802. (5) (SB)

The bluebook demonstrates how several Gothic plots could be shortened and packaged as a unit to yield a saleable shilling shocker. *Shrewtzer Castle* is an utterly typical horrid darling of the circulating libraries. Its Gothic circuits, including the theme of fraternal villainy, are all clumsily ripped from the castles of Reeve and Radcliffe. The hair-raising epilogue or tale of Edmund's ghost is an appendage, which does nothing more than bring the page quota to 96, a common length for a little lurid work of this type.

1–352. Sickelmore, Richard. **Edgar; or, The Phantom of the Castle.** Minerva-Press, 1798. (1)

This diverting and artistically written Gothic novel is a more-than-satisfactory imitation of Radcliffe's prolonged methods of suspense. The work is also a probable source for Ker's *Edric the Forester; or, The Mysteries of the Haunted Chamber* [1–195]. The story has the sort of overt Hamletism that never seems to have made the Gothic readership grow weary. The phantom of the castle instructs young Edgar in the mysteries of his birthright as well as in the dark deeds that led to his father's death. The vociferous phantom is allowed to stalk through several volumes before the long-withheld natural explanation for the ghost dissipates the pleasing atmosphere of terror and wonder. *The Monthly Mirror*, a journal that was often the rational nemesis of Gothic hocus-pocus, gave Sickelmore its accolade for a brisk, yet suspenseful, Gothic.

1–353. Sickelmore, Richard. **Rashleigh Abbey; or, The Ruin on the Rock.** Minerva-Press, 1805. (1)

An orthodox romance of the ruin, which is constructed around the motif of strange and ghostly voices raised in a strange anthem, *Rashleigh Abbey* contains fine night pictures and equally fine night thoughts. The plot is totally conventional. The young heroine is brought to the ruined church by parties unknown for purposes unknown.

1–354. Sickelmore, Richard. **Osrick; or, Modern Horrors: A Romance.** Minerva-Press, 1809. (1)

If the structure of *Rashleigh Abbey* [1–353] is thoroughly conventional, the structure of *Osrick* is thoroughly unconventional and even radical by Gothic standards. The unusual format of this novel would not be seen again until the work of America's John Dos Passos in his *USA* trilogy, for Sickelmore's book is built around headline captions, which move the reader's eye (and hopefully his anxious soul) through a sequence of sensational agonies, entrapments, and distresses. Sickelmore's vivacious captions are not unlike the gory bluntness of the modern tabloid. Instead of polite chapter announcements, we find in bold face such stark advertisements as "A Frightful Abyss," "The Cavern," "A Coffin," and a host of other Gothic teasers and ticklers. The plot too is extraordinary, situating itself in Montevideo and Buenos Aires, where Lieutenant Osrick Somerton of Brighton shields and rescues the ill-fated heroine, Clara, saving her from a pack of vicious dogs and snatching her from the grasp of bloodthirsty Pampas Indians. One would expect Clara to marry the gallant Osrick after all this, but she finally prefers the formidable soldier, Dreadnought, instead. While the novel exhibits its share of legitimate Gothic activity, there is more than just a light touch of satire in the naming of its parts and the speeches of its heroes and victims. Osrick's mannerisms and inflated language will remind devotees of Tobias Smollett of that other invincible comic soldier who has also seen service in the Americas, Lieutenant Obadiah Lishmahago of *Humphry Clinker* (1771).

Given his vitriolic and slightly cruel sense of humor, Sickelmore might well have been the unidentified R. S., the author of *The New Monk* [1–381].

1–355. Siddons, Henry. **The Sicilian Romance; or, The Apparition of the Cliffs.** J. Barker, 1794. (1) (SB)
The title of the Gothic melodrama is misleading, since Siddon's play (an opera) has very little direct relationship to Radcliffe's *Sicilian Romance* [1–314]. The use of a Radcliffean title was simply a ploy to attract Gothic viewers. Siddons shifted the dramatic focus away from the persecuted maiden to the half-evil man whose baseness of character implies the opposite capacity for great good. Thus, Siddons's Ferrand, the Marquis of Otranto, is a forerunner of the Byronic hero in whom moral opposites very often converge. Placed beside his agonies of the soul, the sufferings of the maiden of the cliffs, Alinda, seem pallid. Twisted genealogies, concealed identities, timely strokes of thunder and lightning, melodramatically poised daggers, and pungent rhetoric capped by mad scenes and a Gothic *deus ex machina* in the form of the apparition of the cliffs show Siddons's mastery of Gothic stage mechanics. As Bertrand Evans has pointed out in *Gothic Drama from Walpole to Shelley* (California Univ. Press, 1947), Siddons made sure that Alinda was "menaced in all the favorite horror environs—castle, convent, and cavern."

1–356. Singer, Mr. **The Mystic Castle; or, The Orphan Heir.** Minerva-Press, 1796. (1)
The parricidal tyrant of the castle, Lord Mowbray, must face divine justice at last, but not before he disinherits his brother, Albert, and casts his wife into an obscure underground cell. Coming in right on schedule, the specter of the assassinated father commands Albert to oppose his usurping brother. At the duel to the death between the brothers during a grand tournament, the hand of God delivers a fatal blow to Mowbray and his dishonest ambitions. What we find in the handiwork of this minor Gothic novelist is a transparent canvas behind which can be seen *Hamlet* and Walpole's *Castle of Otranto* [1–398]. The sole attempt at originality is Mr. Singer's management of the *main coupée* or the mighty, sword-wielding hand, which seeks out and punishes injustice with automatic zeal. Without much novelty or original application of the standard Gothic properties, *Mystic Castle* nevertheless sold out quickly and pleased all Minerva-Press patrons.

1–357. **"Sir Bertrand's Adventures in a Ruinous Castle"** in *Gothic Stories*. S. Fisher, 1799. (5) (SB)
Barbauld's famous Gothic fragment, *Sir Bertrand* [1–18], became the object of many bluebook piracies. The anonymous plagiarist fleshed out his collection of Gothic legends with a piece called "The Adventure James III of Scotland Had with the Weird Sisters in the Dreadful Wood of Birnan [*sic*]," indicating that even Shakespeare was not safe from the embalming thefts of the fiend-mongers.

*1-358. Sleath, Eleanor. **The Orphan of the Rhine.** Minerva-Press, 1798; Folio, 1968. (1) (SB)

One of the largest and longest as well as one of the rarest and most elegant of the Northanger Gothics, this Gothic romance in four volumes amounts to more than 1,000 pages in the edition owned by Michael Sadleir. The fascinating story of how Sadleir retrieved this lost Gothic only by chance, while sifting through boxes of books owned by the bibliophile Hutchinson, is one of the great legends of Gothic research. The novel itself is expertly designed to delight the palate of Catherine Morland and her thousands of fellow readers. The period is 1605; the place is the romantic cottage of Julie de Rubine on the shores of Lake Geneva. Here, she lives in poetic solitude with her own child, Enrico, until a second child, the strange and parentless Laurette, is bestowed upon her by the Marchese de Montferrat. When she comes of age, Laurette embarks on the usual Gothic pilgrimage in search of the particulars of her birth while Enrico and Julie travel with her over the Rhine and inevitably closer to the Castle of Elfinbach. The castle approach scene is one of the best in Gothic literature. "The castle, which was seated upon an eminence, about a quarter of a league from the bed of the river, seemed to have been separated by nature from the habitable world by deep and impenetrable woods. Two of the towers, which were all that remained entire, were half secreted in a forest; the others which were mouldering into ruins, opened into a narrow, uncultivated plain, terminating in a rocky declivity at the bottom of which flowed the Rhine, wide, deep, and silent." The gradual Gothic of this familiar setting builds slowly to terror as Laurette (now renamed Chamont), the orphan of the Rhine, matures into a capable Gothic virgin and beautiful hysteric. Spliced into the main story are three complicated insets: Julie's story of her misadventures with her wicked aunt and her awful confederate, Vescolini; the abbess's story; and La Roque's story of separation, suffering, and reunion. Each inset is a kind of Gothic novel by itself, or would be, were it not that each is stitched into the main tale of Laurette's mysterious identity. All the poetic dignities, topographical complexities, and narrative splendor of the Radcliffean Gothic at its highest are present in *The Orphan of the Rhine.*

1-359. Sleath, Eleanor. **Who's the Murderer? or, The Mystery of the Forest.** Minerva-Press, 1802. (1) (SB)

Prophetic dreams, fragmented manuscripts, Gothic moonlight, and obfuscated banditti are accompaniments for the beleaguered orphan Cecilia, who must go forth on a terrifying journey to a dark castle in the depths of the black forest. En route, she undergoes a Burkean education into the sublimities of Gothic landscape. Having also discovered the corpse of her father while proceeding toward the castle, she must also face and solve the fearful question posed in the novel's title. And of course she does answer it and acquires a handsome husband while doing so. In 1810, Minerva-Press pub-

lished Sleath's *The Nocturnal Minstrel; or, The Spirit of the Wood,* another romance of the forest, which shows her sustained abilities as a Gothic writer.
The Nocturnal Minstrel was reissued by Arno Press in 1972.

1–360. Smith, Catherine. **The Castle of Arragon; or, The Banditti of the
Forest.** H. Colburn, 1809–1810. (1) (SB)
An average Radcliffean revival, the novel has an equivalent Emily figure, a
Montoni-ish villain, and a castle in the Pyrenees that is as difficult of access
as the Castle of Udolpho in the Italian Appenines. Bandits lurking in the
landscape were a long-standing expectation of the novel of sublime terror.

*1–361. Smith, Catherine. **Barozzi; or, The Venetian Sorceress: A Romance of the Sixteenth Century.** Minerva-Press, 1815; Arno, 1977. (1) (SB)
The Gothic opens briskly and without Radcliffean delays with an unexplained attack on the maiden Rosalina and her father, Ferrand St. Elmo.
The father is skewered by the two Venetian bravos while the helpless girl is
dragged off. The father's dying shout, "Spare her! oh spare her! I implore
thee," only delights the ruffians. Later rescued from her crude captor, Roldan, by Rosalvo Barozzi, Rosalina is then conveyed to a castle near Pyrano,
which is presided over by the usual mean marchioness, Madame la Rosa.
Whisked back to Palazzo Barozzi to attend a masked ball, Rosalina is
alarmed to confront a hooded sorceress in the guise of Medea, the child-mur-
derer. While she at first appears to be a figure of engaging evil, the Venetian
sorceress will eventually prove an agent of justice against the homicidal designs of Marquis de Barozzi, who has conspired to prevent Rosalina (de Valmont) from gaining her rightful title. The description of the Venetian sorceress has the genuine power of darkness required of the high Gothic: "Her robe
was of white, bordered with various mystic figures; round her head was in-
twined a serpent; her long, black matted hair hung disgustingly on her
shoulders while her piercing dark eyes rolled beneath the raven locks which
half concealed her face, and seemed to read the hearts of the surrounding
spectators." Hellish rites, fratricide, and what Catherine Smith calls "the
horrors of the ruin" complete the Gothic panorama. Confusing, yet exciting,
is one way of appraising this late Gothic, which might have given Poe some
stylistic ideas for his Italianate stories. It is interesting to note, for example,
that Chapter 2 of *Barozzi* is entitled "The Assignation." Poe later stations a
short story bearing this title in the poisonous Venetian atmosphere.

*1–362. Smith, Charlotte. **Emmeline, The Orphan of the Castle.** T. Cadell,
1788; Oxford Univ. Press, 1971. (4) (SB)
Emmeline is the supposedly illegitimate daughter of a deceased nobleman
whose vile and selfish younger brother blocks every attempt at happiness on
the part of the heroine. But Emmeline is consoled in her trials by her handsome cousin, who has declared his love only to be rejected out of maidenly
decency. The oblique suggestion of incest is handled so delicately by Char-

lotte Smith that it retains no shock value whatsoever. In due course, the desolate Emmeline discovers that she is both legitimate and wealthy, but not until she has endured inexplicable noises outside bolted doors and suspicious comings and goings, all of which are sufficient to Gothify her tender sensibilities. Emmeline's prison, the great Castle of Mowbray, which is surrounded by the ruins of a once-powerful abbey, has Gothic possibilities, but it remains almost purely a decorative antique site. Charlotte Smith was not willing to permit the castle to take on a haunted character of its own as the building always does in the high Gothic. Thus we have in *Emmeline* a novel of manners and sensibility that flirts with the current Gothic fashions, but skirts sustained terror.

1–363. Smith, Charlotte. **Ethelinde; or, The Recluse of the Lake.** T. Cadell, 1789. (4) (SB)

The work of Charlotte Smith anticipates in many respects the sort of residual Gothicism to be found in the Brontë sisters several decades later. Although its title is less suggestive of a Gothic ordeal for the maiden than *Emmeline, The Orphan of the Castle* [1–362], the action of *Ethelinde* places the novel more directly under the shadow of the emergent Gothic tradition. Ethelinde Chesterville meets the handsome but mysterious Charles Montgomery beneath the darkened battlements of Castle Newenden on the rustic shores of Lake Grasmere. Together the lovers plan a nocturnal tryst within the castle's inviting interior, which abounds in the usual Gothic apparatus for causing maidens to quake and faint: unaccountable noises, legends of evil, restless specters, and, of course, an abandoned and reputedly haunted chapel. In addition to such Gothic provocations, Ethelinde must also withstand the advances of a married man as well as investigate the origins of the recluse of the lake, whose melancholy history finally reveals her to be Charles's alienated mother. Meanwhile, Charles has strayed off to India, unable to compete as a lover with Ethelinde's new-found curiosity for Gothic distractions. After securing his lost fortune, Charles returns to the shores of Grasmere to reclaim his beloved from her Gothic preoccupations. Although Charlotte Smith gives her readers some glimpse of the Gothic world behind the domestic curtain, she also sees to it that the virtues of common sense and rural living finally win out in the maiden's proper choice of mate. Yet there are elements in the novel that make it an important model of the full-fledged maiden-centered sagas of Radcliffe, which would shortly follow.

*1–364. Smith, Charlotte. **The Old Manor House.** J. Bell, 1793; Oxford Univ. Press, 1969. (4) (SB)

Laced with artfully integrated Gothic elements, *The Old Manor House* is Charlotte Smith's outstanding Gothic achievement in the form of a family saga. Three Victorian Gothicists, Ainsworth, Reade, and Wilkie Collins, acknowledged their debt to this book, which remained a favorite among all classes of readers throughout the nineteenth century. The ancient estate of Raylands is ruled by a proud old lady, the last of the family's illustrious line. As a few presumptive and distant relatives await her demise, Orlando, a virtuous and honorable young man, defies the fortune-hunting vultures sitting on the family fence. His chief heroic service seems to be to fall in love with Monimia, the niece of old Mrs. Raylands's confidante. The young lovers enjoy fleeting moments together in the vast network of rooms in the crumbling old manor house, where their liaisons are occasionally disturbed by Radcliffean tremors and creaks. The wind roars and the lightning flashes as Orlando makes one of his chaste visits to Monimia's hiding place in a secret chamber. All the ghostly and ghastly noises are explained, however, by the presence of a band of smugglers who have taken over the old house's vaults as a hiding place. The lovers' bliss is short-lived, as Orlando volunteers to fight in the American war of independence on the American side and is taken prisoner by the Iroquois. After escaping, he returns to the old manor house to find everything changed. Raylands has fallen into the hands of strangers and Monimia has vanished. The novel's final chapters efficiently correct these adversities; Monimia is found and Orlando is revealed as the true heir of old Mrs. Raylands. The fact that Gothic mayhem could be fused with international adventure impressed James Fenimore Cooper and drew the attention of the American Gothic novelist Isaac Mitchell in *The Asylum; or, Alonzo and Melissa* [1–258].

1–365. Smith, Julia. **The Prison of Montauban; or, Times of Terror: A Reflective Tale.** Craddock, 1810. (1)
Slightly superior to the many bluebooks that condense the dungeon ordeals of the maiden, the work is a nostalgic Gothic that places its action in fifteenth-century France. A hidden heritage and a pining prisoner who is possibly royal give the book its foundations in the historical Gothic tradition.

1–366. Soane, George. **Knight Daemon and Robber Chief.** Sherwood, 1812. (2)
Fluent in German, George Soane had proficiently translated sections of Goethe's *Faust* and had immersed himself in all types of German Gothicism. *Knight Daemon and Robber Chief* is an English fused imitation of the *Räuber-roman* and *Ritter-roman*. While the characters and situations derive from *Rinaldo Rinaldini* [1–390] and various *Schauer-romantik* sources, Soane's anglicization of these popular German Gothic forms is both exciting and superior to the hordes of phony German translations that had been dumped on the Gothic market.

1–367. Le Souterrain; ou, Matilde (The Underground; or, Matilda) (France). Lepetit, 1793. (6)
An anonymous French translation of Lee's popular historical Gothic of 1783, *The Recess* [1–214]. The translation stresses the Gothic action while reducing the historical data.

1-368. The Spectre Mother; or, The Haunted Tower. Dean & Munday, 1800 (5) (SB)

Like *The Mystic Tower; or, Villainy Punished* [1-278], this bluebook takes commercial advantage of the vogue of tower Gothic instigated by John Palmer, Jr., in his 1796 *Mystery of the Black Tower* [1-288]. The tower-haunting apparition of the slain mother in full sanguinary apparel is an unusual variation of the customary paternal ghost; gloomy Gothic towers are generally reserved for assassinated fathers. Here, the aim of the talented bluebooker is to mix the familiar Gothic business of the revenge-demanding parental spirit with dismal doings, secret chambers, and vertical pursuit through the vaults of the tower to yield at least one Gothic thrill or emergency per page. In his classic study of the shilling shockers, W. W. Watt finds that "the most typical specter in the shockers is the murdered lord of the castle," but the anonymous entrepreneur of *The Spectre Mother* thought he was being original (and perhaps he was) by changing the sex of his tower ghost.

1-369. The Spectre of the Mountain of Granada. George Hughes, 1811. (1) (SB)

The three-volume Gothic romance has the appearance of the crude craftsmanship of the bluebook industry greatly enlarged. Even as the emotional climate that had supported the Gothic novel's phenomenal spread was changing, subliterary potboilers of the same ilk as *The Spectre of the Mountain of Granada* continued their tantalization. The plot here is an assortment of basic Gothic plots muddied by a dense style and poor control of the spirit world. It is almost as if the anonymous writer were teaching himself how to write a successful Gothic in this disjointed work. Both the motives and the earthly identity of the mountain ghost remain unclear; in fact, for reasoning known only to the bungling Goth, the specter does not put in an appearance until the middle of the second volume. Regarded in their own day as throwaway titles, books of this kind fetch a huge price among Gothic collectors in the twentieth century. But works of this type should be regarded only as curios or relics, not as readable Gothic literature.

1-370. Spiess, Heinrich Christian (Germany). **Die Löwenritter: Eine Geschichte des dreizehnten Jahrhunderts (The Knights of the Lion: A Tale of the Thirteenth Century).** Leipzig, 1794. (2)

Influenced by Schiller's *Geisterseher* [1-336], Spiess's *Ritter-roman* is a complex romance of chivalry that introduces the supernatural when and where necessary to produce exotic effects. The knights of the lion comprise a brotherhood as worthy as the *Vehmgericht* is sinister. Spiess's romances were popular objects of English translation during the Gothic period and were adored for their fabulous medievalism.

1-371. Stanhope, Louisa S. **Montbrasil Abbey; or, Maternal Trials.** Minerva-Press, 1806. (1) (SB)

A lively specimen of epistolary Gothic, the novel's webwork of letters traces the marital misfortunes and miscalculations of the three Elvington sisters, Elenor, Agnes, and Constance, whose mother, Gertrude Elvington, is an outspoken advocate of celibacy. The most Gothically minded of the sisters, Agnes, writes her letters from Melbourne Castle where she is pursued by the libertine, Major Arbuthnot. Melbourne is a "gloomy piece of Gothic architecture" with a haunted western gallery, a legend of the tyrant Reginald, and a pale spook of the murdered Bertha. After Agnes has perused Radcliffe's *The Mysteries of Udolpho* [1–316], she explores the gallery and is soon terrified by a spaniel. Desiring wealth and position to finance further Gothic thrills, Agnes rejects Arbuthnot and marries the Marquis Montbrasil. In doing so, she acquires a cruel and arrogant master, a harsh husband who is almost the prototype of the brutal rake of Victorian fictions such as *The Tenant of Wildfell Hall* (1848) by Anne Brontë. Her marital trials cause her to run away with Arbuthnot, but the powerful Marquis is soon on their trail. Guilt over the mismatch and her subsequent disloyalty lead to Agnes's emaciation and death. Fragile, fearful, and frenzied, Agnes is the Gothic heroine par excellence: "Her figure is tall and elegantly proportioned; the contour of her countenance Grecian; a bewitching smile playing on her rosy lips, discloses a set of teeth, white as the polished ivory; her nose, aquiline; her blue eyes are soft and expressive, shadowed by long dark lashes; her luxuriant chestnut locks hang in natural ringlets upon the whitest neck I ever beheld." The Victorian heroine would be considerably plainer, but no less a victim of an unwise marriage. Although it is true that Louisa Stanhope has her feet solidly fixed in the Gothic tradition, her hand is on the doorknob of the novel of domestic crisis.

1–372. Stanhope, Louisa S. **The Confessional of Valombre.** Minerva-Press, 1812. (1) (SB)

A reasonably well-conceived monastic shocker, the novel is also a Gothic murder mystery that shows the murder of the decent priest, Abbot Theodore, in his own confessional of Valombre. The novel begins in the official Radcliffean manner of *The Italian; or, The Confessional of the Black Penitents* [1–317] as a mysterious and cowled stranger "paused at the gate of the convent of Valombre. The stilly gloom of the hour, the hollow moaning of the blast, the darkened concave of the heavens, from which no star, no casual reflection of light was emitted, recalled to mind the object of his embassy." From this absolutely familiar Gothic beginning there follow a convent confinement, fantastic persecutions, the assassination of the abbot, and the usual belated unraveling of all the mysteries of the monastery. Stanhope's narrative formula of menace, monastery, murder, and marriage enabled her to produce 14 guaranteed Gothics for the Minerva-Press between 1806 and 1830. Along with "Gabrielli" [1–252], she remained one of Minerva-Press's most cash-worthy authors.

1-373. Stanhope, Louisa S. **Treachery; or, The Grave of Antoinette.** Minerva-Press, 1815. (1) (SB)
Another highly popular Gothic murder mystery, which also reverts to the tearful methods of sentimental fiction. The novel again opens with a stranger in sorrowful posture at the grave of his slain beloved. In imitation of one of the forms of Radcliffe's lyric relief for the reader, this romance also intersperses many rhapsodically morbid pieces of graveyard verse.

1-374. Stanhope, Louisa S. **The Nun of Santa Maria di Tindaro.** Minerva-Press, 1818. (1) (SB)
The three-volume romance depicts the distressed maiden in ecclesiastical garb and takes her through the usual Gothic pains of convent confinement and the enforced taking of the veil. The terrors attendant upon imaginary Catholicism never seem to have lost favor with the Gothic audience as this late work attests. A formulaic Gothic in every aspect, the novel nevertheless pleased immediately.

1-375. Stratton, Jemima Maria. **The Maid of the Castle: A Legendary Tale.** Minerva-Press, 1794. (4)
Written in "Three Cantos," the novel is a semiversified imitation of Charlotte Smith's sentimental romance of 1788, *Emmeline: The Orphan of the Castle* [1-362]. Belinda, the maid of the castle, is a fourteenth-century child of ill fortune who must find her heritage in spite of the elaborate hindrances of jealous relatives.

1-376. Street, Miss. **The Recluse of the Apennines.** Minerva-Press, 1792. (4)
Not attributed to Street until she was listed as the author by a Minerva catalogue of 1814, this obscure sentimental romance owes most of its feeling and material to Charlotte Smith's *Ethelinde; or, The Recluse of the Lake* [1-363] and is also a possible character source for another recluse of a castle in the Apennines, Emily St. Aubert, in *The Mysteries of Udolpho* [1-316].

1-377. Stuart, Augusta Amelia. **Ludovico's Tale; or, The Black Banner of Castle Douglas.** 1807. (1)
Truly a literary orphan, this giant four-volume imitation of Radcliffe's Highland Gothic material shows no publisher. Named for a minor character in *The Mysteries of Udolpho* [1-316], the action of the novel is a Macbethian feast of horrors. The qualities and cast of the German *Räuber-roman* have been transferred to the dark fortresses and eerie glens of medieval Scotland.

1-378. Stuart, Augusta Amelia. **The Cave of Toledo; or, The Gothic Princess: An Historical Romance.** Minerva-Press, 1812. (1)
This five-volume romance, one of the longest Gothic novels ever written, confers upon Stuart the undisputed rank of queen of verbosity. Everything Gothic that had ever been tried is packed tediously into this Gothic sky-

scraper. The Gothic princess herself is lost in a hodgepodge of borrowed themes and characters. Nevertheless, the work belongs in a proper bibliography as a curio of the period and as a death knell for the Gothic novel. Readers could tolerate three volumes or even four, but five volumes of repetitious terror could not be digested.

1–379. Sullivan, Mary Ann. **Owen Castle; or, Which Is the Heroine?** Minerva-Press, 1816. (4)
A second edition of this four-volume Welsh Gothic was called for in 1823. Not strictly speaking a straightforward satire on Gothicism's genealogical complications, the novel does toy with the serious business of the heroine's discovery of her identity. The confusion arising over twin damsels in distress, Ellen and Elaine, is strung out through four volumes of Gothic predicaments and alarms. The question of the subtitle is finally answered by the returning ghost of Owen Castle's murdered master.

1–380. Sykes, Mrs. S. **Margiana; or, Widdrington Tower: A Tale of the Fifteenth Century.** Minerva-Press, 1808. (1) (SB)
A copy of this five-volume Gothic romance was once part of Montague Summers's private collection. The harassed heroine is a typical sensitive sufferer in a typical historical Gothic belonging to the troubled period of Richard II and the usurping Henry IV. Margiana is exposed to the customary predicaments of the maiden, including seizure by ruffians and tower confinement. Her encounters with masked villains is such a regular occurrence that the reader must wonder if all of England in the fourteenth century were wearing the hoods of outlaws.

1–381. R. S., Esq. **The New Monk.** Minerva-Press, 1798. (4)
This novel is a sharp and precise parody of Lewis's famous or infamous Gothic novel of 1796, *The Monk* [1–218]. Its publication by the Minerva-Press indicates that Gothic manufacturer's willingness to deal in lampoons of the very product that had become its profitable trademark among booksellers during the period. Unlike Barrett's *The Heroine* [1–22] or Austen's *Northanger Abbey* [1–11], two later satires that mock the entire Gothic tradition, *The New Monk* sneers at only a single book as it dismantles the old *Monk* almost paragraph by paragraph and scene by scene. Ambrosio is cleverly Protestantized into the Reverend Joshua Pentateuch, a hypocritical Methodist zealot. Lewis's Rosario-Matilda glides into *The New Monk* as Peter, later disclosed as Betsey. The severe convent of St. Clare in whose slimy cellars Agnes undergoes her unspeakable ordeals is modernized into Mrs. Rod's Boarding School, complete with a vicious porter who drags Alice Clottleberry (i.e., Agnes) off to a flogging apartment for some sadistic fun. For Ambrosio's erotic raid on his sister, Antonia, we have Pentateuch's rifling of Ann Maria Augusta's bedchamber—not in search of sexual sport but in quest of some loose banknotes. The trial and gibbet-hanging of Pentateuch

have enough putrid detail to equal Lewis's own emetic style and make these scenes genuinely Gothic if read out of context. Energetically coarse, *The New Monk*'s comic cruelty is based on one of the closest hostile readings of another book in the history of literary satire.

1–382. Thomas, Francis Tracy. **Monk-Wood Priory.** Longman & Rees, 1799. (4)

A morbidly sentimental novel in epistolary form, *Monk-Wood Priory* graphs the anxious career of Mrs. Sullivan in her domestic plights and trials. The Gothic titling of the novel was an obvious falsification to render a book about the self-education of a young lady acceptable to the Gothically oriented audience.

1–383. Thomson, Alexander. **The Three Ghosts of the Forest: A Tale of Horror.** J. Ker, 1803. (5) (SB)

Calling itself "An Original Romance," the bluebook is the usual condensed assortment of pilfered plots and expropriated characters taken freely from several legitimate Gothics. That Gothic bank of the bluebookers, Lewis's *Monk,* seems to be the main object of theft.

1–384. Tieck, Johann Ludwig (Germany). **Abdallah; oder, Das furchtbare Opfer (Abdallah; or, The Dreadful Sacrifice).** Carl August Nicolai, 1795. (2)

Read and plundered by Lewis prior to his composition of *The Monk* [1–218], *Abdallah* is an orientalized *Schauer-roman* full of relentless horror and macabre sufferings. Tieck's strong sense of the malignantly ugly was perhaps the major German Gothic tributary feeding into Lewis's imagination. The nerve-shattering contributions of Tieck to the rise of an English and American Gothic movement have never been adequately measured.

1–385. Tschink, Cajetan (Germany). **Wundergeschichten sammt dem Schlüssel zu ihrer Erklarung (Tales of Wonder Together with the Key to Their Explanation).** Kaiserer, 1789. (2)

A collection of Gothic *Märchen,* these macabre tales are almost always "explained" by supernatural rather than natural causes.

1–386. Tschink, Cajetan (Germany). **Geschichte eines Geistersehers aus den Papieren des Mannes mit Larve (The Story of a Ghostseer from the Papers of the Man in the Iron Mask).** Kaiserer, 1791. Trans. by P. Will as *The Victim of Magical Delusion,* G. G. & J. Robinson, 1795. (2) (SB)

The popular English translation of Tschink's imitation of Schiller's *Geisterseher* [1–336] bore the additional subtitle, *The Mystery of the Revolution of P—L: A Magico-Political Tale.* The theme of the activity of secret societies and political conspiracy is added to the diablerie of corpse-raising in Tschink's work. Tschink had a special talent for supernatural realism, a fact that no doubt caught the attention of Monk Lewis. Summers provides a synopsis of the romance in *The Gothic Quest:* "Miguel, Duke of C——, is sent on his travels under the care of Antonio, a Portuguese count. A most extraordinary and artful impostor, *The Unknown,* and this tutor having deluded the youth by a series of supposed necromancies and wizard charms into a belief that the mysterious being possesses powers of the highest occult order, involve their dupe in a share of the conspiracy by which the revolution of Portugal is to be effected. All too soon Miguel finds that he is bound to the horrid authors of that desperate attempt by every tie of honour, love, pride, and gratitude. There are, it must be acknowledged, certain resemblances between *The Victim of Magical Delusion* and *Horrid Mysteries* [1-139], since in each romance the hero finds himself entangled with clandestine businesses which are murderous and bloody beneath the outworn pretext of liberty."

1-387. Tuckett, T. R. **The Vaults of Lepanto: A Romance.** Minerva-Press, 1814. (1)
This three-volume Gothic romance is catalogued by Dorothy Blakey in her study of Minerva-Press novels, but must be recorded as a "lost" Gothic. From its lateness in the Gothic chronology and the subterranean allusiveness of the title, we may infer that the work imitated the widespread vogue for notes from the underground in Gothic literature.

1-388. Vanzee, Maria. **Fate; or, Spong Castle.** Parsons, 1803. (1)
This orthodox Gothic romance is built around the stock device of the ancient recovered manuscript. The gloomy Yorkshire landscape provides a bleak Gothic locale for the working out of genealogical justice as it is demanded by the ancient parchment. *Fate* in the title signifies the good characters' unnerving discovery of unexplained evil in a close relative. Since fathers are notoriously missing and mothers are generally dead in Gothic fiction, that relative is almost always a displaced uncle or a dowager aunt. In *Spong Castle,* family disclosures come in the form of the long-lost history of a prisoner secluded in a German fortress. Although secret family papers and mislaid manuscripts never seem to lose their Gothic currency, their handling in this romance is more trite than titillating. One artistic test of the competent Goth is his or her ability to make the rusty machinery of Walpole operate smoothly. By such a test, Vanzee's work needs lubrication.

1-389. Viterne, Madame de (France). **Zofloya; ou, Le Maure (Zofloya; or, The Moor).** Barba, 1812.
A French translation of Dacre's explosive Gothic thriller of 1806, *Zofloya; or, The Moor* [1-90].

1-390. Vulpius, Christian August (Germany). **Rinaldo Rinaldini, der Räuberhauptmann: Eine romantische Geschichte unseres Jahrhunderts (Rinaldo Rinaldini, the Robber Captain: A Romantic Tale of Our Century).** Gräff, 1798. Trans. by F. S. A. John Hinckley as *The History of Rinaldo Rinaldini, Captain of Banditti.* Longman & Rees, 1800. (2)

Descending from the vigorous tradition of the noble outlaw found first in Schiller's *Die Räuber* [1–337], *Rinaldo* is a superbly conceived *Räuber-roman* that also incorporates the Gothically popular theme of the *Vehmgericht* or secret tribunal. In Vulpius's other immediate source, Naubert's *Hermann von Unna* [1–279], we read of the secret Fehmic Court that it "was composed of more than 100,000 individuals held together by an invisible chain, known to each other, but indistinguishable from the rest of the world, whose sittings were covered with the most impenetrable secrecy; whose decrees were arbitrary and despotical, and were executed by assassins, whose steel seldom failed to reach the heart of its unfortunate victim." There is a strong element of the picaro or the wandering and roguish antihero in the character of the boisterous brigand Rinaldo. Under a dozen noble disguises and trickeries of costume, Rinaldo's whole life is an imposture in behalf of justice. Also a kind of Gothic Casanova, he helps a lady named Aurelia to avoid the machinations of her sordid husband, Baron Rovezzo. Finally growing weary of the bandit's life, Vulpius's man of a thousand faces nearly finds peace in his retirement to the island of Pantallaria. But fate in the shape of the little old man of Fronteia pursues him. Rather than go to the scaffold after his capture, Rinaldo takes his own life in one of the most honorable suicides in romantic literature. The type of the compassionate criminal, of which Rinaldo is no less a prototype than Schiller's Karl Moor, is a not-too-distant cousin of the Gothic novel's hero-villain. Radcliffe's La Motte in *The Romance of the Forest* [1–315] has traits that may well have been passed along to Rinaldo. Capitalizing on the success of *Rinaldo,* Vulpius also wrote *Fernando Fernandini* (1799) and *Orlando Orlandini* (1802), Gothic offspring of Rinaldo.

1–391. V . . . n, Henri (France). **Le Fermier de la forêt d'Inglewood; ou, Les Effets de la superstition (The Farmer of Inglewood Forest; or, The Effects of Superstition).** Dentu, 1818. (6)
A French translation of the sentimental, agrarian Gothic of Elizabeth Helme, *The Farmer of Inglewood Forest* [1–157]. The French translation's addition of a didactic subtitle is to be noted.

1–392. Wächter, Georg Philipp Ludwig Leonhard (Germany) (used pseud. Veit Weber). **Die Teufelsbeschwörung (The Exorcism)** in *Sagen der Vorzeit (Legends of Ancient Times).* 1795. Trans. by Robert Huish [1–173] as *The Sorcerer.* J. Johnson, 1795. (2)
Veit Weber's demoniac criminal, Francesco, suffers a violent death by a fall from great heights in a spectacular event that is similar to the end of Ambrosio in *The Monk* [1–218]. But Veit Weber's wicked magician is a Faustian figure rather than a lecherous priest. Although the *Monthly Review* for August 1797 accused Lewis of plagiarizing from this German source, this sort of aerial catastrophe was available to Lewis in many other places. Lewis's best twentieth-century biographer, Louis F. Peck, states that "it is quite certain that the conclusion of *The Monk* as it originally appeared was inspired by

Veit Weber's *Teufelsbeschwörung* in his *Sagen der Vorzeit*. Both Francesco in the German story and Ambrosio fall from a great height upon desolate rocks and suffer exactly the same agonies before they are washed away by stormy waters."

1-393. Wächter, Georg Philipp Ludwig Leonhard (Germany) (used pseud. Veit Weber). **Der Schwarze Tal (The Black Valley)** in *Sagen der Vorzeit (Legends of Ancient Times)*. 1796. Trans. Anon. Johnson, 1796. (2)
The tale concerns the grotesque odyssey of one of the most voluptuous of Gothic women, Cunegonde. Lewis's Matilda, the demon of sexuality in *The Monk* [1-218], finds a near sister in Veit Weber's phantom of carnal delight who is described in the English translation as "flushed with the mellow of maturity at thirty, blooming, succulent and exuberant" and quivering with the "gentle impulse of desire in every vein." This erotic portrait might also serve as a basis for Ambrosio himself. Such Germanic beauties were the basis for the corpse bride or decapitated damsel in Irving's "Adventure of the German Student" [1-182].

1-394. Walker, C. E. **The Warlock of the Glen; A Melodrama in Two Acts.** John Lowndes, 1820. (1) (SB)
A late Gothic drama modeled in part on Lewis's *The Wood Daemon; or, The Clock Has Struck* [1-222].

1-395. Walker, George. **The Romance of the Cavern; or, The History of Fitz-Henry and James.** Minerva-Press, 1792. (1)
A first Gothic novel by the accomplished and graceful romancer, George Walker, the title suggests a concentration of the action of Radcliffe's *Romance of the Forest* [1-315] of 1791. The plight of the hidden royal twins also gives this cavern Gothic its strong parallels to Lee's secret daughters of Mary Queen of Scots in *The Recess* [1-214]. Pseudohistorical Gothics featuring the fictitious offspring of romantic monarchs enjoyed a great vogue as a special category of Gothic novel that might be designated the children of the cave or castle.

1-396. Walker, George. **The Haunted Castle: A Norman Romance.** Minerva-Press, 1794. (1) (SB)
A paradigm Gothic romance, *The Haunted Castle* satisfies all the conditions of the high Gothic formula. The preface to the novel reads like a manifesto of Gothicism as Walker declares, "In the choice of subject, I have fallen in with the times." The Gothic subject is the subterranean biography of the orphan hero, Ignatius, and his prolonged search for missing parents in the dark corridors of various haunted castles. Ignatius had been found in childhood by the crusader champion Pierre du Pin, who had come across the child near a lady's body lying in the vicinity of his Mediterranean fortress. The foster father christens the boy Ignatius and raises him to be a warrior against the infidels. Ignatius's talkative servant, Le Moine, the hermit cleric, and the sinis-

ter master of Trone Castle, Count Manfredi, are Gothic regulars all taken directly from the dramatis personae of Walpole's *Castle of Otranto* [1–398]. Reginald Lace, past master of Trone Castle, appears in white armor from time to time to assist the hero in his gropings after his heritage or to extricate him from Gothic hazards. Trone Castle is linked by an underground vault to the haunted castle where strange lights and odd noises have often been reported. Feeling that the haunted castle contains the clue to his identity, Ignatius and Le Moine make the subterranean journey into its interior spurred onward by a bloodstained and beckoning figure. Once within the haunted castle, Ignatius speaks for all Gothic explorers when he wonders: "By what strange fatality have I been conducted to this place—unless indeed—and now for the first time it occurred to him that it perhaps related to the discovery of his birth." The ghostly guide, now revealed as Count Manfredi, reappears to confess that he has had Ignatius's noble father celled up and starved, for which crime he is perpetually condemned to haunt the castle. With birthright clarified and justice satisfied, Ignatius assumes the power and undertakes the renovation of the ruin. Without ever pretending to originality, George Walker showed his Gothic genius by producing an expert replica of Walpole's invention. Eino Railo, who calls his history of the Gothic novel, *The Haunted Castle,* says in the first chapter of his book that "the entire stock-in-trade of horror-romanticism in its oldest and purest form consists, as will be shown in the following pages, chiefly of the properties and staff of this haunted castle, and, as we proceed farther in time, of motives based in the first instance upon these, so that to my mind acquaintance with the materials of horror-romanticism is best begun with this central stage and its appurtenances."

1–397. Walker, George. **The House of Tynian.** Minerva-Press, 1795. (1)
The Sadleir-Black Gothic Collection contains the Irish edition of 1796 published by P. Wogan, P. Byrne, W. Jones, and J. Rice of Dublin in which the original four volumes in Minerva bindings were condensed to two volumes. The novel is a repetition of the formula of *The Haunted Castle* [1–396] with one exception. The ghost of Clara Reeve is brought back to place a forbidden apartment in the path of the hero's search for his father's murderer. Again, Walker was successful in this Gothic refabrication because he did not profess to any originality. His capacities as a Gothicist consisted in knowing how to rewire the haunted castle of Walpole over and over to secure the same set of shocks.

*1–398. Walpole, Horace (used pseud. Onuphrio Muralto in first ed.). **The Castle of Otranto: A Story.** Thomas Lowndes, 1765; in *Three Gothic Novels,* Dover, 1966. Ed. E. F. Bleiler. (1) (SB)
Universally influential and never out of print, *The Castle of Otranto* ranks as the parent form and model for all Gothic novels that conduct their ghastly business behind the walls and beneath the superstructure of a haunted

castle. *Otranto* also contains the indispensable blueprint to which later Gothic novelists would freely turn for notions about the gadgetry of supernatural shock. Walpole's aptitude for Gothic technology enabled him to invent with brilliance and wit all the supernatural plumbing that came to characterize the interior of the haunted castle, Gothic fiction's central symbol and its most durable prop. The plot of *Otranto* exhibits fantastic and melodramatic elements that would shortly become standard in the pages of Gothic romance. These elements include erotic villainy and exotic feelings, a crisis caused by an ancestral curse that places the ownership of the castle in doubt, a "constant vicissitude of interesting passions" among the characters, and a series of "extraordinary positions," many of them absurd or repellent to reason. When Walpole launches the novel by causing an enormous medieval helmet to crash-land from the sky, he shatters the Augustan reader's reliance on common sense and transports him to the irrational freedom of the Gothic world. The great helmet obliterates the sickly young Conrad, son and heir of the tyrant-hero of the tale, Manfred, the sire of a long line of tormented tormentors and the Gothic novel's original half-evil protagonist. Walpole devotes some care to the divided nature of his feudal or Gothic villain: "Manfred was not one of those savage tyrants who wanton in cruelty unprovoked. The circumstances of his fortune had given an asperity to his temper, which was naturally humane; and his virtues were always ready to operate, when his passion did not obscure his reason." With Conrad crushed, Manfred is now confronted with the Gothic villain's classic problem of preserving his lineage and retaining power over the castle that his ancestors had usurped from its rightful lord. The lovely Isabella, who had been scheduled to wed Conrad on the very day the helmet fell upon him, now finds herself the maiden victim of Manfred's dark urges. She whom Manfred had intended for Conrad is now vigorously pursued by Manfred himself through the "long labyrinth of darkness" running through the cloistered vaults of the castle. The Gothic tradition begins with this underground chase through "a vault totally dark" and past the grim relics of a forgotten medieval world imaginatively recreated by a mind bored with the rigidities of reason. Trap-doors that open or close at the wrong times, infernal noises, hideous shrieks, slimy passageways, and unrelieved gloom surround the Gothic virgin (or close in upon her) in her desperate flight from the villain in the hell of the castle's substructure. As the victimization intensifies, the supernatural forces activated by the arrival of the huge helmet begin to consolidate: a statue bleeds; a picture comes alive and deserts its frame; a mighty foot protrudes from the castle walls; a mighty hand fully armored seems to be grasping after a titanic sword. Through these implements and others, Walpole donates to future Gothicists the tools of their trade. He also passes on the idea of the inanimate as animate in the superbiology of the Gothic world. After the cryptic murder of his own daughter, Matilda, the forces of retribution close in on Manfred. In what still remains one of the best catastrophic climaxes in

Gothic literature, he is made to witness the annihilation of the usurped castle when the gigantic body of Alfonso the Good, whose torso had apparently been gathering life within the walls of Otranto, explodes the castle's foundations and stands triumphantly amid the ruins of Manfred's lost seat of power. Literally every feature of Gothic mythology rises with Alfonso in the birth of this new and strange genre. E. F. Bleiler has written that "the Gothic novel is a primitive detective story in which God or Fate is the detective." When Walpole's imitators substituted Satan for God, the Gothicism of *Otranto* underwent its final refinement.

*1–399. Walpole, Horace. **The Mysterious Mother.** Printed privately by Walpole at Strawberry Hill, 1768. Dodsley, 1781; Constable, 1924. (1)
Walpole's Gothic drama adds the Oedipal theme and overtones of incest to the murky genealogy of the Gothic plot. Incest would again appear in Gothic drama in Shelley's powerful play, *The Cenci* (1819), a work in which the father's cruelty to his daughter assumes the form of incestuous passion. In *The Mysterious Mother,* the discovery of true parentage is tantamount to unbearable horror. The Countess of Narbonne has clandestinely assumed the place of her son's mistress and borne him a daughter, Adeliza, who later becomes the object of the son's sexual passions herself. Thus does Edmund unwittingly compound the family malady of incest. From this labyrinth of guilt there is no egress; when the awful secret is made known, the countess follows the example of Queen Jocasta in Sophocles' *Oedipus Tyrannus* and takes her own life. Edmund rushes to find something like an honorable death on the field of battle. The dark sexual transgression hidden from sons and lovers until it surfaces to destroy one and all stalks many Gothic families and becomes an important legacy to the tangled plot of the Gothic novel. Robert Jephson's dramatization of *The Castle of Otranto, The Count of Narbonne* [1–184], drew its character naming from Walpole's drama.

1–400. The Wandering Spirit; or, The Memoirs of the House of Morno. T. Hurst, 1802. (5) (SB)
Compressed terrors and swiftly delivered horrors render *The Wandering Spirit* a high-velocity bluebook. A convent confinement for the trembling heroine, Emma, and a portable ghost who has carefully studied the movements and speeches of Hamlet's father are among the bluebook's functionaries. The young hero, Charles, proudly displays his noble birthmark, a "mark of grapes at his back"—a variation of the usual tattoo of the blue arrow on the back of the Gothic hero. The bluebooker has openly confiscated everything he deemed necessary to manufacture a quick shocker to yield an absolutely stereotypical condensed thriller in blue.

*1–401. Warner, Richard. **Netley Abbey: A Gothic Story.** T. Skelton, 1795; Arno, 1974. (1) (SB)
Germanic materials combined with the traditional mayhem of the monastic shocker insured the instant acceptance of Warner's only Gothic endeavor.

The novel is a sophisticated and artistic arrangement of the customary Gothic stimulants. An abbey specter patrols the chapel; an evil monk, Father Peter, schemes against the happiness of the virtuous characters; a gluttonous abbot supplies the anti-Catholic element. The plot is in the conventional Walpolesque mold. Young Edward is visited in a dream by a man in full armor who demands revenge. The dark depths of the abbey itself must be explored to find the solution to the command of revenge. Thus, young Edward occupies the standard "extraordinary position" of dozens of young Gothic heroes; and, without hesitation, he makes the descent toward his destiny: "When he had arrived a few yards from the phantom, it stretched out its lance, and pointed toward the walls. Edward now thought that he walked toward the walls, and had almost reached them, when he discovered amongst the brambles a trap door, wide open, through which streamed a faint ray of light. A long flight of stairs appeared. These he descended without hesitation, and quickly found himself in a damp and gloomy passage."

1–402. Watkins, Lucy. **Romano Castle; or, The Horrors of the Forest.** Dean & Munday, n.d. (5) (SB)
Of bluebook quality but longer than the normal bluebook, the work is an abridgment of various forest Gothics that place the maiden in suspension between the dungeons of the castle and the caverns in the alien and sullen woods. Names and situations seem to be culled from Radcliffe's *Romance of the Forest* [1–315], which would suggest that the work was written and published in the mid-1790s. The Sicilian setting of the shocker also argues for the writer's Gothic dependencies on Radcliffe.

1–403. Wentworth, Zara. **The Recluse of Albyn Hall.** Minerva-Press, 1819. (4)
A tale of domestic distress with Gothic overtones and undertones, the novel's modification of Gothic extremes suggests the moderating literary climate that would soon lead to Victorian daylight.

1–404. Whalley, Thomas Segwick. **Edwy and Edilda: A Gothic Tale in Five Parts.** S. Colbert, 1783.
Of bluebook length and quality, this historical Gothic is an Irish forgery of the characters and content of Clara Reeve's *Old English Baron* [1–322]. The book advertised itself as "By the Author of the Old English Baron" on the frontispiece.

1–405. White, J. B. **The Mysteries of the Castle; or, The Victim of Revenge.** Larpent Collection MS., 1807. (1)
A late and derivative Gothic melodrama based loosely on Andrews's *The Mysteries of the Castle: A Dramatic Tale in Three Acts* [1–7] and Carr's *The Towers of Urbandine* [1–56]. White's play might be classified as bluebook Gothic drama.

1-406. White, James. **Earl Strongbow; or, The History of Richard de Clare and the Beautiful Geralda.** Crowden, 1789. (4) (SB)
In part a historical fiction and in part a sly burlesque of the evolving Gothic school of Walpole, Reeve, and Lee, the narrative takes the form of a colloquy between a seventeenth-century gentleman and a witty, well-informed ghost on the battlements of Chepstow Castle. In relating the bloody history of the conquest of Ireland, the vociferous phantom imparts much criticism of modern people and manners by comparing the chivalric values of the past with the unmanly attitudes of the present. White's specter of history is less frightening than amusing and more intellectual than ominous. Orates the ghost at one point: "We handled the battle-ax, you wield the dice-box. Our breakfast was beef and ale, yours is toast and chocolate. We were a stately and robust race, you are an enervated and unmajestic generation." The talkative spirit of *Earl Strongbow* is the forefather of the genial and voluble ghosts of the comic Gothic whose appearance can sometimes lead to a friendship between the haunter and haunted, as was the case with *The Spectre* [1-6] by Charles Andrews, also published in 1789.

1-407. White, T. H. **Bellgrove Castle; or, The Horrid Spectre.** White & Jee, 1803. (1)
This very static four-decker Gothic is crammed with Gothic paraphernalia but seems devoid of the true Gothic spirit. We have here an example of subliterary and subliterate amateurism in the bustling field of Gothic novel writing.

1-408. Wilkinson, Sarah. **The Subterranean Passage; or, Gothic Cell.** White Rose Court, 1803. (1)
A first and apprenticeship Gothic novel by one of the most productive and gifted of female fiend-mongers, Wilkinson's novel leads the reader to the awful dungeon of the pining prisoner. All the apparatus of anguish is here: an anxious maiden; a corps of apparitions; a genealogical enigma; an active underground; a dark and enclosed universe of whispering chambers and wailing castles.

1-409. Wilkinson, Sarah. **The Castle Spectre; or, Family Horrors: A Gothic Story.** T. & R. Hughes, 1807. (1) (SB)
Continuing her apprenticeship to the perfection of Gothic techniques, Wilkinson transformed Lewis's Gothic drama, *The Castle Spectre* [1-219], back into a Gothic novel. In 1809, she wrote a competent imitation of Radcliffe's *The Italian* [1-317] entitled *The Mysterious Novice; or, The Convent of the Grey Penitents*. While her Gothic plots and themes remained parasitic, she knew how to rivet the reader's interest and how to imbue her Gothic fantasies with the willing suspension of disbelief.

1-410. Wilkinson, Sarah. **The Castle of Montabino; or, The Orphan Sisters.** Dean & Munday, 1810. (1) (SB)

A high-quality bluebook, *The Castle of Montabino* is a historical Gothic that takes the clichés of the genre—the terrible curse, the missing parents, the dreadful chambers, and the pitiful twins—and elevates these into a satisfactory exercise in suspenseful terror.

1-411. Wilkinson, Sarah. The Spectre of Lanmere Abbey; or, The Mystery of the Blue and Silver Bag. W. Mason, 1820. (1) (SB)

Two decades of continuous Gothic productivity by Wilkinson result in some possible self-parody in this Radcliffean revival. Various passages border on burlesque of the form, as the author makes no pretensions to high seriousness in this amusing shocker. The winking preface sets the tone: "Knowing how eager the fair sex are for something *new* and romantic, I determined on an attempt to *please* my fair sisterhood, hoping to profit myself thereby. If they meet with rapid sale and fill my pockets, I shall be elated." The heroine, Charlotte Bennet, lives in Dickensian squalor with her mother, Agnes, who is in reality the scorned Mary of Lanmere. Sponsored by Lady Cecilia to be trained as a governess at Martimel Castle, feudal seat of Sir Everhard Martimel, Charlotte is literally groomed for Gothic heroism. Near the castle stands Lanmere Abbey, reputed to be haunted by the avenging specter of Albert Godolphin. Martimel Castle is equipped with the "martyr's turret," where the baronet, Sir Everhard, keeps a blue and silver bag containing documents of "incalculable consequence." Mysteries coagulate when the bag vanishes while Charlotte undergoes the standard Gothic crisis by being seized, mantled, and carriaged by rude strangers. In the midst of her ordeal, Charlotte is chided by the pragmatic Amelia Darcy, the novel's denouncer of Gothic experience, who calmly remarks, "I assure you with some heat too, that there are Gothic buildings without spectres or legends of a ghastly nature attached to them; now what is a castle or abbey worth without such an appendage?" In due course, the secret will come forth from the bag. Charlotte will be legitimized as the lost daughter of Sir Everhard, while the explanation of her mother's flight will also be forthcoming from the blue and silver pouch. The Austenesque naming and satiric tone argue strongly that Wilkinson was familiar with both *Northanger Abbey* [1–11] and *Pride and Prejudice,* and that her real intent was to mock the properties of the genre that had made her rich and famous in this late Gothic. Her anti-Gothic voice in the novel, Amelia Darcy, has the last word on the no-longer-tolerable artificialities of the dying form: "A castle, a turret, a winding staircase, an assassin, a suicide, a spectre, an imprisoned damsel, and a variant knight; surely these are ingredients enough, and I want nothing but the pen of Mrs. Radcliffe to give it a descriptive effect."

1-412. Wilkinson, Sarah. Zittaw the Cruel; or, The Woodsman's Daughter: A Polish Romance. B. Mace, n.d. (1) (SB)

Probably published around 1810, the novel is a conscious imitation of that peculiar branch of the Gothic made popular by Charlton in *Phedora; or, The*

Forest of Minski [1–62]. The incredibly sadistic father also has a Gothic ancestor in Moore's vile and violent *Zeluco* [1–268]. Wilkinson knew how to bring into conjunction the extremes of tenderness and brutality so as to produce the maximum sentimental-repulsive excitement.

1–413. Wolfstein; or, The Mysterious Bandit: A Terrific Romance, To Which Is Added, The Bronze Statue: A Pathetic Tale. J. Bailey, 1800. (5) (SB)
The crudest of bluebooks, this plagiarized abridgment of various *Räuber-roman* is two stories in one. The publisher specified an exact number of pages to be filled, and the bluebooker has done just that. Wolfstein is both noble outlaw and vicious charlatan, but the character is etched with the roughest strokes imaginable. The name is significant, however, for P. B. Shelley may well have obtained the name of his morose hero in *Saint Irvyne* [1–350] from this lurid little shocker. In *Shilling Shockers of the Gothic School*, W. W. Watt has noted the fact that in 1803 "Shelley and his schoolmates at Sion House were resorting 'under the rose' to a low circulating library in Brentford for the treasured bluebooks."

1–414. Wood, Mrs. Sally Sayward Barrell Keating (U.S.). **Julia and the Illuminated Baron: A Novel Founded on Recent Facts Which Have Transpired in the Course of the Late Revolution of Moral Principles in France.** Oracle Press, 1800. (3)
Maine's answer to Radcliffe, Godwin, and Lewis, Wood advanced the cause of American Gothic by joining the techniques of the Goths with the radical ideas of the age of revolution. *Julia and the Illuminated Baron* is a terrifying and melodramatic picture of the secret activities of the French society of Illuminati. The baron's enlightenment or illumination resembles the recognition that comes to the Marquis of G. in another Gothic novel of secret revolutionary groups, Grosse's *Horrid Mysteries* [1–139]. Julia too is not an exact reproduction of the standard shrieking maiden of the Gothic, but a young woman of considerable intellectual tenacity who becomes ensnared in the web of radical thought dominating the decade of revolution. Her psychological struggles and force of mind are comparable to the heroines of another American Gothic pioneer and contemporary of Wood, Charles Brockden Brown [1–46]. Very little has been written on Brown's Gothic contemporaries. An old but not outdated survey is Oral Coad, "The Gothic Element in American Literature before 1835," *Journal of English and Germanic Philology* 24 (1925), 72–93.

1–415. Woodfall, Sophia. **Rosa; or, The Child of the Abbey.** J. F. Hughes, 1804. (1)
A sentimental Gothic revival of Regina Maria Roche's 1796 deluxe tale of maidenly distress, *The Children of the Abbey* [1–324].

1-416. C. F. W. (Germany). Die Brautschau; oder, Der Kuss des Schreckens auf der Burg Nothweiler (The Unveiling of the Bride; or, The Kiss of Terror at Castle Nothweiler). Johann Adam Creutz, 1796. (2)

The *Schauer-roman* makes use of the folklore motifs of the icy kiss and the corpse bride. The castle itself is fully furnished with Gothic appliances.

1-417. Yorke, Mrs. R. M. P. The Valley of Collares; or, The Cavern of Horrors: A Romance. Minerva-Press, 1800. (1)

A fake translation from the Portuguese, the romance is a monastic shocker that conveys its heroine from cavern to convent and back to cave again. Yorke drew freely upon various grotto Gothics and also built her awesome abbey of Collares on a number of ready-made foundations. After writing this very conservative religious Gothic, she would break loose into grotesque fantasy in *The Haunted Palace* [1–418] of the following year.

1-418. Yorke, Mrs. R. M. P. The Haunted Palace; or, The Horrors of Ventoliene. Earle & Hemet, 1801. (1) (SB)

Bound in blue covers, Yorke's second Gothic is an album of lurid and sensational moments of horror that breaks away from the moderate terrors of *The Valley of Collares* [1–417]. The story begins with a Gothic roar at the foot of an erupting Mount Vesuvius with old Michael shouting to Edward Fitzallan, "I will pursue the wretch to the confines of hell itself." The island of Ventoliene near Naples is the location of the haunted palace. The bloody trail of his brother-in-law soon leads old Michael and Edward to this colossal and isolated ruin, the abode of the mysterious Vashti and the headquarters as well of the depraved Count St. Prie. Beyond the crumbling portals of the palace await all the unique horrors of Ventoliene. These include a fall through the rotten flooring at one point into an Egyptianized vault, below which Michael suddenly finds himself "astride a marble sphinx." Such a plunge through weakened flooring into a grotesque burial chamber filled with Gothic rubbish is one of Yorke's unique entries in the ledger of Gothic events and would be used later by Sir Walter Scott to precipitate the death of Amy Robsart in *Kenilworth* (1821). A pure Gothic novel in the complimentary sense, *The Haunted Palace* is intricately plotted but defies summary. The book aims at and frequently attains some unmatched blue-fire effects, as in one scene where "the fiends formed a circle round the trembling group, and, while the whole system of nature appeared convulsed by contending elements, the horrid phantoms performed a mystic dance." There is no Radcliffean reticence here—just uninhibited Gothic fantasy done with the zest for the irrational seen earlier in Beckford's *Vathek* [1–25].

1-419. Young, Mary Julia. Rose-Mount Castle; or, False Report. Minerva-Press, 1798. (4)

An average romance of the ruin, this mild-mannered Gothic appears to draw most of its situations from the Radcliffean modifications of Regina

Maria Roche's *Clermont* [1-325], also published by Minerva-Press in 1798. Like so many first Gothic attempts, *Rose-Mount Castle* shows the timidity of the learner along with the potential for better Gothic work to follow.

1-420. Young, Mary Julia. **Moss Cliff Abbey; or, The Sepulchral Harmonist: A Mysterious Tale.** J. F. Hughes, 1803. (1)
Mary Julia Young's Gothic night thoughts reflect the influence of her famous relative, Edward Young. Delight in ruins, eerie music, the pleasures of sorrow, and the morbid sentiments of a pair of runaway lovers who have strayed into the Gothic world, George and Harriet Newton, render the work a novel in the tradition of Henry Mackenzie but dressed in Gothic costume.

1-421. Ziegenhirt, Sophia F. **The Orphan of Tintern Abbey.** Minerva-Press, 1816. (4)
With apologies to Wordsworth, this sentimental Gothic conducts the education of its heroine in the shadow of one of England's most romantic ruins. The work also has the strong features of historical romance and only a fading reminder of the Gothic novel at its most terrific. What we see here and elsewhere in the years after 1814 is a shift away from Gothic excess and a movement toward the pure historical romances of early Scott.

1-422. Zschokke, Johann Heinrich Daniel (Germany). **Aballino, der grosse Bandit (Aballino, the Great Bandit).** Christian Ludwig Friedrich Apitz, 1794. Trans. by M. G. Lewis under the title *The Bravo of Venice*, J. F. Hughes, 1805; *Le Brigand de Venise*, Laffite Reprints, 1978. (2) (SB)
Zschokke's *Räuber-roman* was also condensed into a *Räuber-spiel* or robber play in 1795. Like Vulpius's *Rinaldo Rinaldini* [1-390], Zschokke's work enjoyed an immense wave of imitation and established itself as a model for the figure of the noble outlaw second only in importance to Schiller's notable *Die Räuber* [1-337]. In his clever and innovative translation, Lewis added characters and further Gothified the Venetian setting while retaining Zschokke's simple plot of double identity and patriotic masquerade. Count Rosalvo, a high-minded Neapolitan, arrives in Venice under the guise of Count Flodoardo and offers his services to the republic, which is being undermined by gangs of terrorists. To penetrate their councils and to uncover their evil plans, Rosalvo assumes a second disguise as the hideous Aballino, the fierce rogue chieftain. Goodness masquerading as depravity became a romantic theme that would fasten itself upon the imagination of Gothicists and Byronists alike. After numerous intrigues and near-brushes with death, the ugly Aballino is proclaimed the savior of Venice; casting aside the mask of evil, he wins the niece of the Doge, Rosabella of Corfu, and in an echo of Otway's famous title, Venice is preserved.

2
The Residual Gothic Impulse 1824–1873

Benjamin Franklin Fisher IV

During the period of 1824–1873, the creation of horror fiction remained a vital pursuit, if frequently subordinated to other literary art. The chief overshadowing force was the concern for realism in the great Victorian novel, as it was fashioned by such writers as Charles Dickens, W. M. Thackeray, George Eliot, Anthony Trollope, and George Meredith. Since verisimilitude was linked to the broader Victorian intentness upon "respectability" in fiction, there was little chance that horror could be brought to the fore, except in atypical circumstances. During these years nearly every major and many minor British and American writers—chiefly remembered for other achievements—at some point attempted a few works of horror, mystery, or detection in the Gothic tradition. It is these lesser works by major writers that place them tangentially within the confines of this *Anatomy*. In particular, many British writers, because they brought out works of overt horror, linger today only as minor figures at the peripheries of greater literary currents.

By way of illustration, consider the fiction of Elizabeth C. Gaskell and William Makepeace Thackeray. Both are ordinarily treated as social novelists. Gaskell's tales of terror are cited because they were several and because some are excellent representatives of the horrific, whereas Thackeray's acknowledged respect for the "dark-and-stormy-night" rhetoric typifying tales by W. Harrison Ainsworth, Edward Bulwer-Lytton, and G. P. R. James (in Chapter Six of *Vanity Fair*) does not warrant his inclusion in the period of the residual Gothic impulse. This bit of mock-horrific is too fleeting. Unless more than transient use of horror elements occurs within an individual work, it receives no mention in this chapter. (Thackeray's comic devil stories, which first came out in magazines, but which are not so fine as to merit special citation, are mentioned in entries for recent anthologies including them.)

The significant trend in horror tales of this period mirrored developments in the greater Victorian and American novels then emerging into a solidly artistic and serious genre. There was a shift from physical fright, expressed through numerous outward miseries and villainous actions, to psychological fear. The inward turn in fiction emphasized motivations, not their overt, terrifying consequences. The ghost-in-a-bedsheet gave way, as it did literally in Charles Dickens's *A Christmas Carol,* to the haunted psyche, a far more significant force in the "spooking" of hapless victims.

The years between C. R. Maturin's *Melmoth the Wanderer* (1820) and Dickens's *The Pickwick Papers* (1837) are approached hesitantly by most literary historians because this era is neither conventionally "romantic" nor "Victorian." The period is customarily and uneasily bypassed, with the consequence that much of fruitfulness within the span is left to oblivion. It is true that the original Gothic impulse from the eighteenth century had grown more residual as this generation grew increasingly unable to reconcile art, particularly literary exaggeration, with everyday life. Ironically, two of the long-time publishers of Gothic fiction, through the sheer volume of their output, further weakened the demand for horror tales. Ultimately, the names of this publishing pair, William Lane and A. K. Newman, were taken in vain as a consequence of their hallmark commodity. In *Blackwood's Edinburgh Magazine,* critic Thomas Hamilton deridingly remarked: "But a work more thoroughly absurd and worthless . . . we never met except from the press of Leadenhall Street" (January 1826)—the headquarters of the notorious Minerva-Press, famous as a result of its association with Gothic novels. Hamilton again sniped at the enterprise while reviewing *Matilda: A Tale,* a currently popular work: "There appeared to us something Lane-and-Newmanish about it [*Matilda*], a certain indescribable redolence of Leadenhall Street, by no means tempting to nearer approach."

At this juncture, prior to treating the history of individual currents, writers, or works, we might profitably realize an overall fact about the inherent qualities of fiction during the years covered here. With the deaths of Maturin and Sir Walter Scott in 1824 and 1832 respectively, a feeling that an era in the history of the novel had closed took hold upon many critics and fictionists alike. This notion intensified as a result of the continuing predilection for verse, the generic earmark of the romantic movement. Wordsworth, Coleridge, and Southey were still alive, and the recent deaths of the second-generation romantic poets—John Keats, Percy Bysshe Shelley, and Lord Byron—would perpetuate interest in their poems. The stars of Alfred Tennyson and Robert Browning began to shine within poetry circles during the 1830s and 1840s. In combination with such circumstances, and as a result of the feeble imitations of the Radcliffe-Lewis type of Gothicism, fiction deteriorated into a pretty dreary state. It is no wonder that when a resurgence of the novel began with the advent of Charles Dickens, Edward Bulwer-Lytton, the sisters Brontë, and W. M. Thackeray, a revulsion against shopworn horror tales should mount. With certain few exceptions, Gothic current had to take a back seat until fiction had acquired the status of genuine, high art. By the early 1870s that time had come, and from the time of the apprentice work of Thomas Hardy, a new self-confidence was evident in the works of fiction writers. Thus, the Gothic could once more openly dress in full colors. That it did, with additions from psychological methodology wending their way through the novels and tales of the day. The chronicling of such works thus influenced—like Le Fanu's masterpiece, "Green Tea" (1873)—is, however, the province of another literary historian. Nevertheless, the Gothic flame continued to burn, if with low heat in many cases, during the years from James Hogg's *Confessions of a Justified Sinner* [2–48] through the appearances of Thomas Hardy's *Desperate Remedies* [2–44] and Rhoda Broughton's *Twilight Stories* [2–12].

One agency more than any other kept Gothicism alive from the 1820s through the 1840s: the horror fiction of *Blackwood's Edinburgh Magazine,* known more simply as *Blackwood's* or "Maga." In the face of rivals, the Scottish periodical enjoyed a steadily accruing popularity. An editorial prefacing the 1826 volume immodestly sums up the magazine's growth: "We may say without fear of contradiction, that our magazine has excited more attention, whether for praise or blame, than any periodical which ever existed in this country." *Blackwood's* published some of the best brief horror tales of the era, and the name of the magazine is indissolubly linked with this type of fiction in the minds of many. Mudford, Bulwer-Lytton, Hogg, and MacNish, as well as a host of other major and minor names, were numbered among its authors; and Poe, on the American literary scene, lauded the tales "in those earlier numbers of Blackwood . . . relished by every man of genius." High praise indeed, but it was merited.

The *Blackwood's* school of fiction is varied so far as theme and form are concerned, but several types stand out. Horror was linked with "sensations" in many of the better tales; that is, although physical pain, torture, and discomfort were staples, the stuff and substance of the works centered on mental predicaments. The first type is demonstrable in such stories as Thomas

Gillespie's "Ann Stavert and Amos Bradley" (February 1824), in which Ann, young wife to an elderly miser, chooses Amos for her lover. Their sexual pleasures are treated fairly overtly for the times, although they suffer considerable emotional anguish, all neatly detailed, after the murder of the miser and again when Ann mounts the scaffold. This tale is fine modified Gothicism in its presentation of a reality that can be as terrible as any supernatural phenomenon. Another piece, "Extracts from Grosschen's Diary," also delineates terrors of nonsupernatural origin. The maniac describes his inner states as he contemplates the murder of his mistress; simultaneously he conveys sensory details when, for instance, he tells the priest about fondling the dead girl's cold, bloody breasts.

"The Man in the Bell" and "The Iron Shroud" [both 2–6] offer psychological dramas of overwrought characters beset by physical torture, which in turn leads to insight and release. In the first, a man is unwittingly trapped beneath a huge bell, high above solid ground, and the sounds and burns caused by the sweeping of the great bell drive him into delirium. In the second, Vivenzio is described in all the intensity of his emotional crisis while realizing that he will be crushed to death. Similarly, Bulwer-Lytton's "Monos and Daimonos" [2–17] depicts emotional horrors, as the narrator attempts again and again, unsuccessfully, to elude his terrifying *Doppelgänger*. Although it first appeared in the *New Monthly Magazine* (1830), it could just as easily have come from *Blackwood's*.

In like manner, the shockers of Elizabeth C. Gaskell [2–37, 2–38] appeared mainly in Dickens's magazines *Household Words* and *All the Year Round*, two later nineteenth-century purveyors of horror tales—and appropriate publications for one whose first piece of writing had appeared years earlier in *Blackwood's*. "The Old Nurse Story" resembles the narrative of Nelly Dean from *Wuthering Heights* [2–11] in its theme of frustrated love and spectral revenge. "Lois the Witch" and "The Grey Woman" offer readers thrills rooted in reality, with no need for ghostly diablerie to create fright. These two stories blend Gaskell's overriding tendencies toward realism with the tale of sensation, making her technique rank with Dickens's own as well as Meredith's (less frequently) and Wilkie Collins's habits of terror.

Another type of *Blackwood's* fiction mingled the horrific with the comic in such a manner that what opens in a seemingly "straight" horrific tone or situation proves in the end to be a spoof—the consequences, doubtless, of many writers' perception that horror was akin to the ludicrous if not properly maintained. Such mockery began just as soon as "Maga" started regularly to feature fiction—witness "Singular Recovery from Death" (1821), "Procurante" (1823), "The Last Man" (1826), and "Crocodile Island" (1833), to cite but a few. The last tale gives us a narrator whose account of adventure on a tropical island piles on horrors to this conclusion: "The fact is . . . I have just got to that point in a tale I am writing for next month's Blackwood, and curse me if I know how to get naturally away from Crocodile Island." The third tale employs the device of dreaming for its effect. The first two contain narrators whose garrishly painted "terrors" result from drunkenness. There are also comic devil stories in abundance during the earlier years of this historical period, and they have had far-reaching effects.

Longer, serialized terror tales ran side by side with shorter items in *Blackwood's,* among the better of them William Mudford's "First and Last" and Samuel Warren's "Passages from the Diary of a Late Physician" [2–100], the last appearing ultimately in volume form. The installments of "Passages" for February 1831 reveal Warren's familarity with Maturin, whose writing "excite[s] the most fearful and horrific ideas in the minds of his readers," a method Warren never drops from his own story, replete as it is with razor-wielding maniacs, dizzying sensations of fear, and supernaturalism. The section centers upon the maniac, whose piercing, eerie laughter might well derive from *Melmoth the Wanderer* [1–244].

Not all novels of the *Blackwood's* stamp were literal progeny of "Maga." James Hogg's *Confessions of a Justified Sinner* [2–48] and James Dalton's *The Gentleman in Black* [2–29] represent the sober and comic varieties. The first, and better known, presents the theme of the evil double, so fascinating to Gothic writers. Religious and social currents infiltrate this book, written by one whose affiliation with *Blackwood's,* as the "Ettrick Shepherd," produced an active awareness of weird fiction. *The Gentleman in Black* offers variations on the pact-with-the-devil plot in its ironic mastery of Satan by a shrewd old lawyer. A quarter of a century later, George Meredith, usually consigned to nonhorrific categories by historians of the novel, produced another comic masterpiece of outwitting the devil, *Farina: A Legend of Cologne* [2–69].

Across the sea in America, a cultural lag fostered trans-Atlantic dependencies upon the British literary tradition, although dissenting voices could be heard. The fad for literary annuals and gift books allowed those organs to purvey a Gothicism often as gilt-edged and frail-spined as the books themselves. Washington Irving worked in the vein of sportive Gothicism, but his tongue-in-cheek attitude toward the supernatural made for delightful ambiguities. Those standard touchstones in anthologies of American literature, "Rip Van Winkle" and "The Legend of Sleepy Hollow," rightly fall within the purlieus of horror literature, although the author's light touches in the first, with its brief description of majestic but awesome scenery and its grotesque dwarfs with their otherworldly nature, provide a companion piece to *Blackwood's* fiction of alcohol, because Rip's peregrinations in the Catskills are linked with drunkenness. Even "The Spectre Bridegroom" [2–51] is couched in comic circumstances, which, like those in "The Legend of Sleepy Hollow," imply foibles in the personalities of characters or readers who too credulously accept "ghostly" happenings at face value. Child of neoclassic standards that he was, Irving customarily adopted a playful tone in producing Gothic tales. An exception is "The Story of the Young Italian" from

Tales of a Traveller [2–52], a much-neglected book. Here, the balance of physical gruesomeness with heightened emotional states is truly accomplished.

Others on the American literary scene in this era dabbled in the horrific, although they just as emphatically condemned its excesses. The most notable double opinion of Gothicism is found in the writings of James Kirke Paulding. His typical ploy is to deplore the exaggerations of horror writing, and then to suggest that most horror writing *is* overdone and inferior to the productions of a Fielding or some other realist. In Paulding's *Koningsmarke* [2–73], for example, he never hesitates to inveigh against diablerie on one page, or over several, and then to invoke the spectral or apparently supernatural elsewhere. Like Irving, whose brother-in-law he was, Paulding typically adopted a narrative stance to alert readers to his deprecation of the weird and unreal. Two outstanding pieces are "Cobus Yerks" [2–74], which first appeared in the *The Atlantic Souvenir* (1828), and "The Vroucolacas: A Tale" [2–75] from *Graham's Magazine* (1846). Both point up the gullibility of characters who subscribe too literally to "ghostly" visitants, the first involving drunkenness, the second an unquestioning superstition about vampires. "Cobus Yerks" enjoyed great popularity and was reprinted many times. The great black dog with the phosphorescent head may well provide a model for Doyle's more famous *Hound of the Baskervilles*, whose supernatural nature is finally disproved. "The Vroucolacas" merits reprinting as a comic treatment of vampirism, which occurs fairly early in the history of vampire stories (John William Polidori's *The Vampyre* [1–304] is generally recognized as the first vampire story in English literature).

The name of William Gilmore Simms flickers among those of greater luminaries in American literature. His ventures into Gothicism merit attention. Much of his horrific writings appeared in annuals and other periodicals in the 1820s and 1830s, a period when many American critics were quick to censure "German" productions. This term is synonymous with "Gothic," and many hair-raising tales elicited the disapprobation of those who bracketed such work with the lesser names of German literature, as Poe noted some years later in his preface to *Tales of the Grotesque and Arabesque* [2–80]. Simms was eager to establish his reputation as a man of letters. He adapted popular models in such works as *Martin Faber* [2–90], *Carl Werner* [2–89], and *The Book of My Lady* [2–88]. The first reveals an increasing strength in psychological dimension within Gothic fiction, as the criminal psyche and its origins are unfolded. "The Plank," in *The Book of My Lady*, approaches Poe's visions of demons and cosmological upheaval. From *The Wigwam and Cabin* [2–92], we might notice "Grayling; or, Murder Will Out," which Poe called the best American ghost story of his day, in which a spectral visitant informs on his murderer; and "Sergeant Barnacle; or, The Raftsman of the Edisto," which demonstrates the absurd lengths to which Gothicism could go. A seduced girl hangs herself with a pocket handkerchief, and her former lover produces the same item when he hangs the pathetic villain. Many of Simms's other works included Gothic elements, and his interest in criminal mentality and whatever environmental influences affect it are especially significant as pioneer work in that vein, but too many false echoes sound through his horror tales.

Two Americans who adapted Gothicism to American themes and characters were William Cullen Bryant—not one generally placed within a Gothic context—and George Lippard, a friend of Poe, whose work is seldom mentioned in other than Gothic contexts. Bryant's forays into the supernatural or pseudosupernatural were part of a trend during America's formative years so far as a native literature is concerned, but they stand out from the morasses of hollow-sounding terror fiction of the marketplace. "The Indian Spring" [2–14], "A Border Tradition" [2–14], "The Skeleton's Cave" [2–13], and "Medfield" [2–13] do not create terror for terror's sake. They transfer the haunted castles in the Apennines to American cabins or camps in the wilderness, and the Gothic villains are Americanized into recognizable national types, with native superstitions replacing centuries-old family curses.

George Lippard's *The Quaker City* [2–66] provides the best example of American literary Gothicism inextricably linked to pornography, a bond that is part of the tradition from Walpole to the present, with Phyllis A. Whitney's *The Glass Flame* (1978) a legitimate descendant of *The Castle of Otranto* [1–398]. Lippard's horrors are not otherworldly; indeed, public outcry against him resulted from his sensational realities. To the mid-1840s the sex scenes in *The Quaker City* would have cast those in *The Monk* [1–218], a shocker in its day, into shade, and they titillated numbers of readers, despite critical objections to the work. Lippard's method of approaching the supernatural—but just approaching and then steering his reader onto another course—added appeal to his novel, although the primary emphasis is on the horrific grounded in realism, as Lippard himself embodied a great deal of the social critic.

The primary names of residual Gothic fame in America are Nathaniel Hawthorne, Herman Melville, and Edgar Allan Poe. All were readers of older Gothic works, and Poe turned to the writing of horror fiction with his lesson manual setting out *Blackwood's* formulae and attitudes in hand. Along with Henry James, whose major achievements in horror fiction belong to the next chapter (although two of his tales from the 1860s are cited here [2–54]), these three represent the high-watermark of nineteenth-century American Gothicism.

Eager to produce a genuine American mode, Hawthorne adapted the Gothic romance of Maturin and his predecessors to New England regions. *Fanshawe,* Hawthorne's first novel and published fiction, borrows from Gothic villainy in the ineffectual seducer, Butler, but character motivation is lamely developed in this apprentice work. More substantial efforts appear particularly in the shorter tales as attested by "Alice Doane's Appeal" [2–

45], too seldom reprinted, and "The Hollow of the Three Hills" [2–47]. The visionary elements in both place them in the nightmare conventions of Gothicism, and psychological portraiture indicated the paths into which Hawthorne was later to turn this tradition. Hints of forbidden, perhaps perverse, sexuality are embedded in "The Minister's Black Veil" [2–47] and other stories of this period. Later, "Ethan Brand" and "Young Goodman Brown" maintain such substance, although the second story far surpasses the first, and may be Hawthorne's finest tale.

The Scarlet Letter [2–46] artistically mingles wide-ranging moral and emotional questions with probings of Gothic properties, such that one vitalizes the other. Roger Chillingworth, the aged leech and husband of Hester, is more than a simple version of the Gothic villain with an evil eye and threatening manner who viciously pursues innocence. His machinations could easily fit into a novel by Radcliffe or Lewis, but they stem from far more subtly characterized emotions and have further-reaching implications. Hester, too, is created after the dusky, alluring women in older Gothic fiction; but her physical beauty, ambiguous though it is, furnishes a fit emblem for the inner richness of her character.

Herman Melville's *Moby-Dick* [2–68], along with Hawthorne's *The Scarlet Letter*, marks the full flowering of the Gothic novel in America. Whereas Hawthorne substituted the dark forest, the old jail, and the gloomy environs of Salem Village for European Gothic settings, Melville chooses the omen-ridden ambience of New England seaports, forecastle of the *Pequod*, and the treacherous sea itself. The figures of Ahab and the great white whale embody the traits of evil and destructive passions. Fedallah and his consorts add a note of supernaturalism to this tale, and the sailors' superstitions add substance to the glittering "lights," the terrifying storm, and the unsettling whale itself. As in previous Gothic novels, the "villain," as Ahab is in part, meets destruction at the close; and at the end, like the Gothic villain, Ahab is a "grand, ungodly, god-like man."

Although his successes lay outside the novel form, the tales of Edgar Allan Poe are accepted as the peak in American Gothicism during the nineteenth century. Poe is "residual" because his tales were considered anachronistic in an age when Americans were moving toward the sunnier thinking of an Emerson, or along lines of realism, which featured the common man as hero. Poe is also residual in an ironic frame: he modified the previous generation's shopworn Gothicism into the flesh and blood of psychological and symbolic literature that has influenced nearly every subsequent writer of horror, fantasy, and detective fiction.

Aiming above all else to succeed as a poet, Poe was forced to turn his hand to prose fiction in order to earn a living. A reader of Gothics from his youth, Poe gave himself a thorough course in how to write a *Blackwood's* article, and his works often seem to out-Walpole Walpole in this respect. From such apprentice pieces as "Metzengerstein," a fairly unoriginal if well-written piece based on "German" models, Poe moved to mockery of the very type of terror tale that brought success to many. Readers frequently still misunderstand his intentions in "Bon-Bon," "Loss of Breath," or "King Pest," unless they comprehend that these, and other early pieces such as his prize-winning "Ms. Found in a Bottle," were once slated for publication as *Tales of the Folio Club*, a book containing parodies of then-current fictional modes and writers. The book *qua* book was never published because established writers and publishers discouraged the young writer, stating that his humor was so subtle as to go unnoticed by all but a few. Consequently, he circulated in periodicals and newspapers work that, detached from its context, accumulated greater ambiguity.

From his early blending of the serious and comic, Poe moved to far greater higher Gothicism. "Ligeia," "William Wilson," "The Fall of the House of Usher," "The Masque of the Red Death," "The Tell-Tale Heart," "The Black Cat," "The Cask of Amontillado"—standard anthology choices from his corpus—are horror tales, although to state merely this and no more is to do Poe an injustice. "Usher" in particular provides, among its other elements, a telling portrait of the romantic artist in the character of Roderick, himself named appropriately for the last of the great Gothic rulers of western Europe. Conversely, a comic reading is possible, in which the symbolic names, character types, and settings function as spoofs of traditional Gothic trappings.

Another infrequently analyzed Poe tale, "The System of Dr. Tarr and Professor Fether," published late in 1845, ought not to suffer neglect. Whatever else it may be, it serves by means of its sanity-insanity theme as a parody on those very Gothic devices Poe so deftly manipulated elsewhere—in "Mystification," "Usher," and "Masque," as well as throughout the detective or ratiocinative tales. The ingenuous narrator is readily misled by horrific surfaces, and his rueful end is couched in terms suggestive of the foolishness so frequently overtaking those too eager for, and too unquestioning about, horror fiction.

Haunted minds come to the fore more and more in Poe and his successors. The vision of desolation and fear in "Silence—A Fable" sires children in such spots as the opium visions in Dickens's *Edwin Drood* [2–34]. Poe was not simply joking in "How to Write a *Blackwood* Article" when he wrote: "Sensations are the great things after all. . . . If you wish to write forcibly . . . pay minute attention to the sensations." Equating the intangible, the emotional, and the psychic with the physical is, above all, his central artistic method. Readers who deplore the wealth of "description" in Poe's writing overlook its symbolic texture, a texture that gives concreteness to psychic phenomena, exemplified in an early tale, "Shadow—A Parable." In Poe's work a thing is never merely a "thing"; it is language. We may profitably see this method as his attempt to link essence with everyday comprehension. Poe's great contribution to the Gothic tradition is his ability to take the familiar shilling shocker and recast it into literature with frighteningly realistic implications. In most of his so-called supernatual tales lies evidence that no ghost is intended at all, but that such specters derive from the distorted consciousness of the narrators.

Now, we return once more to the British literary scene. Here the novel becomes the dominant form for the remainder of the nineteenth century, and developments in the horrific aspects of fiction are significant (not that short fiction enjoyed no successes during this period, either as worthwhile general literature or as fine ware in horror). An outstanding collection is Rhoda Broughton's *Twilight Stories*, published first as *Tales for Christmas Eve* [2–12], obviously a ploy to gain the holiday ghost story market. Her effort, gathered from the magazines, places her as a link between Poe and M. R. James. Her cameos present Poe's "terror of the soul," and one story, with its epistolary Mrs. Montresor, betrays a direct debt to "Amontillado." Her greater gift for sharp dialogue in more realistic social situations, however, overshadows her bent for weird creations.

The novels of William Harrison Ainsworth, G. P. R. James, and Edward Bulwer-Lytton are many, their unqualified successes are few, and their output of well-wrought horror fiction is minuscule. The old-fashioned novel of terror for terror's sake persisted throughout this period, although Ainsworth and Bulwer-Lytton modified its situations to contemporary scenes. From the later 1850s on into the 1870s critics affixed the label "sensation novel" to the heirs of the Ainsworth-Bulwer crime novel. Real-life horrors (such as bigamy, arson, poisoning, forging wills) take the place of supernaturalism, although there are dalliances with the weird in the works of Wilkie Collins, Le Fanu, and Braddon. Ainsworth attempted in *Rookwood* [2–1] to vie with the successes of Radcliffe. Chiefly a novel of horrors, *Rookwood* is important because its brutal realism aligns it with Bulwer-Lytton's crime fiction and Dickens's early work.

Similar in kind, although different in degree—because they do not move beyond the horrific, or if they do it is into sentimentality—are G. W. M. Reynolds's *Wagner, the Wehr-Wolf* [2–82], T. P. Prest's *Varney, the Vampire* [2–81], and G. P. R. James's *The Castle of Ehrenstein* [2–53], all dating from the later 1840s, the same period that brought forth *The Quaker City*, mentioned earlier. James departs from his typical sort of historical fiction—although the occurrences in *Ehrenstein* date from centuries past—to produce a good story. The vicissitudes of the young lovers, affected as they are by ghostly visitations, the evil pursuit of innocence, and the astounding revelation at the end, where the "supernaturalism" is explained, give this novel a Radcliffean overlay. So does the sentimentality, which verges at times on the mawkish. Mawkishness of tone is even more noticeable through pages of Wagner's plight (he exchanges infirmities of age for the horrors of werewolfery), although the sensationalism is painted in garish shades. Supernaturalism of even deeper dye adds thrills to the opening portion of *Varney*, as the vampire is introduced in fearsome terms because of his bloodlust *and* his rapacious sexual lust. Not much else makes for artistic appeal in such novels, although the penny-dreadful craze that swept Britain during these years accounts for the eagerness with which the works of Prest and Reynolds were sought.

A move toward the mainstream of British fiction, as we now survey it, occurs in Bulwer-Lytton. His crime novels, such as *Paul Clifford* [2–18], desensationalize the Faustian Gothic villain, à la Byron's heroes, into criminals of admirable parts. Bulwer, however, retained a fascination with situations of a beyond-life nature, and in *Zanoni*]2–20] and *A Strange Story*]2–19] he explores occultism of the sort pertinent to Rosicrucianism—although his characters move beyond the doctrines of that organization. The sympathetic criminal appears in subsequent fiction, perhaps the most famous personage being Lady Audley, the femme fatale of Mary Elizabeth Braddon's bestseller and semidetective novel, *Lady Audley's Secret* [2–9], whose madness is at last startlingly revealed, after bigamy, near-murder, and hatred have been paraded before us.

Poesque in their abrupt style, of which violence is the essence, Charlotte Brontë's *Jane Eyre* [2–10] and her sister Emily's *Wuthering Heights* [2–11] adapt the haunted castle to scenes common in the Yorkshire moors at the time. Like Poe, the Brontës' imaginations sensed the impact of horrors that occurred to plausible character creations in ordinary places. Rochester and Heathcliffe take Gothic passion and suffering of incredible dimensions and make it all the more devastating because they are real human beings suffering genuine emotional torments, such as any of us might. What seems mysterious about these characters and their environments is ultimately explainable in terms of strict realism, or psyches overwrought to planes of hysteria, evident at times in Jane, Catherine Earnshaw Linton, and Lockwood. No wonder there are visions to be seen! Nature's ambiguities abound in these books, doubtless the personal outlet for the authors' feelings about their wild Yorkshire surroundings. Furthermore, the natural scenes shift according to thoughts of beauty or terror within the characters, and neither exists in simplistic terms.

Charles Dickens's interest in the Gothic remained alive in his works for 35 years, and if he used to be touted as a realist, recent criticism recognizes the abundant use of fantasy (fantasy that does not avoid horrors) in his canon, and applauds it. Crime and criminals fascinated Dickens, and his novels point up his increasing employment of both as important, often central, strands in fiction skillfully woven. *Oliver Twist* takes its place—although it betrays greater psychological sophistication in the handling of narrative—with the crime stories, the "Newgate Fiction," of Ainsworth and Bulwer-Lytton. The wicked Jonas's guilt and dream of murder in *Martin Chuzzlewit* [2–33] pave the way for the opium visions and other bizarre sensations of Jasper in *Edwin Drood* [2–34]. *Bleak House* [2–30] builds biting social criticism upon Gothic foundations, intensified by frightening villains, or villainous types, such as Krook, Hortense, or Tulkinghorn. Their evil countenances, speeches, and machinations make them fit companions for so-called good or respectable types embodying less sensational but no less powerful or terrifying inclinations. Vholes, the vampire lawyer; Mrs. Jellyby, the philanthropist; Skimpole, the greedy and thoughtless—all add to the creation of horror in the social and legal spheres. *Bleak House* is also part detective novel, a transition piece between the tales of Poe and the mystery-detective fiction of Wilkie Collins.

The social arena is again furnished victims in *Little Dorrit* [2–32] and *Our Mutual Friend* [2–35]. Both draw heavily on Gothicism, although old Mrs. Clennam's house, decaying and unsound, is much more than just another Gothic castle. Like the hypocritical, masochistic old woman herself, and the facet of society she symbolizes, the house *seems* imposing. Both fall in sensational circumstances. Rigaud (alias Blandois, a devil figure) may remind us of the bygone foreign villain, but he also rises to proportions larger than those of a cardboard ranter and plotter. *Our Mutual Friend*, Dickens's last completed novel, piles fear and suspense fairly high. The lost will, the mystery of Rokesmith's past, the night journeys during which Bradley Headstone dogs the footsteps of Eugene Wrayburn, his rival for Lizzie Hexham's hand, the attack on Wrayburn, and the final murder-suicide of Headstone and Riderhood are calculated to hold the reader's attention. Headstone comes to us with a subtly developed psychological makeup, and his rages provide terrors of the soul—his own and the reader's.

The Mystery of Edwin Drood, left incomplete when Dickens died, indicates his abiding impulse toward the Gothic, highlighted by the use of the cathedral as Gothic setting. The opium visions of John Jasper involve eroticism mingled with violence, and they provide us with an anatomy of a tempestuous psyche. Apparently, Jasper strangles his nephew, Edwin Drood, as a consequence of the uncle's frustrated love for Rosa Bud. Just where he may have deposited the corpse is a matter for speculation, as is the identity of the detective, Dick Datchery, who appears in later chapters. The depths of the criminal mind, however, are crucial in this novel, more so than the surfaces of sensationalism in sex, drug addiction, and murder. How far Dickens exceeds a work like Meadows Taylor's *The Confessions of a Thug* [2–96], a part-fictional, part-factual account of criminal atrocities, is clear on every page.

Dickens's contribution to the supernatural field is critical, as Mike Ashley reminds us, "in that more than almost any other editor in the nineteenth century, Dickens encouraged spooky stories for the Christmas issues of his magazines (*Household Words* 1850–59; *All the Year Round* 1859–70)" (*Who's Who in Horror and Fantasy Fiction*, 1978). His own stories contain elements of the macabre, occult, and supernatural; these stories, taken with the terrors found in his novels, "all reflect the greater horror of life in Victorian London."

The final examples of residual Gothicism are Wilkie Collins, J. Sheridan
Le Fanu, and Thomas Hardy. All wrote much, Collins's later work suffering
from his inclinations toward social criticism. Le Fanu's work is uneven because of repetitiousness in character types and plotting, not to mention dullness in many spots. A close associate of Dickens, Collins published many of
his earlier short stories in the older writer's magazines, with many appearing
regularly in Dickens's Christmas annuals. These short works owe debts to
Poe, whose tales had become popular in England during the 1850s. They are
frequently concerned with emotional sensation in the *Blackwood's* manner,
particularly with dreams, and they generally furnish plausible foundations
for the apparent ghostliness that maintains suspense.

Collins's most notable successes, *The Woman in White* [2–26] and *The
Moonstone* [2–24], blend detection with atmospheric elements fashioned to
create uneasiness in readers, just as guilt, power, lust, and outrage dog the
characters. *The Woman in White* is no detective novel proper, in that no official sleuth appears. Walter Hartwright's quest after the welfare of his wom-
enfolk, tense with adventure, terror, and near-death, approximate the course
of a detective's quest. The journeys into the past, however, take on symbolic
qualities that do not appear as usual provender in most present-day detective fiction. The use of documentary testimony for clarification of the plot
here, as well as in *The Moonstone,* did become popular methodology in horror
fiction, giving the *outré* a degree of verisimilitude unknown in the Walpole-
Lewis school. A contemporary of Collins who seized upon this method to
produce a gruesome mystery story of poisoning for insurance money is
"Charles Felix," and *The Notting Hill Mystery* [2–36] delighted readers of its
serial installments in *Once a Week* in 1892. Poe's influence may also be detected in this work, for his Dupin tales had given realism to atrocities by
means of documentary evidence (see, for example, "The Murders in the Rue
Morgue" in *Collected Works* [2–77]). Another work that charts the Victorians'
eagerness for works mixing horrors with mundaneness is Catherine Crowe's
The Night Side of Nature [2–27], first published in 1849, which sets forth factual and fictional accounts.

Sheridan Le Fanu at his best is indeed the evil genius of later Victorian
horror fictions, and his better work draws a fitting close to an epoch. His literary career parallels that of Dickens, extending from the late 1830s through
the early 1870s. Le Fanu stands out as one who remained too constrictively
within the confines of the melodramatic, much to the detriment of his lasting artistry. His first ghost story, "The Ghost and the Bone-Setter" [2–62], is
comic, as are others, notably "The Drunkard's Dream" and "The Vision of
Tom Chuff" [2–62], all of them cast in the mold of *Blackwood's* and Poe's alcoholic tales. A more sober note sounds in "The Evil Guest," "Schalken the
Painter," and "The Murdered Cousin" [all 2–60], this last a study for the
later *Uncle Silas* [2–63]. Le Fanu's method of low-keyed innuendo produces a

terror that mounts steadily, although he may descend from Poe in certain features of "sensations."

Le Fanu's novels are a motley lot, many padded or otherwise tailored to suit the needs of magazine publication. *The House by the Churchyard* [2–61] and *Uncle Silas* overshadow the other novels, although *Checkmate* [2–59], *Wylder's Hand* [2–64], and *All in the Dark* [2–57] are worthwhile. Because the events in *The House by the Churchyard* occur in times past, the horrors effect greater plausibility than they might were they to occur in the midnineteenth century. Crime is intensified in this novel by means of the Gothic machinery of cryptic sensationalism, curses that doom their victims, and dark-and-stormy-night scenes.

In *Uncle Silas* the timeworn theme of the persecuted maiden recurs, but Le Fanu, in an unusually creative burst, gives it new life. Maud Ruthyn's emotional states, as well as those of others, are portrayed with a depth and skill that is not ordinarily found in many Gothic novels. Her first view of Bartram, which contrasts its one-time pomp and opulence with the present "forlorn character of desertion and decay," as well as her confronting Uncle Silas's bewildering expression—"was it derision, or anguish, or cruelty, or patience"?—give us rhetoric of rich texture. Silas's controlled balance of his courtly mask and his evil aims are a tribute to Le Fanu's art at its greatest, and the old man's wickedness is accorded heightened relief because of the flatter characterization in Mme. de la Rougierre or Dudley Ruthyn. *Uncle Silas* marks a high point along the way to later, greater depths of abnormal psychology in fiction.

Le Fanu's *Checkmate* and Thomas Hardy's first novel, bearing the intriguing title *Desperate Remedies* [2–44], both appeared in book form in 1871. They are detective novels in several respects, and *Checkmate* bears the marks of the Poe-Dickens-Collins school, although with the matter of Walter Longluse's plastic surgery the identifying hands and voice take this novel outside the earlier writer's limits of mystery. *Desperate Remedies,* refashioned after the advice of George Meredith from a social criticism tract into more palatable fare, takes us from realms of Gothic suspense of the type produced by Radcliffe and Braddon into the regions of the modern British novel. An admirer of Ainsworth and Collins, as well as of the sensual poetry of Swinburne, Hardy unfolds bigamy with particular hints of incest and lesbianism, illegitimacy, and thrilling crime. Cythera Graye's dream of trouble prior to her wedding and her waking nightmarish visions, horrific though they be, move us toward areas usually considered the territories of a Henry James or a William Faulkner. The persecuted protagonist of Gothic tradition is hybridized with those of classical tragedy in Hardy's great novels, and the product is a character of new emotional constitution. *Desperate Remedies* is one of the last great Gothic novels of the nineteenth century; its Janus face closes one era in literary history as it begins another.

Bibliography

The titles chosen for this bibliography follow the overriding principle discussed earlier concerning Elizabeth Gaskell as opposed to W. M. Thackeray. That is, each title contributes toward a larger composite of the horrific during the Victorian Age, as tiny bits coalesce to form a great mosaic. Indubitably, such works as Thomas P. Prest's *Varney, the Vampire* [2-81] and the tales of Edgar Allan Poe belong in this literature. These works also illustrate two applied selection criteria. Besides being horrifically significant, they demonstrate historical importance—in the case of *Varney,* because it flouted conventions of realism in its unabashed horrors at a time when novelists and critics alike were giving palms to ordinary life and characters—and literary excellence in the case of Poe's fiction. These criteria govern other entries. For example, one might not expect the name of James Kirke Paulding to crop up here, but it merits some mention because he ventured time and again toward those regions that he so roundly, and satirically, condemned when done to excess. At times the rubric of the horrific makes for strange bedfellows.

I have also tried to remember the availability of texts when selecting these titles. Nearly all have appeared in reprints after the first edition. Bibliographical tangles too complex to be noted in a guide such as this are the customary opponents of direct, rapid access to many horrific titles from the nineteenth century. Consequently, the cream of voluminous outpourings, like those of Mary Elizabeth Braddon or G. W. M. Reynolds, has been skimmed for the benefit of modern readers. With short fiction we encounter even more frustrating bibliographical snarls, although the anthologies of Everett F. Bleiler, Hugh Lamb, G. Richard Thompson, and Peter Haining, as well as those from the trenchant editorial labors of Montague Summers in a bygone day, allow us access to some of the important short fiction in the genre from the past century. Another type of complication arises because many writers of more "respectable" fiction hid behind shelters of anonymity when they penned their thrillers. Pirated editions create worse problems— James Dalton's novelette, *The Gentleman in Black* [2-29], for example. Although first editions are immensely rare, a piracy of 1840 could mislead the unwary into believing that George Cruikshank, the famous nineteenth-century illustrator, wrote a book by this title, for it is frequently catalogued as his. *The Gentleman in Black and Tales of Other Days,* published in 1840 by the obscure London firm of Charles Daly, is shelved in many good libraries, but that it relates in any way to Dalton is usually not evident on the cards that provide keys to authorship as well as to repository location.

I remark again that although this list may seem brief, it represents in my judgment the important and reasonably obtainable horror fiction from most of the nineteenth century. No listing of this sort is ever complete. I include certain warhorses, as well as titles that might not immediately come to mind when thinking about horror fiction. Core titles are chosen because they (a) provide representative coverage of the period and (b) show literary merit or historical significance. (Unless noted otherwise, all authors are American.)

Although the era of residual Gothicism witnessed the continuation of sensationalism from earlier horror writing, there were departures that modified and revitalized the tradition. Who can read Nathaniel Hawthorne's *The Scarlet Letter,* Herman Melville's *Moby-Dick,* or Charles Dickens's *The Mystery of Edwin Drood* without recalling not only their Gothic heritage, but also the freedom sired by that tradition's probing of the irrational? Overall, the core list indicates the various directions taken by literary Gothicism, so divergent in spots as to become well-nigh obliterated as the nineteenth century wore on.

2-1. Ainsworth, William Harrison (U.K.). **Rookwood: A Romance.** Bentley, 1834; AMS Press, 1979.

A Radcliffean revival in the "bygone style of Mrs. Radcliffe," *Rookwood* opens with a charnel-house scene rarely duplicated in Victorian fiction and reminiscent of the atrocities of *The Monk* [1–218]. The decrepit sexton, Luke Bradley, is the presiding evil personage of the story. His malign eye and piercing laugh denote his Gothic lineage, while his belated revelation as Alan Rookwood is clearly a restoration of the overworked device of the masquerading relative. Ainsworth's plotting is convoluted to the point of unintelligibility, and his application of Radcliffe's formula of the "explained supernatural" [1–316] is only intermittently effective, as in the ghostly charade of Jack Palmer. The ancestral curse, awful prophecies, skeletal hands, secret panels, and cloacal vaults appear in great profusion and suggest that Ainsworth believed that the Gothic novel could be revived merely by restoring its apparatus of anguish. One grand episode, Dick Turpin's famous ride to York aboard Black Bess for his own hanging as a highwayman, has enough dark energy to offset Ainsworth's execrable style. Dick Turpin's ride aligns *Rookwood* with the long-standing tradition of "Newgate Fiction," a naturalized branch of the Gothic in which the supernatural was routinely reduced to the brutalities of the prison. Ainsworth was familiar with *The Newgate Calendar; or, Malefactor's Bloody Register* (1774), a sourcebook of sensational crimes and punishments whose material furnished characters and ideas for *Rookwood* and for Ainsworth's antiquarian masterpiece, *The Tower of London* (1840).

2-2. Alcott, Louisa May. **Behind a Mask: The Unknown Thrillers of Louisa May Alcott.** Ed. by Madeline B. Stern. Morrow, 1975; Bantam, 1978.

Best described as quaintly spooky, Alcott's four forgotten stories of the supernatural are taken from various periodicals. Although each of the tales in this modern collection has its lurid moments, Alcott's powers as a writer were clearly toward the successful juvenilia of *Little Women* and not toward the hackneyed and second-hand "household Gothic" of these pieces. One of the four, "Pauline's Passion and Punishment," won the short story competition sponsored by *Frank Leslie's Illustrated Newspaper*. The other three tales appeared originally in the Boston weekly, *The Flag of Our Union*, a paper that often offered its readers cheap Gothic fare, as evidenced by the fact that Poe's grisly story of the vengeful jester, "Hop-Frog," was published here. Securing herself behind the nom de plume "A. M. Barnard," Louisa May Alcott tried her hand at the profiteering Gothic thriller, but proved at the same time that her literary genius lay far afield from the haunted castle.

2–3. Alcott, Louisa May. **Plots and Counterplots: More Unknown Thrillers of Louisa May Alcott.** Ed. by Madeline B. Stern. Morrow, 1976; Popular Library, 1978.

A supplementary collection to *Behind the Mask* [2–2], *Plots and Counterplots* exhumes five additional undertakings by Alcott in the busy field of periodical Gothic fiction. Undistinguished and utterly typical of the magazine trade's repetitive modes of terror, these stories feature such stock Gothic situations as drug-induced visionary extravaganzas, intense but latent sexual savagery, repressed or warped mental states, cadaverous lovers, fatal women, mesmerically endowed males, and the whole range of Gothic appliances and sinister settings. Although these stories demonstrate an aptitude for the technology of the Gothic, they lack the force of sincerity that the committed Gothicist usually brings to his or her fantasies. Labored and derivative, the five tales in this collection are of little more than historical interest. Alcott's occasional Gothic digressions neither enhance nor detract from her deserved place as a creator of fine works for children. Specialists who wish to know everything written by Alcott will find some value in this collection. Readers who are concerned chiefly with the Gothic curios of American magazine fiction can avoid this phase of her work without missing anything of significance.

2–4. Allston, Washington. **Monaldi: A Tale.** Little, Brown, 1841; Scholar's Facsimiles & Reprints, 1967.

A painter, poet, and intimate of Coleridge, Allston produced an Italianate romance full of fatal Gothic passions operating in a lurid atmosphere of revenge and erotic villainy. The frenzied tone, the fatal rivalry of artistically gifted lovers, and the near-madness of several of the characters all carry strong reminders of *The Passions* [1–92], a late Gothic work by "Rosa Matilda" or Charlotte Dacre. The shy and gentle painter-hero, Monaldi, attends a seminary in Bologna; with him is Maldura, a bold and potentially criminal figure whose Gothic heritage shortly manifests itself when the two young men both fall in love with the stereotypical Mediterranean beauty, Rosalia Landi. When Monaldi wins her, the envious Maldura moves with Iago-like precision to ruin both lives. He hires the libertine Fialto to feign an affair. Succumbing to the ruse, Monaldi stabs his beloved and retires from the scene in an anguish of remorse. But Rosalia recovers and seeks out the now insane Monaldi with the news of Maldura's plot against their love. Her appearance only exacerbates Monaldi's madness, for he is convinced that he is receiving a visit from his dead and spectralized beloved come back to torment him. Unable to free themselves from their Gothic delusions and the terrible emotional tangle of their lives, good and bad alike gradually waste away. Even though his gloomy Gothic stage lacks the customary props, all the morbid excesses of feeling and the horrifying grandeur of self-destructive love are vigorously present. Allston appears to have written a novel of tragic passion whose Gothic aspects weaken the book's genuine portrayal of the destructive nature of love and friendship.

2–5. Banim, John, and Michael Banim (U.K.). **Revelations of the Dead Alive.** Simpkin & Marshall, 1824.
John Banim (1798–1842) is remembered in Irish literature as a dramatist, poet, and novelist. His chronicles of the Irish peasantry have a great deal of melodramatic suffering as well as frequent touches of the supernatural. The novel *Revelations of the Dead Alive* is a clever contribution to the field of Gothic satire and accomplishes for the excesses of sensation literature what Jane Austen's *Northanger Abbey* [1–11] does for the extremes of Radcliffean Gothic romance. The plot develops from the recollections of a protagonist-narrator who inexplicably "dies" for a duration of 198 days; each day elongates itself in memory into a single year of life. Writers and literary conventions of the 1820s are satirized through the time-warped consciousness of the narrator. Entrapment within time recalls the situation of Melmoth in the famous Gothic novel by another Irish writer, Charles Robert Maturin, in *Melmoth the Wanderer* [1–244].

2–6. Blackwood, John (U.K.). **Tales from "Blackwood."** First and Second Series. Blackwood, 1858–1861, 1879–1881.
Twelve volumes comprise each series. The 1858–1861 "run" includes tales appearing in "Maga" from 1821 to 1859; the second series contains tales taken from the 1850 to 1878 period; a third series extends beyond the period covered in this segment of the bibliography. *Blackwood's* specialized in sensational and horrific fiction and particularly so in that type of story—a hideous predicament stimulated the entrapped narrator to flights of analytic agony. G. R. Thompson comments, "*Blackwood's* was the most influential of the nineteenth-century British magazines insofar as the development of Gothic fiction is concerned, setting a trend in the 'sensation' and 'predicament' tale. In these, the protagonist gets himself into some kind of impossible situation (such as being buried alive, caught under a huge bell, baked in a copper vat, imprisoned in a shrinking room) and then proceeds to analyze his sensations in detail." Poe simulated *Blackwood's* formula for a successful tale of lethal sensations in "The Pit and the Pendulum" and mocked the

same pattern of heightened distress in "A Predicament," a tale of gradual and comic decapitation.

2–7. Bleiler, Everett F., ed. **A Treasury of Victorian Detective Stories.** Scribner, 1979.
This valuable anthology makes available some of the best supernatural short fiction of eminent Victorian novelists. By its very selection and arrangement, the chronology of stories also shows the evolution of detective fiction, the literary heir-apparent to the Gothic tale. The anonymous "Woman with the Yellow Hair" is an expert presentation of the psychological effects of anxiety. Here, the reader is enticed into a close or detective reading to discover whether and how the frauds will be exposed and what retribution awaits the overcurious brother of the groom. Other selections are taken from the crime fiction of Charles Dickens, Andrew Forrester, Jr., Mary Elizabeth Braddon, and Charles Martel. Although some of these figures fall outside the period of residual Gothicism, the volume is still a recommended starting point for tracing the rise of the story of detection as well as recognizing its Gothic ancestry.

2–8. Booth, Bradford Allen, ed. **A Cabinet of Gems: Short Stories from the English Annuals.** Univ. of California Press, 1938.
Nineteen selections chosen by Booth to represent trends in horror fiction in the period from 1826, when C. R. Maturin's "Leixlip Castle" appeared, to the publication of Wilkie Collins's "Your Money or Your Life" in 1880. Also included are scarce examples of the work of James Hogg, William Harrison Ainsworth, William Maginn, Claire Clairmont, Allan Cunningham, and, quite unexpectedly, W. S. Gilbert. The claim was that writing for the annuals usually did not evoke authors' best efforts or results. But each gem exhibits its own Gothic edge in support of the generalization that Gothicism never actually disappeared, but became a residual impulse after 1824. Even the consummate punster and vitriolic wit, W. S. Gilbert, could turn his comic talents to horrific themes.

*2–9. Braddon, Mary Elizabeth (U.K.). **Lady Audley's Secret.** Tinsley, 1862; Dover, 1974.
Author of some 80 novels and many plays, Mary Elizabeth Braddon's success was first credited to this horror novel.

*2–10. Brontë, Charlotte (U.K.). **Jane Eyre.** Smith, Elder, 1847; Norton, 1971.
A series of imprisonments and distressing experiences at the hands of all-powerful and occasionally demonic males gives the novel *Jane Eyre* certain affinities with the Radcliffean branch of the Gothic romance. Jane's moral consciousness and her will to overcome adversity separate her from such Gothic heroines as Emily St. Aubert in *The Mysteries of Udolpho* [1–316], but

other psychological properties of her character and her ordeals as a kind of prisoner at Lowood School and at Thornfield Hall suggest how thoroughly Brontë's work is grounded in the maiden-centered Gothic novel. For the older ordeal of enclosure of body, Brontë substitutes enclosure of spirit as the orphaned maiden tests her moral will against a closed world of towering male egos that forces her into unwanted roles. When summarized, many elements of the novel's plot strike the reader as domestications of Gothic situations and spectral experiences. Jane's saga of self-growth is confined to various chambers of horror and forbidding houses. Confined as a child to the awful "Red Room" by her nefarious Aunt Reed, she is later packed off to Mr. Brocklehurst's austere academy at Lowood. Brocklehurst himself is a figure of sinister and superhuman strength, "a narrow, sable-clad shape" and "a black pillar." Finally escaping Lowood, Jane must face a second reincarnation of the Gothic villain or satanic hero in the person of Edward Rochester, mysterious master of Thornfield Hall and a neo-Byronic man of dark past, piercing eye, arrogant manner, and lustful inclinations. Locked away in one of Thornfield's forbidden turrets is Rochester's mad wife, whose secret existence is kept from Jane and the world as Rochester prepares to marry Jane. Like the castle specter of earlier Gothic romance, the insane Bertha Mason Rochester periodically breaks loose to seek revenge against Rochester and eventually succeeds in burning down Thornfield. Bertha functions symbolically and is no mere reproduction of the ghost of the castle, for she represents the dark and uncontrolled passions of both Rochester and Jane. Leaving Thornfield after the interrupted wedding ceremony and the exposure of Rochester's bigamy, Jane makes her way to the household of the clergyman St. John Rivers, a saint of ice who is as passionless as Rochester is full of dark passions. Rivers poses another threat to Jane's freedom of spirit, since he stands for a rejection of all carnality. Realizing that a life with Rivers could end only in martyrdom or in a denial of her own fleshly self, Jane refuses his hand to return to Rochester. The summons to return to Thornfield is done through a refurbished Gothic device—that of the enigmatic and telepathic voice or mysterious warning that calls her to her destiny. Originally, this Gothic acoustic was used simply to terrify or to cause a shudder, as in W. H. Ireland's *Bruno; or, The Sepulchral Summons* [1–179]. Jane's sepulchral summons, however, operates as the voice of moral destiny and spiritual duty, bringing her to the blinded Rochester's side. Rochester and Jane finally shed their Gothic identities as villain and maiden or pursuer and pursued to become man and wife as well as spiritual partners in the happy struggle for higher sensitivity to life. Far from departing from the mechanics of the Radcliffean Gothic romance, Brontë refined its melodramatic improbabilities into a parable of the moral life. Her considerable debt to the Gothic tradition is explored and acknowledged by R. B. Heilman in "Charlotte Brontë's 'New Gothic,' " in *Victorian Literature: Modern Essays in Criticism* (Oxford Univ. Press, 1961).

*2-11. Brontë, Emily (U.K.). **Wuthering Heights: A Novel.** Newby, 1847; Clarendon, 1976.
The concentric narrative arrangement, the elaborate and complicated gene-alogy of the Lintons and the Earnshaws, and the violence of both the set-tings and the characters in Emily Brontë's tragedy of the passions all point to the writer's acquaintance with the schools of horror and terror and the methods of the Gothic novelists. The central figure of the somber story and the child of chance is the stormy Heathcliff, a waif picked up in the streets of Liverpool and brought back to Wuthering Heights by Earnshaw to be raised with his own children. Bullied by Hindley Earnshaw, the strange and some-what demonic Heathcliff falls in love with Catherine Earnshaw. The tem-pestuous relationship is almost parallel to the erotic union between the devil and a femme fatale in Gothic fiction. Marrying the insipid Edgar Linton, Cathy later dies while Heathcliff's love intensifies into a vindictive urge to possess her and to devastate the Earnshaws even in death. Heathcliff is something of a composite of Byronic Gothic villain and outlaw hero. His love is both deadly and vampiristic, while at the same time it has a mystical energy that transcends mortal limits. Cathy is less a woman than a person-ification of the wild spirit of nature seeking to unite its own ferocity with the dark force of life embodied in Heathcliff. The novel frequently echoes the rhetoric or the situational shock of the Gothic. When enraged, Heath-cliff's "sharp cannibal teeth, revealed by cold and wrath, gleamed through the dark." Told through a combination of narrators, *Wuthering Heights* draws upon the traditions of Gothic fiction to depict the peculiar mixture of beauty and terror inherent in tempestuous love. If the Gothic originates in the love of terror, perhaps it can be said that Emily Brontë reversed this premise while preserving the conditions of terror to produce a novel that depicts the terrors of love.

*2-12. Broughton, Rhoda (U.K.). **Tales for Christmas Eve.** Bentley, 1873; reissued in 1879 as *Twilight Stories,* Transatlantic, 1948.
These five eerie tales place Broughton in a direct line of descent from Poe and the ultimate terror of soul that Poe's baroque fantasies sometimes achieve. The introductory story, "The Whole Truth, and Nothing but the Truth," retaps Poe's "Cask of Amontillado" in christening its urbane narra-tor Mrs. Montresor. The closing tale "Under the Cloak," exploits the me-dium of the dream state to secure its narcoleptic effects. Adhering to Poe's principle of brevity, Broughton's stories are never prolix. For a writer who "began her career as Zola and ended as Miss Yonge," as Broughton herself summed it up, these brief forays into the opium-tainted world of the Gothic were a form of writer's diversion and perfection of her clipped style. In her pursuit of Gothic sensations and her tracings of the soul's terror in these di-minutive pieces, Broughton earns for herself a transitional place between Poe and Montague Rhodes James—certainly an appropriate niche for the niece of Sheridan Le Fanu.

2-13. Bryant, William Cullen, ed. **Tales of the Glauber Spa.** Harper & Brothers, 1832; Mss Information Corp., 1978.

The ingeniously contrived story "The Skeleton's Cave" can be regarded as an extension of grotto or cavern Gothic, a subspecies of the tale of terror that often had furnished subject matter for the shilling shocker. The scene is the western frontier in the late 1800s. A party of explorers consisting of Father Ambrose, the hard-bitten Frenchman Le Maire, and the delicate Miss Emily are suddenly entombed when a fierce storm causes a rock to seal the cavern's only entrance. But just as an unfortunate accident of nature had brought about their entrapment, so an equally fortunate stroke of nature liberates the trio of subterranean curiosity-seekers, who vow that they have paid their final visit to the legendary cave where Indians' foes had once sought shelter and perished. There is perhaps a touch of the predicament of Charles Brockden Brown's Edgar Huntly [1–49] and his stranded situation in the darkness of the frightful forest pit in the tale. A second story, "Medfield," has a titular hero who is closely akin to the brutal Zeluco of John Moore [1–268], a destroyer of wives. Like the vicious Zeluco, Medfield deliberately causes the premature deaths of his wife and children while exulting in their demise. Entering politics, he is on his way to a successful career when a visitation from his wife's phantom reminds him of his crimes. Morally redeemed by the gentle ghost, he becomes humane, melancholy, and contrite, ultimately dying before his prime. There are curious parallels here with Hawthorne's rather Kafkaesque tale of wife abuse, "Wakefield," whose titular character stumbles into cruelty and spies upon his mourning wife for a period of 20 years.

2-14. Bryant, William Cullen. **William Cullen Bryant: Representative Selections.** Ed. by Tremaine McDowell. American Book, 1935.

Radcliffean ingenuity and topography underlie the two tales in this set of what might be designated as "Vermont Gothic." The first tale, "A Border Tradition," acquires its naturalized Gothic setting from the dismal swamp regions of Great Barrington. The atmosphere here threatens death while the terrain itself is a close transcription of one of Radcliffe's castle exteriors. Bizarre noises and a lurking figure in white build the mood of terror. Typically, the thing in white is associated with the English Gothic's standard ghost of the murdered maiden who stalks her oppressors. An additional source for Bryant may well be Sir Walter Scott's phantasmagoric White Lady of Avenel in *The Monastery* [1–342]. "The Indian Spring" (1830), the second tale, brings the narrator to a ghastly confrontation with a spectral Indian, but in the prescribed Radcliffean manner, all actual horror is dispersed when it is revealed that the narrator has been in the throes of a nightmare. Judging by the questionable dexterity of these two Gothic tales, we may conclude that Bryant's competency in frenetic literature lay in his power as poet in the graveyard school in such famous moral celebrations of death as "Thanatopsis."

2-15. Buckler, William E., ed. **Minor Classics of Nineteenth-Century English Fiction.** Houghton Mifflin, 1967.

Several of the minor classics in Buckler's argosy have residual Gothic characteristics. Included are the important novel of the double life, James Hogg's *Confessions of a Justified Sinner* [2-48]; Edward Bulwer-Lytton's "The Haunted and the Haunters" was first published in *Blackwood's* in 1859.

*2-16. Bulwer-Lytton, Edward George Earl (U.K.). **"The Haunters and the Haunted."** *Blackwood's* (August 1859). In *Minor Classics of Nineteenth-Century Fiction,* ed. by William E. Buckler. Houghton Mifflin, 1967.

Also published under the alternate title "The House and the Brain," the tale has links by way of incident and character with Poe's "The Fall of the House of Usher" (1839). The nameless narrator recalls his desire to rent a strange house. Taking up residence, he finds himself disturbed by sinister sounds. Upon investigating, he discovers a hidden chamber containing a tablet inscribed with a curse against all those daring to inhabit the house. Bulwer's republication of the story under the title "The House and the Brain" deleted all the passages ascribing the mysteries of the house to an occultist from the sixteenth century.

*2-17. Bulwer-Lytton, Edward George Earl (U.K.). **"Monos and Daimonos."** *The New Monthly Magazine* (May 1830). In *Romantic Gothic Tales 1790-1840,* ed. by G. R. Thompson. Saunders & Otley, 1835; Harper & Row, 1979.

The gloomy hero, a wealthy Byronic misanthrope, yearns for solitude. He is tormented by a mysterious double, a being he can neither evade nor kill—although he attempts both. Seeking the advice of a physician or leech, the wanderer trembles when he realizes that he can never disengage himself from his secret sharer. "And must I never be alone again," cries the narrator while the word NEVER is etched in the sand at his feet. This tale influenced Poe's weird miniature, "Silence—A Fable," and also suggested some details for Poe's story of the assassination of the good twin by his evil brother in "William Wilson."

2-18. Bulwer-Lytton, Edward George Earl (U.K.). **Paul Clifford.** Colburn & Bentley, 1830; Routledge, 1902.

A reformist novel with Gothic gadgetry and overtones, *Paul Clifford* was written to arouse sentiment for change in the English penal code. In this respect, its residual Gothicism bears comparison with Godwin's use of the Gothic in *Caleb Williams* [1-128] as a vehicle for sensationalizing the horrors of the law and the inhumanity of various institutions. Brought up by an innkeeper, Paul is arrested for a crime of which he is guiltless and imprisoned with hardened thieves. Escaping, he rises to leadership of a robber band and falls in lover with Lucy Brandon, the delicate niece of the imperious Judge William Brandon. Eventually, Paul is brought to trial before the severe Brandon, but before the death sentence is pronounced news reaches the court that Paul is the judge's own lost son. With inflexible cruelty, the judge pronounces death upon his own son as a demonstration of "justice." But Paul's sentence is commuted to transportation; Lucy and he embark for America to devote themselves to philanthropic enterprises in the New World. There is more of the noble outlaw of the *Räuber-roman* of Schiller [1–337] and Vulpius [1–390] in Paul's situation and temperament than the Gothic hero-villain. Scenic touches of Gothic weather and landscape are evident, although these are generally not so functional or fearsome as those in Radcliffe's novels or the later work of Hardy. *Paul Clifford* is doctrinary fiction with some Gothic overlay.

2–19. Bulwer-Lytton, Edward George Earl (U.K.). **A Strange Story.** Serialized in *All the Year Round* (1861–1862). Blackwood, 1862.
Closer to the authentic spirit of the Gothic than *Paul Clifford,* this long story successfully introduces the occult mood. The narrator, Allen Fenwick, is a rational skeptic who resents all things he deems strange or inexplicable. The pragmatic Allen encounters Lilian and Margrave, two characters who represent the world of the mystic and the occult that fascinates and baffles Fenwick. Thus begins Fenwick's initiation into a dimension beyond the rational, a punishment prophesied by the aged mesmerist and Fenwick's dying rival, Dr. Lloyd. Victimized by Margrave and protected by Lilian, Fenwick endures spells, fiery circles, nocturnal visions, and alchemical performances, and nearly tastes the elixir of life. The malicious Margrave is deprived of immortality at the crucial moment when the elixir spills. Fenwick, however, is made wiser by his new knowledge of things unnatural and unexplainable.

2–20. Bulwer-Lytton, Edward George Earl (U.K.). **Zanoni.** Saunders & Otley, 1842; Multimedia, 1971.
As a Rosicrucian novel drenched in the cabalistic lore of secret societies, *Zanoni* has very interesting connections with such Gothic works as Karl Grosse's *Horrid Mysteries* [1–139] and Godwin's *Saint Leon* [1–129]. Zanoni, the supernaturally endowed hero, resembles the Gothic villain by virtue of his unknown past, his affiliation with strange powers and places, and his inability to translate his colossal emotions into love of any kind on a human plane. Zanoni is loved by Viola, but because he cannot or will not love on a merely human level he encourages her to return the affections of young Glyndon. Mystifications follow as Zanoni draws a dreadful horoscope for Glyndon. Like Zastrozzi and Ginotti in Shelley's Gothic novels [1–349; 1–350], Zanoni appears doomed to pursue evil even though he can apprehend the good. Glyndon's education into the occult ways of the brotherhood is assumed by Mejnour upon Zanoni's disappearance. The action of the novel then shifts to the tumultuous underground activities of the French Revolution. In the midst of the terror, Zanoni suddenly reappears to take Viola's place at her

execution and by this act of selfless sacrifice to become human again through the power of love. Grand in conception and saturated at the same time with Gothic melodrama, *Zanoni* remains a novel of spectacle whose artistic category is peculiarly its own.

2-21. Collins, V. H., and Montague R. James, eds. **Ghosts and Marvels.** Oxford Univ. Press, 1924, 1925.
The accomplished supernaturalist Montague Rhodes James contributes an introduction to this useful Gothic sampler. The anthology itself offers tales by Frederick Marryat, Edward Bulwer-Lytton, Edgar Allan Poe, Nathaniel Hawthorne, Sheridan Le Fanu, and George Eliot. Because these figures are among the masters of the residual Gothic period, the Collins-James collection is an imperative source.

*2-22. Collins, Wilkie (U.K.). **After Dark.** Smith, Elder, 1856; AMS Press, 1970.
The pieces in this collection are best classified as tales of mystery rather than horror or terror. Supernatural horror in the vein of the older Gothic novel gives way to emotional anxiety and psychological uneasiness as Collins's art works by innuendo rather than by jolt or shock. Two of the stories, "A Terribly Strange Bed" and "The Yellow Mask," still hold a place in modern anthologies, while the third piece, "The Lady of Glenwith Grange," seems outmoded. "The Yellow Mask" bears comparison with Poe's "The Masque of the Red Death," while "A Terribly Strange Bed" occupies a lighter vein and can be read as a comic fable for gamblers. After an evening at the gaming tables, the narrator is threatened by an animated bed that moves to crush him to death. "I turned on my back and looked up. Was I mad? drunk? dreaming? giddy again? or was the top of the bed really moving down— sinking slowly, regularly, silently, horribly, right down throughout the whole of its length and breadth—right down upon me, as I lay underneath?"

2-23. Collins, Wilkie (U.K.). **Armadale.** Serialized in *The Cornhill Magazine* (1864–1866). Smith, Elder, 1866; Dover, 1977.
Young Allan Armadale discovers to his dismay that he is being stalked by a wicked twin whose name is Ozias Midwinter. For unknown motives or for sheer delight in evil, Midwinter hounds young Armadale nearly to the point of insanity. Midwinter is assisted in his vicious schemes by a true Victorian femme fatale, Lydia Gwilt, whole Gothic ancestry may be traced to such feminine demons as Matilda in Lewis's *The Monk* [1–218] and to amorous imps such as Biondetta in Cazotte's *Le Diable Amoureux* [1–61]. The tale also features candid depictions of sexuality that turn increasingly violent when thwarted.

*2-24. Collins, Wilkie (U.K.). **The Moonstone.** Serialized in *All the Year Round* (1867–1868). Tinsley, 1868; Penguin, 1966.

British plunderers seize a stone, the eye of a Hindu idol, and it ultimately reaches Britain. Priests follow the stone, as do generations of their successors. When Rachel Verinder, the heroine, inherits the moonstone, strange consequences befall her and her lover, Franklin Blake, the retarded Rosanna Spearman, and the hypocritical Godfrey Ablewhite, villain in this tale. Ezra Jennings, a drug addict whose mysterious aura links him with the foreboding villains of past Gothic fiction, assists in clearing Blake's name after suspicion for the stone's disappearance falls on him. In this novel, a "domestication" of the Gothic haunted castle occurs by means of Rachel's pleasant yet disturbed country residence. And the "Shivering Sands"—quicksand—contributes in its very realism the greater impact of horror and foreboding; for the reader, through Blake's eyes, witnesses the rolling of the sands, knowing they will claim a victim. Anxiety in this famous sensation novel depends not so much upon supernaturalism as it does upon very realistic situations that produce fears of the cold-chill variety.

2-25. Collins, Wilkie (U.K.). **The Queen of Hearts.** Hurst & Blackett, 1859; Arno, 1970; AMS Press, 1976.

A gathering of stories, of which "Mad Monkton" (originally "The Monktons of Wincot Abbey," *Fraser's*, 1885) is the most horrific, with hereditary insanity substituting for family curses. Alfred Monkton's journey to bury the body of an uncle, in order to ward off the prophecy that if a family member remains buried outside the abbey all the others will pass away, provides suspense, grotesque and unpleasant scenes (his coming upon the rotted corpse), and a sensational denouement. "The Dream House" combines near-grisly murder in a dreamlike state (for the protagonist) with violence and high-pitched plotting. "The Dead Hand" provokes uncertain reader responses to the indecisiveness of the narrator, who cannot decide whether he confronts life or death in the next bed in his room rented for the night. All these stories reveal Collins's technique of grounding his horrors in fact, and domesticating the old ghost-in-a-bedsheet into realistic characters, and the supernatural, or apparently supernatural, elements into everyday phenomena.

*2-26. Collins, Wilkie (U.K.). **The Woman in White.** Sampson, Low, 1860; Oxford Univ. Press, 1980.

The destinies of Walter Hartright, Laura Fairlie, Marian Halcombe, and the mentally ill Anne Catherick are tragically complicated by the horrifying machinations of Sir Percival Glyde, Laura's husband, and the sinister, yet captivating Count Fosco. A series of imprisonments in country houses, a burning church, forgery for high station, and near murder combine with the author's inimitable social satire to make this work one of his most appealing.

*2-27. Crowe, Catherine (U.K.). **The Night Side of Nature; or, Ghosts and Ghost Seers.** Newby, 1848; Folcroft, 1976.
Not entirely fiction (with ghost accounts and supernatural visits), this remains popular with aficionados.

2-28. Curran, Ronald T., ed. **Witches, Wraiths & Warlocks: Supernatural Tales of the American Renaissance.** Fawcett, 1971.
In addition to the customary representation of Poe and Hawthorne, there are less frequently anthologized tales that are good samples of periodical fiction of the times—several of them anonymous and for that reason, doubtless, not generally known.

*2-29. Dalton, James (U.K.). **The Gentleman in Black.** Kidd, 1831; Arno, 1976.
For money, entertainment, and long life, Louis Desonges makes a pact with Satan, whereby he will sin once the first year, twice the second, and so on. Along with his friend Maxwell, he engages in a long career of travel and debauchery throughout Europe. Both men eventually decide to settle on more normal lives, and they marry lovely women. Realizing the consequences of their pact, both sinners enlist the aid of old Bagsby, Maxwell's solicitor. Ultimately Bagsby cheats the devil, who, in a comic conclusion, decides to employ the old man for his own dealings.

*2-30. Dickens, Charles (U.K.). **Bleak House.** Bradbury & Evans, 1853; Penguin, 1971.
The ponderousness of the Court of Chancery works to evil and terrifying ends, as numerous persons involved are ruined, go mad, and die because of its effects. The physical horrors of London slums are concrete phenomena that enhance the psychic and social horrors so pointedly unfolded in this story.

2-31. Dickens, Charles (U.K.). **A Christmas Carol.** Chapman & Hall, 1843; Penguin, 1971, in *The Christmas Books.*
Miserly old Ebenezer Scrooge, a man for whom the Christmas season and its overtones of human charity have become humbug, sees the ghost of his late partner, Jacob Marley. From this foreboding opening, Scrooge goes on to meet three additional spirits, those of Christmas past, the Christmas present, and the Christmas future. The last of these visions terrifies him with the prediction of his own death. Ultimately, Scrooge awakens from what, we realize, has been a series of dream hallucinations. A changed man, he discerns that the third "spirit" is nothing more than his bedsheet wrapped around the bedpost. He leaves behind his visions of death as he goes forth motivated by quickened impulses of humaneness.

2–32. Dickens, Charles (U.K.). **Little Dorrit.** Bradbury & Evans, 1857; Clarendon, 1979.

Gothicism infiltrates this novel. The sneaking, insinuating, grasping Rigaud recalls a long gallery of diabolic foreign villains populating earlier Gothics. Little Dorrit herself and Arthur Clennam resemble those put-upon innocents from tradition. Old Mrs. Clennam, with her mysterious secrets from the past, shut up, crippled, in her gloomy room in an altogether gloomy mansion, controls, or tries to control, events in the lives of those under her command. Flintwinch, her faithful old retainer, combines familiar traits of the good and bad servant, helpful at times, hindering at others. His wife's "dreams" add a touch of other-worldliness to this novel of imprisonment within physical and spiritual walls.

2–33. Dickens, Charles (U.K.). **Martin Chuzzlewit.** Chapman & Hall, 1844; Penguin, 1975.

Dicken's interest in dream psychology as a means for sophisticating older Gothic terror is evident here, as Jonas envisions the murder of his victim.

*2–34. Dickens, Charles (U.K.). **The Mystery of Edwin Drood.** Chapman & Hall, 1870; Penguin, 1974.

Young Edwin Drood's wicked uncle, John Jasper, wants Edwin dispatched so that he, Jasper, may openly love Rosa Bud, Edwin's betrothed. A combination of oriental horrors in which opium visions run to the violent and erotic, murderous tendencies embodied in several of the characters, and the eerie cathedral environs in Cloisterham (Walpole's milieu) make this one of the hallmark descendants of the Gothic tradition, as well as a first-rate detective novel—a mystery in many senses, not the least of which is its incomplete state. Jasper's violent temper and his devious pursuits are matched in Neville Landless, who styles himself "tigerish." This novel indicates that, had Dickens lived longer, he might well have matched others—such as George Eliot and Henry James—in the field of psychological fiction. Jasper's opium dreams are masterfully presented, and they terrify by means of their violent eroticism related to murderous consequences. The horrors of the mouldering castle are transmuted into more mundane British surroundings, and the realization of the evil lurking near sunny doorsteps and the sacred precincts of the cathedral itself deepen our sense of terror.

*2–35. Dickens, Charles (U.K.). **Our Mutual Friend.** Chapman & Hall, 1865; Penguin, 1971.

Drownings and attempted murders open this chronicle of social disaster and disorder, and a murder-suicide drowning of the two villains occurs near the close. Bradley Headstone, appropriately named, is madly in love with Lizzie Hexam—or passionately lusts after her—but is so harassed by his rival, Eugene Wrayburn, that he rages like a maddened animal. His pursuit of Wrayburn produces sensational consequences, and the psychological element of the pioneer Gothic novels advances with giant steps in this work.

*2-36. "Felix, Charles" (U.K.). **The Notting Hill Mystery.** Serialized in *Once a Week* (November–December 1862). In *Novels of Mystery from the Victorian Age,* ed. by Maurice Richardson. Pilot Press, 1946; Arno, 1976.
The framing narrator is Ralph Henderson, secretary of a life insurance association that has insured the life of Mme. R., wife of Baron R. The plot advances by means of documentary testimony from persons involved. A series of poisonings, generally with slow-acting antimony, bring ever greater wealth to the Baron. When suspicion is raised against him in the death of his wife's sister, his own wife temporarily "recovers" from the poison he has been administering. But, upon threats of jealous vengeance from his French mistress, he evidently provides a horrible, swift acid poison from which Mme. R. takes her nightly draught—inspired perhaps by the Baron's mesmeric powers. This tale is Poesque in its foreboding, suggestive atmosphere.

2-37. Gaskell, Elizabeth C. (U.K.). **The Grey Woman.** Serialized in *All the Year Round* (January 1861).
Travelers take shelter from a storm with a prosperous German miller, who relates this story. His sister Anna had been rushed into marriage with the wealthy but sinister M. de la Tourelle, owner of a chateau in the Vosges Mountains. Anna's maid, Amante, becomes her sole confidante; they discover a corpse (de la Tourelle is a member of the chauffers, who torture, plunder, and murder their victims) and flee. Anna bears a daughter. This child grows to love a M. Lebrun, although his real name is Maurice de Poissy, son of the man whose corpse the two women had stumbled upon in the chateau. Consequently, the mother dissuades her daughter from marriage with him. The conclusion also mentions de la Tourelle's execution. This story is a tale of sensations akin to those so popular in *Blackwood's* and imitative periodicals a quarter-century earlier.

2-38. Gaskell, Elizabeth C. (U.K.). **Mrs. Gaskell's Tales of Mystery and Horror.** Ed. by Michael Ashley. Victor Gollancz, 1978; Scribner, 1978.
Seven stories appear here, all from periodicals of the 1850s and 1860s. "The Old Nurse's Story" is one of thwarted love, pride, and revenge. A "foreign" musician is loved by two sisters. He marries one and they have a daughter. The proud old Mr. Furnivall, at his scorned daughter's behest, drives the young mother and child into a bitter winter night. They perish, and their ghosts return to haunt the aging spinster to a terrifying death in the presence of witnesses.

2–39. Haining, Peter, ed. (U.K.). **A Circle of Witches: An Anthology of Victorian Witchcraft Stories.** Hale, 1971.

Factual and fictional accounts of witchcraft are reprinted here, notably Mrs. H. L.'s "The Magic Ring" (1839), Lady Duff-Gordon's translation from the German of Meinhold's "The Amber Witch" (1843), "The Witch Spectre" (anon. 1845), Catherine Crowe's "Possessed by Demons" (1848), and Amelia Edwards's "My Brother's Ghost Story" (1860).

2–40. Haining, Peter, ed. (U.K.). **The Gentlewomen of Evil: An Anthology of Rare Supernatural Stories from the Pens of Victorian Ladies.** Hale, 1967.

There are tales antedating and postdating the period, but among those from the times proper are Mrs. Oliphant's "The Open Door," Catherine Crowe's "The Italian Story," Amelia B. Edwards's "The Phantom Coach," George Eliot's "The Lifted Veil," and M. E. Braddon's "Eveline's Visitant."

2–41. Haining, Peter, ed. (U.K.). **Great British Tales of Terror: Gothic Stories of Horror & Romance.** Gollancz, 1972; Penguin, 1973, as *Gothic Tales of Terror: Classic Horror Stories from Great Britain.*

Contains good samplings from the lesser known short fiction of W. Harrison Ainsworth, Edward Bulwer-Lytton, T. P. Prest, W. M. Thackeray, G. W. M. Reynolds, and Thomas De Quincey, as well as selections from anonymous writers. Strangely, Haining's table of contents and headnote indicate, if one does not read carefully to the end of the latter, an anonymous author for the famous tale, "The Iron Shroud" [2–72], although William Mudford's authorship is established.

2–42. Haining, Peter, ed. (U.K.). **Great Tales of Terror from Europe and America.** Gollancz, 1972; Penguin, 1973, as *Gothic Tales of Terror: Classic Horror Stories from Europe and the United States.*

Germany, France, and the United States yield treasures of terror in this volume. Haining wisely chooses from among the less widely anthologized tales of Washington Irving ("The Adventure of the German Student"), Nathaniel Hawthorne ("The Christmas Banquet"), and Edgar Allan Poe ("Shadow— A Parable," although the oft-anthologized "Cask of Amontillado" also appears). The foreign pieces make this collection especially helpful for readers wishing to survey horror fiction from the angle of comparative literature.

*2–43. Haining, Peter, ed. (U.K.). **The Penny Dreadful; or, Strange, Horrid & Sensational Tales!** Gollancz, 1975.

A survey of horror fiction (complete tales and excerpts from longer works) published in the British "penny magazines" from 1825 through the 1970s. Contains a brief but invaluable bibliography of items relevant to the penny dreadful.

2-44. Hardy, Thomas (U.K.). **Desperate Remedies.** Tinsley, 1871; St. Martin, 1977.
This novel of the Collins sensational variety features situations of vicious pursuit of innocence, lesbianism, violence, and detection. The exploration of incest is deftly handled, and the work has a psychological sophistication. Hardy manages to present, albeit not so clearly or comprehensively, dream and symbolic structures that he subsequently handled more efficiently.

*2-45. Hawthorne, Nathaniel. **"Alice Doane's Appeal."** First reprinted as part of *Hawthorne's Works,* XIII, ed. George Parsons Lathrop. Houghton Mifflin, 1883; *Centenary Edition,* XI. Ohio State Univ. Press, 1974.
This early tale was never collected by Hawthorne. It relates the story of Alice and Leonard Doane, her jealous brother, who murders Walter Brome, her apparent seducer. Brome is also their half-brother, and hard upon murdering him Leonard recalls the terrible memories of his father. The narrator relates the tale of two girls on Gallows Hill. The genealogical tangle is pure Gothic.

*2-46. Hawthorne, Nathaniel. **The Scarlet Letter.** Ticknor, 1850; Norton, 1978.
Hawthorne's most famous novel employs many elements from Gothic fiction: the appealing heroine with a stained soul; the hero, a man of divided soul; and the villain of deepest eye. This last, Chillingworth, combines deviltry, or so it seems, with a keen knowledge of human psychology, with which combination he tortures hellishly his clergyman friend Dimmesdale. Eerie journeys into foreboding forest wilderness, suggestions of witchcraft, and supernatural, or seeming supernatural, occurrences in nature add to the book's appeal to readers of horror fiction.

*2-47. Hawthorne, Nathaniel. **Twice-Told Tales.** American Stationer's, 1837; *Centenary Edition,* IX. Ohio State Univ. Press, 1974.
Hawthorne's first collection of stories open with "The Gray Champion," a modified ghost story that symbolizes the spirit of liberty. Other excellent Gothic qualities are evident in "The Hollow of the Three Hills," a tale that centers upon witchcraft, adultery, and pride. The use of aural instead of visual devices makes fine art, and the atmosphere of the desolate hollow, with its stunted vegetation and stagnant pond, is intense. "The Wedding Knell" brings the horrific to everyday environs in the old groom's surprise wedding plan to reduce the foolish egotism of his bride by reminding her of the closeness of death (see Francis Lathom's *Midnight Bell* [1-206]). "The Minister's Black Veil" also keeps the horrors at a symbolic, psychological plane instead of hurling sensationalism at the reader. "The White Old Maid" chronicles the story of embittered love, frustrated passion, and imprisoned emotions, along with claustral surroundings. "Fancy's Show Box" and "The Haunted

Mind" also draw long-established Gothic props into psychic regions to dramatize the effects of pressures upon human emotional life.

*2-48. Hogg, James (U.K.). **The Private Memoirs and Confessions of a Justified Sinner, Written by Himself.** Longmans, 1824; Oxford Univ. Press, 1969.
Protagonist Robert Wringham Colwan (a transparent name) wrangles with his traditional Calvinistic faith. His double torments him with pleasures and pains of the flesh and free-thinking—resulting in an early and bad end for the youth.

2-49. Irving, Washington. **The Alhambra: A Series of Tales and Sketches of the Moors and the Spaniards, by the Author of "The Sketch Book."** Carey & Lee, 1832; Gordon Press, 1976.
Several stories have brush strokes of the Gothic or supernatural, but one, "The Legend of the Arabian Astrologer," stands out. Because of his supernatural powers, the old astrologer grants certain wishes of his greedy, power-mad king. Finally, a dispute between the two aged men over an enticing young Gothic princess ends when the astrologer disappears with her and the king's rule and land subsequently fall into sad decay. There are enough hints of violence and lurid eroticism to place this "oriental" story in the line of *Vathek* [1-25] and other eastern tales.

2-50. Irving, Washington. **Bracebridge Hall; or, The Humorists: A Medley, by Geoffrey Crayon.** C. S. Van Winkle, 1822; AMS Press, 1977.
Most of the stories included here are not horror fiction, but some qualify. "The Student of Salamanca," the longest tale, employs the old device of the stained, blotted manuscript, produced for round-the-fire reading. In the tale, young Antonio meets a singular old scholar, so diligent in his pursuit of wisdom that he desires isolation and rebuffs the cordiality of the youth. Antonio follows the old man to his decaying home, where he is smitten by his beautiful daughter, and where he learns from gypsies that mysterious circumstances surround the family. Antonio saves the old man's life when an explosion occurs in his laboratory, and they fall to discussing alchemy as the elder convalesces. Then Antonio, who has become the old man's pupil, saves the girl from an abductor. This man, Don Ambrosio, shortly thereafter delivers the alchemist to the inquisition in order to cement his suit for the daughter. Hints of awful tortures ensue. Ultimately, the troubles are dispersed, the student proves to be other than what he appears, and a typical Irvingesque sentimental, happy ending closes the tale. "Dolph Heyliger," another lengthy story, relates the history of the title character. Touches of supernaturalism, such as Dolph's spending nights in a "haunted" house and his learning about the storm ship, a nautical phantom ship of Hudson legend, add serio-comic elements.

2-51. Irving, Washington. **The Sketch Book of Geoffrey Crayon, Gent.** C. S. Van Winkle, 1819–1820; Twayne, 1978.

Three stories of the supernatural are included in this collection. "The Spectre Bridegroom" pays respects to "Germanism" so much discussed during this period. "Rip Van Winkle" and "The Legend of Sleepy Hollow" first appear here, and have since become classic examples of the early treatment of the fantasy of the supernatural in America.

*2-52. Irving, Washington. **Tales of a Traveller, by Geoffrey Crayon, Gent.** Carey & Lea, 1824; Arno, 1973.

"The Adventure of My Uncle" features a female ghost, the Duchess, who had occupied the chateau where the uncle of the story now resides. Apparently she and a lover held a midnight assignation, although some of the travelers scoff at the notion of supernaturalism, commenting that noises must have been made by the housekeeper. "The Adventure of My Aunt" centers upon the widowed aunt's portrait of her late husband, which seems suddenly animated. The "life" is caused by a marauder concealed behind it, one who had designs on the aunt's wealth. "The Bold Dragoon; or, The Adventure of My Grandfather" has supernatural furniture—perhaps the consequence of a dream. And "The Adventure of the German Student" is set in the French Revolution, its hero Gottfried Wolfgang. He meets a mysterious, enchanting girl, who converses about the guillotine, makes love to her after he has eternally pledged himself to her, and then goes mad upon discovering that she was yesterday beheaded and that he had made love to a corpse. "The Adventure of the Mysterious Picture" rings changes upon a familiar Gothic theme, although there is no explanation of the sinister eyes and face of the picture. "The Adventure of the Mysterious Stranger" has a protagonist imbued with Byronic good looks, and melancholy as well. This is really no story at all, but leads into "The Story of the Young Italian," in which the young and handsome hero becomes an apprenticed painter. He falls in love with Bianca, a convent pupil. The artist becomes the ward of a wealthy noble, who is also Bianca's guardian, and frustration rises for the lovers. While the hero is away caring for his aged father, young Filippo, the Count's son, intercepts his friend's letters because he, too, desires Bianca, whom he eventually marries and mistreats. The artist murders him, then flees; remorse dogs him like an evil spirit.

2-53. James, George Payne Rainsford (U.K.). **The Castle of Ehrenstein: Its Lords Spiritual and Temporal; Its Inhabitants Earthly and Unearthly.** Smith, Elder, 1847.

Beginning on "an awfully dark and tempestuous night," this story alternates pastiche of Mrs. Radcliffe (by way of Ainsworth but without his soaring sensationalism and brutalities) with Victorian sentimentality in chronicling the vicissitudes of the young lovers Ferdinand and Adelaide. He comes from uncertain origins, and she is daughter to the Count of Ehrenstein, a strangely uneasy nobleman with an awe-inspiring castle, wherein strange occurrences stem apparently from otherworldly sources.

2–54. James, Henry. **The Ghostly Tales of Henry James.** Ed. by Leon Edel. Rutgers Univ. Press, 1948.

Two stories fall within the period: "The Romance of Certain Old Clothes" and "De Grey: A Romance," both of which appeared originally in 1868. In the first, Arthur Lloyd marries Perdita Wingrave, much to the disappointment of her elder sister Rosalind. Perdita dies shortly after the birth of a daughter. Suspicious of the relations between her husband and her sister, Perdita had elicited an oath from Arthur to lock up all her clothes for her daughter until she came of age. Rosalind, who marries Arthur, desires those fine garments. One evening she mysteriously disappears. Arthur finds her in the attic, dead before the opened chest, with ten livid finger marks disfiguring her face. In "De Grey," a curse hovers over the men in the De Grey family, originating with an ancestor who had returned from the Crusades with the plague and caused his beloved's death. Our hero, Paul, wants to marry Margaret, who defies the curse. Paul sickens and dies. Neither story affects sensationalism, but each calmly builds to a terrible climax.

2–55. Lamb, Hugh, ed. **Terror by Gaslight: More Victorian Tales of Terror.** Taplinger, 1975.

The 14 selections contain all the elements of Victorian Gothicism in their range. Predictably, the names of Grant Allen, Rhoda Broughton, FitzJames O'Brien appear.

2–56. Lamb, Hugh, ed. **Victorian Tales of Terror.** W. H. Allen, 1974; Taplinger, 1975.

The 15 hair-raisers included are from the pens of M. E. Braddon, Sheridan Le Fanu, Mary Louisa Molesworth, Charlotte E. Riddell, Guy de Maupassant, Emile Erkmann, and Alexandre Chatrian, among others.

2–57. Le Fanu, Joseph Sheridan (U.K.). **All in the Dark.** Bentley, 1866; Arno, 1977.

This novel by Le Fanu satirizes the table-rapping and spiritualism that were so often staples in sensation fiction of the author's day. And it is interesting to note that Le Fanu, the great creator of Victorian horrors, was able to laugh at what is generally presented with considerable seriousness. In this respect he resembles Robert Browning, who, in his poem "Mr. Sludge the Medium," ridicules what he considered the bogus elements in seances.

*2–58. Le Fanu, Joseph Sheridan (U.K.). **Best Ghost Stories of J. Sheridan Le Fanu.** Ed. by E. F. Bleiler. Dover, 1964.

This collection gathers 16 of Le Fanu's tales, most from scarce periodicals. They typify their creator's predilections for characters dogged by guilt, often pursued by evil forces and beings. They date primarily from the 1850s

through the early 1870s, and as later productions offer more subtle variations on themes and characters of a horrific nature than do most of Le
Fanu's early tales.

*2-59. Le Fanu, Joseph Sheridan (U.K.). **Checkmate.** Hurst & Blackett,
1871; Arno, 1977.
Checkmate is an engrossing mystery, whose plot centers on the pursuit of Alice
Arden by wealthy, devious Walter Longcluse. Formerly known as Yelland
Mace, he had been involved in the murder of Alice's uncle and had sub-
mitted to plastic surgery to avoid criminal charges. His voice and hands be-
tray him, and he is sent off to prison, where he eventually commits suicide.
This novel of detection is something of a derivation from Poe, Dickens, and
Collins, and it merits careful reading because of its perpetuation of those tra-
ditions.

2-60. Le Fanu, Joseph Sheridan (U.K.). **Ghost Stories and Tales of Mystery.** James McGlashan, 1850; Arno, 1977.
Ghost Stories was published in 1851, after Le Fanu had ceased writing historical romances. The book was, in fact, his only publication for a period of 15
years, during which time the author pursued journalism. The volume included "The Evil Guest," "The Watcher," "The Murdered Cousin," and
"Schalken the Painter." "The Evil Guest" was the most gory of Le Fanu's
tales, a melancholy romance brimming with bloodshed and pain. It depicts
a typical Le Fanuesque scene of a misty night, the waning moon shining
through the avenue of tall poplars throwing slanting shadows on a sinister
mansion. Of "Schalken the Painter," a superb masterpiece of the horrible,
there appeared two variant texts. One was published in *The Dublin University
Magazine* in 1839, and the other version was in the second volume of *The Purcell Papers* (1880). The real Godfried Shalken was an artist born in Dordrecht
in 1643, who acquired a reputation for domestic scenes and especially for
candlelight effects. Samples of his work can be seen in the National Gallery,
London.

2-61. Le Fanu, Joseph Sheridan (U.K.). **The House by the Churchyard.**
Tinsley, 1863; Arno, 1977.
The House by the Churchyard, a most terrifying ghost shory by Le Fanu, is acclaimed for its uncanny force and absolute orginality. It pulls together in a
concentrated form all the best qualities of Le Fanu as a storyteller. It builds
up the haunting of The Tiled House, young Mervyn's dwelling, where the
evil presence eventually manifests itself. The varied wealth of picturesque
details and scenic descriptions recalls the art of Maturin. The influences of
nature are attuned with the atmosphere of menace that envelopes the tale.
Strangely enough the book is not a gloomy piece; it sparkles with buoyant
and gay characters, and a current of rollicking farce runs parallel to hauntings and murder, while a somber ballad has a decisive bearing on the catas-

trophe. Le Fanu places the story in the romantic setting of Chapelizod, a pleasant village on the outskirts of Dublin, during the days of the French Revolution. In a complicated vortex of intrigue and mystery, the plot keeps swirling in a masterly reconstruction of a historical period and explodes with heart-rending episodes. A prime sample of the illimitable majesty of death and its train of incurable devastations, its narrative stirs up an orchestrated variety of sensations, and a sense of the unexpected tickles the reader's nerves, while things tender and beautiful touch the senses and delight the spirits. The pages of the novel are crimsoned in gore with seasonings of hauntings, apparitions, and brooding menace. There are conoisseurs of the ghostly who put it first among Le Fanu's works.

2-62. Le Fanu, Joseph Sheridan (U.K.). **J. S. Le Fanu: Ghost Stories and Mysteries.** Ed. by E. F. Bleiler. Dover, 1975.
Most of these 14 tales date from early in Le Fanu's career. A comic note intrudes into these stories, making them companion pieces for many of the comic horror stories in *Blackwood's* and in the canon of Edgar Allan Poe. "A Chapter in the History of a Tyrone Family" (1839) is interesting because of the violence of the blind Bertha's violent attack—circumstances that may have influenced Charlotte Bronte while she composed *Jane Eyre*, with its vengeful madwoman.

*2-63. Le Fanu, Joseph Sheridan (U.K.). **Uncle Silas: A Tale of Bartram-Haugh.** Bentley, 1864; Arno, 1977.
Published in 1864, *Uncle Silas* is perhaps Le Fanu's most celebrated work, superior in atmosphere and emotional power. Draped in black, it is a psychological thriller with a highly concentrated small cast. The mounting force of stealing doom and darkness, and gloomy reflections on life beyond death, bring forth a pressure and a spiritual urgency. This terrifying tale centers on a beautiful young heiress who falls into the clutches of a wicked uncle who is a gambler, a libertine, and a murderer shunned by society. But the girl, having courage and presence of mind, becomes aware of these dangers and escapes the assassin, while the accomplice of the villainous uncle's murderous plan meets his doom in the end. All of the characters are well integrated; all play their determined roles and are never superfluous. And what a character portrait we get of Uncle Silas! He remains an image of power and bewildering expression, a queer mixture of derision, anguish, and cruelty. And even more terrifying than Uncle Silas is the figure of his French housekeeper, Madame de la Rougierre, perhaps Le Fanu's most powerful creation, a fit inhabitant of the eerie atmosphere that prevails in Bartram-Haugh. Le Fanu takes peculiar note of the external weather in *Uncle Silas*. The pitched mood and orchestral range of the novel's weather is dominated by one single autumnal tint—the season of mists and mellow fruitfulness. This perpetual autumn has a hypnotizing effect upon the reader.

2–64. Le Fanu, Joseph Sheridan (U.K.). **Wylder's Hand: A Novel.** Bentley, 1864; Arno, 1977.

Wylder's Hand is a superb mystery tale of murder and retributive fate. At the height of his powers, Le Fanu weaves an intricate plot and keeps the readers breathless with expectation and excitement. The doom of Mark Wylder is foretold by a mysterious oriental ring, and the dread secret of somber Redman's Dell is deferred until the end with artistic use of suspense. The scientific descriptions are all in tune—the sad yellow evening lights over the dells and wooded slopes; the gloomy old house whose windows open against a faded green sky; or at nightfall, the somber old trees waving like gigantic hearse plumes, black and awful; the chapel and the tombstones looking strange and motionless under a cold bright moon throwing sharp lights and shadows. This is a bizarre tale, which in its raw, jagged power almost equals *Wuthering Heights.* Captain Stanley Lake is of the same implacable lineage as Heathcliff. Elements of misfortune and doom are strong points.

2–65. Le Fanu, Joseph Sheridan (U.K.). **The Wyvern Mystery.** Tinsley, 1869; Arno, 1979.

The Wyvern Mystery is Le Fanu's version of *Jane Eyre* where the fall of a supernatural black veil sends up clouds of illusionary dust, presaging the evil to come. A powerful tale, strangely beautiful and abounding in scenes of horror, *The Wyvern Mystery* was the last of Le Fanu's novels to be issued as a serial in the *Dublin University Magazine.* Its happy ending is achieved at the expense of no fewer than four deaths. The central point of the plot is taken from an early story of Le Fanu's entitled "Episode in the History of a Tyrone Family." Apart from that thrilling moment when a blind Dutchwoman makes a murderous attack on Mrs. Fairfield—a bizarre scene from beginning to end—the book is memorable for the number and quaintness of the homely sayings that garnish the talk of Mildred Tarnley and Harry Fairfield. An ordinary plot is concealed behind a many-colored screen of sensationalism. The beauty of the novel comes out in the character of old Squire Wyvern; in the loving devotion of Marjorie Trevellian; in the gaunt, unlovely, brusque Mildred Tarnley who could have modeled for Rembrandt or Hals. There is also beauty in the descriptions of nature in the somber and serious moods that Le Fanu favored—descriptions of mysterious forest depths and of the strange melancholy of a watery sunset.

2–66. Lippard, George. **The Quaker City; or, The Monks of Monk Hall.** T. B. Peterson, 1846; Odyssey, 1970.

A lengthy, incoherent plot makes synopsis of this work difficult. There are many descriptions of illicit assignations at Monk Hall, Agamin House, and Brothel, as Lippard wished to expose vice in Philadelphia. There is a deformed, apelike figure, neither villain nor hero, Devil-Bug, who inhabits regions beneath Monk Hall, and at one point buries alive an unconscious victim. Devil-Bug is not altogether depraved. His tasks of protecting his daughter, Mabel Pyne (who is unaware that he is her father), and providing her ultimately with a decent husband form a complex plot strand. Another intricacy involves the triangle of Dora Livingstone, her husband, and her paramour, Fitz-Cowles. Livingstone discovers their liaison and poisons his wife, then presents her with a coffin and two locks of hair he had snipped from the lovers while they slept. He duels with Fitz-Cowles, who escapes. Livingston's necrophiliac scene with his wife's corpse makes lurid reading, as does his death in a great fire that brings down the mansion. Additional plotting concerns the affair of the licentious Lorimer with innocent Mary Byrnewood, whom he dupes into a fake marriage. Learning of her violation, her brother seeks revenge, is foiled for a time by Devil-Bug, but eventually kills Lorimer and fulfills a prophecy delivered early in the novel about one of the youths slaying the other. *The Quaker City* is a handbook for Gothicism in all its most exaggerated forms, although Lippard's social conscience provides humanitarian interest throughout.

2–67. Marryatt, Frederick (U.K.). **The Phantom Ship.** Colburn, 1839; Arden Library, 1978.
This reworking of the Flying Dutchman legend is erratic but compelling. Philip hears the history of his companion, Krantz, who tells of his father's flight from Transylvania to the Hartz Mountains after he has murdered his wife and her clandestine defiler, his noble lord. There the elder Krantz is duped into marrying a strangely beautiful lady, who is a werewolf, and for whom he promises to sacrifice himself and his children—whose "bones shall bleach in the wilderness," should the lady be harmed. After his new wife kills two of his children, old Krantz shoots her, is immediately confronted by her father and his reminders of the awful penalties, flees with his remaining son to Holland, and dies raving in a madhouse. Young Krantz departs for a sailor's life, and after regaling Philip with his terrifying history, is carried off in the Orient by a huge, ferocious tiger, leaving Philip to recall the fearsome prophecy passed along to him by Krantz. The conflicts between Philip and the one-eyed, evil mate, Schriften, add further touches of horror. The switches involving the reality or the visionary qualities of the ship, depending on the circumstances changing throughout the book, may put off some readers.

*2–68. Melville, Herman. **Moby-Dick.** Harper, 1851; Norton, 1976.
Horror arises as we witness the increasing dementia of Ahab, in whose personality the traits of Faust and the Byronic hero-villain are modified into a native American obsessive personality. Fedallah and his crew add a sinister oriental note to this voyage into regions that become far more important for their religious, psychological, and social qualities than for actual geographical locale. The figure of the white whale itself is ambiguous, as if Melville

had endowed it with both heroic and frightening characteristics from Gothic fiction. Ishmael, the narrator, partakes of the anxiety of Gothic protagonists.

2–69. Meredith, George (U.K.). **Farina: A Legend of Cologne.** Smith, Elder, 1857; Random House, 1950, rev. ed., 1968.
More a grotesque mixing of humor and horror than terror-filled, this novella satirizes human pacts with the devil, who figures here in comic fashion. The mirthful treatment of supernaturalism shows the influence of Meredith's father-in-law, Thomas Love Peacock, whose *Nightmare Abbey* [1–295] held a place in the late history of Gothic fiction "as an antidote against the runaway rhetoric of horror and the emotional absurdities of the high Gothic."

2–70. Meredith, George (U.K.). **The Ordeal of Richard Feverel: A History of Father and Son.** Chapman & Hall, 1859; Random, 1968.
Experimenting for a medium, Meredith toyed with such Gothic clichés as the family curse, omens (foreboding cypress tree shadows), ghosts (who prove to be only too human), and the devil—here clearly marked as an inner emotional force of individuals, not a demon with a tail, horns, and pitchfork, and all the more terrible because it is real and close to home. Sir Austin Feverel functions as a much-muted Gothic villain, hounding the innocence of his son and lovely, if weak, daughter-in-law because of his own "demon," wounded pride.

*2–71. Mudford, William (U.K.). **The Five Nights of St. Albans.** Blackwood, 1829.
Another Gothic novel of desultory planning, this is a veritable supper of horrors. The old abbey of St. Albans is on five successive nights the scene of sensational supernatural visitations. The characters include the wizard Fitz-Maurice, who conjures visions, one of which, the ravishing of Overbury's daughter, causes considerable uproar. Gondoline's spirit appears to her terrified father, who then attempts to murder Fitz-Maurice. The dwarf, Mephosto, adds grotesqueness to the novel, for we are never certain if he is evil or good—his appearance being far from prepossessing.

*2–72. Mudford, William (U.K.). **The Iron Shroud.** *Blackwood's* (August 1830). *Gothic Tales of Terror,* Vol. I, ed. by Peter Haining. Penguin, 1973.
Vivenzio, "the pride of Naples," is imprisoned by the Prince of Tolfi in a vast iron cage, which collapses by means of hidden machinery, finally crushing the victim to death. The sensations of physical and mental torture are recorded in detail.

*2–73. Paulding, James Kirke. **Koningsmarke, The Long Finne: A Story of the New World.** Charles Wiley, 1823; Scholarly, 1976.
This novel centers on the Swedish settlement at Delaware, Elsingburgh, and has as its hero Koningsmarke, who is a cross between a type like James Fenimore Cooper's Natty Bumpo, with his love for American nature, and the By-

ronic hero of the overpowering eye and the mysterious past. Naturally, Koningsmarke loves and is loved by the governor's daughter Christina. Trials
with old Bombie of the Frizzled Head, who hints that Koningsmarke was involved in the death of Christina's mother years before, are finally laid to
rest. Troubles with Indians and with the possibility of Koningsmarke's sale
into slavery, when the English take over the colony, add zest to this novel.
Paulding, an outspoken critic of the Gothic-Byronic modes, remained unde-
cided in his fiction, presenting on one page or in a chapter strictures against
its excesses, while employing its methods and characters elsewhere.

***2-74. Paulding, James Kirke. Tales of the Good Woman, by a Doubtful
Gentleman; otherwise James Kirke Paulding.** Charles Scribner, 1867.
Several selections among these tales of the 1820s–1840s contain elements of
terror—for example, "The Azure House," which satirizes excessive By-
ronism, notably in the character Fitzgiles Goshawk, who inclines to melancholy, gloom, and misanthropy. The most interesting story in the collection,
"Cobus Yerks," an oft-reprinted tale, stands as the transitional piece between "The Legend of Sleepy Hollow" and "The Hound of the Baskervilles."

*2-75. Paulding, James Kirke. "The Vroucolacas: A Tale." *Graham's Magazine* (June 1846).
Prefaced wtih a disquisition on vampirism, this tale has for its hero an enterprising young lover who pretends to be a vroucolaca, tormenting his beloved's reluctant father until the old man removes all obstacles to their wedding. A treatment of vampirism different from the usual horrific angle of
presentation.

2-76. Paulding, James Kirke. Westward Ho! A Tale. J. & J. Harper, 1832;
Scholarly, 1968.
This novel blends westward adventures with an interest in psychology, centering on the circumstances of Cuthbert Dangerfield and his family. Dudley
Rainsford, a religious fanatic, loves Virginia Dangerfield, Cuthbert's daughter, and the hereditary madness dogging his family is where the themes of
insanity and incarceration from earlier Gothicism enter this story—at times
all too clumsily.

*2-77. Poe, Edgar Allan. Collected Works of Edgar Allan Poe. Vol. II.
Tales and Sketches. Ed. by Thomas O. Mabbott et al. Harvard Univ. Press,
1978.
All of Poe's shorter tales are included here, along with the 45 years research
of the late Professor Mabbott and the 10 additional years work on the part
of his collaborators. No one interested in horror fiction should neglect the
notes, a veritable mine of irformation about this type of writing produced
during the second quarter of the nineteenth century. A chronological ordering of Poe's tales makes clear this development.

*2-78. Poe, Edgar Allan. **The Narrative of Arthur Gordon Pym of Nantucket.** Harper, 1838; Penguin, 1976.
Arthur Gordon Pym narrates his own story, a series of incredible nautical adventures followed by equally bizarre circumstances in the south polar regions. He suffers physical and mental tortures. He and the strange half-breed Dirk Peters wind up among savages in the south, where their deaths are planned, but finally do not occur. The story closes in a haze of eerie claustral whiteness, with strange noises surrounding the men in the boat.

2-79. Poe, Edgar Allan. **Prose Romances No. 1, Containing "The Murders in the Rue Morgue" and "The Man That Was Used Up."** William H. Graham, 1843; St. John's Univ. Press, 1968.
This is the first book form of "Murders," which first appeared in *Graham's Magazine* (April 1841). In this tale, which introduces M. C. Auguste Dupin, the French detective who traces the atrocious murders to their actual cause, we witness the modification of older Gothic horrors into their refined form, the detective story.

2-80. Poe, Edgar Allan. **Tales of the Grotesque and Arabesque.** Lea & Blanchard, 1840; Peter Smith, 1965.
The large majority of tales in this first collection of Poe's fiction are Gothic. In serious, comic, or mixed tones, they modify old-fashioned terror tales into subtle literary art, refining psychological horrors to a sophisticated degree.

*2-81. Prest, Thomas P. (U.K.). **Varney, the Vampire; or, The Feast of Blood.** E. Lloyd, 1847; Arno, 1970; Dover, 1972.
Sometimes attributed to J. M. Rymer (see the introductions to the Arno and Dover editions, as well as the remarks of Christopher Frayling), this long novel, 220 chapters, is inescapably associated with Prest. The first appearance of the vampire Sir Francis Varney marks a lurid achievement of the horrific; his tinlike eyes, taloned hands, and terrifying teeth are calculated to elicit shudders and revulsion. His victimization of young lovelies places him in line with Stoker's *Dracula* and a host of other vampires whose intentions are undeniably sexual. The interest of the novel weakens after the first few chapters, as too many digressions mislead the reader and the intricate plot thread confuses more often than not. A prime example occurs late in the story when the identities of Sir Francis Varney and Marmaduke Bannerworth, a suicidal ancestor, blur so as to make their characters downright indistinguishable. A pulp classic no aficionado of horror fiction can ignore.

*2-82. Reynolds, George William MacArthur (U.K.). **Wagner, the Wehr-Wolf.** *Reynold's Miscellany* (Nov. 6, 1846–Jul. 24, 1847); Reynolds & Dick, n.d.; Dover, 1975.
The hero as we first see him is an old man who, in a fit of desperation, agrees to accept the curse of werewolf-dom in order to grow young once more. Love

finally brings a positive if oversententiously sentimental conclusion to a chronicle of amazing transformations. These changes sensationalize the werewolf's havoc, and the carnage he leaves behind anticipates such contemporary ravages in fiction as Michael Maryk and Brent Monahan's *Death Bite* (1979). In *Wagner,* horrors mount when the machinations of the Inquisition begin, which ought to recall the ancestry of this novel in Matthew G. Lewis's *The Monk* [1–218], W. H. Ireland's *The Abbess* [1–177], or C. R. Maturin's *Melmoth the Wanderer* [1–244]. The unconcealed undertones of sensual sexuality accompanying many of the love scenes add interest to this fast-moving story.

2–83. Roberts, H. C., ed. (U.K.). **Tales from "Blackwood."** 10 vols. Doubleday & Page, 1902.
Ten volumes, much from the second half of the nineteenth century. Makes accessible fiction from this period that would otherwise require time and searching.

2–84. Rudwin, Maximillian, ed. **Devil Stories: An Anthology.** Knopf, 1921.
Selections span the medieval period through early twentieth century. Of interest from the residual Gothic period are two comic devil tales by W. M. Thackeray, as well as Washington Irving's "The Devil and Tom Walker" and the infrequently anthologized but excellent Poe tale, "Bon-Bon." There are other interesting choices from lesser writers in English, as well as foreign authors. Rudwin provides notes relating each tale to specific aspects of devil lore—although he errs in dating the first appearance of "Bon-Bon" to the *Broadway Journal* for 1845. It had first appeared in a Richmond, Virginia, magazine, *The Southern Literary Messenger,* in 1835. An even earlier variant, "The Bargain Lost," appeared in *The Philadelphia Saturday Courier,* the newspaper ancestor of today's *Philadelphia Inquirer,* in 1832.

2–85. Sayers, Dorothy L., ed. **Great Short Stories of Detection, Mystery and Horror.** Gollancz, 1929; in U.S. as *The Omnibus of Crime.*
This splendid anthology features works from ancient oriental and classical writers through the early twentieth century. Sheridan Le Fanu, Margaret Oliphant, Charles Dickens, Edgar Allan Poe, and Mrs. Henry (Ellen) Wood represent the residual Gothicists. Sayers's introduction has become a classic in its own right, being the best short sketch of a general nature on the subject of mystery-detection fiction.

2–86. Sayers, Dorothy L., ed. **Great Short Stories of Detection, Mystery and Horror: Second Series.** Gollancz, 1931; in U.S. as *The Second Omnibus of Crime.*
Sayers's second collection offers from our field Edward Bulwer-Lytton, Wilkie Collins, Sheridan Le Fanu, Frederick Marryatt, and Edgar Allan Poe. Sayers's choice of Poe's "Berenice" is deft; it was the American's first tale to draw critical attention, most of it hostile, to his horrific tendencies. Respond-

ing to this negative criticism, Poe wrote a letter that has often been quoted as a chart of the types of fiction he produced—and in its evasion of clarity it stands as yet another masterpiece of flummery by which means Poe had the last laugh at his detractors.

2-87. Search, Pamela, ed. (U.K.). **The Supernatural in the English Short Story.** Bernard Hanison, 1959.
Although this anthology begins with Daniel Defoe in the eighteenth century, and concludes with Algernon Blackwood, years after the period of residual Gothicism ends, there are good representations of Edward Bulwer-Lytton, Frederick Marryatt, Charles Dickens, and Wilkie Collins. Although he is not English, Poe is included, on grounds justified by Search in her perceptive introduction, which is a model in concise treatment of horror fiction.

2-88. Simms, William Gilmore. **The Book of My Lady: A Melange.** Allen & Ticknor, 1833.
The preface mentions "German diablerie," and several tales contain horrific elements. The selections that open and close the book, respectively "A Dream of Earth" and "Dreams and Dreaming," discuss ghosts, demon lore, and fantasy. "The Plank" is a Poesque tale, in which the narrator ships aboard an unlucky vessel, *The Three Cherubs,* where he undergoes a series of terrifying adventures. After visions of demons, storms, and other horrors, the narrator and a comrade grapple for safety on a plank because their ship has been stove in by *The Flying Dutchman* during a storm. "The Spirit Bridegroom" centers on the common theme of a demon lover's abduction of some desirable beauty; but here a comic note is struck because we realize, as the other characters in the tale do not, that the principals have fooled others into believing them supernatural in order to be left alone. See Irving's "Spectre Bridegroom" [2-51].

2-89. Simms, William Gilmore. **Carl Werner, an Imaginative Story; With Other Tales of Imagination.** George Adlard, 1828.
The title story is set in Germany. Carl and his friend make a pact whereby the friend is to return to him after death. Instead, an evil spirit appears, but is driven off with the aid of an old friend. A similar occurrence enlivens "Conrad Weickhoff," in which the hero, Rudolph Steinmyer, and the devil, disguised as Steinmyer's friend Weickhoff, agree on terms. Steinmyer ultimately loses his life and soul because of the arrangement. He is overtly compared with Faust and Weickhoff with Mephistopheles.

2-90. Simms, William Gilmore. **Martin Faber, the Story of a Criminal and Other Tales.** Harper, 1837; Arno, 1976.
In the title story, the criminal intellect of Faber is the center of interest. The impact of childhood education, in this case of bad environment on an essentially good, or neutral, psyche, is stressed. The other tales are generally revised versions of *Book of My Lady* [2-88] selections.

2-91. Simms, William Gilmore. **Southward Ho! A Spell of Sunshine.** Redfield, 1856; AMS Press, 1970.

"The Bride of Hate" is told by a German traveller against a backdrop of an ancient castle and sterile, decaying surroundings. Herman, the hero, is the illegimate son of the present baroness, although she refuses to acknowledge him. A servant knows the truth and tries to force her to turn over her property to Herman. A previous heir to the barony had been thrown from a tower parapet at his mother's order. The conclusion shows a sensational re-enactment of the former crime, with the wicked baroness as the victim.

2-92. Simms, William Gilmore. **The Wigwam and Cabin.** First and Second Series. Wiley & Putnam, 1845; AMS Press, 1970.

Two tales in this collection are especially interesting: "Grayling; or, Murder Will Out" centers on the remorse associated with criminal proceedings, and the suspense is well handled. "Sergeant Barnacle; or, The Raftsman of the Edisto" exemplifies the absurdities to which residual Gothicism could go. Barnacle Sam has long loved Margaret Cole, but, seduced by her false lover, Wilson Hurst, she hangs herself with a pocket handkerchief. Sam pursues Hurst and hangs him—with the same handkerchief.

*2-93. Summers, Montague, ed. (U.K.). **The Grimoire and Other Supernatural Stories.** Fortune Press, 1936.

This anthology of stories written toward the end of the eighteenth and during the first decades of the nineteenth centuries stresses the influence of the German romantic and macabre schools on English literature. Writers included are Joseph Sheridan Le Fanu ("Schalken the Painter," "Wicked Captain Walshawe," "Dickon the Devil"), Alexander Sergeyevich Pushkin ("The Queen of Spades"), Charles Ollier ("The Haunted House of Paddington"), and Mrs. Hartley ("Chantry Manor-House").

*2-94. Summers, Montague, ed. (U.K.). **Supernatural Omnibus.** Doubleday, Doran, 1932, 1962.

Le Fanu, Wilkie Collins, Dickens, Amelia B. Edwards, Richard H. Barham, and Frederick Marryat are representative of our period.

*2-95. Summers, Montague, ed. (U.K.). **Victorian Ghost Stories.** Fortune Press, 1934.

The period 1838–1869 is represented by Le Fanu, Sutherland Menzies, Catherine Crowe, Mark Lemon, and Tom Hood.

2-96. Taylor, Philip Meadows (U.K.). **The Confessions of a Thug.** Bentley, 1839; Eyre & Spottiswoode, 1938.

The narrator recounts his experiences in India, furnishing particularly detailed accounts of Thuggee practices and beliefs. The ritual treatment and strangling of victims reads like the atrocities in Gothic novels, and the relentless pursuit of victims is emphasized. Interestingly, Bulwer-Lytton encouraged Taylor to write a romance on this subject, and Dickens apparently drew upon the finished work for *The Mystery of Edwin Drood* [2–34].

*2–97. Thompson, G. Richard, ed. (U.K.). **Romantic Gothic Tales, 1790–1840.** Harper, 1979.
Ainsworth's "The Spectre Bride," a selection of tales from *Blackwood's* and the *New Monthly,* Balzac's "The Elixir of Life," Gautier's "The Dead Lover," Mary Shelley's "Transformation," as well as tales by Hawthorne, Irving, and Poe, fill in the items from our era. The introduction and bibliography are among the best scholarship concerning this period produced by modern scholars.

2–98. Van Thal, Herbert M., ed. (U.K.). **Told in the Dark: A Book of Uncanny Stories.** Pan, 1950.
From our period Van Thal presents tales by such worthies as Mrs. J. H. (Charlotte E.) Riddell, Catherine Crowe, Mary Louisa Molesworth, and Mary Elizabeth Braddon. This book merits reprinting.

2–99. Wagenknecht, Edward, ed. **Murder by Gaslight: Victorian Tales.** Prentice-Hall, 1949.
For many years this volume provided the only convenient reprinting of Mary Elizabeth Braddon's *Lady Audley's Secret* [2–9]. Wagenknecht's introduction furnishes additional bibliographical information on Braddon's novel, a work that has a confusing publishing history. Wagenknecht also includes shorter writings by Victorians such as Charles Dickens, Wilkie Collins, and others who fall outside the confines of our time span.

2–100. Warren, Samuel (U.K.). **Passages from the Diary of a Late Physician.** *Blackwood's* (Aug. 1830–Aug. 1837). Harper, 1831.
The late physician's predilection for situations that draw upon Gothic thrills, such as murder, the attempts of the physician to pacify a razor-wielding maniac (and the recollections of Maturin that this scene recalls), or the account of one character trapped in an industrial oven, make this lively reading. Like many other *Blackwood's* serial works, this is loosely structured.

2–101. Wise, Herbert A., and Phyllis Fraser, eds. **Great Tales of Terror and the Supernatural.** Random, 1944.
Not restricted to nineteenth-century fiction, the contents include tales by Edgar Allan Poe, Nathaniel Hawthorne, Sheridan Le Fanu, Charles Collins, Charles Dickens, and Edward Bulwer-Lytton. Because they are positioned as parts of greater types or schools of thrillers, these tales can be seen as significant contributions to the broad spectrum of horror fiction.

3
Psychological, Antiquarian, and Cosmic Horror
1872–1919

Jack Sullivan

In the introduction to his famous 1942 collection of ghost stories, editor and literary critic Philip Van Doren Stern declared the late nineteenth and early twentieth centuries to be the "golden age" of the genre. Although the statement may at first seem hyperbolic, one has only to begin recalling names from the period—Kipling, Machen, Henry James, M. R. James, Wharton, Bierce, de Maupassant—to recognize its essential accuracy, at least as an aesthetic proposition. An unprecedented eruption of first-rate ghostly tales began in 1872 with Le Fanu's *In a Glass Darkly* [3–139] and continued unabated through World War I. The genre has enjoyed other high points in terms of popularity and quantity of tales produced, but never has it enjoyed such a happy coincidence of quantity and quality.

For it is precisely the literary quality of fiction from this period that is its most immediately striking feature. It is a particular kind of quality, a distinctly modern dexterity and unity that originated to a large extent in the work of Edgar Allan Poe and Sheridan Le Fanu, the first short story writers in English to work out carefully planned aesthetic strategies of horror. They

221

were also among the first to write modern short stories. Their habitual strict attention to unity of mood and economy of means is a quality we take for granted in short fiction today, but it was virtually unknown to their more didactically inclined contemporaries. The creation of mood for its own sake and the sustaining of that mood without moralistic or occultist interruptions was their specialty, one they cultivated in relative isolation.

In a sense, Le Fanu was more revolutionary than Poe, for he began the process of dismantling the Gothic props and placing the supernatural tale in everyday settings. His stories, especially those in *In a Glass Darkly*, have surprisingly quiet surfaces and ominous undertones; they rely on genuinely *ghostly* scenes, many of them unapologetically supernatural, rather than melodramatic ones. Thematically, they represent the first serious attempt to abandon the Gothic villain who gets his just deserts in favor of the innocent victim who is mysteriously or randomly persecuted by demons who refuse to be exorcised. Le Fanu's early and obsessive preoccupation with helplessness in a malign universe becomes the major theme of later horror fiction and of much mainstream fiction as well. Indeed, the dark, apocalyptic quality of early modern horror fiction is absolutely contiguous with a spirit of restlessness and malaise that some historians, citing the works of Freud, Huysmans, Schoenberg, and others, view as an emotional key to the age and as a premonition of World War I.

Stephen Spender, T. S. Eliot, and many others have written eloquently about the atmosphere of trauma that darkened this period and manifested itself in increasingly bizarre and subjective modes of expression. This was a transitional age characterized by convulsive social changes, ugly repercussions from an unpopular war, economic instability, a sneering cynicism about government and the established order, and a fascination with counter-cultures and occult societies. Since this is the cataclysmic climate in which the tale of terror seems to flourish, it is perhaps no accident that the Vietnam and Watergate periods also witnessed a spectacular revival of the genre.

Le Fanu and other early masters were able to communicate this terror most tellingly in the short tale, and it is fascinating how closely and consistently connected are the developments of modern supernatural fiction and modern short fiction. A remarkable number of early modern writers who pioneered the short story as a major form had, like Le Fanu, a penchant for the weird and the horrific. Hardy, Kipling, de Maupassant, Conrad, Stevenson, Turgenev, and others produced some of their finest work in the genre. To understand why the birth of the modern supernatural tale and the modern short story are so intermeshed, one need only think about the intent of modern supernatural horror. There are more supernatural stories with unity of mood than other kinds of early stories precisely because mood is fundamental to the genre. H. P. Lovecraft, one of the most astute critics of horror, wrote in *Supernatural Horror in Literature* (1927) that "atmosphere is the all-important thing," more important, for example, than plot. In some of the more original stories of Machen and Blackwood, amazingly little happens, just as little happens in the mainstream short stories of Anton Chekhov and James Joyce; tiny attenuations and crescendos of emotion provide the drama and terror.

There is, thus, a powerful emphasis on psychology in the supernatural fiction of this period, an emphasis characteristic of mainstream fiction as well. Poe and Le Fanu are again impressively forward-looking in this respect; their careful blending of hallucinatory psychosis and supernatural malevolence, so that the distinction between the two is ominously effaced, has a striking counterpart in the work of de Maupassant, Henry James, Bierce, and others. In James's *The Turn of the Screw* [3–123] and *The Jolly Corner* (1908), what happens is not as significant as how a character perceives it happening—an emphasis that by no means denies the possibility of a supernatural interpretation. The drama of the story lies in the registering of the effect of the horrific happening on the mind—as in Poe's "The Black Cat" and Le Fanu's "Green Tea"—rather than the happening itself. Taken to an extreme, as it is in the work of James, Wharton, and de Maupassant, the *mind* becomes the locale of the tale, rather than England, America, or France.

This is perhaps the crucial explanation for the curiously international quality of much of the best horror fiction from this period. Turgenev's stories do not seem single-mindedly "Russian" (even though a Russian setting and sensibility are unobtrusively and tellingly present) any more than Le Fanu's genuine masterpieces ("Carmilla," "Green Tea") are "Irish." Rendering the nuances of terror on the mind of the victim—a recognizable, vulnerable mind with which the reader can identify—is what is important, much more so than an anthropologically accurate disquisition on the particular region, culture, or legend from which the horror springs. Even writers who specialized in myth and legend, such as E. L. White and F. Marion Crawford, were careful to relegate that specialty to the background and focus on the psychology of fear. E. F. Bleiler is right to maintain in his introduction to Le Fanu's *Best Ghost Stories* (1964) that Le Fanu's weakest work is his most parochially Irish, and we could make the same point about later writers. To cite the most obvious example, nothing is more irritating or more certain to compromise the mood of terror than a story heavily peppered with dialect. One approaches whole pages of Stevenson, Quiller-Couch, and even M. R. James (not to mention Van Helsing's diatribes in *Dracula* [3–234]) with a feeling of dread that has nothing to do with the supernatural.

The issue of psychology in these tales is put into admirable perspective by M. R. James in the introduction to his anthology, *Ghosts and Marvels* (1927): "It is not amiss sometimes to leave a loophole for a natural explanation, but I would say, let the loophole be so narrow as not to be quite practicable."

The "loophole" usually involves the possibility that the victim of an ostensibly demonic persecution was either mad or temporarily deluded. Since James has an abiding interest in the supernatural per se in his fiction, his loophole is extremely narrow. For other writers, it is much wider, sometimes to the point of making a *supernatural* reading "not quite practicable." By the end of a given tale, we usually know which reading the author wants us to adopt, but not always. De Maupassant, Henry James, Turgenev, and Charlotte Perkins Gilman (in her single and singular masterpiece, "The Yellow Wall Paper") lead us into a modern world of nightmarish ambiguity, which is not resolved by the ending of the story.

Thus, psychology does not comprise a separate category of tale but a preoccupation that spreads into all the weird fiction of this period. Henry James's statement in "The Art of Fiction" on the importance of the narrative point of view reflected a concern with psychological realism in the very form of fiction from which few major writers dissented. At the same time, a few artists, such as James, Wharton, Stevenson, de Maupassant, and Bierce, had a special, almost single-minded interest in psychological nuance, and it is possible to categorize them as "psychological" writers, even though the supernatural appears frequently in their work. The *cante cruel* writers, with their spectacularly morbid interest in the extremities of mental and physical suffering, also fit into this category. Still, the classification is at best a tricky one. Even the most unambiguously demonic works have fascinating, sometimes central psychological aspects, as Leonard Wolf has shown in his self-consciously cute but perceptive book, *A Dream of Dracula* (1972); Stoker's *Dracula* lends itself almost irresistibly to a Freudian reading.

A classificiation more clear and distinct is the "cosmic" or "visionary" tendency in supernatural horror. This emphasis on visionary experience both in plot and narrative attitude marks the work of Algernon Blackwood, Arthur Machen, W. B. Yeats, Grant Allen, Elliot O'Donnell, William Hope Hodgson, Charles Willing Beale, Mrs. Campbell Praed, Oliver Onions, and R. W. Chambers; it also appears fairly frequently in the work of Stoker, M. P. Shiel, Sir Arthur Conan Doyle, Jonas Lie, William Clark Russell, G. S. Viereck, and many others.

By definition, all supernatural horror involves the occult and the mystical to some extent. In the cosmic tale, however, rarefied otherworldly visions are presented as part of an antimaterialist ideology that indicts Victorian scientism and technology and presents mystical experience as an alternative to the grayness and mechanized tedium of modern life. An aesthetically treacherous didactic strain mars much of this fiction, but in the masterpieces of cosmic horror, such as Blackwood's "The Willows" and Machen's "The White People," the creative strain is happily stronger. Unfortunately, this period is filled with oppressively preachy "true believer" works, most of them long occult novels, and most of them mercifully obscure. The most charitable thing we might say is that the average occult novel had little sense of terror or wonder. As Lovecraft points out in *Supernatural Horror in Literature,* the "trade jargon of modern occultism" has ruined many a tale.

Nevertheless, the flowering of occult and "psychical" societies, such as the Order of the Golden Dawn and the Society for Psychic Research, provided a favorable milieu for supernatural fiction. Machen, Yeats, Blackwood, O'Donnell, Blavatsky, and many others were members of such groups. For the real artists, the cosmologies of Rosicrucianism and other exotic belief systems provided a backdrop of imagery and incidents; for hacks and polemicists, it provided a ready-made jargon, a substitute for good writing. It should be added that most of the superior occult mythologies—those with a powerful literary resonance—were invented: Arthur Machen may have been a member of the Order of the Golden Dawn, but his Great God Pan mythos was a product of his own imagination.

Stylistically, the more mystically inclined writers favored lyricism and expansiveness. There is a seriousness of tone, an implied connectedness to apocalyptic forces and secrets, that is worlds removed from the urbanity of M. R. James or the acid humor of Ambrose Bierce, even though they both deal with occult themes. Renouncing the detached irony so characteristic of modern fiction, writers like Blackwood and William Hope Hodgson attempted to infuse their language with an intensity consistent with their concepts. It is a risky strategy, one that sometimes results in ponderousness and overwriting. When it works, however, it delivers an enormously sensual and poetic glimpse of other worlds and other modes of perception.

The cosmic vision in this fiction is complex, for it often fuses ecstasy and horror. There is a curious ambivalence in these stories; the characters want desperately to rid themselves of the routine and mechanization of their daily lives, but the weird and enticing otherworlds they escape to are usually self-destructive or unendurably frightening. Some, like E. F. Benson's archetypal "Man Who Went Too Far," never make it back and die hideous deaths. Others, like the narrator of Blackwood's "May Day Eve," desperately negotiate a re-entry into the same modern world that previously looked so grubby and dull.

Another major tendency in the fiction of this period, more modest in its intent and more straightforward in its thematic thrust, is the antiquarian school of M. R. James. The James school represents a liberation from Gothic melodrama and Victorian allegory in its most insistent and entertaining form. In an October 1923 interview for the *Morning Post,* James took a swipe at the hyperbole of the Gothic writers, the "vagueness" of Poe, and the "trivial and melodramatic" effects of Lord Lytton and his Victorian contemporaries. In his introduction to *Madame Crowl's Ghost* (1923), his pioneering collection of Le Fanu tales, he stated that Le Fanu was the only Victorian worth imitating. And in the introduction to his own *Ghost Stories of an Antiquary* [3–125] he insisted that the sole purpose of his ghostly tales was to make his readers feel "pleasantly uncomfortable."

The aesthetic strategy of the James school is summed up in the introduction to *Madame Crowl's Ghost* with typically Jamesian lucidity:

> Let us, then, be introduced to the actors in a placid way; let us see them going about their ordinary business, undisturbed by forebodings, pleased with their surroundings; and into this calm environment let the ominous thing put out its head, unobtrusively at first, and then more insistently, until it holds the stage.

For the most part, James is true to his Le Fanu-inspired principles: the openings are low-keyed and full of "ordinary business" (as much as antiquarian pursuits can be called "ordinary"); the characters are stolid or cheerful rather than hysterical or neurotic; the invading presence sneaks gradually into the shadows of the story; and the horror that finally holds the stage is usually an "ominous thing" indeed. James's style, like Le Fanu's, is leisurely and careful, but it is also much more economical and urbane. The same qualities, with delightful variations, characterize James's disciples in the period, such as E. G. Swain and Sir Arthur Gray, as well as such later writers as Eleanor Scott, Frederick Cowles, and E. H. W. Meyerstein. Some (Swain and Gray, for example) were conscious imitators of James and worked contentedly in his shadow; others, particularly later artists like Wakefield and Hartley, had antiquarian styles and themes, but were much too individual and idiosyncratic to be conveniently placed in a "school."

One trait all the antiquarian writers shared was erudition. A major medieval scholar and church historian, James filled his tales with allusions to history, architecture, and all manner of antiquarian minutiae. His characters are learned collectors whose collections get them into trouble, and James is careful to make the demons that pounce on them seem chillingly authentic through the use of exact (although often invented) names and scholarly references. This antiquarianism only superficially resembles the antiquarianism in Poe, where collectors' exotica are linked with dramatically deranged psyches such as Roderick Usher's. The characters of James and his followers are at least sane enough to know that their ghosts are real, especially since the apparitions are often seen by more than one of them.

Nevertheless, if antiquarian characters do not, like Poe's, hallucinate their demons, or do not, like Chambers's and Machen's, chase after them, they do set themselves up for disaster. Related to the narrative detachment of the James school is a half-hidden *Wasteland* ambience, a sense of cultivated boredom and ennui, which has its roots in the 1890s "decadence" languors of Wilde's *The Picture of Dorian Gray* [3–257] and Yeats's early weird fiction (a movement prefigured with exacting prescience by Poe). The haunted antiquaries in these tales surround themselves with rarified paraphernalia from the past (books, dollhouses, even ancient whistles) seemingly because they cannot connect with the present. For them, the modern world scarcely exists. The endless process of collecting gives these Edwardian reactionaries an illusory sense of order and stability—illusory because it is exactly this process that unleashes the horror. Because the characters are people of leisure, this gentlemanly horror fiction represents a sophisticated version of the old warning that idleness is the devil's workshop.

Again, it should be noted that neither antiquarian nor cosmic tales are entirely separate from the psychological ones. The psychology of the interaction between viewer and apparition was something most of the better writers were careful to depict. Also, it should be emphasized that "antiquarian" and "cosmic" refer to imaginative tendencies, not rigid categories. The wit, subtlety, and compression of the one and the mysticism, intensity, and otherworldliness of the other represent a basic emotional and stylistic division, but many writers, especially the more richly creative and complex, stubbornly resist codification. H. G. Wells, Arthur Conan Doyle, and the Bensons, to name only a few, have a fluidity of temperament and imagination that moves them sometimes in one direction, sometimes in another. Because of the occult interests of the time, the visionary group is the larger. Indeed, the antiquarian school is limited mainly to British writers, although its voice and sensibility are approximated in the work of Wharton, E. L. White, and others. It should be added that the most conservative writers, such as E. Nesbit, Mrs. Molesworth, and Sir Arthur Quiller-Couch, spin out a combination of terror and fairy-tale enchantment in such a charmingly old-fashioned storytelling manner that they seem to belong in none of these "modern" categories, but in a longed-for past.

Some devotees of the genre may object to the lack of a separate "Christian" category, but close examination reveals that Christianity makes a strangely feeble and fragmentary impression in the quality horror fiction of this period. Christian motifs do appear in works such as Stoker's *Dracula* [3–234], Machen's *The Great God Pan* [3–156], E. F. Benson's "Negotium Perambulans," and R. H. Benson's "The Watcher," but their basic movement is usually toward a vision more pagan or animistic than Christian. Despite Russell Kirk's assertion (in the Afterword to *The Surly Sullen Bell*, 1962) that ghost stories are Christian allegories, Lovecraft was surely right to maintain that orthodoxy of any stripe, Christian or occult, tends to have a deadening effect on the genre. Indeed, the weaker Christian stories of R. H. Benson, Charlotte Riddell, Oliver Onions (in his post-*Widdershins* phase), and Kirk himself fail precisely because they are hemmed in by orthodox allegory.

The reader can hardly fail to notice the heavy emphasis in this chapter on short stories and novelettes. As Poe and others have noted, a convincing mood of terror is much easier to sustain in a short tale than in a full-length novel. Since the major enterprise of this period *was* to create and sustain new worlds of terror—with a concomitant renunciation of heavy-handed allegory, sentimental love interest, needless subplots, irrelevant ratiocination, and other devices of earlier horror fiction—it is no accident that the major genre writers tended to edit out extraneous matter and produce shorter works. A large number of short stories from this period are peerless masterpieces, and it would be false to pretend that the novels, taken as a group, constitute a comparable achievement.

Nevertheless, several impressive supernatural horror novels were produced, often by the same writers who specialized in short stories. Considered solely on the basis of its power as a horror novel, Stoker's *Dracula* is perhaps the most spectacularly successful, as well as the most influential and popular. It has a singularly terrifying and poetic opening, a magisterial supernatural villain, and consistently vivid imagery. It also, unfortunately, falls apart near the end, as do most long horror novels.

Lovecraft makes the rather charitable point that a flawed supernatural narrative should be savored for its "isolated sections" of genuine horror "no matter how prosaically it is later dragged down." By that criterion, a number of novels in this period pass muster, including Hodgson's *The House on the Borderland* [3–106] and *The Night Land* [3–110], Beale's *The Ghost of Guir House* [3–8], Crawford's *The Witch of Prague* [3–64], Buchan's *Witch Wood* [3–48], O'Donnell's *The Sorcery Club* [3–184], Ewers's *Alraune* [3–80], Lee's *A Phantom Lover* [3–143], Marsh's *The Beetle* [3–162], Phillpotts's *A Deal with the Devil* [3–198], Riddell's *The Uninhabited House* [3–219], and Viereck's *The House of the Vampire* [3–241]. These novels have melodramatic or sentimental lapses that detract from their atmosphere, but they also have memorable moments of dread and wonder. Many novels of the period, such as Robert Hichens's *The Dweller on the Threshold* and Marie Corelli's *The Problem of a Wicked Soul* are so saturated in fashionable spiritualist rhetoric that they do not qualify as horror fiction. Even the novels of Algernon Blackwood, as E. F. Bleiler points out in his introduction to Blackwood's *Best Ghost Stories* (1973), fall into the category of "mystical" rather than horror fiction.

The supernatural novelette, however, was one of the great forms of the period. Some of its most innovative pioneers were also pioneers of horror fiction. Beginning with Le Fanu's "Carmilla" and "Green Tea," the Victorian and early modern periods saw the publication of such enduring masterworks as Stevenson's "The Strange Case of Dr. Jekyll and Mr. Hyde" [3–230], Conrad's *Heart of Darkness* [3–55], James's "The Turn of the Screw" [3–123], Machen's "The White People" [see 3–153 to 3–161], Onions's "The Beckoning Fair One" [see 3–187 to 3–190], Turgenev's "Clara Militch," and Housman's *The Were-Wolf* [3–111]. The novelette offered an ideal compromise, a way of painting on a wider canvas of horror than was possible in a short story without risking the hazards of a full-length novel. It is small wonder that it was a favored form.

It should be emphasized that most of the major works from this period, no matter what their length or category, have a basic theme: inexplicable presences and forces exist, both supernatural and psychological, that are aggressively hostile to humanity and can break into our world to create chaos and tragedy. The fundamental darkness of this fiction needs to be asserted to counteract the erroneous claim, perpetrated in numerous anthology introductions, that the horror story is not really horrible and does not really mean business, but instead is a form of allegory about the triumph of good over evil—or at worst a roundabout means of implying the existence of good by showing us evil. The reality is that the early modern masters, beginning with Le Fanu, present ominous visions of the universe in which good conspicuously does *not* triumph and is often absent altogether. The most powerful and ambitiously serious stories by writers such as Machen, Bierce, Hardy, Lie, and Hodgson portray panicked, often pathetic characters who are hounded and cruelly destroyed by forces they often never understand. As much as Kafka's Joseph K., they are persecuted for no clear reason. Nor do the representatives of science or religion (frequently an uneasy and unconvincing melding of the two) offer much relief. In Turgenev's archetypal "Father Alexyei's Story," one of the great Le Fanuesque pursuit tales from the period, a young man studying for the priesthood is persecuted to death by a jeering demon who has the power, among other things, to make him spit out the Eucharist and grind it underfoot when he attempts to take Communion. Not a shred of evidence exists to indicate that the young man has done anything to deserve such a fate. Indeed, he is a devout, earnest, orthodox believer who continually prays for, and does not get, God's help. It scarcely matters whether the demon is supernatural or psychological or whether, as is likely, Turgenev meant the reader to have either option: the sense of vulnerability in a threatening world is the same. When the despairing father, who never recovers from his son's tragedy, breaks down in tears and asks, "How have I deserved such wrath from the Lord?" the reader can only echo him—how indeed?

This is not to suggest that all the writers in the period have a vision as severe as Turgenev's (nor are all of Turgenev's horror tales this unremittingly horrible), but the most seriously intended works surely move in this direction. The tendency is apparent even in Blackwood, the most optimistic and upbeat writer of the period. Although his characters generally survive their horrific ordeals (in itself an unusually positive turn of affairs, given the tragic endings of most stories by Blackwood's contemporaries), they find themselves plunged back into an everyday reality they have already renounced as being profoundly cold and alienating. Neither the ghostly nor the empirical world is presented as a hospitable place.

Because the darkness in this fiction is difficult to sustain for very long, it generally erupts in a more disturbing and uncompromising way in short stories than in novels. The short stories of Bram Stoker, for example, tend to be bleaker than *Dracula,* which at least has a happy ending. Indeed, some of the darkest writers, such as Bierce (and earlier, Poe) did not write novels at all.

What makes the darkness bearable, indeed richly pleasurable, is the artfulness of this fiction—its subtle atmosphere, haunting imagery, and tragicomic sense of humor. The literary quality of an astonishing amount of this fiction continues to go unrecognized by even the more savvy commentators.

In the December 5, 1980, issue of the *Times Literary Supplement,* A. N. Wilson exemplifies a dismally typical attitude when he writes: "We do not judge whether a horror film or ghost story is 'good' by the same standards by which we judge a real work of literature. All that matters here is whether we have been frightened." As anyone who has read even a smattering of James, Wharton, Onions, or any number of other first-rate writers can attest, this pronouncement presents a false dichotomy. Certainly in the horror fiction of the late nineteenth and early twentieth centuries, "whether we have been frightened" is entirely a function of whether the story is well written and imaginatively conceived. The stories that do not frighten are invariably those with no style and no vision. The best of these fascinating and powerful works reach beyond the boundaries of horror and Gothic fandom to all readers who enjoy and value beautifully crafted fiction.

Bibliography

This bibliography covers short stories, novelettes, and novels from 1872–1919 published in England and the United States. It also includes several anthologies as well as selected continental and Russian works in translation. A variety of horror modes are described, from the "pleasantly uncomfortable" chills of the M. R. James school to the extravagant nightmares of the visionaries. (Authors are American unless noted otherwise.) Because short stories and novelettes were the major forms of the period, the annotations consist of unified essays on each writer that attempt to pinpoint his or her distinctive stylistic and thematic contribution as revealed in a number of works. (Individual commentary on each work—many are collections of stories—would have been needlessly fragmented and repetitive.) In the case of borderline works, decisions to include were made on the basis of whether horror is a dominant focus or subsidiary motif. In a period that saw the publication of numerous bona fide horror works—works in which horror and terror are sustained and do not play second fiddle to other concerns—the distinction is well worth making. Thus, the detective and adventure novels of Sax Rohmer are excluded, despite occult episodes, as are the fantasy works of H. Rider Haggard and Lord Dunsany. Many of the short story collections listed are not devoted exclusively to horror fiction; they are included because they have a supernatural slant and contain a generous or at least a reasonable sampling of the writer's work in the genre. For the sake of comprehensiveness, *cante cruel* works are reluctantly included, even though the compiler of this chapter agrees strongly with Elizabeth Bowen that the genre should inspire "not so much revulsion or shock as a sort of awe."

3-1. Allen, Grant (U.K.). **The Desire of the Eyes.** Digby, Long, 1895.

3-2. Allen, Grant. **Strange Stories.** Chatto & Windus, 1884.

3-3. Allen, Grant. **Twelve Tales: With a Headpiece, a Tailpiece, and an Intermezzo.** Grant Richards, 1899.

Notorious for his blistering attacks on Victorian social mores, Canadian-born Grant Allen is the author of the enticingly titled *The Woman Who Did* and other social fictions. His short stories reflect an interest in anthropology, especially his science fiction tales involving lost worlds and time travel. Almost entirely neglected are his supernatural tales, concentrated mainly in the collections cited above, which include such forgotten items as "The Mysterious Occurence in Piccadilly," "The Reverend John Creedy," and "A Confidential Communication."

The ideas in Allen's supernatural tales, which encompass voodoo, pagan rites, esoteric Buddhism, pantheism, and all manner of "elfin visions," are exotic and memorable. His language, however, despite moments of great vividness, is often crude and overwrought: "They cut themselves with flint knives. Ghostly ichor streamed copious. . . . Rudolph bent his head to avoid the blows. He cowered in abject terror. Oh! what fear would any Christian ghost have inspired by the side of these incorporeal pagan savages! Ah! mercy! mercy! They would tear him limb from limb! They would rend him in pieces!" (from "Pallinghurst Barrow"). Allen is a classic example of a writer whose style is not up to his concepts, a visionary who gets carried away with his visions. His mysticism prefigures Blackwood's, but he lacks Blackwood's poetic imagery and ability to evoke cosmic horror. An excellent sample of these fascinating but frustrating stories can be found in Hugh Lamb's *Terror by Gaslight, Victorian Tales of Terror,* and *The Thrill of Horror.*

3-4. Atherton, Gertrude. **The Bell in the Fog and Other Stories.** Harper, 1905.

3-5. Atherton, Gertrude. **The Foghorn.** Houghton Mifflin, 1934; Arno, 1977.

The great-grandniece of Benjamin Franklin, the indefatigable Gertrude Atherton, who wrote books into her ninetieth year, was known for her vibrant style, daring sexual explicitness, and unshakable feminism. Her ghostly tales include "Death and the Countess," "Crowned with One Crest," and her masterpiece, "The Striding Place," which is found in both of her supernatural collections.

3-6. Baring, Maurice (U.K.). **Half a Minute's Silence and Other Stories.** Heinemann, 1925; Arno, 1977.

3-7. Baring, Maurice. **Orpheus in Mayfair.** Mills & Boon, 1909.

Immortalized mainly in the title *For Maurice,* Vernon Lee's collection of weird stories dedicated to him, Maurice Baring has received little attention for his own supernatural tales. Among these forgotten stories are "The Anti-christ," "Shadow of a Midnight," and "The Silver Mountain." He is also the author of *The Glass Mender* (1910), a collection on the borderline of super-natural horror, which consists of recapitulated ghostly legends. Baring's style is lyrical, graceful, and disarmingly musical. He is especially skillful at de-picting the supernatural from the point of view of frightened children. Ghostly motifs and episodes also appear in his mainstream fiction, such as *Robert Peckham* (1930), which opens with a little boy's vision of a corpse sit-ting up in its coffin.

3–8. Beale, Charles Willing. **The Ghost of Guir House.** Editor Publishing, 1897, in *Five Victorian Ghost Novels.* Ed. by E. F. Bleiler. Dover, 1971.

Although most of the many overtly occultist novels published during the late nineteenth and early twentieth centuries were poorly written and in-sufferably didactic, this one, by an obscure American writer, has been praised by Bleiler for its "excellent local color" and "firmness of character-ization." The plot involves hypnotism, a haunted house, a kink in time, and a variety of occultist machinery. As is the case with all too many spiritualist novels, the dialogue is often stilted and preachy: " 'Not only two things, but ten million things, can occupy the same space at the same time; for what is space, and what is time? They are mental conditions, as are all the phenom-ena of nature. Even your scientist will tell you that the infinite ether pene-trates all substances. . . .' " Beale's imagery, however, is powerful and haunt-ing, with a striking sense of desolation and loneliness that makes the reader, like the protagonist, feel he or she has been "snatched back to earth" at the end of the fantastic plot, having had "the ecstatic visions of a drowning man cut short by rescue."

3–9. Benson, A. C. (U.K.). **Basil Netherby.** Hutchinson, 1927.

3–10. Benson, A. C. **The Hill of Trouble and Other Stories.** Isbister, 1903.

3–11. Benson, A. C. **The Isles of Sunset.** Isbister, 1904.

3–12. Benson, A. C. **Paul, the Minstrel, and Other Stories.** Smith, Elder, 1911; Arno, 1977.

Although they are virtually eclipsed by the contributions of his two brothers (E. F. Benson and R. H. Benson), the ghostly tales of essayist A. C. Benson have a unique atmosphere and mood. Lacking the wit and polish of his brothers, A. C. Benson chose to emphasize somber, darkly oppressive states of mind and experience. His stories are haunted by half-seen malevolent creatures that often well up as a consequence of moral depravity or empti-ness. Indeed, the weakness in these otherwise memorable tales is overobvious allegory. (As M. R. James pointed out, it is difficult to be spooked when you are being preached at.) Nevertheless, Benson's wild, elemental imagery and his sure sense of atmosphere make these tales worth searching for, although they are quite rare. Especially worth finding is *Paul, the Minstrel,* as it reprints the stories in *The Hill of Troubles* and *The Isles of Sunset.* Benson is also known for *The Child of the Dawn,* an allegorical novel with supernatural elements. A good sample of the short stories can be found in Hugh Lamb's anthologies.

*3–13. Benson, E. F. (U.K.). **"And the Dead Spake"** and **The Horror Horn.** Doran, 1923.

*3–14. Benson, E. F. **More Spook Stories.** Hutchinson, 1934.

*3–15. Benson, E. F. **The Room in the Tower and Other Stories.** Mills & Boon, 1912.

*3–16. Benson, E. F. **Spook Stories.** Hutchinson, 1928; Arno, 1976.

*3–17. Benson, E. F. **Visible and Invisible.** Hutchinson, 1923.

E. F. Benson's numerous ghostly tales fall into two categories: visionary outdoor stories that attempt to communicate a romantic sense of place, and grim, claustrophobic stories that frequently involve supernatural revenge in haunted-house settings. In both categories he is a master of imagery and a consummate craftsman, although his stories have a curious tendency to fall apart at the end ("And No Bird Sings," "The Face," "The Room in the Tower"). His celebrated skill in characterization and social commentary, especially praised by critics in his revived Lucia novels, is always brought to bear in his ghost stories, making them some of the most sophisticated in the genre.

The outdoor stories are in the mystical tradition of Blackwood and Machen: nature, which is both dazzling and sinister, has animistic qualities that suggest supernatural forces. "The Man Who Went Too Far," Benson's most famous tale in this category, unleashed a Pan-like deity similar to Machen's "The Great God Pan." "A Tale of a Deserted House," a more obscure work, has a vast sense of space that recalls Blackwood. Although Benson is less magical and surreal than Machen and less original in his elemental imagery than Blackwood, he has a deft sense of contrast: his stories have a healthy out-of-doors quality, a relentless prettiness, that suddenly becomes stained with the onslaught of vampires ("Mrs. Amworth"), mummies ("Monkeys"), or giant slugs ("Caterpillars," "Negotium Perambulans," "And No Bird Sings"). Although Benson stocks his forests and landscapes with all manner of demons and ghosts, he has a special, charmingly perverse fetish for monstrous slugs and wormlike creatures.

His claustrophobic haunted-house tales are as gray and grim as any in the genre. Especially powerful is "The Bath-Chair," the story of a man haunted by the ghost of a crippled, vengeful father. Others include "Naboth's Vinyard," "The Corner House," and "James Lamp." Even the stories that do not quite come off have a strong sense of cumulative buildup and invariably contain memorable apparition scenes. The control and understatement in Benson give him an affinity with M. R. James, as does his flair for sardonic humor. His collections are uniformly high in quality, despite the critical carpings of August Derleth and Edmund Wilson. The stories have also appeared in *Weird Tales* and in numerous anthologies, notably Lady Cynthia Asquith's collections.

3–18. Benson, R. H. (U.K.). **The Light Invisible.** Isbister, 1903.
3–19. Benson, R. H. **The Mirror of Shalott.** Pitman, 1907.
3–20. Benson, R. H. **The Necromancers.** Hutchinson, 1909.

A priest and a private chamberlain to Pope Pius X, R. H. Benson wrote ghost stories infused with theological allusions. Occasionally these detract from the ghostly element, but for the most part he keeps them under admirable control. At his best, Benson was capable of creating a highly original version or even inversion of a hackneyed theme. "My Own Tale," for example, is a haunted-house story about a house haunted by nothingness: "I don't think that I felt there was any presence there or anything of the kind. It was rather the opposite; it was the feeling of an extraordinary emptiness. . . . Like a Catholic cathedral in Protestant hands. . . . " Benson's most inventive storytelling device is found in *The Mirror of Shalott,* which consists of stories recounted by a group of haunted priests, who gather together to tell their terrifying experiences. These tales are hard to find (see Hugh Lamb's *A Wave of Fear* and *Return from the Grave*), but worth the search. Benson is also the author of a forgotten supernatural novel, *The Necromancers,* an allegorical indictment of spiritualism in the form of a tale involving a man's desire to communicate with a dead lover.

*3–21. Bierce, Ambrose. **Can Such Things Be?** Cassell, 1893.
*3–22. Bierce, Ambrose. **Ghost and Horror Stories of Ambrose Bierce.** Dover, 1964.
*3–23. Bierce, Ambrose. **In the Midst of Life: Tales of Soldiers and Civilians.** E. L. G. Steele, 1891.

The short fiction of Bierce, one of the masters of American horror, is of two types: supernatural horror tales that emphasize an unpleasant charnel-house gruesomeness, and psychological horror tales that rely, sometimes excessively, on trick endings. The most famous story in the latter category is "An Occurrence at Owl Creek Bridge," a Civil War tale that is one of the most perfect short stories in American fiction. The only authentic American Civil War writer (in the sense that he was the only fiction writer who actually fought in the war), Bierce wrote numerous war tales that have generous doses of psychological horror. One of these, "Chickamauga," is an almost surreal description of the ravages of war as seen from the point of view of a deaf-mute child. Bierce's supernatural tales, notably "The Death of Halpin Frayser" and "The Eyes of the Panther," focus more on the terror and suffering of the victim than on the supernatural pursuer. Thus, even in these stories the psychological element is made central. Nevertheless, Bierce's supernaturalism is memorable; his apparitions are "bodies without souls" (instead of the reverse)—malevolent animated corpses whose presence reminds us of physical corruption and the inevitability of death. When Bierce's ghosts have a story to tell, it is invariably one of loneliness and desolation; the horror of death is that it is merely a continuation of life.

Bierce's pessimism would probably be intolerable were it not for his mastery of black humor. Indeed, he is one of the most successful writers of all time in fusing humor and horror in a way that increases the power of the story rather than diluting it. This humor is frequently, and intentionally, tasteless: the first chapter of "The Damned Thing," a grisly description of an autopsy, is called "One Does Not Always Eat What Is on the Table"; a later chapter, a description of a mutilated corpse, is called "A Man Though Naked May Be in Rags." Often Bierce's humor is brutally ironic—a way of emphasizing that his world is one where things refuse to fit together, where terrible things happen to the wrong people for the wrong reasons, where horrors leap out of the most trivial or absurd circumstances. In this context, Bierce is an early absurdist writer, one of the first to master a black humor that has become endemic in American literature and culture. The structure of his horror fiction is equally forward-looking; frequently, as in "The Moonlit Road" or "The Suitable Surroundings," his tales are told in a fragmented, nonchronological fashion, which evokes the chaotic randomness Bierce saw in the world. His stories are dark collages that have a curiously delayed but desolating impact.

3-24. Biss, Gerald (U.K.). **The Door of the Unreal.** Eveleigh Nash, 1919.
An obscure English writer who dropped out of sight in the 1920s, Biss (often misspelled "Bliss") left one notable mark with this powerful werewolf novel. Some enthusiasts of the genre regard this work as one of the finest werewolf tales ever written. Its qualities include an original plot and a skillful use of the psychic detective theme.

*3-25. Blackwood, Algernon (U.K.). **Ancient Sorceries and Other Tales.** Collins, 1927.
*3-26. Blackwood, Algernon. **Best Ghost Stories of Algernon Blackwood.** Dover, 1973.
*3-27. Blackwood, Algernon. **The Dance of Death and Other Tales.** Dial Press, 1928.
*3-28. Blackwood, Algernon. **Day and Night Stories.** Cassell, 1917.
*3-29. Blackwood, Algernon. **The Doll and One Other.** Arkham House, 1946.
*3-30. Blackwood, Algernon. **The Empty House and Other Ghost Stories.** Eveleigh Nash, 1906.
*3-31. Blackwood, Algernon. **Incredible Adventures.** Macmillan, 1914.
*3-32. Blackwood, Algernon. **John Silence, Physician Extraordinary.** Eveleigh Nash, 1908.
*3-33. Blackwood, Algernon. **The Listener and Other Stories.** Eveleigh Nash, 1907; Arno, 1977.

*3-34. Blackwood, Algernon. **The Lost Valley and Other Stories.** Eveleigh Nash, 1914; Arno, 1977.

*3-35. Blackwood, Algernon. **Pan's Garden: A Volume of Nature Stories.** Macmillan, 1912.

*3-36. Blackwood, Algernon. **Shocks.** Grayson & Grayson, 1935.

*3-37. Blackwood, Algernon. **Strange Stories.** Heinemann, 1929; Arno, 1977.

*3-38. Blackwood, Algernon. **The Tales of Algernon Blackwood.** Martin Secker, 1939.

*3-39. Blackwood, Algernon. **Ten Minute Stories.** John Murray, 1914; Arno, 1977.

*3-40. Blackwood, Algernon. **Tongues of Fire and Other Sketches.** Jenkins, 1924.

*3-41. Blackwood, Algernon. **The Willows and Other Queer Tales.** Collins, 1934.

The unrivaled master of a visionary tradition of ghostly tales that he helped inaugurate, Blackwood is probably the most prolific ghost story writer in English. During his long life, he invented an astonishing variety of ghostly concepts, but he is best known for his nature stories, especially "The Willows," which tells of a group of campers on a Danube island who are beseiged by elusive forces of "bewildering beauty" and mounting terror. In this and other nature stories, Blackwood emerges as a freewheeling pantheist: nature is a thoroughly ambiguous divinity, impossible to pin down, both seductive and terrifying, spreading out into everything. The deadly willow bushes in "The Willows," the snow apparition in "The Glamour of the Snow," and the vampiric patch of earth in "The Transfer" do not in themselves constitute the central "horror" in these stories, but are satellites of larger unseen forces, reminders of the smallness and "utter insignificance" of humanity. Blackwood's imagery, in which he frequently throws out chains of conditional metaphors to capture a transcendental experience, is lyrical and strikingly original. Lacking the wit and suavity of M. R. James and his antiquarian followers, Blackwood goes for majestic, cosmic effects. He often overwrites, but when he succeeds he sweeps the reader into an alternate world in a way that James and other more careful, smaller scaled writers do not attempt. As Jacques Barzun and Wendell Taylor point out in *A Catalogue of Crime,* Blackwood sometimes "repeats his données"; but as H. P. Lovecraft states, he is also "the one absolute and unquestioned master of weird atmosphere."

Less well known but equally masterful are Blackwood's indoor, haunted-house stories, which emphasize physical horror to a far greater extent than the more ephemeral outdoor tales. The most shuddery story in this category is "The Listener," which recounts the fearful experiences of a man haunted by the ghost of a leper. Several of Blackwood's stories, both indoor and outdoor, involve the cases of John Silence, Blackwood's psychic detective, a sometimes overtalkative character who resembles Stoker's Van Helsing, Le Fanu's Dr. Hesselius, and especially Hodgson's Dr. Carnacki. John Silence represents the didactic side of Blackwood, and his overlong occultist disquisitions sometimes bring down these otherwise magical stories.

Compared to the antiquarian tradition of James, Blackwood belongs to a more mystical, didactic tradition that includes Arthur Machen and William Butler Yeats. These writers, members of the Order of the Golden Dawn and other occult societies, placed a strong value on subjective experience and continually indicted the "materialism" of the modern world both in their fiction and in their essays. Some of Blackwood's most sustained mystical writing can be found in his novels, especially *The Centaur* (1911), *The Promise of Air* (1918), and *The Human Chord* (1910). As Bleiler points out, these longer works cannot be classified as "terror stories," but "must be called mystical for want of a better term." They do develop themes, however, which appear in brief flashes in the short stories.

3-42. Blavatsky, Helena P. **Nightmare Tales.** Theosophical Publishing Society, 1892.

A professional occultist and the founder of Theosophy (after emigrating to the United States in 1873), Russian-born Madame Blavatsky is better known for her occult nonfiction, such as *Key to Theosophy*, than for her supernatural fiction. Nevertheless, she did publish occasional short fiction, along with this single collection of stories. The most famous of these is "The Ensouled Violin," but none of her stories is well known to general readers. Perhaps this is just as well, for those who do know her fiction accuse her of heavy-handed didacticism and scant creativity. She is sometimes presented as a textbook case of what is wrong with "true believer" occult fiction. Lovecraft, among others, has written that the best supernatural fiction is actually written by skeptics and nonbelievers who maintain a necessary aesthetic and emotional distance from their material.

3-43. Broughton, Rhoda (U.K.). **Tales for Christmas Eve.** Bentley, 1873; reissued and enlarged as **Twilight Stories** in 1879.

Broughton produced occasional ghost stories under the prodding of Le Fanu; indeed, he bought her first novel. Despite her closeness to Le Fanu (she was his niece by marriage) and her admiration of his style, she lacked her uncle's ability to terrify. Nevertheless, her work is witty, cultivated, and —in the best Le Fanu tradition—sardonically attenuated. Especially impressive is "Nothing but the Truth," an epistolary haunted-house story reprinted in Hugh Lamb's *Terror by Gaslight* (1975).

3-44. Buchan, John (U.K.). **Grey Weather: Moorland Tales of My Own People.** John Lane, 1899.

3-45. Buchan, John. **The Moon Endureth: Tales and Fancies.** Blackwood, 1912.

3-46. Buchan, John. **The Runagates Club.** Hodder & Stoughton, 1928.
3-47. Buchan, John. **The Watcher by the Threshold and Other Tales.** Blackwood, 1902.
3-48. Buchan, John. **Witch Wood.** Hodder & Stoughton, 1927.

The music of John Buchan's horror fiction has an archaic, mythlike tonality. Intensely lyrical and spectral, these stories are eminently worthwhile as long as the reader is willing to wrestle with the difficulties posed by Buchan's insistence on using Scottish dialect in both the dialogue and the narrative of stories set in his native land. Buchan is known among horror enthusiasts for his ability to depict evil lurking in ancient cultures. His most popular horror tales are "The Green Wildebeest," involving African witchcraft, "The Wind in the Portico," which tells of ancient Britano-Roman terrors coming to life, "The Watcher by the Threshold," involving a malignant supernatural presence, and "Skule Skerry," which has what Lovecraft calls "touches of sub-arctic fright." Buchan's leisurely paced horror novel, *Witch Wood,* set in Scotland, tells of the survival of the Witch's Sabbat. An exceptionally poetic story, "The Outgoing of the Tide," is reprinted in Peter Haining's *The Clans of Darkness* (1971).

*3-49. Chambers, Robert W. **The King in Yellow.** F. T. Neely, 1895; Arno, 1977.
*3-50. Chambers, Robert W. **The King in Yellow and Other Horror Stories.** Dover, 1970.
*3-51. Chambers, Robert W. **The Maker of Moons.** Putnam, 1896; Arno, 1977.
*3-52. Chambers, Robert W. **The Mystery of Choice.** Appleton, 1897.
*3-53. Chambers, Robert W. **The Slayer of Souls.** Doran, 1920.
*3-54. Chambers, Robert W. **The Tree of Heaven.** Appleton, 1907.

One of the most exotic and powerful of American horror writers, Chambers is best known for a unifying mythos that provides the underpinning for his best tales. In "The Yellow Sign," "In the Court of the Dragon," and others, his doomed heroes evoke Corcosa, "the awful abode of lost souls," by reading from a demonic book called "The King in Yellow." Corcosa is actually an inventive variation on Bierce's tour de force, "An Inhabitant of Corcosa," but the sensibility of Chambers, with his saturation in metaphysical evil and his obsession with a central mythos, is actually closer to Arthur Machen than to Bierce. "The King in Yellow," Chamber's imaginary demonic book, is similar to Lovecraft's "Necronomicon," M. R. James's "Canon Alberic's Scrapbook," and other lethal tomes in ghostly fiction. Chambers is not a subtle writer; his stories abound with mawkish love-interest sequences, excessively perfumed decadence imagery, and stagey dialogue. But they have numerous unforgettable moments that deliver a combination of physical revulsion and metaphysical wonder. The corpselike apparitions in "The Messenger" and "The Yellow Sign" embody both of these qualities, and the darkly dissonant organ music in "In the Court of the Dragon" evokes a spectral musical effect that is chilling and utterly original.

The strengths and weaknesses in Chambers can be seen most clearly in "The Maker of Moons," a wordy but ultimately powerful horror story. The buildup to this tale is tedious, but the double climax is spellbinding: the first phase involves a man with a skull-like face sending lunar bodies into the night sky; the second introduces us to the Xin creature, a "nameless, shapeless mass," with "thousands of loathsome satellites," which resemble "spidery, crab-like creatures"—clearly a forerunner of the monstrosities of Lovecraft, who admired and championed Chambers's work. Many of Chambers's stories are erratic and read rather badly, but they leave a strong, fantastic image in the mind. Chambers also wrote a number of largely forgotten historical and biographical works.

*3-55. Conrad, Joseph (U.K.). **Heart of Darkness.** Blackwood, 1902; Norton, 1963.

3-56. Conrad, Joseph. **A Set of Six.** Methuen, 1908.

3-57. Conrad, Joseph. **The Shadow Line.** Dent, 1917.

3-58. Conrad, Joseph. **Tales of Unrest.** Doubleday, 1908; Penguin, 1977.

Edmund Wilson first hit upon the happy idea of classifying *Heart of Darkness* as a horror tale. Overanalyzed as a political allegory about imperialism, a religious allegory about the loss of innocence, and a Freudian allegory about a journey into the unconscious (to name only a few), the story has a more immediate appeal based on its unique atmosphere of dread and the grotesque eeriness of its jungle imagery. The plot involves the efforts of Marlowe, Conrad's famous narrator, to find Kurtz, a mysterious and much-feared imperialist, who has in some terrible way been "claimed" by the darkness of the African jungle. A horror story in the most literal sense, *Heart of Darkness* builds toward Kurtz's climactic final words, "The horror! The horror!"—a statement about human existence that is at once chilling and enigmatic. The entire convoluted narrative, with its labyrinth of tales within tales, is permeated with "the terrific suggestiveness of words heard in dreams, of phrases spoken in nightmares." Black magic is insinuated with the appearance of "fiend-like" sorcerers and "the drone of weird incantations," but the real horror is the relativity and dumb mystery of all human perception—what Marlowe in another classic novel, *Lord Jim,* calls "the terrible vagueness of human thought."

Although few of Conrad's shorter tales are supernatural, they consistently have an atmosphere and tone of mystery and dread. "The Idiots," his most explicitly supernatural horror tale (in *Tales of Unrest*), tells of a group of idiot children who haunt the landscape, drifting "according to the inexplicable impulses of their monstrous darkness"; the climax, with its "unappeased" apparition from the grave, moves the story from material to supernatural horror. All of these tales are distinguished by masterful imagery and an exacting sense of place.

3–59. Corelli, Marie (pseud. of Mary McKay) (U.K.). **The Strange Visitation of Josiah McNason: A Christmas Ghost Story.** Newnes, 1904; Arno, 1976.

Although the prolific Marie Corelli wrote in the field of religious fantasy rather than supernatural horror, she did contribute this offbeat ghostly tale about a miserly millionaire, a pathetically crippled ex-employee, and a beautiful young woman jilted because of her poverty. What is peculiar about this novel is its remarkably close imitation of Dickens's *A Christmas Carol.* The story does have one horrific variation: the cold-hearted miser is plunged into his visions of past and future not by a ghost but by a winged goblin.

3–60. Craddock, C. E. (pseud. of Mary N. Murfree). **The Fair Mississippian.** Houghton Mifflin, 1908.
3–61. Craddock, C. E. **The Phantom of the Foot Bridge and Other Stories.** Harper, 1895.

C. E. Craddock wrote folkloric supernatural stories in the American tall tales tradition. Some are folksy and humorous, and thus do not really belong in the genre, but others have touches of horror. All are obscure and rarely mentioned, even by genre enthusiasts. *The Fair Mississippian,* however, was singled out for inclusion in August Derleth's ground-breaking bibliography, "The Weird Tale in English Since 1890," his senior thesis at the University of Wisconsin.

3–62. Cram, Ralph Adams. **Black Spirits and White: A Book of Ghost Stories.** Stone & Kimball, 1895.

An expert in Gothic architecture in America—he designed the Cathedral of St. John the Divine in New York City—Cram wrote only one collection of weird tales, but it has been cited by horror enthusiasts as an exceptionally fine one. Lovecraft has praised "The Dead Valley," Cram's most famous tale, for its suggestiveness, subtlety, and "vague regional horror."

*3–63. Crawford, F. Marion. **Wandering Ghosts.** U.K. title: **Uncanny Tales.** T. Fisher Unwin, 1911.
3–64. Crawford, F. Marion. **The Witch of Prague.** 3 vols. Macmillan, 1891.

A prolific writer in several genres, Crawford is mainly remembered for *Wandering Ghosts,* his volume of supernatural horror tales, a book that by itself established him as one of the premier American horror writers. "The Upper Berth," his most frequently anthologized tale, tells of a ship haunted by the ghost of a suicide. Crawford pulls off the rare feat of having his protagonist physically wrestle with the apparition without diminishing the ghostliness or subtlety of the tale. "The Dead Smile," which involves an Irish banshee, blends ghoulish humor and horror in a manner not unlike Bierce. "For the Blood Is the Life," an unusually poetic and chilling vampire tale, takes place in Italy, where Crawford was born and spent a great deal of time.

Crawford's special talent is an ability to unleash intense, visceral horrors without compromising the poetry and suggestiveness of the overall atmosphere. In *The Witch of Prague,* a forgotten weird novel, the horror involves hypnotism, which is seen as more of a black art than a science. The plot depicts the attempts of Unorna, the "witch" in the novel, to extend human life by keeping an old man continually hypnotized. As Dorothy Scarborough points out, this concept owes much to Poe's "The Facts in the Case of M. Valdemar." Unorna uses hypnotism for other nefarious purposes as well; in one scene, she causes a young man to re-experience the life and violent death of a Jew martyred for converting to Christianity. Although *The Witch of Prague* is on the borderline of science fiction, Crawford's admirers tend to regard it as a gripping horror story, one far more immersed in black magic than in science.

3–65. Dawson, Emma. **An Itinerant House and Other Stories.** William Doxey, 1897.
A pathetic and obscure figure, Dawson was praised by Ambrose Bierce as "head and shoulders" above her contemporaries, but was forgotten by virtually everyone else. It is commonly believed that she starved to death. An opium-dream tale, "The Dramatic in My Destiny," was reprinted in the winter 1973 *Weird Tales.* Her other ghostly tales, such as "Are the Dead Dead?" and "The Singed Moths," are in the hard-to-find *An Itinerant House.*

3–66. Donovan, Dick (pseud. of Joyce E. Preston-Muddock) (U.K.). **Tales of Terror.** Chato & Windus, 1899.
Although he wrote mainly espionage and detective stories, Donovan occasionally delved into the weird and fantastic. *Tales of Terror,* which collects his short horror tales, contains such forgotten chillers as "A Night of Horror," "The Corpse Light," and "The Spectre of Rislip Abbey." His narrative style has an attractive vigor and simplicity, as well as a pleasantly old-fashioned storytelling ambience. Unfortunately, it is also weakened by clichés and crudities, including a tendency toward literal repetition of phrases that are not very striking in the first place. In "The Corpse Light," for example, which involves a haunted mill, the narrator tells of being touched in the face by a "cold and clammy something," a "cold clammy something," and "invisible something," and "the something"—all in the space of two pages. An enormously prolific writer, Donovan was sometimes careless, but his supernatural stories are a great deal of fun. A nice sampling can be found in Hugh Lamb's anthologies, including *Victorian Nightmares, Terror by Gaslight,* and *Victorian Tales of Terror* (1977, 1975, and 1974).

3–67. Doyle, Arthur Conan (U.K.). **The Black Doctor and Other Tales of Horror and Mystery.** Doran, 1919.
3–68. Doyle, Arthur Conan. **The Captain of the "Polestar" and Other Tales.** Longmans, 1890.

3-69. Doyle, Arthur Conan. **Danger! and Other Stories.** John Murray, 1918.

3-70. Doyle, Arthur Conan. **The Great Keinplatz Experiment.** Rand McNally, 1894.

3-71. Doyle, Arthur Conan. **The Last Valley: Impressions and Tales.** Smith, Elder, 1911.

3-72. Doyle, Arthur Conan. **My Friend the Murderer and Other Mysteries and Adventures.** Lovell, Coryell, 1893.

3-73. Doyle, Arthur Conan. **Round the Fire Stories.** Smith, Elder, 1908.

3-74. Doyle, Arthur Conan. **Round the Red Lamp.** Methuen, 1894.

3-75. Doyle, Arthur Conan. **Tales of Terror and Mystery.** Murray, 1922; Doubleday, 1977.

Famous for his Sherlock Holmes series, Doyle also wrote numerous supernatural horror stories, many of them published in the 1890s, long before his later obsession with spiritualism. His weird fiction is characterized by many of the qualities familiar to fans of Sherlock Holmes—sharp characterization, witty dialogue, a careful sense of place. What is less familiar is the visionary imagery of "The Horror of the Heights," a story of gigantic bell-shaped creatures encountered in the sky during a monoplane flight; or the cold and ferocious cruelty of "The Case of Lady Sannox," a revenge story; or the sense of "the marvellous and the monstrous" communicated in "The Leather Funnel," an antiquarian tale worthy of M. R. James. Doyle wrote tales in several categories—antiquarian, mystical, psychological, science fiction/horror—all worth consideration. Even the efforts that don't quite succeed are distinguished by controlled, civilized prose.

3-76. Erckmann, Emile, and Alexandre Chatrian (France). **The Best Tales of Terror of Erckmann-Chatrian.** Millington (planned pub.).

3-77. Erckmann, Emile, and Alexandre Chatrian. **The Man-Wolf and Other Tales.** Ward, Lock & Tyler, 1876; Arno, 1976.

3-78. Erckmann, Emile, and Alexandre Chatrian. **The Polish Jew.** J. H. Hotten, 1871.

3-79. Erckmann, Emile, and Alexandre Chatrian. **Strange Stories.** Appleton, 1880.

Erckmann-Chatrian is the combined pseudonym of two French writers who collaborated for more than 30 years. Most of their fiction, including their weird fiction, is currently neglected and hard to find. Not all their horror stories are supernatural. Indeed, H. P. Lovecraft has complained of "a tendency toward natural explanations and scientific wonders" in their work. However, Lovecraft has also praised their "shuddering midnight atmosphere" and "engulfing darkness and mystery." Dorothy Scarborough, in *The Supernatural in Modern English Fiction,* finds Erckmann-Chatrian to be highly influential: "The Owl's Ear," claims Scarborough, inspired Blackwood's "With Intent to Steal," while "The Waters of Death," the story of "a loathsome, enchanted crab," influenced Wells's "The Strange Orchid." Other notable Erckmann-Chatrian stories include "The Man-Wolf," a werewolf tale complete with a Gothic castle and a thousand-year curse; and "The Spider Crab," a favorite of M. R. James. The latter, the story of an oversize spider crab who develops an appetite for bathers in a French health spa, is characteristic of Erckmann-Chatrian's weird fiction: the buildup is gradual, the science element is overwhelmed by horror and black magic, and the monster that erupts at the end is truly fearsome: "It was as big as my head and a violet crimson; I can only describe it as a bladder full of blood." Readers who wish to obtain a sample of these stories should look for the selections in Hugh Lamb's *Best Tales of Terror* as well as his anthologies, *The Taste of Fear, Victorian Tales of Terror,* and *Terror by Gaslight.*

*3–80. Ewers, Hanns Heinz (Germany). **Alraune** (English tr.). John Day, 1929; Arno, 1976; German version, 1911.
*3–81. Ewers, Hanns Heinz. **The Sorcerer's Apprentice** (English tr.). John Day, 1927; German version, 1907.
*3–82. Ewers, Hanns Heinz. **"The Spider"** (1931 short story). In *Wolf's Complete Book of Terror.* Potter, 1979.
*3–83. Ewers, Hanns Heinz. **Vampire** (English tr.). John Day, 1934; German version, 1921.

Solidly in the German Gothic tradition of Hoffman, Tieck, and Meinhold, Ewers surpasses them in sustained terror. To the romantic supernaturalism of his predecessors, he added a strain of dark psychology from Poe and Freud and a languid decadence from Huysmans and Baudelaire. The desolating power of his work, however, is distinctly his own. Of the novels noted above, *Alraune,* the story of an artificially created female monster, is the most famous. *The Sorcerer's Apprentice,* a favorite of Lovecraft's, has a satanic motif. The most original Ewers novel is *Vampire,* which tells of the unconscious vampiric blood-lust of Frank Braun, a charismatic German patriot living in New York during World War I. Of Ewers's short horror stories, the most famous is "The Spider," a splendid tale that presents a distillation of Ewers's style and major themes in a narrative of spellbinding intensity. Ewers was fond of femme fatale creations, and in "The Spider" he gives us one of the most nightmarish and original evil females in literature, a spidery woman with quivering nostrils and dark eyes full of light, who appears in black gloves and a black dress with purple dots before she lures men to a grisly death. In one scene, the doomed hero watches in appalled fascination as a female spider in his room attracts, flirts with, and finally devours a male spider, prefiguring what is to happen to him. Ewers's characteristic mingling of ecstasy and revulsion in a single death wish is evident throughout.

3–84. Falkner, J. Meade (U.K.). **The Lost Stradivarius.** Blackwood, 1895. This rare novel, known only to connoisseurs of the weird, involves a young musician haunted by the ghost of a dead violinist. The rest of Falkner's sparse output has been forgotten; even *The Lost Stradivarius,* cited by Mike Ashley and others as an important work, does not appear in the critical surveys of Lovecraft, Birkhead, or Scarborough.

3–85. Fraser, Phyllis, and Wise, Herbert. **Great Tales of Terror and the Supernatural.** Modern Library, 1944.

In its tastefulness, erudition, and awesome thoroughness, this landmark anthology of ghost and horror tales remains one of the finest collections of its kind in print. Although selections range from the early nineteenth through the midtwentieth centuries, the overwhelming emphasis is on stories from the late Victorian and early modern periods. Included are such rarities as Blackwood's "Confession" and de Maupassant's "Was It a Dream?" and such classics as Jacobs's "The Monkey's Paw" and White's "Lukundoo." Especially valuable is the inclusion in full of Onions's "The Beckoning Fair One" and Machen's "The Great God Pan." The introduction, although not especially scholarly or profound, is sensible and attractive, as are the brief introductions to each story. This volume has long served as a model of how to organize a quality supernatural anthology.

*3–86. Gilchrist, R. Murray (U.K.). **The Stone Dragon and Other Tragic Romances.** Methuen, 1894.

A Victorian novelist, Gilchrist wrote occasional ghost stories of surpassing vividness and musicality. *The Stone Dragon* is his sole collection, but individual tales ("A Night on the Moor") were written after the turn of the century. His supernatural tales do not appear to have been influential or even widely read, but they are highly original, self-contained masterpieces. Exotic, otherworldly, and richly metaphorical, his style evokes a highly perfumed decadence dreamscape of subtly suggested horrors, which often take deadly and seductive female forms. His diction is elaborate and brilliantly artificial, but his apparitions are deeply felt and genuinely terrifying: "The Thing was lying prone on the floor, the presentiment of a sleeping horror. Vivid scarlet and sable feathers covered its gold-crowned cock's-head, and its leathern dragon-wings were folded. Its sinuous tail, capped with a snake's eyes and mouth, was curved in luxurious and delighted satiety. A prodigious evil leaped in its atmosphere" (from "The Basilisk"). For a generous sampling of these gripping and poetic stories, see the Hugh Lamb anthologies: *The Thrill of Horror* (1975—for "Witch In-Grain"), *Return from the Grave* (1977—for "Roxana Runs Lunatick"), *Terror by Gaslight* (1975—for "The Basilisk"), and *Victorian Nightmares* (1977—for "The Return"). Gilchrist is an almost totally forgotten master of horror who deserves the widest possible circulation and revival.

3–87. Gray, Sir Arthur (U.K.). **Tedious Brief Tales of Granta and Gramarye.** W. Heffer & Sons, 1919.

A fabulously rare item, this cleverly illustrated volume of period pieces is solidly in the M. R. James antiquarian tradition. Gray, a Master of Jesus College, had a style distinctive for its graceful narration and unpretentious erudition. Especially satisfying is "The Everlasting Club," fragments from the Minute Book of an eighteenth-century Libertine Club devoted to "unholy revelry." Also chilling is "The Necromancer," a seventeenth-century tale of black magic in Jesus College. The werewolf in this story, its eyes "smoking with dull malevolence," is perhaps Gray's most memorable apparition.

3–88. Halidom, M. Y. (U.K.). **The Spirit Lovers and Other Stories.** Simpkin, 1903.

3–89. Halidom, M. Y. **Tales of the Wonder Club** (published under pseud. Dryasdust, later under Halidom). Harrison, 1899, 1900.

Halidom and Dryasdust were pseudonyms that may have covered the identities of more than one writer. (One frequently made guess is Edward Heron-Allen, who also had the alias of Christopher Blayre.) Today these tales are as obscure and unknown as their real author. The Dryasdust style is notable for its wide-ranging erudition and pleasing sense of humor. Among the tales collected here are "The Pigmy Queen" and "Lost in the Catacombs: The Antiquary's Story."

*3–90. Hardy, Thomas (U.K.). **Wessex Tales.** Harper, 1896; St. Martin, 1978.

With his fatalistic sensibility, ghostly atmosphere, and unparalleled sense of doom and gloom, Hardy was a natural for horror stories. Hardy's Hap, an agent of cosmic persecution, bears a haunting resemblance to Le Fanu's "enormous machinery of hell," a remorseless supernatural machine that drives the doomed characters to madness or death. Touches of supernatural horror occur in his novels (especially *Tess of the d'Urbervilles*), but his shorter pieces are sometimes devoted exclusively to the ghostly and horrific. Most notable among these tales is "The Withered Arm," the story of a pathetic peasant woman who attempts to cure a horrible affliction by laying her arm on the corpse of a hanged man, not knowing that the corpse is her husband's secret son. Dark irony, a definitive characteristic of modern supernatural horror, is manipulated more masterfully by Hardy than perhaps by any other English writer.

3–91. Hawker, Mary E. (U.K.). **Cecilia De Noel.** Macmillan, 1891.

Hawker, a forgotten Scottish writer, was known during the Victorian period as a writer of considerable refinement and intelligence. *Cecilia De Noel,* her popular spook novel, was highly regarded in its day, but is now extremely rare.

3–92. Hawthorne, Julian. **David Poindexter's Disappearance and Other Tales.** Chatto & Windus, 1888.

3–93. Hawthorne, Julian. **Ellice Quentin and . Other Stories.** Chatto & Windus, 1880.

3-94. Hawthorne, Julian. **The Laughing Mill and Other Stories.** Macmillan, 1879.

3-95. Hawthorne, Julian. **Six Cent Sam's.** Price-McGill, 1893.

Almost totally eclipsed by his famous father, Julian Hawthorne is remembered by only a few enthusiasts of weird fiction. Nevertheless, his output is large and generously laced with occult themes. Dorothy Scarborough praises his skill in symbolism and his "quite modern concept of diabolism." He is also known for inventive plots. In "Lovers in Heaven," a newly dead man searches for a long-dead lover, but instead meets Satan in the form of his double. Other Hawthorne themes include possession and witchcraft.

3-96. Hearn, Lafcadio. **Fantastics and Other Fancies.** Houghton Mifflin, 1914; Arno, 1976.

3-97. Hearn, Lafcadio. **Kwaidan: Stories and Studies of Strange Things.** Houghton Mifflin, 1904; Dover, 1968.

3-98. Hearn, Lafcadio. **Some Chinese Ghosts.** Roberts Brothers, 1887.

Hearn was born in Greece, emigrated to the United States at the age of 19, and settled in Japan in 1890. His American stories, collected in *Fantastics,* have been praised by Lovecraft as containing "some of the most impressive ghoulishness in all literature"; while his later tales of the East have been noted for their more delicate and lyrical texture of spookiness. The latter, which are saturated in legend and history, have a unique beauty and conciseness. From the magical cherry tree in "Ubazakura"—with its flowers "like the nipples of a woman's breast, bedewed with milk"—to the vengeful decapitated head in "Diplomacy," Hearn's supernatural concepts evoke a wide range of emotions, from light enchantment to gruesome horror.

3-99. Hichens, Robert (U.K.). **The Black Spaniel and Other Stories.** Methuen, 1905.

3-100. Hichens, Robert. **Bye-Ways.** Dodd, Mead, 1897.

3-101. Hichens, Robert. **Snake-Bite and Other Stories.** Cassell, 1919.

3-102. Hichens, Robert. **Tongues of Conscience.** Methuen, 1900.

Difficult to classify, the ghostly fiction of Robert Hichens deals with a variety of themes. His most pervasive interest seems to have been in psychic phenomena. A few of his novels (*Flames,* 1897; *The Dweller on the Threshold,* 1911), although not strictly horror works, involve psychic and supernatural ideas such as personality transference and reincarnation. Sometimes, as in the allegorical sections of *The Dweller on the Threshold,* Hichens is clumsy and moralistic: "A little science sends a man away from God. A great deal of science brings a man back to God." His most careful and horrific work is found in his short stories; the most famous is "How Love Came to Professor Guildea," about a man haunted by a horrible, fawning female ghost who is in love with him. The most striking aspect of this remarkable apparition is that its horror is absolutely contiguous with its pathetic devotion to the victim. This is a chilling tale of terror, but it is also a psychological allegory about fear of physical intimacy. The tale is reprinted in Wise and Fraser's *Great Tales of Terror & the Supernatural* (1944).

*3–103. Hodgson, William Hope (U.K.). **The Boats of the Glen Carrig.** Chapman & Hall, 1907; Hyperion, 1976.

*3–104. Hodgson, William Hope. **Carnacki the Ghost Finder.** Eveleigh Nash, 1913.

*3–105. Hodgson, William Hope. **The Ghost Pirates.** Stanley Paul, 1909.

*3–106. Hodgson, William Hope. **The House on the Borderland.** Chapman & Hall, 1908.

*3–107. Hodgson, William Hope. **The Luck of the Strong.** Eveleigh Nash, 1916.

*3–108. Hodgson, William Hope. **Masters of Terror, Vol. 1: William Hope Hodgson.** Corgi, 1977.

*3–109. Hodgson, William Hope. **Men of Deep Waters.** Eveleigh Nash, 1914.

*3–110. Hodgson, William Hope. **The Night Land.** Eveleigh Nash, 1912.

Hodgson's favorite horror setting is the sea, which he evokes with a mastery unrivaled by anyone else in the genre. Organized around a central mythos, many of Hodgson's short pieces chronicle the misadventures of sailors on the Sargasso Sea, a vast breeding ground of weedlike and fungoid creatures that emerge sometimes from ghostly islands, sometimes from the sea itself. The most famous of these tales is "The Voice in the Night," one of the most artful and horrifying weird stories in English. No one who reads it will have an easy time forgetting the pathetic, ultimately tragic story of a young couple lost after a shipwreck on a fantastic fungus isle who are gradually consumed by, then consume, then become, the thing they fear most. Hodgson's descriptive powers, which embody a kind of repugnant lyricism, are at their height here: "I gradually became aware that here the vile fungus, which had driven us from the ship, was growing riot. In places it rose into horrible, fantastic mounds, which blew across them. Here and there, it took on the forms of vast fingers. . . . Odd places, it appeared as grotesque stunted trees, seeming extraordinarily kinked and gnarled—the whole quaking vilely at times." Other sea tales include "A Tropical Horror," "The Mystery of the Derelict," "The Thing in the Weeds," and "From the Tideless Sea." Often overrated by genre promoters, these lesser stories are compromised by triteness and rarely approach the power and freshness of "The Voice in the Night." Nevertheless, they all have superb atmosphere and memorable comic touches.

Another notable Hodgson creation is Carnacki, a psychic detective in the tradition of Stoker's Van Helsing, Machen's Dr. Black, and Blackwood's John Silence. The most imaginative of the Carnacki stories, which are collected in *Carnacki the Ghost Finder,* is "The Whistling Room," the story of a haunted room that transforms itself into a gigantic face with "enormous, blackened lips, blistered and brutal." This story, like the others that feature

Carnacki, is overburdened with occult machinery and clumsy dialogue, but the imagery is exceptionally vivid. Also vivid are Hodgson's weird novels, although, as Lovecraft points out, they are marred by extraneous romance and adventure sequences and a "nauseous" sentimentality. The tightest Hodgson novel is perhaps his first, *The Boats of the Glen Carrig,* an elaboration of his Sargasso Sea mythos. Another sea novel is *The Ghost Pirates,* the story of an apocalyptic voyage of a ship besieged by quasi-human ocean demons. Even more apocalyptic is *The House on the Borderland,* with its otherworldly but repulsively physical "Swine-things" and its vision of the ultimate destruction of the solar system. *The Nightland,* which picks up billions of years later, after the death of the sun, finds Hodgson's always dark world reduced to an infinite nighttime on a dead planet. All of these extraordinarily original and visionary works disappeared after Hodgson's death (in World War I), to be revived later in America by August Derleth and H. C. Koenig.

3-111. Housman, Clemence (U.K.). **The Were-Wolf.** John Lane, 1896; Arno, 1976.
The wife of Laurence Housman, the fantasy writer, Clemence Housman wrote this single chiller, a tale of lycanthropy, to entertain her fellow London art students. Praised by Lovecraft as attaining "a high degree of gruesome tension," *The Were-Wolf* has gained a reputation as one of the most skillfully written works on this popular subject. Housman is particularly deft at capturing the folklore of lycanthropy.

3-112. Hunt, Violet (U.K.). **More Tales of the Uneasy.** Heinemann, 1925.
3-113. Hunt, Violet. **Tales of the Uneasy.** Heinemann, 1911.
A journalist by profession, Hunt wrote only two collections of ghostly tales. Her themes and plots are traditional, with recognizable Victorian ghosts. Her individual treatment of this clichéd material, however, is fresh and original, especially in "The Corsican Sisters," a short novel (in *More Tales of the Uneasy*) about an avenging supernatural eye. Some readers may object to Hunt's ornate, sometimes swooning, Victorian style: "His breathing was loud and full like the rhythm of a steam piston under her little airily bounding, frivolous heart." Others, however, will find her to be a rich exponent of a style that was soon to go out of fashion. Other Hunt stories of interest include "The Night of No Weather," "The Memoir," and "The Coach."

3-114. Jacobs, W. W. (U.K.). **The Lady of the Barge.** Harper, 1902.
3-115. Jacobs, W. W. **Night Watches.** Hodder & Stoughton, 1914.
3-116. Jacobs, W. W. **Sailor's Knots.** Methuen, 1909.
3-117. Jacobs, W. W. **Sea Urchins.** Lawrence & Bullen, 1898.
Author of "The Monkey's Paw," one of the most famous ghost tales in English, Jacobs also wrote more obscure ghost stories such as "Jerry Bundler," "The Unknown," and "My Brother's Keeper." In its intimation of unseen horror, "The Monkey's Paw" is a peerless masterpiece; especially remarkable

for being based so overtly on a seemingly trite fairy motif involving a paw that grants three wishes. Jacobs demonstrates conclusively that commonplace material, if handled in a subtle and fresh way, can generate tremendous emotional intensity. Here, a magical wish that a dead son be brought back to life is the prelude to a hauntingly indirect spectral episode that plays on an ambivalence between a love for one's kin and a horror of the dead. If none of Jacobs's other tales (many of them sea stories) are this artful, they are all nevertheless rich in atmosphere and folklore.

*3–118. James, Henry. **The Lesson of the Master and Other Stories.** Macmillan, 1892.

*3–119. James, Henry. **The Sense of the Past.** Collins, 1917.

*3–120. James, Henry. **The Soft Side.** Macmillan, 1900.

*3–121. James, Henry. **Stories of the Supernatural.** Ed. by Leon Edel. Taplinger, 1970; Paperback, 1980.

*3–122. James, Henry. **Terminations and Other Stories.** Heinemann, 1898.

*3–123. James, Henry. **The Two Magics: The Turn of the Screw. Covering End.** Heinemann, 1898; Norton, 1966.

Known for his fanatical aesthetic refinement and psychological complexity, James wrote the most convoluted and intellectually challenging ghost stories of all time. Most famous is *The Turn of the Screw*, which involves the possible possession of two children, Miles and Flora, by the corrupting spirits of two dead servants, and the efforts of their young governess to save them. Reviewed initially as a supernatural tale of demonic possession, with the then-novel device of depicting evil in children, the work was soon pounced upon by Freudian critics, especially Edmund Wilson, and reinterpreted as a horror story about madness in which the ghosts are eruptions of repressed sexual desire. According to this reading, the governess represses her desire for her employer, fixes the displaced desire onto Miles, imagines herself as a romanticized protector of her would-be lover's children, terrifies the children so that they really *do* behave strangely, and finally frightens Miles to death trying to wring an admission from him to clear herself with her employer. Seen from this point of view, *The Turn of the Screw* becomes the first *consciously* Freudian horror work, by a writer aware of Freud's theories. Nevertheless, many critics and general readers continue to see the work as unabashedly supernatural, and the controversy sputters on to this day, making *The Turn of the Screw* the most argued-over of all ghostly tales. Any careful reader can see that the novel works on both levels, that James deliberately makes both options available.

This doubleness of vision is characteristic of James, who insisted in work after work that life is never as simple as it seems. Even his early ghostly fiction is obsessively intricate. In "The Ghostly Rental," for example, a vicious circle of guilt generated from a father's curse on his daughter results in circular hauntings and reverse hauntings, in ghosts who persecute only to be persecuted by their former victims. As Leon Edel, James's biographer, puts it, "the haunter in the end becomes the haunted." Readers who insist on unambiguously "real" ghosts should try "Sir Edmund Orme," in which the ghost is seen by the narrator and two other characters. Here too, however, the psychological focus is sharp: the apparition is supernatural, but is also an embodiment of guilt. More complicated—indeed one of the most sophisticated and difficult of all ghost stories—is "The Jolly Corner," the story of a man who returns home after living abroad to confront his double in his old house. The double is what he would have been had he stayed home; it is so different, such a "horror," that he does not recognize himself. The crippling nostalgia, the sense of "shame" over having left home, and the final purgation and relief at having done the sane thing after all, are commonly seen as autobiographical, for James wrote of his decision to emigrate to Europe from America and to become a British citizen in much the same terms. All of James's work in the genre is characterized by an attempt to render every psychological nuance of the interaction between the viewer and the apparition. Readers interested in James's surprisingly large contribution to ghostly fiction should look for Edel's generous sampling cited above.

*3–124. James, M. R. (U.K.). **The Collected Ghost Stories of M. R. James.** Longmans, Green, 1931; Arnold, 1931; St. Martin, 1974.
*3–125. James, M. R. **Ghost Stories of an Antiquary.** Arnold, 1904; Dover, 1971.
*3–126. James, M. R. **More Ghost Stories of an Antiquary.** Arnold, 1911; Penguin, 1974 (also includes *Ghost Stories of an Antiquary*).
*3–127. James, M. R. **A Thin Ghost and Others.** Arnold, 1919.
*3–128. James, M. R. **A Warning to the Curious and Other Ghost Stories.** Arnold, 1925.

One of the most prodigious medieval scholars of the early twentieth century, Montague Rhodes James was also, according to the poet John Betjeman, "the greatest master of the ghost story." James both inaugurated and perfected the antiquarian ghost story. His personae are upper-class British antiquaries who have the unfortunate habit of invoking lethal apparitions. Since the conjurings are accidental, readers have the unsettling sensation that the same thing could happen to them. James's style, which has many imitators, is characterized by restraint rather than Gothic hyperbole. Terse, cumulative, and insidiously understated, his prose suggests a half-seen world of supernatural presences who require only a brief invocation to pounce. A typical James tale—one admired by Lovecraft and favored by James himself—is "Count Magnus," the story of a collector who dooms himself by peering at a terrifying sarcophagus engraving that should have remained unseen and opening a moldy volume of demonology that should have remained closed. By doing these things, he summons from the sarcophagus the dreaded and long-dead Count Magnus. To make matters worse, the count's hooded, tentacled companion also appears. In James's fiction, and the fiction of the school he spawned, such creatures are easier summoned than eluded.

James once wrote of his fiction that its sole purpose was to make the reader feel "pleasantly uncomfortable." For James's narrators, the adverb is as important as the adjective. Even the most gruesome moments in these stories—the cannibalism in "Lost Hearts" or the vampirism in "Wailing Well"—are told with an odd detachment and urbanity. The narrators seem determined to maintain impeccable manners, especially when presenting material they suspect to be in irredeemably bad taste. As much as the collectors' lore, it is this contradiction between scholarly reticence and fiendish perversity that characterizes the antiquarian ghost story. Masquerading as fireside amiability, the almost pathological aloofness of the narrators is as chilling as the horrors they recount.

The originality of James's style is at odds with his statement that he was merely an imitator of Le Fanu, whose works he helped revive in his famous edition of Le Fanu stories, *Madam Crowl's Ghost* (1923). Although James was influenced by what he calls Le Fanu's "deliberateness" and "leisureliness," he departs from Le Fanu in his suaveness of tone, his economy of means, and his radical emphasis on unseen—or very briefly seen—horrors. The compact, chilling, and extremely indirect glimpse of a giant spider (first mistaken for a squirrel) in "The Ash Tree" is typical: "The vicar looked and saw the moving creature, but he could make nothing of its color in the moonlight. The sharp outline, however, seen for an instant, was imprinted on his brain, and he could have sworn, he said, though it sounded foolish, that, squirrel or not, it had more than four legs." James's late work becomes increasingly indirect and enigmatic, sometimes to the point of real obscurity, but a second reading of such puzzling tales as "Two Doctors" or "Rats" invariably reveals new terrors and delights.

James was a much more influential writer than he pretended, and the imprint of his personality can be seen in the antiquarian ghost stories of E. F. Benson, L. P. Hartley [4-112, 4-113], R. H. Malden [4-171], E. G. Swain, A. N. L. Munby [4-180], Sir Arthur Gray, and others. To a contemporary audience conditioned by the monotonous brutality of so many occult novels and films, James's use of innuendo to evoke horror is likely to seem puzzling at first encounter. Nevertheless, readers who are even remotely interested in the genre should treat themselves to the handsome St. Martin's reissue of James's *Collected Ghost Stories*—or at the very least to the Penguin paper edition of *Ghost Stories of an Antiquary*, which, unlike the Dover edition, also includes *More Ghost Stories of an Antiquary*.

*3-129. Kipling, Rudyard (U.K.). **Actions and Reactions.** Macmillan, 1909.

*3-130. Kipling, Rudyard. **The Phantom Rickshaw.** Wheeler, 1888.

*3-131. Kipling, Rudyard. **Phantoms and Fantasies.** Doubleday, 1965.

*3–132. Kipling, Rudyard. **Plain Tales from the Hills.** Thacker & Spink, 1888.

*3–133. Kipling, Rudyard. **They.** Macmillan, 1905.

*3–134. Kipling, Rudyard. **Traffics and Discoveries.** Macmillan, 1904.

Long out of fashion because of his imperialist politics, Kipling was revived by critics in the 1970s as a master of the modern short story. Nowhere is the subtlety, suggestiveness, and complexity of Kipling's short fiction more in evidence than in his ghost stories, many of which he calls "a collection of facts that never quite explained themselves." "They," a long tale about ghostly children, is especially striking in its evocation on the supernatural through the tiniest of hints. More explicit and horrific, although equally controlled, is "The Mark of the Beast," a werewolf tale. Kipling is an example of a major writer (Henry James is another) whose contributions to the genre are rendered in the author's finest prose, making them landmarks of ghostly fiction.

3–135. Lamb, Hugh (U.K.). **Terror by Gaslight.** Taplinger, 1975.

3–136. Lamb, Hugh. **Victorian Nightmares.** Taplinger, 1977.

3–137. Lamb, Hugh. **Victorian Tales of Terror.** Taplinger, 1974.

Like all Hugh Lamb's anthologies, these Victorian collections are full of enticingly rare items. Included are Broughton's "Nothing but the Truth," Lie's "The Earth Draws," and Allen's "The Beckoning Hand" (in *Terror by Gaslight*); Donovan's "The Corpse Light," E. Heron and H. Heron's "The Story of Baelbrow," and Marsh's "The Haunted Chair" (in *Victorian Nightmares*); and Shiel's "Xelucha," Mrs. Molesworth's "The Shadow in the Moonlight," and Mrs. Riddell's "The Last of Squire Ennismore" (in *Victorian Tales of Terror*). Especially welcome are "The Return" and "The Basilisk" (in *Nightmares* and *Gaslight*, respectively) by R. Murray Gilchrist, one of the most sadly neglected masters of Victorian terror. Lamb is a connoisseur of quality supernatural fiction, and these anthologies are typical of his excellent work in the field.

3–138. Landon, Percival (U.K.). **Raw Edges: Studies and Stories of These Days.** Heinemann, 1908.

The little-known Percival Landon was capable of considerable suspense, terror, wit, and insight into Edwardian technology. The stories collected in *Raw Edges* are a decidedly mixed bag (and not all of them supernatural). According to Jacques Barzun and Wendell H. Taylor in *Catalog of Crime* (1974), "There is much to admire, as well as much to disappoint." The most often reprinted Landon tale is the superb "Thurnley Abbey."

*3–139. Le Fanu, Sheridan (U.K.). **In a Glass Darkly.** Bentley, 1872.

*3–140. Le Fanu, Sheridan. **The Purcell Papers.** Bentley, 1880.

In a Glass Darkly, a collection published a year before Le Fanu's death, features the author at the height of his powers—which is to say that it features the most masterful and multilayered ghost stories found anywhere. (See the introduction to this chapter for more commentary on Le Fanu.) The most surprising aspect revealed in *In a Glass Darkly* is Le Fanu's modernity, a quality apparent not only in the depiction of certain characters—Carmilla, the sympathetically drawn lesbian vampire, or Dr. Hesselius, the first psychotherapist in English fiction—but in a consistent vision. Le Fanu's penchant for grim absurdity and black humor gives his fiction a peculiarly contemporary ring. Coming out of nowhere, choosing their victims for their own mysterious reasons, Le Fanu's horrors are a personal mythos rather than recyclings of the familiar folkloric specters from his Irish background. The randomness of the persecutions gives the reader the queasy sensation that he or she could be next. In "Green Tea," for example, a clergyman is persecuted with remarkable tenacity by a demon monkey who stares balefully and communicates threatening obscenities through a psychic "singing." All attempts to exorcise the demon through prayer and the therapeutic ministrations of Dr. Hesselius fail, and the victim finally cuts his own throat.

In his stubborn refusal to provide a revenge motive, an allegorical resolution, or a comforting moral, Le Fanu conjures a horror vision closer to Kafka and Conrad than to this contemporaries. Also modern is his startling use of narrative distance and ambiguity. "Green Tea" and "Mr. Justice Harbottle" in particular contain multiple narratives and tales within tales, which force the reader to make his or her own decisions about what actually occurs. Like many "modern" writers, Le Fanu repays and indeed requires careful rereading. "Carmilla," for example, implies the possible vampirism of the female narrator in such a subtle way that the reader may miss it altogether at first glance. Less refined but equally powerful are the earlier tales published posthumously in *The Purcell Papers,* an ingeniously organized work that collects the papers of Father Purcell, a priest whose parish was decidedly unholy.

3–141. Lee, Vernon (pseud. of Violet Paget) (U.K.). **For Maurice, Five Unlikely Stories.** John Lane, 1927; Arno, 1976.

3–142. Lee, Vernon. **Hauntings, Fantastic Stories.** Heinemann, 1890.

3–143. Lee, Vernon. **A Phantom Lover: A Fantastic Story.** Blackwood, 1886; in *Five Victorian Ghost Novels,* ed. by E. F. Bleiler, Dover, 1971.

3–144. Lee, Vernon. **Pope Jacynth and Other Fantastic Tales.** Grant Richards, 1904.

3–145. Lee, Vernon. **The Snake Lady and Other Stories.** Grove Press, 1954. The supernatural (as well as mainstream) fiction of Violet Paget is set in Italy, where she lived most of her life. Written under the pen name of Vernon Lee, much of it seems dated now, cluttered with too many ghosts and too much Victorian sentimentality. Nevertheless, the Italian settings are evocative, and some of the ghost scenes, especially those in old churches, have a magisterial creepiness: "It struck me suddenly that all this crowd of men and women standing all round, these priests chanting and moving about the altar, were dead—that they did not exist for any man save me. I touched, as if by accident, the hand of my neighbor; it was cold, like wet clay. He turned round, but did not seem to see me: his face was ashy, and his eyes staring, fixed, like those of a blind man or a corpse" (from "Amour Dure"). An excellent compilation of Lee's ghostly fiction is *The Snake Lady*, which contains an extensive introduction by Horace Gregory. Her single novel, *A Phantom Lover*, is atypical. According to E. F. Bleiler, "Its calculated ambiguities and subtleties are more in the manner of the earlier Henry James than her later work." This early novel was reprinted in *Hauntings, Fantastic Stories*, as "Okè of Okehurst."

3-146. Level, Maurice (France). **Crises.** Philpot, 1920. Alternate titles: *Grand Guignol Stories, Tales of Mystery and Horror.*
3-147. Level, Maurice. **The Grip of Fear.** Kennerley, 1911.
3-148. Level, Maurice. **Those Who Return.** McBride, 1923.
French writer Maurice Level is often compared to Villiers de l'Isle Adam as a perpetrator of the *cante cruel,* the fictional equivalent of Grand Guignol. A doctor by profession, Level specialized in clinically gruesome charnel-house horror in his novels and short stories. *The Grip of Fear* and *Those Who Return* are forgotten novels. His dark, sadistic short stories include "Night and Silence" (involving physical deformity and premature burial), "The Kiss," "The Empty House," and "The Maniac." Touches of the *cante cruel* can be found in the work of Edwardian English horror writers (as in H. G. Wells's "The Cone"), and it emerges full blown in the stories of Charles Birkin. For an example of Level at his grimmest, see "Blue Eyes," reprinted in Hugh Lamb's *Return from the Grave* (1976). This story of a prostitute who accidently sleeps with her true love's executioner reveals Level's fondness for elaborate cruelty jokes and gruesome surprise endings.

3-149. Lie, Jonas (Norway). **Weird Tales from the Northern Seas.** Paul, Trench, Truebner, 1893; Arno, 1977.
Lie was one of Norway's most noted novelists. A writer of sea lore, he specialized in fusing realism with mysticism. This edition of tales, which is illustrated by Laurence Housman, focuses on the magic and folklore of the Lapp races in such stories as "The Wind-Gnome," "Finn Blood," and "The Huldrefish." Lie's supernatural concepts tend to be elusive, ambiguous, and shrouded in tantalizing mystery. In "The Earth Draws," for example (reprinted in Hugh Lamb's anthology *Terror by Gaslight,* 1975), a young salesman is gradually and inexplicably seduced into a vampiric society located in a kingdom inside the Earth. The story has Lie's characteristic rhythmic flow and mythlike conciseness.

3-150. London, Jack. **Moon-face and Other Stories.** Macmillan, 1906; Arno, 1977.

3-151. London, Jack. **The Strength of the Strong.** Macmillan, 1914.

One of America's great outdoor writers, London is known for his stunning physical descriptions, his empathy with wild nature (especially the sea and the Yukon), and his environmental determinism. His short fiction is laced with fantasy and horror, although he is generally not associated with either genre. London also wrote science fiction, with an emphasis on Marxian and Darwinian themes. These two collections contain a good smattering of tales that have touches of the supernatural.

3-152. Lowndes, Marie Belloc (U.K.). **Studies in Love and Terror.** Methuen, 1913.

A mystery writer, Lowndes occasionally wrote horror stories that appeared, among other places, in the anthologies of Lady Cynthia Asquith [4-244, 4-245, 4-246]. Her work has strong moments, but it is weakened by clumsy melodrama and gimmicky plot twists.

*3-153. Machen, Arthur (U.K.). **The Children of the Pool and Other Stories.** Hutchinson, 1936; Arno, 1976.

*3-154. Machen, Arthur. **The Cosy Room.** Rich & Cowan, 1936.

*3-155. Machen, Arthur. **The Glorious Mystery.** Covici-McGee, 1924.

*3-156. Machen, Arthur. **The Great God Pan and The Inmost Light.** John Lane, 1894; Arno, 1977

*3-157. Machen, Arthur. **The House of Souls.** Grant Richards, 1906; Arno, 1977.

*3-158. Machen, Arthur. **The Shining Pyramid.** Covici-McGee, 1923.

*3-159. Machen, Arthur. **Tales of Horror and the Supernatural.** 2 vols. Knopf, 1949; Pinnacle, 1971.

*3-160. Machen, Arthur. **The Terror: A Mystery.** Duckworth, 1917.

*3-161. Machen, Arthur. **The Three Imposters.** John Lane, 1895.

One of the most lyrical of all horror writers, Machen possessed a trancelike sense of rhythm and imagery. His landscape descriptions, especially those depicting his native Wales, are often as sensuous and musical as those of D. H. Lawrence. Machen strikes a highly original note of dissonance, in which beauty and horror ring out at precisely the same moment. This style reaches its apex in "The White People," his masterpiece, which is written from the point of view of a little girl who is being initiated into the diabolical mysteries of the White People, an otherworldly race that forms the central mythos of Machen's short fiction. In "The White People," Machen's mysticism is dramatized in the language of the story, as form and content dissolve into one. The narrative, which consists of memories within memories, is almost entirely nonchronological and at times approaches stream of consciousness. By destroying chronological time, Machen puts the reader in touch with a world beyond space and time.

More conventional in structure and overt in language is "The Shining Pyramid," where the reader is allowed a rather direct glimpse of the creatures referred to by one character as the Little People: "At his heart something seemed to whisper ever 'the worm of corruption, the worm that dieth not,' and grotesquely the image was pictured to his imagination of a piece of putrid offal stirring through and through with bloated and horrible creeping things . . . the things made in the form of men but stunted like children hideously deformed, the faces with the almond eyes burning with evil and unspeakable lusts." The most notorious version of the Machen mythos is the novelette "The Great God Pan," which, with its demonic Aubrey Beardsley frontispiece, was described this way by the *Manchester Guardian* in 1894: "The book is the most acutely and intentionally disagreeable we have yet seen in English." Contemporary readers may well wonder what all the fuss was about, for although the tale does have a fairly horrific transformation scene as its climax, the visions of the evil Pan are extremely attenuated and indirect. Indeed, Machen was later criticized by Edmund Wilson for fudging his horror scenes with excessive indirection and timidity.

The furthest Machen goes in the direction of physical horror is "The Novel of the White Powder," from *The Three Imposters* (a series of related stories that can be read as self-contained pieces), which describes the hideous consequences that befall a man who accidently takes a drug used in Witches' Sabbat ceremonies. The ugly climax of this tale recalls the climax of Edgar Allan Poe's "The Facts in the Case of M. Valdemar," but the narrative is filled with typically Machenesque touches of lyricism and elegance. It is also filled—indeed somewhat bloated—with a metaphysics found in all Machen's short fiction, which concerns itself with "the secrets of an evil science which existed long before Aryan man entered Europe," and with the Little People, who are not explicitly named here, but referred to as "beings well qualified to assume, as they did assume, the part of devils." Although "The Novel of the White Powder" is as a whole one of Machen's tighter, more economical tales, it is weakened somewhat by his besetting faults: essaylike mysticism and heavy-handed occultist dialogue. But Machen's empathy with the outdoors, his ability to make landscapes come alive with singing prose, and his feel for cosmic horror make him one of the greatest writers of visionary ghost fiction. With Blackwood, he is one of the major exponents of fiction that indicts the "materialism" of the modern world and plunges its readers and characters into an alternate world both nightmarish and ecstatic.

3–162. Marsh, Richard (U.K.). **The Beetle.** Skeffington, 1897; Arno, 1976.
3–163. Marsh, Richard. **Both Sides of the Veil.** Methuen, 1901.
3–164. Marsh, Richard. **Marvels and Mysteries.** Methuen, 1900.
3–165. Marsh, Richard. **The Seen and the Unseen.** Methuen, 1900.
Marsh is known mainly for his mysteries, but he was an occasional contributor to weird fiction. These collections are little known except to fans of British fantasy and contain only a smattering of genuine supernatural horror

stories (such as "The Photograph" and "The Violin"). *The Beetle*, however, is considered an offbeat classic by Lovecraft and other commentators. Dorothy Scarborough calls it "the most curdling example" of "entomological supernaturalism." The plot, which focuses on ancient Egypt, features a priestess of Isis who haunts the modern world in both human and beetle manifestations. In addition to terror, the novel offers humor, suspense, and memorable minor characters. Lovecraft ranks it on the same level as Stoker's *Dracula* [3–234].

*3–166. Maupassant, Guy de (France). **Allouma and Other Tales.** Holland, 1895.

*3–167. Maupassant, Guy de. **The Life Work of Henri René Albert Guy de Maupassant.** 17 vols. Dunne, 1903.

A master of psychological horror, de Maupassant is also one of the early masters of the modern short story, a writer known for his incisive prose and ingenious plots. Although his reputation rests primarily on his contribution to the French naturalistic school, he wrote numerous horror stories, some of which border on the supernatural. Supernaturalism per se did not concern him. His primary interest lay in madness and the finer nuances of psychological anguish, a preoccupation that is not surprising given his own encroaching, ultimately fatal insanity. "The Horla," de Maupassant's most frequently anthologized tale, tells of an invisible being that is either a "rover of a supernatural race" or a manifestation of the narrator's much-feared insanity. "Was It a Dream?" is a less-known but equally powerful story, which implies the definitive de Maupassant ambiguity in its title, contains a superior visionary sequence in which the dead rise from their graves to rub out the pious lies inscribed on their tombstones and to substitute the unflattering truth with their skeletal fingers. Other de Maupassant stories with similarly enticing titles include "Was He Mad?" and "Who Knows?" The intensity of mental suffering depicted in de Maupassant with such merciless authenticity makes him a decidedly unpleasant writer, but an unforgettable one as well. A few of his stories, such as "The Mother of Monsters," have a physical repulsiveness close to *cante cruel*.

3–168. Menville, Douglass, and Reginald R. Menville. **Ancient Hauntings.** Arno, 1976.

3–169. Menville, Douglass, and Reginald R. Menville. **Phantasmagoria.** Arno, 1976.

Both these anthologies feature fascinatingly obscure ghostly tales, many by writers not often associated with the genre. Although *Phantasmagoria* contains a few midtwentieth-century items, the bulk of these tales come from the Victorian and early modern periods. *Phantasmagoria* features E. F. Benson's "The Sanctuary," Doyle's "Playing with Fire," Pain's "The Moon Slave," and Richard Garnett's "The Demon Pope"; *Ancient Hauntings* includes Blavatsky's "The Ensouled Violin," Turgenev's "Ghosts," and Robert McNish's

"The Metempsychosis." Unlike Arno's typical productions, most of which are reprints, these are original anthologies.

3-170. Middleton, Richard (U.K.). **The Ghost Ship and Other Stories.** Unwin, 1912.

3-171. Middleton, Richard. **The Pantomime Man.** Rich & Cowan, 1933.

Known mainly for his humorous ghost stories, "The Ghost Ship" and "On the Brighton Road," Middleton also wrote several little-known straight horror tales. Some of the most grisly and striking of them can be found in John Gawsworth's anthology, *New Tales of Horror by Eminent Authors* (1934). Others include the pathetic "The Passing of Edward," the story of a child who dies because of the neglect of a drunken father and returns as an invisible ghost to help tend the sheep, and "The Coffin Merchant," an ambiguously supernatural story about a coffin merchant who seems to know which of his potential customers will die. One of the most interesting stylists in British ghostly fiction, Middleton is rich and exuberant in his more traditional ghost stories (especially the humorous ones), lean and concise in his more original psychological tales. He was a sad, neglected figure, and is still not well known. He was also a tragic figure: he killed himself at the age of 29.

3-172. Molesworth, Mrs. Mary (U.K.). **Four Ghost Stories.** Macmillan, 1888.

3-173. Molesworth, Mrs. Mary. **Uncanny Tales.** Hutchinson, 1896; Arno, 1976.

These stories convey only low-intensity chills, but they are charming, atmospheric, and original. Known mainly for her children's literature, Molesworth featured children in her ghost stories and invested her style with a childlike conciseness that contrasts strikingly with the highly embellished diction of Vernon Lee, Violet Hunt, and Rhoda Broughton. "I must tell it simply," says one of her first-person narrators, and so she does. Another attractive quality is Molesworth's sense of humor. One of her ghosts, for example, continues to appear on a tapestry that originally concealed a crime, even after the tapestry is moved: "He could not get over the ghost's sticking to the *tapestry*—and indeed it does rather lower one's idea of ghostly intelligence." These are simple, unambiguously supernatural stories, often involving ghosts with terrible secrets to reveal. Refreshingly uncluttered by the fashionable rhetoric of psychic societies and occult ideologies, they move along briskly and unaffectedly. Especially notable is "The Shadow in the Moonlight," included in Hugh Lamb's *Victorian Tales of Terror* (1975). For anyone interested in Molesworth's work in the genre, the Arno Press reprint of the delightful *Uncanny Tales* is essential. Disappointments in the collection include "At the Dip of the Road," an excessively simple and abrupt tale, and the marvelously titled "The Clock That Struck Thirteen," an atmospheric but sentimental antifeminist allegory.

3–174. Morrow, W. C. **The Ape, the Idiot, and Other People.** Lippincott, 1897.

An obscure American writer, Morrow is remembered primarily for his single collection of horror stories. Although not all the stories are supernatural, the more famous ones, such as "His Unconquerable Enemy" and "Over an Absinth Bottle," are highly regarded by genre specialists. Other stories in the collection include "The Monster Maker" and "A Story Told by the Sea."

3–175. Munro, H. H. (pseud. Saki) (U.K.). **Beasts and Super-beasts.** John Lane, 1914; Core Collection, 1978.

3–176. Munro, H. H. **The Chronicles of Clovis.** John Lane, 1911.

3–177. Munro, H. H. **Complete Works.** Doubleday, 1976.

3–178. Munro, H. H. **Reginald.** Methuen, 1904.

3–179. Munro, H. H. **Reginald in Russia and Other Sketches.** Methuen, 1910.

3–180. Munro, H. H. **The Toys of Peace and Other Papers.** John Lane, 1919.

Writing under the pseudonym Saki, Munro was the author of some 136 short stories. He is noted for his clever plots, jolting endings, and dryly ironic style. Saki is a polished, epigrammatic writer. Each sentence is carefully composed for full ironic weight; each small incident is invested with psychological symbolism. Nowhere is Saki's style more insidiously controlled than in his horror stories, which are cold, nasty, and beautifully written. The most often anthologized is "Sredni Vashtar," the tale of a little boy who takes revenge on his authoritarian female guardian through the passive but brilliantly orchestrated use of a vicious ferret, which he worships as the god of "the fierce, impatient side of things." Another famous Saki offering is "Gabriel-Ernest," a cruel, grimly humorous story about what happens when a werewolf accompanies children home from Sunday school. Other horror stories scattered through these collections include "The Open Window," "Laura," "The Music on the Hill," and "Lois." Although Saki is not primarily a supernatural horror writer, his contributions to the genre are of jewel-like quality.

3–181. Nesbit, E. (U.K.). **Fear.** Paul, 1910.

3–182. Nesbit, E. **Grim Tales.** Innes, 1893.

Edith Nesbit, whose pseudonyms included E. Bland and Mrs. Hubert Bland, was primarily a writer of children's books. She also wrote more than a few short ghost stories, including "The Head," a prototype of modern wax museum tales, and "Man-Size in Marble," her best-known horror story. A particularly satisfying Nesbit tale is "John Charrington's Wedding," a supernatural variation on Hawthorne's "The Wedding Knell." In Hawthorne's tale, a bridegroom shows up at his wedding dressed like a corpse in a shroud; in Nesbit's tale, the bridegroom *is* a corpse, as the young bride discovers in a moment of fatal horror: "We carried her into the house in her bridal dress and drew back her veil. I saw her face. Shall I ever forget it? White, white and drawn with agony and horror, bearing such a look of terror as I have never seen since except in dreams. And her hair, her radiant blonde hair, I tell you it was white like snow." This passage is characteristic of Nesbit in its simplicity, clarity, and storytelling ambience. Her rhythmic prose and fairy-tale metaphors parallel the style of her children's fiction. The combination of childlike wonder and agonizing terror makes her one of the most enticing British writers of her period.

3–183. O'Donnell, Elliot (U.K.). **Dread of Night: Five Short Ghost Stories.** Pillar, 1945.

3–184. O'Donnell, Elliot. **The Sorcery Club.** Rider, 1912; Arno, 1976.

Like William Butler Yeats, O'Donnell was not only an avid researcher, but a committed believer in Irish supernatural lore. He regarded himself as an expert "ghost hunter" and devoted most of his writing to true-believer "nonfiction" rather than ghostly fiction. Like most occult believers and apologists who wrote fiction on the side, O'Donnell could not resist didacticism. He very much wants us to *believe* in the supernatural, not merely experience it as an imaginative projection in a work of fiction. Thus, his style—like that of Yeats and Blackwood, and unlike that of M. R. James and his followers—is characterized by earnestness and intensity rather than wit and subtlety. Only three sentences into "The Haunted Spinney," for example, we find this passage: "To my left was a huge stone wall, behind which I could see the nodding heads of firs, and through them the wind was rushing, making a curious whistling sound, now loud, now soft, roaring and gently murmuring. The sound fascinated me. I fancied it might be the angry voice of a man and the plaintive pleading of a woman, and then a weird chorus of unearthly beings, of grotesque things that stalked along the moors, and crept behind huge boulders." The jump to "unearthly beings" comes almost out of nowhere and is not really prepared for by the description of the wind. Like most of O'Donnell's visionary fiction, "The Haunted Spinney" has characters (all eager to make such a jump) who are involved in psychic research. It also has the obligatory blast against the modern world: "There were rows and rows of chimneys everywhere, a sea of chimneys, an ocean of dull, uninviting smoke. I began to hate London, and to long for the wide expanse of the Atlantic, and the fresh resin-laden air of the woods. . . ." For O'Donnell and other visionary ghost story writers, occult experience is a way of cleansing oneself of the modern world. In *The Sorcery Club*, a novel that some critics regard as O'Donnell's masterpiece, this theme of plunging headfirst into the wierd and fantastic is taken to an extreme. Capitalizing on the popularity of early twentieth-century occult societies, *The Sorcery Club* tells of the horrific consequences of one such society's exploration into the lost powers of Atlantis. Not all critics agree on the quality of this work: Elsa J. Radcliffe, in her *Gothic Novels of the Twentieth Century* (1979), calls it "a dated and dull horror Gothic."

3–185. Oliphant, Mrs. Margaret (U.K.). **A Beleaguered City.** Munro, 1879; Greenwood, 1979.

3–186. Oliphant, Mrs. Margaret. **Stories of the Seen and Unseen.** Roberts Brothers, 1889; Arno, 1977.

An obscure historical novelist, Oliphant is mainly remembered for a handful of Victorian ghost stories. Despite touches of sentimentality, her style has a leisurely, languid spookiness that is quite attractive. Dorothy Tomlinson has accurately described Oliphant's style as one that "needs to take its time." Particularly lyrical and satisfying are her lengthier stories, such as "The Open Door" and "The Library Window." Although Oliphant builds her effects slowly, the simplicity and musicality of her prose make the wait worthwhile: "What did it mean? Oh, what did it mean? I turned round again to the open window at the east end, and to the daylight, the strange light without any shadow that was all round about this lighted hall, holding it like a bubble that would burst, like something that was not real. The real place was the room I knew, in which that picture was hanging, where the writing-table was, and where he sat with his face to the light. But where was the light and the window through which it came? I think my senses must have left me. . . . The hall swam in a dazzle of shining and of noise round me" (from "The Library Window"). Oliphant's delicate, spectral writing is also evident in *A Beleaguered City,* a short novel about a haunted French village.

*3–187. Onions, Oliver (U.K.). **The Collected Ghost Stories of Oliver Onions.** Nicholson & Watson, 1935; Dover, 1971.

*3–188. Onions, Oliver. **Ghosts in Daylight.** Chapman & Hall, 1924.

*3–189. Onions, Oliver. **The Painted Face.** Heinemann, 1929.

*3–190. Onions, Oliver. **Widdershins.** Martin Secker, 1911; Arno, 1976.

A railer against what he called "the groans and clankings of the grosser spook," Onions spent a long career creating wispy, subtle spooks who are quite capable, in their underplayed way, of being malignant and evil. Onions is a master of the English ghost story; his *Collected Ghost Stories* is a must for any supernatural fiction collection, and his *Widdershins* is a classic rare item. The most famous piece in the latter—and one of the most beautifully written ghost stories in English—is "The Beckoning Fair One," the tale of a novelist who falls in love with his unfinished, ultimately murderous heroine. Like Yeats, Onions identifies ghostly experience with the world of art, a world both ecstatic and demonic. Unlike the narrator's prosaic "real" girl friend, the Beckoning Fair One is a principle of transcendence, a ghostly personification of what Coleridge calls the Imagination; she is in the "category of absolute things," and as such fuses the extremities of joy and terror. She is also dangerous and eventually lethal; when the narrator submits to the Beckoning Fair One, he also submits to the loss of his sanity. The victim of one of the most subtle vampires in literature, he becomes an emaciated, ghostly figure himself. The unexpectedly ugly ending, with an image of the murdered rival woman as "a large lumpy pudding," demonstrates the consequences of what is otherwise a wondrous transcendental experience, a visionary alternative to the dullness of the modern world. The same ambivalence can be found in Machen and Blackwood, where the "other" world is enticing but destructive.

An alternative perspective is presented in Onions's "The Cigarette Case," a rare example of a ghost story that manages to be chilling without any horror element whatsoever. In this tale, the ghostly experience is a timeless moment—but *only* a moment—and the characters who experience it accept it as such. More typical is "The Lost Thyrsus" (alternately titled "Io"), in which the vision—one very close to Machen—overwhelms reality and induces madness: "They came down, mad and noisy and bright—Maenades, Thyades, satyrs, fauns—naked, in hides of beasts, ungirdled, dishevelled, wreathed and garlanded, dancing, singing, shouting. The thudding of their hooves shook the ground. . . ." Occasionally, Onions's work is marred by dated Victorian piety (such as in "The Woman in the Way"), but at his best he is one of the most intelligent and careful of the visionary ghost story writers. Indeed, the characterization and dialogue in "The Beckoning Fair One" far outdistance in naturalness and realism anything found in Machen or Blackwood.

3–191. Pain, Barry (U.K.). **Collected Tales.** Vol. 1 (no more published). Martin Secker, 1916.

3–192. Pain, Barry. **More Stories.** T. Werner Laurie, 1930.

3–193. Pain, Barry. **Short Stories of Today and Yesterday.** Harrap, 1928.

3–194. Pain, Barry. **Stories and Interludes.** Henry, 1891.

3–195. Pain, Barry. **Stories in Grey.** T. Werner Laurie, 1911.

3–196. Pain, Barry. **Stories in the Dark.** Grant Richards, 1901.

3–197. Pain, Barry. **Stories without Tears.** Mills & Boon, 1912.

A curious mixture of humor, satire, and cruelty, the supernatural stories of Barry Pain rely heavily on allegory. "The Celestial Grocery," which tells of a place where one may buy desires, makes a psychological and moral point about the ambiguities of human happiness; "The Glass of Supreme Moments," which tells of a witch who presents her victims with a mirror reflecting the supreme ecstasies in their lives, is an allegory about the lure of death. Despite his flair for whimsy and satire, Pain is well named, for many of his tales are agonizing and horrifying, with a strong sense of diabolical evil. "The Moon Slave," for example, describes what happens to a young girl who dances in the moonlight with a creature that turns out to have a cloven hoof. In praising this story, Scarborough says: "The reader feels a miasmatic atmosphere of evil, a smear on the soul. . . ." Dorothy L. Sayers includes Pain's "The End of a Show" in the "Tales of Blood and Cruelty" section of her *Omnibus of Crime* (1929, Vol. 1). This story of a quack doctor who helps a female freak in a carnival to commit suicide is all the more insidious for being told in Pain's civilized, elegant style.

3-198. Phillpotts, Eden (U.K.). **A Deal with the Devil.** Bliss, Sands & Foster, 1895; Arno, 1976.

3-199. Phillpotts, Eden. **Fancy Free.** Methuen, 1901.

3-200. Phillpotts, Eden. **Loup-Garou.** Sands, 1899.

3-201. Phillpotts, Eden. **Peacock House and Other Mysteries.** Hutchinson, 1926.

Like *Wuthering Heights* and *Lorna Doone,* the fiction of Eden Phillpotts is steeped in the dark folklore of the Dartmoor peasants. Phillpotts has a special interest in satanic motifs: in "Another Little Heath Hound," a pack of ghostly dogs, each the spirit of a damned soul, chases the devil without cease until Judgment Day, in a reversal of the usual chase dynamic in horror fiction; in "The Witch," a peculiar old lady named Mother Tab has devil-worshipping paraphernalia that includes toad corpses and cat mummies; in *A Deal with the Devil,* a short novel that exploits an ever-popular theme with surprisingly droll humor, the hero bargains with Satan to grow younger each day. An astonishingly prolific writer, with some 250 books to his credit, Phillpotts wrote considerably more fantasy than horror. His folkloric horror tales are scattered through several collections, chiefly those listed.

3-202. Praed, Mrs. Campbell (Australia). **The Brother of the Shadow.** Routledge, 1886; Arno, 1976.

3-203. Praed, Mrs. Campbell. **The Soul of Countess Adrian: A Romance.** Trischler, 1891.

The forgotten weird novels of this Australian writer are full of the occult trappings so common in late nineteenth-century fiction (see [3-8] and [3-42]). *The Brother of the Shadow* includes Hindu mysticism, astral projection, Egyptian black magic, and a villainous doctor. *The Soul of the Countess Adrian* is a tale of psychic vampirism in the tradition of Blackwood and W. F. Harvey.

3-204. Prichard, Hesketh, and Kate Prichard (pseud. E. and H. Heron) (U.K.). **Ghosts.** Arthur Pearson, 1899.

A mother-son collaboration, this collection of psychic detection tales was originally published in *Pearson's* in 1898 as "Real Ghost Stories," complete with photographs of the allegedly haunted houses. Among these forgotten English ghost stories are "The Story of the Grey House" and "The Story of the Moor Road." The hero in both tales is Flaxman Low, a psychic detective in the tradition of Hodgson's Dr. Carnacki and Blackwood's John Silence. Unlike his long-winded colleagues, Professor Low keeps his theorizing to a minimum and invariably manages to make it charming and imaginative. These are thoroughly pleasant, skillfully written ghost stories with genuine chills as well as considerable wit. Especially endearing is "The Story of Baelbrow," reprinted in Hugh Lamb's *Victorian Nightmares* (1977), which combines mummy and vampire motifs in a ghost of singular grotesqueness.

3-205. Q. (pseud. of Arthur Quiller-Couch) (U.K.). **I Saw Three Ships and Other Winter's Tales.** Cassell, 1902; Arno, 1977.

3-206. Q. **Noughts and Crosses.** Cassell, 1891; Arno, 1977.

3-207. Quiller-Couch, Arthur. **Old Fires and Profitable Ghosts.** Cassell, 1900; Arno, 1973.

3-208. Quiller-Couch, Arthur. **Two Sides of the Face: Midwinter Tales.** Arrowsmith, 1903.

3-209. Q. **Wandering Heath: Stories, Studies, and Sketches.** Cassell, 1895.

3-210. Quiller-Couch, Arthur. **The White Wolf and Other Fireside Tales.** Methuen, 1902.

The ghost stories of Sir Arthur Quiller-Couch, a prolific Cornish writer and scholar, are beguiling and enchanting, if not especially frightening. Quiller-Couch specializes in simple, folkloristic concepts that recapitulate Cornish legends in new, imaginative contexts. Eschewing the psychological ambiguities so popular with his contemporaries (Henry James, Walter de la Mare), Quiller-Couch gives us real ghosts, which are often fully visible to several characters. Yet the magical simplicity of his prose imparts a subtlety to his apparitions that persists in spite of their explicitness. This quality is especially apparent in "The Haunted Dragoon," a rare example of an effective ghost tale told in dialect, in which the ghost of a "naked babe" wails its way into the reader's imagination. Other stories in which Quiller-Couch gets away with being explicit through an unassuming lyricism include "The Roll Call of the Reef," which evokes the ghosts of soldiers rising from the sea to recount their individual damnations; "Old Fires and Profitable Ghosts," which combines the same motif of dead men rising from the sea with witchcraft; and "Old Aeson," which features an originally conceived vampire. The most often collected Quiller-Couch stories are "A Pair of Hands" (which features a disembodied hand motif in the manner of Le Fanu's "Ghost Stories of the Tiled House") and "The Seventh Man." In the main, however, the rather large output of this writer is sadly neglected.

3-211. Riddell, Mrs. J. H. (U.K.). **The Banshee's Warning and Other Tales.** Remington, 1894.

3-212. Riddell, Mrs. J. H. **The Collected Ghost Stories of Mrs. J. H. Riddell.** Dover, 1977.

3-213. Riddell, Mrs. J. H. **The Disappearance of Mr. Jeremiah Redworth.** Routledge, 1878.

3-214. Riddell, Mrs. J. H. **Fairy Water.** Routledge, 1873; as *The Haunted House at Latchford* in *Three Supernatural Novels of the Victorian Period*, ed. by E. F. Bleiler, Dover, 1975.

3-215. Riddell, Mrs. J. H. **Frank Sinclair's Wife and Other Stories.** Tinsley, 1874.

3-216. Riddell, Mrs. J. H. **Handsome Phil and Other Stories.** F. V. White, 1899.

3-217. Riddell, Mrs. J. H. **Idle Tales.** Ward & Downey, 1888.

3-218. Riddell, Mrs. J. H. **Princess Sunshine and Other Stories.** Ward & Downey, 1889.

3-219. Riddell, Mrs. J. H. **The Uninhabited House** and **The Haunted River.** Routledge, 1883; in *Five Victorian Ghost Novels,* ed. by E. F. Bleiler, Dover, 1971.

3-220. Riddell, Mrs. J. H. **Weird Stories.** James Hogg, 1882.

Until an interest in her work was revived by S. M. Ellis's ground-breaking book, *Wilkie Collins, Le Fanu and Others* (1931), Charlotte Eliza (known as Mrs. J. H.) Riddell was little known as a writer of supernatural fiction. Her work is typically Victorian in its leisurely pace, its close observation of social mores, its moralistic tone (although she is considerably less aggressive in this respect than many of her contemporaries), and its ornate syntax. As E. F. Bleiler points out, Riddell was "constricted in technique and ideas," but had a persuasive sense of verisimilitude. Her ghostly scenes, such as the following description of the cry of a banshee in "The Banshee's Warning," are careful and often lyrical:

> . . . then, with a start and a shiver, and a blanched face, he turned sharply round, whilst a low, sobbing, wailing cry echoed mournfully through the room. No form of words could give an idea of the sound. The plaintiveness of the Aeolian harp— that plaintiveness which so soon affects and lowers the highest spirits—would have seemed wildly gay in comparison with the sadness of the cry which seemed floating in the air. As the summer wind comes and goes amongst the trees, so that mournful wail came and went—came and went. It came in a rush of sound, like a gradual crescendo managed by a skillful musician, and died away in a lingering note, so gently that the listener could scarcely tell the exact moment when it faded into utter silence.
>
> I say faded, for it disappeared as the coast line disappears in the twilight, and there was total stillness in the apartment.

Surprisingly, "The Banshee's Warning" is one of the few of Riddell's many ghost stories that deals with Irish themes; although she was born in Carrickfergus, she referred to the Irish only rarely in her work. In her own day, she was noted mainly as a novelist, but her work in this form is now virtually forgotten. Her short ghostly tales have enjoyed something of a revival, especially in E. F. Bleiler's welcome edition of her collected ghost stories and two of her four supernatural novels. The latter offer realistic renderings of Victorian middle-class life in which the supernatural manifestation strikes only a mildly chilling note. Nevertheless, Bleiler regards her as "in many ways the Victorian ghost novelist *par excellence.*"

3-221. Russell, W. Clark. **The Death Ship: A Strange Story.** 3 vols. Hurst & Blackett, 1888; Arno, 1976.

3-222. Russell, W. Clark. **The Frozen Pirate.** Sampson, Low, Marston, 1887; Arno, 1975.

3-223. Russell, W. Clark. **The Phantom Death.** Chatto & Windus, 1895.

Russell's penchant for horror stories on the sea makes him an American equivalent of William Hope Hodgson. *The Death Ship* his best-known novel, combines motifs from the Flying Dutchman and the Ancient Mariner. Both the hero and the heroine are hurled aboard a ship, whose crew appears to consist entirely of zombies. (Poe's "Ms. Found in a Bottle" has a similarly haunted ship.) After a dramatic escape, in which the heroine is killed, the hero attempts to tell his fantastic tale to anyone who will listen. *The Frozen Pirate*, Russell's other weird novel, is a tale of suspended animation involving a pirate from the eighteenth century who survives death by freezing himself. Russell's short horror tales, collected in *The Phantom Death*, include such forgotten items as "The Secret of the Dead Mate" and "A Nightmare of the Doldrums."

3-224. Shiel, M. P. (U.K.). **Here Comes the Lady.** Richards Press, 1928.

3-225. Shiel, M. P. **The Pale Ape and Other Pulses.** T. Werner Laurie, 1911.

3-226. Shiel, M. P. **Xelucha and Others.** Arkham House, 1975.

Although Matthew Phipps Shiel has been revived as a neglected horror writer, it should not be forgotten that he wrote primarily in the fields of fantasy and science fiction. In his scattered supernatural stories, found mainly in the collections cited, Shiel writes in a perfumed 1890s Decadence style, which relies heavily on alliteration, assonance, and literal repetition to achieve its rhythmic effects. At his best, Shiel achieves a mesmeric intensity and sense of rapture; at his worst, he is awkward and self-consciously archaic. As H. P. Lovecraft puts it, he "occasionally attains a high level of horrific magic." His greatest horror story, according to Lovecraft and others, is "The House of Sounds" (originally "Vaila"), which describes a Norwegian island assaulted by otherworldly forces. This tale was apparently too ornate and overwrought even for Shiel, who revised it in the direction of conciseness and restraint, changing the title in the process. Other notable stories include "Xelucha," "The Bride," and "The Tale of Henry and Rowena," all of which involve one of Shiel's favorite supernatural themes, the return from the grave of a deadly female. Shiel's admirers include Rebecca West, who calls him "a writer of imperial imagination."

3-227. Stenbock, Eric (U.K.). **Studies of Death: Romantic Tales.** Nutt, 1894.

One of the most strikingly audacious oddballs of the Victorian period, Count Stanislaus Eric Stenbock was sometimes seen at dinner seated in a coffin with a pet toad or snake. He wrote only a handful of horror stories, but those collected in *Studies of Death*, six tales of demons and vampires, have been frequently anthologized.

*3-228. Stevenson, Robert Louis (U.K.). **Island Night's Entertainment.** Cassell, 1893; Scholarly, 1970.

*3-229. Stevenson, Robert Louis. **The Merry Men and Other Tales and Fables.** Chatto & Windus, 1887.

*3–230. Stevenson, Robert Louis. **The Strange Case of Dr. Jekyll and Mr. Hyde.** George Munro, 1886; Dutton, 1954 (includes *The Merry Men*).
*3–231. Stevenson, Robert Louis. **Tales and Fantasies.** Tauchnitz, 1905.
*3–232. Stevenson, Robert Louis. **Thrawn Janet: Markheim.** Thomas Mosher, 1906.

The celebrated moral complexity of Stevenson makes him one of the most distinguished masters of the horror story. In *The Strange Case of Dr. Jekyll and Mr. Hyde*, surely the most famous dual-personality tale in English fiction, Stevenson presents a poignant moral and psychological dilemma: the responsible, moral Dr. Jekyll side of the doomed hero's chemically induced double personality is "safe of all men's respect, wealthy, beloved"; it is also, however, characterized by excessive restraint and repression, by "effort, virtue and control" and "self-denying toils." The evil Mr. Hyde side, on the other hand, is "a sea of liberty," a "current of disordered sensual images." Hyde is a man of violence, depravity, and "utter selfishness," but he is no more an extreme than the relentlessly normal Dr. Jekyll, whose repressiveness explodes into the destructive behavior of Hyde. Both represent self-destructive extremes, an inability to accept the messy ambiguities of reality. Thus, the tale is not the simple allegory of the good and evil in each person, as it is often misconstrued, but a sophisticated psychological study of the consequences of reducing all behavior to those simple labels. In terms of the history of literature, *Jekyll and Hyde* represents the breakdown of the stable ego in late Victorian fiction and a fascination with irrationality that prefigures the works of Conrad, Joyce, and Woolf. However, as Vladimir Nabokov has pointed out, the charm and greatness of Stevenson lie not so much in his themes as in his language, in his "rich tone" and "delightful winey taste." He is a master of atmosphere and imagery whose sense of the fantastic and the bizarre is grounded in careful, subtly developed characters and settings. These same qualities are evident in his shorter horror pieces, especially "The Body Snatchers" and "Markheim."

*3–233. Stoker, Bram (U.K.). **The Bram Stoker Bedside Companion.** Taplinger, 1973.
*3–234. Stoker, Bram. **Dracula.** Constable, 1897; Doubleday, 1959.
*3–235. Stoker, Bram. **Dracula's Guest.** Routledge, 1914; Zebra, 1978.
3–236. Stoker, Bram. **The Lair of the White Worm.** Heinemann, 1902; Zebra, 1909.

Stoker's *Dracula* is perhaps the greatest and most enduring full-length supernatural horror novel in English fiction. Its flaw in pacing and structure, particularly in the second half of the book, are eclipsed by a spellbinding narrative power and by a genuinely awesome and magisterial supernatural villain. The historical source for *Dracula* is Vlad the Impaler, the original Count Dracula, a ruthless fifteenth-century Transylvanian ruler who is reputed to have impaled some 30,000 of his enemies on stakes. Stoker was also influenced by the Roumanian peasant myth of the *nosferatu*, a vampire that can be fought only with such exotic devices as garlic, decapitation, and wooden stakes driven through the heart. Thoroughly steeped in East European folklore, Stoker faithfully recreated such beliefs as the vampire's ability to transform himself into animals, his inability to cast reflections in mirrors, and his fear of the sign of the cross.

It was Stoker's ingenious idea to combine the historical Count Dracula and Vlad the Impaler with the mythological vampire, to interweave history with myth in such a way as to create a new mythos of his own, which has been endlessly recycled in films, plays, and other novels. The structure of *Dracula* takes the form of an epistolary novel, a device that allows Stoker to present the encroaching horror of vampirism from radically different points of view, creating the variety necessary to sustain the reader's interest in a long narrative about fantastic events. Each character writes his or her sections of the novel in a distinctive style: Jonathan Harker is terse and gripping; Nina Harker is flowery and metaphorical; Dr. Seward is cold and prosaic; and Dr. Van Helsing is assertive and dogmatic. The most memorable passages, no matter in whose style they are rendered, are those that evoke the dreaded Count and his vampiric female entourage. Stoker's horror scenes are overwhelmingly vivid and imaginative:

> There lay the Count, but looking as if his youth had been half renewed, for the white hair and moustache were changed to dark iron-grey; the cheeks were fuller, and the white skin seemed ruby-red underneath; the mouth was redder than ever, for on the lips were gouts of fresh blood, which trickled from the corners of the mouth and ran over the chin and neck. Even the deep, burning eyes seemed set amongst swollen flesh, for the lids and pouches underneath were bloated. It seemed as if the whole awful creature were simply gorged with blood; he lay like a filthy leech, exhausted with his repletion.

The only man capable of combating this powerful force of evil is the novel's hero, Dr. Abraham Van Helsing, a "philosopher and a metaphysician" who is an expert on vampires. Van Helsing is a fusion of two characters in the fiction of another Irish horror writer, Sheridan Le Fanu: Baron Vordenburg, the vampire expert in Le Fanu's *Carmilla*, a work that, according to Stoker himself, greatly influenced *Dracula*; and Dr. Hesselius, the Doctor of Metaphysical Medicine in "Green Tea" and other Le Fanu stories. Like his literary antecedents, Van Helsing is part psychiatrist and part philospher, a unified force of light against an implacable force of darkness. The struggle between good and evil, between Christ and Antichrist, is an obvious, theme in *Dracula*. Recently, however, there has been a tendency to view the *Dracula* novel as a sexual rather than a theological allegory. George Stade, Leonard Wolf, and other critics have made a strong case for Dracula as an initiator of sexuality, whose bite injects his victims with sexual desire. There is no question that Stoker's women, once they are bitten, become attractive and alluring, especially those who were plain and nonsexual to begin with. Words such as "voluptuous" and "beautiful" are consistently used to describe them in their vampiric manifestations. Indeed, Dracula himself, the Prince of Darkness, has an animal attractiveness that has been emphasized in recent film and theatrical versions of the story. The real triumph of the novel, however, as Leonard Wolf points out in *A Dream of Dracula* (1972), is Dracula's aura of mystery and evil. Stoker has the good sense to keep his monster half hidden in the shadows of the novel, encroaching on London gradually through dreams and through apocalyptic freaks of nature, emerging luminescent only in key dramatic scenes.

This sense of repressed evil and violence lurking just under the quiet surface of a narrative, always ready to explode, is also found in Stoker's short fiction. His most striking short story is "Dracula's Guest," originally intended to be a chapter in *Dracula*, a lyrical and chilling description of the Count's ability to manipulate the forces of nature. Other notable Stoker horror stories include "The Squaw," a surprisingly cruel revenge tale, and "The Judge's House," a haunted-house tale. The wonderfully titled *The Lair of the White Worm* is a forgotten horror novel about an evil force lurking in the vault of an English castle. According to H. P. Lovecraft, its obscurity is at least partly deserved; in Lovecraft's judgment, Stoker "ruins a magnificent idea by a development almost infantile."

3–237. Sullivan, Jack. **Lost Souls: A Collection of English Ghost Stories.** Ohio University Press (planned pub.).
This large collection of classic and rare English ghost stories is a companion volume to Sullivan's *Elegant Nightmares: The English Ghost Story from Le Fanu to Blackwood*, a critical and historical study of the genre. The basic division of antiquarian and visionary stories proposed in *Elegant Nightmares* is used organizationally in *Lost Souls*. Antiquarian stories include classics such as M. R. James's "Count Magnus" and E. F. Benson's "Negotium Perambulans," and rarities such as Swain's "The Man with the Roller"; visionary stories include classics such as Hodgson's "The Voice in the Night" and rarities such as Blackwood's "A Haunted Island." Also in the book are two Le Fanu stories and, to round out the collection, a sampling of contemporary tales. Short introductions are provided for each story, along with an overall introduction and a bibliography.

3–238. Swain, E. G. (U.K.). **The Stoneground Ghost Tales.** Heffer, 1912.
Affectionately dedicated to M. R. James, this delightful and extremely rare collection of ghost stories is resolutely in the James antiquarian mode. Swain's Reverend Roland Batchel, the hero, is the quintessential antiquary, a man who obsessively collects and arranges artifacts, partly out of a worship of the past, partly out of a need to create the illusion that nothing is ever out of its place: "He almost determined to have the sashes 'seen to,' although he could seldom be induced to have anything 'seen to.' He disliked changes,

even for the better, and would submit to great inconvenience rather than have things altered with which he had become familiar." Unfortunately, Reverend Batchel must submit to more than inconvenience, for these very artifacts act as a magnet for a variety of ghosts and unearthly emanations. Swain breaks James's cardinal dictum by refusing to make all of his ghosts malignant. Nevertheless, there is a graceful, delicate spookiness in Swain's ghost scenes that delivers a distinctive chill of its own. The plots, however, are often unflinchingly close to James: in "The Man with the Roller," for example, a figure with an "indescribably horrible suffering face" appears in a supernaturally animated photograph, unmistakably recalling James's "The Mezzotint." In his dedication, Swain calls James "the indulgent parent of such tastes as these pages indicate"; James could not have asked for more delectable progeny.

*3–239. Turgenev, Ivan (Russia). **Phantoms and Other Stories.** Tr. by Isabel F. Hapgood. Scribner, 1904; Arno, 1977.

*3–240. Turgenev, Ivan. **A Reckless Character and Other Stories.** Tr. by Isabel F. Hapgood. Scribner, 1904; Arno, 1977.

Written in the 1870s and 1880s, during his last years, the neglected ghostly tales of Turgenev are somber, austere, deeply moving, and surprisingly terrifying. According to Scarborough, they are also highly influential: in *The Supernatural in Modern English Fiction* (1917), she cites Turgenev's use of dream imagery, "mystical supernaturalism," and the psychic vampire theme as having influenced English supernatural fiction in the early twentieth century. Whether this is true (and it may not be, given the relative obscurity of Turgenev's ghostly tales), there can be no doubt about Turgenev's originality and uniqueness, his ability to blend terror and compassion in a manner that universalizes his evocative Russian settings. Nowhere is this mixture more powerful than in "Father Alexyei's Story" (1877), about a young man pursued to madness and a grave by a black elflike apparition, with white eyes and grinning teeth. Although this tale bears a superficial resemblance to Le Fanu's "Green Tea," Turgenev's simple storytelling ambience and paradoxical warmth are radically unlike Le Fanu's narrative convolutions and icy aloofness. Also memorable is the novel-length "Clara Militch" (1882), an early tale of psychic vampirism. His shorter horror tales include "The Dream" (1876) and "The Song of Love Triumphant" (1881). His terror fiction is laced with Russian folklore, but the overwhelming effect is one of intense social and psychological realism.

3–241. Viereck, G. S. **The House of the Vampire.** Moffat, Yard, 1907; Arno, 1976.

Born in Munich, Viereck settled in America where, in collaboration with Paul Eldridge, he wrote a notable Wandering Jew fantasy trilogy. His first novel was *The House of the Vampire*, a forgotten horror tale now revived in the United States. Unlike *Dracula*, Stoker's unabashedly supernatural tale, Viereck's novel is a psychological thriller about a psychic vampire. The concept of the vampire as a pathological personality with psychic powers, who drains and deadens his victim without fangs or flapping wings, was a popular one in the early twentieth century, especially with short story writers. Examples of this theme can be found in Blackwood's "The Transfer" and Harvey's "Miss Avenal." An important precursor is Turgenev's "Clara Militch."

3-242. Villiers de l'Isle Adam (France). **Sardonic Tales** (English version). Knopf, 1927. French volumes published 1883, 1889.
Jean-Marie Phillipe Auguste Mathias Villiers de l'Isle Adam is sometimes cited as the first French symbolist writer. A friend of Huysman, Villiers had an interest in satanic ideas, which he worked into his fiction. The collection listed is an English translation of his *cante cruel* tales published in two volumes in the 1880s. The most famous is "The Torture of Hope," a typically sadistic tale of the Inquisition.

*3-243. Wells, H. G. (U.K.). **Complete Short Stories.** Ernest Benn, 1927; St. Martin, 1974.
*3-244. Wells, H. G. **The Country of the Blind and Other Stories.** Nelson, 1911; Arno, 1977.
*3-245. Wells, H. G. **The Plattner Story and Others.** Methuen, 1897.
*3-246. Wells, H. G. **The Stolen Bacillus and Other Incidents.** Methuen, 1895.
*3-247. Wells, H. G. **Thirty Strange Stories.** Arnold, 1897; Arno, 1977.
*3-248. Wells, H. G. **Twelve Stories and a Dream.** Macmillan, 1903; Arno, 1977.
*3-249. Wells, H. G. **The Valley of Spiders.** Fontana, 1974.
Although Wells is generally classified as a science fiction writer, he also wrote some of the most original and finely wrought ghost and horror stories in English fiction. His supernatural tales include "The Door in the Wall," "The Red Room," "The Story of the Late Mr. Elvesham," "The Stolen Body," and many others. When he was in the mood, Wells could write surprisingly grisly and grim horror tales: "Pollock and the Porroh Man," the story of a man pursued by a decapitated head, is as relentless and fatalistic as Le Fanu's "Green Tea"; "The Cone," a revenge tale, has a description of a man's blood boiling in his veins that will curdle the reader's own; "The Sea Raiders" unleashes an attack of octopoid creatures as loathsome and fearsome as anything in H. P. Lovecraft or Clark Ashton Smith. For the most part, however, Wells's stories are witty and urbane, with dark terrors half-concealed by bright surfaces. His dialogue, as in this passage from "The Strange Orchid," is fluent and often sparkling:

> "Nothing ever does happen to me," he remarked presently, beginning to think aloud. "I wonder why? Things happen enough to other people. There is Harvey. Only the other week, on Monday, he picked up sixpence, on Wednesday his

chicks all had the staggers, on Friday his cousin came home from Australia, and on Saturday he broke his ankle. What a whirl of excitement—compared to me."

"I think I would rather be without so much excitement," said his housekeeper. "It can't be good for you. . . ."

"That orchid-collector was only thirty-six—twenty years younger than myself—when he died. And he had been married twice and divorced once; he had had malarial fever four times, and once he broke his thigh. He killed a Malay once, and once he was wounded by poisoned darts. And in the end he was killed by jungle leeches. It must have all been very troublesome, but then it must have been very interesting, you know—except, perhaps, the leeches."

"I'm sure it was not good for him," said the lady with conviction.

Mr. Wedderburn, the speaker in this passage, is a typical Wells hero; complaining that his life is dull, he is delighted later on in the story to find himself attacked by what turn out to be vampiric orchids.

Wells was one of the early creators of the antihero, the ordinary "little man" who seeks out weird adventures to enliven his tedious life in the modern world. This compulsion to escape modern life is also found in Blackwood's fiction, although Blackwood's characters are more outgoing, more conventionally "heroic" than in Wells. Wells is fond of beginning a story with a drab or unpleasant domestic scene (as in "The Crystal Egg" and "The Purple Pileus") and having the mundane dissolve into something bizarre and fantastic: in "The Crystal Egg," the strange vision comes from outer space; in "The Purple Pileus," it comes from psychedelic mushrooms.

There is no question that Wells had a keen and enduring interest in science and that he wrote some of the masterworks of science fiction. In his more weird and spectral stories, however, science is merely an excuse, a momentary vehicle to get his imagination stimulated and to move it into the realm of awe and terror. "The Plattner Story," for example, begins with a dryly scientific explanation of the fourth dimension only to move into the otherworld of the "Watchers of the Living," where dead people hover and swirl around tomblike monuments and cities. The science fiction fan would undoubtedly call these creatures inhabitants of another dimension; the horror addict would simply call them ghosts.

*3-250. Wharton, Edith. **The Ghost Stories of Edith Wharton.** Scribner, 1973.

*3-251. Wharton, Edith. **Ghosts.** Appleton-Century, 1937.

*3-252. Wharton, Edith. **Here and Beyond.** Appleton, 1926.

*3-253. Wharton, Edith. **Tales of Men and Ghosts.** Scribner, 1910.

*3-254. Wharton, Edith. **Xingu and Other Stories.** Scribner, 1916.

An admirer of Henry James and Walter de la Mare, Edith Wharton was committed to the proposition that the modern world is a perfectly congenial habitat for ghosts. In "All Souls," one of her most beautifully controlled ghost stories, she has her narrator put it this way: "As between turreted castles patrolled by headless victims with clanking chains, and the comfortable suburban house with a refrigerator and central heating where you feel, as soon as you're in it, *that there's something wrong*, give me the latter for sending a chill down the spine!" "All Souls" is an admirable demonstration of this bias: the heroine's suburban house is thoroughly modern, but what happens there, involving witchcraft and possession, is every bit as creepy and shuddery as a haunting in a conventional Gothic setting.

Wharton put her ghost stories "under the special protection" of de la Mare, in a dedication in which she described them as "ghostly straphangers." A giant in the field of American supernatural fiction, she brought the same sophistication and mastery of psychological nuance to her ghost stories as she did to her distinguished novels, such as *Ethan Frome*. Like the tales of de la Mare, Wharton's are dense in texture and challenging in the amount of intelligence and close attention they demand of the reader. Indeed, a story like "Pomegranate Seed," which involves letters sent from the grave, is so ambiguous and open-ended that the reader who expects neat resolutions or even tidy ambiguities will probably be frustrated. The reader should also avoid looking for anything peculiarly American in Wharton's ghost stories. Occasionally, as in "Bewitched," a Hawthornian horror tale with a superb rendering of New England dialect, Wharton reveals her American background. Usually, however, she is careful to universalize her stories, to make them represent the modern rather than the American condition. Her ghostly fiction spans her entire career, beginning in 1904 with "The Lady's Maid's Bell" and concluding with "All Souls" in 1937, the year of her death. Readers who desire a comprehensive, easily available sampling of these excellent stories should look for the 1973 Scribner edition, which, with one change, reprints the 1937 *Ghosts*.

3–255. White, E. L. **Lukundoo and Other Stories.** Doran, 1927.
3–256. White, E. L. **The Song of the Sirens and Other Stories.** Dutton, 1919.

The horror stories of Edward Lucas White are distinguished by a dreamlike ambience pierced by sharp, often loathesome touches of realism. The dreaminess undoubtedly comes from White's practice of basing his tales, as did Le Fanu, on actual dreams. The realism comes from a careful attention to historical, anthropological, and anatomical detail, a quality found in White's historical novels (featuring ancient Greece and Rome) as well as his short horror fiction. The combination of nightmare intensity and coldly exact detail is especially telling in "Lukundoo," a story of African sorcery and White's most often anthologized tale: "Then we three sat about Stone and watched that hideous, gibbering prodigy grow out of Stone's flesh, till two horrid, spindling little black arms disengaged themselves. The infinitesimal nails were perfect to the barely perceptible moon at the quick, the pink spot on the palm was horribly natural. These arms gesticulated and the right plucked toward Stone's blond beard." "Lukundoo" falls into a subgenre of African black magic tales that includes bloodcurdling items such as Wells's "Pollock and the Porroh Man" and Wakefield's "Death of a Poacher." Other notable White tales are "The Song of the Sirens" and "The Snout." Although none of White's other stories have achieved the popularity of "Lukundoo," the latter has been anthologized with such dependable frequency that it alone has put him on the map of American horror fiction.

*3-257. Wilde, Oscar (U.K.). **The Picture of Dorian Gray.** Ward, Lock, 1891; Penguin, 1949.

Like Poe, the pioneer of aestheticism, Wilde argued tirelessly and brilliantly that didacticism was the enemy of literature. *The Picture of Dorian Gray*, Wilde's delightful and profoundly influential weird novel, opens with the proposition that "there is no such thing as a moral or an immoral book. Books are well written, or badly written. That is all." Wilde's book, like all his books, is well written. A precursor of Joyce, he showed that prose could be as hard and glittering and precise as poetry. The overall atmosphere of the book, however, is silken and languid: "The studio was filled with the rich odour of roses, and when the light summer wind stirred amidst the trees of the garden there came through the open door the heavy scent of the lilac, or the more delicate perfume of the pink-flowering thorn." This is the imagery of the Decadence movement, an imagery of wilting flowers and hedonistic opulence. The young protagonist, Dorian Gray, who wishes to preserve this world of uncompromised pleasure, finds himself with a portrait that ages as he remains young. Gray pays a horrific price for this arrangement, but for the reader the pleasures remain uncompromised from beginning to end. Indeed, the sheer immediate enjoyment of reading Wilde makes him the perfect spokesman for this aesthetic of "the pleasure of the moment."

The Picture of Dorian Gray has some of Wilde's most scintillating, epigrammatic, brilliantly artificial dialogue. "Being natural," says one character, "is simply a pose, and the most irritating pose I know." Indeed, all the characters talk like Wilde himself, whose brilliant conversation was once described by E. F. Benson as being "like the play of a sunlit fountain." But the novel is also a persuasive tale of terror, with a powerful and chilling climax at its abrupt end. For Wilde, the theme of the novel, the idea of growing old yet not growing old, was ideally suited for his obsession with paradox, with uniting two completely different points of view. This paradoxical bent usually takes the form of humor: "A bad sort of man is the sort of man who admires innocence." "To love oneself is to begin a lifelong romance." *The Picture of Dorian Gray*, however, moves from bright comedy to dark tragedy. In fact, given Dorian Gray's hideous end, the novel seems as much a warning against the seeking out of new sensation as an embracing of it.

Lady Windermere's Fan and other early Wilde plays also have curiously moralistic endings. Only in *The Importance of Being Ernest* (1895) did Wilde create a plot that consistently echoed his hedonistic philosophy. It is the atmosphere of the Decadence, the emphasis on what Poe earlier called "the grotesque and arabesque," that makes Wilde a significant figure in the evolution of the horror tale. A similar fondness for rich, highly perfumed imagery can be found in the 1890s horror tales of Arthur Machen and William Butler Yeats, as well as, of course, in the tales of Poe himself.

3–258. Wilkins-Freeman, Mary. **The Collected Ghost Stories.** Arkham House, 1974.

3–259. Wilkins-Freeman, Mary. **The Wind in the Rose Bush and Other Stories of the Supernatural.** Doubleday, Page, 1903.

Described by H. P. Lovecraft as a "New England realist," Mary Wilkins-Freeman is best known for her ability to invest her ghost stories with a powerfully regional authenticity. Happily lacking in the melodrama characteristic of their period, these stories are notable for their subtlety of mood, depth of character development, and careful evocation of New England as an imaginative and distinctly physical place. The most famous are "The Shadows on the Wall" and "The Wind in the Rose Bush." Given the quality of these tales and their relative neglect, the Arkham House compilation is welcome.

3–260. Yeats, William Butler (U.K.). **Mythologies.** Macmillan, 1959; Collier, 1972.

This volume collects the ghost stories written by Yeats in the 1890s and scattered through tiny collections such as *The Celtic Twilight* (1893) and *The Secret Rose* (1897). Yeats was always ambivalent about these stories. In 1925 he described them as having originally been written in "that artificial, elaborate English so many of us played with in the 'nineties." The revised versions collected in *Mythologies* make one wonder whether they should have been tampered with. Consisting mainly of Irish folk tales recast in the affectedly "simple" English of Lady Gregory, they sometimes read more like propagandistic vehicles for the Celtic revival than finished works of fiction. Nevertheless, some of these tales, especially the later ones, are striking and original. Yeats was an early practitioner of a peculiar kind of ghost story that fuses horror and ecstasy in a single intense moment of vision. Like Arthur Machen and Algernon Blackwood, who were his fellow members in the Order of the Golden Dawn, Yeats fills his stories with occult doctrines and diatribes, sometimes to a debilitating extent. In "Rosa Alchemica" and "The Tables of the Law," however, the doctrines are part of a fascinatingly complex, self-recoiling vision. Like the characters of Blackwood, Yeats's Michael Robartes and Owen Aherne denounce the material world for the "higher space" of occult experience only to discover that they need the lower spaces after all. Aherne speaks of the desire for otherworldly experience as ultimately a "thirst for destruction"; he finds in the spirit world only a random succession of "wild shapes rushing from despair to despair."

4
The Modern Masters
1920–1980

Gary William Crawford

Modern fiction of supernatural horror is a literature of consciousness, and the genre itself manifests this attitude toward its own existence as a genre. Twentieth-century literature of terror looks back toward history and regards the human as an isolated being in an indifferent cosmos who has only this: consciousness of self. As modern fiction of cosmic and psychological horror almost ritually reminds us, we must always face the dark; and this element of ritual, of conscious invocation of our demons so that we may exorcise them, of repetitive form and language, makes the literature of terror in this century a reflection of itself, a conscious form produced by a conscious being.

Recent studies of the development of the Gothic tradition into this century and of the formal elements and historical background of the English ghost story [1] argue that the fiction of ghosts, the supernatural, and cosmic and psychological terror parallel developments in other fiction, the sciences, and the history of the ideas of the period. Elizabeth MacAndrew writes that "the development of the study of the mind into the science of psychology has

276

continued to affect concepts of human nature and their reflection in Gothic literature. . . . In addition, there has been a great proliferation of forms as a result of the upsurge in popular literature, the introduction into our culture of films, television, and comic books, and the appearance of a 'youth culture.' " [2] While cultural and scientific advances affect all literature of the era, modern fiction influenced by the Gothic tradition is pervasive, not only within a strict, formal, popular genre such as the proliferation of "women's Gothics" [3] or the tale of cosmic alienage in the Lovecraft mold, but in much of literature as a whole. One finds a covert tale of the doppelgänger within Conrad's *The Secret Sharer,* and his *Heart of Darkness* is not so far removed in setting and theme from the generic horror tales of Henry S. Whitehead. Flannery O'Connor's work is filled with the kind of Gothic grotesques that inhabit, if less convincingly, the novels of best-selling horror writer Stephen King. Themes of psychological alienation, of the human alone in an absurd universe, find expression in such works as Carson McCullers's "The Ballad of the Sad Cafe," with its physical aberrations peopling a Gothic castle domesticated into a cafe. The novels of Iris Murdoch are openly advertised as Gothic works, [4] and the short stories of Joyce Carol Oates, above all the collection *Night-Side* [4-184], are as psychologically Gothic and profoundly mysterious as anything in the recent tales of Robert Aickman.

Faulkner's "A Rose for Emily" and his early psychological horror story "The Leg" [4-107] not only contain Gothic motifs and techniques of realistic fiction, but show humans as utterly alone in a meaningless, and therefore horrifying, mental and material universe. Faulkner's entire Yoknapatawpha saga, as has been amply demonstrated by Elizabeth M. Kerr in her recent *William Faulkner's Gothic Domain,* explores American Gothicism, "the transmogrification of the American dream into the American nightmare." [5] Nor does it require a considerable stretch of one's critical faculties to perceive, in its broadest outlines, similar motives behind Lovecraft's mythical Arkham and its environs.

The fiction of the English ghost story tradition, to turn once again to the generic form, particularly the ghostly tales of the Edwardian era, manifests intellectual concerns found in the works of Lawrence, Joyce, Hardy, and Woolf. As Jack Sullivan argues in his study of the Edwardian ghost story, the peculiar power of the form is its "Hardyesque blending of supernaturalism and skepticism" [6] and its struggle to place meaning on what seems a chaos that must be kept in check. In this sense, the English ghost story as a form never seems to resolve itself, for it cannot keep these forces in abeyance, Sullivan implies, and it remains something of an enigma. This quality is what compels Julia Briggs to write, "The ghost story seems to look back over its own shoulder. It has become a vehicle for nostalgia, a formulaic exercise content merely to recreate a Dickensian or Monty Jamesian atmosphere. It no longer has any capacity for growth or adaptation." [7]

There are cultural, historical, and intellectual changes, however, that in turn change the focus of the English ghost story and, by implication, the larger body of generic terror fiction up to the present. The best writers in the genre are acutely sensitive to their milieu, and it no longer needs to be asserted that the genre has some serious concerns, its eye resting speculatively on the human condition. By the turn of the century, fiction of horror and the supernatural had arrived at consciousness. Humans are able, with all of the methods of modern science, to see the human psyche as a microcosm of the universe, to see that all things are possible. The anthropological writings of Tylor and Frazer, the almost fabulous connections perceived by Freud and Jung between the human psyche, human perception of reality, and human heritage as an evolved species as charted by Darwin, all converge with concepts opened up by Einstein in his theory of relativity, his assertion that time is curved space, the theories that led to nuclear physics and the space age. The genre of the tale of horror in this century is indeed looking over its shoulder, as Briggs says in specific reference to the English ghost story, but it is not dead. It has merely looked backward, inward, to the reaches of inner space, and beyond, to a consciousness of a truly stupendous and alien dimension in which we find ourselves alone.

Simultaneously, the rigid dichotomies of good and evil explored in late eighteenth-century Gothicism have given way to moral ambiguity and, in the works of H. P. Lovecraft, anarchy. Modern fiction of horror is saying that the ghosts of guilt of the past fictions are no longer important; the true horror is in the subconscious, in inner space, in a mysterious realm beyond morality where the horror is all there is.

So commonplace are such ideas in twentieth-century culture that their expression in the horror tale seems, at first glance, trivial. But in our era, popular culture has become the new subject matter for serious speculation. It often rings true in ways that serious art does not because it is a pop culture absorbed by a large middle-class audience that is, particularly since the mid-1950s, educated and truly aware.

This conscious awareness is what distinguishes horror fiction as a twentieth-century genre that is forever pointing to itself for its meaning. Since everyone now knows that we must face the dark, and the darkness is *us*, we must ritually invoke it, give it meaning, and banish it, for by now we know that the genre, the manner of speaking, is all there is.

As the genre becomes conscious in our century, it begins to talk about itself. The number of writers in the form who write about horror story writers facing horrors evoked by other horror story writers is simply uncanny in itself. For example, references to Lovecraft himself abound in the long line of Cthulhu Mythos stories based on his cosmic outsiders. In a story such as Robert Bloch's "The Ghost Writer" [4–27], a horror author bequeaths his typewriter to a younger writer in the genre after his death, and as revenge for the ideas stolen by his protégé, *lives on* in the typewriter and eventually kills the literary thief. Such conscious irony is a major way of saying anything about ourselves in this century, and the modern tale of terror is so deeply enmeshed in a tradition from which it cannot escape that, unfortunately, it frequently falls into self-parody.

By the same token, however, the intense isolation many writers find in humankind collectively in our era lends to the best contemporary horror tales an awareness of character and motivation unsurpassed in earlier ones. In these works, the horrors evoked grow spontaneously out of situation and character and point to themselves, much like the forms of poetry, for their meanings. The reader returns from the story knowing what he or she knew at the outset: The alienation, the horror, is a manner of reminding oneself again that the form of life and its quality are its only meanings. At this juncture, the genre itself *is* its meaning.

After World War I, writers in the genre already display a considerable awareness of the concerns of literature as a whole with advances in psychology and anthropology. As Julia Briggs and Jack Sullivan demonstrate, the widespread human restlessness and discontent in an age that continuously opens up new vistas of soul-shattering knowledge find expression in the English ghost story in particular. Donald Whitelaw Baker, as well, charts the specific impact of the writings of Charles Darwin, Edward Tylor, Sir James Frazer, Sigmund Freud, and even of the theosophists, most notably Madame Blavatsky, on the tale of terror. There is, quite clearly, a shift to the internal, to the isolated psyche, where we attempt to fend off the shattering truth and keep it in check. [8]

The emphasis on psychological states of conflict, on the breakdown of psychological time and space, on ancient, anthropomorphic cosmic horror, is evident in the United States as well in the terror fiction of Ambrose Bierce and Robert W. Chambers. [9] Moreover, this consciousness of moral and psychological ambiguity in the face of new scientific knowledge gives to our terror fiction, in its more conscious manifestations, a sharp-edged irony. As the form becomes conscious of our position in the universe, it becomes conscious of its role as a popular form speaking to the general reader of the same discontents that the major writers deal with in their fields.

In England, more so than in the United States, the horror story is distinctly realistic and psychological by the 1920s. Those writers working within the form of the English ghost story are Walter De La Mare, L. P. Hartley, W. F. Harvey, R. H. Malden, A. N. L. Munby, L. T. C. Rolt, M. P. Dare, H. Russell Wakefield, Elizabeth Bowen, May Sinclair, and Cynthia Asquith. More importantly, Arthur Machen and Algernon Blackwood before them speak of humans in an absurd cosmos. The cosmic strain in their works links them to U.S. writers such as Bierce and Chambers, and their impact on H. P. Lovecraft signals a new departure in horror fiction as the term *weird* begins to be applied to fiction of this type in a conscious way.

Some key tales by W. F. Harvey, L. P. Hartley, and Walter De La Mare after World War I demonstrate certain thematic concerns of the English writers that shape the form of U.S. and English fiction later in the century. The fiction of W. F. Harvey blends the psychological and the supernatural in a manner that is the distinctive feature of the English ghost story and much recent fiction in the genre. Harvey's fiction presents characters whose previous moral and psychological conceptions of reality are shattered by evidence of the paranormal, or of psychological revelation, or, more importantly, of disintegration. In this way, Harvey's work demonstrates the human's increasing sense of self-conscious irony toward a universe over which he or she has no control.

In Harvey's "The Beast with Five Fingers" [4–114], one of his most famous tales, the milieu is the upper-middle-class landed gentry of Edwardian England. The Borlsover family is, like many a family of the day, disintegrating from within; their status is changing as the Great War and its political and economic aftermath force them into new, and frequently terrifying, revelations, both psychological and social. In this tale, Adrian Borlsover's blindness has endowed him with an extraordinary sensitivity, and his writing hand seems to possess a mind of its own, since it has the gift of automatic writing. After Adrian dies, the hand lives on, severed from his dead body, and arrives for his nephew Eustace in a package in the evening post.

What is significant in this tale, because it manifests itself in much later U.S. and English terror fiction, is that the living severed hand functions in a poetic way, much like the symbolism of poetry, for the irrational side of human nature that is our inheritance from the ancient past; and the terror fiction of our era repeatedly finds us attempting to confront this aspect of ourselves. Harvey's beast with five fingers is the human; and as his tale bears out, humans have built a scientific and rational world that, for all of its benefits for a better life, seems unable to fend off what becomes in Lovecraft, for example, new vistas of the terrifying knowledge it has opened up.

Such knowledge lends to English terror fiction of the 1920s and 1930s an awareness of the genre's ability to speak of the uncertain position of the human in the universe with a skeptical materialism that is the hallmark of the form. The works of L. P. Hartley retain the haunting wit and irony, black humor, and sensitivity to the Absurd found in the best tales of the period. Hartley's best-known story of black humor, "The Travelling Grave" [4–113], shows the effects of a mechanical horror, quite literally "a travelling grave," on a group of British gentlemen in a country house who play a game of hide-and-seek with a late-arriving guest. What the late-arrival Hugh Curtis discovers in an upstairs room of the house is an Absurd horror that, in its ironic way, is even more shattering than the horrors of the Great War. A pair of host Dick Munt's shoes are fixed to the floor upside down. What ensues is a delightfully witty scene that, in its sense of Absurd humor, reverberates through much terror fiction of our century. Hugh Curtis, veteran of the Great War, his neurotic companion Valentine, and Munt's man Franklin disintegrate in a kind of hysterical amusement as they try to pull the slippers off the floor, only to discover that host Dick Munt is a victim of his own "travelling grave," his stocking-feet exposed to the night air from beneath the floor.

If Hartley's and Harvey's tales epitomize the ironic wit of much terror fiction up to the present, they have their antecedents in a great tradition that has become truly conscious. The strikingly modern stories of *In a Glass Darkly* [3–139] by the Victorian master Sheridan Le Fanu, the stiff-upper-lip imperialism of Hodgson's Carnacki [3–104], and the unfortunate hero of Machen's "The Novel of the White Powder," who, after taking a mysterious drug, drips through the floor of his bedroom as a liquescent, putrescent horror, are all harbingers of the truly conscious generic tales after World War I. In the United States, Robert Bloch is perhaps the leading exponent of such Absurdist, psychological horror.

The literature of terror becomes aware of itself in other ways. As the general populace becomes increasingly better educated, there emerges a popular culture that gives rise to numerous anthologies of terror fiction. In Britain, the most noted among these are Lady Cynthia Asquith's *Ghost Books* [4–244 to 4–246], the first of which appeared in 1926. These anthologies, like the tales of M. R. James before them, also enjoyed tremendous popularity among intellectuals. James himself was a biblical and medieval scholar of some note, and his tales, like Lovecraft's in the United States, spawned a series of imitations, all of variable quality. In addition, Algernon Blackwood, who wrote only a few works of pure terror after the 1920s, read his works aloud over the BBC radio after World War II.

In Britain, motion pictures reflected this tradition, which the nation has always regarded with pride. Britain's first great contribution to the horror film was *Dead of Night,* in which some of the country's leading actors, directors, camera crews, and musicians combined talents to produce an extraordinary anthology of cinematic terror based on some of the writings of the great masters of the form. In the late 1950s, a small production company with its own set of sound stages, built on the lot surrounding a country house at Bray near Windsor, gave itself the name Hammer Films and produced a long series of Gothic films that made enormous sums worldwide and led to the knighting of its board chairman, Sir James Carreras, for his philanthropies and for his company's role in improving Britain's balance of payments. [10]

In the 1930s and 1940s, however, the one writer who stands as a transitional figure between the Edwardian ghost story and the recent tales of Robert Aickman and Ramsey Campbell is Walter De La Mare. He gives to the form an evocative prose style and a sensitive delineation of character that the most recent masters have attempted to emulate. His unique achievement in the genre far exceeds the works of the Jamesian imitators of his time, such as R. H. Malden, A. N. L. Munby, and L. T. C. Rolt, or the single collection by M. P. Dare—*Unholy Relics* [4–85], which consists of nothing more than a pastiche of James with minimal characterization and a marked stylistic deficiency. [11]

De La Mare's fiction, on the other hand, contains little that is imitative. As Julia Briggs has noted, he stands somewhat outside the tradition, observing it with a visionary eye. His work foreshadows what is best in the most recent British writers in the genre and looks back toward Henry James because he regards the ghostly "not merely as an end in itself, but also as a subordinate element" in the tale. [12] Two of De La Mare's best-known stories, "Seaton's Aunt" [4-90] and "A Recluse" [4-88], contain, in concentrated form, elements that point to later developments in the form. Moreover, De La Mare's supernaturalism grows out of characters who are utterly alone in an almost timeless world, which speaks of alien forces "on the edge" that subvert the human's all-too-tenuous grasp of reality.

"Seaton's Aunt" is reminiscent of Henry James's concern with the uncertain, shifting mental universe of children seeking to grow into adult responsibility. On a holiday from school, the narrator Withers travels with his friend Seaton to his aunt's home in the country. There, he discovers that Seaton's inability to interact socially with the other boys at school may be due to the almost alien world that is his home and the almost alien, supernatural creature that is his aunt. Seaton's aunt is reminiscent of Dickens's Miss Havisham, and the house she inhabits is of Gothic gloom, and it appears, at least, that Seaton and his aunt communicate, albeit silently, with another world than this. This realm, however, appears to grow out of their loneliness, their silent hatred for each other, and it is filtered through the perceptions of the narrator Withers, a technical device in ghostly fiction from LeFanu onward. Moreover, out of character and incident, the mysterious realm grows until the mystery and terror is all there is. Here, as in other generic terror fiction of our century, this form begins to point to itself as it becomes its meaning, and the form, like the forms of poetry, contains its meanings.

Similarly, in De La Mare's "A Recluse," Mr. Dash, the narrator, is mysteriously drawn to and forced to spend the night with Mr. Bloom, who resides completely alone in an old country house. Mr. Bloom is an occultist, Mr. Dash discovers, and the male secretary who resided with him has recently died. Like Seaton's aunt, Mr. Bloom and his secretary seem to have gone over the edge to that mysterious and alien realm that all the writers of the era grapple with to some degree. De La Mare says it really is there, but only people like Mr. Bloom and Seaton and his aunt ever enter it completely. The mysterious realm of which De La Mare speaks is never specified, for in typical ghost story fashion, it comes to us filtered through the perceptions of Mr. Dash, a common enough English gentleman of his day.

Furthermore, the constant innuendo and suggestion of alien forces we find in so much British ghostly fiction is transformed into cosmic and scientific terms in the United States during a somewhat later period. In this respect, De La Mare's work marks a transitional phase in supernatural fiction in

Britain, for later British writers, such as Campbell and Aickman, who turn to the genre again in the 1960s and 1970s, look back to De La Mare in particular for their sources.

The interim period in Britain is relatively inactive. When Campbell and Aickman look back to De La Mare and others for inspiration, they also are cognizant of, if not directly influenced by, the radical departure that U.S. terror fiction becomes in the meantime. The almost cosmic, but distinctly mystical and psychological, quality of De La Mare's work undergoes an enormous change into a world of utter cosmic chaos in Lovecraft, Clark Ashton Smith, and Frank Belknap Long.

If previous terror writers were only interested in edges of consciousness, so to speak, American horror fiction after World War I is certainly not interested in edges any more. For there is clearly a movement in horror fiction in the United States toward outward, cosmic terror. The movement outward, which reflects the horror tale's concern with the new vistas of soul-shattering scientific knowledge opened up by Einstein, is also counterpoised by a deeper movement inward, psychologically speaking, to the archetypal realms of inner space, where new findings in psychology, particularly the writings of Carl Jung on what he calls the collective unconscious, reveal our ancient links with the past. The writer who charts these new dimensions of the horror story form with such intensity is H. P. Lovecraft.

However, the opportunities that Lovecraft takes to explore these dimensions arise from his reading in a generic form that is already conscious of itself. From Lovecraft's reading of Poe, Machen, Blackwood, Bierce, and Chambers and his fortuitous rise to prominence in a circle of writers all publishing in a pulp magazine called *Weird Tales*, which was itself a conscious manifestation of an emerging pop culture, a new era of horror fiction develops. So powerful is the impact of Lovecraft and *Weird Tales* on the modern horror form that, to this day, no new writer in the genre can quite escape their combined influence.[13]

At its inception, *Weird Tales* was an effort to promulgate further the tradition of the terror tale. J. C. Henneberger, a long-time Poe enthusiast who was also familiar with Lovecraft's work in various amateur and little magazines, founded *Weird Tales* with a view to publishing stories that were, in the words of Poe's lines from "Dream-Land":

> From a wild weird clime that lieth, sublime,
>   Out of SPACE—out of TIME. [14]

No writer in *Weird Tales* remained more sensitive to Poe, the Gothic tradition, and his elder masters of the form—Blackwood and Machen—than Lovecraft. As Barton Levi St. Armand has suggested, Lovecraft is the Aristotle of horror fiction, for he wrote his own *Poetics* of the form, "Supernatural Horror in Literature." [15] In this essay, Lovecraft speaks most clearly of what the fully developed modern "weird tale" becomes: "A certain atmosphere of breathless and unexplainable dread of outer, unknown forces must be present; and there must be a hint, expressed with a seriousness and portentousness becoming its subject, of that most terrible conception of the human brain—a malign and particular suspension or defect of those fixed laws of Nature which are our only safeguard against the assaults of chaos and the daemons of unplumbed space." [16]

In Lovecraft's fiction, and in much horror fiction to the present, the realm of terror on the borderline of consciousness found in such writers as De La Mare has given way to an utter cosmic chaos that is, at least in its present-dimensional earthly manifestations, acutely visceral. Lovecraft's realistic descriptions of putrescent physical horror abound; and Algernon Blackwood is said to have remarked of his work that spiritual terror seemed completely absent. [17] However, in his critical study *The Roots of Horror in the Fiction of H. P. Lovecraft,* St. Armand explores Lovecraft's Gothic sources, noting his use of Radcliffe's distinction between terror and horror, which in Lovecraft becomes a fusion of the two. St. Armand finds that in Lovecraft "terror leads to cosmic awe, dread of the abyss," [18] while horror looks backward and inward to the workings of the psyche, where the viscous horror of Lovecraft's stories takes on a symbolic resonance analogous to Carl Jung's archetypes of the collective unconscious. [19] Lovecraft's fusion of outer, cosmic terror and inner, archetypal psychological horror marks the arrival of the generic terror story as a conscious form that begins to invoke as in a ritual the terror and horror that is our heritage from the past and our link to the future.

As Lovecraft's tales mature from the Poe-esque "The Outsider" (1921) [4–160] and the cosmic outsideness of "The Music of Erich Zann" (1921) [4–160] through "The Rats in the Walls" (1923) [4–160], which represents in St. Armand's view the confluence of Lovecraft's ideas, to the birth of the Cthulhu Mythos in "The Call of Cthulhu" (1926) [4–160] and his later explorations of science fiction and pure fantasy, there emerges a mythical world in Arkham and its environs, which, in its self-allusiveness, serves as a truly conscious evocation of a generic form that looks back on itself to its Gothic foundations and to its future as a form closely allied to the forms of science fiction and fantasy. [20]

Moreover, the mythical, timeless quality of Lovecraft's transformed New England, which seems poised between the terrors of the cosmos on the outside and the viscous symbols of psychological horror on the inside, links it to the Gothic realm of Faulkner's Yoknapatawpha saga, which is also self-allusive and reflective of a particularly social and psychological Gothicism. As Elizabeth M. Kerr argues throughout her study of the Gothic in Faulkner, ". . . the South provided William Faulkner . . . with a reality which could be depicted with the strong contrasts of the Gothic genre to reveal social and psychological truths less accessible to purely objective and realistic treatment. . . . With a foundation of realistic displacement which conceals Gothic structure beneath the representation of modern society, all the strategies of point of view, discontinuity, ironic inversion, exaggeration, and parody are employed to give new meaning to old formulas. . . ." [21]

Clearly, Lovecraft is no Faulkner, for he lacks Faulkner's insights into character and motivation; and, more importantly, his achievement lies only within the generic form. There are, however, broader ideological concerns in Lovecraft's works, which arise from both Faulkner's and Lovecraft's awareness that the Western concept of a moral universe with a teleology centered on human liberation from fear and superstition was being undermined subconsciously by human primitive, instinctual nature: our progression has opened up such stupendous vistas of knowledge and power that we instinctively retreat, as in the teleological regression of schizophrenia, into a new dark age. Faulkner's regressive grotesques are not so far removed from the denizens of Lovecraft's Innsmouth, who possess "the Innsmouth look" [22] because they have, like the narrator of Lovecraft's "The Shadow over Innsmouth" [4–160], regressed teleologically, after having partaken of the blasphemous knowledge of The Esoteric Order of Dagon and incestuously propagated themselves. Such similarities between Lovecraft's and Faulkner's fictional worlds invite other, perhaps more odious, comparisons. Grotesque indeed would be a side-by-side lineup of Lovecraft's and Faulkner's grotesques, with Benjy Compson and Wilbur Whateley leading the ranks. As Elizabeth Kerr has pointed out, "Faulkner was both a Gothic and a comic novelist and combined the horror story with the comic tall tale, a combination . . . of the regressive and the progressive in art." [23]

Similarly, Lovecraft's fictional world is distinctly self-conscious, ironic, and Absurdist. His art is, like Faulkner's, both progressive and regressive, for his themes grow out of the genre in which he chose to work; and he is, like the early Gothicists, unconcerned with character development or complexity of motivation. He is, however, concerned with the intellectual milieu of his day, but he views it with a sense of comic irony that disarms the reader, negating all pretensions to high seriousness. [24] Lovecraft regarded his work as a commercial product, but even if it actually is, it speaks as much pop culture does—with a voice that is, in its twentieth-century manifestations, clearly ironic.

Still, Lovecraft's intellectual concerns have become the subject of much recent speculation. Aside from St. Armand's work, Paul Buhle [25] and the psychologist Dirk W. Mosig [26] have explored the sociological and psychological ramifications of his writings. If any aspect of Lovecraft's fiction embodies these concerns, it is his formation of the Cthulhu cycle of stories. In these tales, Lovecraft's principal concern is the continual dramatization of the Western teleological progression toward liberation from ignorance and fear, which, ironically, opens up new vistas of soul-shattering truth. The dramatic tension of these tales, however, lies not in one complex character's struggle with a personal confrontation with the truth that is horror, but in a timeless, psychosymbolical world where an epic conflict is enacted. In this conflict, the human discovers that teleological progression can, because of our primitive, instinctual, and unconscious urges, simultaneously bring about teleological regression to a new dark age that, as St. Armand has demonstrated in Jungian terms [27] in "The Rats in the Walls," parallels a descent into the collective unconscious.

If Lovecraft's "daemons of unplumbed space," the entities of the Cthulhu stories, are evoked from the ancient past of human prehistory as a result of the actions of the Cthulhu cultists investigated by Professor Angell in "The Call of Cthulhu" [4–160], they represent one scientist's confrontation with new vistas of knowledge about alien dimensions. In other tales of the Cthulhu cycle, such as "The Whisperer in Darkness" [4–160]—in which Professor Wilmarth, a student of folklore, happens to correspond with a Vermont recluse and amateur scientist who stumbles on the dreaded Necronomicon by the mad Arab Abdul Alhazred and links it to the appearance of strange, winged creatures with buzzing voices he calls the nameless Outsiders [28]—they represent one man's regression into a state similar to psychosis. The awesome suggestion of horrifying forces on the outside engulfs Wilmarth until, on his correspondent's disappearance, his discovery of the microscopic reproduction of his correspondent's hands and face left by the Outsiders forces him "to half-accept the scepticism of those who attribute my whole experience to dream and nerves and delusion" (p. 277).

Implicit, then, in Lovecraft's Cthulhu stories is the idea that insanity, or teleological regression, is the instinctual reaction to the truth that science posits. As in the mind of a psychotic, the truth becomes so intolerable that a regressive reaction sets in, building a tight, concentric world of primitive logic, or paleologic, that takes over; and this primitive world of infantlike thought seems real, seems scientifically valid. [29] In "The Shadow Out of Time" [4–160], Professor Nathanial Wingate Peaslee discovers where science will lead: As he enters a strange, psychic, and perhaps delusory world, deep within the earth beneath western Australia, he goes into the ancient past of humans to a primal realm where he discovers amid "cyclopean, buried ruins" a book within a metal case in "the dust of a million centuries" whose "queerly pigmented letters on the brittle, aeon-browned cellulose pages were not indeed any nameless hieroglyphs of earth's youth," but "the letters of our familiar alphabet, spelling out the words of the English language in my own handwriting." [30]

Lovecraft's terror fiction represents a dramatic change in the form. His work is far from the morally disintegrating world of the Gothic novelists, or of the darkly romantic world of Poe's guilt-ridden madmen. He has transcended the clouded, interior world of LeFanu's protagonists in *In a Glass Darkly*, who suffer because they can see reality only in a distorted way, and has plunged headlong beyond the findings of science to a place where we come face to face, as does Professor Peaslee, with ourselves.

Many of the writers who cluster around Lovecraft (and become known as the *Weird Tales* circle) are acutely aware, like the narrator of Lovecraft's "The Call of Cthulhu," that "the piecing together of dissociated knowledge will open up such terrifying vistas of reality, and of our frightful position therein, that we shall either go mad from the revelation or flee from the deadly light into the peace and safety of a new dark age." [31]

Curiously, however, what follows Lovecraft in the United States and is later taken up from him in England in the 1970s may be likened to a renaissance of horror that is far from over. Lovecraft's vision, itself supremely ironic and self-aware, since it was the vision of a reclusive *poseur* who fancied himself an eighteenth-century English gentleman and who never faced the responsibilities of life, is his bequest to his adulators and detractors. Moreover, Lovecraft is often more profoundly interesting than his stories, and he is a pop culture figure without parallel in America, the hero of a youth culture very conscious of the outsideness of his vision and the outsider that he was. [32]

Much of the writing of the major contributors to *Weird Tales* follows the Lovecraftian formula, and the staggering number of Cthulhu Mythos stories produced during his life and after his death in 1937 may, it seems, never end. [33] What evolves, however, as a result of Lovecraft's voluminous correspondence with other *Weird Tales* writers, is a conscious, almost ritual evocation in the form of the "weird tale" of the chaos Lovecraft saw as human heritage. [34]

If any writers serve to offer within some of their fiction a commentary on Lovecraft and his contribution to the weird tale, they are Frank Belknap Long and August Derleth. Long's "The Hounds of Tindalos" [4–154] may be regarded as a more concrete scientific expansion of the science fantasy aspects of Lovecraft's Cthulhu stories. In this tale, Halpin Chalmers is a journalist and amateur scientist, like Lovecraft himself, although Long's "The Space Eaters" [4–154] contains a character named Howard who actually is modeled after Lovecraft, a close friend of Long's. Chalmers's character aligns with the tradition of the metaphysical scientist found in terror fiction from LeFanu's Dr. Hesselius to Blackwood's John Silence.

"The Hounds of Tindalos" retains in almost purely scientific terms the metaphysicals of Lovecraft's mythos. Long uses these same terms again in his short novel *The Horror from the Hills* [4–153], in which another metaphysical scientist, Roger Little, defeats another Outsider, Chaugnar Faugn, with a fourth-dimensional weapon. Later Cthulhu Mythos stories repeatedly use the same motifs and concepts to the extent that Cthulhu Mythos fiction becomes a subgenre itself, although it is largely the result of August Derleth's coining the term to market a certain type of story.

With a very conscious reverence, Derleth takes assorted fragments and notes left by Lovecraft after his death and composes a series of Cthulhu stories later collected in the volume *The Watchers Out of Time* [4–101]. Derleth's use of the mythos, however, is unimaginative, for his work contains few passages that approach the prose style Lovecraft employs; and Lovecraft's style serves to displace what little complexity lies in his characters. "The Lurker at the Threshold" [4–100] and "The Shuttered Room" [4–101] are the best of the Derleth-Lovecraft "collaborations." Derleth's Cthulhu novels *The Mask of Cthulhu* [4–94] and *The Trail of Cthulhu* [4–99] retain nothing of the feverish intensity of Lovecraft's mythology.

At this juncture, the genre of the tale of "cosmic dread," and by implication the larger body of generic horror fiction, begins to talk about itself, so to speak, and to indicate that the form, not necessarily the horror, is its own meaning. At the same time, Cthulhu Mythos stories continue to abound. Some of Robert Bloch's early tales, and more notably his recent *Strange Eons* [4–34], are in this subgenre. In the 1960s and 1970s, Brian Lumley is the leading writer in the mythos, and some of his more recent fantasy works in the Titus Crow series *The Clock of Dreams, Spawn of the Winds* [4–168], and *In the Moons of Borea* [4–167] extend Lovecraft's later, mature fantasies, while *The Burrowers Beneath* [4–164] and *Beneath the Moors* [4–163] are more traditional mythos novels. Basil Copper's *The Great White Space* [4–77] is a conscious tribute to Lovecraft and Clark Ashton Smith.

Smith, long-time correspondent of Lovecraft's, takes his own route into the realms of fantasy in the pages of *Weird Tales*. His fantasies contain occasional references to Lovecraft's work, but he is most noted for the creation of such mythical, fantastic realms as the polar continent of Hyperborea, the futuristic world of sorcery Zothique, and, finally, Xicarph, another planet dominated by a magician. [35] Smith however, produced a few supernatural horror tales that, for sheer power in the evocation of cosmic horror, are without equal. In his "Genius Loci" [4–201] and "The Seed from the Sepulchre" [4–205], one finds that the chaos to which Lovecraft alludes is in the dimensions of inner and outer space simultaneously, a concept already explored by other writers. In Smith, however, the carefully controlled yet expansive prose style evokes this chaos and points to what the surfaces of the genre accomplish, as in some decadent poetry: The manner of evocation, and its form, are the only meanings that can be placed on the chaos. The dissolving surfaces of descriptive language, evoking a strangely ancient, cosmic horror, which is by now the domain of much modern horror fiction of our era, is also a conscious manifestation of a phenomenon that might be called "horror for horror's sake." These stories by Smith are, like much of his poetry, distinctly decadent in the Baudelairian sense, for Smith wrote his own translations of Baudelaire. [36]

Unfortunately, the type of decadent, cosmic horror, of which Smith is one of the few unique voices, lapses into cliché after World War II. There are other writers of the *Weird Tales* period, however, most notably Derleth, Carl Jacobi, and Robert Bloch, whose fiction explores more human and personal values because they look back to the English ghost story tradition or to folklore for more immediate themes. At the same time, there is an effort to bring the weird tale to a more mature, literate, and sophisticated audience.

To achieve this end, August Derleth founded Arkham House. With Donald Wandrei, a minor writer in the genre, Derleth created a small press that produced handsome, uniform, limited editions of the works of Lovecraft, Long, Smith, Bloch, and a number of British writers. Even today, Arkham House is the major publisher of quality weird fiction in the world, even though it has never been a profitable venture. If Arkham House did more to promulgate the works of cosmic horror produced by Lovecraft and his followers, it also promoted fine works from a number of lesser talents.

Derleth himself produced several volumes of his own ghost stories from the pages of *Weird Tales,* but as he admitted, most of his enormous body of short macabre fiction is derivative and written in the simple, clear prose of his regional mainstream fiction, which remains his best work. Nevertheless, Derleth possessed a deep respect for the genre. The stories collected as *Someone in the Dark* [4–97] reveal Derleth's admiration for M. R. James. The best of these stories are "Glory Hand" and "The Guardian." Other Derleth stories show the considerable impact of the ghost stories of Mary E. Wilkins-Freeman, such as "The Patchwork Quilt" from *Dwellers in Darkness* [4–92]. Derleth must, however, be considered a genuine devotee and a capable publisher and editor above all, for without Arkham House there would be no weird fiction as we know it today. Derleth's fiction, with the exception of his Cthulhu stories, reveals a particular concern for the simple values of human life, and in this respect his achievement resembles that of Val Lewton's horror films in the 1940s. This similarity is nowhere more evident than in the ghost stories he wrote under the pseudonym Stephen Grendon, collected as *Mr. George, and Other Odd Persons* [4–95].

A kindred spirit, in many respects, to August Derleth is Carl Jacobi. Like the largest portion of Derleth's imitative weird tales, Jacobi's stories are remarkable for their simplicity and serve as a counterpoint to the cosmic outsideness of much *Weird Tales* fiction. Jacobi's best-known story, "Revelations in Black" [4–124], excels the best of Derleth's work because out of the well-worn materials of the vampire myth he creates an uncanny atmosphere of subtle, impending schizophrenia, and his early use of the phenomena of the psychoses links him to later writers like Robert Bloch and Fritz Leiber. In this story, the implicit alienation of the characters in a world that is psychically tainted, in this case by World War I, makes it a subtle, haunting tale.

In Jacobi's tale, as in others of the period, the fascination of the writers with the psychoses of course is a reaction to the maturation of the science of psychology, which, in many ways, has roots in the realms of much nineteenth-century Gothic fiction (for example, Freud's exploration of Hoffmann's "The Sandman" in his essay "The Uncanny") and in such seemingly occult phenomena as mesmerism, later taken up by Charcot to cure illnesses from hysteria to homosexuality. The concept of teleological regression implicit in Lovecraft's work is a reflection of the impact of psychology, and no writer of modern terror fiction can avoid its influence. W. F. Harvey's story "Miss Cornelius" [4–114] is an early, humorous attempt to combine the kind of psychological horror and humor later found in the works of Robert Bloch. In this ironic tale, a gentleman becomes obsessed with a medium.

Psychology, combined with a grim Absurdist irony, is the starting point of much of Robert Bloch's fiction; and although the bulk of his tremendous output is contrived, flippant, and repetitive, his work contains a vision of the beast with five fingers that is human; consciously ironic toward his own existence as a creature who must confront the truth about himself, even though that truth may eventually split him in two. Bloch's early tale "Yours Truly, Jack the Ripper" [4–30] is about an Englishman whose mother was murdered by Jack the Ripper and who believes the Ripper to be alive in the United States. He engages a psychiatrist to aid him, and, in an ironic twist, the psychiatrist himself turns out to be Jack the Ripper or, implicitly, split into a personality who may be as deluded as the patient. Bloch's short fiction contains a number of variations of this formula, but this best work remains *Psycho* [4–32], about a schizoid personality who is both his dead mother and the proprietor of an out-of-the-way motel, an apt modern Gothic setting for his murder of a young woman escaping with stolen money.

Bloch's career spans the entire modern era of the weird tale. His work consists of Cthulhu Mythos stories in addition to fantasy, science fiction, and mysteries. Like many other writers in the genre in the 1950s and 1960s, such as Richard Matheson and Charles Beaumont, he has written scripts for horror films. Bloch epitomizes the horror dimension of today's pop culture.

Due in large part to the impact of horror films, the tradition of horror fiction has reached industry heights. The success of such novels as Ira Levin's *Rosemary's Baby* [4–150], William Peter Blatty's *The Exorcist* [4–24], Thomas Tryon's *The Other* [4–211], Jeffrey Konvitz's *The Sentinel* [4–140], Fred Mustard Stewart's *The Mephisto Waltz* [4–207], and, more recently, Stephen King's *Carrie* [4–129], *Salem's Lot* [4–133], and *The Shining* [4–134] is due more to the box office hits they become when transformed into films than to their merits as works in the best tradition of terror fiction.

Stephen King is probably the best-known figure in the genre today, but he does acknowledge his debt to the American Gothic tradition.[37] *The Shining* and *Salem's Lot* are the most Gothic of his works, although his use of Poe's "Masque of the Red Death" in *The Shining* reveals what is perhaps his only instinctual insight into Poe's brand of Gothicism. King's best work is in the short story form, his collection of stories *Night Shift* [4–132] containing such memorable stories as "Gray Matter," which is reminiscent of Machen's "The Novel of the White Powder," and the credible story of a romance between a sophisticated girl-on-campus and a lowly, homely "dorm rat" with psychic powers, "I Know What You Need."

King's sudden and extraordinary rise to popularity and the amazing resurgence of interest in Lovecraft and *Weird Tales* by a youth culture obsessed with "consciousness," whether through drugs, pop psychology, music, or a combination, has given rise to a proliferation of works in the genre. The revival of such early *Weird Tales* writers as Hugh B. Cave, E. Hoffman Price, and Manly Wade Wellman, and the announcement of a new paperback revival of *Weird Tales* mark the flowering of a fully conscious genre that has become its own meaning, since it imposes on the alien worlds within and without, or the chaos of terrifying possibilities opened up by science—without which we cannot survive as a civilization, a meaning that must be invoked so that we can come to terms with ourselves. Three writers of our era who remain most sensitive to the times are Fritz Leiber, Robert Aickman, and Ramsey Campbell.

The work of Fritz Leiber spans the fields of science fiction, heroic fantasy, and horror. His knowledge of the hard sciences, reflected both in his numerous articles in *Science Digest* and in his fiction, and of psychology, philosophy, and sociology, gives to his horror fiction a number of pointed thematic concerns. More importantly, however, his terror fiction manifests the tendency of the best writing in the genre today to move away from the tales of cosmic outsideness to more personal and immediate concerns. In Leiber's fiction, as in the work of Ramsey Campbell and Robert Aickman, the elements of the weird or supernatural grow naturally and convincingly as a poetic, almost metaphorical, expression of the chaos within and without that the characters must come to terms with. When they do, the supernatural horror evoked becomes a means of allowing the characters, and the reader by extension, to perceive that the form of life and its quality are its only meanings.

Leiber's early terror tale "Smoke Ghost" [4–146] contains the theme of psychological regression as a result of an advanced urban environment devoid of humanity, a theme later developed in "The Black Gondolier" [4–145] and *Our Lady of Darkness* [4–147]. In this story, as in a number of Leiber's other works, such as "A Bit of the Dark World" and "The Terror from the Depths," he places an emphasis on humanity and love united against the cosmic chaos without and the microcosmic chaos within; and overall he seems to be a positive rationalist. If the regression to psychosis can be countered by human love, as in "Smoke Ghost," Leiber remains aware, like Lovecraft, that the teleological progression toward freedom from superstition can also bring about its opposite, regression.

In "The Dreams of Albert Moreland" [4–146], and to a lesser extent "Belsen Express" [4–144], Leiber dramatizes the phenomenon as a commentary on regression into war. Albert Moreland is, like the protagonist of Leiber's "Midnight by the Morphy Watch" [4–144], a chess player who gradually plunges into a dream world, or cosmic dimension, in which the thought processes of a chess game, with progression to an end, take on the regressive form of a psychosis. Here Leiber equates human involvement in war with a regression in which we may exchange our souls as in some cosmic chess game. Implicitly, Albert Moreland does so. George Simister meets a similar fate when he ignores the impact or significance of war to the larger concerns of humanity in "Belsen Express."

Leiber's concern with love and sexuality as a logical extension of his use of the supernatural as a metaphor for his themes finds expression in *Conjure Wife* [4–143]. Aside from the fact that the book would serve as a useful textbook for faculty wives new to the game, it is a sensitive attempt to explore the power of feminine sexuality and love in terms of its supernatural metaphor: witchcraft. The mystical power of feminine sexuality becomes a dangerous force as it spirals down the regressive path to impending madness and death.

In Leiber's fiction, human beings can make a false move, as does Albert Moreland in his cosmic chess game, but can also achieve insight in the moment of confrontation with outer forces. This insight occurs, however, on the personal level in most of Leiber's work, as it does in the best writers of the genre today.

The narrator of Leiber's "The Black Gondolier" [4–145], too, achieves insight into the apparently supernatural disappearance of his drifter friend Daloway, who appears to have been carried off by the "black gondolier" of his vivid dreams. Daloway's vision of the world seems dangerously paranoid, yet curiously true. He speaks with the vocabulary of a paranoid, of a mysterious "they" who possess some greater knowledge. What Daloway fears, however, in the town of Venice, California, and throughout the world by extension, is the consciousness of *oil*. Although Daloway's thinking, which the narrator suspects is a symptom of mental illness, resembles the underlying concepts of much cosmic horror fiction, the insight the narrator achieves at Daloway's apparent disappearance with the black gondolier in his dreams of alien worlds of black, organic slime is conveyed in personal terms. After Daloway's near death in an accident with an oil truck, the two men are drawn into a more personal involvement motivated by fear that Daloway's dream is reality. Finally, this narrator, like that of "The Dreams of Albert Moreland," achieves a deeper insight into the nature of the intimate connection between human life and the powers of darkness.

The cumulation of all of Leiber's concern with themes of sexuality and urban alienation occurs in *Our Lady of Darkness* [4–147], which is also a conscious tribute to the U.S. weird tale. Its protagonist is widowed horror-story writer Franz Westen, who lives alone in a high-rise apartment complex in San Francisco. After writing horror novels under the series title Weird Underground, Westen becomes enmeshed in a widening realm of terror as he discovers the existence of "paramental entities" in the city. As he pieces together the clues that lead him to Mater Tenebrarum—Our Lady of Darkness—Westen encompasses a circle of past relationships, including such masters of the weird tale as Clark Ashton Smith and Ambrose Bierce. Westen's quest leads him to the writings of de Castries, who seems to have invoked or had some consort with these paramental entities surrounding Mater Tenebrarum at the turn of the century. As the reader becomes absorbed in Westen's delvings into the past, he or she realizes that Leiber is making a conscious statement about the thematic concerns of such writers as Lovecraft and Smith.

More important, however, is Leiber's final epic confrontation with the alienage and horror of which Lovecraft and Smith speak, for it is expressed in pointedly human terms. In his love for Calpurnia, a musician who lives in Franz's building, Westen achieves insight that saves him from the terrors of de Castries's paramentals. Here, as in *Conjure Wife* and, to a lesser extent, the story "Dark Wings" [4–144], the mystery that feminine sexuality embodies is for Leiber the key that will open the door to wisdom.

Leiber's work, then, represents a fusion of the cosmic horrors of Lovecraft with the more intimate, personal concerns found in other writers. It serves, as well, as a conscious statement about what Lovecraft, Smith, and other writers do for weird fiction. Leiber, however, above all manages to endow his supernatural events with richly symbolic meanings, such as the appearance of Mater Tenebrarum as formed of the fine, powderlike paper of the books of *Weird Tales* writers Westen keeps in his room in *Our Lady of Darkness*. Here, the mature, modern horror tale points to itself and to the tradition from which it springs for its meaning.

Such consciousness of the genre may be found in more recent British fiction as well. Robert Aickman's work, in particular, embodies a conscious awareness of the English ghost story tradition. His work appears in the 1950s and 1960s at roughly the same time that Leiber reaches maturity and is a product of the same period in which Cynthia Asquith produced her second and third ghost book anthologies. Significantly, however, Aickman's work, like Leiber's, concerns itself with more personal and intimate themes at the same time that it uses the supernatural like forms of poetry to point to its own meanings. As Aickman says in his introduction to *The Fontana Book of Great Ghost Stories* [4–236], the form is "allied to poetry." [38]

In keeping with this concept of the genre, Aickman's work looks back to the stories of Walter De La Mare, who is most noted perhaps for his poetry. Similarly, Aickman seems to ignore all U.S. weird fiction of the *Weird Tales* era, for his work in the form is distinctly English. Yet because he regards the ghostly tale as a genre using forms like those of poetry, his work transcends that of all of his English predecessors, with the exception of De La Mare.

The most striking resemblance between the art of De La Mare and that of Aickman lies in their creation of what Peter Penzoldt calls "the inconclusive tale of terror." [39] The technique of such a tale consists in the writer's suggesting "a supernatural danger lurking directly behind our back, or just outside the range of our five senses, but ready at any moment to pounce upon its victim." [40] In such stories as "Seaton's Aunt" [4–90], "A Recluse" [4–88], and "Out of the Deep" [4–90], the supernatural never appears in any outward manifestation. Similarly, in Aickman's fiction, the supernatural possibilities, if not actualities, grow out of character development naturally and, much like symbolism and metaphor in poetry, carry the meaning of the stories. Rarely does Aickman write about a traditional ghost, werewolf, or vampire (the vampire tale "Passages from a Young Girl's Journal" [4–1] is an exception), but he evokes an uncanny realm of implicit terror, violence, and death, always counterpoised by human love. Like Leiber, Aickman, even in his darkest fictions, conceives of a humanity that can achieve insight into its infections of the soul, even though, frequently, it means willful entrance into those realms.

Particularly in such stories as "Into the Wood" and "Never Visit Venice" [both 4–5], Aickman creates characters who achieve a delicate yet profoundly transforming insight into the loneliness and alienation in the modern world and willfully forsake the common and everyday realities for the utter mystery, which becomes in Aickman a force of pure love.

Love for something in humanity greater than what husband and family offer compels Margaret Sawyer in "Into the Wood" to forsake the world of the suburbs of Manchester and to go "into the wood" at the Kurhus, a sanitorium in Sweden that she visits with her husband during a business trip. Her final decision to remain at the Kurhus even after learning that willful entrance into that world means death for some of the patients, since they walk the woods without sleeping, takes on the quality of a descent into the unconscious; but for Sawyer it is a descent motivated by love for something greater and perhaps more honest than the stifling life she leads with her husband.

Aickman's concerns in his ghostly tales arise from his awareness of the human struggle to come to terms with the discontents that subvert modern civilization. He admits allegiance to Freud, who in his *Civilization and Its Discontents* speaks in psychological terms of the same concerns as those in Aickman's art. Aickman writes of the ghost story's indebtedness to Freud in his introduction to *The Fontana Book of Great Ghost Stories:*

> Dr. Freud established that only a small part, perhaps one-tenth, of the human mental and emotional organisation is conscious. Our main response to this discovery has been to reject the nine-tenths unconscious more completely and systematically than ever before. Art reflects disintegration on the one hand, and commercialized fashion on the other. Religion concerns itself more and more exclusively with ethics and politics. The most advanced psychologists have begun even to claim that the unconscious mind has no existence, and that unhappiness can be cured physically, like, say, cancer. The trouble, as we all know, is that the one-tenth, the intellect, is not looking after us: if we do not blow ourselves up, we shall crowd ourselves out; above all, we have destroyed all hope of quality in living. The ghost story, like Dr. Freud, makes contact with the submerged nine-tenths. [41]

Aickman's attitude toward his genre consists in his awareness of its conscious restoration of the hidden truths in life that give it quality and meaning. Like Aickman's Margaret Sawyer, one can come to terms with the darkness and utter mystery. Similarly, in "Never Visit Venice" [4–5], Aickman's Henry Fern is, like Leiber's Haloran in "The Black Gondolier," a loner and a dreamer. Fern dreams of riding on a gondola in Venice with a beautiful woman, who remains vaguely mysterious and threatening. At a significant juncture in his life, Fern decides to leave England to visit Venice and perhaps confront the truth beneath the surface of his life. The Italian city symbolizes for Fern, as it has for Europe of the past, the gateway between two worlds; and as the story bears out, Fern's dreamworld comes true. He does, like Sawyer and Leiber's Haloran, enter that other world. And interestingly, since the modern Venice that Fern visits seems to have lost its past charm, Aickman is speaking for a civilization that has, one hesitates to admit, died to itself.

This aspect of Aickman's work, its conscious awareness of a culture—and specifically an English culture—that may be dying from its collective psychic infections, also finds expression in "A Choice of Weapons" [4–2]. This tale, like nearly all of Aickman's stories, ends on an ambiguous note. Nothing seems to be quite resolved in any logical way, and the stories appear on the verge of breaking into time and space, like the spring of a watch wound too tight. However, at the moment of breaking, Aickman's stories speak of an unconscious truth that may rise to the surface as a symbol that points to itself.

The work of Ramsey Campbell reflects, to a large extent, the unresolved ghost story in the manner of Aickman and De La Mare, but reflects U.S. writers as well. As T. E. D. Klein has pointed out, there is little resemblance between Campbell's work in the collection *Demons by Daylight* [4–57] and his early Cthulhu Mythos stories collected as *The Inhabitant of the Lake and Less Welcome Tenants* [4–60], which he wrote when he was 18. [42] One must credit the metamorphosis to maturity, to an extent, but the most apparent impact on Campbell's best work is the "youth culture": that amorphous mass of bowdlerized Zen, acid rock, and drugs. Campbell's fiction is most often set in this milieu of the youth of Liverpool, England, itself haunted by the Beatles, whose mature music virtually spoke for a culture it helped to create. Transforming this setting into a neo-Gothic realm, Campbell remains most sensitive to a culture obsessed with alienation, Dharma psychology, strange states of consciousness, and sexual and moral anarchy. He renders this world in some of the most effective prose of modern terror fiction: As in a "bummer," minute elements of the environment convey a potent, terrifying meaning; news headlines of mass murder, suicide, and rape, snatches of radio dialogue, and flashes of television images are pregnant with subversive meaning; statues, automobiles, neon signs collude as in a psychotic state; and the images that Campbell creates can be labeled quite simply those of paranoia.

From the blackest story, "Potential" [4–57], to the sexually potent evil of

The Doll Who Ate His Mother [4–58], Campbell's world remains one in which humans must come to terms with their potential for evil, and quite simply live with their paranoia, which, as T. E. D. Klein has suggested, arises from the wells of superstition in Campbell's own Catholic upbringing.[43]

Campbell's art is a conscious manifestation of a culture and an era obsessed with "turning on" its denizens to new realities amid a meaningless cosmos. And in other stories, such as "Missing" [4–59], in which a young Liverpool student moves deeper into a psychosislike state mingled with drugs and apparently ghostly manifestations of a young girl missing since World War II, Campbell depicts in human terms a culture attempting to come to terms with the moral evil and anarchy that is its heritage.

In many of Campbell's works, the theme of sexuality as a power of destructiveness and evil emerges, and in these cases, his characters must learn to come to terms with it, even though it frequently implies a confrontation with violence or death. In "The Telephones" [4–59], a young man named Tim fears an apparently threatening homosexual caller, and the story depicts his confrontation with what lies within his fear.

The theme of the potentially evil power of sexuality born of innocence finds expansive form in Campbell's *The Doll Who Ate His Mother* [4–58]. The novel's structure resembles that of the detective novel, and one cannot help but think of its resemblance to Stoker's *Dracula* [3–234], because, as in that novel, the evil character lives and walks among and becomes intimate with those who attempt to destroy him. Chris Kelley, himself born of what the reader learns is a satanic conception, is, like Stoker's vampire, a very human, victimized, yet potently evil creature whose innocence has been corrupted.

Ultimately, in these most recent fictions, we must all face the darkness within and without, evoke it, give it a name, and banish it. Our best writers of the genre of the terror tale thus ritually invoke its forms to observe the human struggle to become conscious and thus more human.

Our present-day writers of the genre who are most sensitive to their art show that we can face our demons. Earlier works of our era, such as those by Hartley, Harvey, and De La Mare, display a somewhat puzzled, disconcerted, and ironic attitude toward those demonic dreads, because they are not sure they can be kept in check. In Lovecraft, Long, and Smith, the demons momentarily hold us in the power of their alien dimensions.

The future of the tale of terror, then, lies in its ability to remain sensitive to the world in which we live. At the same time, it may very likely continue to remain fascinated with itself as a genre. For in such works as Anne Rice's *Interview with the Vampire* [4–194], we find a young man with a tape recorder interviewing a centuries-old vampire: We are fascinated with the darkness within us. And as we grow into another age, we will no doubt be forced to look deeper within, where our art will produce new symbols to render us conscious again.

Notes

1. See Elizabeth MacAndrew, *The Gothic Tradition in Fiction* (New York: Columbia University Press, 1979); Jack Sullivan, *Elegant Nightmares: The English Ghost Story from LeFanu to Blackwood* (Athens: Ohio University Press, 1978); and Julia Briggs, *Night Visitors: The Rise and Fall of the English Ghost Story* (London: Faber, 1977).
2. MacAndrew, *The Gothic Tradition in Fiction*, pp. 241–242.
3. I do not cover here or in my annotated bibliography the "women's Gothics," with varied mixtures of romance, suspense, and horror. For a bibliographical guide to this form, see Elsa J. Radcliffe, *Gothic Novels of the Twentieth-Century: An Annotated Bibliography* (Metuchen, NJ: Scarecrow Press, 1979).
4. See Zohreh T. Sullivan, "The Contracting Universe of Iris Murdoch's Gothic Novels," *Modern Fiction Studies* 23 (1978): 557–569.
5. Elizabeth M. Kerr, *William Faulkner's Gothic Domain* (Port Washington, NY: Kennikat Press, 1979), p. 52.
6. Sullivan, *Elegant Nightmares,* p. 130.
7. Briggs, *Night Visitors,* p. 14.
8. See Donald Whitelaw Baker, "Themes of Terror in Nineteenth-Century English Fiction: The Shift to the Internal" (Ph.D. diss., Brown Univ., 1955).
9. See, in particular, Phillip M. Rubens, "The Gothic Foundations of Ambrose Bierce's Fiction," *Nyctalops* 2, no. 7 (1978): 29–31.
10. See David Pirie, *A Heritage of Horror: The English Gothic Cinema, 1946–1972* (New York: Avon, 1974).
11. For a swift, jaunty guided tour of the Jamesian imitators, see Mike Ashley, "Shadows of the Master," in *Ghosts and Scholars* (Liverpool, England: Rosemary Pardoe, 1979).
12. Briggs, *Night Visitors,* p. 186.
13. For an in-depth history of *Weird Tales,* see Robert Weinberg, *The Weird Tales Story* (West Linn, OR: FAX Collector's Editions, 1977).
14. L. Sprague de Camp, *Lovecraft: A Biography* (Garden City, NY: Doubleday, 1975), p. 177.
15. Barton Levi St. Armand, *The Roots of Horror in the Fiction of H. P. Lovecraft* (Elizabethtown, NY: Dragon Press, 1977), p. v.
16. H. P. Lovecraft, "Supernatural Horror in Literature," in *Dagon and Other Macabre Tales* (Sauk City, WI: Arkham House, 1965), pp. 349–350.
17. In Peter Penzoldt, *The Supernatural in Fiction* (New York: Humanities Press, 1965), p. 169.
18. St. Armand, *The Roots of Horror,* p. 8.
19. Ibid., pp. 8–33; and Penzoldt, *The Supernatural in Fiction,* pp. 168–169.
20. For a discussion of the increasingly blurred distinctions in this century between what is called Gothic fantasy, further broken down into "high" and "low" Gothic fantasy (the latter inclusive of nearly all fiction discussed here), and science fantasy, see Marshall B. Tymn, Kenneth J. Zahorski, and Robert H. Boyer, *Fantasy Literature: A Core Collection and Reference Guide* (New York: R. R. Bowker, 1979), pp. 15–19.
21. Kerr, *William Faulkner's Gothic Domain,* p. 28.
22. H. P. Lovecraft, "The Shadow over Innsmouth," in *The Dunwich Horror and Others* (Sauk City, WI: Arkham House, 1963), p. 368.

23. Kerr, *William Faulkner's Gothic Domain,* p. 229.
24. For a delightful sidelong glance at Lovecraft's ironic attitude toward the intellectual concerns of his day, see Barton Levi St. Armand and John H. Stanbury, "H. P. Lovecraft's *Waste Paper:* A Facsimile and Transcript of the Original Draft," *Books at Brown* 36 (1978): 31–52. *Waste Paper* is Lovecraft's version of T. S. Eliot's *The Waste Land.*
25. Paul Buhle, "Dystopia as Utopia: Howard Phillips Lovecraft and the Unknown Content of American Horror Literature," *Minnesota Review* 6 (1976): 118–131.
26. See especially Mosig's "Lovecraft: The Dissonance Factor in Imaginative Literature," *Gothic* 1 (1979): 20–26.
27. See St. Armand, *The Roots of Horror,* pp. 8–33.
28. H. P. Lovecraft, *The Dunwich Horror, and Others* (Sauk City, WI: Arkham House, 1963), p. 274. All citations are to this edition.
29. See Silvano Arieti, *Interpretation of Schizophrenia* (New York: Basic Books, 1955), pp. 192–193.
30. Lovecraft, *Dunwich Horror,* p. 431.
31. Lovecraft, *Dunwich Horror,* p. 130.
32. For two contrasting views of Lovecraft the man, see L. Sprague de Camp, *Lovecraft: A Biography* (Garden City, NY: Doubleday, 1975), and Frank Belknap Long, *Howard Phillips Lovecraft: Dreamer on the Nightside* (Sauk City, WI: Arkham House, 1975).
33. See R. E. Weinberg and E. P. Berglund, *Reader's Guide to the Cthulhu Mythos* (Albuquerque, NM: Silver Scarab Press, 1973).
34. For a well-researched yet critically superficial history of Lovecraft's Cthulhu Mythos and its use by other writers, see Lin Carter, *Lovecraft: A Look behind the Cthulhu Mythos* (New York: Ballantine, 1972).
35. See Lin Carter, *Imaginary Worlds: The Art of Fantasy* (New York: Ballantine, 1973), pp. 61–65.
36. See also Barton Levi St. Armand, *H. P. Lovecraft: New England Decadent* (Albuquerque, NM: Silver Scarab Press, 1979), esp. pp. 36–44.
37. Kenneth Gibbs, in the forthcoming essay "Stephen King and the Tradition of American Gothic," argues that King's fiction is more closely aligned to the positive transcendental Gothicism of Melville's *Moby Dick,* since his novel *The Shining* has parallels with Melville rather than Poe.
38. Robert Aickman, ed., *The Fontana Book of Great Ghost Stories* (London: Fontana, 1964), p. 7.
39. Penzoldt, *The Supernatural in Fiction,* p. 203.
40. Ibid., p. 205.
41. Aickman, *The Fontana Book,* p. 7.
42. T. E. D. Klein, "Ramsey Campbell: An Appreciation," *Nyctalops* 13 (1977): 19–25.
43. Klein, "Ramsey Campbell," p. 23.

Bibliography

This bibliography on the modern masters contains major and minor examples of all categories of supernatural or nonsupernatural horror fiction published between 1920 and 1980. Several of the writers represented here wrote some works before 1920, and these are included; for purely critical reasons, these writers are considered "modern masters." (All authors are from the United States unless noted otherwise.)

The following categories of horror fiction have been used as criteria for a representative sampling of modern works in the genre:

1. Modern Gothic novels and stories retaining the trappings of late eighteenth-century Gothic works. Excluded are the popular "women's Gothics," which are regarded as outside the scope of this chapter.
2. Cthulhu Mythos stories based on H. P. Lovecraft's cycle of stories beginning with "The Call of Cthulhu."
3. The psychological horror story with no supernatural elements. These works use mental aberration as a source of horror.
4. The modern weird tale involving no Gothic trappings but containing elements of supernatural horror.
5. The *contes cruel*, using no supernatural elements but invoking horror by physical aberration or grotesquerie.
6. Anthologies represent terror fiction in all its varieties from 1920 to 1980. Criteria for inclusion involves this bibliographer's judgment as to what constitutes the finest anthology selections.

I am indebted to Hugh Lamb for information about a number of rare British editions.

*4–1. Aickman, Robert (U.K.). **Cold Hand in Mine.** Scribner, 1975; Berkeley, 1979.
One of Aickman's best collections of macabre tales, it contains the chilling, atmospheric story of a young girl's gradual metamorphosis into a vampire, "Passages from a Young Girl's Journal," which won a 1975 World Fantasy Award for best short fiction. Other tales—such as "The Swords," about a young man's first sexual encounter, which partakes of the supernatural, and "Meeting Mr. Millar," which centers on a struggling young writer's fascination with a mysterious member of an accounting firm that has its offices below his attic dwelling—reveal Aickman's gift for endowing the most ordinary circumstances with a subtle supernatural quality. On the surface, these tales appear deceptively simple, but in a story like "The Hospice," in which Lucas Mayberry, while traveling on business in the north of England, runs out of gasoline and is forced to spend the night at an isolated home for the terminally ill, there is an undercurrent of the supernatural that is expressed indirectly by means of implication.

*4–2. Aickman, Robert (U.K.). **Dark Entries.** Collins, 1964.

All of these stories, with the exception of "A Choice of Weapons" and "Bind Your Hair," appear in Aickman's 1979 collection [4–3]. *Dark Entries* is, however, his first collection, if one does not include *We Are for the Dark* [4–7], in which he published three stories. "A Choice of Weapons" is a carefully produced ghostly tale about a young architectural student named Malcolm Fenville who falls in love at first sight with Dorabelle, who lives alone in the house of her dead parents. Dorabelle leads Malcolm on, but later reveals that she is in love with and will marry an eighteenth-century gentlemen she has met in the supernatural mirror in her room. Malcolm comes under the influence, meanwhile, of Dr. Bermuda, who says that he will cure Malcolm of love. Eventually Malcolm encounters Dorabelle's eighteenth-century fiancé in her house and duels with him, his choice of weapons being a rapier. Malcolm kills the man, only to discover that he has killed Dorabelle. Bermuda, a mysterious presence throughout this mysterious tale, arrives and says that he has failed to cure Malcolm. The story ends in an equally strange manner when Bermuda extracts some unnamed object from behind the supernatural mirror in Dorabelle's room. "Bind Your Hair" is a more accessible if less chilling tale. Clarinda, a young London secretary, agrees to marry a co-worker and goes to visit his family in the country. There, she meets a neighbor, Mrs. Pagani, who lives in a remodeled chapel overlooking a churchyard. Clarinda ventures out to this place on a foggy night and discovers that the neighbor is the leader of a mysterious cult. No explanation for the strange ritual-like activities Clarinda witnesses is ever offered.

*4–3. Aickman, Robert (U.K.). **Painted Devils: Strange Stories.** Scribner, 1979.

This collection of nine stories exhibits Aickman's careful maintenance of character and realistic settings out of which grows the most delicate hint of the supernatural. "Ravissante" concerns a painter of mystical and supernatural themes who leaves a manuscript about a visit to a woman painter, Madame A, who ravishes him with a kind of ghostly sexuality that leaves him marked for life. In this story, as in others such as "The View"—about another painter who stays with a woman in her country house while attempting to paint a seaside landscape that continually changes—and "Ringing the Changes"—about a couple on honeymoon in a strange coastal town where once every year the inhabitants ring all the bells in the vicinity in order to wake the dead—Aickman equates love and sexuality with the supernatural. And in all cases, the vaguely elusive quality of the supernaturalism of these stories suggests that, for Aickman, there is nothing in life but mystery and the unknowable. In "Larger than Oneself," Mrs. Iblis joins a weekend house party that seems a microcosm for human search for some supernal truth about existence, a truth that, for Aickman, lies in the mystery just under the surface of daily affairs.

*4-4. Aickman, Robert (U.K.). **Powers of Darkness.** Collins, 1966.
Three of the stories in this collection are available in other of Aickman's collections and three are first published here. "The Wine-Dark Sea" is about a man who becomes fascinated by a mysterious island in the Aegean. When he visits it, he finds himself possessed by what appear to be three sorceresses from Greece's past. "The Visiting Star" is a weird tale about a Victorian actress who makes a comeback amid ghostly company. Equally strange is "Your Tiny Hand Is Frozen," about a mysterious telephone caller who haunts Edmund St. Jude during a lonely Christmas season.

*4-5. Aickman, Robert (U.K.). **Sub Rosa: Strange Tales.** Gollancz, 1968.
This collection of eight tales, two of which are also available in *Painted Devils* [4-3], reflects Aickman's concern with characters who must confront the inexplicable mystery at the heart of their lives and come to terms with it. In "The Inner Room," a woman narrates her early childhood and her life with her struggling family, which later splits apart. As a birthday gift, she receives an enormous doll house, which is a source of almost supernatural mystery for her because it contains an inaccessible inner room. Later in life, in a curious episode, she visits what is apparently the actual model of the house and comes close to discovering what seems a nameless horror in the inner room. In "Never Visit Venice," Henry Fern, a lonely, single English businessman, dreams of an episode of romance in Venice and travels there only to discover that he should have never visited the place, since he lives his dream and is carried out in a gondola to isolated terror at sea. "No Stronger Than a Flower" is the story of a young, homely, newlywed woman who, after visiting a sort of beauty spa, changes into a devastatingly beautiful and terrifying female in what amounts to a supernatural transformation that dissolves her relationship with her husband. "The Cicerones" is an episode in the life of Englishman John Trant, who undergoes a strange, apparently supernatural ordeal with the inhabitants of a cathedral in Italy. "Into the Wood" concerns Margaret Sawyer, who, while traveling in Sweden with her husband on business, stays for a few evenings at a sanitorium near a wood in the Swedish countryside where the inhabitants cannot sleep. After Margaret leaves the place, she finds that she, too, can no longer sleep, and she returns to the sanitorium to walk the wood with the other patients, forever sleepless.

*4-6. Aickman, Robert (U.K.). **Tales of Love and Death.** Gollancz, 1977.
This collection of seven stories is one of Aickman's best. While the story "Marriage" is available elsewhere, six stories are new within this volume. The best are "Growing Boys," about twins who grow to a monstrous size; "Le Miroir," in which a woman physically disintegrates to her death as her mirror retains her youthful image; and "Residents Only," the history of the inhabitants of a cemetery. All of these weird tales once again demonstrate Aickman's ability to create an atmosphere of the supernatural from seemingly ordinary situations.

*4-7. Aickman, Robert, and Elizabeth Jane Howard (U.K.). **We Are for the Dark.** Jonathan Cape, 1951.

This volume contains Aickman's earliest work in the genre. "The Trains," one of his best uncanny tales, is widely available in anthologies, and "The View" is available in *Painted Devils*. [4-3]. Elizabeth Jane Howard's best contribution here is "Three Miles Up."

4-8. Aiken, Joan (U.K.). **A Bundle of Nerves.** Gollancz, 1976; Peacock, 1978.

One critic has written of Joan Aiken: ". . . rather as though Iris Murdoch had gone into partnership with Agatha Christie." This collection of grim, ironic tales remains the best of Aiken's work in the genre. The finest of these 19 stories are "Cricket," "Smell," "The Cold Flame," and "Lodging for the Night."

4-9. Arlen, Michael (U.K.). **Ghost Stories.** Collins, 1927; Arno, 1976.

Although Michael Arlen is considered a mainstream writer, he produced one volume of ghostly tales. His best-known story from this book is "The Gentleman from America," about a man who is frightened into a madhouse after a supernatural experience. Other stories of note are "The Prince of the Jews," "To Lamoir," and "The Ancient Sin."

*4-10. Asquith, Cynthia (U.K.). **This Mortal Coil.** Arkham House, 1947.

Asquith is noted for her anthologies of supernatural horror tales, but she has also produced one fine volume of ghost stories. Perhaps the best from this volume are "In a Nutshell," concerning a guilt-ridden woman who is haunted by dreams of her husband's death by angina, dreams that once again become reality as her son dies of the same disease; "The White Moth," about a plain, simple young woman who produces magnificent poetry by ghostly telepathy; and "God Grante That She Lye Stille," a doctor's account of the possession of his beautiful patient by an ancestor. All the stories in the volume, however, reveal Asquith's command of the ghost story form. A revised edition of this volume appeared in 1951 as *What Dreams May Come*.

4-11. Baker, Denys Val (U.K.). **The Face in the Mirror.** Arkham House, 1971.

These unusual fantasy and macabre stories are among Baker's best work in the genre. A whimsical fantasy tale is "The Trees," while "The Face in the Mirror" and "Passage to Liverpool" are remarkable macabre pieces.

4-12. Beaumont, Charles (pseud. of Charles Nutt). **The Hunger, and Other Stories.** Putnam, 1958; Bantam, 1959.

None of these stories is a supernatural horror tale, but they fall loosely into the category of the *contes cruel*. "Miss Gentibelle" is the story of a mother who, having wanted a girl instead of a boy, inflicts cruel punishment on her boy-child. "The Hunger," perhaps the best and most gruesome of these 17 stories, centers on a young girl who unconsciously yearns for a lover and is murdered by a rapist. These stories are similar to those by Charles Birkin [4–13 to 4–19].

4–13. Birkin, Charles (U.K.). **Death Spawn.** Tandem, 1968.
These stories include some of Birkin's earliest and perhaps best work. There is the title story in addition to tales based on actual experience, such as "Waiting for Trains." Birkin is essentially a Grand Guignol writer.

4–14. Birkin, Charles (U.K.). **Devil's Spawn.** George Allen, 1936.
This is Birkin's first collection of stories, most of which are available in revised versions in his later collections.

4–15. Birkin, Charles (U.K.). **The Kiss of Death.** Tandem, 1964.
This book marked the return of Birkin to horror fiction after nearly 30 years. "Some New Pleasures Prove" is perhaps the finest work about a sex maniac ever penned. Some of the stories are redrafted from Birkin's earliest collection and are, again, in the Grand Guignol tradition.

4–16. Birkin, Charles (U.K.). **My Name Is Death.** Panther, 1966.
This collection again features Birkin's work in the Grand Guignol tradition. The best story is "My Name Is Death," which concerns a girl caught alone on an island "possessed by the sea."

4–17. Birkin, Charles. (U.K.). **The Smell of Evil.** Tandem, 1965.
Birkin's second modern collection again features stories from the 1930s, but carefully remodeled to avoid anachronisms. "Text for Today" is an ironic comment on the dangers of too much religion in the wrong hands. "Ballet Negre" is a fine zombie tale, and "The Godmothers" deals with a grim child murder.

4–18. Birkin, Charles (U.K.). **So Pale, So Cold, So Fair.** Tandem, 1970.
Dennis Wheatley has written of Birkin: "I feel we may claim for him a definite touch of the old master, Edgar Allan Poe." This volume again reveals Birkin's gift for ironic twists of the Grand Guignol variety. The best stories are "The Godsend," "Circle of Children," and "A Haunting Beauty."

4–19. Birkin, Charles (U.K.). **Spawn of Satan.** Award, 1970.
This volume contains some of Birkin's most recent work. "The Beautiful People" is his attempt, although not a wholly successful one, to depict modern youth.

4–20. Bishop, Zealia B. **The Curse of Yig.** Arkham House, 1953.
This book is noteworthy in that the three stories it contains, "The Curse of Yig," "Medusa's Coil," and "The Mound," were largely revised by H. P. Lovecraft. "The Mound" is perhaps the most Lovecraftian of the three, since it incorporates some elements of his myth cycle. Also contains useful profiles of Lovecraft and August Derleth.

4–21. Blackburn, John (U.K.). **Bury Him Darkly.** Cape, 1969; Sphere, 1970.
Blackburn's fourteenth novel is one of his best. Like so many of his stories, this concerns ancient evil loosed on the world through stupidity, in this case, evil from another planet. Where modern masters like Stephen King write at length on their original ideas, Blackburn instead chooses traditional legends based on half-truths, adds his own well-structured plot with many ironic twists, and produces minor masterpieces.

4–22. Blackburn, John (U.K.). **Children of the Night.** Cape, 1966; Panther, 1968.
Another of Blackburn's studies of ancient evil resurrected. In this work, peopled by a number of colorful characters, explorer Moldon Mott investigates strange happenings centering on the potential end of the world.

4–23. Blackburn, John (U.K.). **Nothing but the Night.** Cape, 1968; Panther, 1971.
This novel, successfully filmed with Christopher Lee, contains Blackburn's series characters microbiologist Sir Marcus Levin and intelligence chief General Kirk. It combines elements of the thriller and the horror novel.

4–24. Blatty, William Peter. **The Exorcist.** Harper and Row, 1971; Bantam, 1972.
This best-selling novel of the supernatural, later made into one of the biggest money-making horror films of the 1970s, concerns the daughter of a divorced actress and delineates the process of her gradual possession by the devil. It depicts the classic struggle of modern science—specifically psychiatry—and twentieth-century religion—specifically Catholicism—to come to terms with the irrational. A young priest beset by his own doubts about his faith and an aging detective attempt to confront the mystery of the possessed girl. Eventually, the priest beckons the devil to transfer itself into him after a ritual exorcism proves a failure. This novel is among the several books of the late 1960s and early 1970s, all successfully filmed (such as *Rosemary's Baby* [4–150] and *The Sentinel* [4–140], which treat the occult from a religious standpoint.

4–25. Bloch, Robert. **American Gothic.** W. H. Allen, 1975.
Set in Chicago during the 1893 World's Fair, *American Gothic* is a grim novel centered on G. Gordon Gregg, a pharmacist who builds a castle near the fair and carries on death-bringing experiments with women and young girls.

4–26. Bloch, Robert. **Atoms and Evil.** Fawcett, 1962; Corgi, 1977.
Although this collection contains some of Bloch's science fiction stories, the tales of horror that figure here display his not inconsiderable knowledge of psychology, which is frequently the starting point in his tales of terror. The

best stories are "Try This for Psis," about parapsychology, and the similar tale "The Professor Plays It Square."

4-27. Bloch, Robert. **Bogey Men.** Pyramid, 1963.
The most successful stories in this volume are "The Skull of the Marquis de Sade" [see 4-33] and "The Man Who Collected Poe," in which Bloch parodies Poe's style in the story of a Poe collector, who has in fact collected Poe himself and kept him alive. "The Ghost Writer" is a humorous yet grisly tale of two horror story writers, one who dabbles in black magic, dies, and leaves his typewriter to his friend. The typewriter continues to produce stories by itself and eventually kills the recipient of the legacy. An essay on Bloch by Sam Moskowitz is appended to the volume.

4-28. Bloch, Robert. **Chamber of Horrors.** Award, 1966; Corgi, 1977.
This collection of grotesque tales of abnormal psychology contains one of Bloch's most ironic stories. "The Screaming People" concerns a young advertising copywriter named Steve, who, after a near-fatal automobile accident, suffers from amnesia and is treated by a psychiatrist using hypnotic suggestion. The psychiatrist has built a clinic where he "cures" hopeless psychotics, but in the end is killed by his amnesia patient, who then becomes one of the psychiatrist's "screaming people." In this story, as in others such as "Frozen Fear"—about a man who butchers his wife and carves up her body into packages of beef to go in his freezer—and "Fat Chance"—about a man who tries to kill his overweight wife with arsenic-filled chocolates in order to marry his mistress, only to have his mistress eat the chocolates by mistake—Bloch repeatedly asserts that the horror is in the mind of the person.

*4-29. Bloch, Robert. **Cold Chills.** Doubleday, 1977.
This collection, which also contains some of Bloch's science fiction horror tales, features two horror stories that were selected for the Year's Best Horror Stories series. The first of these, "The Double Whammy," takes place in a third-rate traveling carnival. The protagonist Rod is barker for a sideshow attraction in which an old drunk dressed up like a monster called a geek feeds on dead chickens to the delighted horror of the spectators. Rod has recently discovered that the granddaughter of Madame Sylvia, a fortune-telling gypsy who travels with the carnival, is pregnant by him. When Madame Sylvia discovers this, she places a curse on him that transforms him into a chicken about to be fed to the geek. In a similar vein, "The Animal Fair" unfolds from the point of view of Dave, a drifter who comes upon Captain Ryder, a one-time Hollywood stunt-man who travels the country with a carnival showing a gorilla. The gorilla, Dave discovers, is in reality a hippie named Dude who murdered Ryder's daughter years earlier; Dude has been physically altered and eventually dies insane, since he has been transformed into a genuine gorilla. In these two stories, as in others such as "See How

They Run" (a stream-of-consciousness narrative about an alcoholic writer regressing into schizophrenia), the horror is within the human mind.

*4–30. Bloch, Robert. The Opener of the Way. Arkham House, 1945; Neville Spearman, 1974.
This collection of 21 stories is a representative sampling of Bloch's early formative tales. The collection contains a number of tales that may be regarded as pastiches of early Gothic fiction. "The Fiddler's Tune," "The Mandarin's Canaries," and "The Feast in the Abbey" come under this heading. Other tales, such as "The Dark Demon," "The Faceless God," and particularly "The Shambler from the Stars" show the influence of H. P. Lovecraft, the latter tale containing a character modeled after Lovecraft himself. Lovecraft's "The Haunter of the Dark" was a reply to Bloch's tale. The most important stories in the book, however, are "Yours Truly, Jack the Ripper" and "The Cloak." Both of these tales are the essential Bloch in that they contain his gift for wit and ironic twists in addition to his frequent use of concepts from psychology.

4–31. Bloch, Robert. Pleasant Dreams. Arkham House, 1960; Jove, 1979.
This volume contains stories that are among the best written by Bloch during the late 1940s and 1950s. Perhaps the finest item is his completed version of Poe's unfinished tale "The Light-House." Other stories of note are "Hungarian Rhapsody," "The Sorceror's Apprentice," and "Sweets to the Sweet."

*4–32. Bloch, Robert. Psycho. Simon & Schuster, 1959.
This, Bloch's most famous novel of psychological horror, has become a household name largely because of the excellent film version directed by Alfred Hitchcock. The novel follows Marian Crane, a secretary in love with a divorced man, who decides to leave her unhappy world behind and escape with money stolen from the company in which she works. She ends her flight in an out-of-the-way motel run by Norman Bates, a split personality who at times takes on the murderous personality of his dead mother. This novel is a profound psychological study of human innocence and human evil, a modern Gothic thriller of the first rank.

4–33. Bloch, Robert. The Skull of the Marquis de Sade, and Other Stories. Robert Hale, 1975; Corgi, 1976.
Although this collection contains stories available elsewhere, the title story is one of Bloch's best, about Christopher Maitland, a collector of occult curios, who comes upon the haunted skull of the Marquis de Sade, which drives him to murder, madness, and finally death.

4–34. Bloch, Robert. Strange Eons. Whispers Press, 1978.
This fine Cthulhu Mythos novel is a conscious tribute to Lovecraft himself, since his fiction serves as a part of its plot. In the novel, Albert Keith and his friend Simon Waverley discover that Lovecraft's work is not fiction after all.

Keith and Waverley then set out to combat The Great Old Ones in an epic battle of wits.

*4–35. Bloch, Robert. **Such Stuff as Screams Are Made Of.** Ballantine, 1979.
This collection spans 30 years of Bloch's career and contains a useful afterword by Bloch himself plus a number of his best short stories. "The Unspeakable Betrothal," one of his best tales, centers on a young woman, about to be married, who lives alone in her family's old house. In her attic bedroom is a high window through which creatures based on Lovecraft's Cthulhu Mythos entities enter, fill her dreams, and eventually take her with them into the outside. "The Weird Tailor" is the moving story of a drunken tailor who is hired by an apparently wealthy man to construct a suit for his son. The tailor is provided with material that is like no earthly fabric, and in the end the suit's occult powers animate a dummy in the tailor's shop, bringing death to the tailor and his wife. "Lucy Comes to Stay" is an ironic tale that contains a theme Bloch later develops in *Psycho* [4–32], split personality. "The Pin" is a fascinating tale about a man who discovers that death is nothing more than a tiny pin, which, when dropped on the printed name of anyone in the world, ends life. "The Final Performance" is the grisly story of a has-been ventriloquist who murders the girl he keeps in his country saloon and uses her dead body as his dummy.

4–36. Bloch, Robert. **Tales in a Jugular Vein.** Pyramid, 1965.
Although the tales in this volume represent some of Bloch's psychological thrillers with macabre overtones, the best stories reveal his wit and irony and his deft and horrifying psychological twists. In "Double-Cross," an actor employs his double to play a horrifying practical joke on his studio boss; the boss murders the double, and then the real actor plots diabolical revenge. In one of Bloch's *contes cruel*, "The Deadliest Art," a murderer disposes of the corpse of his victim by serving it to his guests as the main course of a meal.

*4–37. Block, Lawrence. **Ariel.** Arbor House, 1980.
One of the best horror novels in recent years, *Ariel* uses some stereotypical Gothic material, such as a precocious child, an old, foreboding house, aged portraits, and the death of a child, to produce an atypical masterpiece. One critic has written: "*Ariel* taunts the reader by the absence of direct information, thereby building not only a fascinating and disturbing mystery, but a portrayal of very human characters in situations that . . . seem humanly possible."

4–38. Bowen, Elizabeth (U.K.). **The Cat Jumps, and Other Stories.** Jonathan Cape, 1934.
Although not all the stories in this volume are in the genre, the most note-

worthy is the title story, a grim, ironic tale of a party of housewarming guests who find themselves in ghostly company.

*4–39. Bowen, Elizabeth (U.K.). **The Demon Lover, and Other Stories.** Jonathan Cape, 1945.

This collection contains the best of Bowen's ghostly tales. Julia Briggs writes of them: "These haunted stories take place against the background of war-time London, ghostly in the blackout with sandbags and bombed-out houses, broken windows, drifting smoke and wailing sirens." The best is "Pink May," about a woman who narrates the dissolution of her love affair and marriage against the background of a haunted bedroom and its ghost. Other fine tales are "The Happy Autumn Fields" and "The Demon Lover," about a woman who sees the ghost of a soldier who loved her. As Briggs goes on to say, "The stories express all those ambivalences so characteristic of the ghost story, its awakenings longed for yet dreaded, fearful yet reassuring, long ago yet here and now, subjective and objective by turns."

4–40. Bowen, Marjorie (pseud. of Mrs. Gabrielle M. V. Long) (U.K.). **Black Magic.** The Bodley Head, 1909; Sphere, 1974.

This novel centers on two students of black magic who participate in bringing about the rise of the Antichrist. Set in the Middle Ages, the novel follows the rise of Satan in the form of the pope to his eventual destruction. It remains one of the best novels of satanism written and is comparable to the best of Dennis Wheatley's work.

*4–41. Bowen, Marjorie (pseud. of Mrs. Gabrielle M. V. Long) (U.K.). **Kecksies, and Other Twilight Tales.** Arkham House, 1976.

Bowen writes in the preface to this volume: "Some of these tales have some foundation of truth, in as much as they are based on some ancient tradition that the author chanced to hear or read, but most of them are inventions, expressions of the desire to relate the terrible, the monstrous, or the incredible that some story-tellers ardently feel." In keeping with such a thesis, the collection reflects her careful delineation of character, as in "Florence Flannery," or the carefully wrought period pieces, such as "Kecksies" or "Scoured Silk." These are some of the best stories by this neglected author.

4–42. Bradbury, Ray. **Dark Carnival.** Arkham House, 1947.

These 27 short pieces are essentially macabre word-pictures that appeared in *Weird Tales* during Dorothy McIlwraith's editorship. The best is the lead story, about a sickly child in a family of vampires, called "The Homecoming." Other tales of note are "The Scythe" and "Skeleton."

4–43. Brennan, Joseph Payne. **The Casebook of Lucius Leffing.** Macabre House, 1973.

This collection purports to be true stories narrated by Brennan concerning his relationship with the metaphysical detective Lucius Leffing. Leffing is in the great tradition of the metaphysical detectives beginning with Le Fanu's Hesselius in *In a Glass Darkly* [3–139] and carried through Hodgson's Carnacki stories [3–104], and Blackwood's *John Silence* [3–32].

4–44. Brennan, Joseph Payne. **The Chronicles of Lucius Leffing.** Grant, 1977.
This second collection of eight case histories of Lucius Leffing's confrontations with the supernatural is noteworthy for its excellent illustrations by John Linton. The best story of the volume is "The Dead of Winter Apparition."

4–45. Brennan, Joseph Payne. **Nine Horrors and a Dream.** Arkham House, 1958.
These simple, well-crafted tales of supernatural horror are effective pieces. Their minimal characterization and sparse plotting liken them to the tales of August Derleth. "Slime" is perhaps the most original work, about an enormous rolling mass that terrorizes a small town.

4–46. Brennan, Joseph Payne. **Stories of Darkness and Dread.** Arkham House, 1973.
This collection of short pieces reveals Brennan's gift for creating credible tales of the supernatural with an economy of words. The best stories are "Delivery on Erdmore Street," "Apprehension," and "Black Thing at Midnight."

4–47. Broster, D. K. (U.K.). **Couching at the Door.** Heinemann, 1942.
"Couching at the Door," the title story of this collection, is the tale of a poet whose decadent past life in Prague haunts him in the snakelike and apparently living form of a feather boa. Also noteworthy is "From the Abyss."

4–48. Bullett, Gerald (U.K.). **The Street of the Eye, and Nine Other Tales.** John Lane, 1923.
These sophisticated, ironic tales reveal Bullett's gift for creating a mystical atmosphere of impending horror. The best is the title story, about a religious fanatic who communicates with other worlds. Also noteworthy is "Dearth's Farm," which focuses on the terror engendered by a horse with an evil grin.

4–49. Burke, Thomas (U.K.). **Dark Nights.** Herbert Jenkins, 1932.
Burke is best remembered for his series of books that popularized the Chinatown area of London, such as *Limehouse Nights*. However, this collection contains a few stories that approach the category of the weird, such as "Roses Round the Door," "The Yellow Box," and "Beautiful Doll."

4–50. Burke, Thomas (U.K.). **Night-Pieces.** Constable, 1935.
A few of the stories in this volume approach the domain of the weird. "The Horrible God" has been anthologized in Boris Karloff's famous *And the Dark-*

ness Falls [4–276]. Other stories of note are "Johnson Looked Back" and "The Watcher."

4–51. Burks, Arthur J. **Black Medicine.** Arkham House, 1966.
Mike Ashley has noted that Arthur J. Burks has been dubbed "Speed Merchant of the Pulps" because of his tremendous output in all types of fiction. This volume contains the best of his supernatural horror stories. "The Ghosts of Steamboat Coulee," "Bells of Oceana," and "Vale of the Corbies," all represented here, were among the most popular stories in *Weird Tales* history.

4–52. Burrage, A. M. (U.K.). **Between the Minute and the Hour.** Herbert Jenkins, 1967.
This posthumous collection of some of Burrage's best macabre pieces includes such noteworthy entries as "Between the Minute and the Hour," "Playmates," and "Smee."

4–53. Burrage, A. M. (U.K.). **Some Ghost Stories.** Cecil Palmer, 1927.
This early collection of ghostly tales contains some effective pieces. In them, Burrage suggests the supernatural with delicacy, and often with a wry sense of humor. The best stories are "Between the Minute and the Hour," and the touching story of a bachelor and the supernatural surroundings of his home, "Playmates."

4–54. Burrage, A. M. (U.K.). **Someone in the Room.** Jarrolds, 1931.
These 14 stories purport to be the case histories of "Ex-Private X," an occult investigator. The best are "Through the Eyes of a Child," about a house haunted by the spirit of a little boy, and "The Strange Case of Dolly Frewan," about a murdered girl's getting revenge by possessing her murderer's new lover.

4–55. Caldecott, Andrew (U.K.). **Fires Burn Blue.** Edward Arnold, 1948.
This collection of 13 ghost stories is, according to Mike Ashley, "much in the vein of M. R. James." These often-humorous enigmatical stories sometimes center on clergy faced with evidence of the supernatural. In "An Exchange of Notes," a dead man's apparition appears to affect the musicians at a clergyman's parish concert. In "His Name Was Legion," a local church bulletin contains items by a man with the gift of automatic writing.

4–56. Caldecott, Andrew (U.K.). **Not Exactly Ghosts.** Edward Arnold, 1947.
This collection once again displays the not inconsiderable influence of M. R. James. "Branch Line to Benceston" is the story of the mysterious death of Adrian Frent, who dies under seemingly supernatural circumstances. Similarly, there is the apparently supernatural puzzle of "A Victim of Medusa."

Also noteworthy are "Whiffs of the Sea," "Autoepitaphy," and "Light in the Darkness."

*4–57. Campbell, Ramsey (U.K.). **Demons by Daylight.** Arkham House, 1973.

This collection of stories reveals Campbell's maturation as a writer and solidifies his vision of human instability and paranoia within a culture saturated with the media and its conflicting, shifting moral attitudes. Campbell's attention to realistic detail, which is filtered through the hazy, almost psychotic minds of his characters, lends to his work a quality of perception that transcends most horror fiction of this century. "Potential" is perhaps the finest story of the volume because it brings into sharp focus all the qualities of Campbell's technique. Charles, a young civil servant, enters the world of Britain's drug culture, and in a brief episode at a party at which he expects to partake of his first drug experience, he finds himself participant in a mind game during which he is taken in by a staged scene of torture and sexual sadism, and commits murder, thus realizing his potential. "The End of a Summer's Day" concerns a young woman and her lover on a tour in a cave in the country. In what amounts to a nightmare experience, the lover is transformed in the darkness of the cave into an old man who is blind. In "The Guy," a young boy becomes involved with a playmate from a lower class and, while participating at a bonfire in his playmate's backyard, witnesses the apparently supernatural murder of his friend. In "Concussion," a man travels to Liverpool, meets a girl, falls in love, and, as a by-product of his possible insanity, causes an accident in which he is killed and in which the girl, Anna, receives a concussion. In the latter story, as in others in the book, the deliberate vagueness, the suggestion of possible psychosis, leave a vague impression of the kind of supernaturalism Campbell sees in the human perception of reality. Like many a horror tale, these stories have much to do with "what is reality?" Their masterful technique links them to another British master, Robert Aickman [4–1 to 4–7].

*4–58. Campbell, Ramsey (U.K.). **The Doll Who Ate His Mother.** Bobbs-Merrill, 1976; Jove, 1978.

Stephen King has written of Ramsey Campbell: "He is literate in a field that has attracted too many comic book intellects, cool in a field that tends toward panting melodrama by virtue of its subject-matter, fluid in a field where many of the best practitioners often fall prey to cant and stupid 'rules' of fantasy composition." This novel is one of Campbell's best works. With a masterful prose style and an attention to detail, Campbell creates the story of Clare Frayn, whose brother is killed and loses an arm in an auto accident. The severed arm is stolen, and *eaten,* by a psychopath, Chris Kelley, and the remainder of the novel concerns the revelation of his implied satanic conception and his eventual tracking down by a circle of Clare's friends.

*4–59. Campbell, Ramsey. (U.K.). **The Height of the Scream.** Arkham House, 1976.

Campbell's vision of humans in a universe where the bizarre can occur reaches full maturity in this collection. The best-wrought tale is "The Scar," about Jack Rossiter, whose brother-in-law Lindsey finds he has a murderous doppelgänger with a scar. "Missing" is told in the form of the diary of a young man in Liverpool whose life takes on the qualities of a psychosis. He becomes obsessed with a strange, elusive girl he sees at a party, and he later discovers that she murdered her husband in a ritual involving voodoo and disappeared during World War II. As the young man appears to disintegrate, the girl becomes a part of his life and leads a ghostly existence with him. In "Reply Guaranteed," a young girl responds to an advertisement in a local newspaper for a man seeking an "unconventional relationship." Then she is increasingly haunted by what appears to be a man in a wheelchair who seems to have murderous intent. In its deliberate vaugueness, this tale maintains a careful balance between concrete description and psychological detail reminiscent of Aickman's stories. "The Cellars," one of the most effective tales in the volume, concerns a young girl who ventures into the cellars of a deserted warehouse with a boy who works with her. The boy is exposed to an unearthly fungus and is eventually forced to leave work as the horrifying details of his physical disintegration accumulate. "The Height of the Scream" centers on the suicide of an artist and his friend's ability to foresee his death. Eventually, this ability transmits itself to the narrator, who foresees another death. In each of the above tales, a vague sexual theme is submerged, which finds its fullest realization in "The Telephones," about a young man whose uncertainty about his sexual identity becomes intensified as a homosexual caller haunts him along the phone boxes of a Liverpool street.

4–60. Campbell, Ramsey (U.K.). **The Inhabitant of the Lake and Less Welcome Tenants.** Arkham House, 1964.

Campbell's first book reveals something of the talent he has displayed to better advantage in recent years. The book is a collection of Cthulhu Mythos stories set in mythical locales in England. The best of the stories is still a rather typical Cthulhu Mythos tale about a creature from another dimension and the artist who confronts him by means of a book called *The Revelations of Glaaki*.

*4–61. Campbell, Ramsey (U.K.). **The Parasite.** Macmillan, 1980.

Peter Straub has written of Ramsey Campbell: "Horrors in his fiction are never merely invented, they are felt and experienced, and affect the reader for days afterward." This most recent novel concerns Rose Tierney, who is haunted by an amorphous, unnameable, but malignant being from her childhood. Untroubled by such visitations until she is mugged in New York

City, her adult life is changed into a nightmare world of out-of-body traveling and communication with the outer being of her youth.

4–62. Cave, Hugh B. (U.K.). **Legion of the Dead.** Avon, 1979.
Hugh B. Cave is one of the most prolific writers of the pulp era. This novel, his most recent full-length work, is about Cary Connoway, who arrives on the Caribbean island of San Marlo, where he comes face-to-face with a zombie cult.

4–63. Cave, Hugh B. (U.K.). **Murgunstrumm, and Others.** Carcosa, 1977.
Cave produced stories in all genres, but he is best known for his weird stories. This collection won a World Fantasy Award in 1978. It includes some excellent vampire stories, such as "Stragella," "The Brotherhood of Blood," and the novella "Murgunstrumm." Cave has returned to the form again with new stories in *Whispers* [4–294, 4–295] and his novels *Legion of the Dead* and *The Nebulon Horror* [4–64].

4–64. Cave, Hugh B. (U.K.). **The Nebulon Horror.** Dell, 1980.
This novel centers on the terrifying horror unleashed in a small Florida town. A number of its children are possessed to perform acts of physical cruelty and murder. Finally, the seeds of the possession lead to the evil within the house of Gustave Nebulon.

4–65. Chetwynd-Hayes, R. (U.K.). **Cold Terror.** Pyramid, 1975.
Chetwynd-Hayes is a fairly new figure in macabre fiction. He is prolific, but his work is of variable quality. The best story here is "The Door," about an antique doorway that haunts its owner by unspeakable evil from its past history. Other works of note are "Neighbors," about a family of vampires, "The Shadow," and "The Fourth Side of the Triangle."

4–66. Chetwynd-Hayes, R. (U.K.). **The Night Ghouls.** Fontana, 1975.
This collection of ten stories deals with supernatural entities known as ghouls. In "The Ghouls," Mr. Goldsmith finds himself alone in a world where everyone is a ghoul. In "Danger in Numbers," a wife is visited by the multiple ghoulish ghosts of her husband, even after she buries him a second time.

4–67. Chetwynd-Hayes, R. (U.K.). **Tales of Fear and Fantasy.** Fontana, 1977.
This collection utilizes folklore for its sources. "Manderville" concerns Paul Wheatley, who goes to the site of Manderville, a village since destroyed, to commit suicide, but finds himself drawn into the village's ghosts of the past. "The Resurrectionist," another of the better entries, concerns a young boy who is resurrected in ghostly fashion when a highway is built where he rests in his grave. Another worthy, but predictable, story is "The Changeling."

4–68. Chetwynd-Hayes, R. (U.K.). **Terror by Night.** Tandem, 1974; Pyramid, 1976.

The best tales in this collection are "Lileas and the Water Horse," which concerns the ghostly Water Horse, who appears "in a tiny Scottish village in the guise of a tall dark man" who leaves "behind a dreadful warning" for the living; "Under the Skin," which tells of the manner in which Carl Blackwood, an actor famed for his role as the Beast Man, lives out his part in supernatural fashion; and "Lord Dunwilliam and the Cwn Annwn," in which the lord meets a young woman whose lover has cast a terrible spell on any who attempt to gain her hand.

4–69. Chetwynd-Hayes, R. (U.K.). **The Unbidden.** Pyramid, 1975.

This collection contains 16 stories that are among Chetwynd-Hayes's earliest works, and all are of variable quality. The best is "No One Lived There," about an English house occupied by Nazi agents during World War II, discovered by a man who is eventually haunted by the almost humanly intelligent rats of the place. Other stories of note are the amusing "A Family Welcome" and "The Head of the Firm."

*4–70. Cobb, Irvin S. "Fishhead" in **Cobb's Cavalcade.** World, 1945.

This tale is perhaps closest in its vision to the work of Lovecraft. It is gruesome like Lovecraft's Cthulhu cycle of stories, since it deals with freaks of nature and the horror of what is unimagined by humans. Lovecraft writes, "Fishhead . . . is banefully effective in its portrayal of unnatural affinities between a hybrid idiot and the strange fish of an isolated lake, which at the last avenge their biped kinsman's murder."

*4–71. Collier, John (U.K.). **Fancies and Goodnights.** Doubleday, 1951.

Collier's talent for grim irony reminds one of L. P. Hartley's work. This collection contains some of his finest work, from "Green Thoughts," about a carnivorous plant, to his best-known story "Thus I Refute Beelzy," about a little boy whose playmate is Beelzebub. The collection won the 1952 International Fantasy Award.

*4–72. Cooper, Louise (U.K.). **Blood Summer.** New English Library, 1976.

This excellent novel concerns Marion and Roland Huws, who, while on a holiday in Cornwall, meet a recluse, Keith Sharwood. Marion's involvement with Keith brings about a' widening circle of supernatural horror that leads to "an insane and bloody murder" and the evocation of a 5,000-year-old Assyrian demon. *In Memory of Sarah Bailey* is the interesting sequel.

*4–73. Coppard, A. E. (U.K.). **Fearful Pleasures.** Arkham House, 1946.

This collection of Coppard's best ghostly tales reveals his use of the superstitions and folklore of the English countryside. The best known of the stories is "Adam and Eve and Pinch Me," about a man who lives, for a brief time, a dual existence as his own double, and in this state he sees his unborn child.

Herbert A. Wise and Phyllis Frazer have called this story "a delicate and beautiful symbolization . . . , in the person of the still-unborn little boy, of the miracle of true poetic genius." Of the other tales, the best is "Old Martin," about a retired seaman whose daughter returns as a spirit troubled by another lecherous spirit. The book contains a useful introduction delineating Coppard's rationale of the ghost story.

4–74. Copper, Basil (U.K.). **And Afterward, the Dark.** Arkham House, 1977.
A collection of macabre pieces that contains such items as "The Janissaries of Emilion," which concerns a group of ancient horsemen who wreak supernatural vengeance on a modern man. "The Cave" is set in lower Germany, as the terrified denizens of an inn are besieged by a monster. "Archives of the Dead" is a subtle tale of a Satan cult. All of these stories reveal Copper's gift for a variety of supernatural themes expressed in markedly different styles.

4–75. Copper, Basil (U.K.). **The Curse of the Fleers.** St. Martin, 1977.
This modern Gothic thriller concerns the elderly Sir John Fleer and his family, who are driven to unspeakable heights of terror when an ancient curse come true enters their lives. A widening circle of fear involves their servants and neighbors, and finally an enormous killer ape, Konga.

*4–76. Copper, Basil (U.K.). **From Evil's Pillow.** Arkham House, 1973.
These five macabre tales mark Copper's first U.S. publication. "The Gossips" is a story of demonic evil from the Renaissance period of Sicily's history let loose in the exhibition halls of London. "Amber Print" is the best, a chilling story with the classic silent films conveying a potent, supernatural meaning. Copper is noted for his versatility in the horror tale.

*4–77. Copper, Basil (U.K.). **The Great White Space.** St. Martin, 1975.
Copper's only novel in the tradition of Lovecraft's Cthulhu cycle involves a great northern expedition into the arctic regions and beneath the ice-covered surface. The narrator Plowright and Professor Clark Ashton Scarsdale find deep within the earth the home of ancient beings from another dimension filled with insects like slugs. Finally, Plowright discovers Professor Scarsdale in the Great White Space, and there he appears to have become one of the ancient creatures of evil.

*4–78. Copper, Basil (U.K.). **Necropolis.** Arkham House, 1980.
Set in the gaslight era of London, this novel is in the great tradition of such masters of the Gothic thriller as Wilkie Collins, Sheridan Le Fanu, and Arthur Conan Doyle. The story concerns Clyde Beatty, who is hired to investigate the death of the father of Angela Meredith. In this expertly constructed Gothic mystery, the environs of London are likened to a city of the dead as Copper's style conveys an atmosphere of grim corruption.

4–79. Copper, Basil (U.K.). **Voices of Doom.** Robert Hale, 1980.
Although this collection of macabre tales contains some items available in other volumes of his short stories, two original tales figure here: "The Stranger" is a study of growing paranoia in the tradition of Poe, and "The Madonna of the Four-Ale Bar" is the story of a beautiful barmaid and her murder of a lonely bachelor.

4–80. Cowles, Frederick (U.K.). **The Horror of Abbot's Grange.** Frederick Muller, 1936.
Cowles's work is most sought after by collectors. The collection contains many reworkings of old themes, but the title story is the best.

4–81. Cowles, Frederick (U.K.). **The Night Wind Howls.** Frederick Muller, 1938.
This collection contains much stronger material than Cowles's first. Two of the tales, "The Cadaver of Bishop Louis" and "Death in the Well," smack of M. R. James. "Rats" deals with the awful fate of a hanging judge who sentences a witch to death. All of Cowles's work is derivative, however.

*4–82. Cross, John Keir (U.K.). **The Other Passenger.** John Westhouse, 1944; Ballantine, 1961.
The original edition contains 18 stories and fine surrealist paintings by Bruce Angrave. The title story is a classic doppelgänger tale, with its image of a composer who may or may not be haunted by himself. The strangest story is "Petranella Fan," a unique variation on the Frankenstein theme, in which a mother deliberately keeps her baby from physical development in order to continue winning baby shows. This book is definitely among the finest volumes of macabre and weird tales to appear in the 1940s.

4–83. Daniels, Les. **The Black Castle.** Scribner, 1978; Berkley, 1979.
This tale of the macabre has been called "a readable, credible novel of Gothic proportions." It takes place in the Spain of 1496 during the Inquisition and centers on the efforts of Sebastian of Villanueva and his witch-consort Margarita to stop the horrors engendered by it.

4–84. Daniels, Les. **The Silver Skull: A Novel of Sorcery.** Scribner, 1979.
This, Daniels's second novel, does not match the quality of *The Black Castle* [4–83]. Alfonso Martinez escapes from the Spanish Inquisition and comes to Mexico, where he takes the skull of Don Sebastian of Villanueva, a known vampire. Don Sebastian is resurrected and begins a new reign as a vampire.

4–85. Dare, M. P. (U.K.). **Unholy Relics, and Other Uncanny Tales.** Edward Arnold, 1947.
This delightful set of pastiches of M. R. James's antiquarian supernatural horror tales is, although lacking in James's subtle sense of the uncanny, clearly a conscious tribute to the ghostly tale of the English variety. There are touches of Arthur Machen here also, and in Mike Ashley's view Dare,

like Malden, Munby, and Rolt, "achieve[s] the most success in blending James's techniques with [his] own narratives."

4–86. De La Mare, Walter (U.K.). **The Conoisseur, and Other Stories.** Collins, 1926.
This collection of general fiction includes a few ghostly tales: "Mr. Kempe," "Missing," "All Hallows," and "The Wharf."

4–87. De La Mare, Walter (U.K.). **Eight Tales.** Arkham House, 1971.
Eight of De La Mare's earliest stories appear here for the first time in book form, reflecting the author's growing abilities in the genre. "A: B: O:" is the best tale, about a monster being dug up in a buried chest.

*4–88. De La Mare, Walter (U.K.). **On the Edge.** Faber, 1930.
Julia Briggs writes of De La Mare's work in the ghost story form: "His imaginative world is essentially subjective, an intensifying gaze focussed on a sequence of curious, perhaps inexplicable events." In the tales of this collection—such as "A Recluse," about the mysterious and seemingly supernatural death of a man who dabbles in black magic, and "Crewe," about a suicide and murder with supernatural overtones—what is left unsaid gives these stories a vaguely supernatural quality. In this respect, they serve as models for the work of Ramsey Campbell [4–57 to 4–61] and Robert Aickman [4–1 to 4–7].

*4–89. De La Mare, Walter (U.K.). **The Return.** Edward Arnold, 1910; Collins, 1922.
According to Edward Wagenknecht, "*The Return* was written as a 'potboiler,' a 'shocker' and designed to earn money for its author; instead it brought him the Polignac Prize." De La Mare's novel is a moving yet subtle story of the supernatural. Like all of his best work in the genre, its evocative language suggesting other worlds on the edge of consciousness lends a misty poetry to the story of Arthur Lawford, who falls asleep on the grave of a suicide and takes on the physical appearance of the dead man. What follows is the moving account of Lawford's family and friends, as well as Lawford himself, to come to terms with the supernatural. The 1922 edition of this novel is a revised version.

*4–90. De La Mare, Walter (U.K.). **The Riddle, and Other Stories.** Selwyn and Blount, 1923.
This collection contains two of De La Mare's most compelling ghostly tales, which suggest the supernatural while not presenting it directly. "Seaton's Aunt" is the mysterious story of young Seaton and his aunt, who appears to communicate with another world. After Seaton's marriage is called off, he seems to die under unknown, but suggestively supernatural, circumstances. "Out of the Deep" is the story of Jimmie, ill with tuberculosis, who inherits

an old and haunted house and must exorcise its ghosts before he can die peacefully. Both stories are types of the inconclusive ghost tale.

*4–91. De La Mare, Walter (U.K.). **The Wind Blows Over.** Faber, 1936.
Peter Penzoldt has declared Walter De La Mare the master of the inconclusive ghost story. The ghostly tales of this volume, "What Dreams May Come," "Cape Race," "In the Forest," "A Forward Child," and "A Revenant," reveal this elusive quality. The best of the collection, "A Revenant," presents the appearance of a stranger at the lecture on Edgar Allan Poe as a borderline supernatural manifestation. Professor Monk, an English professor, is haunted and eventually confronted by a man who takes on the appearance, in Monk's view, of a revenant from the past. All these supernatural tales evoke a near-mystical realm out of which grows a subtle hint of the supernatural.

4–92. Derleth, August. **Dwellers in Darkness.** Arkham House, 1976.
This recent collection of Derleth's macabre tales that appeared in magazines such as *Weird Tales* and *Strange Stories* again shows his precise, realistic approach to the macabre and to psychic phenomena. In "The Ghost Walk," a British architect is hired to remodel a country house and discovers that it has a ghost walk that is haunted by the murdering spirit of a former servant. "The Ormulu Clock" has as its supernatural engine an antique clock that triggers the apparition of a murder committed in its vicinity. "A Knocking in the Wall" is a ghostly love story in which the spirit of a murdered wife is released from the place in which she was walled up by her husband. As a middle-aged bachelor and his secretary come to terms with the supernatural presence, they discover their love for each other. "The Lost Path" concerns a young boy who is carried off by the shining, monstrous entity that occupies a garden path behind his house; and "Man in the Dark" is a ghost story about a British traveler who comes upon the spirit of a murderer at a deserted railway station. All of these tales are simple, straightforward supernatural stories that reveal Derleth's precise command of the genre.

*4–93. Derleth, August. **Lonesome Places.** Arkham House, 1962.
This collection of Derleth's regional supernatural stories set in the Sac Prairie region of Wisconsin consists of atmospheric macabre pieces. "The Lonesome Place" concerns two young brothers and their secret of "the lonesome place," where a faceless monster lurks. "The Extra Child" is about a painting that supernaturally changes, and "The Dark Boy" is perhaps the best, about the ghost of a young boy killed in an accident who returns to see his widowed father remarry.

4–94. Derleth, August. **The Mask of Cthulhu.** Arkham House, 1958; Neville Spearman, 1974.
This collection of five novellas and one short story stems, in large part, from Lovecraft's Cthulhu cycle. "The Return of Hastur" was suggested by Love-

craft before his death. However, these stories contain nothing of the power of Lovecraft's original creations of the mythos.

*4–95. Derleth, August. **Mr. George, and Other Odd Persons.** Arkham House, 1963.
This collection of 17 stories written by Derleth under the pseudonym Stephen Grendon contains the finest of his supernatural stories. Many of these tales have been successfully filmed for television. The best stories are "Mr. George," about a little girl and what may or may not be the ghost of one of her dead relatives (Mr. George). "A Gentleman from Prague" concerns a stolen relic and ghostly revenge; "Mrs. Manifold" is the grisly tale of an out-of-the-way London inn and its terrifying proprietress.

4–96. Derleth, August. **Not Long for this World.** Arkham House, 1948.
These 31 brief tales are not as powerful as those of *Mr. George,* but they reflect, in their simple yet effective prose, Derleth's devotion to the macabre in fiction. The best stories are "Birkett's Twelfth Corpse," "Lesandro's Familiar," and "He Shall Come."

*4–97. Derleth, August. **Someone in the Dark.** Arkham House, 1941; Jove, 1978.
Next to *Mr. George* [4–95], this is Derleth's best collection of macabre tales. Divided into three groups, the stories show the influence of M. R. James, Mary E. Wilkins-Freeman, and H. P. Lovecraft. The tales in the first category, collectively titled "Not Long for This World," contain such Jamesian stories as "Glory Hand," about the legend of the hand of glory, and "Altimer's Amulet." The second category, under the collective title "A House with Somebody in It," contains such items of ghostly vengeance as "The Sheraton Mirror" and "The Panelled Room." The Lovecraftian tales under the heading "Visitors from Down Under" contain "The Return of Hastur" and "The Sandwin Compact."

4–98. Derleth, August. **Something Near.** Arkham House, 1945.
Some of Derleth's short stories from *Weird Tales*—they are of variable quality, the best being character studies about unusual people who, in one way or another, experience the supernatural as a confrontation with some aspect of themselves. "Mr. Ames' Devil" involves Mr. Ames's conjuring of a devil who may or may not cause a number of supernatural occurrences, thus leaving open the question of Ames's own role in his apparently supernatural experiences. "No Light for Uncle Henry" raises like questions. "Carousel" is the haunting tale of a little girl's confrontation with the evil that lies within her relationship with her stepmother. "Beyond the Threshold" is a moderately effective Cthulhu Mythos story.

4-99. Derleth, August. **The Trail of Cthulhu.** Arkham House, 1962; Neville Spearman, 1974.
This epic Cthulhu Mythos novel begins in Curwen Street in legendary Arkham, Massachusetts, and delineates the pursuit of Cthulhu to his lair in sunken R'lyeh. It spans continents as the scenes follow Cthulhu to a mysterious island in the South Pacific. Written as a series of eyewitness accounts, the novel ends on an ambiguous note as narrator Horwath Blayre wonders who will be the next victim of Cthulhu.

4-100. Derleth, August, and H. P. Lovecraft. **The Lurker at the Threshold.** Arkham House, 1945.
This novel is built on Lovecraft's notes and is nothing more than a so-called posthumous collaboration. It is available in the later collection of collaborations by Derleth, *The Watchers Out of Time* [4-101].

4-101. Derleth, August, and H. P. Lovecraft. **The Watchers Out of Time, and Others.** Arkham House, 1974.
This collection of 15 short stories and one novel comprises all of the so-called posthumous collaborations of Derleth and Lovecraft. These works must properly be considered in the Derleth canon because they were written for the most part by him. He took assorted fragments and notes left by Lovecraft and created his own stories from them. The best items are the novel and "The Shuttered Room."

4-102. Derleth, August, and Mark Schorer. **Colonel Markesan, and Less Pleasant People.** Arkham House, 1966.
These collaborations by Derleth and Schorer from the earliest days of their careers cover a wide variety of themes. "The Woman at Loon Point" is an interesting werewolf tale, while "The House in the Magnolias" is a story of zombies.

4-103. Dinesen, Isak (pseud. of Karen Blixen) (Denmark). **Seven Gothic Tales.** Modern Library, 1939.
These stories by Karen Blixen resemble fables that approach the domain of the Gothic. William Rose Benét wrote of these tales on their first publication: "A book of unique atmosphere and scenes indelibly delineated, a book bringing the psychological insight of a Henry James to the material of a Northern Boccaccio, a book of extraordinary fantasy that yet takes us intimately into a vivid variety of human lives." The best stories are "The Dreamers" and "The Poet."

4-104. Dinesen, Isak (pseud. of Karen Blixen) (Denmark). **Winter's Tales.** Random House, 1942.
Christopher Morley has described these tales as "Hans Anderson writing with the pen of Maupassant." The stories, subtle and haunting, thus resemble fables. They hint darkly at other worlds that bloom poetically from a

language and style of sinister magic. In "The Sailor-Boy's Tale," a young boy commits murder and is haunted by a woman with yellow eyes like those of a trapped bird he had once seen. "The Pearls" concerns a young bride who teaches her husband fear with a necklace she owns. "The Dreaming Child" is the ghostly tale of a house filled with a little boy's imaginings. These stories evoke the most subtle hint of the supernatural, and they compare well with the work of Joyce Carol Oates [4–184] and Robert Aickman [4–1 to 4–7].

4–105. Du Maurier, Daphne (U.K.). **Echoes from the Macabre.** Doubleday, 1977.
This fine collection of terror tales by the famous novelist contains such well-wrought stories as "Don't Look Now," successfully filmed, about a couple on holiday in Venice who meet a psychic who predicts danger ending in tragedy. "The Apple Tree" concerns a forlorn apple tree that takes on the character of a man's deceased wife. "The Blue Lenses" is also a noteworthy supernatural tale of a young girl who undergoes an eye operation and is fitted with lenses that reveal people as they really are.

4–106. Endore, Guy. **The Werewolf of Paris.** Farrar & Rinehart, 1933; Sphere, 1974.
This excellent novel of lycanthropy concerns young Bertrand, who as a child, and later to an even greater extent, suffers from terrible urges to roam the woods and hunt and kill animals. As his symptoms begin to show his tendencies to turn into a wolf, he fights his disease until his sexual urges overpower him and aggravate the condition. His only savior is his uncle and guardian, Galliez.

4–107. Faulkner, William. **Collected Stories.** Random House, 1948.
Some of Faulkner's work may be properly called "Southern Gothic," since it contains numerous Gothic motifs, such as the old mansion or house, the grotesque, and occasionally the macabre. In this collection, the famous story "A Rose for Emily" and the psychological horror tale "The Leg" clearly fall into this category.

4–108. Grant, Charles L. **The Hour of the Oxrun Dead.** Doubleday, 1977; Popular Library, 1978.
This, the first of Grant's horror novels centering on a small New England town called Oxrun, approaches the work of Stephen King [4–129 to 4–135] in its delineation of occult forces unleashed. The novel deals with Natalie Windsor, who becomes the focus of a supernatural conspiracy.

4–109. Grant, Charles L. **The Last Call of Mourning.** Doubleday, 1979.
This novel set in Oxrun centers on Cynthia Yarrow, who, on her return to the town, finds her family possessed by evil forces and herself followed by "the glaring dead eyes of the lurking Greybeast."

4–110. Grant, Charles L. **The Sound of Midnight.** Doubleday, 1978; Popular Library, 1979.

This second novel of Oxrun centers on its children, who begin to take on supernatural powers. They go to a tiny toy shop in the town and use the toys as occultists use tarot cards, to manipulate the adults of the village.

4–111. Grubb, Davis. **Twelve Tales of Suspense and the Supernatural.** Scribner, 1964.

This collection contains Grubb's best-known story from the pages of *Weird Tales,* "One Foot in the Grave." Grubb has begun writing weird fiction again. A sample of his most recent work may be found in two anthologies compiled by Kirby McCauley [4–283, 4–284].

4–112. Hartley, L. P. (U.K.). **Night Fears, and Other Stories.** Putnam, 1924.

Hartley's early tales do not, for the most part, represent his work in the weird or the supernatural. However, the stories "Night Fear," about a night watchman murdered by a mysterious companion, and "The Island," about a confrontation of a man with his wife's lover, reveal his use of the uncanny as an expression of the conflicts that develop within his characters.

*4–113. Hartley, L. P. (U.K.). **The Travelling Grave, and Other Stories.** Arkham House, 1948; Hamish Hamilton, 1957.

This excellent selection of Hartley's tales of grim, Absurdist terror contains his best-known stories. "The Travelling Grave" is undoubtedly the most famous, about a collector of coffins who owns "a travelling grave," which causes its occupant to disappear. "A Visitor from Down Under" and "Podolo" are also effective. "The Killing Bottle" is an ironic and witty shocker about a man who comes upon a wealthy family in the English countryside whose occupation is murder. All of Hartley's short pieces of macabre fiction reveal his cool, calculating style, wit, and grim irony.

*4–114. Harvey, W. F. (U.K.). **The Beast with Five Fingers, and Other Tales.** Dent, 1928.

This collection of early supernatural tales contains one of Harvey's best known, "The Beast with Five Fingers." In it, Harvey creates a world in which the supernatural occurs with an unnerving sense of reality. With unusual clarity of mind, Eustace Borlsover combats the apparently living severed hand of his dead uncle until it finally causes his death in what appears to be an accidental fire. The story was transformed into a fine horror film by Robert Florey in the 1940s. The next most effective tale is "Miss Cornelius," a subtle psychological study of a man who becomes obsessed with a certain woman who is reported to have contact with the spirit world. When he begins to suspect he is losing his sanity, Miss Cornelius is killed in a car accident. With the skill of the master, Harvey leaves the question of the actual supernatural quality of the occurrences in the story with the reader.

*4–115. Harvey, W. F. (U.K.). **Midnight Tales.** Dent, 1946.
This collection, published after Harvey's death, is a selection of his best work. "Midnight House" is about an inn called Midnight House. The narrator spends an uncomfortable night there and comes away with the vague, ill-defined feeling that it is haunted. This note of psychological uncertainty lends Harvey's characters a depth lacking in similar tales. "Mrs. Ormerod," in particular, is an example of Harvey's ability to create a lingering uncertainty in the reader's mind. In this tale a woman writes a letter to a friend about her acquaintance with Mrs. Ormerod, the housekeeper of a friend. The narrator is convinced that Mrs. Ormerod is a supernatural and malignant force, although one wonders how reliable a narrator she is. "August Heat," Harvey's most famous tale, is about an artist who foresees his own murderer in the gallows and draws him, only to discover that the man is carving a tombstone carrying the artist's name.

4–116. Howard, Robert E. **The Dark Man, and Others.** Arkham House, 1963.
Macabre tales that represent the best of Howard's work in the genre: "The Voice of El-Lil" is told in the oral tradition; "The Dark Man" is typical of his heroic fantasy tales. Most of the other tales in this volume fall into the category of fantasy, not supernatural horror.

*4–117. Jackson, Shirley. **The Bird's Nest.** Farrar, Straus, & Giroux, 1954; Popular Library, 1976.
Lenemaja Friedman notes that Jackson "spent many hours studying dissociation, schizophrenia and the multiple personality" before writing *The Bird's Nest.* This novel reads like a fascinating mystery that spirals downward into a widening circle of psychological terror. Narrated from the point of view of the main character's four personalities, it excels in many ways Robert Bloch's own psychological Gothic novel, *Psycho* [4–32].

*4–118. Jackson, Shirley. **Hangsaman.** Farrar, Straus, & Giroux, 1951; Popular Library, 1976.
Jackson's novel deals with mental aberration, particularly schizophrenia; her early collection *The Lottery* is only a pale shadow by comparison with this. Here, Jackson delineates the disintegration of Natalie Waite, an intelligent girl whose personality splits in two, one, her shy self, the other, her imagined girl friend Toni.

*4–119. Jackson, Shirley. **The Haunting of Hill House.** Viking, 1959; Popular Library, 1975.
Jackson's novel centers on the experiences of a group of psychic investigators who explore the ghostly manifestations of Hill House. According to Lenemaja Friedman, the explorers in this house "are and remain very much alone. Each, concerned with his own thoughts, fancies, and problems, does not seek to understand the others." The novel is thus essentially a study of

character, and the evil spirits of Hill House reflect the evil of the living characters. The tale has been transformed to the screen as a highly effective horror film by Robert Wise.

4-120. Jackson, Shirley. **The Sundial.** Farrar, Straus, & Giroux, 1958; Popular Library, 1976.
Jackson's moderately successful modern Gothic novel reflects her fascination with some eighteenth-century Gothic works, most notably *The Castle of Otranto* [1-398]. Readers of the original Gothic novels will delight to such touches as a mysterious portrait whose glass shatters supernaturally, statues that feel warm with life, a mysterious sundial that takes hold of the family, and the characterizations of the Halloran family. Here, their supernatural trials resemble those of Walpole's Montoni family.

*4-121. Jackson, Shirley. **We Have Always Lived in the Castle.** Viking, 1962; Popular Library, 1975.
This is Jackson's best and most critically acclaimed book; it received the National Book Award. Narrated in the first person, the novel unfolds as Merricat Blackwood reveals a sociopathic personality disguising the murder of several members of her family. This *is* Merricat Blackwood's story of horror. As one reviewer has put it, "Shirley Jackson looks at the world as practically nobody else does and describes it in a way almost everybody would like to emulate. Her story has so much suspense a reader may not see at first how beautifully she has avoided the textbook case-history in showing us the fascinating workings of Mary Katherine Blackwood's surprising mind."

4-122. Jacobi, Carl. **Disclosures in Scarlet.** Arkham House, 1972.
Fritz Leiber has called Carl Jacobi "a more northern Derleth." Indeed, Jacobi's work resembles Derleth's tales in its simple, clear prose. However, in many respects, Jacobi's macabre sense is more sinister. The best stories in this collection are undoubtedly "The Aquarium," with its grotesque occupant, and "The Unpleasantness at Carver House."

4-123. Jacobi, Carl. **Portraits in Moonlight.** Arkham House, 1964.
This second fine collection of Jacobi's work contains such outstanding items as "Portraits in Moonlight," "Witches in the Cornfield," and "The La Prello Paper." All reveal his gift for creating a sense of the uncanny in clear, vivid prose.

*4-124. Jacobi, Carl. **Revelations in Black.** Arkham House, 1945; Neville Spearman, 1974.
These 21 stories make up Jacobi's first collection and one of his best. One critic wrote that Jacobi "is a traditionalist; that is to say his horrors are the traditional ones and his treatment of them is by and large in the accepted pattern. But his restraint, his refusal to pad, his background care, his often surprising originality all combine to make this book a very satisfactory col-

lection for the *aficionado*." In addition to the excellent tale of vampirism, "Revelations in Black," there are "Carnaby's Fish" and the chilling "Mive."

4-125. Keller, David H. **The Folsom Flint, and Other Curious Tales.** Arkham House, 1969.

Although the bulk of Keller's work is in the field of science fiction, he produced a few stories of supernatural horror that are minor classics. Keller was a psychiatrist in a mental hospital, and his knowledge of mental aberration no doubt gave him added insight into the horror engendered by the human personality. Some of the stories in this volume reflect such concerns, such as "The Thing in the Cellar," from the pages of *Weird Tales,* about a boy who fears that some nameless and invisible horror lurks in the cellar. "The Dead Woman" reveals similar concerns, about a man who is convinced that his wife is dead, even though others do not believe him.

4-126. Keller, David H. **Tales from Underwood.** Arkham House & Pellegrini & Cudahy, 1952; Neville Spearman, 1974.

Although only a few horror stories figure in this volume, they represent Keller's sources from his career as a psychiatrist. In fact, he claimed to have written several of these tales, such as "A Piece of Linoleum," under self-hypnosis. Other weird stories of note are "The Moon Artist" and "The Door."

4-127. Kerruish, Jessie Douglas (U.K.). **The Undying Monster.** Heath, Cranton, 1922; Tandem, 1975.

This modern Gothic novel concerns the Hammond family, which lives under an ancient curse. A psychic detective discovers that the cause is hereditary lycanthropy.

4-128. Kersh, Gerald (U.K.). **The Horrible Dummy, and Other Stories.** Heinemann, 1944.

During Kersh's varied career, he produced very few volumes of weird fiction. This collection contains some of his best work. In addition to the title story, "Comrade Death" serves as his commentary on war.

4-129. King, Stephen. **Carrie.** Doubleday, 1973; Signet, 1975.

King's first novel reflects his fascination with psychic phenomena, in this case telekinesis. Carrie, a young girl brought up by a mother who is a religious fanatic, thinks her own psychic powers are a result of her sins. As Carrie reaches puberty, her psychic powers mature and, through a complex series of Carrie's frustrating and dangerous relationships, become destructive. The novel has been successfully filmed by Brian de Palma.

4-130. King, Stephen. **The Dead Zone.** Viking, 1979.

King returns to the terror experienced by those possessed with psychic powers. John Smith's ability to foresee the future and experience the past of others by merely touching them lies within the "dead zone" of his brain, a portion blanked by an automobile accident that left him in a coma for several years. On this premise, King weaves a fascinating tale of fate and its consequences, of human helpless isolation in a world we cannot control. Eventually, Smith meets Guy Stillson, an aspiring politician. In one of his visions, Johnny foresees this man's dangerous rise to power and attempts to alter his fate.

4–131. King, Stephen. **Firestarter.** Viking, 1980.
This 1980 novel concerns a little girl named Charlie, whose parents participated in a 1969 drug experiment run by a government agency known as The Shop. As Charlie matures, her ability to set anything on fire by looking at it becomes more pronounced. What follows is a story of terror as The Shop hunts Charlie and her father to use her as a new weapon.

*4–132. King, Stephen. **Night Shift.** Doubleday, 1978.
This, Stephen King's only collection of short stories, excels the best of his novels, which tend to be prolix. "Jerusalem's Lot" is a period piece much in the manner of Lovecraft. "Graveyard Shift" is the grim tale of a rat-infested warehouse, and "Gray Matter" is a grisly story reminiscent of Machen's "Novel of the White Powder." "Children of the Corn" and "I Know What You Need" are perhaps the best tales of the volume.

*4–133. King, Stephen. **'Salem's Lot.** Doubleday, 1975; Signet, 1976.
An excellent novel of vampirism; it concerns Ben, a writer who lived for four years as a boy in a small New England town called Jerusalem's Lot. As a man, he returns to find the deserted Marston House is the home of a vampire. As the vampire infection spreads in the community, Ben enlists the aid of others to help him combat the evil force. He comes upon a young boy and together they leave Salem's Lot to travel the country and seek out other vampires. Although the plot of the novel is relatively simple, it succeeds largely as a result of its fine characterizations. As Ben Mears comes to terms with the horror of Salem's Lot, he comes to terms with his own life and destiny.

*4–134. King, Stephen. **The Shining.** Doubleday, 1977.
This popular novel of modern Gothic horror, filmed by Stanley Kubrick, draws on key motifs from the Gothic romance of the late eighteenth century and fuses them with motifs borrowed from Poe, and perhaps even Melville. Jack Torrance, an alcoholic writer, is fired from his position as an English teacher in a small New England college and takes a job at the Overlook, a resort hotel in the Colorado Rockies, as the winter caretaker. He travels there with his wife, Wendy, and little boy, Danny. As Jack discovers the grim and ghostly past of the hotel, Danny's propensities for psychic visions, or "shinings" as he learns to call them, increase. Out of the grisly past of the Overlook and the psychological conflicts of Jack and his wife, King weaves a complex tale of psychological horror as the hotel, the counterpart of the isolated mountain castle in many an old Gothic novel, becomes a symbol for

the psychological and moral evil within Jack. Echoes of Poe's tale "The Masque of the Red Death" figure in the book as it moves to its typcially Gothic climax.

4–135. King, Stephen. **The Stand.** Doubleday, 1978.

This novel is a modern-day narrative that is partly derived from the Gothic tradition in its delineation of good and evil, but it approaches the domain of science fiction. It deals with a possible horror of today—the accidental release of a deadly germ that almost destroys the human race. Those who survive not only fight death, but struggle with vivid dreams of good and evil. The good is symbolized in these dreams by an old black woman named Mother Abigail, the evil by Randall Flagg, known as the "Dark Man," the "Walkin' Dude," or "the man with no face." The conflict between good and evil takes on epic proportions as the evil ones are destroyed by a nuclear explosion.

4–136. Kirk, Russell. **Lord of the Hollow Dark.** St. Martin, 1979.

Kirk's first foray into mystical romance, a rich, allusive work based on some of T. S. Eliot's poetry (Eliot having been a close personal friend of Kirk's). Here, the characters dabble in the occult for an experience of what they call the "timeless moment," produced by the drug kalanzi. Mark Hennelly writes, "The overall virtue of *Lord of the Hollow Dark* is its ability to blend credibly together the sceptical and spectral strains of Gothicism." The novel is a success in terms of its intellectual richness, but it loses power for the reader new to such intellectual allusiveness in terror fiction.

4–137. Kirk, Russell. **Old House of Fear.** Fleet, 1961.

Kirk, in his dedication to this novel, calls it a "Gothick tale, in unblushing line of direct descent from *The Castle of Otranto*." Kirk's work is thus a modern Gothic novel set in Scotland, an ancient castle called Old House of Fear as the symbol of the political and moral themes that run through the novel. Hugh Logan, an American, travels to Carnglass, the locale of the Old House, to investigate its sordid past, and finds himself in a widening mesh of political terrorism formed by Dr. Jackman, the villain of the piece. Mary MacAskival is the damsel in distress and the guiding force of good behind Hugh Logan.

*4–138. Kirk, Russell. **The Princess of All Lands.** Arkham House, 1979.

Although this collection contains two stories available in *The Surley Sullen Bell* [4–139], the new stories are "The Last God's Dream," a fantasy in which an ancient Roman emperor returns in a sepulchral setting, and "There's a Long, Long Trail A-Winding," which won a 1977 World Fantasy Award. Also noteworthy is "The Princess of All Lands," in which a woman experiences a strange cosmic event. Kirk's work is always well written in clear, careful prose, and while he is not prolific, his works in the short story form are minor masterpieces.

*4–139. Kirk, Russell. **The Surley Sullen Bell.** Fleet, 1962.

In this, Kirk's first collection of ghostly tales, the influence of M. R. James, Machen, LeFanu, and Blackwood is revealed throughout. In "Uncle Isaiah," a laundry owner evokes the spirit of his dead uncle to do justice to those who have done him an injustice. This tale, like its companion "Off the Sand Road," has its supernatural incidents arise from a more secure past to shatter the denizens of the present. The title story concerns a man who comes to visit a former girl friend and her husband, only to find that she is dying; her husband has been administering strychnine over a period of weeks, gives the same to her visiting lover, and then kills himself. In the finest of the collection, "Soworth Place," a drifter falls in love with a mysterious woman whose dead husband returns to claim her. And in the Jamesian tale "What Shadows We Pursue," a bookseller comes to terms with the ghost of the man whose books he is purchasing. Out of the past, the truth alters the lives of those in the present; time, dreams, and hate are the essences of the fear of the supernatural in Kirk's vision. The book concludes with a fine essay, "A Cautionary Note on the Ghostly Tale," in which Kirk delineates a sensible rationale of the form.

4–140. Konvitz, Jeffrey. **The Sentinel.** Simon & Schuster, 1974; Ballantine, 1976.

This novel is the spiritual child of such supernatural horror novels as *Rosemary's Baby* [4–150] and *The Exorcist* [4–24]. In this work, Allison Parker takes a brownstone apartment near that of a blind priest who guards the gateway to hell. As her new world disintegrates into one in which everyone she meets seems possessed by evil, she becomes engulfed in a widening circle of supernatural horror and religious terror.

4–141. La Spina, Greye. **Invaders from the Dark.** Arkham House, 1960.

Originally appearing in *Weird Tales,* this novel centers on a young researcher who becomes involved with a werewolf princess. It remains one of the few noteworthy werewolf novels written in the modern era.

4–142. Lawrence, Margery (U.K.). **Number Seven, Queer Street.** Mycroft & Moran, 1969.

This collection of five tales purports to be the chronicles of one Miles Pennoyer, who is described by his fictional biographer Jerome Latimer as "a 'psychic doctor'—one who deals in ills that beset the soul rather than the body of man." Pennoyer is thus in the great tradition of fictional psychic doctors beginning with LeFanu's Hesselius. The best of the five "cases" by Pennoyer are "The Case of the Bronze Door," "The Case of Ella McLeod," and, finest of all, "The Case of the Moonchild."

*4–143. Leiber, Fritz. **Conjure Wife.** Twayne, 1953; Award, 1968.

Called "the definitive novelistic treatment of witchcraft," the story centers on Tanzy Saylor and her professor husband, Norman. Tanzy, like other of the faculty wives, has been practicing witchcraft to further her husband's career. Another critic has written that the novel "is easily the most frightening (and necessarily) the most thoroughly convincing of all modern horror stories. Its premise is that witchcraft still flourishes, or at any rate survives, an open secret among women, a closed book to men. Under the rational overlay of twentieth-century civilization, this sickly growth, uncultivated, unsuspected, still manages to propagate itself."

*4–144. Leiber, Fritz. **Heroes and Horrors.** Whispers Press, 1978.
Leiber's collection contains some of his fantasy stories and excels, in many ways, the fine horror tales gathered in *Night's Black Agents* [4–146]. The showpieces of the horror tales are "Belsen Express," "Midnight in the Mirror World," "Midnight by the Morphy Watch," and, perhaps the best, "Dark Wings." "Belsen Express" is an expertly crafted horror tale of a wealthy businessman, George Simister, who is haunted by a strange "rat-faced" man who is linked with Simister's irrational fear of the Nazi depravities and mass killings during World War II as an express train by the name of Belsen takes on a similarly threatening meaning. An expertly done shift to an omniscient viewpoint in this story gives its climax a chillingly appropriate psychic resonance. "Midnight in the Mirror World" centers on a reclusive dilettante, Giles Nefandor, whose fascination with the repeating images formed by the opposite mirrors in a hallway in his home leads to a ghostly encounter with a failed actress whom he spurned. As he learns of her suicide, he meets her finally as an essence in the mirror world he has created. "Midnight by the Morphy Watch" is a brilliant study in which the paleologic of paranoid psychosis is brilliantly linked to the obsessive thought processes of a chess player. The chess player comes upon a bizarre watch that has been passed down among the world's greatest chess champions, each of whom experienced paranoid psychoses. This same player, Richter-Rebil, is himself on the verge of a psychosis and saves himself at the last minute by destroying the watch, but by implication he remains a changed man because of the experience. "Dark Wings" is the unique horror tale of Leiber's career. Two orphaned twin sisters who have lived apart meet for the first time in a single night of devastating psychosexual revelation, which, in a sense, is the twentieth-century parallel to Le Fanu's Victorian vampire tale "Carmilla."

*4–145. Leiber, Fritz. **Night Monsters.** Ace, 1969; Gollancz, 1974; Panther, 1975.
Although this collection contains some of Leiber's science fiction, it is noteworthy for the inclusion of a few supernatural tales unobtainable elsewhere in book form. "The Black Gondolier" is narrated by a sensitive young man who befriends an intelligent drifter named Daloway, who believes, as a result of his vivid dreams, that the world's oil is an organic substance that controls all human life. Daloway's dreams center on "a black gondolier," an unidentifiable boatman who seems aptly placed, since Daloway lives in Venice,

California; and this dream figure apparently becomes real when Daloway mysteriously disappears. "The Oldest Soldier" deals with one of Leiber's important themes: the human adjustment to war. In this story, the narrator's fascination with war draws him to an old soldier whose personality becomes absorbed into his own. In one of Leiber's most interesting tales, "The Girl with the Hungry Eyes," Leiber creates a beautiful girl who, like a vampire, seems an almost supernatural manifestation of all women. In this respect, this story deals with themes similar to *Conjure Wife* and *Our Lady of Darkness*. In "I'm Looking for Jeff," another mysterious and apparently supernatural girl haunts a barroom looking for her dead lover.

*4-146. Leiber, Fritz. **Night's Black Agents.** Arkham House, 1947; Neville Spearman, 1975.

Leiber's first collection of horror and fantasy tales from the pages of *Weird Tales* and *Unknown* reflects his concern with supernatural and quasi-scientific horror in modern settings. "Smoke Ghost" is a carefully wrought story delicately poised between psychological and supernatural themes. Catsby Wran is haunted by a sooty black ghost he encounters in the labyrinthine factories and office buildings of Chicago. A similar theme is treated in "The Inheritance," in which a young man inherits his uncle's meager possessions as well as his three-month's lease on a small apartment. The young man begins to experience a series of vivid dreams about his uncle, who was a policeman and a murderer. The best horror tale is "The Dreams of Albert Moreland," about a professional chess player who experiences a series of vivid dreams in which he plays a chess game with alien beings. As the shattering universal implications of the game become apparent, Moreland is overcome with fear, beginning to suspect that the future of human existence in the universe is threatened.

*4-147. Leiber, Fritz. **Our Lady of Darkness.** Putnam, 1977; Berkley, 1978.

This tale, which won the World Fantasy Award in 1977 for best novel, deals with widowed horror-story writer Franz Westen's search for the solution to the mystery of de Castries's occult investigation of paramental entities in San Francisco at the turn of the century. When Westen finds that the entities still exist in the city, he links them to the tragic deaths of writers Ambrose Bierce and Jack London. The novel itself is a tribute to the tradition of the U.S. weird tale, and through Westen's love for a beautiful young musician, it links the occult with love and sexuality; for Westen, the special allure of feminine sexuality is an occult force itself.

4-148. Leiber, Fritz. **The Secret Songs.** Rupert Hart-Davis, 1968; Panther, 1975.

This collection of science fiction, horror, and fantasy includes some of Leiber's best-known supernatural tales, such as "Smoke Ghost" and "The Girl with the Hungry Eyes," which are available in other collections. "The Secret Songs" is one of the most original of Leiber's tales.

4-149. Leiber, Fritz. **Shadows with Eyes.** Ballantine, 1962.
A horror collection containing six stories, most of which are available in other Leiber collections. The most noteworthy are "The Power of Puppets," "Schizo Jimmie," and "A Bit of the Dark World."

*4-150. Levin, Ira. **Rosemary's Baby.** Random House, 1967.
This novel of satanism presents an antithesis to the Christian birth of Christ as a New York actor becomes acquainted with a group of satanists. He uses his wife, Rosemary, to further his career, as he drugs her and admits her, without her knowledge, to a sexual encounter with the devil. Unknown to her, Rosemary carries the Antichrist, and as she gradually pieces together the puzzle of her baby's conception in what amounts to a deepening paranoia, she willingly accepts her motherhood. The success of this novel, however, is largely due to the excellent film version directed by Roman Polanski.

4-151. Lewis, L. A. (U.K.). **Tales of the Grotesque.** Philip Allan, 1934.
The identity of L. A. Lewis has never been ascertained. He or she never wrote anything else except one story in Christine Thompson's *Not at Night* series [4-297 to 4-307]. Still, this volume contains more originality than many others from the same period. A man is crossed with a bird in "Hybrid." An abandoned baby lives on in a house in the forest to eat living things in "The Child." In "The Tower of Moab," a religious cult builds a tower to heaven, and the narrator's madness completes it. Despite the mystery surrounding the authorship of this book, it is a creditable collection of weird tales.

*4-152. Long, Frank Belknap. **The Early Long.** Doubleday, 1977.
Although this collection contains Long's earliest work, which is also available in other collections, it is most useful for its lengthy introductions and the informative personal essay at the beginning of the book.

4-153. Long, Frank Belknap. **The Horror from the Hills.** Arkham House, 1963.
This short novel, which has affinities with Lovecraft's tales of cosmic horror, reflects Long's concern with modern scientific theory and the supernatural. When Algernon Harris, archaeological student, acquires the idol of the god Chaugnar Faugn, after the mysterious and grisly death of one of his associates, more murders occur in the vicinity. With the help of a mystical scientist and his fourth-dimensional weapon, Chaugnar Faugn is sent back to his dimension.

*4-154. Long, Frank Belknap. **The Hounds of Tindalos.** Arkham House, 1946; Panther, 1975. Part of contents in a companion volume, *The Black Druid*, Panther, 1975.

Here is Long's most famous collection of weird tales. It contains his acclaimed story of cosmic horror, "The Hounds of Tindalos," about Halpin Chalmers, author and journalist, whose researches into the occult lead him to experiment with a new drug Liao, which allows him to perceive other dimensions of time and space. As his experiences become more disturbing, he is compelled to prevent beings from the other dimensions he calls the Hounds of Tindalos from penetrating through angular space to this dimension. There follows a mysterious earthquake that the narrator believes is related to Chalmer's experiences and mysterious death. This tale has its origins in the mythos created by Lovecraft. Another tale, "The Space Eaters," is a story based on Lovecraft himself. A character named Howard, who is a writer of cosmic tales, and the narrator succeed in banishing beings from another dimension who feed on the brains of the living. A number of other stories contain science fiction elements, but the most noteworthy tales of horror are "A Visitor from Egypt," about a mysterious stranger who appears to be the messenger of an ancient curse and takes grim revenge on the curator of a New England museum, and "The Black Druid," about a scholar of Druidic folklore who experiences a supernatural manifestation transforming him into a personality from the past. "Dark Vision" is the interesting tale of Ronald Horn, who, after an accident in which he is almost electrocuted, has a degree of psychic sensitivity. This story is especially interesting when compared with King's *The Dead Zone* [4–130].

4–155. Long, Frank Belknap. **Night Fear.** Zebra, 1979.
Although this collection represents Long's work in the genre of science fiction, "The Man from Nowhere" is the only tale, aside from *The Horror from the Hills*, [4–153], that approaches his other tales of cosmic horror. It is about an artist who is also a being from another dimension. He has the power to alter time and space and even human will. When he interferes in the relationship of his friend and his friend's fiancée, he destroys his dwelling and returns to his dimension of space and time.

4–156. Long, Frank Belknap. **The Rim of the Unknown.** Arkham House, 1972.
Spanning the genres of science fiction, fantasy, and the macabre, the best weird stories of the volume are "Humpty Dumpty Had a Great Fall," "The Last Man," and "The House of Rising Winds."

*4–157. Lovecraft, H. P. **At the Mountains of Madness, and Other Novels.** Arkham House, 1964.
This collection of eight of Lovecraft's short novels spans his entire career. The best, "At the Mountains of Madness," is about a professor at mythical Miskatonic University who travels to the Antarctic, where he finds a ruined city of the Ancient Ones. "The Case of Charles Dexter Ward" is a fantasy about the revival of the dead and the black-magic evocation of Lovecraft's

famous Outsiders. "The Shunned House," based for the most part on actual events in the history of Providence, Rhode Island, is a story about "a gelatinous thing" that absorbs human lives into itself. "The Dreams in the Witch House" concerns Walter Gilman, who spends a night in an old house in Arkham once inhabited by a witch. This novella stands as a unique blend of Lovecraft's familiar alien dimensions and witchcraft. "The Statement of Randolph Carter" centers on a narrator who, according to L. Sprague de Camp, "is a fictional idealization of Lovecraft himself." The narrator Carter goes with Harley Warren on a nocturnal mission to an ancient cemetery where beneath a tomb Warren enters and never returns. "The Dream-Quest of Unknown Kadath" is an elaborate fantasy influenced by Lord Dunsany. Similarly, "The Silver Key" is another fantasy of Randolph Carter, as is "Through the Gates of the Silver Key."

*4–158. Lovecraft, H. P. **Beyond the Wall of Sleep.** Arkham House, 1943. This second volume of Lovecraft's fiction and poetry is widely sought by collectors. It contains a representative selection of his minor works and an essay on Lovecraft by W. Paul Cook.

*4–159. Lovecraft, H. P. **Dagon, and Other Macabre Tales.** Arkham House, 1965.
A collection of 37 short pieces and the essay "Supernatural Horror in Literature," for the most part secondary works in the Lovecraft canon. The best is undoubtedly "Beyond the Wall of Sleep," about a criminally insane man who has visions of other dimensions. Other stories of note are "Herbert West—Reanimator," "Arthur Jermyn," and the Dunsanian fantasy "The Doom That Came to Sarnath."

*4–160. Lovecraft, H. P. **The Dunwich Horror, and Others.** Arkham House, 1963.
Here is a selection of Lovecraft's best stories. "In the Vault" is the simple story of an undertaker, George Birch, who cuts off the feet of a corpse to make it fit a smaller coffin; the corpse takes supernatural revenge. "Pickman's Model" centers on an artist who paints pictures of feasting ghouls from actual photographs. "The Rats in the Walls," one of Lovecraft's best-known tales, is narrated by de la Poer, an American of English descent. He buys a crumbling English mansion infested by an army of rats, and discovers an ancient altar in the cellar. Beneath the altar is a cavern used by a cannibal cult from prehuman times. Gradually, de la Poer goes mad. "The Outsider" is a conscious imitation of Poe narrated by "an outsider," a monstrous being who lives alone in a castle beneath the earth. When he travels to another castle and finds a ball in progress, the revelers flee in horror, and "the outsider" sees himself in a mirror for the first time. "The Colour Out of Space" is a story from the Cthulhu cycle about a mysterious, leathery meteorite that lands in New England. It gives off a gaseous substance that kills all

living things within its vicinity. "The Music of Erich Zann" concerns a musician who composes "other worldly" music and eventually becomes absorbed into another dimension. "The Haunter of the Dark" concerns Robert Blake, Lovecraft's version of fellow-writer Robert Bloch, who becomes fascinated by an old desecrated church. "The Picture in the House" is a simple tale of a man traveling on research in genealogy through Miskatonic Valley who comes upon an old, lonely man gloating over a picture of a butcher cleaving a corpse in two. As the picture takes on a supernatural existence of its own, the house in which the old man lives is destroyed supernaturally. "The Call of Cthulhu" is the first story in the Cthulhu cycle, while "The Dunwich Horror," which centers on Wilbur Whateley and his alien twin brother, solidifies the Cthulhu cycle. "Cool Air" is the horrifying story of a man who must live in cold temperatures to survive. Eventually, his cold air machine breaks down and he dies, a loathsome, shapeless mass. "The Whisperer in Darkness" is another story of Lovecraft's nameless Outsiders, in this case winged creatures with buzzing voices. "The Terrible Old Man" is reminiscent of some of Dunsany's work, while "The Thing on the Doorstep," "The Shadow over Innsmouth," and "The Shadow Out of Time" are all contributions to the Cthulhu cycle.

4–161. Lovecraft, H. P. **The Horror in the Museum, and Other Revisions.** Arkham House, 1970.
Throughout his career, Lovecraft produced a number of revised versions of other writers' stories. He did so in large part to earn money, and in many cases his revisions excel in quality the original works. In addition, a number of these stories are almost entirely Lovecraft's work. This volume contains 20 stories that he revised. The most noteworthy is C. M. Eddy, Jr.'s "The Loved Dead," about necrophilia. It created a minor sensation when published in *Weird Tales.*

***4–162.** Lovecraft, H. P. **The Outsider, and Others.** Arkham House, 1939.
This volume was the first one produced by Arkham House and the one that put both the publishing company and H. P. Lovecraft on the map. It contains a representative selection of Lovecraft's work also available in the three later volumes, *The Dunwich Horror* [4–160], *Dagon* [4–159], and *At the Mountains of Madness* [4–157]. This book is one of the most sought after by collectors. Some of Lovecraft's work was published in paperback editions by Ballatine in the 1970s: *The Dream Quest of Unknown Kadath,* 1970; *The Doom That Came to Sarnath,* 1971; *The Lurking Fear, and Other Stories,* 1971; *At the Mountains of Madness, and Other Tales of Terror,* 1971; *The Tomb, and Other Tales,* 1970.

4–163. Lumley, Brian (U.K.). **Beneath the Moors.** Arkham House, 1974.
Like all of Lumley's work, this is derived from Lovecraft's Cthulhu cycle of stories. It concerns Professor Ewart Masters, who after an automobile accident, spends his convalescence at the home of his nephew Jason Masters,

where he discovers the existence of an ancient city beneath the Yorkshire moors. What follows is a series of a dream-adventures in which Masters travels through the realms of the Old Ones.

4–164. Lumley, Brian (U.K.). **The Burrowers Beneath.** DAW, 1974.
Related through a series of letters and diaries, this is the story of Titus Crow, who discovers the existence of Lovecraft's Old Ones beneath the earth. It involves such well-known Lovecraftian characters as Wingate Peaslee from "The Shadow Out of Time" and is an extension of Lovecraft's work.

4–165. Lumley, Brian (U.K.). **The Caller of the Black.** Arkham House, 1971.
Lumley's first collection of stories, all loosely based on H. P. Lovecraft's work. The best story is "The Caller of the Black," and other noteworthy tales are "The Thing from the Blasted Heath" and "The Mirror of Nitocris."

4–166. Lumley, Brian (U.K.). **The Horror at Oakdeene, and Others.** Arkham House, 1977.
This collection of short stories again reveals Lumley's indebtedness to Lovecraft for sources. "The Horror at Oakdeene" begins in Oakdeene Sanatorium, and out of this setting Lumley weaves a respectable Cthulhu tale. "The Statement of Henry Worthy" is another Cthulhu Mythos tale, which centers on a primeval cavern that contains a breed of hideous funguslike creatures. "Born of the Winds" takes place in the arctic regions and resembles Basil Copper's novel *The Great White Space* [4–77].

4–167. Lumley, Brian (U.K.). **In the Moons of Borea.** Jove, 1979.
Another novel featuring the quester de Marigny and his timeclock as well as Titus Crow. They travel via the timeclock to a parallel universe where they come to Borea, an ice planet, where they witness a psychic combat between the Warlord of the Plateau, his regal mate Armandra, and her father Ithaqua the wind-walker.

4–168. Lumley, Brian (U.K.). **Spawn of the Winds.** Jove, 1978.
This novel is in the tradition of Lovecraft's fantasies such as "The Silver Key" and "Through the Gates of the Silver Key" [4–157]. It begins with Lovecraft's character Professor Wingate Peaslee and spans time and space to an alien dimension beyond the outer reaches of the Arctic.

4–169. Lumley, Brian (U.K.). **The Transition of Titus Crow.** DAW, 1975.
One of Lumley's earlier novels in the Lovecraft tradition, it establishes characters used later in the series, such as de Marigny and Titus Crow, and involves their transition into Lovecraft's alien dimensions.

4–170. Macardle, Dorothy. **The Uninvited.** Doubleday, 1942.
A delightful ghost story that focuses on the haunting of an English country house called Cliff End and the owners' attempts to exorcise the spirit of one

Mary Meredith. It remains an interesting novel of the supernatural since its ghost is essentially harmless. Readers will delight at Macardle's characterizations and the scenes involving séances that conclude the book.

*4–171. Malden, R. H. (U.K.). **Nine Ghosts.** Edward Arnold, 1943.
These stories are clearly influenced by the work of M. R. James. Malden himself was acquainted with James at King's College, Cambridge, and later became a minister in the Church of England. Nearly all of the nine stories deal with antiquarians who, while delving into the past, release some host or revenant into the present. The best are "The Sundial," in which a sundial is placed over a revenant's *genius loci,* and "The Priest's Brass," about a collector of brass rubbings who encounters a sexton who may or may not be the ghost of a fifteenth-century priest who practiced the black arts.

4–172. Marasco, Robert. **Burnt Offerings.** Delacorte, 1973.
It is said that *Burnt Offerings* "rivals *The Turn of the Screw* in the artistry of its construction of evil." The novel centers on the Rolfes, who abandon their New York apartment and take up residence in a summer home with a secret haunted room. It remains a successful modern Gothic novel, evocative in its atmosphere of almost magnetic evil. The book, like many other full-length horror novels following *Rosemary's Baby* [4–150], has been filmed to critical acclaim.

4–173. Matheson, Richard. **Hell House.** Viking, 1971.
This novel of paranormal terror matches Shirley Jackson's *The Haunting of Hill House* [4–119]. In similar fashion, a group of psychic investigators spend time in reputedly haunted Hell House. The investigators confront aspects of their own personalities as the psychic phenomena take hold of their lives. This work has been successfully filmed with a screenplay by Matheson himself.

4–174. Matheson, Richard. **Shock Waves.** Dell, 1970; Berkley, 1979.
Not all of these stories are supernatural horror tales, but they fall easily into the category of the weird tale. In some cases, such as "Finger Prints," "The Thing," and "A Drink of Water," they are comparable to the works of Robert Aickman [4–1 to 4–7]. "Come Fygures, Come Shadows" is a portion of a novel about extrasensory perception.

4–175. Matheson, Richard. **Shock I.** Berkley, 1979.
Although a few of these tales fall into the category of science fiction, the best of the weird stories are "Long Distance Call," about phone calls from the dead, and "The Children of Noah," about the strange people of Zachry, Maine, who cook human visitors alive.

4–176. Matheson, Richard. **Shock II.** Berkley, 1979.
The essentially weird story of this collection is Matheson's original treatment of the vampire theme in "No Such Thing as a Vampire."

4–177. Matheson, Richard. **Shock III.** Dell, 1966; Berkley, 1979.
The only supernatural story of this volume is "Slaughter House," which originally appeared in *Weird Tales*. It is presented as a report by a society for psychical research and concerns the spirits of the Slaughter family.

4–178. Metcalfe, John (U.K.). **The Feasting Dead.** Arkham House, 1954.
This short novel centers on a young boy, Denis, who while vacationing in France comes under the influence of a ghoulish revenant from the past. Eventually, the boy runs away from his father's house in England to return to France, where a final encounter with the ghoul causes his hair to turn white from shock.

4–179. Metcalfe, John (U.K.). **The Smoking Leg, and Other Stories.** Jarrolds, 1925.
These fantasy tales reflect Metcalfe's interest in Eastern mysticism. The best Eastern tales of supernatural horror are "The Smoking Leg," "Nightmare Jack," and "The Double Admiral." In each, British citizens living in India must come to terms with superstition and fear.

*4–180. Munby, A. N. L. (U.K.). **The Alabaster Hand, and Other Ghost Stories.** Dennis Dobson, 1949.
Mike Ashley describes Munby as the one writer who comes "closest to inheriting the mantle of M. R. James." This collection of stories, written in a World War II prison camp, reads beautifully in that Munby's style often resembles the King James version of the Bible. Most of the stories, such as "Herodes Redivivus," "The Tregannet Book of Hours," and "The Devil's Autograph," are antiquarian tales that equal those of James. Others, such as "The Alabaster Hand," "The Four-Poster," and "The Tudor Chimney," reveal Munby's fascination with architectural details that haunt his protagonists.

*4–181. Munn, H. Warner. **Tales of the Werewolf Clan: Vol. I. In the Tomb of the Bishop.** Donald M. Grant, 1979.
These seven tales are a sequel to Munn's early story from *Weird Tales* "The Werewolf of Ponkert." They center on the revenge of the "master" on the descendants of Wladislaw Brenryk of Ponkert.

*4–182. Munn, H. Warner. **Tales of the Werewolf Clan: Vol. II. The Master Goes Home.** Donald M. Grant, 1980.
Six final stories in the Werewolf clan saga complete Munn's work in the series.

*4–183. Munn, H. Warner. **The Werewolf of Ponkert.** Centaur, 1976.
This is the original *Weird Tales* story that began Munn's Werewolf series. Here, along with "The Werewolf of Ponkert," is its sequel, "The Werewolf's Daughter."

*4-184. Oates, Joyce Carol. **Night-Side.** New American Library, 1977; Fawcett, 1980.

Although these tales fall into the category of mainstream fiction, they contain the essence of the modern tale of terror. In such stories as "Night-Side," about a New England professor exploring the realm of spirits and mediums, and "A Theory of Knowledge," about a scholar who, while attempting to systemize a lifetime of research in philosophy, becomes obsessed with a strange retarded boy who is abused by his family, Oates offers her vision of an uncertain, shifting mental universe in which the human gropes frantically for understanding. The most Gothic, "The Dungeon," centers on the isolated mental state of a frustrated artist. "Famine Country" presents a young man who has apparently been hospitalized for a psychotic reaction to a poisoned hallucinogen. He experiences a kind of mental absorption into matter and a vague dreamlike state in which a pet turtle speaks to him with the voice of God. These often difficult, obscure, and enigmatic tales are clearly thematically related to more traditional horror tales of this century. They are compellingly mysterious, almost in the manner of the tales of Robert Aickman [4-1 to 4-7].

4-185. Petaja, Emil. **Stardrift.** Fantasy, 1971.

This collection of Petaja's stories of science fiction, fantasy, and horror contains some of the finest stories by this neglected author. In the best tale, "Dark Balcony," the theme of a demon lover is linked with concepts of Lovecraft's Cthulhu Mythos.

4-186. Quinn, Seabury. **The Adventures of Jules de Grandin.** Popular Library, 1976.

Seabury Quinn was perhaps the most popular writer among *Weird Tales* readers. He is best known for his "Sherlock Holmes of the supernatural," Jules de Grandin, whose exploits continue the tradition of the metaphysical detective as established by Le Fanu, Hodgson, and Blackwood (see Chapter 1). This selection of stories includes the first and most popular Jules de Grandin tale, "Terror on the Links."

4-187. Quinn, Seabury. **The Casebook of Jules de Grandin.** Popular Library, 1976.

Another selection of Jules de Grandin tales. Noteworthy are "Children of Ubasti," "The Silver Countess," and "The Serpent Woman."

4-188. Quinn, Seabury. **The Devil's Bride.** Popular Library, 1976.

This novel is a Jules de Grandin adventure about a devil-worship cult. It is comparable to some of the work of Dennis Wheatley [4-224 to 4-228].

4-189. Quinn, Seabury. **The Hellfire Files of Jules de Grandin.** Popular Library, 1976.

Noteworthy de Grandin adventures in this volume are "The Devil People," "The Wolf of St. Bonnot," and "The Hand of Glory."

4–190. Quinn, Seabury. **The Horror Chambers of Jules de Grandin.** Popular Library, 1977.
The best Jules de Grandin tales in this volume are "The Poltergeist," "The Jest of Warburg Tantavul," and "A Gamble in Souls."

*4–191. Quinn, Seabury. **The Phantom-Fighter.** Mycroft & Moran, 1966.
This original collection of Jules de Grandin stories from Arkham House's sister imprint contains "Terror on the Links," "The Dead Hand," "Children of Ubasti," "The Jest of Warburg Tantavul," "The Corpse-Master," "The Poltergeist," "The Wolf of St. Bonnot," "Restless Souls," "The Silver Countess," and "The Doom of the House of Phipps."

*4–192. Quinn, Seabury. **Roads.** Arkham House, 1948.
This fine Christmas ghost story was one of the most popular stories in *Weird Tales*. The volume features five interior illustrations by noted macabre artist Virgil Finlay.

4–193. Quinn, Seabury. **The Skeleton Closet of Jules de Grandin.** Popular Library, 1976.
Another volume of Jules de Grandin stories; noteworthy are "The Doom of the House of Phipps" and "Daughter of the Moonlight."

*4–194. Rice, Anne. **Interview with the Vampire.** Knopf, 1976; Ballantine, 1978.
This extraordinary novel of a hero-vampire has become a cult classic. The novel begins with a boy's interviewing Louis, a vampire, with a tape recorder. What the boy records is the personal narrative of the vampire's life and travels from New Orleans to Paris. Rice sustains a convincing portrait of the vampire Lestat with a wealth of period detail, making it one of the most readable vampire novels of our era. An interesting comparison may be drawn with Chelsea Quinn Yarbro's recent vampire trilogy [4–233, 4–234, 4–235].

4–195. Rolt, L. T. C. (U.K.). **Sleep No More.** Constable, 1948.
L. T. C. Rolt was by trade an engineer (he helped build railways and waterways in England) and his knowledge of engineering is reflected in this, his one volume of supernatural tales. The best stories are "The Mine," "Bosworth Summit Pound," and "Music Hath Charms."

4–196. Russell, Ray. **Unholy Trinity.** Bantam, 1967.
This collection consists of three novellas of terror: "Sanguinarius," based on the legend of Elizabeth Bathory, who was reputed to be a vampire; "Sardonicus," successfully filmed by William Castle, about a man whose face is fixed in a hideous grin; and "Sagittarius," based on the legend of Gilles de Rais. All three are effective modern Gothic tales that tend toward the pornographic.

4–197. Sinclair, May (U.K.). **The Intercessor, and Other Stories.** Hutchinson, 1931.

May Sinclair was a confirmed spiritualist, and this serious interest in the supernatural as a reality is reflected in her fiction. The best stories in this collection are "Jones's Karma," "The Intercessor," and "The Villa Desiree."

4–198. Sinclair, May (U.K.). **Uncanny Stories.** Macmillan, 1923.

Noteworthy are "The Token" and "The Flaw in the Crystal," both of which reflect Sinclair's serious interest in spiritualism.

4–199. Smith, Basil A. (U.K.). **The Scallion Stone.** Whispers Press, 1980.

These delightful stories by clergyman Basil A. Smith are written in the tradition of M. R. James. The best are "The Scallion Stone" and "The Propert Bequest." In the words of Russell Kirk, who provides an introduction to the volume, "These stories are parables, after a fashion, of that fascinating perilous darkness, which suddenly may close about the fallen or the unwary."

*4–200. Smith, Clark Ashton. **The Abominations of Yondo.** Arkham House, 1960; Neville Spearman, 1972.

The three horror tales of this collection, "The Nameless Offspring," "The Devotee of Evil," and "The Epiphany of Death," again reveal Lovecraft's influence on Smith, the latter tale being dedicated to Lovecraft's memory. "The Third Episode of Vathek" builds on the Oriental Gothic tale by William Beckford [1–25], while the rest of the volume contains Smith's fantasies with macabre elements. "The Devotee of Evil," however, is one of his best traditional horror tales; Jean Armand creates a mechanical device that evokes another realm of pure evil, and eventually freezes Armand into a statuelike form of malignity.

*4–201. Smith, Clark Ashton. **Genius Loci, and Other Tales.** Arkham House, 1948; Neville Spearman, 1972.

One of the finest macabre tales of Smith's career, and the only true macabre tale of the volume, is "Genius Loci." It concerns Amberville, an artist of supernatural and mystic works, who becomes deeply fascinated by a landscape he paints. The landscape is near the house of Chapman, who may himself have been driven mad by the *genius loci* of the place. Gradually, Amberville, and later his fiancée, become obsessed even more by the place and eventually commit suicide amid mysterious, supernatural surroundings.

*4–202. Smith, Clark Ashton. **Lost Worlds.** Arkham House, 1944; Neville Spearman, 1971.

Most of these tales exemplify Smith's use of fantasy rather than horror. Certain of the fantasies, however, incorporate elements of Lovecraft's Cthulhu Mythos: "The Beast of Averoigne," "The Coming of the White Worm," "The Door to Saturn," and "The Tale of Satanpre Zeiros" elaborate or echo Lovecraft's other-dimensional beings. The two stories in the volume that are more clearly traditional horror tales, or tales of low Gothic fantasy, are "The Gorgon," a Medusa tale set in modern London, and the chilling "The Hunters from Beyond," in which Lovecraft himself is mentioned. This tale of a sculptor whose creatures are based on actual models of other-dimensional beings is reminiscent of Lovecraft's "Pickman's Model" [4–160].

4–203. Smith, Clark Ashton. **Other Dimensions.** Arkham House, 1970.
This book contains some of Smith's minor macabre pieces. "The Necromantic Tale" is a study of a modern man's absorption into the personality of his ancestor, who was a warlock. "The Supernumerary Corpse" is a grisly macabre tale about a corpse and its doppelgänger, and "The Ghoul" is a Gothic tale in the tradition of *Vathek* [1–25].

*4–204. Smith, Clark Ashton. **Out of Space and Time.** Arkham House, 1942; Neville Spearman, 1971.
Smith's gift for language evocative of fantastic worlds of alien beauty and horror is without parallel. In this respect, his work falls into the category of high Gothic fantasy, a term defined by fantasy scholars Robert Boyer and Kenneth Zahorski. This collection of tales chosen by Smith himself from his early writings in *Weird Tales* exemplifies his approach to the weird by his use of imaginative, secondary worlds expressing his vision of cosmic beauty and horror in human existence. "The End of the Story" and "A Rendezvous in Averoigne" are Gothic fragments in medieval settings, while "The Second Interment" is a man's dream of premature burial, all the more final because it does not resemble the actual one from which he was rescued. "The Dark Eidolon" is one of Smith's best weird fantasies; it has no parallel except, perhaps, in Lovecraft's dream fantasies.

*4–205. Smith, Clark Ashton. **Tales of Science and Sorcery.** Arkham House, 1964; Panther, 1976.
Of the few supernatural horror tales in this collection, the best is "The Seed from the Sepulchre," in which two orchid hunters on an expedition in Venezuela travel down the Orinoco River. The older of the men is dying of a fever in which he babbles about his defilement of a sacred Indian sepulchre. As their journey progresses, a monstrous, sentient plant grows out of the dying man's brain and eventually spreads itself to grow into his companion. Smith's other-worldly fantasies have been grouped into volumes under the heading of place names by Lin Carter in the Ballantine Adult Fantasy series. They are: *Hyperborea*, 1971; *Poseidonis*, 1973; *Xiccarph*, 1972; and *Zothique*, 1970.

*4–206. Stewart, Desmond. **The Vampire of Mons.** Harper & Row, 1976; Avon, 1977.
John Fowles has written of *The Vampire of Mons:* "the most interesting Gothic novel I have read for some time." This novel is reminiscent of *A Separate Peace* and *Lord of the Flies* as two gifted boys in a run-down public school be-

come involved with their eccentric schoolteacher and dabble in the occult and vampirism. The background is the breakout of World War II; the blood lust of the young becomes mindless violence as German bombers hover over the city.

4-207. Stewart, Fred Mustard. **The Mephisto Waltz.** Coward-McCann, 1969.
Emerging from the same period as novels such as *Rosemary's Baby* [4-150] and *The Exorcist* [4-24] this novel has also been successfully filmed. It centers on pianist Duncan Ely and his protégé Miles Clarkson. While Ely is dying, he dabbles in satanism to live on in Clarkson's body. Thus, Miles Clarkson becomes famed pianist Duncan Ely and carries on his tradition by transmigration of souls.

4-208. Straub, Peter. **Ghost Story.** Coward, McCann, & Geoghegan, 1979.
This highly successful modern Gothic novel deals with the bizarre connections between three separate people in different parts of the United States, a supernatural connection unraveled by a young novelist in California. Straub utilizes his Gothic sources well in this chilling novel.

***4-209.** Sturgeon, Theodore. **Some of Your Blood.** Ballantine, 1961.
Sturgeon's novel remains one of the most original variations of the vampire myth. Presented as a psychological case history with a number of humorous off-the-record letters between two army psychiatrists, the story of an overgrown orphaned boy named Bela, or George as he is later called, unfolds in a witty and ironic manner. Although George appears to be criminally psychotic, he is in fact a vampire, but with this difference: He feeds on menstrual blood only. This "shocker" is similar to some of Robert Bloch's fiction [4-25 to 4-36].

4-210. Tryon, Thomas. **Harvest Home.** Knopf, 1973.
This modern-day horror story centers on Ned Constantine and his dream of an idyllic life away from the city. He comes to the village of Cornwall Coombe where he becomes enmeshed in a web of horror as he discovers that the denizens of the place still practice fertility rites.

***4-211.** Tryon, Thomas. **The Other.** Knopf, 1971; Fawcett Crest, 1972.
Hailed on its appearance as one of the best supernatural horror stories written in many years, this novel, successfully filmed by Robert Mulligan, centers on the Perry twins, one of whom dies but lives on in the demented personality of his twin brother. This unique horror novel, told from the viewpoint of the demented child, is a psychological thriller reminiscent of the work of Shirley Jackson [4-117 to 4-121].

4–212. Wakefield, H. Russell (U.K.). **The Clock Strikes Twelve.** Arkham House, 1946.
Wakefield remains an unjustly neglected author of ghostly tales. This, his first Arkham House collection, contains such fine macabre pieces as "Into Outer Darkness," "Ingredient X," and "In Collaboration."

4–213. Wakefield, H. Russell (U.K.). **Ghost Stories.** Jonathan Cape, 1932; Arno, 1976.
This early collection of Wakefield's ghostly tales contains such fine stories as "A Peg on Which to Hang," "Used Car," "Damp Sheets," "An Echo," and "Old Man's Beard."

4–214. Wakefield, H. Russell (U.K.). **Strayers from Sheol.** Arkham House, 1961.
This last collection by Wakefield includes such memorable tales as "Ghost Hunt," "The Sepulchre of Jasper Sarasen" and "Four-Eyes."

*4–215. Walter, Elizabeth (U.K.). **In the Mist, and Other Uncanny Encounters.** Arkham House, 1979.
This collection contains the best of Walter's ghostly fiction. Noteworthy tales are "The Concrete Captain," about a solitary seaman haunted by a ghost from the sea; the title story; and also "The Sin-Eater," which utilizes Welsh folklore to chilling effect. "The Hare" is a fine story of a modern-day witch, and "Davy Jones's Tale" is another ghost story set at sea.

4–216. Walton, Evangeline. **Witch House.** Arkham House, 1945; Ballantine, 1979.
This fine horror novel centers on a New England house as the setting for the haunting of a little girl. Dr. Gaylord Carew, a character in the tradition of the psychic-doctor-detective, is called in to expel the evil presence in Witch House.

4–217. Wandrei, Donald. **The Eye and the Finger.** Arkham House, 1944.
Donald Wandrei is best known today as the co-founder with August Derleth of Arkham House. This collection consists of his early work in *Weird Tales* and other magazines. There is much science fiction material here, and the collection reflects Wandrei's reading of Lovecraft and Clark Ashton Smith. The best horror tales are "The Eye and the Finger," which concerns a man haunted by a living eyeball, and "The Lives of Alfred Kramer," about a man whose sleepless existence encompasses all the past of humankind. "A Scientist Divides" is the science fiction account of a scientist who formulates a protoplasm that causes him to divide endlessley into smaller versions of himself. This book is also noteworthy for its introduction by Wandrei himself.

4-218. Wandrei, Donald. **Strange Harvest.** Arkham House, 1965.
This second collection of Wandrei's short stories from *Weird Tales* and other magazines includes such noteworthy items as "Spawn of the Sea," "Strange Harvest," and "The Whisperers."

4-219. Wandrei, Donald. **The Web of Easter Island.** Arkham House, 1948.
An interesting novel loosely related in spirit to Lovecraft's Cthulhu Mythos. It follows the exploits of one Graham from England to Easter Island, where ancient, anthropomorphic horror is discovered.

4-220. Wellman, Manly Wade. **After Dark.** Doubleday, 1980.
This Silver John novel centers on an ancient humanoid race, the Shonokins, who are revived.

4-221. Wellman, Manly Wade. **The Old Gods Waken.** Doubleday, 1979.
This is the first full-length novel centering on Wellman's well-known character, the balladeer John, who is called to stop the reawakening of the Voths, Old World Druids who attempt to evoke once again the spirits of Wolter Mountain. This novel signals Wellman's comeback.

*4-222. Wellman, Manly Wade. **Who Fears the Devil?** Arkham House, 1963; Star, 1975.
A collection of 11 tales that purport to be the experiences of a North Carolina mountain traveler named John. Each tale of the supernatural is written in John's folksy manner, and all the tales stand as fine essays in the strange and uncanny. Most noteworthy are "O Ugly Bird," "One Other," "Vandy, Vandy," and "Nine Yards of Other Cloth."

*4-223. Wellman, Manly Wade. **Worse Things Waiting.** Carcosa, 1973.
An excellent collection of Wellman's weird fiction from the pages of *Weird Tales, Unknown,* and *Strange Stories,* including two stories of Silver John in addition to such tales as "The Terrible Parchment," a story of the Necronomicon, and "The Undead Soldier," a terrifying tale published here in its original version. Also of note are "Come into My Parlor," "The Devil Is Not Mocked," and "School for the Unspeakable."

*4-224. Wheatley, Dennis (U.K.). **The Devil Rides Out.** Hutchinson, 1934; Ballantine, 1972.
This is justly Dennis Wheatley's most widely read occult novel. It concerns the struggle of occult investigator Duc de Richlieu against the forces released by the satanist Mocata. Wheatley steeped himself in occult lore before writing this, the first and most successful of his occult novels. According to Glen St. John Barclay, the novel "is totally successful as a painless introduction to the occult sciences." It is thus filled with a wealth of occult detail, is fast-paced and well-plotted with shocking and terrifying events as de Richlieu brings Mocata to his doom. A superb film version of this novel has been made by noted horror film director Terence Fisher.

4–225. Wheatley, Dennis (U.K.). **Gateway to Hell.** Hutchinson, 1970; Ballantine, 1973.
Another of Wheatley's black-magic novels featuring Duc de Richlieu, this centers on the disappearance of Rex van Ryn, Richlieu's aid, who has been accused of embezzling funds from a Buenos Aires bank and is suspected of murder. Richlieu comes to the rescue as the mystery leads to a mysterious place in the Bolivian Andes, where he discovers a satanist plot calculated to plunge the world into a race war.

4–226. Wheatley, Dennis (U.K.). **The Haunting of Toby Jugg.** Hutchinson, 1948.
Glen St. John Barclay writes of this novel: "Dennis Wheatley's literary talents and occult perceptions reached their highest expression in *The Haunting of Toby Jugg,* which is in every way his best story, and is certainly comparable with *Dracula,* in terms of its success both as an exercise in literary technique and as a study in the occult." The plot involves Albert Abel Jugg, who is incapacitated by a war injury. He is continually haunted by an evil manifestation during his convalescence, and as his family betrays him, his fortune falls into their hands to be used in the service of Satan.

4–227. Wheatley, Dennis (U.K.). **The Satanist.** Hutchinson, 1960; Ballantine, 1972.
This novel is the story of Barney Sullivan, who indulges in satanic rites in order to penetrate a group of satanists. He is actually a secret agent who attempts to penetrate the cult after the horrifying death of one of his colleagues.

4–228. Wheatley, Dennis (U.K.). **To the Devil—a Daughter.** Hutchinson, 1953; Ballantine, 1972.
This, one of Wheatley's better occult novels, has been successfully filmed with Christopher Lee as Canon Copely-Syle, who goes "to the blue skies and gay life" of the south of France "to achieve his life's ambition—the transfer of a virgin's soul, by ceremonial sacrifice" to the birth of the Devil on earth.

4–229. Whitehead, Henry S. **Jumbee, and Other Uncanny Tales.** Arkham House, 1944; Neville Spearman, 1974.
Whitehead was a minister in the Episcopal Church and archdeacon of the Virgin Islands in the West Indies from 1921 to 1929. There, he learned much about native superstitions, particularly voodoo, and this knowledge is reflected in nearly all the stories of this volume. In addition to the fine title story, other tales of note are "The Shadows," "Sweet Grass," "The Tree-Man," and "Hill Drums."

*4–230. Whitehead, Henry S. **West India Lights.** Arkham House, 1946.
This second collection by Whitehead contains 17 stories that are matchless for their authenticity. Whitehead brings firsthand knowledge of occult phe-

nomena to his stories, as in his earlier collection *Jumbee* [4–229]. "Black Terror" and the title story are highly effective pieces set in the West Indies. "The Trap" is perhaps the most outstanding work in the volume. It centers on a fourth-dimensional mirror in which a young student becomes trapped.

4–231. Williamson, Jack. **Darker Than You Think.** Fantasy Press, 1948; Sphere, 1976.
This novel centers on Will Barbee, who falls in love with beautiful April Bell, whose occult powers cause him to turn into a wolf.

4–232. Wilson, Colin (U.K.). **The Mind Parasites.** Arkham House, 1967.
A science fiction horror novel, Lovecraftian in theme, about Professor Gilbert Austin and his conflict with the Tsathogguans, invisible mind parasites that menace the most brilliant people of the world.

4–233. Yarbro, Chelsea Quinn. **Blood Games.** St. Martin, 1979; Signet, 1980.
Chelsea Quinn Yarbro has written three historical vampire novels comparable to the work of Les Daniels [4–83, 4–84]. This novel, the third in the trilogy that began with *Hotel Transylvania* [4–234], centers on the vampire hero St. Germain during the period of Rome under Nero.

4–234. Yarbro, Chelsea Quinn. **Hotel Transylvania.** St. Martin, 1978; Signet, 1979.
This is the first novel in Yarbro's trilogy, which deals with his vampire hero St. Germain and his love for Madelaine De Montalia. The plot is set in Paris in 1744.

4–235. Yarbro, Chelsea Quinn. **The Palace.** St. Martin, 1978; Signet, 1979.
Another historical horror novel centering on the life and loves of the vampire St. Germain, set in fifteenth-century Florence.

Anthologies

*4–236. Aickman, Robert, ed. (U.K.). **The Fontana Book of Great Ghost Stories.** Fontana, 1964.
"The Travelling Grave," by L. P. Hartley; "The Ghost Ship," by Richard Middleton; "Squire Toby's Will," by Sheridan Le Fanu; "The Voice in the Night," by William Hope Hodgson; "Three Miles Up," by Elizabeth Jane Howard; "The Rocking-Horse Winner," by D. H. Lawrence; "The Wendigo," by Algernon Blackwood; "The Crown Derby Plate," by Marjorie Bowen; "The Trains," by Robert Aickman; "The Old Nurse's Story," by Mrs. Gaskell; "Seaton's Aunt," by Walter De La Mare.

*4-237. Aickman, Robert, ed. (U.K.). **The Second Fontana Book of Great Ghost Stories.** Fontana, 1966.

"Playing with Fire," by Arthur Conan Doyle; "Man-Size in Marble," by Edith Nesbit; "How Love Came to Professor Guildea," by Robert Hichens; "The Demon Lover," by Elizabeth Bowen; "A. V. Laider," by Sir Max Beerbohm; "The Facts in the Case of M. Valdemar," by Edgar Allan Poe; "Our Distant Cousins," by Lord Dunsany; "The Inner Room," by Robert Aickman; "Thurnley Abbey," by Perceval Landon; "Nightmare Jack," by John Metcalfe; "The Damned Thing," by Ambrose Bierce; "Afterward," by Edith Wharton.

*4-238. Aickman, Robert, ed. (U.K.). **The Third Fontana Book of Great Ghost Stories.** Fontana, 1966.

"Negotium Perambulans," by E. F. Benson; "The End of the Flight," by W. Somerset Maugham; "The Beckoning Fair One," by Oliver Onions; "The Dream," by A. J. Alan; "The Stranger," by Hugh MacDiarmid; "The Case of Mr. Lucraft," by Sir Walter Besant and James Rice; "The Seventh Man," by Sir Arthur Quiller-Couch; "No Ships Pass," by Lady Eleanor Smith; "The Man Who Came Back," by William Gerhardi; "The Visiting Star," by Robert Aickman.

*4-239. Aickman, Robert, ed. (U.K.). **The Fourth Fontana Book of Great Ghost Stories.** Fontana, 1967.

"The Accident," by Ann Bridge; "Not on the Passenger-List," by Barry Pain; "The Sphinx without a Secret," by Oscar Wilde; "When I Was Dead," by Vincent O'Sullivan; "The Queen of Spades," by Alexander Pushkin; "Pargiton and Harby," by Desmond MacCarthy; "The Snow," by Hugh Walpole; "Carlton's Father," by Eric Ambrose; "A School Story," by M. R. James; "The Wolves of Cernogratz," by Saki; "Mad Monkton," by William Wilkie Collins.

*4-240. Aickman, Robert, ed. (U.K.). **The Fifth Fontana Book of Great Ghost Stories.** Fontana, 1969.

"The Firmin Child," by Richard Blum; "Lord Mount Prospect," by John Betjeman; "The Library Window," by Mrs. Oliphant; "The Dancing Partner," by Jerome K. Jerome; "The Swords," by Robert Aickman; "The Mysterious Stranger," Anonymous; "A Question of Time," by Elizabeth Walter; "Venus," by Maurice Baring; "Jerry Bundler," by W. W. Jacobs; "The Great Return," by Arthur Machen.

*4-241. Aickman, Robert, ed. (U.K.). **The Sixth Fontana Book of Great Ghost Stories.** Fontana, 1970.

"Clarimonde," by Theophile Gautier; "The Grey Ones," by J. B. Priestley; "The Door in the Wall," by H. G. Wells; "Priscilla and Emily Lofft," by George Moore; "Soworth Place," by Russell Kirk; "Where Their Fire Is Not

Quenched," by May Sinclair; "Oke of Okehurst," by Vernon Lee; "The Lips," by Henry S. Whitehead.

*4-242. Aickman, Robert, ed. (U.K.). **The Eighth Fontana Book of Great Ghost Stories.** Fontana, 1972.
"The Haunted Haven," by A. E. Ellis; "The Red Lodge," by H. R. Wakefield; "Midnight Express," by Alfred Noyes; "Meeting Mr. Millar," by Robert Aickman; "The Gorgon's Head," by Gertrude Bacon; "The Tree," by Joyce Marsh; "The Haunted and the Haunters," by Lord Lytton; "Bezhin Lea," by Ivan Turgenev; "The Last Seance," by Agatha Christie.

4-243. Ashley, Mike, ed. (U.K.) **Weird Legacies.** Star, 1977.
"Skulls in the Stars," by Robert E. Howard; "The Three Marked Pennies," by Mary Elizabeth Counselman; "He That Hath Wings," by Edmond Hamilton; "The Distortion Out of Space," by Francis Flagg; "The Utmost Abomination," by Clark Ashton Smith and Lin Carter; "External Rediffusion," by Eric Frank Russell and Leslie J. Johnson; "The Ducker," by Ray Bradbury; "The Black Kiss," by Robert Bloch and Henry Kuttner; "The Survivor," by H. P. Lovecraft and August Derleth.

*4-244. Asquith, Cynthia, ed. (U.K.). **The Ghost Book.** Hutchinson, 1926. Pan, 1970.
"The Villa Desiree," by May Sinclair; "Chemical," by Algernon Blackwood; "The Duenna," by Mrs. Belloc Lowndes; "A Visitor from Down Under," by L. P. Hartley; "The Lost Tragedy," by Denis Mackail; "Spinsters' Rest," by Clemence Dane; "Mrs. Lunt," by Hugh Walpole; "Munitions of War," by Arthur Machen; "The Rocking-Horse Winner," by D. H. Lawrence; "A Recluse," by Walter De La Mare; "The Corner Shop," by C. L. Ray; "Two Trifles," by Oliver Onions; "Twelve O'Clock," by Charles Whibley; "The Amorous Ghost," by Enid Bagnold; "Mr. Tallent's Ghost," by Mary Webb; "Pargiton and Harby," by Desmond MacCarthy.

*4-245. Asquith, Cynthia, ed. (U.K.). **The Second Ghost Book.** James Barrie, 1952; Pan, 1956.
"Captain Dalgety Returns," by Laurence Whistler; "Christmas Meeting," by Rosemary Timperley; "Danse Macabre," by L. A. G. Strong; "The Memoirs of a Ghost," by G. W. Stonier; "The Bewilderment of Snake McKoy," by Nancy Spain; "A Story of Don Juan," by V. S. Pritchett; "The Guardian," by Walter De La Mare; "Whitewash," by Rose Macaulay; "The Chelsea Cat," by C. H. B. Kitchin; "W. S.," by L. P. Hartley; "The Amethyst Cross," by Mary Fitt; "Bombers' Night," by Evelyn Fabyan; "Spooner," by Eleanor Farjeon; "Autumn Cricket," by Lord Dunsany; "The Restless Rest-house," by Jonathan Curling; "Back to the Beginning," by John Connell; "Possession on Completion," by Collin Brooks; "Hand in Glove," by Elizabeth Bowen; "The Lass with the Delicate Air," by Eileen Bigland; "One Grave Too Few," by Cynthia Asquith.

The Modern Masters 349

*4–246. Asquith, Cynthia, ed. (U.K.). **The Third Ghost Book.** James Barrie, 1955; Pan, 1957.

"The Telephone," by Mary Treadgold; "The Claimant," by Elizabeth Bowen; "Napoleon's Hat," by Evelyn Fabyan; "The Bull," by Rachel Hartfield; "The House That Wouldn't Keep Still," by L. A. G. Strong; "The Doctor," by Mary Fitt; "On No Account, My Love," by Elizabeth Jenkins; "The Ghost of the Valley," by Lord Dunsany; "The Day of the Funeral," by Margaret Lane; "Take Your Partners," by Ronald Blythe; "Someone in the Lift," by L. P. Hartley; "Ringing the Changes," by Robert Aickman; "The Tower," by Marghanita Laski.

4–247. The Avon Ghost Reader. Avon, 1946.

"The Dunwich Horror," by H. P. Lovecraft; "The Panelled Room," by August Derleth; "The Fireplace," by Henry S. Whitehead; "The Haunted Doll's House," by M. R. James; "The Squaw," by Bram Stoker; "Wingless Victory," by H. F. Heard; "Through the Dragon Glass," by A. Merritt; "Naked Lady," by Mindret Lord; "The Curious Case of Benjamin Button," by F. Scott Fitzgerald; "The Bottle Party," by John Collier; "By the Waters of Babylon," by Stephen Vincent Benét; "The Salamander," by William B. Seabrook.

4–248. Bensen, D. R., ed. **The Unknown.** Jove, 1963.

"The Misguided Halo," by Henry Kuttner; "Prescience," by Nelson S. Bond; "Yesterday Was Monday," by Theodore Sturgeon; "The Gnarly Man," by L. Sprague de Camp; "The Blead Shore," by Fritz Leiber; "Trouble with Water," by H. L. Gold; "Double and Redoubled," by Malcolm Jameson; "When It Was Moonlight," by Manly Wade Wellman; "Mr. Jinx," by Robert Arthur; "Snulbug," by Anthony Boucher; "Armageddon," by Fredric Brown.

*4–249. Campbell, Ramsey, ed. (U.K.). **New Tales of the Cthulhu Mythos.** Arkham House, 1980.

"Crouch End," by Stephen King; "The Star Pools," by A. A. Attanasio; "The Second Wish," by Brian Lumley; "Dark Awakening," by Frank Belknap Long; "Shaft Number 247," by Basil Copper; "Black Man with a Horn," by T. E. D. Klein; "The Black Tome of Alsophocus," by H. P. Lovecraft and Martin S. Warnes; "Than Curse the Darkness," by David Drake; "The Faces at Pine Dunes," by Ramsey Campbell.

*4–250. Campbell, Ramsey, ed. (U.K.). **New Terrors.** Pan, 1980.

"The Stains," by Robert Aickman; "City Fishing," by Steve Rasnic; "Sun City," by Lisa Tuttle; "Yare," by Manly Wade Wellman; "A Room with a View," by Tanith Lee; "Diminishing Landscape with Indistinct Figures," by Daphne Castell; "Tissue," by Marc Laidlaw; "Without Rhyme or Reason," by Peter Valentine Timlett; "Love Me Tender," by Bob Shaw; "Kevin Malone," by Gene Wolfe; "Time to Laugh," by Joan Aiken; "Chicken Soup," by Kit Reed; "The Pursuer," by James Wade; "Bridal Suite," by Graham Masterton; "The Spot," by Dennis Etchison and Mark Johnson; "The Gingerbread House," by Cherry Wilder; "Watchers at the Straight Gate," by Russell Kirk; "220 Swift," by Karl Edward Wagner: "The Fit," by Ramsey Campbell.

*4–251. Campbell, Ramsey, ed. (U.K.). **New Terrors Two.** Pan, 1980.
"The Miraculous Cairn," by Christopher Priest; "The Man Whose Eyes Beheld the Glory," by John Brunner; "The Rubber Room," by Robert Bloch; "Drama in Five Acts," by Giles Gordon; "The Initiation," by Jack Sullivan; "Lucille Would Have Known," by John Burke; "Teething Troubles," by Rosalind Ashe; "The Funny Face Murders," by R. A. Lafferty; "Femme Fatale," by Marianne Leconte; "Big Wheels," by Stephen King; "Richie by the Sea," by Greg Bear; "Can You Still See Me?" by Margaret Dickson; "A Song at the Party," by Dorothy K. Haynes; "One Way Out," by Felice Picano; "The Ice Monkey," by M. John Harrison; "Symbiote," by andrew j. offutt; "Across the Water to Skye," by Charles L. Grant; "The Dark," by Kathleen Resch.

*4–252. Davis, Richard, ed. (U.K.). **The Year's Best Horror Stories: I.** DAW, 1972.
"Double Whammy," by Robert Bloch; "The Sister City," by Brian Lumley; "When Morning Comes," by Elizabeth Fancett; "Prey," by Richard Matheson; "Winter," by Kit Reed; "Lucifer," by E. C. Tubb; "I Wonder What He Wanted," by Eddy C. Bertin; "Problem Child," by Peter Oldale; "The Scar," by Ramsey Campbell; "Warp," by Ralph Norton; "The Hate," by Terri E. Pinckard; "A Quiet Game," by Celia Fremlin; "After Nightfall," by David Riley; "Death's Door," by Robert McNear.

*4–253. Davis, Richard, ed. (U.K.). **The Year's Best Horror Stories: II.** DAW, 1974.
"David's Worm," by Brian Lumley; "The Price of a Demon," by Gary Brandner; "The Knocker at the Portico," by Basil Copper; "The Animal Fair," by Robert Bloch; "Napier Court," by J. Ramsey Campbell; "Haunts of the Very Rich," by T. K. Brown III; "The Long-Term Residents," by Kit Pedler; "Like Two White Spiders," by Eddy C. Bertin; "The Old Horns," by J. Ramsey Campbell; "Haggopian," by Brian Lumley; "The Events at Poroth Farm," by T. E. D. Klein.

*4–254. Davis, Richard, ed. (U.K.). **The Year's Best Horror Stories: III.** DAW, 1975.
"The Whimper of Whipped Dogs," by Harlan Ellison; "The Man in the Underpass," by J. Ramsey Campbell; "S. F.," by T. E. D. Klein; "Uncle Vlad," by Clive Sinclair; "Judas Story," by Brian M. Stableford; "The House of Cthulhu," by Brian Lumley; "Satanesque," by Allan Weiss; "Burger Creature," by Steve Chapman; "Wake Up Dead," by Tim Stout; "For-

get-Me-Not," by Bernard Taylor; "Halloween Story," by Gregory Fitz Gerald; "Big, Wide, Wonderful World," by Charles E. Fritch; "The Taste of Your Love," by Eddy C. Bertin.

*4–255. Derleth, August, ed. **Dark Mind, Dark Heart.** Arkham House, 1962.
"Under the Horns," by Robert Bloch; "Come Back, Uncle Ben!" by Joseph Payne Brennan; "The Church in High Street," by Ramsey Campbell; "Hargrave's Fore-Edge Book," by Mary Elizabeth Counselman; "Miss Esperson," by Stephen Grendon; "The Habitants of Middle Islet," by William Hope Hodgson; "The Grey God Passes," by Robert E. Howard; "The Aquarium," by Carl Jacobi; "The Man Who Wanted to Be in the Movies," by John Jakes; "In Memoriam," by David H. Keller; "Witches' Hollow," by H. P. Lovecraft; "The Ideal Type," by Frank Mace; "The Firing-Chamber," by John Metcalfe; "The Green Vase," by Dennis Roidt; "Xelucha," by M. P. Shiel; "The Animals in the Case," by H. Russell Wakefield; "Caer Sidhi," by George Wetzel.

4–256. Derleth, August, ed. **Dark Things.** Arkham House, 1971.
This collection of Derleth's tales includes: "The Funny Farm," by Robert Bloch; "The Eyes of Mme. Dupree," by P. H. Booth; "The Peril That Lurks Among Ruins," by Joseph Payne Brennan; "Napier Court," by Ramsey Campbell; "The Dweller in the Tomb," by Lin Carter; "Shaggai," by Lin Carter; "The House by the Tarn," by Basil Copper; "The Knocker at the Portico," by Basil Copper; "Lord of the Depths," by David Drake; "Omega," by Alice R. Hill; "The House in the Oaks," by Robert E. Howard; "The Singleton Barrier," by Carl Jacobi; "The Case of the Double Husband," by Margery Lawrence; "Innsmouth Clay," by H. P. Lovecraft; "Rising with Surtsey," by Brian Lumley; "The Deep-Sea Conch," by Brian Lumley; "Company in the Orchard," by Frances May; "Beryondaril," by John Metcalfe; "The Manterfield Inheritance," by Charles Partington; "The Storm King," by Emil Petaja; "The Elevator," by James Wade; "Appointment with Fire," by H. Russell Wakefield; "The Rings of the Papaloh," by Donald J. Walsh, Jr.; and "Requiem for Earth," by Donald Wandrei.

*4–257. Derleth, August, ed. **The Night Side.** Rinehart, 1947.
"The Colour Out of Space," by H. P. Lovecraft; "The First Sheaf," by H. Russell Wakefield; "The Moon-Caller," by MacKinlay Kantor; "The Extra Passenger," by Stephen Grendon; "Bethmoora," by Lord Dunsany; "The Smoking Leg," by John Metcalfe; "The Exalted Omega," by Arthur Machen; "Joshua," by H. Creighton Buck; "Enoch," by Robert Bloch; "Cheese," by A. E. Coppard; "Mr. Minchin's Midsummer," by Margery Lawrence; "Mimsy Were the Borogoves," by Henry Kuttner; "The Eerie

Mr. Murphy," by Howard Wandrei; "The Smiling People," by Ray Bradbury; "The Face in the Mirror," by Denys Val Baker; "Professor Pfaff's Last Recital," by Alan Nelson: "Seaton's Aunt," by Walter De La Mare; "The Mask of Medusa," by Nelson Bond; "One Head Well Done," by John D. Swain; "Sammy Calls a Noobus," by Henry A. Norton; "The Night Wire," by H. F. Arnold; "The Three Marked Pennies," by Mary Elizabeth Counselman; "Nightmare," by Marjorie Bowen.

4-258. Derleth, August, ed. **Night's Yawning Peal.** Arkham House & Pellegrini & Cudahy, 1952; Signet, 1974.
"Mr. George," by Stephen Grendon; "The Sign," by Lord Dunsany; "The Loved Dead," by C. M. Eddy, Jr.; "The La Prello Paper," by Carl Jacobi; "The Gorge of the Churels," by H. Russell Wakefield; "Dhoh," by Manly Wade Wellman; "The Churchyard Yew," by J. Sheridan LeFanu; "Technical Slip," by John Beynon Harris; "The Man Who Collected Poe," by Robert Bloch; "Hector," by Michael West; "Roman Remains," by Algernon Blackwood; "A Damsel with a Dulcimer," by Malcolm Ferguson; "The Suppressed Edition," by Richard Curle; "The Lonesome Place," by August Derleth.

4-259. Derleth, August, ed. **Over the Edge.** Gollancz, 1967; Arrow, 1976.
"The Crew of the Lansing," by William Hope Hodgson; "The Last Meeting of Two Old Friends," by H. Russell Wakefield; "The Shadow in the Attic," by H. P. Lovecraft; "The Renegade," by John Metcalfe; "Told in the Desert," by Clark Ashton Smith; "When the Rains Came," by Frank Belknap Long; "The Blue Flame of Vengeance," by Robert E. Howard; "Crabgrass," by Jesse Stuart; "Kinkaid's Car," by Carl Jacobi; "The Patchwork Quilt," by August Derleth; "The Black Gondolier," by Fritz Leiber; "The Old Lady's Room," by J. Vernon Shea; "The North Knoll," by Joseph Payne Brennan; "The Huaco of Senor Perez," by Mary Elizabeth Counselman; "Mr. Alucard," by David A. Johnstone; "Casting the Stone," by John Pocsik; "Aneanochian," by Michael Bailey; "The Stone on the Island," by J. Ramsey Campbell.

*4-260. Derleth, August, ed. **Sleep No More.** Farrar & Rinehart, 1944.
"Count Magnus," by M. R. James; "Cassius," by Henry S. Whitehead; "The Occupant of the Room," by Algernon Blackwood; "The Return of the Sorcerer," by Clark Ashton Smith; "Johnson Looked Back," by Thomas Burke; "The Hand of the O'Mecca," by Howard Wandrei; "He Cometh and He Passeth By," by H. R. Wakefield; "Thus I Refute Beelzy," by John Collier; "The Mannikin," by Robert Bloch; "Two Black Bottles," by Wilfred Blanch Talman; "The House of Sounds," by M. P. Shiel; "The Cane," by Carl Jacobi; "The Horror in the Burying Ground," by Hazel Heald; "The Kennel," by Maurice Level; "The Yellow Sign," by Robert W. Chambers; "The Black Stone," by Robert E. Howard; "Midnight Express," by Alfred

Noyes; "A Gentleman from Prague," by Stephen Grendon; "The Black Druid," by Frank Belknap Long; "The Rats in the Walls," by H. P. Lovecraft.

*4–261. Derleth, August, ed. **The Sleeping and the Dead.** Pellegrini & Cudahy, 1947.
"A View from a Hill," by M. R. James; "Glory Hand," by August Derleth; "The Lady Maid's Bell," by Edith Wharton; "The Shadows," by Henry S. Whitehead; "Out of the Eons," by Hazel Heald; "The Jar," by Ray Bradbury; "The Bully of Chapelizod," by J. Sheridan Le Fanu; "Over the River," by P. Schuyler Miller; "Carnaby's Fish," by Carl Jacobi; "The Painted Mirror," by Donald Wandrei; "The Double Shadow," by Clark Ashton Smith; "The Ocean Leech," by Frank Belknap Long; "Anima," by Edward Lucas White; "Farewell Performance," by H. Russell Wakefield; "One Way to Mars," by Robert Bloch; "Out of the Picture," by Arthur Machen; "The Canal," by Everil Worrell; "The Postman of Otford," by Lord Dunsany; "Deaf, Dumb, and Blind," by C. M. Eddy, Jr.; "Spider-Bite," by Robert S. Carr; "Brenner's Boy," by John Metcalfe; "Mr. Lupescu," by Anthony Boucher; "Masquerade," by Henry Kuttner; "Seventh Sister," by Mary Elizabeth Counselman; "In Amundsen's Tent," by John Martin Leahy; "Man in a Hurry," by Alan Nelson; "The Last Pin," by Howard Wandrei; "The Doll," by Algernon Blackwood; "The Tool," by William F. Harvey; "The Dreams in the Witch-House," by H. P. Lovecraft.

*4–262. Derleth, August, ed. **Tales of the Cthulhu Mythos.** Arkham House, 1969.
"The Call of Cthulhu," by H. P. Lovecraft; "The Return of the Sorceror," by Clark Ashton Smith; "Ubbo—Sathla," by Clark Ashton Smith; "The Black Stone," by Robert E. Howard; "The Hounds of Tindalos," by Frank Belknap Long; "The Space-Eaters," by Frank Belknap Long; "The Dwellers in Darkness," by August Derleth; "Beyond the Threshold," by August Derleth; "The Shambler from the Stars," by Robert Bloch; "The Haunter of the Dark," by H. P. Lovecraft; "The Shadow from the Steeple," by Robert Bloch; "Notebook Found in a Deserted House," by Robert Bloch; "The Salem Horror," by Henry Kuttner; "The Haunter of the Graveyard," by J. Vernon Shea; "Cold Print," by Ramsey Campbell; "The Sister City," by Brian Lumley; "Cement Surroundings," by Brian Lumley; "The Deep Ones," by James Wade; "The Return of the Lloigor," by Colin Wilson.

4–263. Derleth, August, ed. **Travellers by Night.** Arkham House, 1967.
"The Cicerones," by Robert Aickman; "Episode on Cain Street," by Joseph Payne Brennan; "The Cellars," by J. Ramsey Campbell; "The Man Who Rode the Trains," by Paul A. Carter; "A Handful of Silver," by Mary Elizabeth Counselman; "Denkirch," by David Drake; "The Wild Man of the Sea," by William Hope Hodgson; "The Unpleasantness at Carver House,"

by Carl Jacobi; "The Terror of Anerley House School," by Margery Lawrence; "The Horror from the Middle Span," by H. P. Lovecraft; "Not There," by John Metcalfe; "Family Tree," by Frank D. Thayer, Jr.; "Death of a Bumblebee," by H. Russell Wakefield; "The Crater," by Donald Wandrei.

4-264. Derleth, August, ed. **When Evil Wakes.** Souvenir Press, 1963. Sphere, 1977.

"The Eye and the Finger," by Donald Wandrei; "The Feasting Dead," by John Metcalfe; "Death Waters," by Frank Belknap Long; "An Invitation to the Hunt," by George Hitchcock; "The Tsanta in the Parlour," by Stephen Grendon; "Moonlight-Starlight," by Virginia Layefsky; "The Kite," by Carl Jacobi; "Sweets to the Sweet," by Robert Bloch; "A Thin Gentleman with Gloves," by Simon West; "The Horror at Red Hook," by H. P. Lovecraft; "The Triumph of Death," by H. Russell Wakefield; "The Lips," by Henry S. Whitehead; "A Piece of Linoleum," by David H. Keller; "The Seed from the Sepulchre," by Clark Ashton Smith; "Canavan's Back Yard," by Joseph Payne Brennan; "The Shuttered Room," by H. P. Lovecraft and August Derleth.

*4-265. Derleth, August, ed. **Who Knocks?** Rinehart, 1946.

"The Shadows on the Wall," by Mary E. Wilkins-Freeman; "Running Wolf," by Algernon Blackwood; "Old Martin," by A. E. Coppard; "Alannah," by Stephen Grendon; "The Shunned House," by H. P. Lovecraft; "The Lake," by Ray Bradbury; "The Seventeenth Hole at Duncaster," by H. R. Wakefield; "The Ankardyne Pew," by W. F. Harvey; "It," by Theodore Sturgeon; "The Phantom Farmhouse," by Seabury Quinn; "Squire Toby's Will," by J. Sheridan Le Fanu; "Negotium Perambulans," by E. F. Benson; "The Intercessor," by May Sinclair; "The Dear Departed," by Alice-Mary Schnirring; "The House of the Nightmare," by Edward Lucas White; "A Reversion to Type," by Edgar Lloyd Hampton; "The Follower," by Cynthia Asquith; "The Ravel Pavane," by Henry S. Whitehead; "The Ghosts of Steamboat Coulee," by Arthur J. Burks; "The Woman at Seven Brothers," by Wilbur Daniel Steele.

*4-266. Grant, Charles L., ed. **Nightmares.** Playboy, 1979.

"Suffer the Little Children," by Stephen King; "Peekaboo," by Bill Pronzini; "Daughter of the Golden West," by Dennis Etchison; "The Duppy Tree," by Steven Edward McDonald; "Naples," by Avram Davidson; "Seat Partner," by Chelsea Quinn Yarbro; "Camps," by Jack Dann; "The Anchoress," by Beverly Evans; "Transfer," by Barry N. Malzberg; "Unknown Drives," by Richard Christian Matheson; "The Night of the Piasa," by George W. Proctor and J. C. Green; "The Runaway Lovers," by Ray Russell; "Fisherman's Log," by Peter D. Pautz; "I Can't Help Saying Goodbye," by Ann Mackenzie; "Midnight Hobo," by Ramsey Campbell; "Snakes and

Snails," by Jack C. Haldeman II; "Mass without Voices," by Arthur L. Samuels; "He Kilt It with a Stick," by William F. Nolan; "The Ghouls," by R. Chetwynd-Hayes.

*4-267. Grant, Charles L., ed. **Shadows.** Doubleday, 1978.

"Naples," by Avram Davidson; "The Little Voice," by Ramsey Campbell; "Butcher's Thumb," by William Jon Watkins; "Where All the Songs Are Sad," by Thomas F. Monteleone; "Splinters," by R. A. Rafferty; "Picture," by Robert Bloch; "The Nighthawk," by Dennis Etchison; "Dead Letters," by Ramsey Campbell; "A Certain Slant of Light," by Raylyn Moore; "Deathlove," by Bill Pronzini; "Mory," by Michael Bishop; "Where the Spirits Gat Them Home," by John Crowley; "Nona," by Stephen King.

*4-268. Grant, Charles L., ed. **Shadows 2.** Doubleday, 1979.

"Saturday's Shadow," by William F. Nolan; "Night Visions," by Jack Dann; "The Spring," by Manly Wade Wellman; "Valentine," by Janet Fox; "Mackintosh Willy," by Ramsey Campbell; "Dragon Sunday," by Ruth Berman; "The White King's Dream," by Elizabeth A. Lynn; "The Chair," by Alan Dean Foster and Jane Cozart; "Clocks," by Barry N. Malzberg and Bill Pronzini; "Holly, Don't Tell," by Juleen Brantingham; "The Old Man's Will," by Lee Wells; "The Closing Off of Old Doors," by Peter D. Pautz; "Dead End," by Richard Christian Matheson; "Seasons of Belief," by Michael Bishop; "Petey," by T. E. D. Klein.

*4-269. Grant, Charles L., ed. **Shadows 3.** Doubleday, 1980.

"The Brown Recluse," by Davis Grubb; "To See You With, My Dear," by Bruce Francis; "Avenging Angel," by Ray Russell; "The Ghost Who Limped," by R. Chetwynd-Hayes; "Janey's Smile," by Juleen Brantingham; "Opening a Vein," by Barry N. Malzberg and Bill Pronzini; "The Partnership," by William F. Nolan; "Wish Hound," by Pat Murphy; "Ant," by Peter D. Pautz; "Tell Mommy What Happened," by Alan Ryan; "At the Bureau," by Steve Rasnic Tem; "Cabin 33," by Chelsea Quinn Yarbro.

*4-270. Haining, Peter, ed. (U.K.). **The Black Magic Omnibus.** Taplinger, 1976.

This anthology is divided into two sections: Part one reprints portions of actual black-magic texts. Part two contains fiction as follows: "An Appointment for Candlemass," by Robert Graves; "Double Hex," by Samuel M. Clawson; "In Letters of Fire," by Gaston Leroux; "Vampire's Prey," by Hanns Heinz Ewers; "Invoker of the Beast," by Feodor Sologub; "Night of the Leopard," by William Sambrot; "The Circular Ruins," by Jorge Luis Borges; "The Wedding Guests," by W. B. Seabrook; "The Power of Every Root," by Avram Davidson; "By Appointment Only," by Richard Matheson; "The Witch Doctor of Rosy Ridge," by MacKinlay Kantor; "Writer's Witch," by Joan Fleming; "The Power of the Job," by Larry M. Harris; "Dr. Muncing, Exorcist," by Gordon MacCreagh.

4-271. Haining, Peter, ed. (U.K.). **Deadly Nightshade.** Taplinger, 1978.
"Lost Hearts," by M. R. James; "The Doll's Ghost," by Francis Marion Crawford; "Nurse's Tale," by H. R. Wakefield; "The Attic," by Algernon Blackwood; "The Thing in the Cellar," by David H. Keller; "The Dabblers," by W. F. Harvey; "The Tortoise-Shell Cat," by Greye La Spina; "The Looking-Glass Tree," by Joan Aiken; "The Human Angle," by William Tenn; "Gabriel-Ernest," by Saki; "Sweets to the Sweet," by Robert Bloch; "The Witch of Ramoth," by Mark Van Doren; "Twilight Play," by August Derleth; "Mr. Lupescu," by Anthony Boucher; "Silent Snow, Secret Snow," by Conrad Aiken; "Midnight Express," by Alfred Noyes; "The October Game," by Ray Bradbury.

*4-272. Haining, Peter, ed. (U.K.). **The Lucifer Society: Macabre Tales by Great Modern Writers.** Taplinger, 1972; Signet, 1973.
"Man Overboard," by Sir Winston Churchill; "Timber," by John Galsworthy; "The Angry Street," by G. K. Chesterton; "The Call of Wings," by Agatha Christie; "The Cherries," by Lawrence Durrell; "A Man from Glasgow," by Somerset Maugham; "Earth to Earth," by Robert Graves; "The Grey Ones," by J. B. Priestley; "The Man Who Didn't Ask Why," by C. S. Forester; "All but Empty," by Graham Greene; "Animals or Human Beings," by Angus Wilson; "Something Strange," by Kingsley Amis; "The Post-Mortem Murder," by Sinclair Lewis; "The Dance," by F. Scott Fitzgerald; "A Rose for Emily," by William Faulkner; "The Bronze Door," by Raymond Chandler; "A Man Who Had No Eyes," by MacKinlay Kantor; "The Affair at 7 Rue de M——," by John Steinbeck; "The Snail Watcher," by Patricia Highsmith; "Inferiority Complex," by Evan Hunter; "The Terrible Answer," by Paul Gallico; "Miriam," by Truman Capote; "Exterminator," by William Burroughs; "During the Jurassic," by John Updike.

*4-273. Haining, Peter, ed. (U.K.). **Weird Tales.** Neville Spearman, 1976; Sphere, 1978. Part of contents in a companion volume, *More Weird Tales,* Sphere, 1978.
The original hardcover edition of this book is a facsimile of the original stories as they appeared in *Weird Tales.* The contents are: "The Man Who Returned," by Edmund Hamilton; "Black Hound of Death," by Robert E. Howard; "The Shuttered House," by August Derleth; "Frozen Beauty," by Seabury Quinn; "Haunting Columns," by Robert E. Howard; "Beyond the Wall of Sleep," by H. P. Lovecraft; "The Garden of Adompha," by Clark Ashton Smith; "Cordelia's Song," by Vincent Starrett; "Beyond the Phoenix," by Henry Kuttner; "The Black Monk," by G. G. Pendarves; "The Passing of a God," by Henry S. Whitehead; "They Run Again," by Leah Bodine Drake; "The Eyrie" (readers' letters); "The Valley Was Still," by Manly Wade Wellman; "A Weird Prophecy," by Ken Gary; "Winter Night," by Alice Olsen; "San Francisco," by Caroline Evans, "Heart of Atlantan," by Nictzin Dyalhis; "The Phantom Slayer," by Fritz Leiber; "The

Eyrie" (more readers' letters); "The Beasts of Barsac," by Robert Bloch; "Bang! You're Dead!" by Ray Bradbury; "The Eyrie" (more readers' letters); "Cellmate," by Theodore Stugeon; "The Familiars," by H. P. Lovecraft; "The Pigeon Flyers," by H. P. Lovecraft; "Roman Remains," by Algernon Blackwood; "Displaced Person," by Eric Frank Russell; "To the Chimera," by Clark Ashton Smith; "From the Vasty Deep," by H. Russell Wakefield; "The Shot Tower Ghost," by Mary Elizabeth Counselman; "Take the Z-Train," by Alison V. Harding; "The Little Red Owl," by Margaret St. Clair; "Ooze," by Anthony M. Rud.

4-274. Hammett, Dashiell, ed. **Creeps by Night.** John Day, 1931.
"A Rose for Emily," by William Faulkner; "Green Thoughts," by John Collier; "The Ghost of Alexander Perks, A. B.," by Robert Dean Frisbie; "The House," by André Maurois; "The Kill," by Peter Fleming; "Ten O'Clock," by Philip MacDonald; "The Spider," by Hanns Heinz Ewers; "Breakdown," by L. A. G. Strong; "The Witch's Vengeance," by W. B. Seabrook; "The Rat," by S. Fowler Wright; "Faith, Hope and Charity," by Irvin S. Cobb; "Mr. Arcularis," by Conrad Aiken; "The Music of Erich Zann," by H. P. Lovecraft; "The Strange Case of Mrs. Arkwright," by Harold Dearden; "The King of the Cats," by Stephen Vincent Benét; "The Red Brain," by Donald Wandrei; "The Phantom Bus," by W. Elwyn Backus; "Beyond the Door," by Paul Suter; "Perchance to Dream," by Michael Joyce; "A Visitor from Egypt," by Frank Belknap Long.

4-275. Harre, T. Everett, ed. (U.K.). **Beware after Dark!** Emerson, 1942.
"Negotium Perambulans," by E. F. Benson; "Back There in the Grass," by Gouverneur Morris; "The Mollmeit of the Mountain," by Cynthia Stockley; "Fishhead," by Irvin S. Cobb; "The Fountain of Gold," by Lafcadio Hearn; "The Shadowy Third," by Ellen Glascow; "Lukundoo," by Edward Lucas White; "Rappaccini's Daughter," by Nathaniel Hawthorne; "Lazarus," by Leonid Andreyeff; "The Lame Priest," by S. Carleton; "The Call of Cthulhu," by H. P. Lovecraft; "Novel of the White Powder," by Arthur Machen; "The Devils of Po Sung," by Bassett Morgan; "The Isle of Voices," by Robert Louis Stevenson; "The Sunken Land," by George W. Bayly; "Two Spinsters," by E. Phillips Oppenheim; "The Monster-God of Mamurth," by Edmond Hamilton; "Huguenin's Wife," by M. P. Shiel; "The Coconut Pearl," by Beatrice Grimshaw; "The Quest of the Tropic Bird," by John Fleming Wilson; "The Striding Place," by Gertrude Atherton.

*4-276. Karloff, Boris, ed. **And the Darkness Falls.** World, 1946.
"The Test," by Maurice Level; "John Gladwin Says . . . ," by Oliver Onions; "The Black Pool," by Frederick S. Greene; "The Scoop," by Leonora Gregory; "Femme et Chatte," by Paul Verlaine; "The Hanging of Alfred Wadham," by Edward F. Benson; "The Departure," by Selma Robinson; "The

Adventure of Second Lieutenant Bubnov," by Ivan Turgenev; "In the Wheat," by Maurice Level; "The Madman," by Guy de Maupassant; "The Storm," by McKnight Malmar; "Rizpah," by Alfred Lord Tennyson; "One Who Saw," by Ex-Private X; "My Favorite Murder," by Ambrose Bierce; "The Grove of Ashtaroth," by John Buchan; "The Case of Lady Sannox," by Arthur Conan Doyle; "The Black Godmother," by John Galsworthy; "The Stranger," by Algernon Blackwood; "The Panelled Room," by August Derleth; "The Mask," by Tennyson Jesse; "Richard Cory," by Edwin Arlington Robinson; "The Witness," by Violet Hunt; "The Caged White Werewolf of the Saraban," by William B. Seabrook; "Footsteps," by Eileen Verrinder; "The Island," by L. P. Hartley; "The Red Lodge," by H. R. Wakefield; "The Cyprian Cat," by Dorothy L. Sayers; "An Official Position," by W. Somerset Maugham; "The Garden of Prosperine," by Algernon C. Swinburne; "Little Louise Roque," by Guy de Maupassant; "The Sutor of Selkirk," Anonymous; "The Idol with Hands of Clay," by Sir Frederick Treves; "Another American Tragedy," by John Collier; "The Razor of Pedro Dutel," by Richard M. Hallet; "The Crucifixion of the Outcast," by William B. Yeats; "Ulalume," by Edgar Allan Poe; "Where Their Fire Is Not Quenched," by May Sinclair; "The Ghost," by Richard Hughes; "Jenshih, or the Fox Lady," by Shen Chi-chi; "Three O'Clock," by William Irish; "The Mortal," by Oliver Onions; "The Listeners," by Walter De La Mare; "The Well," by W. W. Jacobs; "The Horrible God," by Thomas Burke; "Mrs. Adis," by Sheila Kaye-Smith; "Telling," by Elizabeth Bowen; "The Death of the Poor," by Charles Baudelaire; "A Maniac," by Maurice Level; "An Illusion in Red and White," by Stephen Crane; "A Modest Proposal," by Dean Jonathan Swift; "The Chaser," by John Collier; "Where the Tides Ebb and Flow," by Lord Dunsany; "My Last Duchess," by Robert Browning; "Out of the Deep," by Walter De La Mare; "Perchance to Dream," by Michael Joyce; "The Empty House," by Maurice Level; "Browdean Farm," by A. M. Burrage; "Breakdown," by L. A. G. Strong; "The Weird of Avoosl Wuthoqquan," by Clark Ashton Smith; "The Angelus," by William Younger; "Song of the Skirt," by Thomas Hood; "The Silver Mask," by Hugh Walpole; "Viy," by Nikolai Gogol; "Death," by Dorothy Richardson; "Prospice," by Robert Browning; "The Woman's Ghost Story," by Algernon Blackwood; "The Brute," by Joseph Conrad; "The Thing on the Doorstep," by H. P. Lovecraft.

*4–277. Lamb, Hugh, ed. (U.K.). **Cold Fear: New Tales of Terror.** Taplinger, 1978.

"In the Bag," by Ramsey Campbell; "The Music in the House," by Eleanor Inglefield; "In the Glow-Zone," by Brian Lumley; "The Papal Magician," by Ken Alden; "Laura," by Robert Aickman; "An Emissary for the Devil," by Robert Haining; "A Little Bit of Egypt," by David Sutton; "Aunty Green," by John Blackburn; "All the Amenities," by Kathleen Murray;

"The Demon in the Stone," by Adrian Cole; "Dinner in a Private Room," by Charles Birkin; "The House in the Forest," by Frederick Cowles; "The Man Who Wouldn't Eat," by Arthur Porges; "The Darkhouse Keeper," by Rosemary Timperley; "After the Queen," by Ramsey Campbell.

*4–278. Lamb, Hugh, ed. (U.K.). **Return from the Grave.** Taplinger, 1977.
"Waxworks," by W. L. George; "Ingredient X," by H. R. Wakefield; "In the Tomb," by Arthur Porges; "Roxana Runs Lunatick," by R. Murray Gilchrist; "The Sistrum," by Alice Perrin; "The Coffin of Lissa," by August Derleth; "The Slype House," by A. C. Benson; "The Watcher," by R. H. Benson; "The Other Woman," by Rosemary Timperley; "Snow Time," by Oswell Blakeston; "The Tower of Moab," by L. A. Lewis; "Blue Eyes," by Maurice Level; "In the Shadows," by Ramsey Campbell; "Some Words with a Mummy," by Edgar Allan Poe; "Dad," by John Blackburn; "Composed of Cobwebs," by Eddy C. Bertin; "Death in the Well," by Frederick Cowles; "The Legion of Evil," by Warden Ledge; "The Wall," by Robert Haining; "At Simmel Acres Farm," by Eleanor Scott.

*4–279. Lamb, Hugh, ed. (U.K.). **The Taste of Fear: Thirteen Eerie Tales of Horror.** Taplinger, 1976.
"Three Shall Meet," by Frederick Cowles; "The Fetch," by David Sutton; "Manfred's Three Wishes," by H. F. W. Tatham; "From the Tideless Sea," by William Hope Hodgson; "Benjamin's Shadow," by Michael Sims; "The Final Trick," by John Blackburn; "The Queen of Beauty," by E. H. Visiak; "The Uttermost Farthing," by A. C. Benson; "Ash," by Ramsey Campbell; "The House of Vengeance," by L. T. C. Rolt; "Late," by Les Freeman; "The Crab-Spider," by Erckmann-Chatrian; "Interim Report," by Roger Parkes.

*4–280. Lamb, Hugh, ed. (U.K.). **The Thrill of Horror.** Taplinger, 1975.
"Only a Dream," by H. Rider Haggard; "The Meerschaum Pipe," by L. A. Lewis; "The Life-Buoy," by A. Erskine Ellis; "The Lady of Rosemount," by Sir T. G. Jackson; "How It Happened," by John Gawsworth; "In the Mirror," by Valery Bryusov; "Calling Miss Marker," by Joy Burnett; "A Night of Horror," by Dick Donovan; "The Shouting," by L. T. C. Rolt; "The Happy Dancers," by Charles Birkin; "The Weed Men," by William Hope Hodgson; "Eyes for the Blind," by Frederick Cowles; "Mr. Ash's Studio," by H. R. Wakefield; "Montage of Death," by Robert Haining; "Pallinghurst Barrow," by Grant Allen; "Randalls Round," by Eleanor Scott; "The Skeleton at the Feast," by E. H. Visiak; "Medusan Madness," by E. H. Visiak; "Out of the Sea," by A. C. Benson; "Witch In-Grain," by R. Murray Gilchrist; "The Tudor Chimney," by A. N. L. Munby; "The Experiment," by M. R. James.

*4–281. Lamb, Hugh, ed. (U.K.). **A Tide of Terror: An Anthology of Rare Horror Stories.** Taplinger, 1973.

"The Red Lodge," by H. R. Wakefield; "His Unconquerable Enemy," by W. C. Morrow; "On the Elevator," by Joseph Payne Brennan; "The Closed Window," by A. C. Benson; "The Step," by E. F. Benson; "Father Brent's Tale," by R. H. Bensen; "Some New Pleasures Prove," by Charles Birkin; "The Dogs of Pemba," by Margery Lawrence; "Full Circle," by Algernon Blackwood; "The Tregannet Book of Hours," by A. N. L. Munby; "The Master of Hollow Grange," by Sax Rohmer; "The Trapdoor," by C. D. Heriot; "The Sign of the Spider," Bertram Mitford; "Some Haunted Houses," by Ambrose Bierce; "The Eyes," by T. O. Beachcroft; "Johnson Looked Back," by Thomas Burke; "The Twelve Apostles," by Eleanor Scott; "Mrs. Lunt," by Sir Hugh Walpole.

*4–282. Lamb, Hugh, ed. (U.K.). **A Wave of Fear.** Allen, 1973; Coronet, 1976.

"The Child," by L. A. Lewis; "Celui-la," by Eleanor Scott; "A Resumed Identity," by Ambrose Bierce; "Huguenin's Wife," by M. P. Shiel; "Blind Man's Bluff," by H. R. Wakefield; "Marjorie's on Starlight," by Charles Birkin; "Hawley Bank Foundry," by L. T. C. Rolt; "Twilight," by Marjorie Bowen; "Basil Netherby," by A. C. Benson; "The Wishing Well," by E. F. Benson; "The Traveller," by R. H. Benson; "Phantom Silhouette," by Joy Burnett; "Terrible Mrs. Greene," by Frederick Cowles; "Clairvoyance," by D. K. Broster; "The Late Occupier," by J. D. Beresford; "The Messenger," by Robert W. Chambers; "A Honeymoon in Hate," by Vivian Meik.

*4–283. McCauley, Kirby, ed. **Dark Forces.** Viking, 1980.

"The Late Shift," by Dennis Etchison; "The Enemy," by Isaac Bashevis Singer; "Dark Angel," by Edward Bryant; "The Crest of Thirty-Six," by Davis Grubb; "Mark Ingestre: The Customer's Tale," by Robert Aickman; "Where the Summer Ends," by Karl Edward Wagner; "The Bingo Master," by Joyce Carol Oates; "Children of the Kingdom," by T. E. D. Klein; "The Detective of Dreams," by Gene Wolfe; "Vengeance Is," by Theodore Sturgeon; "The Brood," by Ramsey Campbell; "The Whistling Well," by Clifford D. Simak; "The Peculiar Demesne," by Russell Kirk; "Where the Stones Grow," by Lisa Tuttle; "The Night before Christmas," by Robert Bloch; "The Stupid Joke," by Edward Gorey; "A Touch of Petulance," by Ray Bradbury; "Lindsay and the Red City Blues," by Joe Haldeman; "A Garden of Blackred Roses," by Charles L. Grant; "Owls Hoot in the Daytime," by Manly Wade Wellman; "Where There's a Will," by Richard Matheson and Richard Christian Matheson; "Traps," by Gahan Wilson; "The Mist," by Stephen King.

*4–284. McCauley, Kirby, ed. **Frights: New Stories of Suspense and Supernatural Terror.** St. Martin, 1976.

"There's a Long, Long Trail A-Winding," by Russell Kirk; "The Whisperer," by Brian Lumley; "Armaja Das," by Joe Haldeman; "The Kitten," by Poul Anderson and Karen Anderson; "Oh Tell Me Will It Freeze Tonight," by R. A. Lafferty; "Dead Call," by William F. Nolan; "The Idiots," by Davis Grubb; "The Companion," by Ramsey Campbell; "Fireflight," by David Drake; "It Only Comes Out at Night," by Dennis Etchison; "Compulsory Games," by Robert Aickman; "Sums," by John Jakes and Richard E. Peck; "The Warm Farewell," by Robert Bloch; "End Game," by Gahan Wilson.

*4–285. Marguiles, Leo, ed. **Weird Tales.** Pyramid, 1964.
"The Man Who Returned," by Edmond Hamilton; "Spider Mansion," by Fritz Leiber; "A Question of Etiquette," by Robert Bloch; "The Sea Witch," by Nictzin Dyalhis; "The Strange High House in the Mist," by H. P. Lovecraft; "The Drifting Snow," by August Derleth; "The Body-Masters," by Frank Belknap Long; "Pigeons from Hell," by Robert E. Howard.

*4–286. Marguiles, Leo, ed. **Worlds of Weird.** Jove, 1965.
"Roads," by Seabury Quinn; "The Sapphire Goddess," by Nictzin Dyalhis; "The Valley of the Worm," by Robert E. Howard; "He That Hath Wings," by Edmond Hamilton; "Mother of Toads," by Clark Ashton Smith; "The Thing in the Cellar," by David H. Keller; "Giants in the Sky," by Frank Belknap Long.

*4–287. Mazzeo, Henry, ed. **Hauntings: Tales of the Supernatural.** Doubleday, 1968.
This volume is noteworthy for its illustrations by Edward Gorey. "The Lonesome Place," by August Derleth; "In the Vault," by H. P. Lovecraft; "The Man Who Collected Poe," by Robert Bloch; "Where Angels Fear," by Manly Wade Wellman; "Lot No. 249," by Arthur Conan Doyle; "The Haunted Dolls' House," by M. R. James; "The Open Door," by Mrs. Olliphant; "Thus I Refute Beelzy," by John Collier; "Levitation," by Joseph Payne Brennan; "The Ghostly Rental," by Henry James; "The Face," by E. F. Benson; "The Whistling Room," by William Hope Hodgson; "The Grey Ones," by J. B. Priestley; "The Stolen Body," by H. G. Wells; "The Red Lodge," by H. Russell Wakefield; "The Visiting Star," by Robert Aickman; "Midnight Express," by Alfred Noyes.

4–288. Page, Gerald W., ed. **Nameless Places.** Arkham House, 1975.
"Glimpses," by A. A. Attanasio; "The Night of the Unicorn," by Thomas Burnett Swann; "The Warlord of Kul Satu," by Brian Ball; "More Things," by G. N. Gabbard; "The Real Road to the Church," by Robert Aickman; "The Gods of Earth," by Gary Myers; "Walls of Yellow Clay," by Robert E. Gilbert; "Businessman's Lament," by Scott Edelstein; "Dark Vintage," by Joseph F. Pumilia; "Simaitha," by David A. English; "In the Land of Angra Mainyu," by Stephen Goldin; "Worldsong," by Gerald W. Page; "What

Dark God?" by Brian Lumley; "The Stuff of Heroes," by Bob Maurus; "Forringer's Fortune," by Joseph Payne Brennan; "Before the Event," by Denys Val Baker; "In 'Ygiroth," by Walter C. DeBill, Jr.; "The Last Hand," by Ramsey Campbell; "Out of the Ages," by Lin Carter; "Awakening," by David Drake; "In the Vale of Pnath," by Lin Carter; "Chameleon Town," by Carl Jacobi; "Botch," by Scott Edelstein; "Black Iron," by David Drake; "Selene," by E. Hoffman Price; "The Christmas Present," by Ramsey Campbell; "Lifeguard," by Arthur Byron Cover.

*4-289. Page, Gerald W., ed. **The Year's Best Horror Stories: IV.** DAW, 1976.
"Forever Stand the Stones," by Joe Pumilia; "And Don't Forget the One Red Rose," by Avram Davidson; "The Christmas Present," by Ramsey Campbell; "A Question of Guilt," by Hal Clement; "The House on Stillcroft Street," by Joseph Payne Brennan; "The Recrudescence of Geoffrey Marvell," by G. N. Gabbard; "Something Had to Be Done," by David Drake; "Cottage Tenant," by Frank Belknap Long; "The Man with the Aura," by R. A. Lafferty; "White Wolf Calling," by C. L. Grant; "Lifeguard," by Arthur Byron Cover; "The Black Captain," by H. Warner Munn; "The Glove," by Fritz Leiber; "No Way Home," by Brian Lumley.

*4-290. Page, Gerald W., ed. **The Year's Best Horror Stories: V.** DAW, 1977.
"The Service," by Jerry Sohl; "Long Hollow Swamp," by Joseph Payne Brennan; "Sing a Last Song of Valdese," by Karl Edward Wagner; "Harold's Blues," by Glen Singer; "The Well," by H. Warner Munn; "A Most Unusual Murder," by Robert Bloch; "Huzdra," by Tanith Lee; "Shatterday," by Harlan Ellison; "Children of the Forest," by David Drake; "The Day It Rained Lizards," by Arthur Byron Cover; "Followers of the Dark Star," by Robert Edmond Alter; "When All the Children Call My Name," by C. L. Grant; "Belsen Express," by Fritz Leiber; "Where the Woodbine Twineth," by Manly Wade Wellman.

*4-291. Page, Gerald W., ed. **The Year's Best Horror Stories: VI.** DAW, 1978.
"At the Bottom of the Garden," by David Campton; "Screaming to Get Out," by Janet Fox; "Undertow," by Karl Edward Wagner; "I Can Hear the Dark," by Dennis Etchison; "Ever the Faith Endures," by Manly Wade Wellman; "The Horse Lord," by Lisa Tuttle; "Winter White," by Tanith Lee; "A Cobweb of Pulsing Veins," by William Scott Home; "Best of Luck," by David Drake; "Children of the Corn," by Steven King; "If Damon Comes," by Charles L. Grant; "Drawing In," by Ramsey Campbell; "Within the Walls of Tyre," by Michael Bishop.

*4-292. Page, Gerald W., ed. **The Year's Best Horror Stories: VII.** DAW, 1979.

"The Pitch," by Dennis Etchison; "The Night of the Tiger," by Stephen King; "Amma," by Charles Saunders; "Chastel," by Manly Wade Wellman; "Sleeping Tiger," by Tanith Lee; "Intimately, with Rain," by Janet Fox; "The Secret," by Jack Vance; "Hear Me Now, My Sweet Abbey Rose," by Charles L. Grant; "Divers Hands," by Darrell Schweitzer; "Heading Home," by Ramsey Campbell; "In the Arcade," by Lisa Tuttle; "Nemesis Place," by David Drake; "Collaborating," by Michael Bishop; "Marriage," by Robert Aickman.

4-293. Parry, Michel, ed. (U.K.). **Great Black Magic Stories.** Taplinger, 1977.

"Potential," by Ramsey Campbell; "The Snake," by Dennis Wheatley; "They Bite," by Anthony Boucher; "The Vixen," by Aleister Crowley; "He Cometh and He Passeth By," by H. R. Wakefield; "The Invoker of the Beast," by Feodor Sologub; "Witch War," by Richard Matheson; "The Ensouled Violin," by Madame Blavatsky; "Nasty," by Frederic Brown; "The New People," by Charles Beaumont; "In the Valley of the Sorceress," by Sax Rohmer; "The Devil's Debt," by James Platt; "The Hand of Glory," by Seabury Quinn.

*4-294. Schiff, Stuart David, ed. **Whispers.** Doubleday, 1977.

"Sticks," by Karl Edward Wagner; "The Barrow Troll," by David Drake; "The Glove," by Fritz Leiber; "The Closer of the Way," by Robert Bloch; "Dark Winner," by William F. Nolan; "Ladies in Waiting," by Hugh B. Cave; "White Moon Rising," by Dennis Etchison; "Graduation," by Richard Christian Matheson; "Mirror, Mirror," by Ray Russell; "The House of Cthulhu," by Brian Lumley; "Antiquities," by John Crowley; "A Weather Report from the Top of the Stairs," by James Sallis and David Lunde; "The Scallion Stone," by Basil A. Smith; "The Inglorious Rise of the Catsmeat Man," by Robin Smyth; "The Pawnshop," by Charles E. Fritch; "Le Miroir," by Robert Aickman; "The Willow Platform," by Joseph Payne Brennan; "The Dawka," by Manly Wade Wellman; "Goat," by David Campton; "The Chimney," by Ramsey Campbell.

*4-295. Schiff, Stuart David, ed. **Whispers II.** Doubleday, 1979.

"Undertow," by Karl Edward Wagner; "Berryhill," by R. A. Lafferty; "The King's Shadow Has No Limits," by Avram Davidson; "Conversation Piece," by Richard Christian Matheson; "The Stormsong Runner," by Jack L. Chalker; "They Will Not Hush," by James Sallis and David Lunde; "Lex Talionis," by Russell Kirk; "Marianne," by Joseph Payne Brennan; "From the Lower Deep," by Hugh B. Cave; "The Fourth Musketeer," by Charles L. Grant; "Ghost of a Chance," by Ray Russell; "The Elcar Special," by Carl Jacobi; "The Box," by Lee Weinstein; "We Have All Been Here Before," by Dennis Etchison; "Archie and the Scylla of Hades Hole," by Ken Wisman; "Trill Coster's Burden," by Manly Wade Wellman; "Conversation Piece," by Ward Moore; "The Bait," by Fritz Leiber; "Above the World," by Ramsey Campbell; "The Red Leer," by David Drake; "At the Bottom of the Garden," by David Campton.

*4–296. Schiff, Stuart David, and Fritz Leiber, eds. **The World Fantasy Awards: Vol. 2.** Doubleday, 1980.
This volume is the second in a series begun by Gahan Wilson commemorating the annual World Fantasy Convention. It contains the following fiction: "The Whimper of Whipped Dogs," by Harlan Ellison; "Jerusalem's Lot," by Stephen King; "The October Game," by Ray Bradbury; "Smoke Ghost," by Fritz Leiber; "Belsen Express," by Fritz Leiber; "The King's Shadow Has No Limits," by Avram Davidson; "The Ghastly Priest Doth Reign," by Manly Wade Wellman; "A Visitor from Egypt," by Frank Belknap Long; "It Only Comes Out at Night," by Dennis Etchison; "The Barrow Troll," by David Drake; "Two Suns Setting," by Karl Edward Wagner; "The Companion," by Ramsey Campbell; "There's a Long, Long Trail A-Winding," by Russell Kirk. An introductory essay by Fritz Leiber is noteworthy.

*4–297. Thompson, Christine Campbell, ed. (U.K.). **At Dead of Night.** Selwyn & Blount, 1931.
"Creeping Fingers," by Loretta C. Burrough; "The Owls," by F. A. M. Webster; "Four Doomed Men," by Geoffrey Vace; "The Curse of the House of Phipps," by Seabury Quinn; "His Beautiful Hands," by Oscar Cook; "The Seeds of Death," by David H. Keller; "Passing of a God," by Henry S. Whitehead; "Prince Borgia's Mass," by August Derleth; "Pussy," by Flavia Richardson; "The Wonderful Tune," by J. K. Kerruish; "The Scourge of Mektoub," by Paul Ernst; "Rats," by Michael Annesley; "The Idol of Death," by Richard Jackson and A. Edward Chapman; "The Grey Killer," by Everil Worrell; "Guardians of the Guavas," by Charles Henry Mackintosh.

*4–298. Thompson, Christine Campbell, ed. (U.K.). **By Daylight Only.** Selwyn & Blount, 1929.
"The Chain," by H. Warner Munn; "The Fates," by John Dwight; "Pickman's Model," by H. P. Lovecraft; "The Last Laugh," by C. Franklin Miller; "At Number Eleven," by Flavia Richardson; "Devils of Po Sung," by Bassett Morgan; "The Rose Window," by Charlton Lawrence Edholm; "Panthers of Shevaon," by Morgan Johnson; "Medusa," by Royal W. Jimerson; "Piece-Meal," by Oscar Cook; "Bells of Ocean," by Arthur J. Burks; "The Devil's Martyr," by Signe Toksvig; "The Cave of Spiders," by William R. Hickey; "The Witch-Baiter," by R. Anthony; "The Trimmer," by Douglas Newton; "Blood," by Rupert Grayson; "The Tenant," by August Der-

leth; "White Lotus Flower," by Harold Markham; "In Kashla's Garden," by Oscar Schisgall; "The Copper Bowl," by Captain George Fielding Eliot.

*4–299. Thompson, Christine Campbell, ed. (U.K.). **Grim Death.** Selwyn & Blount, 1932.

"If You Sleep in the Moonlight," by J. Leslie Mitchell; "Island of Doom," by Bassett Morgan; "Flies," by Anthony Vercoe; "Lord of the Talking Heads," by Arthur Woodward; "Helvellyn, Elivilion or Hill of Baal," by Rosalie Muspratt; "The House of the Living Dead," by Harold Ward; "The Wings," by J. Dyott Matthews; "The Great White Fear," by Oscar Cook; "The Black Stone," by Robert E. Howard; "The Ghost That Never Died," by Elizabeth Sheldon; "Behind the Blinds," by Flavia Richardson; "The Thing in the Cellar," by David H. Keller; "Dorner Cordaianthus," by H. H. Gorst; "Night and Silence," by Maurice Level; "The Inn," by Guy Preston.

*4–300. Thompson, Christine Campbell, ed. (U.K.). **Gruesome Cargoes.** Selwyn & Blount, 1928.

"Dead Man's Luck," by Lockhart North; "When Hell Laughed," by Flavia Richardson; "The Black Spider," by Edmund Snell; "The Hunting on the Doonagh Bog," by Anthony Wharton; "Drums of Fear," by Dora Christie-Murray; "The Hand from the Ruins," by Harold Markham; "A Celestial Hell," by Harry de Windt; "The Children of Bondage," by Dagney Major; "The Man Who Ordered a Double," by Rupert Grayson; "When Glister Walked," by Oscar Cook; "Offspring of Hell," by H. Thompson; "The Tomb," by Francis Beeding; "The Creeping Horror," by A. R. Rawlinson; "The Green Eyes of Mbuiri," by Benge Atlee; "The Padlocked House," by L. Outon.

*4–301. Thompson, Christine Campbell, ed. (U.K.). **Keep on the Light.** Selwyn & Blount, 1933.

"The Library," by Hester Gaskell Holland; "Golden Lilies," by Oscar Cook; "The Chadbourne Episode," by Henry S. Whithead; "Worms of the Earth," by Robert E. Howard; "The Black Hare," by Flavia Richardson; "Tiger Dust," by Bassett Morgan; "The House of Shadows," by Mary Elizabeth Counselman; "Green Slime," by J. Dyott Matthews; "The Seven-Locked Room," by J. D. Kerruish; "The Legion of Evil," by Warden Ledge; "The Head of Wu-Fang," by Don C. Wiley; "The Way He Died," by Guy Preston; "The Cult of the White Ape," by Hugh B. Cave; "Althorpe Abbey," by Rosalie Muspratt; "Isle of the Torturers," by Clark Ashton Smith.

*4–302. Thompson, Christine Campbell, ed. (U.K.). **Nightmare by Daylight.** Selwyn & Blount, 1936.

"Scarred Mirror," by Charles Cullum; "One Alaskan Night," by Barrett Willoughby; "The Dead Woman," by David H. Keller; "The Crimson Head-Dress," by Oscar Cook; "Little Red Shoes," by Gordon Chesson; "The Yellow Paw," by Zayn Konstanz; "The Flute of the Seven Stops," by Dion

Fortune; "The Scream," by Hester Holland; "Mirabel Houston," by Nicholas Stafford; "The Horror of the Cavern," by Walter Rose; "The Gold of Hermodike," by Jessie Douglas Kerruish; "The Cossaks," by E. M. P. Inglefield; "Grannie," by Ralph Dawson; "Empty Stockings," by Flavia Richardson; "The Crack," by Oswell Blakeston.

*4–303. Thompson, Christine Campbell, ed. (U.K.). **Not at Night.** Selwyn & Blount, 1925.

This series of anthologies edited by Christine Campbell Thompson is significant because, like Cynthia Asquith's *Ghost Books* [4–244, 4–245, 4–246], it contains new work by emerging authors as well as work by established writers in the genre. Moreover, Thompson reprinted stories from the pages of *Weird Tales,* and often such reprintings were the first appearance of some writers in hardcover. This volume contains: "Monsters of the Pit," by Paul S. Powers; "Four Wooden Stakes," by Victor Roman; "The Third Thumb-Print," by Mortimer Levitan; "Lips of the Dead," by W. J. Stamper; "The Devil Bed," by Gerald Dean; "Death-Waters," by Frank Belknap Long; "Black Curtains," by G. Frederick Montefiore; "The Plant-Thing," by R. G. Macready; "His Family," by C. Franklin Miller; "A Hand from the Deep," by Romeo Poole; "The Tortoise-Shell Cat," by Greye La Spina; "The Case of the Russian Stevedore," by Henry V. Whitehill; "The Leopard's Trail," by W. Chisell Collins; "The Last Trip," by Archie Binns; "The Purple Cincture," by H. Thompson Rich.

*4–304. Thompson, Christine Campbell, ed. (U.K.). **More Not At Night.** Selwyn & Blount, 1926.

"The Hooded Death," by Joel Martin Nichols, Jr.; "The Man Who Was Saved," by B. W. Sliney; "Fidel Bassin," by W. J. Stamper; "Teeth," by Galen C. Colin; "Vials of Wrath," by Edith Lyle Ragsdale; "The Experiment of Erich Weigert," by Sewell Peaslee Wright; "The Mystery under the Sea," by Donald Edward Keyhoe; "The Horror on the Links," by Seabury Quinn; "The Yellow Spectre," by Steward van der Veer; "Swamp Horror," by Will Smith and R. J. Robbins; "The Dead Soul," by Raoul Lenoir; "The Sea Thing," by Frank Belknap Long; "The Black Box," by H. Thompson Rich; "Bat's Belfrey," by August Derleth; "The Phantom Drug," by A. W. Kapper.

*4–305. Thompson, Christine Campbell, ed. (U.K.). **Switch on the Night.** Selwyn & Blount, 1931.

"The Curse of Yig," by Zelia Brown Reed; "Murder by Proxy," by Richard Stone; "Haunted Hands," by Jack Bradley; "The Flame Fiend," by N. J. O'Neail; "Boomerang," by Oscar Cook; "The Tapping," by J. Dyott Matthews; "The Red Fetish," by Frank Belknap Long; "The Pacer," by August Derleth and Mark Schorer; "Flower Valley," by J. S. Whittaker; "The Rats in the Walls," by H. P. Lovecraft; "Suzanne," by J. Joseph Renaud; "The

Thought Monster," by Amelia Reynolds Long; "The Red Turret," by Flavia Richardson; "Pigmy Island," by Edmond Hamilton; "Bhuillaneadh," by R. F. Broad.

*4–306. Thompson, Christine Campbell, ed. (U.K.). **Terror by Night.** Selwyn & Blount, 1935.
"King Cobra," by Joseph O. Kesselring; "The Chamber of Death," by Armiger Barclay; "The House of the Worm," by Mearle Prout; "The Flying Head," by Ernest Bonney; "The Man Who Saw Red," by J. Wilmer Benjamin; "The Horror in the Museum," by Hazel Heald; "Dog Death," by Oscar Cook; "The Metronome," by August Derleth; "The Accursed Isle," by Mary Elizabeth Counselman; "The Watcher in the Green Room," by Hugh B. Cave; "Rogues in the House," by Robert E. Howard; "The Closed Door," by Harold Ward; "The Death Plant," by Michael Gwynn; "Behind the Yellow Door," by Flavia Richardson; "The Author's Tale," by L. A. Lewis.

*4–307. Thompson, Christine Campbell, ed. (U.K.). **You'll Need a Light.** Selwyn & Blount, 1927.
"The Last Horror," by Eli Colter; "The Life Serum," by Paul S. Powers; "The Girdle," by Joseph McCord; "Si Urag of the Tail," by Oscar Cook; "The Beast," by Paul Benton; "His Wife," by Zita Inez Ponder; "Laocoon," by Bassett Morgan; "Out of the Earth," by Flavia Richardson; "Ti Michael," by W. J. Stamper; "The House of Horror," by Seabury Quinn; "The Coffin of Lissa," by August Derleth; "The Parasitic Hand," by R. Anthony; "The Death Crescents of Koti," by Romeo Poole; "Ghosts of the Air," by J. M. Hiatt and Moye W. Stephens; "The Horror at Red Hook," by H. P. Lovecraft.

*4–308. Wagner, Karl Edward, ed. **The Year's Best Horror Stories: VIII.** DAW, 1980.
"The Dead Line," by Dennis Etchison; "To Wake the Dead," by Ramsey Campbell; "In the Fourth Year of the War," by Harlan Ellison; "From the Lower Deep," by Hugh B. Cave; "The Baby-Sitter," by Davis Grubb; "The Well at the Half Cat," by John Tibbetts; "My Beautiful Darkling," by Eddy C. Bertin; "A Serious Call," by George Hay; "Sheets," by Alan Ryan; "Billy Wolfe's Riding Spirit," by Kevin A. Lyons; "Lex Talionis," by Russell Kirk; "Entombed," by Robert Keefe; "A Fly One," by Steve Sneyd; "Needle Song," by Charles L. Grant; "All the Birds Come to Roost," by Harlan Ellison; "The Devil behind You," by Richard A. Moore.

*4–309. Wilson, Gahan. **First World Fantasy Awards.** Doubleday, 1977.
This volume commemorates the First World Fantasy awards and includes a number of fiction items: "The Bat Is My Brother," by Robert Bloch; "Beetles," by Robert Bloch; "Passages from a Young Girl's Journal," by Robert Aickman; "The Events at Poroth Farm," by T. E. D. Klein; "A Fa-

ther's Tale," by Sterling E. Lanier; "Sticks," by Karl Edward Wagner; "Come into My Parlor," by Manly Wade Wellman; "Fearful Rock," by Manly Wade Wellman; "The Bait," by Fritz Leiber; "The Shortest Way," by Dave Drake. The volume contains information about the awards and a number of interesting essays.

*4-310. Wise, Herbert A., and Phyllis Fraser, eds. **Great Tales of Terror and the Supernatural.** Modern Library, 1944.

"La Grande Breteche," by Honoré de Balzac; "The Black Cat," by Edgar Allan Poe; "The Facts in the Case of M. Valdemar," by Edgar Allan Poe; "A Terribly Strange Bed," by Wilkie Collins; "The Boarded Window," by Ambrose Bierce; "The Three Strangers," by Thomas Hardy; "The Interruption," by W. W. Jacobs; "Pollock and the Porroh Man," by H. G. Wells; "The Sea Raiders," by H. G. Wells; "Sredni Vashtar," by Saki; "Moonlight Sonata," by Alexander Woollcott; "Silent Snow, Secret Snow," by Conrad Aiken; "Suspicion," by Dorothy L. Sayers; "The Most Dangerous Game," by Richard Connell; "Leiningen versus the Ants," by Carl Stephenson; "The Gentleman from America," by Michael Arlen; "A Rose for Emily," by William Faulkner; "The Killers," by Ernest Hemingway; "Back for Christmas," by John Collier; "Taboo," by Geoffrey Household; "The Haunters and the Haunted, or, The House and the Brain," by Edward Bulwer-Lytton; "Rappaccini's Daughter," by Nathaniel Hawthorne; "The Trial for Murder," by Charles Collins and Charles Dickens; "Green Tea," by Sheridan Le Fanu; "What Was It?" by Fitz-James O'Brien; "Sir Edmund Orme," by Henry James; "The Horla," by Guy de Maupassant; "Was It a Dream?" by Guy de Maupassant; "The Screaming Skull," by F. Marion Crawford; "The Furnished Room," by O. Henry; "Casting the Runes," by M. R. James; "Oh, Whistle, and I'll Come to You, My Lad," by M. R. James; "Afterward," by Edith Wharton; "The Monkey's Paw," by W. W. Jacobs; "The Great God Pan," by Arthur Machen; "How Love Came to Professor Guildea," by Robert Hichens; "The Return of Imray," by Rudyard Kipling; "They," by Rudyard Kipling; "Lukundoo," by Edward Lucas White; "Caterpillars," by E. F. Benson; "Mrs. Amworth," by E. F. Benson; "Ancient Sorceries," by Algernon Blackwood; "Confession," by Algernon Blackwood; "The Open Window," by Saki; "The Beckoning Fair One," by Oliver Onions; "Out of the Deep," by Walter De La Mare, "Adam and Eve and Pinch Me," by A. E. Coppard; "The Celestial Omnibus," by E. M. Forster; "The Ghost Ship," by Richard Middleton; "The Sailor-Boy's Tale" by Isak Dinesen; "The Rats in the Walls," by H. P. Lovecraft; "The Dunwich Horror," by H. P. Lovecraft.

4-311. Wollheim, Donald A. **Terror in the Modern Vein.** Hanover House, 1955.

"The Croquet Player," by H. G. Wells; "They," by Robert Heinlein; "Fritzchen," by Charles Beaumont; "The Girl with the Hungry Eyes," by Fritz

Leiber; "The Fishing Season," by Robert Sheckley; "The Crowd," by Ray Bradbury; "He," by H. P. Lovecraft; "The Strange Case of Lemuel Jenkins," by Phillip M. Fisher, Jr.; "The Rag Thing," by David Grinnell; "The Burrow," by Franz Kafka; "Gone Away," by A. E. Coppard; "The Silence," by Venard McLaughlin; "Shipshape Home," by Richard Matheson; "The Dream Makers," by Robert Bloch; "The Republic of the Southern Cross," by Valery Brussof; "The Inheritors," by Robert W. Lowndes and John Michel.

5
The Horror Pulps
1933–1940

Robert Weinberg

The first pulp magazine was published in the United States by Frank A. Munsey in 1896. Reasoning that people were more interested in content than in paper quality, Munsey took his slick *Argosy* magazine, printed it entirely on cheap wood pulp paper, filled it completely with fiction, and priced it at ten cents. Lower in price than most magazines, *Argosy*'s only competition came from the dime novels of that period. The magazine, however, had one tremendous advantage: it could be mailed more cheaply than the dime novel. Munsey, who had been $20,000 in debt in 1889, soon became a millionaire as his pulp magazine concept caught on with the public.

Competition from other publishers developed in the early twentieth century, but it was Munsey again who came up with the next revolutionary idea—a pulp magazine featuring stories in one particular field. *Railroad Man's Magazine* debuted in 1906 and was another success for the now-burgeoning Munsey chain of pulps. Within a few years, other publishers followed his lead with such titles as *Detective Story Magazine, Action Stories, Sea Stories, West, Adventure,* and numerous others.

The 1920s saw a tremendous growth in the pulps. Specialization increased as magazines fought for space on the newsstands. The first all-science fiction magazine, *Amazing Stories,* began during this decade and led the way for others in the field of fantastic fiction. Detective fiction flourished with the advent of *Black Mask,* which, under editor Joseph Shaw, championed the "realistic" school of detective writing, or the "hard-boiled detective story" as it was later called. There were pulps for every taste, ranging from *Wild West Weekly* to *Submarine Stories* to *Zeppelin Stories.*

The Depression actually fueled the growth of the pulp market. More than ever people wanted cheap, light reading, and the pulps specialized in that. Many printers with expensive equipment had nothing to publish in the depressed economy and publishing a pulp magazine for low rates, or even on credit, was better than idle machinery with no chance to make a dollar. Pulp authority Robert Jones pointed out in his book, *The Shudder Pulps,* how easy it was to start a magazine:

> All you need is some credit from a dealer in pulp paper and from a printer, and an arrangement with a distribution company. You can promise to pay authors after publication. You can pay the printing and paper bills when the check for sold copies comes in from the distributor.[1]

In some cases, the printers even published their own magazines, usually pulps owned by bankrupt clients. It was a time of speculation and experimentation. In 1930, Street and Smith left the American News Company distributors to handle its own distribution of magazines. Street and Smith was the biggest chain of pulp magazines, and ANC encouraged any other publishers they could find to fill in the gap. Many responded. As long as the credit was there, so was hope. If one magazine did not do well, it was discontinued and another started, often using the same numbering as the first and the same second-class mail permit. It was a time when people with ambition could get rich. Into this volatile market came Henry Steeger, who would become one of the giants of the pulp publishing field.

Steeger started in the pulp field with Dell Publishing Company in 1927. A graduate of Princeton, he worked on several pulps during the next few years, rising to editor of *Sky Birds* and *War Birds,* two popular aviation pulps. However, Steeger always wanted to publish his own magazines, not to work for someone else. "I was very anxious to get into the pulp publishing business on my own," he said, "regardless of any external conditions such as a depression."[2] In 1929, Steeger contacted Harold Goldsmith of Ace Publications and proposed a partnership. Goldsmith would handle the business side of the new company (he was doing just that at Ace) and Steeger would manage the editorial end. The new chain was Popular Publications, and its first four magazines appeared in 1930.

The new partnership was typical of the time. Steeger recalled, "Goldsmith and I each put up $5,000, which we borrowed, and I remember we were able to obtain about $125,000 worth of credit with this initial investment." [3] Of the four magazines, *Battle Aces*, an air war pulp, was an immediate success. *Western Rangers, Gang World,* and *Detective Action Stories* all ran in the red for the first few years. Inventory was kept low by the limited budget. "We never had a large backlog of stories," said Steeger, "because we didn't have the money to buy them and I was very careful to buy only the stories I liked for those initial issues." [4]

Although not a rousing success, Popular Publications made enough money to start two more titles in 1931. *Dime Detective*, whose first issue appeared in November 1931, featured stories in the *Black Mask* tradition—fast, tough, and hard-boiled. Steeger managed to lure Erle Stanley Gardner away from *Black Mask* by paying him the astonishing rate of four cents a word. Other *Black Mask* regulars, including Carrol John Daly, were soon writing for *Dime Detective* as well. The new magazine was an immediate success. *Black Mask,* the premier detective pulp, featured static, plain covers, usually with a white background and one figure prominent. *Dime Detective* sported action paintings by William Reusswig, filled with violence and bizarre happenings. Strong, dynamic covers with lots of action were always the hallmark of a Popular magazine. Said Steeger, "I would agree . . . to a certain extent that the covers were actually what sold the pulp magazine. I devoted more time and attention to covers than to anything else because I figured they were our salesman and so they should be just right." [5] The success of *Dime Detective* helped finance an entire wave of expansion at Popular, which was beginning to make itself felt as a force in the pulp field.

Dime Mystery was one of a number of pulps started in 1932 by Popular Publications. It was intended as a companion magazine to *Dime Detective,* which featured a number of novelettes and short stories in each issue. *Dime Mystery* contained a complete novel; the idea was to give the readers "A New $2.00 Detective Novel" complete in each issue. To further push this book-length concept, each cover of *Dime Mystery* featured a cover within a cover. The magazine cover contained a painting of a book, complete with title and spine, with the featured novel done as the jacket art for the book. Unfortunately, even fine cover paintings could not make *Dime Mystery* a success. The idea of a complete novel in every issue was not new. It had been used successfully for years by Fiction House in *Detective Novels Magazine* and *Detective Classics.* Both magazines specialized in reprints of current mysteries by top writers and featured long stories by Ellery Queen, Leslie Charteris, and Edgar Wallace. Priced at 20 cents each, these magazines had a firm grip on the market that Popular could not break, even with its lower price and novels with such "come-on" titles as "The Bride's House Horror" and "The Purple Eye."

Steeger was not one to drop a magazine or lose a second-class mail permit, however, so he searched for a new format for *Dime Mystery*. Part of the answer came from the lurid covers that were featured on *Dime Detective*. Pulp authority Ron Goulart speculated that the new wave of monster movies gave Steeger his concept.[6] Henry Steeger credited an unusual source: "My inspiration came from having watched the Grand Guignol Theater in Paris. This theater had been popular for so many years that it seemed like a good starting point for a pulp magazine."[7]

October 1933 was the date of the first issue of *Dime Mystery* featuring Steeger's new format. No longer was the lead novel 50,000 words. The lead story was half that length, backed up with a bunch of novelettes and short stories. The old cover format was gone, and in its place was the final creation that had begun to evolve with the first *Dime Detective* cover by Reusswig. According to Jones, "It was the first in a pictorial gallery . . . of man's inhumanity to woman, with the heroines being pursued down dark corridors, nailed into coffins, whipped, choked, clubbed by cowled fanatics, hunchbacked cretins, gibbering idiots and gnarled seniles, all this taking place . . . without mussing up their carefully coiffured hair or smudging their penciled eyebrows and mascara'd eyes."[8]

Inside the magazine, the editor's page stated the magazine's new slant: "No magazine, to our knowledge, has ever combined these two elements of mystery and terror and devoted its pages exclusively to stories of this one heart-quickening type."[9] In the months that followed, this policy of mystery-horror stories was refined and redefined by the editor of *Dime Mystery*, Rogers Terrill, until it was a standard formula that served as a basis for all the horror pulps that followed.

Basically, the mystery-horror story of *Dime Mystery* was a direct descendant of the Gothic novels of the nineteenth century and an indirect ancestor of the Gothic romances so popular in the 1960s. There was a mystery, usually a murder, often many murders. The cause of the crimes was seemingly a supernatural or supernormal agency. Hero and heroine were threatened by a variety of terrible death and torture possibilities. Frequently the hero suspected that he had caused the crime during a fit of madness, or that the heroine had. In the end, a hidden villain was revealed and the supernatural manifestations were shown to be some clever plotting or machinery used by the plotter. The stories featured a strong streak of morality—good always triumphed over evil. The heroine was threatened, but rarely harmed.

The lead novel for the first of the new issues of *Dime Mystery* offered a telling insight into the plotting of such a story. "Dance of the Skeletons" was written by Norvell Page, one of the leading writers working for the pulps. Originally a reporter on the *New York World-Telegram*, Page began writing detective and gangster stories for the pulps in the early 1930s. By 1934, he was making so much money writing for the pulps that he quit his newspaper job to concentrate full time on his fiction. Page wrote more than 100 novels featuring The Spider, one of Popular's continued magazine characters, during the 1930s and 1940s, as well as hundreds of other stories for the pulps of that period. During World War II, he wrote government reports, starting in 1943. After he left government service, Page tried fiction writing again, but the pulp market was dying. He returned to writing for the government and prepared a number of papers for the Atomic Energy Commission. When he died in 1961, he received a column-length obituary in the *New York Times,* one line of which said that he wrote "detective stories" before starting to write for the government.

In an article for *Writer's Yearbook* for 1935, Page documented step-by-step how he wrote "Dance of the Skeletons." This breakdown gave a clear outline to the basic format of the mystery-horror story. Using a clipping about piranhas as his main gimmick, Page declared that "the maximum of terror would be obtained by converting living men into nice white skeletons within a few minutes and concealing the method by which this was done. . . . To have the horror of the story to the full, these skeletons must be flaunted in the face of the city, they must appear at the festive board, thud at the feet of the police commissioner entering headquarters." [10] Motive and mystery proved to be a little more challenging for Page, but he came up with both through logical thinking:

> An unscrupulous capitalist who has fallen on hard times sets out to clean up on the stock market by foul means. He kills off certain captains of industry to make the stock of their companies decline. However, mere murder of these men would not depress the stocks. He must contrive to kill them and make it seem they have merely disappeared because the financial condition of their companies is no longer sound. To accomplish this, he kidnaps them and feeds them to piranha. . . . The villain then places the skeletons in various conspicuous places. By this means, he not only depresses stocks . . . but he distracts the attention of the police from the stock market manipulations. [11]

As in all the mystery-horror stories, along with the diabolical villain there was a resourceful hero and a beautiful heroine. Stories were written by men like Norvell Page, full-time pulp authors who could turn out a 20,000-word story in a week or less. Like most pulp fiction, the basic plot line remained the same, with editors discouraging invention other than in the narrow, acceptable band they were using. It was formula stuff, but it sold.

The revived *Dime Mystery* was a success. Within a year, Popular came out with its second magazine using the same type of story. *Terror Tales* began publication in September 1934. Soon after, it was followed by *Horror Stories* (January 1935). These first three Popular Publications horror pulps remained the leaders in the pulp horror field throughout their entire existence.

Rogers Terrill served as editor for all three of the horror pulps published by Popular. He started in the pulp field working for Fiction House. When that company had financial troubles in the early 1930s, he began to work for Popular, where he ended up editing more than a dozen magazines and being paid one of the top salaries of any editor in the pulp field. Terrill stayed with Popular through the 1940s, becoming an editor for *Argosy*. He left there to form his own literary agency, and died in 1964.

Like most people connected with the pulps, Terrill considered his work a job and nothing more. "My husband did not keep a single example of his pulp work," stated Gean Purcell, widow of Norvell Page, "and whenever he met with those who worked with him in the pulps, such as Rogers Terrill, the conversation *never* turned to the pulps." [12]

It was Terrill who defined the three key words for his magazines. "According to Terrill," related Wyatt Blassingame, one of the most prolific contributors to the horror pulps, "*horror* is what a girl would feel if, from a safe location, she watched the Ghoul practise diabolical rites upon a victim. *Terror* is what the girl would feel, if, on a dark night, she heard the steps of the Ghoul coming toward her and knew she was marked for the next victim. *Mystery* is the girl wondering who-done-it-and-why." [13]

Using these basic terms and the formula plot standard of the Popular magazines, pulp writers working for Terrill filled his three magazines with some of the most grotesque and gruesome stories ever written. Titles were often changed by Terrill to fit the mood of the pulps. Readers were treated to such works as "The Dead Hate the Living," "The Molemen Want Your Eyes," "Satan's Roadhouse," "The Chair Where Terror Sat," "The Corpse Factory," "Slaves of the Blood Wolves," "The Flame Things Are Hungry," "Our Host, the Madman," "Cathedral of Horror," and dozens of others. Unlike most popular fiction of the time, the stories often outdid their titles in sheer bizarre imagery.

The strength of the stories came from those who plotted and wrote them. Although all three magazines were an open market for new writers, full-time professional pulp authors dominated the contents page. These were people who were writing and selling tens of thousands of words per year, sometimes as much as a million words or more in 12 months. Many of the smaller pulps paid only one-half cent *or less* a word, often on publication, and sometimes long after publication. However, Popular and Street and Smith and several of the other major chains paid a penny or more a word, on acceptance. As Frank Gruber put it, "My income in 1935 was ten thousand dollars. And that was very, very good money." [14]

Some of the very best pulp writers worked for Popular, and it was their polished, professional writing that made their terror pulps the leaders in the field. Among them were Wyatt Blassingame, Hugh B. Cave, Paul Ernst, Arthur Leo Zagat, Nathan Schachner, Bruno Fischer (writing under the name Russell Gray), Arthur J. Burks, and Frederick C. Davis.

Blassingame began writing for *Dime Mystery* in 1933 with "Horror in the Hold." During the next six years, he sold over one million words to the mystery-horror magazines. Blassingame used a number of plot devices. In an article for *Writer's Digest*, he detailed some of the devices that enabled him to sell consistently to the horror pulps:

> In plotting a mystery story for any of these magazines, I begin by trying to get two things: a new and evilish method of murder, and a good motive which will allow the villain to use this method. Once I have a *way* for the villain to commit his crimes, and a reason for him to commit them, I rarely have much trouble working out the remainder of the story. . . . In explaining these methods you need a basis of fact on which to build. A single definite fact can be stretched to amazing proportions and will be accepted, but you must make your explanation sound and convincing.[15]

Blassingame moved on to the slick magazines from the pulps after World War II, and later wrote juveniles. He now lives in Florida, occasionally writing nonfiction articles for magazines.

Hugh B. Cave was another writer who began in the pulps and made the transition into the slicks. Cave, who was born in England and raised in New England, began writing in 1931 and was one of the most prolific contributors to the horror pulps. Now residing in Florida, as do many of the "old-time" pulp writers, Cave not long ago returned to the supernatural horror field with several prize-winning short stories and a number of novels.

Paul Ernst, who also lives in Florida, estimated he wrote a million words a year for the pulps from 1934 through 1940.[16] Ernst was one of the few writing for *Horror Stories* who managed to sell the magazine some straight supernatural stories. Now in his seventies, Ernst admitted to Robert Jones that writing for the horror pulps was a job and nothing more. "I sold ninety percent of my material. But I never read anything I wrote. I had no interest in it. You could throw it out the window, as long as I got the check."[17]

Arthur Leo Zagat was one of the mainstays of the Popular horror magazines, writing 25 short novels for the terror pulps. Born in New York in 1896, Zagat received a law degree from Fordham in 1929. The Depression made any thought of a law career impossible, and his wife, Ruth, suggested that he try writing instead. Within a short time, Zagat was one of the best-selling authors in the pulp field. In World War II, Zagat worked for the Office of War Information, where he devoted all his time to nonfiction writing. He was a member of the Council of the Authors League of America. He died in 1949, a few months before the first hardcover publication of one of his novels.

Nat Schachner was a close friend of Zagat, and his first story was a collaboration with Zagat published in 1930 in a science fiction magazine. Schachner was also trained in the law, but unlike Zagat, he became a practicing attorney. His first few stories were all science fiction and all written in collaboration with Zagat. Schachner soon branched out and began writing for the horror pulps, although he also kept up his science fiction writing. After World War II, Schachner wrote several well-known biographies about major historical figures that were critical successes. He died in 1955.

Bruno Fischer began writing for the horror pulps in 1936. Within a year, he left newspaper work for the pulp field. "I found the horror-terror market wide open, and, on the whole, paying [as high a rate] as more sedate detective magazines," he recalled. "Evidently I had the knack for handling the breathless atmosphere and bizarre plot patterns required in those yarns, for I started selling at once and kept right on through all the gyrations of editorial demands." [18] Fischer later moved into the detective field, where he gained recognition for his hard-boiled novels featuring ordinary people as the main characters.

Arthur J. Burks served as a lieutenant in the Marines during World War I and was later stationed in Haiti and the Dominican Republic. Burks began writing in 1920, but it was not until 1924, when he started to sell to *Weird Tales,* that he had any success with the pulps. By 1928, Burks had resigned from the Marines to write full time. Soon he achieved almost legendary status among his fellow writers as "the Speed Merchant of the Pulps." Burks tried to average 18,000 words a day and rarely missed his mark. Nearly everything he wrote sold, and he bragged that one month his name was on the cover of 11 different pulp magazines. He never was able to make 12. Not primarily known for his novels, Burks once wrote a science fiction novel in a week. When an editor refused to see it because no work written so fast could be any good, Burks held the novel for three more weeks and then resubmitted the story as one he had taken a month to write. Needless to say, the unsuspecting editor bought the novel. Burks contributed numerous short stories to all the horror pulps during the 1930s. He later helped form the American Fiction Guild and was a professional lecturer on a number of topics. He died in 1974.

Fred C. Davis was another million-words-a-year man for the pulps. He began writing for them while attending Dartmouth in 1924. Davis specialized in continued characters, and along with his numerous stories for the horror pulps he wrote the Operator 5 novels each month for the magazine with that same title for Popular, contributed the Oke Oakley and Carter Cole stories to *Dime Detective,* wrote the Moon Man stories for *Ten Detective Aces,* and the Ravenwood series for *Secret Agent X.* When the pulps began to die, Davis switched to writing mystery novels and wrote dozens of them under his own name and the pen name Stephen Ransome. He died in 1978.

These were just some of the many writers who wrote for the horror pulps. They had nothing in common other than the fact that they wrote for a living, and thus had to sell what they wrote. They were able to write for a market and slant their stories to suit an editor's wants.

During the first years of their existence, *Horror* and *Terror* stressed a Gothic-style mystery-horror story. Certain themes dominated. The villain was usually after money. As Wyatt Blassingame put it, "The villain must be sane and working for some sane and logical motive. Financial gain is the best one since your readers won't have any trouble understanding it." [19] His victims were ordinary people who unknowingly stood in his way to financial fortune. Working in the guise of some monster or legendary creature, the villain would try to kill or scare away all those in his path. This theme was the most popular used in the early horror pulps. A variation had the young hero or heroine being driven to the brink of madness by a relative or friend who wanted to gain control of the main character's financial holdings or forgotten bequest. Logic was never a major requirement for the stories as long as they were fast-paced and all the major loose ends were explained at the conclusion. Often these explanations came in dying confessions made by the villains, who rarely escaped their just reward.

These early stories were important reflections of the time. They expressed an optimism that was prevalent in all pulp fiction. Good triumphed over evil. People had courage and fought for what they believed in. The heroes struggled against the evil villains not only for love of the heroine, but because it was the right thing to do.

At the same time, there was a dark side to the stories. Mistrust of big business was a common theme and implicit in nearly all the stories. The city was presented as a vast, uncaring metropolis, where people died and no one noticed. Small towns were glorified as places where the common person could make good (if only free of the evil capitalists bent on possessing the land for its wealth). Big cities were constantly represented as vast slums where evil lurked in every alley and crawled through the subway stations at night.

Although sex was advertised with half-clad women on the covers and near-naked females within, the Popular magazines of the mid-1930s did not feature any sexually explicit material. Women were threatened by evil villains, but the worst that happened was that the heroine was tied up and perhaps tortured for an instant before her rescue. She was never sexually abused or attacked.

This was not the case with another major magazine that had its start during this period. Frank Armer's Culture Publications began with one title in 1934—*Spicy Detective Stories*. It was followed in short order by *Spicy Mystery, Spicy Adventure,* and *Spicy Western.* Armer had a different approach to pulp publishing from Steeger's. Under the banner of Trojan Publications, Armer gathered together a stable of writers who monthly filled the pages of his magazines with stories under their names and various house names owned by the magazines. The Spicy magazines were rarely copyrighted and often were sold "under the counter" as racy publications. Needless to say, by today's standards, the Spicy magazines were anything but.

The Spicy pulps were long on sex and short on mystery. Covers were done by H. J. Ward and R. Parkhurst and were masterpieces of erotic art—stunning oil paintings that had little or nothing to do with the stories in the magazine. Each story was liberally illustrated with excellent line drawings featuring scantily clad women in various threatening circumstances. As to contents, Wyatt Blassingame stated it best in 1936: "You've got to get hot here. Use lush anatomical descriptions of your heroines and other female characters and make your heroes virile. The women, however, must be essential parts of the story. You can't just drag them in. The supernatural story goes here as well as the logically explained one. Quite a few first person stories. All the stories are short, 5,500 words being their top." [20]

Debuting in early 1935, *Spicy Mystery* was the other side of the coin from *Horror* and *Terror*. Where the lead stories in the Popular pulps were long, those in the Spicy magazine were short. Atmosphere was built up gradually in the Popular stories, but there was no room for that in the Spicy magazine. The stories zipped along with a minimum of plot or deception. There was little mystery or suspense, but there was horror and often supernatural occurrences. Women were beaten, abused, and attacked. Even here, however, explicit sex was never featured; it was suggested, but never spelled out in detail.

Lawrence Cadmen was editor for Armer, and the Spicy magazines were located in Wilmington, Delaware. Most pulps had their offices located in New York, and most pulp writers lived in Manhattan so they would have an inside line with editors and publishers. Regulars got assignments just by going to the offices of the magazine. This was not the case for Trojan Publications in their Delaware office. They did not need walk-in contributions nor were they after submissions through the mail. Their stable of writers provided them with all the fiction they needed.

The Spicy magazines were priced at 25 cents each, a good deal higher than the dime charged for most Popular magazines, or the 15 cents for *Horror* or *Terror*. With large print and many pictures, the Spicys offered nowhere near the amount of words per issue that the Popular magazines featured. Yet they evidently sold well as they continued into the 1940s, even expanding their line into the detective field.

Chief among the writers for *Spicy Mystery* was Robert Leslie Bellem. A professional journalist, Bellem worked part time writing stories for the pulps from the late 1920s on. He teamed up with Armer in 1933 and was soon able to leave the newspaper field. By 1936, Bellem had joined the million-words-a-year group. [21] During his career for the pulps, Bellem wrote over 3,000 stories. His most famous creation was private detective Dan Turner, who even had his own pulp magazine featuring stories reprinted from *Spicy Detective* as well as new Turner adventures. Bellem later turned to television and wrote TV scripts until his death in 1968.

Also working for Armer were E. Hoffmann Price, Norvell Page, Wyatt Blassingame, Norman Daniels, and Hugh Cave (under the novel pseudonym Justin Case).

Popular was the champion of the long, Gothic horror-mystery tale; *Spicy Mystery* offered sex and horror in short format. Both types sold and were successful. In the pulps, success meant competition. Other publishers soon had imitations on the stands, although rarely did they capture the flavor or sales of the originals.

The Standard Group entered the field in late 1935 with *Thrilling Mystery*.

The publisher was Ned Pines, and the editor of the pulp (and of all the Standard magazines) was the "Little Giant" of the pulps, Leo Margulies. Frank Gruber, who began in the pulp magazines, characterized Margulies as "a short man, not over five feet five. He was a dynamic, forceful man with a low boiling point." [22] Margulies began in the pulps as an office boy for the Munsey magazines. He left them to work for Tower Publications and for a short time ran a literary agency. In the early 1930s he went to work for his friend Pines when the latter began Standard Publications. Margulies knew just about everyone in the pulp field and was a shrewd editor.

Ned Pines followed his brother, Robert, into the magazine field with *College Life* in 1927. Robert Pines was already the successful publisher of *College Humor* magazine. In 1930, when Street and Smith left American News to handle its own magazine distribution, Pines was asked by American to fill the gap. [23] Working with Margulies, he launched his Standard magazines, which became known throughout the field as "the Thrilling Group." This was because nearly all their magazines used *Thrilling* as part of their title. The first three magazines published by Pines were *Thrilling Detective, Thrilling Love,* and *Thrilling Adventures.* By the late 1930s, the Standard chain listed more than 20 titles.

In early 1935, Popular published one issue of a new magazine titled *Thrilling Mysteries.* Ned Pines complained to Steeger that his company was "trying to develop the 'Thrilling Line' and he would appreciate it if we abandoned our effort." [24] Popular dropped the magazine. Strangely enough, no mention was made of the fact that Standard was publishing *Popular Detective* and *Popular Western* during this same period without any complaints from Popular Publications.

In any case, *Thrilling Mystery* began in October 1935. "We had seen the success of some other magazines, like *Horror Stories* and *Terror Tales,*" Leo Margulies was quoted as saying. "It was the only type we didn't have at the time; that's why we started *Thrilling Mystery.*" [25] The format of the new magazine was similar to the Popular Big Three, with several novelettes or short novels as well as a number of short stories in each issue. Covers were lurid and garish, though not as well done as the Popular artwork. The authors were familiar. Arthur J. Burks, of course, and Wyatt Blassingame, Ray Cummings, Paul Ernst, John Knox, and others who wrote for *Horror* and *Terror.* As to the actual contents of the stories, there were cosmetic differences. Margulies never allowed an actual fantasy or supernatural story in his magazine. Rogers Terrill sometimes did. Popular went in more for the dark, Gothic type of mystery. Standard featured more of the fast action type with less introspection or mood development. *Thrilling Mystery* featured a number of stories written by science fiction authors who wrote for some of their other pulps like *Thrilling Wonder Stories,* but even these stories were the usual fare. Richard Tooker, who wrote a number of stories for *Thrilling Mystery,* described the formula he used in these terms: "A fearful menace, apparently due to supernatural agencies, must terrify the characters at the start, but the climax must demonstrate convincingly that the menace was natural after all." [26] It was a description that would work as well for Popular as for Standard magazines.

Another competitor, but one that lasted for only three issues, was *Ace Mystery*. The title made it clear that it was part of the Ace Magazine chain owned by A. A. and Rose Wyn. Wyn, like Henry Steeger, began work at Dell in the late 1920s. He started his own company in the early 1930s, buying several failing pulp magazines from Harold Hersey Publications. Taking *Detective Dragnet,* a Hersey pulp, Wyn changed the title to *Ten Detective Aces,* featuring ten complete detective stories for a dime. The new magazine sold well and Wyn soon had a dozen different magazines on the stands. His wife Rose did a good deal of editing for him, handling all the love and romance pulps. Harry Widmer served as editor for his detective and horror pulps. *Ace Mystery* was Wyn's first attempt at a horror pulp, but not his last.

Fred Davis had the featured novel in all three issues of *Ace Mystery*. Along with Davis, the magazine featured stories by Hugh B. Cave, John Knox, Paul Ernst, and Henry Treat Sperry, who had all contributed to Popular. However, even with garish Norman Saunders covers, *Ace Mystery* did not sell. It was killed after three issues. What hurt Wyn was the fact that he paid on publication. In a field where a penny a word was the norm, having to wait for months to get paid for a story was not something that attracted many top authors. *Ace Mystery* did feature some of the better horror writers, but the stories were obvious rejects from other magazines that the authors felt were better sold—even if they had to wait for payment—than destroyed. In any case, payment on publication put Wyn's magazines well below the Popular and Standard chains in author interest and enthusiasm.

Wyn did not give up. In 1937 he published *Eerie Stories*. This lasted but one issue. Robert Jones explained why the second magazine might have folded: "The most exciting thing about it was the cover by Saunders. . . . Unfortunately, Ace magazines often followed up these stimulating artistries with some of the poorest illustrations of just about any pulp." [27] Even worse was the poor typeface and reproduction. Pulps were printed on the cheapest paper, and a poor typeface could make a magazine unreadable, no matter what the contents. None of the Ace magazines was noted for readability, and *Eerie* had to be the worst.

Wyn tried one more time, with *Eerie Mysteries*. This fared slightly better than the two previous attempts, lasting four undistinguished issues. He finally got the message and stopped trying to conquer the horror field.

In 1937, the contents of *Horror, Terror,* and *Dime Mystery* began to change. Faced with increasing competition from numerous detective pulps, the magazines began to feature stories to match their covers. The Gothic elements of the lead stories disappeared. There was less introspection and much less mystery. The fast pace and menacing villain remained, but there was something else as well—sex. The stories in all three pulps featured more nude women threatened by villains with lust as well as greed on their minds. The illustrations in the magazines still featured beautiful women, but where they used to be fully or partially clothed, they were now totally nude. Stories, while not sexually explicit, were filled with good amounts of sadism and torture, usually aimed at women. In earlier days, the heroine was threatened but rarely harmed. In the late 1930s, it was rare that the heroine was not tortured or humiliated by the villain. Even the covers reflected the change. Women who once were threatened by fiends were now being tortured by these creatures. Typical of the period was "Revolt of the Circus Freaks" by Donald Graham from 1938. It told of a group of deformed sideshow performers who paid the mysterious villain money to be supplied with normal humans for them to torture in their twisted revenge against the world. The story had little plot or sense, but it did have torture and sadistic death on nearly every page. Neither the hero nor the heroine were spared from the tortures of the misshapen monsters of the story until the masked villain and his employers were destroyed at the conclusion of the tale. Graham soon was working for the most successful of the sex-and-sadism horror pulps.

The Red Circle magazines offered readers what the other pulps only promised. Manvis Publications had been started by Martin Goodman in 1932, publishing Western pulps. Featuring a red bullet surrounded by a circle, these Red Circle pulps soon broke into the mystery and detective field. The editor for Goodman was Robert O. Erisman, who handled all their entries into the mystery-horror line.

Goodman's first try in the horror field was *Mystery Tales* in March 1938. He followed it with *Uncanny Tales* the following month. In 1940, he published two issues of *Real Mystery*, but the first issue consisted primarily of retitled stories from his earlier entries in the field. All three magazines featured stories that were strong on sex and sadism and had little plot or mystery. Some of the regulars for the other terror pulps worked for Red Circle, which paid competitive rates, but many of their stories were by unknowns or were done under house names. The magazines featured stunning covers by Norman Saunders and also had competent interior artwork. The stories, however, were rough material for the pulps, and that signaled trouble.

Donald Graham fit in perfectly with Red Circle and wrote a number of their lead stories. Among them were "Scourge of the Corpse Clan," "Mates for Hell's Half-World Minions," and "Revelry in Hell," based on an idea similar to that used in "Circus Freaks" and perhaps qualifying as the most gruesome, torture-filled story ever published in any of the horror pulps.

Mystery Novels and Short Stories, published by Winford Magazines, began early in 1939, featuring the same brand of sex and sadism that was popular in all the magazines in the field. It was cheaply produced and had low rates. Evidently it made a profit, since the publisher continued it on an irregular basis through 1940. However, Winford joined the game as it was winding down to its inevitable conclusion.

The first step was taken in 1938 when *Dime Mystery*, the first into the field, became the first out of it. Rogers Terrill switched the magazine from mystery-horror to detective-horror. Before, the heroes of *Dime Mystery* were *never* detectives. Now, all of them were. Terrill kept the same type of plotting masterminds with their fiendish death devices, but now featured them battling equally strange detectives. To further capture the reader, Terrill featured these new detectives in series roles.

There was Nat Perry, the hemophiliac detective, for whom even one scratch might mean death. Nicholas Street, an amnesiac named after the location where he was found, searched for his identity and found crime instead. Russell Gray had Ben Byrn, five feet tall but with arms like steel bands. There were many others. The villains were as diabolical as ever, but the sex-and-sadism element was gone. The emphasis was now on detective fiction.

The war in Europe changed things for Popular. A common practice for the pulps was to ship returns to England as ballast and then sell the magazines there. However, English censors frowned on any sex in the horror pulps, so it was kept to a minimum. Then, with new competition and overseas problems, emphasis switched again. "One day sex went out because the British market wouldn't stand for it, in which case I kept on the clothes of the full-bodied heroine throughout the adventure," explained Bruno Fischer. "War in Europe and the loss of the foreign market brought sex back, laid on with a trowel." [28] Unfortunately, the increased emphasis on sex also brought the reformers out.

Mayor Fiorello La Guardia of New York and the American Legion began a campaign to clean up the newsstands in 1939. La Guardia put pressure on all the publishers located in the city. "Cleanup organizations started to throw their weight around and gave editors jitters," Fischer stated. "Artists and writers were instructed to put panties and brassieres on the girls." [29]

Red Circle ran into trouble with the government for using reprints without clearly labeling them as such. Winford's *Mystery Novels and Short Stories* ran into the same problem. Both publishers agreed not to continue the practice, and both dropped their horror titles shortly afterward. [30]

Popular remained in the field somewhat longer. In 1940 it began two new magazines, *Sinister Stories* and *Startling Mystery*. Neither lasted the year. Sex was effectively removed from all the Popular horror titles on instructions coming from the top. "Popular always had a policy of steering away from the so-called sex or spicy titles," declared Henry Steeger. "When *Horror Stories* and *Terror Tales* were started, they were clean from start to finish and the editors were told to keep them that way. However, . . . the editors began to pull sex into the stories and it was quite some time before I realized how far they had gone." [31] *Horror* and *Terror* continued without the sex into early 1941, when both magazines were finally discontinued.

Thrilling Mystery followed the lead of *Dime Mystery* and converted into a regular detective mystery pulp featuring weird villains and unusual heroes.

By the middle 1940s, even those gimmicks were dropped and both magazines were standard detective pulps.

The end was sudden and complete. Bruno Fischer summed it up best: "In the fall of 1940, I followed the example of other word slingers and went with my family to Florida for the winter. We had hardly got settled when the clean-'em up boys and girls won their fight. Horror-terror was out, with or without sex." [32]

Of the horror pulps, only *Spicy Mystery* remained. Even that magazine encountered newsstand pressure, and in January 1943 changed its title to *Speed Mystery*. Stories grew much tamer until the magazine was nothing more than another detective pulp.

It was not just through the efforts of La Guardia and the American Legion that the horror pulps died. Their time was coming to an end before the reformers ever got started. New publishing ideas were already beginning to spell an end for the pulps. Martin Goodman readily dropped his pulp magazines as his comic book sales soared into the millions during the early days of 1940. Winford Publications went the same path. Paperbacks started in 1939, and they spelled death to the reprint pulps. Many of the mainstays of the field began to drop out. Popular bought up each title as the publishers sold it, and by the middle 1940s was publishing *Argosy, Adventure,* and *Black Mask,* the big three name titles in the pulp field. Popular was the undisputed leader. The horror pulps were an episode of pulp history that had come to an end.

Notes

1. Robert Jones, *The Shudder Pulps* (West Linn, Ore.: FAX Collector's Editions, 1975), p. 115.
2. Nils Hardin, "An Interview with Henry Steeger," *Xenophile,* July 1977, p. 3.
3. Ibid.
4. Ibid., p. 4.
5. Ibid., p. 6.
6. Ron Goulart, *Cheap Thrills* (New Rochelle, N.Y.: Arlington House, 1972), p. 178.
7. Hardin, p. 5.
8. Jones, p. 6.
9. *Dime Mystery,* October 1933, p. 4.
10. Norvell Page, "How I Write," *Writer's Yearbook 1935,* p. 17.
11. Ibid., p. 18.
12. Letter from Mrs. Gean Purcell, March 1980.
13. Wyatt Blassingame, "Plotting and Writing the Terror Story," *Writer's Digest,* July 1936, p. 13.
14. Frank Gruber, *The Pulp Jungle* (Los Angeles: Sherbourne Press, 1967), p. 69.
15. Wyatt Blassingame, "Kill Them the Hard Way," *Writer's Digest,* August 1940, p. 32.
16. Jones, p. 221.
17. Ibid.

18. Bruno Fischer, "The Writer Was Too Successful," *Writer's Digest,* July 1945, p. 30.
19. Blassingame, "Plotting and Writing the Terror Story," p. 14.
20. Ibid., p. 17.
21. Stephen Metz, "Robert Leslie Bellem, the Great Unknown," *Xenophile,* February 1976, p. 49.
22. Gruber, p. 89.
23. Goulart, p. 14.
24. Hardin, p. 7.
25. Jones, p. 25.
26. Richard Tooker, "Writing the Terror Story," *Author and Journalist,* June 1936, p. 17.
27. Jones, p. 130.
28. Fischer, p. 32.
29. Ibid., p. 32.
30. A. A. Mathieu, "The Good Fight Is Won," *Writer's Digest,* March 1942.
31. Hardin, p. 8.
32. Fischer, p. 32.

Historical Bibliography

This historical bibliography has been arranged sequentially by date of first publication. Thus, the first weird-menace pulp magazine is listed first (*Dime Mystery,* 1933), and the final published magazine is listed last (*Real Mystery,* 1940). In this way, the interested reader can follow the history of the field through the beginning of each magazine, as described in the first part of this chapter.

5-1. Dime Mystery (1933).

Dime Mystery was the first of the horror pulps and, for that reason alone, the most important. This magazine set the standard and the example for all those to follow. It signaled the change to the horror motif, and when it switched format back to straight detective stories (even with a horror orientation) it marked the beginning of the end of the terror period.

Rogers Terrill was the chief editor of *Dime Mystery,* and he served as the main architect of the story type that appeared in that magazine, and thus in all the horror magazines. Terrill's definitions of "horror," "terror," and "mystery" (see beginning of this chapter) served as a basis for the stories in all three of his major horror publications. The stories were solicited in issues of *Writer's Digest,* a major market source for pulp contributors in the 1930s. In the August 1933 issue, Terrill spelled out what he wanted in terms of fantastic mysteries with seemingly supernatural or supernormal events. However, he clearly stated, "No matter how grotesque, there must be a logical explanation" (p. 6).

In the same magazine in November 1933, Terrill stressed that he wanted stories with "mystery, horror and credibility." These terms served as basic ground rules for all the stories in the Terrill-edited pulps.

The first issue of the new *Dime Mystery* appeared in October 1933. The lead story was "The Dance of the Skeletons" by Norvell Page, a short novel taking up approximately half the magazine. Also included were two other short novels and three short stories. In years to come, the novel shrank in size until it was only 25 pages or so (about 15,000–18,000 words). Medium-length stories in the 8,000- to 10,000-word range dominated the contents, and some issues featured three or four novelettes along with a group of shorts.

Along with the Page story were contributions by Hugh Cave, Franklin H. Martin, and Edgar Wallace. The November issue of *Dime Mystery* featured a long novel by Cave (as well as a short story by him under his Geoffrey Vace pen name). Page returned in December with "The Death Beast," the lead novel, which featured a giant wolf that fed on blood. Wyatt Blassingame followed in January with "Death Underground."

The writing was brisk and pulpy, always with explanations for the unbelievable events. Unfortunately, the explanations often left major holes in the plot glaringly revealed, as authors were not always adept at tying up loose ends. But no one seemed to care.

The villains were often masked, always disguised, and usually out for some sort of financial reward. Madmen were plentiful, but were usually "red herrings" to draw suspicion from the coldly calculating master plotter. Typical villains included greedy guardians, power-crazy inventors, and rejected suitors. Trying to drive the hero or heroine insane was the most popular pastime, and leprosy was the most popular threat other than death. Subterranean torture vaults were the most common location.

Early covers were done by Walter M. Baumhofer. In later years, Baumhofer went on to do covers for *Field and Stream.* Interior art was usually by Amos Sewell, who became a cover artist for *The Saturday Evening Post.* Later, Tom Lovell took over the cover chores, although Sewell continued to do the interiors.

Typical story beginnings were: "She was afraid—but she did not know what it was she feared. It was nothing, yet it was a dread that haunted her every waking hour." * "Darkness lay heavily on Maury Bay and invested Oak Point with Stygian gloom. Against the faint glow of rippling water, the squat bulk of a house showed visible only because of the more solid quality of its blackness, a blackness somehow ominous." †

---

* Frederick C. Davis, "Necklaces for the Dying," *Dime Mystery,* March 1936, p. 8.
† Arthur Leo Zagat, "Garden of the Dying," *Dime Mystery,* July 1934, p. 11.

Unlike the science fiction and fantasy magazines of the same period, the menaces and plots were not awesome. Often, unbelievably complex traps were conceived just to wrest a few hundred dollars away from the hero. "The Tongueless Horror" as depicted by Wyatt Blassingame (and faithfully executed by Walter Baumhofer on the cover for April 1934) killed using "a poison only recently discovered and based in tetra-ethyl lead" and then cut the tongue out of his victim, in the quest of $5,000 extortion money. He was brought to justice the same night he made his demand by a detective and a hospital technician. Stories were local, not national in scope.

Formula was the order of the day, but some nonformula stories and writing did manage to make it into *Dime Mystery*. The magazine featured a small number of fantasy stories. Most famous was the series by Chandler Whipple, "The Curse of the Harcourts." The six stories began in the February 1935 issue and ran through October 1935. Together, they formed an episodic novel. In the first, "The Son of Darkness," the evil Signor Pirelli curses the d'Harcourt family and their ancestral line in the year 1000. Each of the succeeding stories details how future Harcourts battle the curse as they are pursued by reincarnations of the devilish Pirelli. "Curse of the Harcourts" (March 1935) takes place in thirteenth-century Wales. "Shadow of the Plague" takes place in London at the time of the Black Death. "White Lady of Hell" has sixteenth-century Florence as the setting. Puritan New England is the location and time of "A Child for Satan" (September 1935), and the modern day brings Lionel Harcourt, in "The Last Harcourt" (October 1935), face to face with the monster Pirelli for the last time. The Harcourt series was reasonably popular with the readership of *Dime Mystery,* but it was the only continued series featured in the magazine. Popular Publications was strongly against continued stories or serials, often proclaiming "All Stories Complete," so the Harcourt series was a one-time occurrence. Whipple served as an editor at Popular during the time that his stories appeared, and that fact might have helped sell the grouping. He later left the company and took over as editor of *Argosy*.

Paul Ernst also succeeded in selling several fantasy stories to *Dime Mystery*. Ernst, who was living in rural Pennsylvania at the time, wrote a number of weird fantasies set in rural areas. The best of these was "The Devil's Doorstep" (October 1935), coincidentally the same issue with the last Harcourt story, in which a young couple buys an old home that contains a fireplace opening into a chasm that leads directly to hell. However, such stories were rare, and by 1936 had all but disappeared from the magazine.

First-person narration was used in about half the stories, and surprisingly enough for the time, women were often the narrators or the main characters in the stories. Arthur Leo Zagat often had a female lead in his short novels and novelettes for all the Popular magazines. Some sort of logical explanation was always given, with all the supposedly supernatural elements explained away, usually at the end of the story; often the villain would gloatingly explain his methods to the helpless heroine and hero just before fate, the police, or a convenient earthquake saved the couple from terrible death.

September 1938 was the last horror issue of *Dime Mystery*. The editorial announced the format change that brought in detectives battling weird criminals. Soon, even that idea had degenerated into straight detective fiction. In the 1940s, *Dime Mystery*, by then strictly a mystery and detective magazine, published a number of Ray Bradbury's earliest stories. The magazine continued through October 1950, running for a total of 159 issues, of which 60 were mystery-horror.

PUBLISHING HISTORY. Published (horror issues) October 1933 (vol. 3, no. 3) through September 1938 (vol. 18, no. 2). Monthly, four issues per volume, total of 60 horror issues. Titled *Dime Mystery Magazine* throughout this run. Editor: Rogers Terrill; associate editors included Henry Treat Sperry and Loring Dowst. Publisher: Popular Publications, New York. Price: 10 cents.

5–2. Terror Tales (1934).

Soon after the success of *Dime Mystery* [5–1] was firmly established, Popular Publications brought out *Terror Tales*. Unlike the first magazine, there could be no mistaking the contents of this one by its title. Where *Dime Mystery* featured murky dark covers, primarily by Baumhofer, *Terror* had bright yellow lettering and violent, fantastic covers mostly done by John Howitt. The featured stories were the same style and work as in the other two major Popular Publications horror pulps.

Of the early contributors, Arthur Leo Zagat probably was the most influential. He wrote a number of excellent lead novels, beginning with "House of Living Death" in the first issue and including such titles as "When Love Went Mad," "Chains of the Living Dead," and "Crawling Madness." Zagat often used the heroine as his lead character and effectively built up scenes where she was alone and frightened waiting for something to happen—and it always did. Madmen were popular villains in Zagat stories, but they usually had the profit motive spurring them on.

Nat Schachner, Zagat's friend and one-time collaborator, also wrote a number of excellent stories for the early issues of *Terror Tales*. He featured strange cultists and bands of evil old men in his stories, some of which included "They Dare Not Die," "Death Takes a Bride," "Death Teaches School," and "Railroad to Hell." Also appearing frequently in these issues were Wyatt Blassingame, Hugh Cave, and Paul Ernst (under both his own name and his pen name, George Edson).

One of the very best stories to appear in *Terror* was written by an author who had only one story in the Popular horror titles. "Satan's Roadhouse" by Carl Jacobi was an excellent short novel in which a detective encounters voodoo not far from New Orleans. Jacobi was a regular contributor to *Weird Tales* and did write a number of mystery-horror stories for *Thrilling Mystery* [5–6].

An early story by Wyatt Blassingame, "The Unholy Goddess," featured a theme that the author was to repeat several times in his work for the Popular horror pulps. The narrator encounters a beautiful woman, often nude, who tempts him and promises him evil rewards if he will do her bidding. Her bidding usually involves torture and death, often with those whom the hero loves best as the victims. The hero tries to obey, his actions getting wilder and wilder. At the end of the story, the hero is locked in an asylum after trying to kill himself, and his actions are explained by the doctors as due to dope, insanity, or some other affliction. However, there is always some physical evidence that he was driven into his mad state by a supernatural creature. "Satan Sends a Woman" (January 1936) featured this same theme.

Later issues of *Terror Tales* featured much more sex and sadism than the early issues, and stories from that period did not hold up as well or make any great impression. One of the best was "Salves for the Wine Goddess" by Russell Gray, with its possibility of fantasy. "Test-Tube Frankenstein" by Wayne Robbins had the best cover of all the later issues of *Terror*. It also was the best story to appear in the later issues (May 1940). In this science fiction tale, a scientist creates artificial life that can imitate anything it sees. The monster kills the scientist and then tries to kill the hero, the one person that realizes it exists. Able to take on the appearance of any person, the creature has a distinct advantage over the hero, who doesn't know what the creature even looks like—or who. However, when it disguises itself as the main character's wife, the monster betrays itself in an unusual way. Trying to entice him closer, the creature begins disrobing. But having never seen a naked human body, it creates breasts without nipples. The creature escapes the hero, however, and at the end the hero kills the creature (using a knife to hack it to shreds), which has kept the form of his wife. As usual, the story concludes with the hero wondering whether he has killed the monster or his wife. It was an effective, well-written (if somewhat overdone) horror story combining the best elements of science fiction and horror.

PUBLISHING HISTORY. First published September 1934. Monthly through July 1936, then bimonthly through March–April 1941, last publication date. Four issues per volume, total of 51 issues. Editor: Rogers Terrill. Publisher: Popular Publications, New York. Price: 15 cents.

5–3. Horror Stories (1935).

Horror Stories was the third of the "Big Three" (after *Dime Mystery* and *Terror Tales*) horror fiction pulps published by Popular Publications. Rogers Terrill served as chief editor on all three magazines, and stories were substantially the same in all of them. By the time the first issue of *Horror* was published, the lead novel had shrunk to about 28 pages, and it leveled off at about 25–26 pages, or 12,000–15,000 words.

The first issue of *Horror Stories* featured a stunning cover by John Newton Howitt, probably the best artist for the mystery-horror pulps and the mainstay of the Popular line. Howitt was known for his grim depictions of wild scenes of madness. His women were perfect "damsels in distress," and his menaces were evil madmen whose eyes seemed to glow right out of the covers. Howitt made brilliant use of colors and backgrounds and was a master of detail—the Hieronymous Bosch of the pulps.

Howitt was born in 1885 and opened his studio in New York when he was 22 years old. He became an established portrait painter and illustrator, listed in many major reference books on modern American artwork. He began doing pulp paintings when he was nearly 50 years old and probably did some 200 pulp covers in the span of six or seven years. (As so little research has been done on the pulps of the 1930s, an exact date for the start of Howitt's pulp career is not available, nor is the exact number of his paintings.) Howitt later worked for *Liberty* and then returned to landscapes, having numerous exhibits before his death at age 75. His work was once described in a publicity release from Ainslie Galleries in these glowing terms: "Mr. Howitt is concerned with the American scene. He is fond of peaceful country—Vermont pastures, rocky Rhode Island fields, the hills of Westchester. . . ." Could this be the same artist who did the covers for "Men without Blood," "Death's Bloodstream," and "Hospital of the Damned"?*

By the time *Horror* was published, the Popular mystery-horror pattern was already well established. The first issue of the magazine featured a lead novel by Francis James, novelettes by Arthur Leo Zagat, John Knox, and Wyatt Blassingame, and a group of short stories. Amos Sewell did all the illustrations. There was an editorial of sorts, mainly promoting the stories in that issue, and no letter column. The magazine contained 128 pages.

Authors featured in the next few issues included Arthur J. Burks, Nat Schachner, Paul Ernst, Francis James, and Wyatt Blassingame. There were new names from time to time—but mainly the regulars dominated. John Dickson Carr had one story, "The Door to Doom," in the magazine in 1935.

By 1937, sex had crept into *Horror Stories*. Covers were usually by Howitt, but Don Hewitt also did a number of paintings, as did several other unidentified artists. Women still wore a few shreds of clothing in the interior illustrations, but very few. And the blurbs promised a great deal more: "What seeds of lust were planted in my heart? What grisly power lurked in my soul—that I could summon from the grave the woman of my bygone sins—and feed her with the life blood I stole from my wife's warm body!"† The stories were the same, with logical endings for seemingly supernatural events. Besides Blassingame, Knox, and Ernst, there were new names—Ralston Shields, Donald Graham, and Julius Long, to name a few. Sadism was more in evidence and the stories were shorter and bloodier.

By 1938, the magazine had shrunk to 112 pages, although the number of stories remained about the same, meaning that the length of the lead stories

* William Papalia, "John Newton Howitt, a Discussion," *Xenophile*, July 1977. The definitive article on this artist whose pulp work was among the most influential of all painters in the field.
† Blurb for "Daughter of the Devil" by Ralston Shields, October 1937.

shrank again. The women in the illustrations were rarely clad now, and they were threatened with sexual abuse as well as torture and death. However, the motives remained the same, as we can see from the following exchange:

> "Would you mind telling me your reason for all this?"
>
> "Sure I'll tell you why. You won't be alive much longer! . . . When I was young and stupid I thought I was in love with our dear friend, Helen. But would she have me? No! And why? Because she and you and all the rest of that damned crowd thought you were too good for me. But don't think I'd ever lose my head over any woman," he continued. "Not much! It's money I want. . . ." (from "Things That Once Were Girls" by Donald Graham, August 1938)

Sex and sadism lasted until late 1939, when it disappeared quickly and completely. Horror was back, but it lacked the punch and vitality of the early stories. Covers were bland and did not have the smooth professional look of the earlier work by Howitt. Many of the later stories had a science fiction slant, but the tales were poorly done compared with the science fiction of the time. *Horror Stories* seemed to fade away rather than just die.

PUBLISHING HISTORY. Published January 1935 through April 1941. Issues in 1935 published January, February, March, June through December; following December 1935 issue, ran as bimonthly for rest of its history. Four issues per volume, total of 41 issues. Editor: Rogers Terrill, with help from Steve Farrelly, Leon Byrne, and Loring Dowst. Publisher: Popular Publications, New York. Price: 15 cents.

5-4. Thrilling Mysteries (1935).

The first and only issue of *Thrilling Mysteries* was published by Popular Publications in April 1935. With *Terror Tales* started in September 1934 and *Horror Stories* the following January, the April date seemed to indicate that *Thrilling* was the next in a series of horror pulps. Departments were set up exactly like Popular's other horror titles [5–1, 5–2, 5–3] (with the "Crypt of Terror," a quasi-editorial promoting the stories in the issue being run by the Black Monk) and interior illustrations by Amos Sewell. The cover was by Emery Clarke in the *Dime Mystery* style.

Stories included a short novel, "Army of the Maimed" by Arthur Leo Zagat (a horde of maimed beggars is organized by a masked villain who plans to use them to control a city), and stories by Nat Schachner, Arthur J. Burks, Hugh Cave, and others. All were in the usual Terrill mold and could have been featured in any other Popular horror pulps.

Problems with Standard Publications [see 5–6] caused *Thrilling Mysteries* to be dropped after one issue (it was announced as a monthly).

PUBLISHING HISTORY. One issue, April 1935 (vol. 1, no. 1). Editor: Rogers Terrill. Publisher: Popular Publications, New York. Price: 15 cents.

5-5. Spicy Mystery (1935).

Story quality was never a major goal of the Spicy magazines, published by Delaware-based Culture Publications. Instead, the stories were designed to feature long, loving descriptions of the female characters, with great emphasis on anatomical parts. Explicit sex was never featured in the pulps, but the Spicy magazines focused on soft-core sex throughout their history. Stories were kept short, with a 5,500-word maximum, and most were written under contract. Lew Merrill, Hugh Cave, and Robert Leslie Bellem were a few of the contributors who wrote under both their true names and a host of pseudonyms.

Spicy Mystery featured horror and weird stories, often employing supernatural villains or science fiction trappings such as death rays or creatures from space. Anything was allowed, including unhappy endings, as long as the requisite sex scenes were included. None of the stories were very good; Hugh Cave's work, usually under the name of Justin Case, was the best of the lot. Authors were not above using story ideas from other sources; Han Heinz Ewers's "The Spider" was rewritten several times during the course of the magazine's publication! In the early 1940s, *Spicy Mystery* began featuring reprints of earlier stories, usually with no indication that they were reprints and often under new titles. However, since the magazine was never copyrighted, it never ran into trouble with the government. In the middle 1940s, the title was changed to *Speed Mystery,* and the magazine became much more of a mystery periodical, still with some attempt to publish racier material than most pulps.

PUBLISHING HISTORY. First published June 1935 (vol. 1, no. 1). Monthly through December 1937, six issues per volume. Issues skipped in 1938, 1939, 1940, 1941, and 1942, although no data exists on exactly what issues were published; 1941 probably included January (vol. 9, no. 6); February (vol. 10, no. 1); March (no. 3); April (no. 4); June–July (no. 5); August–September (no. 6); October (vol. 11, no. 1); November (no. 2); and December (no. 3); 1942 included January, February, and March (vol. 11, nos. 4, 5, and 6); April (vol. 12, no. 1); May (no. 2); June–July (no. 3); August–September (no. 4); October (no. 5); November (vol. 13, no. 1); and December (the last issue, no. 2). As one collector stated, "The Spicy magazines exist in an information vacuum all their own." Editor: Lawrence Cadmen. Publisher: Culture Publications, Wilmington, Delaware. Price: 25 cents.

5–6. Thrilling Mystery (1935).

Thrilling Mystery was the major competitor to the Popular Publications magazines. The stories followed much the same pattern as those in the three Popular magazines [5–1, 5–2, 5–3], which was not surprising since many of the same contributors appeared in all the publications. For example, the first issue of *Thrilling Mystery* featured stories by Paul Ernst, Ray Cummings, and Arthur J. Burks. Also included were tales by Robert Wallace and C. K. M. Scanlon, two house names for the chain, and G. T. Fleming-Roberts and Allan Echols, who did nearly all their writing for the *Thrilling* line. Stories were shorter and contained no sex element at all. Heroines were necessary, but the worst that could threaten them was death. Cover art was poor and the interiors not much better. The magazine sold for 10 cents, and this was proclaimed in a big white circle displayed under the title.

Thrilling Mystery changed very little during its entire run as a horror pulp. The covers were uniformly terrible, the cover artist never identified. The authors often were the same writers who appeared in the Popular magazines, although the stories read as if they might have been rejects from Popular. Length never varied, with seven to nine stories per issue, the longest around 10,000 words, the shortest a few thousand.

A few science fiction authors wrote for *Thrilling Mystery,* but most of them contributed only one or two stories before realizing that their work was not what the magazine wanted. Edmond Hamilton appeared with "The Earth Dwellers" in the April 1936 issue. Jack Williamson published "Death's Cold Daughter" in September of that year.

Robert E. Howard, creator of the Conan series in *Weird Tales,* had a number of novelettes in *Thrilling Mystery,* the best of which was "Graveyard Rats" in the February 1936 issue. Howard's florid style might have seemed perfect for the type of story published in *Thrilling Mystery,* but his work proved too grim and cheerless.

Although sex was out, fantasy was in at *Thrilling Mystery* if handled right. The publisher (the Standard group) already had several science fiction magazines and was later to publish one on fantasy, *Strange Stories.* Out-and-out fantasies were rarely published. However, editor Leo Margulies would accept and often publish stories with "Lady-or-the-Tiger" endings—leaving the reader to decide if supernatural elements were at work, or just coincidence. In this fashion, supernatural vengeance could overtake a killer and no one could complain that the story was a fantasy; a logical, possible ending was offered as well.

Margulies was successful in recruiting all types of pulp authors. Thorp McClusky, Carl Jacobi, and Henry Kuttner, regulars for *Weird Tales,* did stories for *Thrilling Mystery;* mystery writers Stewert Sterling and Fredric Brown were contributors; even Joe Archibald, who wrote humorous World War I air stories, did several horror stories for Standard.

By 1940, *Thrilling Mystery* was featuring more and more detective stories in the *Dime Mystery* vein—with unusual detectives battling weird villains. By November 1941, the banner across the top of the magazine stated "Detective Stories That Are Different." By 1942, *Thrilling Mystery* had changed completely into a regular detective pulp, even though that change had been coming gradually from the late 1930s on.

PUBLISHING HISTORY. First published October 1935 (vol. 1, no. 1). Monthly through September 1937, then bimonthly through November 1941 (when it became a detective pulp). There was no issue for November 1935; December 1935 was vol. 1, no. 2. Three issues per volume, total of 48 issues. (*Thrilling Mystery* continued to be published as a detective pulp through May

1947, although the title changed to *Thrilling Mystery Novel Magazine* with the winter 1945 issue. The entire run of the magazine, from the October 1935 issue until May 1947, was 74 issues.) Editor: Leo Margulies (under the pseudonym Harvey Burns). Other editors might have worked under his supervision, but none are known for sure. Publisher: Beacon Magazines (Standard Magazine group), New York. Price: 10 cents.

5-7. Ace Mystery (1936).

The first of Ace's three attempts at a horror pulp [see 5-8, 5-10]; *Ace Mystery* was the best of the three, but still not competitive with either the Popular titles [5-1, 5-2, 5-3] or *Thrilling Mystery* [5-6]. Stories read like rejects from the better paying magazines.

Frederick Davis wrote the lead short novels for all three issues. All three novels were told from the viewpoint of the heroine, but are otherwise undistinguished. *Ace Mystery* did feature a number of stories with science fiction devices or supernatural occurrences, but the writing was uniformly mediocre. Other contributors included Arthur Leo Zagat, John Knox, Hugh Cave, and Paul Ernst. Covers were either by Norman Saunders or Rafael De Soto and were all quite good. Interiors were the usual terrible stuff. Story titles included "Bride for the Half-Dead," "Doomsday Fate," and "Coyote Woman." The last was probably the best of any of the stories in *Ace Mystery*. It is a weird-horror fantasy in which the hero is attacked by three vampires in the middle of the desert. Only the rising sun enables him to escape the monsters' clutches and kill them. By no means a masterpiece, it was nonetheless a most effective mood story laced with some real suspense.

PUBLISHING HISTORY. Published May, July, and September 1936 (vol. 1, nos. 1, 2, and 3). Total of three issues. Editor: Harry Widmer. Publisher: Ace Magazine, New York. Price: 10 cents.

5-8. Eerie Stories (1937).

This pulp—Ace Magazine's second entry [see 5-7, 5-10] into the horror pulp field—was a complete failure. Stories included "Virgins of the Stone Death," "The Pain Master's Bride," and "Mate of the Beast," the final story actually a reprint of "Wolf Vengeance" from *Ace Mystery*. The cover by Norman Saunders, featuring a man threatening a woman with a blowtorch, far exceeded anything inside.

PUBLISHING HISTORY. One issue, August 1937 (vol. 1, no. 1). Scheduled for bimonthly publication. Editor: Harry Widmer. Publisher: Ace Magazine, New York. Price: 15 cents.

5-9. Mystery Tales (1938).

The first of the horror pulps published by Martin Goodman's Manvis Publications, *Mystery Tales* was evidently a retitling of one of Goodman's Western or detective pulps (the numbering of the volume indicated earlier issues). This practice of completely changing the contents, title, and direction of a pulp magazine while keeping the volume and issue sequence intact was common practice where a second-class mailing permit was the most important thing needed to publish a magazine. Once the permit was in hand, publishers did almost anything they could to retain the privilege.

Mystery Tales featured a strong mixture of sex and sadism with very little mystery or suspense. The horror in the stories was the result of gruesome torture and mutilation, not from any skill of the authors in creating an atmosphere of fear. There was no attempt at plot complexity, and the plot lines were the same as in the other horror pulps; a diabolical scheme to drive the hero insane by making him think he was a murderer or maniac was the most common, but the emphasis was on sex and shock.

Donald Graham was the most prolific author, with "Mates for Hell's Half-World Minions" typical of his story title and approach. He was the master of torture stories and wrote the most shocking tales ever to be published in the entire horror pulp genre, filled with lust, degradation, and torture. Other authors working for *Mystery Tales* included Arthur J. Burks, Wayne Rogers, Wyatt Blassingame, and Robert Leslie Bellem. Many authors refused to work for this entire Red Circle line because of the heavy emphasis on sadism.

PUBLISHING HISTORY. First published March 1938 (vol. 2, no. 3). Rarely kept to proposed bimonthly schedule. Remaining issues in 1938 were June (no. 4) and November (no. 5); in 1939, February (no. 6), June (vol. 3, no. 1), September (no. 2), and December (no. 3); in 1940, March (no. 4) and May (no. 5). Total of nine issues. Editor: Robert O. Erisman. Publisher: Western Fiction Publishing (later changed to Manvis Publications), New York. Price: 15 cents.

5–10. Eerie Mysteries (1938).

The third and final Ace entry into the horror field [see 5–7, 5–8], *Eerie Mysteries* featured both new stories and reprints, although reprints were not identified as such and came from other Ace magazines such as *Ten Detective Aces* and *Secret Agent X*. Many of the stories appeared under Ace house names or were by undistinguished or unknown authors. None were noteworthy, and after four issues owner A. A. Wyn must have decided that the horror field was not for him.

PUBLISHING HISTORY. Published August–September 1938 (vol. 1, no. 1); November–December (no. 2); February–March 1939 (no. 3); April–May (no. 4). Bimonthly. Total of four issues. Editor: Harry Widmer. Publisher: Ace Magazine, New York. Price: 15 cents.

5–11. Mystery Novels and Short Stories (1939).

This was one of the last horror pulps to be placed on the market (March 1939). The magazine paid one-half cent a word on publication and was usually not recommended by authors describing the horror market in various writers' magazines. Since it was not a dependable payer, it featured stories by unknowns or under numerous house names. Story titles were typical: "Mate of the Demon," "Satan Takes a Wife," "Mistress of the Murder Madmen," and "Bride of the Ape." Authors who wrote for the magazine included Harold Ward (who contributed to *Weird Tales* for many years), Frank Belknap Long, and Arthur J. Burks. None of their stories were memorable. Covers were usually by Norman Saunders and, as was often the case, were the best things about the magazine.

PUBLISHING HISTORY. Published March 1939 (vol. 1, no. 1), then May, July, September, December 1939, July 1940, and final issue December 1940 (vol. 2, no. 1). Six issues per volume, total of seven issues. Editor: Abner Sundell. Publisher: Double Action Magazines, New York. Price: 15 cents; dropped to 10 cents September 1939.

5–12. Uncanny Tales (1939).

The second Red Circle horror pulp [see 5–9], this magazine's title suggested science fiction or fantasy stories. As usual, the contents were the same blend of sex, sadism, and torture offered by all the Red Circle pulps. *Uncanny* featured stories by Frederick Davis, Arthur J. Burks, and Russell Gray, all regulars with Popular Publications, as well as a number of authors (or author's pseudonyms) who wrote only for the Red Circle magazines.

Uncanny Tales had the dubious honor of publishing "Revelry in Hell" by Donald Graham, probably the most sadistic torture story ever featured in the horror pulps. "The Gargoyles of Madness" by Russell Gray presented an interesting scene. The hero awakens in bed after passing out in a stupor. Going to the clothes closet, he notices a small pool of blood and a strange pair of shoes. On investigation, the hero discovers that there are still *feet* in the shoes. Arthur J. Burks combined fur-fetishism, seduction, and sadomasochism in "Flesh-Hungry Phantoms" in a 1940 *Uncanny*. All in all, the magazine was an advertisement for the worst in the horror pulps.

PUBLISHING HISTORY. Published April–May 1939 (vol. 2, no. 6, another magazine evidently continued from where another pulp ended); then August–September (vol. 3, no. 1), December–January 1939–1940 (no. 2), March 1940 (no. 3), and May 1940 (no. 4). Bimonthly. Total of five issues. Editor: Robert O. Erisman. Publisher: Manvis Publications, New York. Price: 15 cents.

5–13. Sinister Stories (1940).

Published for three issues in 1940, *Sinister* was one of the last horror pulps. By the time it started, sex and sadism had been cut out of the horror magazines, and the three issues published weird-horror stories much in the style of the early issues of *Horror* [5–3] and *Terror* [5–2]. Unfortunately, the authors involved in the stories for *Sinister* had been writing the sex-and-sadism tales, not the early Gothic adventures. None of the stories showed much originality or suspense. The lead stories were so short that there was little chance to build any sort of mood or impact. All three issues reprinted covers used on other Popular horror pulps. Interior illustrations were also reprints.

In an effort to cut costs, Popular set up a Chicago publishing company. Called Fictioneers, this group paid only one-half cent a word (compared to the one cent a word normally paid by Popular). Needless to say, this move did not make Fictioneers pulps very popular markets for the writers. Thus, *Sinister,* which was officially a Fictioneers magazine, probably did not get the same quality of submissions as earlier horror titles. Many authors could easily work for other pulps outside the horror field, and those who could write only horror stories were usually not the best authors anyway.

Of the stories published in *Sinister,* Hugh Cave's long novelette, "School Mistress for the Mad," was probably the best; "The Dead Who Hate the Living" by Francis James was fairly well written when compared to most of the stories in the issues.

PUBLISHING HISTORY. Published March 1940 (vol. 1, no. 1), then April and May 1940 (nos. 2 and 3). Total of three issues. Editor: Costa Carousso. Publisher: Fictioneers (branch of Popular Publications), Chicago. Price: 15 cents.

5–14. Startling Mystery (1940).

Startling Mystery ran for only two issues in 1940. It was another Fictioneers pulp venture from Popular [see 5–13], and featured reprinted covers as well as reprinted interior illustrations. Paying only one-half cent per word, the magazine featured little worth printing. Probably the most famous story to appear was "The Dinner Cooked in Hell" by Mindret Lord, which dealt with a group of people unwittingly participating in a cannibalistic dinner. A gruesome tale, it was reprinted in *The Pulps,* edited by Tony Goodstone, as an example of the mystery-horror story genre. Unfortunately, although it is a horror story, it shows little of the true nature of the genre and is a poor example at best.

PUBLISHING HISTORY. Published February 1940 (vol. 1, no. 1), then April 1940 (no. 2). Total of two issues. Editor: Costa Carousso. Publisher: Fictioneers, Chicago. Price: 15 cents.

5–15. Real Mystery (1940).

Published for two issues in 1940, *Real Mystery* featured reprints from earlier Red Circle horror pulps [see 5–9, 5–12]. Unfortunately, these reprints were presented as new stories, with new titles, and used illustrations from other Red Circle stories. Red Circle ran into trouble with the federal government because of this practice, and the magazine was dropped, as were all their horror pulps, although economics more than government intervention probably canceled the other two magazines.

PUBLISHING HISTORY. Published April 1940 (vol. 1, no. 1), then July 1940 (no. 2). Total of two issues. Editor: Robert O. Erisman. Publisher: Western Fiction Publishing, New York. Price: 15 cents.

Part II
Poetry

6
Supernatural Verse in English

Steve Eng

A study of supernatural poetry? How quaint; we may smile—until we recall the old ballads that still endure, the "graveyard poets," Coleridge's "Christabel," the poems of Poe, and the supernatural verses of mainstream poets such as Masefield, Frost, or Millay, as well as the larger weird output of such bards as Thomas Lovell Beddoes, Clark Ashton Smith, and Joseph Payne Brennan.

But despite recent formal interest in supernatural horror fiction, its poetry counterpart is still neglected. There are two reasons for this: (1) before 1920, the poetry of the weird is scattered through general mainstream collections, and only the rare anthologist has troubled to gather and group it around its supernatural themes (likewise, most of its criticism is diffused through larger studies); (2) after 1920, the poetry of the weird is less common and is usually found in ephemeral pulp magazines, fanzines, special limited editions, or in the journals of the Small Press movement (also, for this modern period there exists almost no criticism).

Facing these problems, we still hope to trace the long tradition of supernatural and weird poetry. For despite changes in book and magazine pub-

Note: In memory of Margaret Widdemer, 1883–1978.

lishing, in literary fashions, and in the forms of poetry, this genre has altered little with the shift of centuries. In fact, it gave rise in large part to horror fiction itself and has nourished it since (just as the attacks on horror poetry after 1720 broadened into attacks on horror fiction, which continue yet today). So for reasons of history alone, our genre deserves special, chronological study.

Aesthetically, there *are* problems. The ususal poetic virtue of terseness may cause unintended humor or flat triteness in a weird poem—whereas in fiction, writers can more slowly weave atmosphere before the climax. But enough poets have triumphed repeatedly to warrant respect and attention.

Selection criteria. Poems cited must have at least some supernatural horror/ terror elements. We have kept out merely mythological or magical poems where the supernatural is calmly taken for granted. We have barred most elf and fairy poetry—excepting older verse, where the creatures were still malign. We have allowed some poems strong only in their supernatural *tone* (but we so state); we have tolerated some poems of more supernatural-horror *rhetoric* than substance; we have picked some poems that are ostensibly funny, but with enough latent horror to qualify; and we have permitted some dragons and sea creatures (*kraken*) once deemed supernatural, but that tomorrow's science may discover to be only survived plesiosaurs. For in most instances we side with the author's original intent, and in borderline cases we weigh secondary elements like atmosphere or mood.

We name some poems we have not seen, risking another author's definition of "supernatural," but each instance is referenced. To omit them in this tentative, preliminary study, we believe, would be the greater ill.

We have been arbitrary. Poetry—densely packed, allusive, connotative, symbolic—is hard enough to analyze completely. The supernatural is even harder: after all, if it were easy to categorize and apprehend, it would lie in the tame, dull lands of the Known.

Methods. We acknowledge imbalance. Better-known poetry we sometimes pass more quickly, so as to tarry with the neglected or completely ignored poets and poetry. Thus, the space given an author or poem does not always signify relative worth. Also, we may skimp on critical analysis, to better stress valuable historical, biographical, or bibliographical lore. For much of this material is seldom or never studied, catalogued, or reprinted; our first duty has been simply to make it more accessible, that others may locate and use it. Thus, here is not a "last word," but a first review only.

Our hope is to stir more academic interest in supernatural poetry and to stimulate libraries to form core collections. Further, we would like in some small way to encourage publishers, editors, and anthologists to publish or reprint materials, and to help collectors and readers acquire and enjoy more of the poetry.

Early Traces

Bardic sources, and later. According to H. P. Lovecraft in *Supernatural Horror in Literature* (1945), "so it is in poetry that we first encounter permanent entry of the weird into standard literature." In primitive, tribal times, *magic* mastered the human mind, and poetry helped voice that magic. Usually it was in easily memorized, rhymed-and-metered verse, to be passed down for generations, such as early Irish poetry with its supernatural mood (especially 600–1100 A.D.), when the bard, or *file*, was almost a medicine man, "a dealer in magic, a weaver of spells and incantations who could blast his enemies with the venom of his verse." Even as late as the seventeenth century, an Irish king or chieftain might keep his own personal poet, although an unrewarded poet just might assail his patron with a satire, or *aer*, aimed at his reputation—or even at his body.

Such bards had become organized; they were often confined to certain families, and they underwent stern self-discipline. Reportedly they fasted, preferred solitary confinement, and practiced rhyming verses in their heads in the dark.[1] They flourished almost into modern times, if barely tolerated: reputedly someone was "rhymed to death" in 1493; an English Lord Lieutenant was "recited to death" for plundering the lands of a poet's family; and some Elizabethan officials grumbled that the poets were "great maintainers of witches and other vile matters."[2]

But Sukumar Dutt reminds us that English weird verse had Teutonic sources as well as Celtic: "Old English heroic poetry inherited a strain of old-world supernaturalism with its monstrous shapes of Grendels, fire-drakes, giants and ogres."[3] And Lovecraft praised the Scandinavian legacy: "The . . . Eddas and Sagas thunder with cosmic horror, and shake with the stark fear of Ymir and his shapeless spawn."[4]

In actual early English verse we see the supernaturalism in *Beowulf*, in Chrestien de Troyes's Arthurian romance, and in medieval lays and old romances ("strange adventures . . . outlandish things," notes Dutt), as well as in Chaucer's "Tale of Meliboeus" and his romantic parody, "Tale of Sir Thopas," with its near-supernatural happenings.

Balladry. The old ballads were in quatrains (alternating four-stress with three-stress lines), and their tragic, usually foreseeable endings made them ideal for the telling of supernatural tales. Events are often unmotivated and unexplained, which only heightens the magical mood; and like their Celtic and Scandinavian models, they take the preternatural for granted—that is, mermaids and mermen, malign elves and fairies, ghosts and witches. Frequently, a ballad follows a character to the grave (or barrow)—and beyond, to the Otherworld.[5] Although the balladists believed in the Unseen World, the best of their lyrics have drama and artistic distance—and timeless worth.

This is the spectral folksong heritage that haunted and enchanted so many who came later: the eighteenth-century ballad collectors and all those who wrote "literary ballads," such as Gothic-romantics Matthew Lewis and Walter Scott, the romantics, the Pre-Raphaelites, the late Victorian aesthetes, and modern lyricists.

Edmund Spenser. His tour de force, *The Faerie Queene* (1590–1596), had supernatural elements. The eighteenth century parodied "Old Spenser" and critics scorned *The Faerie Queene*'s lack of classical "unities," but Bishop Hurd, in 1762, rightly saw it as a "Gothic poem" with *Gothic* unity.[6] The Romantics embraced Spenser (in our genre, Southey and George Darley), and Donald Sidney-Fryer detects his strain of "pure poetry" in those California romantics Ambrose Bierce, George Sterling, and Clark Ashton Smith (see "Late Victorians and After" later in this chapter). As Kenneth Clark observed, "Spenser invented almost all the stage properties of Gothicism which were to furnish the scenery of later poets." [7]

Pre-Gothic: Melancholy and Macabre

The Elizabethans and later

But we must be tormented now with ghosts,
With apparitions fearful to behold?
                              Thomas Kyd
                              The Spanish Tragedy
                              (iii, 6), ca. 1586

Translations of Seneca appeared by 1560, and verse tragedies, often Seneca-influenced, brought ghosts and furies visibly onstage, or at least into spoken poetic dialogue.

At this time there was also a spate of "devil plays" or "witch plays." In nondramatic poetry, we note the *Awntyrs of Arthur* (ghost menacing Guenevere's mother),[8] Milton's disquieting Lucifer in *Paradise Lost,* and his melancholy "Il Penseroso" (foreshadowing the eighteenth-century gloom school of graveyard poets). Also, Dryden told the tale of Nostagio degli Oresti, from Bocaccio's *Decameron,* in his supernatural "Theodore and Honoria." [9]

But literary chills seem tame beside real-life Renaissance horrors: religious heresies, crusades, wars (schisms, revolts, suppressions, the Reformation), plus bloody secular wars of succession and sovereignty, and finally, genocidal plagues of disease. Some seventeenth-century popular ballads echoed these dreads, using supernatural themes. Plots include the devil in disguise, a woman's curse, and various ghosts.

But most of the poetry of the supernatural thrives after the plagues and witchcraft manias, after the supernatural passed from daily belief, and after "rationalism" had begun to flatter the educated. For as Les Daniels suggests, perhaps weird literature needs a logical, waking world to react against. And, as we shall see, the eighteenth century was not as logical as it believed itself to be.[10]

Funerary verse and the spectral

O lead me, queen sublime, to solemn glooms
Congenial with my soul; to cheerless shades,
To ruined seats, to twilight cells and bowers,
Where thoughtful Melancholy loves to muse
Her favorite midnight haunts. . . .

Thomas Warton
Pleasures of Melancholy, 1747

The seventeenth century had at first considered melancholy to be a disease, then later as something profitable to the soul; by the early eighteenth century, religiously oriented "funeral elegies" were common.

The elegies drew much from Virgil's *Aeneid* and *Georgics* and were often set in shaded cemeteries thick with yew, cypress, and ghosts, or, in Kenneth Clark's phrase, "the machinery of melancholy" as in Dyer's *Grongar Hall* (1727):

'Tis now the Raven's bleak abode;
'Tis now the apartment of the toad;
And there the fox securely feeds;
And there the poisonous adder breeds
Concealed in ruins, moss and weeds;
While, ever and anon, there falls
Huge heaps of hoary moldered walls.

Such poems showed a "love of dramatised decay and Gothic architecture" according to Clark, as in Mallet's "The Excursion" (1726):

Behind me rises an awful *Pile*
Sole on this blasted Heath, a Place of Tombs,
Waste, desolate, where *Ruin* dreary dwells,
Brooding o'er sightless Sculls, and crumbling Bones.
Ghastful *He* sits, & eyes with Stedfast Glare
The Column grey with Moss, the falling Bust,
The Time-shook Arch, the monumental Stone. . . .

But as Clark suggests, "We do not think of real Gothic buildings, but of old-fashioned stage scenery; the moonlight streams down from the wings, and the owl's eyes have an unnatural luminosity. The sensationalist requires each dose to be a little stronger." And he believes that the literature affected the architecture of the Gothic revival, as much as vice versa.[11]

Among these gloomy poems we may think of Nahum Tate's "Melancholy" (spectral, charnel imagery), John Hopkins's "Victory of Death" elegy ("Horrid Groans of Ghosts"), Edward Young's early "A Poem on the Last

Day" (with rattling bones and dismembered flying heads), or William Broome's "Melancholy: An Ode" (1723), with a walk by the tombs, past their phantoms.

There was a brief lull around 1715, with Pope, Addison, Steele, and "sensible journalism." Lord Shaftesbury was complaining and cautioning: "Sentiments of *honest Good,* and *virtuous Pleasure,* disappear, and fly before this *Queen of Terrors.* . . . The Vicious Poets employ this *Spectre* too on their side. . . . The Gloomy Prospect of Death becomes the Incentive to Pleasure of the lowest Order. *Ashes* and *Shade,* the *Tomb* and *Cypress,* are made to serve as Foils to Luxury." [12] But soon, even more poets had arisen to exalt melancholy and the supernatural: Alan Ramsay, whose "The Gentle Shepherd" (1728) included a witch, a ghost, and a sorcerer; or John Armstrong with "Imitations of Shakespeare and Spenser" (1726); or John Gay with "A True Story of an Apparition"; or William Collins with "Ode to Fear" (1746). Robert Blair's *The Grave* (1743)—" 'Midst skulls and coffins, epitaphs and worms"—was written at the height of what came to be called graveyard poetry. Richard Glover's popular *Aeneid*-imitation "Leonidas" (1737) referred repeatedly to the supernatural, and even Alexander Pope's "Epistle to a Lady" has at least metaphorical witches and ghosts; his "Elegy to the Memory of an Unfortunate Lady" has a moonlight ghost. Elizabeth Rowe made a supernatural addition to the Old Testament with "The History of Joseph," while David Mallet convinced critics that his new "William and Margaret" was really an old ballad, one critic even comparing it with Shakespeare and Homer (*The Plain Dealer,* 1724). There is, of course, an older, genuine "William and Margaret" ballad.

Sometimes the ghost was only a "token symbol of intense emotion," notes Patricia Spacks—as in "Despair" by John Sheffield (Duke of Buckinghamshire) or Nicholas Rowe's "Colin's Complaint" (a self-pitying ghost). Elsewhere, the weird was still Christianized (Isaac Watts's "The Day of Judgment" and "Songs for Children"). James Thomson mentions ghosts briefly in *The Seasons* (1730), and his balladeer-friend David Mallet ("William and Margaret") treats ghosts at more length in *The Excursion* (1728). [13]

The Age of Benightenment. The "Enlightenment" at once denounced the supernatural *and* indulged it—thrilling to cabalism, alchemy, hell-fire clubs, Rosicrucianism, Martinism, Illuminism, Swedenborgianism, and Mesmerism.

> The Enemy has been here in the Night of our Naturall Ignorance . . . introducing the Demonology of the Heathen Poets . . . such as dead mens Ghosts, and Fairies, and other matter of old Wives Tales. . . . (Thomas Hobbes, *Leviathan,* Ch. 4).

And mystery men and charlatans flitted like phantoms across the age of unreason: Casanova, Chevalier d'Eon, Dr. Falk, le Comte de St.-Germain, Weishaupt, Althotas, Kölmer, Cagliostro. [14]

Meanwhile, critics such as Dr. Johnson were still deploring horror poetry, and poets like William Collins ("Ode to the Popular Superstitions of the

Highlands") were still defending it. In turn, he was hilariously lampooned in "Ode to Horror, in the Allegoric, Descriptive, Alliterative, Epithetical, Fantastic, Hyperbolical, and Diabolical Style of our Modern Ode-Wrights and Monody-Mongers." But such jeers and preachments could not stifle poems like Mark Akenside's "The Pleasures of Imagination" (1744, 1757), or one major graveyard poem, Edward Young's *Night Thoughts* (like Blair's *The Grave,* published in 1743). For as Joseph Warton's "Ode to Fancy" invited, "Let us with silent footsteps go / To charnels and the house of woe / To Gothic churches, vaults and tombs. . . ."

Until that point, supernatural poetry had been mostly generalized, sentimental, and religiously justified, with stock props and ghosts. Patricia Spacks decries the lack of "world view" in the poems. Whereas a Gothicist might sigh: who needs a wider universe than a bat-filled ruined abbey or vaulted musty crypt? But, of course, Spacks is right: the graveyard crew of poets produced no Coleridge, no Christina Rossetti. She also damns the empty language . . . "the words of one poem tend to seem precisely those of another . . . new arrangements of the same adjective-sound combinations, the same verbs." [15] Again, one might defend the funerary lexicon as having a certain charnel charm, as with Lovecraft's notorious eldritch adjectives. But certainly the tombstone school of bards produced no musicians like Shelley or Swinburne, no word sorcerers like Clark Ashton Smith.

As the century passes, certainly the poems *do* get better, with more personification, notes Spacks, and as Eleanor Sickels sees, they move from "restrained sentiment" to the later "intensely imaginative subjectivity," [16] as in, for instance, Robert Dodsley's "Melpomene; or, The Regions of Terror" and Macpherson's *Ossian* forgeries—whose narrative form and exotic setting Spacks praises, and whose specters, says Montague Summers, "have their ghostly progeny in the thousand phantoms of a thousand Castles" (referring to the great impact of *Ossian* upon Gothic novels). [17] For as Devendra Varma observed, "Ossianic poetry contributed a barbaric richness of colour, misty melancholy, and an air of dim and sweeping vastness" to the literature that followed. [18]

Then there was the eighteenth-century "ballad explosion." Percy's famous *Reliques of Ancient English Poetry* (1765) and new—and older—supernatural lyrics, such as Richard Glover's "Admiral Hosier's Ghost" and "The Witch of Wokey" by "Dr. Harrington of Bath." There were ghostly ballads in David Herd's *Ancient and Modern Scottish Songs* (1776), and in Dodsley's 1763 volume, such as Tickell's "Colin and Lucy." William Hamilton's often-reprinted "The Braes of Yarrow" was followed by a poem of the same name by John Logan. And William Mickle's "The Sorceress" was another narrative verse, styled "a ballad" by its author.

Thus, latter-day ballads and other poems show the mere graveyard melancholy darkening into starker supernatural poetry. Increasingly, critics railed against it, as others—Richard Hurd, William Duff, Mrs. Montague, John Aikin, even Edmund Burke—rallied to defend it.

Pre-Romantics and Gothic Balladeers

The close of the eighteenth century cannot be fully understood nor the progress of poetry in the nineteenth, without some study of the plague of ghosts and skeletons which has left its mark. (W. P. Ker, "Lecture on Sir Walter Scott," May 22, 1919)

Beginnings. The Gothic mood in poetry was intensifying. Supernatural elements appeared in James Beattie's "The Minstrel; or, The Progress of Genius" (1770–1774), which was in Spenserian stanzas and was influenced by Percy's *Reliques.* But as late as 1781 George Crabbe was forecasting the end of supernatural poetry in "The Library," just as Anna Seward was yearning for more of it in "Alpine Scenery" (1785). Her own "Louisa" had early used the haunted-castle theme, and later she cast two MacPherson "Ossian" ghost passages into verse.

Meanwhile, with the rise of Gothic novels, Gothic dramas became important, sometimes as dramatizations of novels, sometimes original. Thus, macabre poetry was spoken onstage. Nondramatic horror poetry was no longer mere graveyard verse. The religious pretext was mostly gone, and now the poems had to thrill, convince, and entertain. Ballads came into vogue, in what Sukumar Dutt calls "Scottish Mediaevalism," with such traits as colorful descriptions, glimpses into the otherworld, and a sense of far-off things, of evil in life and destiny, of intense longing.[19] Audibly, now, a wraith named "Romanticism" could be heard howling in the winds. And one of the winds blew from Germany.

Bürger's "Lenore"

Emotional shudders, as only Shakespeare can evoke, I have felt down to the very marrow. Sympathy! Horror!—Shudders, cold shudders, as when the north wind blows! . . . Thank God, now I am finished with my immortal 'Lenore!' (Gottfried August Bürger, in letters, 1773)

Written in 1773, "Lenore" (or "Leonora") soon became known to English poets interested in German letters; translations passed in manuscript in the early 1790s.

It influenced Matthew Gregory Lewis's "Alonzo the Brave, and Fair Imogene," in *The Monk* (1796); and Walter Scott, greatly influenced by it indirectly through Lewis's "Alonzo," translated it for his first published book. Then, in 1796, five English translations appeared (one in three editions), in seven total versions; scores more and many parodies appeared through the decades. The Romantics, especially Coleridge, were in debt to "Lenore." Its acceptance set the stage for Lewis's important ballad collection *Tales of Wonder* [6–32], whose contents were also affected by the poem. J. G. Robertson says it was *the* most influential short poem in all world literature. Never has a foreign poem become "English" so fast, so thoroughly, so lastingly. Yet it is barely recalled today, although it was a best-seller of its time, and of incalculable impact. The hoofbeats of Lenore's wild ride, with the skull-faced horseman, echoed for generations.[20]

"The Monk" and his Muse

O wonder-working Lewis! monk or bard
Who fain would make Parnassus a churchyard!
Lo! wreathes of yew, not laurel, bind thy brow,
Thy muse a sprite, Apollo's sexton thou!

Lord Byron, *English Bards
and Scotch Reviewers,* 1809

As early as 1793, young Matthew Gregory Lewis was writing to his mother from Germany that he had found enough old and new ballads for a collection, and that some of their German authors had praised his translations.

But his successful *The Monk* (1796) interrupted these plans. This novel contained "Alonzo the Brave, and Fair Imogene," a 17-stanza "ballad" (not in ballad stanzas, but rhyming *abaab*), which, like "Lenore," combined "the wedding of the living and dead, the jubilation and revelry of the ghostly rout." [21] Also in *The Monk* was "The Water-King," with unvarying metrics and simple horror plot.

These poems, along with "Lenore," inspired young Walter Scott to write his own ballads. Soon he was Lewis's pupil and found the even younger man to be "a martinet . . . in the accuracy of rhymes and of numbers. . . . few persons have exhibited more mastery of rhyme, or . . . the melody of verse." [22] Now Lewis was still planning his ballad collection, to be called *Tales of Terror,* for, as he said, "a Ghost or a Witch is a sine-qua-non ingredient in all the dishes, of which I mean to compose my hobgoblin repast." [23] But this ballad-banquet was overdue, and the public's hunger for ghost lyrics was waning. Impatiently Scott concocted *An Apology for Tales of Terror,* consisting of nine ballads privately printed (1799). The title was meant to nudge Lewis, whose "hobgoblin repast" was now to be called *Tales of Wonder,* at last appearing in late 1800. This two-volume set was probably the first weird poetry anthology published in English. Among the Lewis originals: "Alonzo," "Osric the Lion," "The Grim White Woman," "The Cloud-King," "Bothwell's Bonny Jane," "The Gay Gold Ring," and the "Alonzo" self-parody "Giles Jollup the Grave, and Brown Sally Green." It also includes eight paraphrase "translations" from German, Danish, and "Runic." Other poems by Scott, Southey, John Leyden, Burns, and cliché traditional ballads bulk out this two-volumed overpriced set. The reaction was shrill and savage; shrieked *The Critical Review* (January 1802):

> . . . translating works from the northern languages, which . . . our better informed ancestors would have been ashamed to have seen written in English. Whether these horror-hunters will incorporate themselves into a society for the sublime rapture of terrifying one another, or to consult in what manner they may still more effectually terrify their readers, we cannot say . . . there is nothing but fiends and ghosts—all is hideous—all is disgusting . . . filth and obscenity . . . will show to what a depth the human mind may be voluntarily degraded.

Several parodies bludgeoned Lewis, the ballad-monger; yet enough editions came out to suggest considerable reader interest too. Scott escaped with the best reviews, and in his memoirs distanced himself from the horror-ballad business; still, *Tales of Wonder* launched Walter Scott. Also, the volumes are an immortal bibliographical horror story. To start with, an 1801 lampoon, *Tales of Terror,* was ever after mislisted as by Lewis and/or confused with Scott's private book of the same title. Publishers have since abridged, wrongly combined, mistitled, and misattributed these down the years, forever misleading cataloguers and reference-work compilers. (The mistakes afflicting the series constitute many "tales of error and blunder," the subject of several articles).[24]

Undaunted, Lewis wrote more successful verse. His poems can be musical, racy, and dramatic, if often marred by moralizing. In his *Romantic Tales* (1808) were the usual free "translations" and some original poems—"Bill Jones: A Tale of Wonder," about a sailor's ghost (once recited at the Lyceum Theater), and "Oberon's Henchman; or, The Legend of the Three Sisters," containing witchcraft and fairy elements, suggesting *Midsummer Night's Dream.* In his final *Poems* (1812), a white-clad mystery lady kisses a sad poet ("Friend, my name is Death"). His posthumous *Journal of a West India Proprietor* (1834) has "The Isle of Devils," done on a trip to his Jamaican plantation (written perhaps to fight feelings of seasickness), which Irwin calls his "crowning achievement as a poetic Gothicist." He died at sea on the trip home, and his sea burial was superbly Gothic: his coffin escaped its weights and, not sinking, floated back toward Jamaica.

Lewis's poetry is forgotten, although some of the best lives within *The Monk.* In his day he was a "hit" songwriter (words and music); he trained Walter Scott; he was a friend of, and poetic influence on, Byron; and his Gothic ballads affected Coleridge and Shelley. His *Tales of Wonder* was the first anthology in this genre.

Scott and his ballad compeers. Like Lewis, Scott was steeped in German balladry; he translated two of Bürger's poems, published as a leaflet in 1796, and translated "The Erl-King" and "The Fire-King."[25] He edited *An Apology for Tales of Terror* and wrote a "ballad trilogy" on Thomas the Rymer (poet who visits Fairyland); his "Eve of St. John" mixes the supernatural with the medieval; and "Alice Brand" sets an elfin world against the world of human love and grief.

After appearing in Lewis's *Tales of Wonder,* Scott launched his own *Minstrelsy of the Scottish Border* (1802, enlarged 1803) with work by John Leyden and James Hogg. His *The Lay of the Last Minstrel* (1805) had medieval supernatural tones (lady's grimoire, a goblin page, and elemental spirits). Dutt feels that Scott drifts in and out of his supernatural mood, but praises *Harold the Dauntless* (1817) as more "gloomy, sinister, fearful," although stilll with unsustained mood. *The Lady of the Lake* (1810) contains demons, hags, goblins, and Druid rites ("The Cross of Fire"), to Dutt the "most weird creation of Scott's imagination." Additional poems touching on the supernatural are *The Vision of Don Roderick* (1811)—a haunted spring; *Rokeby* (1813)—a haunted glen; *The Bridal of Triermain* (1813)—ghosts of those long dead; *The Dance of Death* (1815)—spirits foredooming the souls of the slain, at the Battle of Waterloo.

Scott's verse possessed lyric grace and metrical variety, and employed firm, specific language; it was in poetry that this great novelist first learned dramatic storytelling. He also recruited other ballad men, "literary anti-quarians" like John Leyden (who wrote "Lord Soulis," which Dutt finds labored, and "The Mermaid" and "The Elfin-King," which Sickels believes "makes fine and restrained use of the macabre").[26]

Southey's work. Robert Southey appeared in Scott's *Terror* and Lewis's *Wonder* anthologies; Patricia Spacks says that Southey had a wider range of material than Lewis—for example, his juvenile ode "To Horror" (1797), "Rudiger" (1797), "Lord William" (1799), "Bishop Bruno" (1799), Death personified, "Cornelius Agrippa," and the witchly "The Old Woman of Berkeley." [27]

Southey's more ambitious *Thalaba* is an Oriental "Quest" poem, in something close to free verse. Dutt likes some of the supernatural scenes, but not its ununified whole (geographically, conceptually), with its overcrowding witchcraft, primeval lore, and mythology. But Southey followed Spenser, so perhaps *Thalaba*, like *The Faerie Queene,* has "Gothic unity." In the same vein are George Sterling's "A Wine of Wizardry" [6-54] and Clark Ashton Smith's "The Hashish-Eater" [6-52].

The Curse of Kehama (1810) also blends witchcraft, folklore, and mythology (Arabian, Indian); Dutt finds it more cohesive and geographically centered. A Western witch clashes with Eastern dieties, ghosts appear, and the curse itself makes a good horror piece; the whole poem is in the "Wandering Jew" vein. Dutt still thinks *Kehama* (and *Thalaba*) rank below Scott's medievalism;[28] but Sickels reminds us that both poems impressed .contemporaries with their "pretentious and sombre eloquence." [29]

Burns and Blake. Robert Burns's supernatural verse is lighthearted: "Death and Dr. Hornbook" (village apothecary and phantom death), "Address to the Devil," "Halloween" (terror turns to comedy), and the popular "Tam O'Shanter." William Blake, strange poet, mystic, printer, engraver, and artist, wrote "Fair Elenor" (Gothic terror), which Dutt calls crude juvenilia,[30] but in strange. rhythms no one but Blake would have thought of; Sickels finds that it echoes "The Song of Solomon." Other supernatural traces in Blake are "America," "The First Book of Urizen," "The Book of Ahania," and "Vala," of which Spacks says, "In a sense it is meaningless to speak of the supernatural in poems in which no one seems human," but suggests that this total fantasy effect makes the "supernatural" parts even more plausible: "When he wishes to achieve an effect of horror, it is more intense than anyone else's horror." [31]

The Gothic novels often contained poems, such as Ann Radcliffe's *The Mysteries of Udolpho,* which had eight poems, including the eerie "Shipwreck." [32] And we have seen graveyard verse evolve into bolder and starker poetry and observed the thriving old English ballad tradition and the influx of German balladry affecting collectors and writers of ballads, especially Scottish. Thus, by 1800 the poets, like the fiction writers, were taking the supernatural for granted.

The Romantics

Wordsworth. Even this Lake Poet, with his oversweetened reputation, was touched by the Gothic—"The Thorn" (weird images and a ghostly sight at the end), "An Evening Walk" (spectral horseman, images recalling Thomson's *The Seasons*), "Lucy Gray" (girl lost in snow living after death), "The Haunted Tree" and "The Wishing Gate" (celebrating animistic superstitions), and the long "Peter Bell" with the supernatural throughout, especially in its prologue.

Coleridge. Imaginative since childhood, Coleridge read deeply in the occult and wrote defenses of fanciful literature.[33] Supernatural imagery appeared in his early poems: "Anna and Harland" (slain woman's ghost), "The Raven" (a wronged bird with supernatural intensity, anticipating "The Ancient Mariner"), "The Ballad of the Dark Ladié" (supernatural verse fragment), and "Three Graves" (evil mother's curse on three lives). His opium-atmosphered "Kubla Khan" has at least a "demon-lover" simile; and "The Rime of the Ancient Mariner" is, of course, supernatural. Said Wordsworth: "We agreed to write jointly a poem, the subject of which Coleridge took from a dream which a friend of his had once dreamt concerning a person suffering under a dire curse from the commission of some crime . . . a dream about a skeleton ship, with figures in it." Coleridge revised the poem for years and years; one of the stanzas that he scrapped has a hypnotic eye suggesting Mesmer and "animal magnetism." [34] The published passages about the spirit world and specter ship assure that this literary Flying Dutchman will forever enchant and mystify.

His third famous poem, also worked on for years but never finished, is "Christabel." Shielded by her mother's ghost, Christabel falls under the strange dominion of ethereal Geraldine. Supernatural effects include the psychic power of a dog and the ghosts of dead sextons, as well as Geraldine's seeming psychic-erotic possession of Christabel, making this an early vampire poem.

Critics flailed the unfinished "Christabel," partly for its radical meter—which counted only *stresses,* not syllables, anticipating free verse—and partly for its sensational subject matter.[35] Hacks parodied it, or helpfully "completed" it at least twice. And one legendary evening, around June 16–18, 1816, Byron read it aloud to Percy Shelley, Mary Shelley, his wife, and Dr.

Polidori. As tension rose, excitable Shelley ran shrieking from the room, hallucinating about a hag-woman. Byron then proposed that they each write a ghost story. Byron and Percy Shelley managed only to write fragments, but Dr. Polidori's final result was his novel *The Vampyre* and Mary Shelley conjured up the immortal *Frankenstein*.[36] (Thus even science fiction owes thanks to sweet Christabel and her friend Geraldine.) It also influenced Scott's "The Lay of the Last Minstrel," possibly Keats's "Lamia," and, much later, "Rose Mary" by tragic Pre-Raphaelite Dante Gabriel Rossetti, who was Polidori's nephew. Like the rest of Coleridge's work, this classic weird poem is still being reinterpreted, for as fairy-tale antiquarian Andrew Lang believed, "Christabel" is "a masterpiece of supernatural suggestion."[37]

Shelley

> While yet a boy I sought for ghosts, and sped
> Through many a listening chamber, cave and ruin,
> And starlight wood, with fearful steps pursuing
> Hopes of high talk with the departed dead.
>
> Shelley, "Hymn to
> Intellectual Beauty," 1816

As a child Percy Shelley loved dressing up as a devil to scare his elders, telling "marvellous stories of fairyland and apparitions of spirits" from beyond the grave, looking for ghosts at night and even trying to raise one after reading a magic book.

At Oxford, recalled his friend Hogg, Shelley "had a decided inclination for magic, demonology, incantations, raising the dead, evoking spirits and devils, seeing ghosts, and chatting familiarly with apparitions."[38] We know that Shelley read M. G. Lewis's horror-ballads, *Faust,* and Bürger's "Lenore"—which may have started him writing verse. He copied out by hand W. R. Spencer's translation, planning his own version of it.[39] "Lenore" is echoed in "Sister Rosa," a poem in *St. Irvyne* (1811), of which stanzas XIII–XVIII were picked for an anthology of great *bad* poems.[40] As late as 1817, Shelley was reciting "Lenore" at Christmastime and scaring a neighbor girl with it. Southey's "Thalaba" was a favorite, and he thrilled at Byron's reading of "Christabel."

In the juvenile *Original Poetry by Victor and Cazaire* (1810) were "Revenge" and "Ghasta; or, The Avenging Demon!!!" and "St. Edmund's Eve"—plagiarized from a parody of Lewis, *Tales of Terror*.[41] Other supernatural juvenilia include "Fragment: Omens," "A Dialogue," "The Spectral Horseman," the humorous "The Devil's Walk," and three Wandering Jew poems.

"The Revolt of Islam" has Cynthia's ghost and many haunted, horrible passages; "Rossalind and Helen" contains apparitions; and "Julian and Maddalo" recalls Bürger's and Lewis's ghostly lovers. Other poems wholly or partly supernatural are "The Daemon of the World," the satiric "Peter Bell the Third," "The Witch of Atlas," the spirit in "The Fragments of an Unfinished Drama," "Marrianne's Dream," the "On Death" passages in

"Mount Blanc," "Death" (1817), and "Fragments of a Ghost Story" (inspired by Byron's reading of "Christabel").

Shelley is so macabre that Achibald Strong ranks him "with Baudelaire and Poe as one of the poets of decay. His preoccupation with the charnel...suggests...*The Conqueror Worm*...*Annabel Lee*...." And to many who knew him, Shelley seemed haunted or possessed. Once, his "spirit" was seen when he was really someplace else, and later, close to his death, Shelley felt he had been visited by his own ghost.[42] Certainly, his overtaxed nervous system suggests that he may have been a natural medium.

Keats. Born on All-Hallows Eve, John Keats showed early imagination in "Sleep and Poetry," and his famed "Endymion" has supernatural tones. His "Isabella" summons mysterious Lorenzo's ghost—with the tenderness of the old ballad "The Wife of Usher's Well," says Dutt, although Sickels says Keats is too fond of "bright beauty" to handle the macabre well and that "Isabella" is only sentimental. "The Eve of St. Agnes" begins with an old superstition, and two lovers flee to fairyland during a magical storm, with some resemblance to "Christabel"; some supernatural tragedy marks "La Belle Dame sans merci"; and "Lamia" has an invisible, serpentine wood-nymph (following John Dryden's form and meter), and of course is in the honored vampire tradition.

Lord Byron. Byron's early work, "Oscar of Alva," contains Scottish legendry, plus a scene from Schiller's "Ghost-Seer." Byron—a self-made Gothic hero-villain—wrote his "Byronic" drama *Manfred* with varied spirits, a "phantom," and a quoteworthy incantation (Act I, Scene I). "Lines Inscribed upon a Cup Formed from a Skull" (1814) have a spectral phrase or two ("rhyme and revel with the dead"); "The Destruction of Sennacharib" (1815) reveals the Angel of Death; spirits haunt "The Dream" and other of his works. Although lacking actual ghosts, "Darkness" gloomily foresees the future, while in language, tone, and form anticipates Clark Ashton Smith [6–52].

Beddoes and Darley. Thomas Lovell Beddoes's amazing macabre verses were collected posthumously [6–4].[43] Like Beddoes, solitary, rejected George Darley wrote mainly for himself, and—typically "romantic"—left his masterpiece unfinished: *Nepenthe,* a dream narrative. Its four-stress couplets and more varied rhyme schemes have a haunted, supernatural tone. Like Southey, and later George Sterling [6–54] and Clark Ashton Smith, it derives from *The Faerie Queene.* And from *The Sea-Bride*—a manuscript mostly lost—six Gothic siren songs survive (such as "The Sea-Ritual," and "The Mermaid's Vesper-Hymn"); this might have been his best work.[44]

Hood and Moore. The popular poet Thomas Hood wrote several weird poems, among which are "Pompey's Ghost," "The Ghost," "The Supper Superstition," and "Miss Kilmansegg and Her Precious Leg" (1840–1841), which has death's shadow following a lady on a stair and a bony hand clutching the closing curtain. "The Elm Tree" verges into the "indistinct and indefinite, shading off confusedly into grotesque, fantastic shapes," says

Sukumar Dutt—who still credits it with good atmosphere.[45] "The Haunted House" has a Gothic novel sense of crime and mystery; Poe called this often-reprinted poem one of the truest ever written and one of the most artistic (in theme and execution); he called Hood "one of the most singularly fanciful of modern poets." Hood was a funster-punster, popular in his day and still valued for his wit: his best horror verses are anthologized, often for children.

Like Hood, Thomas Moore was popular and thus often underrated by later critics. This Irish patriot, prolific poet, friend of Byron, and songwriter also wrote several weird verses: "The Ring" (mock-horror), "By That Lake, Whose Gloomy Shore" (ghost on a lake), "Oh, Ye Dead!," "The Mountain," "The Voice," "The Magic Mirror" (wizard aids a knight to see his lover), "The Pilgrim" (a dream leads to death), and "The Legend of Puck the Fairy," including some set in America: "A Ballad; or, The Lake of Dismal Swamp," "Song of the Evil Spirit of the Woods," and "On Passing Dead-man's Island" (ghost ship).

Novelists, playwright, and the poems of a painter. The wind-whipped Yorkshire moors of the Brontës are storybook—and movie-screen—clichés. But we may forget that Emily, author of *Wuthering Heights,* wrote such gloomy verses as "Lines by Claudia" and that sister Anne wrote the ghostly and dramatic "The Captain's Dream." Prolific Gothic playwright Joanna Bailey (*The Phantom* and *Witchcraft*) also wrote poems such as "Malcolm's Heir: A Tale of Wonder," "The Elden Tree," "The Ghost of Fadon," and "Night Scenes of Other Times"—all rather long, in ballad stanzas, melodramatic but intense and real. And J. M. W. Turner, romantic painter of misty skies and water, wrote "A Spectre Boat," in which a "sunset-ship of doom" appears; "A Dream" (specter takes control of a drifting boat); and others. His "Apollo and Python" describes a monster-snake.

Also to be mentioned are vampire and other verses by John Stagg [6–53], and the obscure *The Death-Wake, or Lunacy* [6–55] by Thomas T. Stoddart, which was hilariously parodied by William Aytoun.

Thus, the Romantics—raised on old ballads, exposed to graveyard poetry, remembering Shakespeare and Spenser, and growing up on Gothic novels—became particularly excited by the lurid ballads from Germany and their hectic Scottish and English imitations. Soon they were enthusiastically creating their own horror poems, for as Varma says, "The Romantic poets hark back to the sources of terror, and once again revive the latent feelings of awe, wonder, and fear." All who have written supernatural poetry since have been in their deep debt.

The Victorians
Alfred, Lord Tennyson

> It is perhaps natural for a boy to write gloomy poetry.
> Prof. Thomas Rainsford Lounsbury
> *The Life and Times of Tennyson,* 1915

In his early manuscript notebooks, Tennyson left such poetry as the play *The Devil and the Lady* (with necromancer and devil, in exciting Gothic language), "Armageddon" (supernatural passages and Miltonic tone), and "The Coach of Death," a "Monk" Lewis- (or German)-style ballad, possibly influenced by "The Ancient Mariner" or by "The Death Coach" of T. C. Croker. "The Mermaid" and "The Merman" (both 1830) are delightfully weird, owing perhaps to Leyden's "The Mermaid" and to Thomas Keightley's *Fairy Mythology* (1828). "The Kraken" (1830) probably has the same sources, as has "The Sea-Fairies" (1830).

Other poems relevant to this study include "Song" (1850), which has effective funerary and supernatural touches; "Sonnet" (1830), which has theological aims and sanguine Gothic language; "Hark! the Dogs Howl!" (1833), which is supernatural (unpublished); and "The Mother's Ghost," which has a specter hovering over her daughter whose birth cost the mother her life (1833). Weird lines occur in the many longer poems (such as "The Lady of Shallot"). Throughout his career, Tennyson now and then strayed into the shadow realm of supernatural poetry.

Pre-Raphaelites. These talented painters and poets thought that before Raphael, art had been "freer," and they aspired to greater realism; yet their work seems romantic and imaginative today. Many of their poems are supernatural.

Poet-painter Dante Gabriel Rossetti grew up amid books on alchemy, Swedenborg, freemasonry, and mysticism; as a dreamy, insomniac adult he took chloral hydrate. The start of his poetic career was Poesquely Gothic: bereaved over his wife's death, Rossetti buried his poetry manuscripts with her, only to have them exhumed years later for publication. His verse, like his art, is haunted by *femmes fatales,* recalling his stifled love for William Morris's wife, and it is often spectral-weird. [46] His superb "Sister Helen" curses the lover who spurned her; "The Burden of Nineveh" (1856) muses about the mythical carved creature in the museum; "The House of Life" sonnet series has a few weird passages; and *The King's Tragedy* verse drama has strong supernatural elements. But despite popular success as a painter—after initial virulent attacks—Rossetti sank into alcohol, drugs, and suicide attempts, and his verse grew more complex and florid.

His sister Christina Rossetti's "Goblin Market" is the famous dialogue between supernatural merchant men (selling poisoned fruit) and two sisters; "The Ghost's Return" is a dialogue between wife and dead husband; "At Home" is a beyond-the-grave discourse; and "After Death" has a bitter ghost seeing the husband who did not love her in life; all were published in 1862. Christina's lyric gifts place her high in English letters. Like her brother, she is realistic in use of dialogue and romantic in tone.

Close to their group, Irish folksong collector William Allingham reflected Irish fairy and supernatural legends in his own verse: "The Maids of Elfin-Mere," "The Witch Bride," "A Dream," and the immortal, ever-anthologized "The Fairies." William Bell Scott, one more poet-painter, wrote "The Witch's Ballad" (four witches who each enchant a man).

Multiple man-of-arts and borderline Pre-Raphaelite William Morris also wrote many weird poems. "The Writing on the Image" from *The Earthly Paradise* (1868–1870) is a grim allegory (man seeking riches down a secret staircase); "The Blue Ghost" (1858) has afterlife dialogue; and "The Tune of the Seven Towers" is another dramatic monologue. For others near the Pre-Raphaelites—Meredith, Swinburne—see Hayes [6–25]. Thus, the Pre-Raphaelites and their fringe-followers wrote several effective supernatural poems, and their stance and style generally anticipate the 1890s Aesthetes and Decadents, the California-romantics, and later romantic-weird poets.

Other Victorians (United Kingdom). Versatile fairy-tale collector Andrew Lang sometimes wrote his own supernatural poems, like "A Dream," "Two Sonnets of the Sirens," and "The Bridge of Death." Thomas Gordon Hake, a poet for over 50 years, wrote "The Sibyl." Arthur O'Shaugnessy's "Bisclaveret" (werewolf theme) and Thomas Edward Heath's dramatic, blank verse "The Doom of the Deverils" are noteworthy. For others, see Derleth [6–16], Hayes [6–25], Coblentz [6–13], and Widdemer [6–63]. Then there is disquieting Richard Dadd, exquisite oil painter of ethereal fairy scenes, who slew his father and spent 43 years in an asylum. His most famous picture is "The Fairy Feller's Master-Stroke," used as a cover design for *Fantasy Literature* (Bowker, 1979). The painting may hint at his own parricide and is the theme of his long, unpublished poem (c. 1865). [47]

Longfellow, Poe, and others (United States). Henry Wadsworth Longfellow wrote several poems in this vein: "The Haunted Chamber" (from "Birds of Passage"), "The Beleaguered City," "Two Angels," "Haunted Houses," and "The Phantom Ship." His poems skillfully move from spectral specifics toward generalizations about humans and life—rare in this genre, but welcome.

We barely need even to list Poe's "The Raven," "Ulalume," the last part of "The Bells," "The Haunted Palace," or "The Conqueror Worm"; less remembered are juvenilia like "Dream-Land," "Spirits of the Dead," "Hymn to Aristogeiton and Hamodius," and the later-discovered "Rise, Infernal Spirits" (a probable attribution, written in 1822, unsigned, but found in his stepfather's company files). [48] Critics in the nineteenth century deplored the drunkeness of the poet and the morbidity of his themes, but today Poe's detractors lament his musical and metrical regularity. But his influence may be as important as his poems: on Decadent-aesthetes Swinburne, Arthur Symons, Ernest Dowson (filtered through Baudelaire), and on California romantics Bierce, George Sterling, Clark Ashton Smith, and the later *Weird Tales* school and their Small Press successors. For a Poe hoax, see Charles Gardette [6–19].

Poe's fellow short-story writer and weird-tale master Fitz-James O'Brien wrote "The Enchanted Titan" (about a wizard) and "Minot's Ledge" (asserting God's power over demons in the night). Emily Dickinson's dark, uniquely mystical poems include some that are supernatural: "The Chariot," "I Felt a Funeral," "Witchcraft Has Not a Pedigree," and "She Died at Play." James Whitcomb Riley wrote more than the light dialect poetry for which he is commonly remembered, such as "The Werewife"; James Greenleaf Whittier's "The Dead Ship of Harpswell" is a vivid sea tale; novelist Thomas Bailey Aldrich wrote "Identity" (where two ghosts meet); and *fantasiste* Lafcadio Hearn translated Gautier's "Clarimonde" (haunted by a dead sweetheart).

Some lesser known American poets in this genre are: politician and editor Otway Curry—"To a Midnight Phantom"; Rebecca S. Nichols—"The Shadow"; Caroline A. Chamberlin—"The Soul's Visitants"; John Gibson Dunn—"Spirit of Earthquake" and "Who'll Be the Next to Die?"; Edward Rowland Sill—"A Morning Thought"; and Irish-born Charles Dawson Shanly—"The Walker of the Snow."

Thus, despite the respectable Victorian affirmation of life—or perhaps because of it—the supernatural-macabre was a commonplace to the major and minor poets of the age. After all, the century's faith in a Divine purpose to the universe implied a belief in the malign forces, too.

Fin de Siècle, and After: The British Isles

> Only the brain of a child or of a savage could form the clumsy idea that a century is a kind of living being. . . . To die with expiration of the hundredth year, after being afflicted in its last decade with all the infirmities of mournful serenity. (Max Nordau, *Degeneration*, 1895)

> There are two things to remark in the poets of the 'nineties: the distinction of their work and the tragedy of their lives. (Derek Stanford, *Poets of the 'Nineties*, 1965)

As Queen Victoria's reign and century closed, so died the fashion for lush romantic verse, of which a minor but insistent strain was the supernatural-horrific. The last brilliant display of aesthetic poetry was at its flashiest in the mid-1890s, and we shall notice some of its survivors who straggled into the unwelcoming twentieth century.

Decadents and aesthetes. The romantic origins of Oscar Wilde may be recalled—his Irish mother gave him the middle name *Fingal* after the weird *Ossian* poems of James Macpherson, and she claimed descent from Dante and from Gothic novelist Charles Maturin, who wrote *Melmoth the Wanderer*. [49] Yet it is easy to forget Wilde's supernatural poems, such as "The Dole of the King's Daughter" (horror ballad with ravens and stars that portend death), "The Sphinx" (with mounting Oriental imagery), and "Fabrin dei Franchi" (celebrating the supernatural in Shakespeare).

Wilde was a member of the Rhymers' Club, which met at the Cheshire

Cheese pub, aspiring to a kind of Mermaid Tavern immortality and posturing a Left Bank decadence. Their real, more modest feats included some capable weird poems, such as stereotypically tragic Ernest Dowson's "The Three Witches" and his spectral "In a Breton Cemetery" and "Vesperal." Or such poems by pre-eminent poet and critic, Arthur Symons—"Opium Dream," "Mad," and "Over the Threshold." In 1896 he visited an Irish castle with Yeats and met Yeats's uncle, who cast Symons's horoscope; ever after Symons believed in the magic of numbers and portents. [50] (For his other verse, see *Jezebel Mort* [6–56]). Symons lived like an 1890s ghost as late as 1946, as Benjamin de Casseres observed, "holding firm to the dreamworld as the one thing substantial." [51] Other Rhymers' Club members were Richard LeGalliene ("The Resurrection") and Ernest Rhys ("Ballad of the Buried Sword").

Like Wilde, William Butler Yeats was another member of the Rhymers' Club to become world famous. But he was also an occultist and member of the secret Rosicrucian Hermetic Order of the Golden Dawn (with Arthur Machen, Aleister Crowley, and Algernon Blackwood). Yeats's study of Blake helped him write some of the order's rituals. Nobel Prize-winner Yeats wrote sensible and positive poetry that is yet deeply imbued with the supernatural. [52] His occult life—automatic writing, hermetic magic, the Tarot, and spiritualism—is only beginning to be understood. As Kathleen Raine has said, "For Yeats magic was not so much a kind of poetry, as poetry was a kind of magic." [53]

Two shadowy poets crossed Yeats's path in the 1890s; little is known about Count Stanislaus Eric Stenbock beyond the facts of his occultism, opium and alcohol addiction, zoöphilia, and tragic death. Even for that era he was bizarre. Only his weird fiction is known: of his first two poetry books, merely one or two copies exist (in private hands)—*Love, Sleep and Dreams* (c. 1881) and *Myrtle, Rue and Cypress* (1883)—and some of the poems were probably supernatural. His third book, *The Shadow of Death* (1893), has one known library copy; his poems in this genre are "Sonnet XI," "Sonnet VII," "May Blossom," "All Souls' Even," and versions of Goethe's "Erl-King" and "The Fisher." Stenbock's musical lyrics sigh for sleep and for self-immolation, and even more than Beddoes are of the Oblivionist school. [54]

Yeats also knew Aleister Crowley in their secret Golden Dawn period, before Crowley's exit toward weirder, more infamous occultism. Crowley's early Swinburnian-alliterative verse had lush pageantry and often supernatural morbidity; his later verse is more "magickal," less literary. Supernatural lines appear in his very first poems, *Aceldama* (1898) and *The Tale of Archais* (1898). Said Montague Summers: "Crowley had flashes of genius. He left ... some fine poetry." [55] The best is at least anthologizable; a volume of selected poems is needed—and sober criticism, which is unlikely amid the controversy still blackening "The Great Beast 666."

Fiona Macleod (William Sharp). As a child in Scotland, saw "presences" that his playmates could not see. His Highland nurse taught him Gaelic legendry, and at Glasgow University his studies included mysticism, occultism, magic, mythology, and folklore. Later in London he was near the Rossetti Pre-Raphaelite clique and was a struggling poet (*Romantic Ballads and Poems of Phantasy,* 1888), critic, and editor. Under seven different pen names he wrote the entire first issue of *The Pagan Review* (1892), which failed. But posing as Fiona Macleod, he was soon astounding literary London with a lush Celtic poetry that it would have rejected from staid William Sharp. Several successful books appeared, and although Richard LeGalliene guessed Fiona's identity, he stayed quiet. Sharp's sister even answered Fiona's letters from readers and admirers to provide some feminine handwriting. But such literary schizophrenia seemed to tax Sharp's mental and physical health, for he died in 1905. [56]

Other late romantics. Dora Sigerson Shorter filled many volumes with affecting ballads that pine for the old Ireland of romance; phantoms invade her pages. Claude Houghton was a throwback to the 1890s, and his 1917 *The Phantom Host,* besides the title poem, has "Claire de Lune" in this genre. The volume pines with the mystic tone of Dowson or Symons. Alfred Noyes, a very famous poet, wrote ballads sometimes better than the ancient originals, such as the classic "The Highwayman." Others in *The Enchanted Island and Other Poems* (1910) were the title poem (with its mermaids) and "The Admiral's Ghost." The fiction of E. H. Visiak is being revived, but his stark and active dialect ballads of the sea, such as "The Dead Ship," "The Haunted Pirate," "The Will of Peter Baines," "The Haunted Island," and "The Haunted Key," await discovery. Coleridge was his early inspiration and Masefield his early sponsor; later advocates have included Colin Wilson and John Gawsworth.

The 1890s, with their imported French decadence, certainly encouraged the occasional supernatural poem. As Derek Stanford notes, "Mortality and melancholy marked the poetry of this period," and he quotes Arthur Symons: "I have known twelve men who killed themselves." [57] Yet LeGalliene challenged this sensationalist view of the decade: "Far from being 'decadent,' except in certain limited manifestations," he wrote, "they were years of an immense and multifarious renaissance." [58] And Benjamin de Casseres complained later that "to stigmatize the poets who possess this wonderful vision as 'decadent' is the shriek of an age that is spiritually impotent." [59] Of course, there is truth in both positions—and in others—for the 1890s will ever fascinate and perplex critics, and for the genre of the supernatural the century's close marked the beginning of an ending. Rhymed and metered poetry would soon be under fire, and imaginative subject matter would be dismissed by a new school of criticism. Henceforth romantic poets would have more difficulty publishing poems in major magazines, and popular magazines with literary quality would themselves start to disappear.

Late Victorians and After

America, the native land of Edgar Allan Poe, now and again produced lesser romantics—like Sidney Lanier, whose "The Raven Days" employs ghost imagery and whose "Psalm of the West" contains a ghost passage, or novelist F. Marion Crawford, whose "Song of the Sirens" is among many similarly titled poems in English. The "Carcosa" myth of Crawford's fellow cosmopolite, novelist Robert W. Chambers, influenced many later poets, and his "At the Masked Ball" (1896) has an eerie döppelganger following the narrator through nine terse quatrains.

Bierce, Sterling, and others

California was the first to discover that it is fantasy that leads reality, not the other way around. (William Irwin Thompson, historian, in *The Aquarian Conspiracy*, by Marilyn Ferguson, 1980)

San Franscisco literary mentor Ambrose Bierce is immortal for his epigrams and weird fiction, but he also wrote verse (see *A Vision of Doom* [6–5]). His influence on other California romantics is less remembered.

Bierce praised the verse of fantasy author Emma Frances Dawson, who wrote poems of the supernatural-weird: "Unknown," "Unfulfilled," "Portent," and "Haphazard" (all 1897). [60] Her dreamy music has flashes of unexpected horror and her stronger poems merit reprinting.

But George Sterling was Bierce's leading protégé. He wrote, loved, drank, and even looked like an 1890s aesthete of the London *Yellow Book* days; his vogue came a decade later. His poems contain unreal scenes, unearthly visions, and post-Swinburnian music. [61]

Certainly something remote and mysterious shadows the work of Ambrose Bierce, then Sterling, and more amazingly that of his protégé Clark Ashton Smith. Sterling's most notorious poem was "A Wine of Wizardry" [6–54], but other supernatural poems appear in his collections of verse such as *The Testimony of the Suns and Other Poems* (1909), *The House of Orchids and Other Poems* (1911), *Beyond the Breakers* (1914), *The Caged Eagle and Other Poems* (1916), *Sails and Mirage* (1921), and *After Sunset* (1937). There are several supernatural-macabre passages in the verse-drama *Lilith* (1919), a work praised by Dreiser and Clark Ashton Smith, who compared it with the work of Shelley and Swinburne.[62]

Sterling's romantic verse and bohemian life made him a treasured San Francisco anachronism, and his *fin de siècle* verse had been long out of style by 1926, the year of his probable suicide. For too long he has been remembered only as the overpraised pupil of Ambrose Bierce—to whom Poe and Sterling were not merely the greatest American poets, but simply the greatest two Americans! But after more than 50 years, the first full-length study appeared in 1980 from Thomas Benediktsson. Sterling's fantasy and macabre verses should be separately gathered, and the impact of his poems on

the collateral fields of science fiction stories and science fiction poetry must
be measured.

Other supernatural poems. From this same period we note Genevieve Far-
nell-Bond's "Wind of the Night," "The City of the Dead," and the quaint
"The Book Spirits." We must also recall Baltimore schoolteacher Lizette
Woodworth Reese's ghostly verses, from the 1880–1920 period. She was
praised by Jessie Rittenhouse and by H. L. Mencken, who ranked her with
Poe; her lyric simplicity anticipates de la Mare. [63]

Fantastic novelist George Sylvester Viereck wrote some verses in the 1890s
manner with supernatural effects: "Love in Dreamland" (1908), "A Ballad
of Sin," "Queen Lilith," and "Capri" (1924). Exotic novelist Edgar Saltus
wrote a spectral "History" in 1884; he knew Wilde and Symons in the 1890s
in London, and his lush, often decadent poems appeared posthumously as
Poppies and Mandragora (1926).

A very prolific lyric poet was Madison Cawein, the "Keats of Kentucky"
or "Omar Khayyám of the Ohio Valley." Observed William Henry Hulme:
"He recalls Poe . . . in his weird, uncanny images . . . poems peopled by fairies, pixies, gnomes, elves and fays . . . Persian legends . . . with their enchantment and necromancy seem to have exerted a powerful influence on him." [64]
For Cawein's ghostly poems, see [6–11].

Canadians. As Cawein was popular in Kentucky and Sterling in California, so was Bliss Carman in Canada. Like theirs, his lyric gifts are forgotten
today. Some of his supernatural poems are "The Yule Guest," "The Kelpie
Riders," and "In the Offing." William Archer praised Carman's "weird and
fantastic imagination . . . some of his poems have an eerie strength, and others a haunting charm peculiar to themselves . . . the poems, one and all,
bring home to us with a peculiar and searching power the mystery and terror of a stormy northern seaboard . . . the grim superstitions of a stormy
coast . . . the maligner aspects of the great waters . . . death's head fantasies." [65]

We see, then, late Victorians in North America, raised on Shelley and
Tennyson, also exposed to Swinburne and the Decadents, writing competent
supernatural verse in traditional form. But critical reaction against fixed-
form poetry, and against the fanciful in verse, would soon stunt the genre's
growth permanently.

Modern Romantics: 1920 to Present

After 1910, critical opinion began to harden against beauty of style in poetry, and fixed-form verse became increasingly rare. Florid poetry such as
George Sterling's was banished, like Victorian furniture, to the attic, and
even the plainer traditional poetry of Masefield, de la Mare, Millay, and
Frost was seen as an exception—and was less popular with the critics than
with the public. *Meter* was especially discouraged, even more than rhyme—

yet meter had been the life-beat of most supernatural poetry, with its hypnotic, musical, and incantatory force. [66]

True, some excellent free verse of the supernatural would be written—for example, by Joseph Payne Brennan—but much less often. For another modernist tenet was the rejection of such imaginative themes as the cosmic, the fantastic, and the supernatural. Ghost poems would hardly seem relevant to a post-1920 critic. Nor was narrative verse as common, since the new poetry did not have to have logical sequence and critics preferred that a poem conceal layers of meaning they could strip away in textual analysis. Simultaneously, the tradition of reading poetry aloud in the classroom and at the home fireside, for immediate understanding, entertainment, and escape, was fast passing. [67]

For these and other reasons, fewer and fewer supernatural poems were written, and those that appeared had little chance of permanent publication. As we shall see, however, in America—where the critical move against formal poetry was swifter—there arose the alternative of the pulp magazines, then the Arkham House collections, the fanzines, and the Small Press movement. In addition, horror poetry would be written for the children's market, admittedly in mostly humorous tone. [68] But August Derleth, the century's chief book publisher of macabre verse, rightly observed in 1961 that supernatural poetry, plentiful for hundreds of years, declined sharply after 1900 and even more drastically after 1947—although the slight upsurge after his death in 1971 is partly his legacy, and modest monument. [69]

The British Isles. Some representative works include Laureate John Masefield's "The Rider at the Gate," a ghost-horseman foretelling Julius Casear's death; "The Hounds of Hell," with death-as-a-rider; and "The Haunted," a masterly horror poem. Walter de la Mare's poetry has pleased children and imaginative adults. His most famous, "The Listeners," contains eerie ghosts and was the first of three poems that Thomas Hardy asked to have read to him on his deathbed. Henry Duffin said, "Ghosts have a special place and significance in de la Mare's poetry. Far from being unreal, they are a part of reality itself." [70]

Lord Dunsany wrote "The Lost Trick" (half-humorous card game with Death), the macabre "Nemesis" (both 1929), and the gloomy "To a Spirit Seen in a Dream" (1938). We should also note Siegfried Sassoon's eerie "Goblin Revel" and "Night-Piece" (witches, dryads), and Mervyn Peake's stark and ghastly "Satan," "Caliban," and "At Times of Half-light." Fantastic novelist M. P. Shiel wrote the demoniac "The Cat" (1903), "Shapes in the Fire" (1896), and "Sulphate of Morphia." His friend John Gawsworth wrote "Death, the Evangelist." Laureate John Betjamin's "A Lincolnshire Tale" evokes the old ballads.

Mainstream American poets. Edna St. Vincent Millay wrote the dramatic "Wraith" (1921), "Ode to Silence" (1921), and "Moriturus" (1928), with Death fiercely personified. Equally famed Robert Frost wrote "Two

Witches" (1923), which includes "The Witch of Coös." Margaret Widde-mer's poetry is discussed with her anthology *The Haunted Hour* [6-63]. Other mainstream poets who occasionally wrote in the genre may be found in August Derleth's *Dark of the Moon* [6-15] and *Fire and Sleet and Candlelight* [6-16] anthologies, including several in free verse by Derleth himself.

Many poems by science fiction novelist and man-of-letters Stanton A. Coblentz are supernatural-macabre: "Poe Cottage," "Edgar Allan Poe," "Napoleon among the Shades," "Europe," and "Nephree-Ti-Ta." A Californian who knew George Sterling, Coblentz retains Victorian color, music, and fancy in his poems, but not the archaisms, inversions, and frequent *enjambements*. Dunsany praised his poetry greatly; his many, many poetry books and scores of works in other fields make him a formidable presence. He indirectly affected the preservation of much supernatural poetry with his battling for traditional verse, and his 1949 *Unseen Wings* anthology [6-13] contains many poems in the genre. Born in the last century, Coblentz still publishes at his Redwood Press at Monterey, California. (With Lilith Lorraine, he was also an influence on the field of science fiction poetry.)

Poems from the pulps. Poems were sometimes a magazine space-filler in the pulps as elsewhere, and *Weird Tales* bought many, giving some of them special illustrations. H. P. Lovecraft is credited with challenging its initial "no poems" policy—perhaps one of Lovecraft's more important, far-reaching achievements. [71] For *Weird Tales* printed hundreds of poems, including works by Clark Ashton Smith (48 poems), H. P. Lovecraft (41), Robert E. Howard (37), Leah Bodine Drake (23), Donald Wandrei (17), Frank Belknap Long (12), and Mary Elizabeth Counselman (6). It also published enough verse to inspire later anthologies and book publication of these and other poets, and enough poetry to accustom a fantasy-reading public to weird poetry, indirectly leading to the Small Press movement (late 1960s–1980s). It is likely that many of the *Weird Tales* poems would not have been written without this magazine as a market—many fictioneers doubtless dashed off a poem before mailing a short story manuscript. Poems were likely accepted even as the tales that went with them were rejected. Small checks were welcome—even at the rate of 25 cents a line. Of course many of the poems were not supernatural horror, but exotic, strange, dream fantasy, or Oriental adventure. However, as the Arkham House collections demonstrate, certainly a significant amount was macabre.

Not surprisingly, *Weird Tales'* three most prolific poets—Smith, Lovecraft, and Howard—were also its most enduring weird fiction writers from the 1920s to the 1930s. Each writer's poetry was a compulsion and not a mere hobby or bid for extra notice, and each writer's poetry seems to complement his prose.

Clark Ashton Smith contributed early to *Weird Tales,* and it bridged long decades for him, since between 1925 and 1951 no volume of new Smith poetry would appear. The early praise of Bierce and George Sterling would echo fainter with time—although a knowing few would continue to extol his poems—for example, Samuel Loveman, Vachel Lindsay, Ina Coolbrith, Benjamin de Casseres, Stanton A. Coblentz, Lilith Lorraine, Lovecraft, Robert E. Howard, and Donald Wandrei. [72] In the 1940s he readied his *Selected Poems* [6–52] for publication, but he did not live to see the volume.

Like Smith, H. P. Lovecraft had published much poetry earlier, but only in local papers and amateur press journals. *Weird Tales* became the chief market for his macabre verse, printing many of the *Fungi from Yuggoth* sonnets, some posthumously. Nearly all Lovecraft's supernatural-weird poetry is in *Collected Poems* [6–36]. He also wrote various essays and reviews on poetry for the amateur press. [73]

Robert E. Howard published mainly in *Weird Tales,* leaving much manuscript poetry at his death. The first of his several posthumous collections was *Always Comes Evening* [6–27], but a volume of selected poems is badly needed. [74]

Other *Weird Tales* fiction writers whose supernatural poetry was later collected were Frank Belknap Long [6–34, 6–35] and Donald Wandrei [6–60]. Mary Elizabeth Counselman's simple, dramatic lyrics await publication as *The Face of Fear;* Dorothy Quick also sold many tales and 25 poems to *Weird Tales,* whereas the outstanding Leah Bodine Drake [6–17] was primarily a poet. Others who published a number of poems in the magazine were A. Leslie, Cristel Hastings, Edgar Daniel Kramer, Clarence Edwin Flynn, Page Cooper, Marion Doyle, Yetza Gillespie, Robert Nelson, Harriet Bradfield, and Edith Hurley. Also of interest was the Virgil Finlay Poetry Series (1937–1940)—the famed illustrator who let a few lines from Coleridge, Tennyson, and other poets inspire his drawings.

This *Weird Tales* subrealm of poetry has been indexed by T. G. L. Cockcroft and it deserves a fresh review since August Derleth combed the pages for his anthology of 1947 [6–15].

Arkham House and other specialty presses. Founded in 1939 by August Derleth and Donald Wandrei to preserve Lovecraft in book form, Arkham House published his second omnibus, *Beyond the Wall of Sleep* (1943), with some poetry. Soon Derleth was asking Clark Ashton Smith to ready *The Hashish-Eater and Other Poems,* probably the first Arkham poetry collection to be commissioned. Smith narrowed it from a "collected" to a *Selected Poems* [6–52]—but it was postponed until after his death. Meanwhile, the first Arkham poetry book published was Derleth's vital 1947 anthology *Dark of the Moon* [6–15], and the first one-author collection was Leah Bodine Drake's 1950 *A Hornbook for Witches* [6–17]. Two slender Smith collections appeared: in 1951, *The Dark Chateau and Other Poems,* and in 1958, *Spells and Philtres.* In 1957 Robert E. Howard poems had appeared as *Always Comes Evening* [6–27], another milestone volume. These one-author collections, taking years to sell out their 500-copy runs, from $2.10 and $3 per copy, today fetch prices in the hundreds of dollars.

After 14 years *Dark of the Moon* was still in print, yet in 1961 Derleth edited a new anthology from the 1946–1960 period, *Fire and Sleet and Candlelight* [6–16], typical of his vision and dogged industry in this unpromising poetry market. Other collections published were Lovecraft's 1963 *Collected Poems* [6–36], Donald Wandrei's 1964 *Poems for Midnight* [6–60], and the 1964 *Nightmare Need* [6–7] of Joseph Payne Brennan. This noted mainstream poet and horror fiction writer was a craftsman in free verse who achieved an economy of form that a traditionalist might envy. Stanley McNail's unusual, pleasurable *Something Breathing* [6–41] was the last of this decade, published in 1965.

L. Sprague de Camp's fast-selling *Demons and Dinosaurs* (1971) was outside the genre—but for a few selections like "Ghosts" and "The Sorceress." De Camp's fantasy and horror poems are mostly parodies and satires. More fanciful than weird was *Songs and Sonnets Atlantean* (1971) by Donald Sidney-Fryer; these poems transcend their Sterling-Smith influence with their lighter music and a new sonnet form. Some within the genre are "To Clark Ashton Smith," "Connaissance Fatale," "For the Black Beetles in Amber of Ambrose Bierce," and "Song." This volume became its own tradition. [75] In the 1970s Arkham House published Long's *In Mayan Splendor* [6–34] and Lin Carter's *Dreams from R'Lyeh* [6–9], and, most celebrated, Clark Ashton Smith's long-due *Selected Poems* [6–52]. An excellent "Poets out of Arkham" anthology could be compiled as a tribute to Arkham's four decades of fantasy poetry commitment.

In 1970 Donald M. Grant published Howard's *Singers in the Shadows* [6–30] and in 1972 *Echoes from an Iron Harp* [6–28], both with some horror poems, and in 1980 Bierce's *A Vision of Doom* [6–5]. Morningstar Press brought out Howard's 1976 *Night Images* [6–29], and Whispers Press collected much general and a few fantasy and horror poems in Lovecraft's *A Winter Wish* (1977), which included three of his essays: "The Despised Pastoral," "Metrical Regularity," and "The Allowable Rhyme." H. Warner Munn, a successful fiction writer, had been publishing poems in the Small Press in the 1970s; his *The Book of Munn* (1979) from Outré House contained several horror poems. Each of these specialty editions excelled at design, layout, and art in hard covers, whereas Roy A. Squires produced poetry and other pamphlets in paper covers for collectors—notably, Clark Ashton Smith's lesser verse. Whether such well-produced poetry editions can be sustained by the 1980s market is not clear. An alternative may be the paper-covered chapbook—R. Alain Everts's Strange Company printed several in the 1970s, by G. Sutton Breiding [6–6], Richard Tierney [6–58], Fred C. Adams [6–1], and Joseph A. West [6–61, 6–62]. In whatever format, there are several poetry collections now assembled for print in the 1980s. [76]

The Fan Press. The earliest "fan" publications of the 1930s carried some poetry, but the fantasy verse in general—including the macabre—is largely unremembered through the 1960s. Often the horror poems were mixed with other fantasy, including science fiction poetry. The forgotten publications of the 1940s–1950s especially should be reexamined: Larry Farsace's *Golden Atom,* Lilith Lorraine's *Flame* and *Different,* Robert E. Briney's *Cataclysm,* Orma McCormick's *Star-Lanes,* and W. Paul Ganley's 1953 anthology *Snow-flakes in the Sun.* Meanwhile, these "lost years" of fantasy poetry remain unresearched.

Later journals include Stanley McNail's *Nightshade* (1965–1968), probably an all-macabre verse magazine; Joseph Payne Brennan's *Macabre* (which included fiction) and *Essence,* not confined to weird poetry; Glenn Lord's *The Howard Collector;* and *Coven 13* (becoming Gerald W. Page's *Witchcraft and Sorcery*). These publications are more in the Small Press category—a distinction that is not always clear, but that generally implies more literary quality, and certainly more professional design and printing.

The Small Press Movement. To better reach his Arkham House customers and to have an overflow outlet for fiction and verse, Derleth launched *The Arkham Collector* (1967–1971). It published many poems by Walter Shedlofsky, Walter C. DeBill, Jr., Richard L. Tierney, Donald Sidney-Fryer, and Wade Wellman. Almost simultaneous with Derleth's death—and that of *Collector*—appeared better quality fan journals, seemingly striving to become more than fanzines. Among the many that used macabre poetry were *Ambrosia, Cross Plains Quarterly, Dark Horizons* (U.K.), *The Diversifier, Fantasy and Terror, Fantasy Crossroads, Nyctalops, Space and Time, Weirdbook, Whispers* (of which, the last four still flourish); others came later: *Copper Toadstool, Dark Fantasy, Dragonfields, Eldritch Tales, Equinox, Evermist, Fantasy Tales* (U.K.), *Gothic, Journal Fantome, Myrddin, The Romantist;* and there were a few all-poetry journals: *Bleak December, Fantasae,* and *Amanita Brandy.* In general, the quantity and quality of the poetry increased. Editors became backlogged, and to clear the files would print many poems in one issue—only to trigger even more submissions than before. Subscribers sometimes complained of "too much poetry," which several editors, to their risk, ignored.

Among the poets were older names like Walter Shedlofsky [6–48, 6–49], H. Warner Munn [6–44], Joseph Payne Brennan [6–7], Edith Ogutsch, W. Paul Ganley, and Lucile Coleman (see her *The Lyric Return,* 1977). Among the newer emerging Small Press poets, a representative list might include Eddy C. Bertin, G. Sutton Breiding [6–6], William A. Conder, j. e. coplin, Carol Ann Cupitt, Michael Danagher, K. Allen Daniels, Denise Dumars, Thomas F. Egan, Galad Elflandsson, Michael Fantina [6–18], Joey Froehlich, William Fulwiler, Don Herron, Dwight E. Humphries, George Laking, Gordon Larkin, Frederick J. Mayer, Jim Pianfetti, Jessica Amanda Salmonson, David Schultz, David C. Smith, Steve Sneyd, Stephanie Stearns, David Szurek, Richard L. Tierney, Steve Troyanovich, Neal Wilgus, Billy Wolfenbarger, and more who have escaped this random roster. [77] No doubt the more prolific poets will be publishing collections in the 1980s. Two anthologies from this period have appeared: Bacon and Troyanovich's 1976 *Omnium-*

gathum [6–3], and Anderson's 1980 *Hidden Places, Secret Words* [6–2]. Someday a retrospective selection could be made from this Small Press poetry explosion.

Some fiction writers. Ray Bradbury published verse in his early fanzine days (1937–1940). Novelist Thomas Burnett Swann wrote at least two of interest—"Unhaunted" and "Moonmad." [78] Recent fictioneer Karl Edward Wagner has put poems in stories. There are doubtless other storytellers utilizing macabre poems in the countless novels, trilogies, and series of novels pouring forth since the middle 1970s.

Outlook

> What is the natal country of poets? That country bounded by Nowhere and reached by staying home—the Imagination. (Benjamin de Casseres, *Forty Immortals,* 1926)

Thus, the minor strain of supernatural-macabre poetry persists in the larger "fantasy" field, and will be increasingly collected and studied. When this happens, scholars will be reminded anew—as we noted at the outset— that weird poetry, while presently being a subgenre, historically speaking is a source of horror fiction itself. We think not merely of the old ballads and graveyard poetry leading to the Gothic novel, but of the many modern fiction writers such as Lovecraft, Robert E. Howard, Clark Ashton Smith, Frank Belknap Long, Donald Wandrei, Mary Elizabeth Counselman, Joseph Payne Brennan, and H. Warner Munn, for whom poetry was as natural a craft, and sometimes as important, as their fiction.

Meanwhile, in the early 1980s, there are some favorable portents for survival of this sometimes fragile field.

1. emerging Small Press poets
2. new weird poetry anthologies—for example, Anderson [6–2], Bacon and Troyanovich [6–3], Hayes [6–25].
3. occasional weird poetry appearing in anthologies of mostly fiction; for example, editors Carter, Haining, Lord, Offutt, or sprinkled through novels like Karl Edward Wagner's
4. increasing numbers of weird poems appearing in general fantasy verse single-author collections
5. fantasy publishers featuring poetry (Arkham House, Donald M. Grant) or specializing in it (Fantome Press, Roy A. Squires, The Strange Company)
6. noted fantasy fiction authors with poetry collections published—Bradbury, de Camp, Long, Munn
7. fantasy poetry awards: Balrog, Clark Ashton Smith, Small Press, Writers and Artists Organization, and the corollary Science Fiction Poetry Association "Rhysling"
8. rare book price boom affecting out-of-print weird poetry books
9. increasing number of biocritical studies, such as those on the poetry of Lovecraft, Howard, Smith, and Sterling

10. increasing number of reprints for libraries of romantic-aesthetic poets—Saltus, Sterling, Symons
11. new ancillary field of "speculative" (formerly science fiction) poetry, and its editors and critics: Suzette Haden Elgin, Bob Frazier, Frederick J. Mayer [79]
12. persistent poetry in the children's field, (for example, Jack Prelutsky) as well as anthologizing (William Cole, Daisy Wallace)

So to these propitious signs, we aim to add this survey and hope that this genre may receive new attention and dignity. For there have always been readers for the oldest of arts—poetry—and for the oldest of literary realms—the kingdoms of the Unseen and the Uncanny.

Acknowledgments

Many helpful persons answered inquiries, often supplying documents or books. Their assistance made all the difference: Donn Albright, Michael Ambrose, Jonathan Bacon, Edward Paul Berglund, Ray Bradbury, G. Sutton Breiding, Joseph Payne Brennan, Robert E. Briney, Dr. Madison Cawein, William Cole, Lucile Coleman, Mary Elizabeth Counselman, Gary Crawford, L. Sprague de Camp, Clark Evans (Library of Congress, Rare Books), R. Alain Everts, Kenneth W. Faig, Michael Fantina, Frederick Frank, Phil Garland, Don Herron, C. M. James, S. T. Joshi, Randy Kaebitzche, Fritz Leiber, Glen Lord, Robert W. Lowndes, Stanley McNail, William Pugmire, Duane W. Rimel, J. Vernon Shea, Walter Shedlofsky, David C. Smith, Patricia Spacks, Richard L. Tierney, James Turner, Joe West, and John Widdemer. Countless books were loaned by John C. Moran, and dozens of items tracked by Betsy Fisher, Celia Fogel, and Phyllis Jones of Area Resource Center, Nashville. Mistakes of fact or interpretation, of course, remain our own.

Notes

1. Seán Ó. Súilleabhán, "Poets," *Man, Myth and Magic* 79 (1971), 210–211.
2. Peter Somerville-Sarge, *Irish Eccentrics: A Selection* (New York: Harper & Row, 1975), pp. 37–38.
3. Sukumar Dutt, *The Supernatural in English Romantic Poetry, 1780–1830* (Folcroft, Pa.: Folcroft Library Editions, 1972), p. 2.
4. H. P. Lovecraft, *Supernatural Horror in Literature* (New York: Dover, 1975; reprint of 1945 ed.), p. 20.
5. Lowry C. Wimberly, *Folklore in the English and Scottish Ballads* (New York: Dover, 1965; reprint of 1928 ed.). See throughout this superlative study.
6. Montague Summers, *The Gothic Quest* (New York: Russell & Russell, 1964; reprint of 1938 ed.), p. 43, regarding Hurd's vindication of the Gothic, *Letters on Chivalry and Romance* (1762).
7. Kenneth Clark, *The Gothic Revival: An Essay in the History of Taste* New York: Harper & Row, 1962), p. 28.
8. Charles Edward Whitmore, *The Supernatural in Tragedy* (London: Oxford Univ.

Press, 1915), pp. 203–288; with valuable supernatural-in-Shakespeare bibliography.

9. Montague Summers, *The Supernatural Omnibus* (London: Gollancz, 1931), p. 16.
10. Les Daniels, *Living in Fear: A History of Horror in the Mass Media* (New York: Scribner, 1975), p. 11.
11. Clark, *Gothic Revival*, pp. 30–32.
12. Amy Louise Reed, *The Background of Gray's Elegy: A Study in the Taste for Melancholy Poetry, 1700–1756* (New York: Russell & Russell, n.d.; reprint of 1924 ed.), p. 133. Despite Addison's attack ("The Fairy Way of Writing") in July 1712 in *The Spectator,* he praised Milton, and in November 1712 Steele praised Spenser.
13. Patricia Spacks, *The Insistence of Horror: Aspects of the Supernatural in Eighteenth Century Poetry* (Cambridge, Mass.: Harvard Univ. Press, 1962), pp. 29–66, 132–164, contains an intensive treatment of the period 1700–1750.
14. In lieu of a large, single study of eighteenth-century occultism, see James Webb, *The Occult Underground* (LaSalle, Ill.: Open Court, 1974), Gwendolyn Bays, *The Orphic Vision* (Lincoln: Univ. of Nebraska, 1964), and Auguste Viatte, *Les Sources occultes du romantisme: Illuminisme-Théosophie* (Paris: Librarie Ancienne Honoré Champion, 1928).
15. Spacks, *Insistence of Horror,* pp. 84–85.
16. Eleanor Sickels, *The Gloomy Egoist: Moods and Themes of Melancholy from Gray to Keats* (New York: Octagon, 1969; reprint of 1932 ed.), p. 3.
17. Summers, *Gothic Quest,* p. 47.
18. Devendra P. Varma, *The Gothic Flame* (London: Arthur Baker, 1957), p. 25.
19. Dutt, *Supernatural,* pp. 368–371.
20. J. G. Robertson, *A History of German Literature* (New York: Putnam, n.d.), pp. 307–309; William A. Little, *Gottfried August Bürger* (New York: Twayne, 1974); S. Whyte and E. A. Whyte, *Miscellanea Nova* (Dublin: Robert Marchbank, 1800), pp. 161–171.
21. Dutt, *Supernatural,* pp. 139–141.
22. Sir Walter Scott, *Poetical Works* (London: Oxford Univ. Press, 1926), p. 685.
23. Louis F. Peck, *A Life of Matthew G. Lewis* (Cambridge, Mass.: Harvard Univ. Press, 1961), p. 118.
24. Dan J. McNutt, *The Eighteenth-Century Gothic Novel: An Annotated Bibliography of Criticism and Selected Texts* (New York: Garland, 1975), pp. 232–244, gives summaries of the many articles that sort out the *Terror/Wonder* tangle.
25. Edgar Johnson, *Sir Walter Scott: The Great Unknown* (New York: Macmillan, 1970), pp. 127–128.
26. Sickels, *Gloomy Egoist,* p. 167.
27. Spacks, *Insistence of Horror,* pp. 120–121; also William Haller, *The Early Life of Robert Southey, 1774–1803* (New York: Octagon, 1966; reprint of 1917 ed.), p. 46.
28. Dutt, *Supernatural,* pp. 118–121; also Haller, *Early Life,* Ch. V and App. C, for *Thalaba* and its sources.
29. Sickels, *Gloomy Egoist,* p. 173.
30. Dutt, *Supernatural,* p. 54.
31. Spacks, *Insistence of Horror,* pp. 124–126, 188–189.
32. See also Ann Radcliffe, "On the Supernatural in Poetry," *New Monthly Magazine* (1826), pp. 145–152; and Alan D. McKillop, "Mrs. Radcliffe on the Supernatural in Poetry," *Journal of English and Germanic Philology* 31 (1932), 352–359.

33. See Dougald M. Monroe, Jr., *Coleridge's Theories of Dreams, Hallucinations and Related Phenomena, in Relation to his Critical Theories* (Diss., Northwestern, 1953), also James Volent Baker, *The Sacred River: Coleridge's Theory of the Imagination* (Greenwood, 1969), and Norman Fruman, "Dreams," in *Coleridge: The Damaged Archangel* (Brazilier, 1971), pp. 365–412.

34. Lane Cooper, "The Power of the Eye in Coleridge," *Studies in Language and Literature in Celebration of the Seventieth Birthday of James Morgan Hart, November 2, 1909* (1910), pp. 78–121; also Kathleen Coburn, "Coleridge and Wordsworth and 'The Supernatural,' " *University of Toronto Quarterly* 25 (January 1956), pp. 121–130.

35. See J. R. de J. Jackson, *Coleridge: The Critical Heritage* (New York: Barnes & Noble, 1970).

36. Accounts of this evening vary slightly; see Arthur H. Nethercott, *The Road to Tryermane: A Study of the History, Background, and Purposes of Coleridge's "Christabel"* (New York: Russell & Russell, 1962), pp. 20, 78; and Radu Florescu, *In Search of Frankenstein* (New York: New York Graphic Society, 1975), pp. 162–166.

37. Andrew Lang, "The Supernatural in Fiction" in *Adventures among Books* (London: Longmans, Green, 1905), pp. 273–276.

38. Quoted in Archibald Strong, "The Sinister in Shelley" in *Three Studies in Shelley* (London: Oxford Univ. Press, 1921), pp. 113–114, 120–122.

39. M. Roxana Klapper, *The German Literary Influence on Shelley* (Salzburg: Universität Salzburg, 1975), pp. 12–13.

40. James Camp, et al., eds., *Pegasus Descending: A Book of the Best Bad Verse* (New York: Macmillan, 1971), pp. 217–218.

41. A. B. Young, "Shelley and M. G. Lewis," *Modern Language Review* 1 (1906), 322–324.

42. Strong, "Sinister in Shelley," pp. 124, 136–137.

43. See Horace Gregory, "The Survival of Thomas Lovell Beddoes" in *Spirit of Time and Place* (New York: Norton, 1973), pp. 42–51; Arthur Symons, "Thomas Lovell Beddoes" in *Figures of Several Centuries* (Freeport, N.Y.: Books for Libraries, 1969), pp. 122–129; and H. W. Donner, *Thomas Lovell Beddoes: The Making of a Poet* (Oxford: Basil Blackwell, 1935).

44. Claude Colleer Abbott, *The Life and Letters of George Darley: Poet and Critic* (London: Oxford Univ. Press, 1967; reprint of 1928 ed.), pp. 87–88, 126–135; John Heath-Stubbs, *The Darkling Plain: A Study of the Later Fortunes of Romanticism* (London: Eyre & Spottiswoode, 1950), pp. 24–37.

45. Dutt, *Supernatural*, pp. 326–336; John Clubbe, ed., *Selected Poems of Thomas Hood* (Cambridge, Mass.: Harvard Univ. Press, 1970).

46. Cecil B. Lang, *The Pre-Raphaelites and Their Circle* (Chicago: Univ. of Chicago Press, 1968), pp. 23, 121–122.

47. See Patricia Allderidge, *Richard Dadd* (London: Academy Editions, 1974), and Charles N. Lewis and John Arsenian, "Murder Will Out: A Case of Parricide in a Painter and his Painting," *Journal of Nervous and Mental Disease* 164, No. 4, 273–279.

48. Peter Haining, ed., *The Edgar Allan Poe Scrapbook* (New York: Schocken, 1978), p. 39.

49. J. E. Chamberlin, *Ripe Was the Drowsy Hour: The Age of Oscar Wilde* (New York: Seabury, 1977), pp. 2–3.

50. Roger Lhombreaud, *Arthur Symons* (London: Unicorn, 1963), pp. 9–10, 19, 132, 135.
51. Benjamin de Casseres, "Arthur Symons: An Impression" in *Forty Immortals* (New York: Joseph Lawren, 1926), p. 59.
52. *The Collected Poems of W. B. Yeats* (New York: Macmillan, 1956), *passim.*
53. Kathleen Raine, "Yeats, the Tarot, and the Golden Dawn," *Sewanee Review* 77 (1969), 130; see also her book of the same title (Atlantic Highlands, N.J.: Dolmen Press, 1972), and George Mills Harper, *Yeats's Golden Dawn* (New York: Barnes & Noble, 1974).
54. See John Adlard, *Stenbock, Yeats and the Nineties* (London: Cecil & Amelia Woolf, 1969), with essay by Arthur Symons and bibliography by Timothy d'Arch Smith, and Adlard, *Christmas with Count Stenbock* (London: Enitharmon, 1980); also Smith, *Love in Earnest: Some Notes on the Lives and Writings of English "Uranian" Poets from 1889 to 1930* (London: Routledge & Kegan Paul, 1970), pp. 34–39.
55. Montague Summers, *The Galanty Show* (London: Woolf, 1980), p. 242.
56. Flavia Alaya, *William Sharp—"Fiona Macleod," 1855–1905* (Cambridge, Mass.: Harvard Univ. Press, 1970), *passim;* Richard LeGalliene, "The Mystery of Fiona Macleod" in *Vanishing Roads and Other Essays* (New York: Putnam, 1915), pp. 275–290.
57. Derek Stanford, *Poets of the 'Nineties: A Biographical Anthology* (London: John Baker, 1965), p. 19.
58. Richard LeGalliene, *The Romantic '90s* (Garden City, N.Y.: Doubleday, Page, 1923), p. 136.
59. de Casseres, "Arthur Symons," p. 64.
60. Emma Francis Dawson, *An Itinerant House and Other Stories* (San Francisco: William Doxey, 1897).
61. Lionel Stevenson, "George Sterling's Place in Modern Poetry," *University of California Chronicle* 31 (October 1929), 401–421, sets Sterling in English Late Victorian tradition.
62. Dreiser's introduction to *Lilith* (New York: Macmillan, 1926); also Clark Ashton Smith, "George Sterling: An Appreciation" in *Planets and Dimensions: Collected Essays of Clark Ashton Smith*, ed. by Charles K. Wolfe (Baltimore: Mirage Press, 1973), p. 7.
63. See *Lizette Woodworth Reese, 1856–1935: A Tribute* (Baltimore: Enoch Pratt Free Library, 1944); also Alexander C. Wirth, *Complete Bibliography of Lizette Woodworth Reese* (Baltimore: Proof Press, 1937).
64. William Henry Hulme, "Madison Cawein" in *Southern Writers: Biographical and Critical Studies,* Vol. II (New York: Gordian, 1970; reprint of 1903 ed.), pp. 332–378; also Otto A. Rothert, *The Story of a Poet* (Freeport, N.Y.: Books for Libraries, 1971; reprint of 1921 ed.); John Wilson Townsend, "Has Kentucky Produced a Poet?" in *Kentuckians in History and Literature* (New York: Neale, 1907), pp. 137–152; and Ish Richey, *Kentucky Literature* (Tumpkinsville, Ky.: Monroe County, 1963).
65. William Archer, *Poets of the Younger Generation* (St. Clair Shores, Mich.: Scholarly Press, 1969; reprint of 1902 ed.), pp. 66–79.
66. See Edward D. Snyder, *Hypnotic Poetry: A Study of Trance-Inducing Techniques in Certain Poetry and Its Literary Significance* (New York: Octagon Books, 1970; reprint of 1932 ed.).

67. See "Futurist Manifestoes" of Filippo Marinetti, c. 1909–1922, which demanded the demolition of logic, reason, syntax, morality, and especially beauty of form. Marinetti's most important dogma, though, was that *individual* taste in poetry be subordinated to *collective* taste—that of a critical élite. Though personally derided, histrionic Marinetti worked through Ezra Pound until most of his Manifestoes became accepted. Forgotten today, he deserves recognition for his seminal influence.

68. Poets such as Jack Prelutsky and John Ciardi and anthologists such as William Cole and Daisy Wallace exemplify this. See the quality children's magazine *Cricket;* also see Brewton's *Index to Children's Poetry.*

69. August Derleth, ed., *Fire and Sleet and Candlelight: New Poems of the Macabre* (Sauk City, Wis.: Arkham House, 1961), dust-wrapper blurb.

70. Henry Charles Duffin, *Walter de la Mare: A Study of his Poetry* (Freeport, N.Y.: Books for Libraries, 1969; reprint of 1949 ed.), p. 69; also R. L. Mégroz, *Walter de la Mare: A Biographical and Critical Sketch* (London: Hodder & Stoughton, 1924), especially Chs. 4 ("Poetry as Dream") and 5 ("Psychology of Dream").

71. William Fulwiler, review of S. T. Joshi and Marc A. Michaud, eds., *H. P. Lovecraft in "The Eyrie",* in *Lovecraft Studies* 1 (1979), p. 33; also Lin Carter, *Imaginary Worlds* (New York: Ballantine, 1973), p. 60.

72. As Sterling wrote in a letter to Smith (September 21, 1926), "the whole intellectual (including of course the aesthetic) trend is increasingly against admiration of the demonic, the supernatural. Such elements now seem only to awaken smiles, as being childish in their nature and no part of the future vision of the race." Still, Smith replied (November 4), "My fondest dream is to find a Hyperborea beyond Hyperborea, in the realm of imaginative poetry." From *Nightshade* 4 (1977), 28.

73. For Lovecraft's recommended poets and texts on poetry, see "Suggestions for a Reading Guide" in *The Dark Brotherhood and Other Pieces* (Sauk City, Wis.: Arkham House, 1966), pp. 36–44; for those he owned see S. T. Joshi and Marc A. Michaud, *Lovecraft's Library: A Catalogue* (West Warwick, R.I.: Necronomicon Press, 1980); for his comments on poets and poetry see S. T. Joshi, *An Index to the Selected Letters of H. P. Lovecraft* (Necronomicon, 1980).

74. See Glenn Lord, ed., *The Last Celt* (West Kingston, R.I.: Donald M. Grant, 1976) for statements by Howard and others on his poetry and poetic influences.

75. See *Nyctalops,* Nos. 11/12 (1976), for extended commentaries and reviews.

76. Some book-length manuscripts are already extant: Lucile Coleman, K. Allen Daniels, Michael Fantina, Joey Froehlich, Richard L. Tierney, and Billy Wolfenbarger.

77. See also poetry collections not primarily supernatural, but containing some examples: Frederick J. Mayer, *Where Does the Real Go When It's Gone?* (1975); D. C. Smith, *Born Ready* (1980); James Wade, *Early Voyagers* (1969); Smith's *Chipped Bone* (1976), an anthology including Smith, Breiding, and Fantina; and Stephanie Stearns, *The Saga of the Sword That Sings and Other Realities* (1981).

78. Thomas Burnett Swann, *Wombats and Moondust: Poems, Frolicsome and Serious* (Mill Valley, Calif.: Wings, 1956), p. 22; and *Driftwood* (New York: Vantage, 1952), p. 22.

79. Robert Frazier and Terry Hansen, "A Silent Evolution: Speculative Verse," unpublished; and Frazier, "New Maps—Starry Provinces: The Challenge to the

Speculative Poets," paper read at the Science Fiction Research Association National Conference (1978), University of Northern Iowa; also Dick Allen, "What Rough Beast: SF-Oriented Poetry," *Extrapolation* 17 (1975), 8–17.

Bibliography

This first bibliography of supernatural horror poetry is offered as a pioneer essay. It spans nearly two centuries of an elusive genre that is usually scattered throughout other sources. So the actual list of poetry books that are wholly or significantly supernatural-macabre is short, even with some borderline additions. (These exceptions are plainly marked.) Included in the bibliography are:

1. Collections (single-author) or anthologies whose verse content seems to be at least 50 percent within the genre. Also included are some ephemeral chapbooks, leaflets, and broadsides that, however trivial, might otherwise be lost or forgotten.
2. Collections or anthologies of less than 50 percent supernatural-horror content, but whose dominant tone, relevance to other work, or rarity merits inclusion. Such questionable items are so identified.
3. Translations of Bürger's *Lenore* when they form separate volumes. The genre might not have flourished without "Lenore" and her wild ride, for this German ballad quickly became "English" in countless translations, paraphrases, and parodies.
4. Dramas. Only one or two weird-horror plays that would otherwise be forgotten. Some other plays are mentioned when the poetry in them deserves notice, although the entire play may fail as drama. By contrast, the successful plays of the Irish Renaissance have been ignored, as well as some earlier Gothic plays.
5. M. G. Lewis's *Tales of Wonder*. The many editions in this cycle are routinely mislisted even in today's reference books, directories, and catalogues (even though Gothic specialists and Lewis and Scott biographers have long known the facts). Since *Tales of Wonder* is *the* seminal horror-verse anthology in English, we have chosen to discuss the problem at length, to cut down on future confusion in listing or ordering the volumes.
6. Humor. Several forgotten spoofs or pastiches of horror poems, some of whose literary worth doubtless excels that of their original targets. A few modern comic-macabre books have been included. One hoax is annotated and its spurious nature exposed.

Not included in the bibliography are:

1. Most books whose contents were wholly or mostly absorbed by larger, later editions. Similarly omitted are later, smaller editions taken from larger vol-

umes. Such listings would be duplication, although they are mentioned in passing (exception: the *Tales of Wonder* dynasty of M. G. Lewis, where the known editions have been listed).

2. "Name" or standard authors like Coleridge, Poe, or Christina Rossetti—especially the countless single volumes of *The Raven, The Ancient Mariner,* or *Goblin Market,* which would only clog a list better reserved for the lesser-known author and book.

3. Merely allegorical or occult verse—where the poet (or mage) is writing for the faithful, so that the dieties or devils invoked or exorcised are for magical, not literary purposes (example. the later verse of Aleister Crowley).

4. Collateral fantasy: fairy poems, "speculative" or science fiction poetry, mysticism, reincarnation, and so on. (Sometimes such poetry has *also* included supernatural horror elements, and in such cases the work may be listed.)

Many of the items in this bibliography are out of print, some were never properly distributed, and some were printed but never "published." Some items were published by their author, and some "publishers" were one-time only. Poetry booklets and leaflets are notorious for escaping standard listings, and in fairness, depository libraries will often not accept them for collection. But the public or private locations of nearly all items in this survey are known, and most are accessible for study or copying. We know the addresses of nearly all the contemporary authors and/or publishers. Most of the modern items have been seen. For some of the earlier items *National Union Catalogue* has had to serve. Authors/editors are American unless noted otherwise. We hope that this bibliography, whatever its excesses or lapses, may stimulate the purchasing, lending, and borrowing of material, and may encourage further study and republication. For as Clark Ashton Smith wrote in *The Auburn Journal* for March 5, 1925: "Time has been known to avenge many wrongs and injustices—even those inflicted upon poets."

6-1. Adams, Fred C. **A Bagwyn's Dozen.** Illus. by James E. Faulkenberg. Strange, 1974.
Mostly rhymed-and-metered, often with Lovecraftian themes. Noteworthy are the terse "Danse Macabre" and jolting "The Lesson." Reviewed: *Nyctalops* (April 1976).

6-2. Anderson, Anita Loreta, ed. **Hidden Places. Secret Words: An Anthology of Fantasy Poetry.** Illus. by Nick Forrest Evangelista and Anita Loreta Anderson. Northwoods Press, 1980.
Fifteen poets, 22 poems, most supernatural-horror. Representative are Bruce D. Griffiths ("Rainbow King"), Lucile Coleman ("Sea Ditty"), Michael Fantina ("The Dark Mage"), William R. Barrow ("Hands"); also, veterans W. Paul Ganley and Walter Shedlofsky and emerging Small Press poets William A. Conder, John Taylor. j. e. coplin, Stephanie Stearns, and Neal Wilgus. Compare to Harvey [6–24] and Bacon and Troyanovich [6–3].

*6-3. Bacon, Jonathan, and Steve Troyanovich, eds. **Omniumgathum: An Anthology of Verse by Top Authors in the Field of Fantasy.** Stygian Island Press, 1976.

Landmark volume, reviving obscure verses by Lovecraft, William Hope Hodgson, and others, and rescuing or introducing poems by fantasy-fiction writers like Manly Wade Wellman, H. Warner Munn, Joseph Payne Brennan, and August Derleth, and poets like Donald Sidney-Fryer, Lucile Coleman, Winona Nation, and Richard L. Tierney. Includes some nonfantasy verse by fantasy writers and many nonsupernatural selections amid the 111 verses by 44 poets. Still a signal collection with useful biographical data. Illustrated by many hands. Compare with Anderson [6-2], Derleth's *Fire and Sleet and Candlelight* [6-16], and Harvey [6-24].

*6-4. Beddoes, Thomas Lovell (U.K.). **The Works of Thomas Lovell Beddoes,** ed. by H. W. Donner. Oxford Univ. Press, 1935; AMS, 1976.

Massive, authoritative edition of probably the most morbid poet writing in English. Yet Beddoes also wrote light, happy song lyrics, and his verses shine in children's anthologies. Often compared to his gore-thirsty favorites Marlowe, Webster, Marston, and Tourneur, this "Gothic Keats" is, however, more of a Romantic than a latter-day Elizabethan. "Dream Pedlary" is his most reprinted poem, but almost the only piece published in his troubled lifetime was the weird *The Bride's Tragedy* (1822)—which won immense praise from his generation. Like his father (who had sold drugs to the Coleridge-De Quincey circle), this strange poet was a physician, and he kept a skeleton in his room to invoke his grisly muse. He was a political agitator, close to the secret societies, until he was expelled from Bavaria, and after his suicide a box of papers was found. Its contents shocked Browning and Edmund Gosse, and the latter mutilated the texts for a mangled edition of 1894. Happily, H. W. Donner has rectified the Beddoes canon in an accurate version; he has also written a thorough biography [7-4]. Unfinished is Beddoes's greatest work, *Death's Jest Book,* a favorite of Clark Ashton Smith, which Eleanor Sickels in *The Gloomy Egoist* (1928) calls "undoubtedly the most astonishing *danse macabre* in English literature," praising "the strength and suppleness of its neo-Elizabethan blank verse and the exquisite and eerie music of its lyrics." Verse dramas like *The Second Brother* and *Torrismond* have supernatural lines, as have many of the shorter poems. Beddoes lives on today in anthologies, and his ghost hovers over the woodcuts and pages of C. M. James's Fantome Press (and *Journal Fantome*). But fantasy enthusiasts have yet to really discover this favorite of Clark Ashton Smith. Compare to Brennan [6-7], Smith [6-51, 6-52], and Breiding [6-6].

6-5. Bierce, Ambrose. **A Vision of Doom.** Ed. by Donald Sidney-Fryer. Illus. by Frank Villano. Donald M. Grant, 1980.

Fifty poems, mostly sardonic-sarcastic—one hesitates to call anything by Ambrose Bierce "light." Although only a minority are supernatural, the

morbid tone, the beautiful and horrific color plates, and historically important title piece qualify this overdue book. Among the witty and weird verses
are "Restored," "Tempora Mutantur," "Presentiment," and "Saralthia's
Soliloquy," plus the song of the "dead body" from the verse play "A Bad
Night." More serious are the bizarre-imaged "Basilica," "A Study in Gray,"
and the influential title poem in declamatory, incantatory blank verse. The
detailed introduction, "A Visionary of Doom," reminds us of Bierce's larger,
longer shadow over California late romanticism through his tutelage and
sponsorship of other poets, and in such essays as "Poetry and Verse" and
"Thought and Feeling." A vital weird-horror collection and a poetic California romantic artifact.

6-6. Breiding, (G.) Sutton. **The Crosses of December (After Reading
George Trakl).** Strange Company, 1977.
A ghostly poem-leaflet—three stanzas of free verse. Breiding is a follower of
Poe, Baudelaire, Rimbaud, and California romantics George Sterling and
Clark Ashton Smith. However, his decadent vision is his own and is es-
teemed highly by his compeers and numerous readers. A volume of selected
poems from this author is wanted; see such verses as "Blue November," "The
Dark Breath," and "Halloween Arcane" in Small Press journals like his own
Oracle, and *Nyctalops.* He has edited *Ebon Lute* and numerous ephemeral pub-
lications that merit preservation. Compare to Bierce [6–5], Sterling [6–54],
Smith [6–51, 6–52], Trakl [6–59], and Symons [6–56].

6-7. Brennan, Joseph Payne. **Nightmare Need.** Arkham, 1964.
The noted storyteller and established poet's first horror verse collection.
There is a morbid, macabre intensity in these brief poems; nearly all are of
supernatural horror, none is really weak. "Nocturne Macabre," "The White
Huntress," "The Scythe" are typically excellent among these 57 choices.
The black vision of Brennan, especially in other volumes (which are less
spectral), such as *Death Poems* (1974), *As Evening Advances* (1978), and *Webs of
Time* (1979), suggest Count Stenbock or Beddoes [6–4]. A major fantasy
verse collection is planned—(*Creep to Death*) and a general *Sixty Selected Poems,*
which will inlcude some fantasy-horror poems. Brennan for years edited the
poetry journal *Essence* and fantasy magazine *Macabre.* Compare with McNail
[6–41] and Drake [6–17]; contrast with Smith [6–52].

*6-8. Bürger, Gottfried (Germany). **The Earliest English Translations of
Bürger's Lenore: A Study in English and German Romanticism,** by Oliver
Farrar Emerson. In *Western Reserve University Bulletins, May 1915.* Literary
Section Supplement. Western Reserve Univ. Press, 1915.
This German ghost-ballad became an "English" poem overnight, with seven
versions published in 1796 alone and dozens of subsequent translations and
adaptations, as well as many parodies. "Lenore" may be the single most im-
portant horror poem "in English," since its sensational popularity caused the

spate of ballad writing at the end of the eighteenth century, especially by Sir Walter Scott and Matthew Gregory Lewis. Virtually all the Romantics were deeply influenced by "Lenore," especially Southey, Coleridge, and Shelley. Translations in the Emerson volume include those by J. T. Stanley, William Taylor, and H. J. Pye. The introductory material corrects many errors that occur in existing texts. The volume merits reprinting; conceivably, a massive variorum could also be compiled, gathering all the better "Lenores" together with the parodies. For listings of most of the versions—as separate books or in periodicals, collections, and anthologies—see Evelyn B. Jolles (*G. A. Bürger's Ballade "Lenore" in England,* 1974) and Bayard Quincy Morgan (*A Bibliography of German Literature in English Translation,* University of Wisconsin Studies in Language and Literature, No. 16, 1922). Two Bürger adaptations made up Walter Scott's first published book, *The Chase, and William and Helen* (1796), technically the first known horror poem "collection" (one author) in English. Also of value is Pre-Raphaelite Dante Gabriel Rossetti's *Lenore* (1900). Rossetti modified the stanza's rhyme scheme and line length, and he mutes the gruesome mood in favor of a more colorful, romantic tone. This edition is enhanced by a detailed introduction by William Rossetti.

6-9. Carter, Lin. **Dreams from R'lyeh.** Arkham, 1975.
Versatile editor and fiction writer, Carter's first books were of poetry—*Sandalwood and Jade* (1951), *Galleon of Dream* (1953)—and nonfantasy—*A Letter to Judith* (1959). This volume's title-cycle of 31 sonnets is one more tribute to Lovecraft's "Fungi From Yuggoth" [6-36] using his gods, places, and books; but they also commemorate Robert W. Chamber's "Carcosa" mythos. Other poems include the noteworthy "Once in Fabled Grandeur" and "The Elf-King's Castle." Carter's verse influences were Clark Ashton Smith [6-52], Don Blanding, and John Masefield, although he has preferred reading modern and nonfantasy poetry more recently. (See "Author's Note" at end of volume for Carter poetry-credo.) Reviewed: *The Diversifier* (May 1976). Compare with Lovecraft [6-36], Smith [6-52], Tierney [6-58], and Long [6-34, 6-35].

6-10. Cawein, Madison. **The Poems of Madison Cawein,** Vol. IV *Poems of Mystery and of Myth and Romance.* Illus. by Eric Papé. Small, Maynard, 1908.
Cawein of Kentucky filled many books with colorful, singing verse. His facile, metrical poems are thick with the mist of woodland glens, where ghosts often appear. This volume culls many of the best poems that he wrote in our genre, especially the 69 "Poems of Mystery," such as "Gloramone," "Haunted," "The Headless Horseman," "The Image in the Glass," "The Vampire," and "The Werewolf." Like George Sterling, whom he admired, Cawein was a late romantic in the Victorian tradition, yet happily haunted by his own sense of place, which makes his best work memorable. Compare to Shorter [6-50] and Drake [6-17].

6–11. Cawein, Madison. **The Shadow Garden (A Phantasy) and Other Plays.** Putnam, 1910.

Of the four verse dramas included here, two are within our genre. "The House of Fear: A Mystery," has virtually all ethereal characters. Personifications like "Dead Dreams" and "Shadow of the Past" speak the lines in a very Gothic setting. "The Witch" is likewise allegorical, with "A Demon" and "A Witch" cast as protagonist-villains, and a heavy supernatural aura.

6–12. Christabess, by S. T. Colebritche, Esq.: A Right Woeful Poem, Translated from the Doggerel, by Sir Vinegar Sponge. (U.K.). J. Duncombe, 1816.

Cheapest of all the parodies of "Christabel," Coleridge's vital vampire poem. Published by an erotic bookseller, author luckily unknown. The "doggerel" subtitle points up the offense many took with "Christabel's" *meter*—relying on stress, not syllable count. This innovation, anticipating today's free verse, was bitterly derided at the time. Cited by Nethercott in *The Road to Tryermaine* [8–58].

*6–13. Coblentz, Stanton A. **Unseen Wings: The Living Poetry of Man's Immortality.** Beechurst Press, 1949.

Veteran poet (over a dozen volumes), editor (*Wings,* 1933–1960), and science fiction novelist, Coblentz selects 236 poems for this collection. Not all are in the genre, but sections II "Eerie Visitants" (43 poems) and III "Hauntings" (27 poems) largely qualify. Coblentz's wide-ranging choices expand on those of Widdemer [6–63] and Derleth's *Dark of the Moon* [6–15], although admittedly his scope differs. Included are some nonspectral poems and some spectral but nonhorrific ones; excluded are vampires, werewolves, and such. Many poets left out by Widdemer and Derleth are here—for example, Thomas Bailey Aldrich, the editor's friend George Sterling, Ernest Dowson, and Robert Hillyer. Two helpful additions—introductions to each section and biographical notes—were absent in his predecessors' volumes. An excellent companion volume to theirs; compare also to Derleth's *Fire and Sleet and Candlelight* [6–16] and Hayes [6–25]. Merits reprinting. Reviewed: *San Francisco Chronicle* (September 18, 1949); *Saturday Review of Literature* (June 4, 1949); *Springfield Republican* (July 3, 1949).

6–14. Cooney, Ellen. **The Silver Rose.** Duir Press, 1979.

Full-length free-verse epic poem (in 11 parts) of bizarre mythology stressing bisexuality and androgyny. Fantastic enough to warrant attention, although not conventionally supernatural; still, a consistent but incredible otherworld with horror elements.

*6–15. Derleth, August, ed. **Dark of the Moon: Poems of Fantasy and the Macabre.** Arkham, 1947; Books for Libraries, 1969.

The single most vital volume in any collection of supernatural verse. Lengthy, rich, and representative: 64 poets, 210 poems. Includes some anonymous ballads by Romantics like William Blake, Scott, Keats, Thomas Hood, and Beddoes; and Victorians like Tennyson, William Morris, and Longfellow. Revives other more-neglected Victorians, such as J. Sheridan LeFanu's "The Legend of the Glaive," Fitz James O'Brien's "The Steamship" and "The Demon of the Gibbet," and James Whitcomb Riley's "The Witch of Erkmurden." Derleth is strongest on twentieth-century poets, but Americans outnumber British or Celtic 20 to one (exception: de la Mare, his famed "The Listeners," and two other choices). Some notable modern mainstream selections are Amy Lowell's "A Dracula of the Hills" and "The Paper in the Gate-Legged Table," William Rose Benét's "The Sorceress," Arthur Inman's "Werewolf," Merrill Moore's "Just Then the Door," and Elinor Wylie's "Atavism." Derleth is most loyal to his *Weird Tales*–Arkham House peers: Robert E. Howard, Clark Ashton Smith, H. P. Lovecraft, Donald Wandrei, Leah Bodine Drake, Mary Elizabeth Counselman, Frank Belknap Long, Francis Flagg, and Dorothy Quick. But this imbalance does not sacrifice quality; also, these poets were in greater risk of oblivion, then, than were some of the English poets left out, such as Lord Dunsany. Other omissions: graveyard verse, Shelley, the late Victorian aesthetes and decadents, and Californians Ambrose Bierce and George Sterling. Derleth was in great debt to Widdemer's 1920 *The Haunted Hour* [6–63]; one-third, or 22, of his pre-1921 choices appear in hers. However, she grouped poems by theme, like Coblentz [6–13], and Derleth's run chronologically, like Hayes's [6–25]. A milestone volume from this prodigious editor-poet-publisher and an influence upon the emerging Small Press poets (late 1960s–1980s).

*6–16. Derleth, August, ed. **Fire and Sleet and Candlelight: New Poems of the Macabre.** Arkham, 1961.

An important more recent anthology, an update of *Dark of the Moon* [6–15]. Two hundred forty-seven well-picked poems of the 89 authors, about evenly split between Derleth's mainstream contemporaries, and his *Weird Tales*–Arkham House colleagues. Some noted general names: John Betjamin, Felix Stefanile, Jesse Stuart (like Derleth, a famed regional writer), Harold Vinal, Laura Benét, Mark Van Doren, Grant Code (fellow Wisconsin poet), Loring Williams, and Margaret Widdemer, editor of *The Haunted Hour* [6–63]. Among the better known fantastic poets: Clark Ashton Smith, Vincent Starrett (premier bookman of fantasy and detection), Stanton A. Coblentz (editor of *Wings* and Wings Press), Robert Bloch, Joseph Payne Brennan, Stanley McNail, Robert E. Barlow (Lovecraft friend), Lilith Lorraine (editor of *Flame*, founder of Avalon Poets), Frank Belknap Long, Leah Bodine Drake, Robert E. Howard, Joseph Payne Brennan, and Mary Elizabeth Counselman. Only a few nonspectral or nonweird choices. With useful biographical notes. Important bridge between the *Weird Tales* days and the Small Press movement, which Derleth's own *The Arkham Collector* (1967–1971) helped to intensify. A further collection to capture the next 20 years is now needed. Compare to Bacon and Troyanovich [6–3].

6–17. Drake, Leah Bodine. **A Hornbook for Witches.** Arkham, 1950.
Forty-seven poems in the older English tradition—"All Saints' Eve," "The Tenants," "Wood Wife," "Changling" are but a few facile examples from this Pulitzer Prize winner. Fellow Arkham House poet Stanley McNail says that this volume "set a standard of excellence never equalled, in my opinion, before or since," and poet Richard Tierney links Drake with Mary Elizabeth Counselman as "definitely the best women poets in *Weird Tales*." Deserves reprinting in an expanded version to include "The Undine" from *This Tilting Dust* (1951) and several in Derleth's 1963 *Fire and Sleet and Candlelight* [6–16]. Compare with Shorter [6–50], Brennan [6–7], McNail [6–41], and Munn [6–44].

6–18. Fantina, Michael. **Night Terrors.** Michael Fantina, 1974.
Sonnets (24) in the Lovecraft "Fungi from Yuggoth" tradition, by a skilled verse-maker who also writes effective poems beyond the Lovecraftian mythology. Widely published in the Small Press. Compare with Tierney [6–58], Carter [6–9], and Lovecraft [6–36]. Note also "Demon Wind" and "Night Feast" in Harvey [6–24].

6–19. Gardette, Charles D. **The Fire-Fiend and The Raven: The Story behind a Literary Hoax.** De la Ree, 1973.
Gardette hoaxed contemporary editors, critics, and readers with his "unpublished manuscript of the late Edgar A. Poe." But like many a literary forger, he soon was claiming all the credit. Reproduced in facsimile within this volume is his *The Whole Truth in the Question of "The Fire-Fiend"* (1864). In the best tradition of a Victorian feud, it is enjoyably verbose, sarcastic, learned, and savage, as bombastic as "The Fire-Fiend" poem it defends. The poem, based on "The Raven" (also reproduced for comparison), itself reads like a parody: the fiend "Spat a ceaseless, seething, hissing, bubbling, gurgling stream of gore!" Yet this fooled a Poe scholar as late as 1901! Historical introduction by Gerry De la Ree, appropriately illustrated by Virgil Finlay, Stephen Fabian, Clark Ashton Smith, and others. Other poems in the original *The Fire-Fiend and Other Poems* (1866) that are spectral include "The Treasure-Ships" (pirate lore, in couplets) and "Too Late" (ghost of the beloved by a tomb): these are more sedate and modest than the Poe parodies. Compare to *Golgotha* [6–20].

6–20. Gardette, Charles D. **Golgotha: A Phantasm.** Illus. by Virgil Finlay. Gerry De la Ree, 1973.
Poe-hoaxer Gardette ("The Fire-Fiend") wrote this other pastiche of "The Raven" in apparent seriousness. The still-enjoyable imagery and alliteration are weakened by frenzied, Poesque dashes—and exclamation points!—but craftsmanship and passion are evident. Compare to *The Fire-Fiend* [6–19].

6–21. Garland, Phil. **Moon-Foam: A Fantasy in Two Octaves.** Folly Press, 1975.
Leaflet-chapbook. Blank verse, metaphorical-macabre imagery.

6–22. Garland, Phil. **Night of the Demon: A Fantasy Poem.** Roy A. Squires, 1972.

Twelve well-done blank verse octaves in the late romantic, George Sterling–Clark Ashton Smith tradition. Narrates a sorcerer's horrific incantation. Compare to Breiding [6–6], Fantina [6–18], Smith [6–52], and Tierney [6–58].

6–23. Garland, Phil. **Nocturne: A Fable.** Folly Press, 1974.

Another blank verse horror poem—this one in six octaves. Narrates a were-wolf's last hunt and death, and subsequent eternal life with an immortal pack of lycanthropes. Skillful treatment, sustaining its tone.

6–24. Harvey, Jon M., ed. **Dark Words—Gentle Sounds.** Illus. by David Jackson. Spectre, 1977.

Slender but enduring collection of emerging Small Press poets. Horror verses from Michael Fantina, William A. Conder, A. R. Fallone, and Marion Pitman; of the 16 poems and eight poets, some are nonhorror. Compare to Bacon and Troyanovich [6–3] and Anderson [6–2].

*6–25. Hayes, Michael, ed. (U.K.). **Supernatural Poetry: A Selection, 16th Century to the 20th Century.** John Calder, 1978.

Another vital, representative anthology, bringing forth several poets not in Derleth's *Dark of the Moon* [6–15], such as Andrew Lang, "Fiona Macleod" (William Sharp), and Francis Ledwidge. Differs also by adding five earlier poets and some allegorical (nonspectral) verse; includes no translations; contains only two Americans, and no poet born after 1884. Among the Victorian poets included are: George Meredith ("Will o' the Wisp"), Algernon Swinburne ("After Death"), Richard Henry Horne ("Orion"), Sir Samuel Ferguson ("The Fairy Thorn"), George MacDonald ("Mammon Marriage"), Owen Meredith ("Saturnalia"), Sidney Thompson Dobell ("The Ballad of Keith of Ravelston"), and Robert Buchanan ("The Ballad of Judas Iscariot"). Contains 42 poets and 52 poems, of which seven are in Derleth's *Dark of the Moon;* thoughtful introduction and useful glossary. Not all choices horrific (a fairy poem or two). Compare with Widdemer [6–63] and Coblentz [6–13]. Reviewed: *The Romantist,* No. 3 (1979).

6–26. Hodgson, William Hope (U.K.). **Poems of the Sea.** Illus. Ferret Fantasy, 1977.

Although neglected in his lifetime, Hodgson's prose is widely published today; his verse, like his prose, evokes salt air and echoes the sounds of sad oceans. "Grey Seas Are Dreaming of My Death," "Thou Living Sea," and "The Calling of the Sea" merit notice among the 17 poems; the non-supernatural verses are still weird, somber, and nautical enough to give the volume unity. Excellent black-and-white art.

6-27. Howard, Robert E. **Always Comes Evening.** Comp. by Glenn Lord. Arkham, 1957. 2nd ed. Illus. by Keiko Nelson. Underwood-Miller, 1977.

Initial gathering of the then-known Howard poems (68 in the first edition, 69 in the second). Still a representative volume, capturing Howard's intense, somber poetic talent. As in his fiction, there is color and clamor and story-telling zest. Like Clark Ashton Smith, Howard may have been more instinctively a poet than a prose writer; and as with Smith—and to some extent Lovecraft, Long, Wandrei, and Brennan—the power of his prose had its origin in his verse. Like much *Weird Tales* poetry, Howard's was often merely exotic or fanciful, yet much was supernatural-horrific, too. Howard's mother read him poetry from earliest childhood, and he later visited his many influences—the first three being Robert W. Service, Kipling, and Masefield; their drumming cadences and active verbs certainly resound in his verse. He named over two dozen other poets whom he liked, including Siegfried Sasson (whose war poetry may have inspired him), George Sylvester Viereck (whose pagen pomp evokes Howard), Alfred Noyes Villon (whom he commemorated in a poem), Coleridge (after two readings, he is said to have memorized *The Ancient Mariner*), Swinburne, and Poe. A paraphrased couplet from Ernest Dowson was left as Howard's suicide note. Compare to Lovecraft [6-36], Long [6-34, 6-35], Wandrei [6-60], Munn [6-44], and Beddoes [6-4]. Reviewed: *The Savage Sword of Conan* (Nobember 1980).

6-28. Howard, Robert E. **Echoes from an Iron Harp.** Illus. by Alicia M. Austin. Donald M. Grant, 1972.

Borderline volume whose overall weird and macabre tone merits inclusion. Of the 61 poems, some that qualify are: "Skulls and Dust," "The Dweller in Dark Valley," " 'Feach Air Muir Lio Lionadhi Gealach Buidhe Mar Or,' " "The Sea," and "A Song for Men That Laugh." Some of the poems were headings for short stories; many were reprinted from Glenn Lord's *The Howard Collector* or *Magazine of Horror*. Affecting, subtle illustrations. Reviewed: *Ambrosia* (August 1973) and *The Savage Sword of Conan* (November 1980).

6-29. Howard, Robert E. **Night Images.** Morning Star Press, 1976.

Several of the 57 poems are in our genre, such as "Swamp Murder" and "The Dead Slaver's Tale" (according to Fred Blosser). Some reprinted from *Always Comes Evening* [6-27], others from *Verses in Ebony* (1975), and Roy A. Squires private editions, including *Black Dawn* (1972), this last having much weird imagery and macabre tone. The style of the two introductions evokes the fierce, colorful poetry of the collection itself. Reviewed: *Fantasy Crossroads*, No. 12 (November 1977), *The Savage Sword of Conan* (November 1980).

6-30. Howard, Robert E. **Singers in the Shadows.** Illus. by Robert Bruce Acheson, Donald M. Grant, 1970; 2nd ed. Science Fiction Graphics, 1977.

Twenty poems compiled by the author in 1928 and rejected for book publication; the manuscript was found among Howard's papers in 1966. Many of the poems are nonsupernatural (typically, sword-and-sorcery), but weird illustrations and enough examples of horror poetry qualify the volume for inclusion here. No Howard verse collection appeared during his lifetime, yet this first edition sold out within a year, and the enlarged second edition almost as quickly. Still, there is much uncollected Robert E. Howard poetry that has never seen book publication. Reviewed: *The Savage Sword of Conan* (November 1980).

6–31. Ireson, Barbara, ed. (U.K.). **Shadows and Spells.** Illus. by Gill Simmonds. Faber & Faber, 1969.
Mostly twentieth-century poetry, in such sections as "Who's That Knocking on the Window?," "What Ghosts Could Walk," "The Hag Is Astride."

*6–32. Lewis, Matthew Gregory (U.K.). **Tales of Wonder.** 2 vols. J. Bell, 1801. (Some copies distributed in late 1800.) K. Wogan, 1801; Samuel Campbell, 1801.
The first known published and single most important horror verse anthology in English. Volume One contains 32 poems by Matthew Lewis, Walter Scott, John Leyden, and others. Volume Two contains 28 standard poems by Ben Johnson, Dryden, Burns, Glover, Mallet, Ransay, Dr. Harrington, and Gray. *Tales of Wonder* was a decisive, if not always admitted, influence on the Romantics and is *the* seminal horror poetry volume in English. In its day the lavish, high-priced set was jeered at as *"Tales of Plunder"*—alluding also to the sometimes careless "translations" in Volume One and the padding with commonplace ballads in Volume Two. Yet the very venom of the attacks—and of the scathing parodies—plus the many reprints and new editions, suggest that *Tales of Wonder* was a vital, popular collection. Its forerunner had been Walter Scott's private *An Apology for Tales of Terror* (1799). Other editions with various numbers of ballads were published in 1801, 1805, 1817, 1836, 1869. Also in 1801 came the parody *Tales of Terror,* containing 20 hilarious poems, often mislisted as being authored by Lewis, although he had no known hand in it. The parodies were combined with Volume One of the books Lewis did edit, as *Tales of Terror and Wonder* (1887), as being authored by Lewis, thus creating a new title, a mistake, and more confusion; *Tales in Verse of Terror and Wonder* (1925) was a scaled-down version of this error. There were other parodies: George Watson Taylor's *The Old Hag in a Red Cloak* (1801); Thomas Dermody's *More Wonders!* (1801); James Atkinson's *Rodolpho* (1801); Anne Bannerman's *Tales of Superstition and Cruelty* (1802); and the anonymous *Tales of the Devil* (1801). The parodies could all be reprinted as a period anthology of rare wit and ribald abuse. Lewis's own *Tales of Wonder,* Volume One, needs an annotated reprint to fix its place in Romantic literature more firmly. Too long have all these volumes been prisoners of bibliographic chaos, which Morchard Bishop rightly called "A Terrible Tangle" (*Times Literary Supplement,* October 19, 1967).

6–33. Liddell, Hon. Henry (U.K.). **The Wizard of the North, the Vampire Bride, and Other Poems.** Blackwood, 1833.

"The Vampire Bride" combines vampire and demon-lover themes; presumably other poems in this volume are in our genre. Noted by Summers, *The Vampire: His Kith and Kin* (1928).

6–34. Long, Frank Belknap. **In Mayan Splendor.** Illus. by Stephen E. Fabian. Arkham, 1977.

Forty poems by a noted *Weird Tales* and Arkham House fiction writer, selected from the legendarily rare *A Man from Genoa* (1926), *The Goblin Tower* (1935, 1949), and more recent *The Marriage of Sir John de Mandeville* (1976). Various traditional forms, often ballad stanzas—for example, "A Man from Genoa" and "The Marriage of Sir John de Mandeville," or sonnets—such as "Night Trees," "On Reading Arthur Machen: A Sonnet," and the title poem. This latter piece so impressed poet Richard Tierney [6–58] that he memorized it and visited the site of the poem (Copan, Honduras), reciting the sonnet atop every edifice that he could find to climb, in the late 1960s. Others who have praised the poems are Masefield, George Sterling, and Arthur Machen. Preface by noted poet-critic Samuel Loveman (friend of Bierce, Hart Crane, and Lovecraft). Long's poems have active verbs and *move,* and they are clear and musical. Hopefully his decades of poetic silence will be shattered, like A. E. Housman's, by a sequel volume. Compare with Wandrei [6–60], Lovecraft [6–36], Munn [6–44], and Smith [6–51, 6–52]. Reviewed: *Nyctalops* (March 1978).

6–35. Long, Frank Belknap. **When Chaugnar Wakes.** Two-color blockprint by C. M. James. Fantome Press, 1979.

Collector's item of one poem.

*6–36. Lovecraft, H. P. **Collected Poems.** Illus. by Frank Utpatel. Arkham, 1963; Ballantine, 1971, as *Fungi from Yuggoth and Other Poems* (with one less).

Eighty-one poems that partly reflect the author's fiction, with many of the poems intrinsically valuable, and some fewer significant as an influence. Lovecraft's first poetic models were late seventeenth-eighteenth century: Dryden, Cowper, Dyer, Oldham, Parnell, Tickell, Gray, Joel Barlow, James Thompson, and the Wartons. The "Early Poems" here are mostly in such pre-1800 style. Despite a few weird touches, only a few really fit the genre, such as "Aletheia Phrikodes" in "The Poe-et's Nightmare"; the latter has been explicated by R. Boerem in *H. P. Lovecraft: Four Decades of Criticism,* ed. by S. T. Joshi [8–43]. But these early antiquarian rhymes are amazing anachronisms, and they foretell Lovecraft's later, history-haunted fiction. Shedding his eighteenth-century costume, he wrote more effective horror verses. (We know that his library included such romantics as Scott, Shelley, Keats, Coleridge, Tennyson, and Poe, although he was less fond of late Victorian aesthetes—and he hated Whitman and Eliot.) Several supernatural horror poems are included in the section "The Ancient Track." But the most popular and influential Lovecraft poems are "The Fungi from Yuggoth," a 36-sonnet cycle written mostly in December–January 1929–1930. David Schultz notes that all but three are in Italian form—although we must observe the closing rhyming couplet as being an English compromise. Themes and content of "The Fungi" paralllel Lovecraft's tales (Schultz counts 15 gods, people, and places from the fiction, plus sources of the sonnets in Lovecraft's *The Notes and Commonplace Book*). The cycle captures much of its fantastic author's own yearning, nostalgia, and philosophy. "Fungi" has influenced Carter [6–9], Fantina [6–18], Tierney [6–58], and many in the Small Press movement (late 1960s–1980s). The title of this volume is a misnomer; it is really a *Selected Poems*. Lovecraft enthusiasts originally published *H.P.L.* (1937, eight poems) and *The Fungi from Yuggoth* (1943), which are embraced in this volume. Lesser verse has been collected since: Tom Collins, *A Winter Wish* (1977); and S. T. Joshi and Marc Michaud, eds., *Uncollected Prose and Poetry* (1978), Volume Two (1980); but few in these later collections are within the genre. (Oddly, all of Lovecraft's fantasy verse has never been collected as one volume.) Meanwhile, *Collected Poems* deserves reprinting.

6–37. Lowndes, Robert W. **Annals of Arkya.** Phantagraph Press, 1944.
Six Lovecraftian sonnets in the "Fungi" style, by a noted author and magazine editor. Sonnets 1–2, *Weird Tales* 48, no. 1 (1981); Sonnets 3–4, *Weird Tales* 48, no. 2 (1981).

6–38. Lowndes, Robert W. **New Annals of Arkya.** Phantagraph Press, 1945.
Six more Lovecraftian sonnets. "The Fool" and "The Street" are restrained and effective examples. Compare to Carter [6–9], Fantina [6–18], Lovecraft [6–36], Tierney [6–58], and Wandrei [6–60].

6–39. Macbeth, George, ed. (U.K.). **The Penguin Book of Sick Verse.** Penguin, 1963.
Introduction argues that "the extreme situation . . . can be a source of wisdom in the form of terror," and suggests psychosis as a "voyage" that may enlighten the traveler who survives. Perhaps. Meanwhile, at least the book's title is 100 percent fulfilled, and there are several poems in the genre: James Thomson's "The City of Dreadful Night," William Mickle's eighteenth-century "Cumnor Hall," and others from Beddoes, Thomas Gordon Hake, William Rowley, Thomas Middleton, and more. Total tone of volume suggests its inclusion, if countered by the nonsupernatural but macabre poems; 165 poems, 98 poets.

6–40. McDougle, William. **The Female Demon: 31 Poems of Fantasy and the Unusual.** Illus. by Charles J. Momberger. Shroud, 1955.
Many supernatural-horror poems in this 31-poem collection, usually telling a story. The best in this uneven volume include "The Traitor," "Water,"

and "The Wind Has Risen from the Dead." A forgotten book and author, even for this off-trail genre.

6–41. McNail, Stanley. **Something Breathing.** Arkham, 1965.
Stark, evocative short poems (32) fill this highly readable collection. Author also edited *Nightshade* (1965–1968), a presumed weird poetry journal (if so, the longest-lived), and *The Galley Sail Review* (1958–1971), from his Nine Hostages Press at San Francisco. Earliest influences: Poe, Coleridge, *Macbeth*, and later: Lovecraft, Derleth, Robert Bloch, Donald Wandrei, and *Weird Tales*. Most recent book is a nonfiction "how-to" manual for taping paranormal voices, *Your Haunted Tape Recorder*. An anthology of *Nightshade* poetry is contemplated. Compare with Brennan [6–7]; contrast with Smith [6–51, 6–52].

6–42. Moone, S. (Schuyler), trans. **King Cahal Mor of the Wine-Red Hand.** Fantome Press, 1977.
One-poem collector's edition, 62 lines. Supernatural romance of Old Spain.

6–43. Moore, Lilian, and Lawrence Webster, eds. **Catch Your Breath: A Book of Shivery Poems.** Illus. by Graham Wilson. Garrard, 1973.
Poems of witches, "creepy creatures," and other menaces; also Halloween verses. Includes de la Mare, Sandburg, and Elizabeth Coatsworth among the 26 poets and 42 poems.

6–44. Munn, H. Warner. **The Book of Munn or "A Recipe for Roast Camel."** Illus. by Vandy Vandervoort and Erin McKee. Outré House, 1979.
The best of these 105 poems are haunted with the sound of sea and wind, like the old English or Celtic ballads, such as "Fimmilene, the Spae-Wife," "The Little Glass Ship," or "The Changeling." "Cradle Song for a Baby Werewolf" won the Clark Ashton Smith Poetry Award ("Book of Eibon" division) for 1977. Munn demurred that he writes "spooky," not "horror" poems, but enough of these qualify. Also there are many nonfantasy poems. Munn's first influence was Kipling; he corresponded with Clark Ashton Smith and visited Lovecraft; his short tales and novels have long been popular. His poetry pamphlets have appeared from The Folly Press of Tacoma, and he wrote a nonfantasy poetry book commemorating Joan of Arc, *The Banner of Joan.* Compare to Drake [6–17], Shorter [6–50], Cawein [6–10], and Long [6–34]. Reviewed: *The Romantist*, No. 3 (1979), *The Anthology of Speculative Poetry*, No. 4 (1980), and *Starline* 3, No. 6 (1980), 4, No. 3 (1981).

6–45. Palmer, John Phillips. **The Wizard's Trade and Other Poems.** By the author, 1977.
Thirty poems by the "Imperator of the Bennu Phoenix Temple of the Golden Dawn," an ostensible Rosicrucian order. Enough of the verses have Gothic horror elements to qualify this borderline volume—for example, "The Ballad of the Devil and His Love," "Dark Halloween," "The Tomb-

stone Tells When You Die," and others. Author is today untraceable. (Copy in W. Paul Ganley collection.)

6–46. Pugmire, W. (William) H., ed. **Visions of Khryod'hon.** W. H. Pugmire, 1976.

A slight, ephemeral collection with yet several quality verses by H. Warner Munn, and emerging Small Press poets G. Sutton Breiding, William A. Conder, Michael Fantina, Jessica Amanda Salmonson, Neal Wilgus, and others; 35 poems, 18 poets, mostly supernatural-horror. Note: some copies bound up with *Fantasy and Terror*.

6–47. Rimel, Duane W. **Dreams of Yith.** FAPA (Fantasy Amateur Press Association), July 1943.

Weird-horror poem with stellar setting, influenced by Lovecraft, who read it and suggested the planet Yith, which he later used in *The Shadow Out of Time* novelette. Manuscript at Brown University Library. Compare to Lovecraft [6–36]. Reprinted in Derleth's *Dark of the Moon* [6–15].

6–48. Shedlofsky, Walter. **The Fantastic Acros.** Acrostic Press, 1970.

Rhyming acrostic poems (first letters spelling vertically each poem's title) in varying rhythms and rhyme schemes. The acrostic device can be cloyingly clever in lesser hands, but seems natural in such examples as "Moonglow," "Invisible," and "Draconia," among many of the total 47 poems.

6–49. Shedlofsky, Walter. **Fantastic Echoes.** Acrostic Press, n.d. (1970s).

Nine different weird-fantastic greeting cards, each issued singly, three poems to each card; all published previously, mostly in Small Press journals.

6–50. Shorter, Dora Sigerson (U.K.). **A Legend of Glendalough and Other Ballads.** Maunsel & Roberts, 1921.

Nearly all seven of these Irish lyrics are ghostly and most are horrific, such as "The Woman Who Went to Hell" and "The White Witch." Dora (Mrs. Clement) Shorter was a haunting balladeer, praised in her lifetime by Swinburne, Theodore Watts-Dunton, Francis Thompson, George Meredith, and her fellow Irish partisan Katherine Tynan. Her many verse volumes are gloomed with Irish mist, where the phantoms float and the banshees wail. Compare with Drake [6–17] and Munn [6–44]; well represented in Widdemer [6–63] and Derleth's *Dark of the Moon* [6–15].

6–51. Smith, Clark Ashton. **The Black Book.** Ed. by Donald Sidney-Fryer. Illus. by Andrew Smith. Arkham, 1979.

The notebook of this premier fantasy poet furnishes earlier or variant drafts of many poems and reprints other delicious minutiae. Many of the acerbic epigrams discuss poetry. Invaluable to the scholar and an enjoyable general introduction to Smith. Reviewed: *The Romantist*, No. 3 (1979).

*6-52. Smith, Clark Ashton. **Selected Poems.** Arkham, 1971.

A major twentieth-century poetry collection, and one of the most vital in the genre. Contains over 500 verses picked from other volumes by the poet himself before his death—although some were revised, dropped, or added. Smith creates an unearthly spell with his varied rhyme schemes, rich imagery, antique and rarified vocabulary, and funereal-sad music. The impact is totally weird, perhaps the most macabre in English since Beddoes or Poe, two of his favorites. Compare with Beddoes [6–4], Lovecraft [6–36], Long [6–34, 6–35], Howard [6–27, 6–28, 6–29, 6–30], and Wandrei [6–60]. Contrast with Brennan [6–7] and McNail [6–41].

6-53. Stagg, John (U.K.). **The Minstrel of the North; or, Cumbrian Legends, Being a Poetical Miscellany of Legendary, Gothic and Romantic Tales.** J. Blacklock, 1810; as *Legendary, Gothic and Romantic Tales in Verse,* 2 vols., C. Hulbert, 1825.

Contains "The Vampyre," wherein a vampire is slain by a consecrated sword. Possibly the first vampire poem in English after Coleridge's "Christabel." The poem is so gory that it might be a parody—certainly the prose preface is tongue-in-cheek. Compare to Lewis, *Tales of Wonder* [6–32].

6-54. Sterling, George. **A Wine of Wizardry and Three Other Poems.** A. S. Fick, 1964.

A gaudy 207-line blank verse extravaganza by a California cosmic aesthete and late Romantic. "A Wine of Wizardry" is an exalted riot of pageantry and flaring color. It personifies a pagan "Fancy," who leads the reader on a dizzying, breathless journey past a cowled magician, past a dragon, past an enchantress, and past a *blue*-eyed vampire "sated at her feast" who "smiles bloodily against the leprous moon," and past many other occult and charnel horrors. Sterling's mentor, Ambrose Bierce, said in 1903, "No poem in English has so bewildering a wealth of imagination. Not Spenser himself has flung such a profusion of jewels into so small a casket." The poem was originally sold to *Cosmopolitan* (September 1907), and in 1971 it appeared in *New Worlds for Old*, edited by Lin Carter. Reviewed: *The Romantist*, Nos. 3–4 (1979, 1981). Compare with Smith [6–52].

6-55. Stoddart, Thomas T. (U.K.). **The Death-Wake, or, Lunacy: A Necromaunt in Three Chimeras.** Henry Constable, 1831.

A 20-year-old's serious horror poem, although with a wry subtitle. A monk with worldly desires is coveting a girl when she dies; the poem narrates his unreal voyage with his dead love, past overwhelmingly weird and horrifying scenes—although not technically spectral. *Blackwood's* called it "an ingeniously absurd poem, with an ingeniously absurd title, written in a strange, namby-pamby sort of style, between the weakest of Shelley and the strongest of Barry Cornwall." Importantly, it appeared 11 years later in America in *Graham's Magazine* as "Agatha" by "Louis Fitzgerald Tasistro," and could well have been seen by Poe—whose music and unearthliness it foreshadows. There are other poems in the book, which Andrew Lang in *Adventures among Books* (1905) says "are vague memories of Shelley, or anticipations of Poe." Lang discovered one of the only surviving copies of this curiosity—nearly all the edition had remained in unbound sheets, used slowly by a family cook over 40 years for starting fires! Lang's rare, bound copy possessed marginal cartoons and sarcastic notes by its previous owner, satirist William E. Aytoun. Lang reproduces Aytoun's hilarious parody-sonnet written into the book also ("O wormy Thomas Stoddart, who inheritest / Rich thoughts and loathsome, nauseous words"). As for the precocious poet Stoddart, he quit writing verse, but produced an entire book on his other great love besides the macabre—fishing (although Lang reports that he once combined the two, by driving home in a hearse from a fishing trip).

6-56. Symons, Arthur (U.K.). **Jezebel Mort.** Heineman, 1931.
Its weird tone and many uncanny-supernatural subjects, poems like "The Ghost," "Merlin and Monks," and the demoniac cat poems of Setebos warrant this book's inclusion. The starkness of these verses recalls the author's lapse into madness (*Confessions*, 1930); they contrast with his more ethereal 1890s verse, when he wrote for *The Yellow Book*, knew Dowson, and edited *The Savoy* with Beardsley. There are several nonsupernatural, but weird and erotic, verses. Overall demoniac, decadent tone recalls Beddoes [6-4], and anticipates Clark Ashton Smith [6-51, 6-52] and Breiding [6-6].

6-57. Teskey, F. J., and T. H. Parker, eds. (U.K.). **The Supernatural.** Blackie & Son, 1970.
Twentieth-century poetry under headings: "The Ghost Walks," "Witches and Wizards," and "What Is to Be?" Intended for school use.

6-58. Tierney, Richard. **Dreams and Damnations.** Strange Company, 1975.
Verses (23) by a noted Small Press poet and professional fictioneer. Includes 17 sonnets, one evoking Chambers's "Carcosa" myth, several others owing to Lovecraft's "Fungi" [6-36]—although none are slavish emulations and generally avoid the trap of the jolting final couplet. Euphony, imagery, and taste make the best of Tierney's verse his own, whatever the sources of his inspiration; and much equally good work still awaits book publication, such as "Jack the Ripper," "Minas Morgul," "Mordor," and the "Sonnets of the Outer Dark" cycle, among many from the days of *The Arkham Collector* (1960s) through the last decade in *Whispers, Nyctalops, Fantasy and Terror,* and others. Compare with Fantina [6-18], Long [6-34], Lovecraft [6-36], Wandrei [6-60], and Carter [6-9]. Reviewed: *Nyctalops* (April 1976), *The Diversifier* (May 1976).

6–59. Trakl, George. **In the Red Forest.** Trans. by Reinhold Johannes Kaebitzche. Red Dove Press, 1973.

Intense, brooding images of weird-macabre intensity. Well rendered by a noted mainstream "little magazine" poet; 30 poems evoke Baudelaire and Rimbaud, and anticipate Smith [6–51, 6–52] and Breiding [6–6].

6–60. Wandrei, Donald. **Poems for Midnight.** Illus. by Howard Wandrei. Arkham, 1964.

Sixty-one poems by a popular *Weird Tales* fiction writer and Arkham House cofounder. Includes verses from earlier collections *Ecstasy* (1928) and *Dark Odyssey* (1931). Shorter lines, starker language contrast with Smith [6–51, 6–52]. "The Phantom," "The Woman at the Window," "Incubus," and "The Witches' Sabbath" are typically evocative and macabre. The underrated cycle "Sonnets of the Midnight Hours" may have influenced Lovecraft's "Fungi from Yuggoth" [6–36]. Quatrains, ballad stanzas, and the "In Memoriam" Tennyson-stanza give the volume variety. Stark perfection everywhere. Compare to Howard [6–27, 6–28, 6–29, 6–30] and Long [6–34], and to sonneteers Fantina [6–18] and Tierney [6–58].

6–61. West, Joseph A. **Galloping Pinwheels.** Strange Company, 1974.

Seven poems, nearly all ghostly but humorous; wryly illustrated by the ghoulish author. Reviewed: *Nyctalops* (April 1976).

6–62. West, Joseph A. **Grave Song.** Strange Company, 1975.

Twelve poems, 10 of which are "light" graveyard verse aptly illustrated by this perversely funny author-artist. Compare to McNail [6–41]. Reviewed: *Nyctalops* (April 1976).

*6–63. Widdemer, Margaret, ed. **The Haunted Hour: An Anthology.** Harcourt, Brace, & Howe, 1920.

The first known ghost-verse anthology since Matthew Lewis in 1801 [6–32]. Contains 106 poems selected for entertainment value, not historical representation. Selections are grouped by theme, some innovative (sea ghosts, ghosts of children, soldier ghosts). Noteworthy entries include works by neglected poets Madison Cawein and Lizette Woodworth Reese, and works by well-known poets such as Tom Moore, de la Mare, Quiller-Couch, and Yeats. This collection influenced the conception and many of the actual choices of Derleth's *Dark of the Moon* [6–15]. Widdemer was a Pulitzer Prize-winning poet (1919) who also read pulp magazines (*The Black Cat,* and *Weird Tales* in the 1930s–1940s); she also wrote many spectral poems herself (*The Dark Cavalier,* 1958). Compare to Hayes [6–25] and Coblentz [6–13]. Reviewed: *Nation* (September 4, 1920) and *Springfield Republican* (April 29, 1920).

6–64. Youngson, Jeanne. **The Further Perils of Dracula.** Adams Press, 1979.

Rhymed-and-metered poems (21) by the founder of the International Count Dracula Fan Club. Ostensible horror in every line is almost always a thing of fun: enjoyable morbid light verse. Only "The Child" is serious and restrained. Probably the first all-vampire verse collection. The introduction suggests that we achieve catharsis from reading supernatural horror literature. Compare to McNail [6–41].

Part III
Reference Sources

7

Biography, Autobiography, and Bibliography

Mike Ashley

For ease in reference, the annotations in this chapter are listed in order of the subject of the bio/bibliography. For reference to a particular author, consult the Author Index. Annotations by Richard Dalby are identified by RD in parentheses after the text.

William Harrison Ainsworth (1805–1882)
7-1. Ellis, Stewart Marsh. **William Harrison Ainsworth and His Friends.** 2 vols. Bodley Head, 1911.
The definitive record of the life, work, and friendships of William Harrison Ainsworth was the first of several memorable works by Ellis, once dubbed "the last of the Victorians." It set a model for scholarship and thoroughness that has rarely been excelled. *Rockwood, Windsor Castle, Old St. Pauls, Auriol,* and all the other novels are covered in detail. Excellent bibliography and index (the latter occupies more than 70 double-column pages), plus four photogravure plates and 52 other illustrations. Written with the help of Ainsworth's third daughter and several younger friends and contemporaries, this work is unlikely ever to be superseded. [Note: In 1925, Elkin Mathews

published *A Bibliographical Catalogue of the Published Novels and Ballads of W. H. Ainsworth* by Harold Locke.] (RD)

William Beckford (1760–1844)
7-2. Alexander, Boyd. **England's Wealthiest Son: A Study of William Beckford.** Centaur Press, 1962.
Before his untimely death in 1980, Boyd Alexander was widely regarded as the world's leading authority on Beckford. Although Alexander denies in his preface that this is a biography of Beckford, passing that honor back to Dr. J. W. Oliver (*Life of William Beckford,* 1932) and Professor Guy Chapman (*Beckford,* 1952), this is a splendid and very thorough study of Beckford from his antecedents, birth, and early youth, right through his long life to the sale of Fonthill in 1822 and his death in 1844. His classic, *Vathek,* is well covered in two chapters. Excellent notes and index. (RD)

7-3. Chapman, Guy, and J. Hodgkin. **A Bibliography of William Beckford of Fonthill.** Constable, 1930; Bowker, 1931.
A complete and useful bibliography of the writer's works. (RD)

Thomas Lovell Beddoes (1803–1849)
7-4. Donner, H. N. **Thomas Lovell Beddoes: The Making of a Poet.** Blackwell, 1932, 1935; Folcroft, 1976.
Extensive biography of probably the most morbid poet in the English language and author of *Death's Jest-Book.* Reflects careful research in Bavaria where Beddoes lived, locates his several addresses there, and details his political agitating. Thoroughly treats his important supernatural (and other lyric) poetry, and rightly sees Beddoes not as a "neo-Elizabethan," but as an important romantic. Empathetic, appreciative study by Beddoes's definitive textural editor; see *The Works of Thomas Lovell Beddoes* [6–4].

Ambrose Bierce (1842–1914?)
7-5. O'Connor, Richard. **Ambrose Bierce: A Biography.** Gollancz, 1968.
The best of the modern biographies of Bierce and the first full study of his career for nearly 40 years. [Note: Earlier biographies include *Ambrose Bierce* by Vincent Startett (1920), *Bitter Bierce* by C. Hartley Grattan (1929), and *Ambrose Bierce: The Devil's Lexicographer* by Paul Fatout (1951).] (RD)

Algernon Blackwood (1869–1951)
7-6. Blackwood, Algernon. **Episodes before Thirty.** Cassell, 1923.
Blackwood's autobiography covers the years until 1898 and concentrates on his life in New York, with only occasional references to his writings. Two later editions vary in content. Retitled *Adventures before Thirty* (Jonathan Cape, 1934), it has been slightly edited by Blackwood, but is in a handier pocket-size edition. Reprinted as *Episodes before Thirty* (Peter Nevill, 1950), this reverts to the original text, but includes 13 rare photographs plus an index.

7–7. Hudson, Derek. **Talks With Fuddy and Others.** Centaur Press, 1968. This collection of essays includes a chapter on Algernon Blackwood and is the only readily available biographical item in print covering briefly but adequately Blackwood's life and works, with special emphasis on his often overlooked novels. The first full-length biography of Blackwood has been completed by Professor Jean-Louis Grillou of the University of Limoges, France, for 1981 French publication. An expanded English edition written in collaboration with Michael Ashley is in preparation.

Robert Bloch (1917–)
7–8. Flanagan, Graeme. **Robert Bloch: A Bio-Bibliography.** Canberra, Australia: Privately printed, 1979.
A small but useful 64-page booklet. It includes a brief biography, two interviews, appreciations by Harlan Ellison, Fritz Leiber, Robert Weinberg, and Mary Elizabeth Counselman, plus an extensive bibliography of fiction and nonfiction in magazine and book form, including foreign editions and adaptations for radio, television, and the cinema.

Ray Bradbury (1920–)
*7–9. Nolan, William F. **The Ray Bradbury Companion.** Gale, 1975.
The definitive bibliography of Bradbury.

Wilkie Collins (1824–1889)
7–10. Robinson, Kenneth. **Wilkie Collins: A Biography.** Bodley Head, 1951.
During the flood of Victorian biography in the first half of this century, Wilkie Collins was curiously overlooked (apart from the monographs by S. M. Ellis and C. K. Hyder). This readable biography by the young English politician, later minister of health, made full use of every known source of information, including a substantial number of unpublished letters. Separate chapters are devoted to the major novels. Useful bibliography and index. (RD)

F. Marion Crawford (1854–1909)
7–11. Moran, John C. **Seeking Refuge in Torre San Nicola.** F. Marion Crawford Society, 1980.
A short (86-page) study of the life and works of Crawford as a romanticist and writer of supernatural and horror fiction. A useful basis for a study of this neglected writer. Includes an introduction by Russell Kirk.

Walter de la Mare (1873–1956)
7–12. Brain, Russell. **Tea with Walter de la Mare.** Faber, 1957.
Informal record of conversations between de la Mare and the eminent neurologist. Valuable for the light it throws on de la Mare's thinking during his last years. (RD)

*7–13. McCrosson, Doris Ross. **Walter de la Mare.** Twayne, 1966.
Excellent critical-analytical study of the writings of de la Mare (no. 33 in
Twayne's English Author series). Individual chapters on the short stories,
poetry, and novels (the "pilgrimage of the imagination"), and additional
chapters on each of the novels, including *Henry Brocken* ("The Journey Begins") and *The Return* ("What Dreams May Come"). Good bibliography and
index. (RD)

7–14. Mégroz, R. L. **Walter de la Mare: A Biographical and Critical
Study.** Hodder & Stoughton, 1924.
The first long critical study of de la Mare. Useful for biographical information. Mégroz, a friend of de la Mare, also examined his life and work in a
later book, *Five Novelists—Poets of Today* (1933). (RD)

**7–15. Walter de la Mare: A checklist prepared on the occasion of an ex-
hibit of his books and mss at the National Book League, April 20–May 19,
1956.** Cambridge University Press for the NBL, 1956.
Of special interest to collectors, this book gives full bibliographic details of
the books on show highlighting variant editions and bindings. Also details
original magazine publications. [Note: *Walter de la Mare: An Exploration* by
John Atkins (C. & J. Temple, 1947) and *Walter de la Mare* by Kenneth Hopkins (1953) are excellent but too brief analyses of de la Mare's work. Interesting articles on de la Mare have appeared in the *Fortnightly Review* as follows: October 1927 by R. H. Coats; July 1932 by G. K. Chesterton; and
March 1940 by Richard Church.] (RD)

August Derleth (1909–1971)
7–16. Derleth, August. **100 Books by August Derleth.** Arkham House, 1962.
Detailed checklist of Derleth's 102 hardbound volumes to date, plus several
ephemeral paperbound titles, plus details of recordings, compilations, anthologies, television films, and lectures. Includes a foreword by Donald
Wandrei and appraisals by Sinclair Lewis and others. (RD)

Sir Arthur Conan Doyle (1859–1930)
7–17. Goldscheider, Gaby. **A Bibliography of the Works of Sir Arthur
Conan Doyle, M.D., L.L.D.** Privately printed, 1977.
A short (40 pages) but useful listing of all stories and books by Doyle in al-
phabetical order with original publication and important reprints cited.
Also covers contributions to other books and collected works.

7–18. Reece, Benny R. **A Bibliography of the First Appearances of the
Writings by A. Conan Doyle.** Greenville, 1975.
Lists the earliest periodical publication and book appearance of all Doyle's
prose and poetry, including his writings on politics and spiritualism. Limited
to 300 copies.

Lord Dunsany (1878–1957)
7-19. Armory, Mark. **Lord Dunsany: A Biography.** Collins, 1972.
Comprehensive study of the life and work of Lord Dunsany, with details of his many friends and acquaintances, including the artist Sidney H. Sime. Hastily edited, with a haphazard checklist of his books. (RD)

E. R. Eddison (1882–1945)
7-20. Hamilton, G. Rostrevor. **"E. R. Eddison."** "Hedonicus." **"A Writer of Prose."** Book Handbook No. 1, 1947.
Hamilton's essay is biographical, while the pseudonymous Hedonicus judges Eddison's achievements as a writer. There is also an excellent bibliography of Eddison's books published between 1916 and 1941. (RD)

Sir Henry Rider Haggard (1856–1925)
7-21. Cohen, Morton. **Rider Haggard: His Life and Works.** Hutchinson, 1960.
The first scholarly, critical biography of Haggard. Contains much of interest on the fantastic romances, with copious notes and useful checklists. Cohen was also the editor of *Rudyard Kipling to Rider Haggard: The Record of a Friendship* (1965). (RD)

*7-22. Haggard, Lilias Rider. **The Cloak That I Left.** Hodder & Stoughton, 1951.
Warm and fascinating biography of Rider Haggard by his youngest daughter. It is full of new material from his diaries and letters, and reveals the man from every angle—the novelist, traveler, historian, and agricultural authority. (RD)

*7-23. Scott, J. E. **A Bibliography of the Works of Sir Henry Rider Haggard, 1856–1925.** Elkin Mathews, 1947. Limited to 500 copies.
The definitive bibliography of Rider Haggard, containing, besides the first editions, details of his letters, reviews, dramatizations, interviews, reports of speeches, and the parodies. (RD)

Lafcadio Hearn (1850–1904)
7-24. Wedeck, H. E. **Mortal Hunger.** Sheridan, 1947.
A biographical novel based on the life of Lafcadio Hearn.

William Hope Hodgson (1877–1918)
*7-25. Moskowitz, Sam. **Out of the Storm.** Donald M. Grant, 1975.
Actually a collection of seven previously uncollected stories by Hodgson and edited by Moskowitz, with a long biographical introduction (pp. 9–117) detailing Hodgson's life and works. [Note that the paperback reprint of the collection by Centaur Books in 1980 excludes the introduction.] Moskowitz's biography of Hodgson originally appeared as a series of articles in the *Weird Tales* issues of Summer, Fall, and Winter 1973. Concurrently, researcher R.

Alain Everts published his findings "William Hope Hodgson: Master of Fantasy" in two parts in *Shadow* for April and October 1973 with some hitherto unpublished photographs.

A. E. Housman [see 7–26]

Clemence Housman [see 7–26]

Laurence Housman (1865–1959)
7–26. Hodgkins, I. G. Kenyur. **The Housmans.** National Book League, 1975.
Published to accompany an exhibition of books by the NBL from February 5–19, 1975, it carries brief biographies and useful bibliographies of Laurence Housman and his sister Clemence, plus lesser coverage of their brother, A. E. Housman. The Laurence Housman listing covers his poetry, plays, stories, books, nonfiction, and illustrations.

Robert E. Howard (1906–1936)
7–27. de Camp, L. Sprague. **Dark Valley Destiny.** Forthcoming.
Intended as the authoritative biography of Howard, originally started as a collaboration with the late Dr. Jane Griffin, but now completed with de Camp's wife, Catherine.

7–28. Lord, Glenn. **The Last Celt: A Bio-Bibliography of Robert E. Howard.** Donald M. Grant, 1976.
The definitive bibliography of Howard assembled by the executor of his estate and including all his published, republished, and unpublished stories.

G. P. R. James (1799–1860)
7–29. Ellis, Stewart Marsh. **The Solitary Horseman.** Cayme Press, 1927.
Limited to 800 copies.
The definitive biography of George Payne Rainsford James, author of *The Castle of Ehrenstein* and 90 other titles. Illustrated with an exhaustive bibliography and index. (RD)

Henry James (1843–1916)
7–30. Edel, Leon, and Don H. Laurence. **A Bibliography of Henry James.** Hart-Davis, 1957.
The complete bibliography of all of Henry James's works, citing all variant editions—covers, original works, contributions to books, published letters, contributions to periodicals, translations, and even braille editions.

M. R. James (1862–1936)
*7–31. Lubbock, S. G. **A Memoir of Montague Rhodes James.** Cambridge Univ. Press, 1939.
The best of the many tributes to appear on M. R. James during the three years following his death in the absence of any friends or contemporaries

able to attempt a proper biography. There are only three pages on the ghost stories. A. F. Scholfield supplies an excellent checklist of his writings; it has never really been superseded, although there are a few notable omissions (such as the essay "Some Remarks on Ghost Stories"). (RD)

7-32. Pfaff, Richard William. **Montague Rhodes James.** Scolar Press, 1980. The definitive biography of M. R. James. Superbly researched text backed up by nearly 1,000 footnotes. Regrettably the checklist of James's writings at the rear does not include any of the ghost stories, but there are several fascinating references to this small corner of his career sprinkled throughout the text. Good index. (RD)

Rudyard Kipling (1865–1936)
7-33. Stewart, James McG. **Rudyard Kipling: A Bibliographical Catalogue,** ed. by A. W. Yeats. University Press (Toronto), 1959.
The definitive Kipling bibliography, especially for the bibliophile.

7-34. Wilson, Angus. **The Strange Ride of Rudyard Kipling: His Life and Works.** Secker & Warburg, 1977.
A very readable and detailed biography with special relevance to Kipling's supernatural stories.

Andrew Lang (1844–1912)
7-35. Green, Roger Lancelyn. **Andrew Lang: A Critical Biography.** Edmund Ward, 1946.
The first major study of Andrew Lang, thorough and well researched in the style of S. M. Ellis. Lang's contributions to the fantasy genre are well covered, with chapters devoted to *The World's Desire*, Fairnilee and Pantoufla, the Master of Fairyland, and his work as a mythologist. The short-title bibliography amply covers his wide array of books, essays, and magazine articles, and details his contributions to *The Encyclopaedia Britannica* (apparitions, hauntings, poltergeists, psychical research, second sight, and so on). (RD)

Joseph Sheridan Le Fanu (1814–1873)
7-36. Browne, Nelson. **Sheridan Le Fanu.** Arthur Barker, 1951.
Brief but worthy study of Le Fanu. Together with the 1931 essay by S. M. Ellis [8–24], the most authoritative account of the man and his works so far. Chapters on the life, novels, short stories, and verse, and the summing up. The appendix includes a useful checklist of the 15 novels, 43 short stories, and 10 reprint collections. [Note: completist researchers may also be interested in an essay by E. F. Benson, "Sheridan Le Fanu," in *The Spectator*, February 1931]. (RD)

Vernon Lee (Violet Paget, 1856–1935)
7–37. Gunn, Peter. **Vernon Lee: Violet Paget 1856–1935.** Oxford Univ. Press, 1964.
The definitive biography of one of the most gifted writers of her time, author of 46 highly acclaimed books, including *Hauntings, Pope Jacynth,* and *For Maurice.* Gunn was allowed access to Vernon Lee's private papers at Colby College, Maine, and his book contains fascinating detail concerning her relationships with Henry James, Bernard Berenson, Maurice Baring, H. G. Wells, and many others. Good bibliography and index. (RD)

David Lindsay (1876–1945)
7–38. Wilson, Colin, E. H. Visiak, and J. B. Pick. **The Strange Genius of David Lindsay.** John Baker, 1970.
The three authors, all admirers of Lindsay, hoped that this "definitive life and work" would finally establish Lindsay's genius, strange or not, high in the literary firmament, among both critics and the reading public. Pick describes Lindsay's life as man and writer, and the two unpublished novels *The Witch* and *The Violet Apple;* Wilson discusses Lindsay as novelist and mystic; and Lindsay's contemporary and soulmate E. H. Visiak discusses *A Voyage to Arcturus, The Haunted Woman,* and *Devil's Tor,* and the nature of Lindsay's genius. [*Note:* Wilson's chapter "Lindsay as Novelist and Mystic" is available separately as *The Haunted Man: The Strange Genius of David Lindsay,* Borgo Press, 1979.] (RD)

H. P. Lovecraft (1890–1937)
Note: Lovecraft has had more written about him in recent years than probably any other writer with the exception of Poe and Dickens. The following annotations cover the more general reference aids, which will give further reference to the more detailed specialty publications. [See also 8–54, 8–69, 8–70]

7–39. Carter, Lin. **Lovecraft: A Look behind the Cthulhu Mythos.** Ballantine, 1972.
Useful as a basic introduction to Lovecraft and easily readable, but to be approached with caution because of Carter's generalizations and sweeping statements.

7–40. Conover, Willis. **Lovecraft at Last.** Carrolton-Clark, 1975.
For the specialist this was intended to be the finest book money could buy, with exact holographic reproduction of Lovecraft's letters down to the detail of the color of the ink. Basically a reprinting of the correspondence between Conover and Lovecraft in the last 18 months of Lovecraft's life, but intrinsically an emotional and moving insight into Lovecraft as a person.

*7–41. de Camp, L. Sprague. **Lovecraft: A Biography.** Doubleday, 1975.
Objective, comprehensive, and very well researched study of the strange and
complex life and work of H. P. Lovecraft. Liberal quotations from his letters
and stories are included together with considerable gratis information on
Lovecraft's correspondents and writer-clients. Extensive notes, bibliography
and index. [Note: The paperback edition, Ballantine, 1976, was revised and
abridged by de Camp, but does not contain the index.] (RD).

7–42. Long, Frank Belknap. **Howard Phillips Lovecraft: Dreamer on the
Night Side.** Arkham House, 1975.
A personalized memorial to Lovecraft by the writer with whom Lovecraft
had the longest continuous association.

7–43. Lovecraft, H. P. **Selected Letters: I (1911–24).** Arkham House, 1965.
Selected Letters: II (1925–29). Arkham House, 1968. **Selected Letters: III
(1929–31).** Arkham House, 1971. **Selected Letters: IV.** Arkham House,
1976. **Selected Letters: V (1934–37).** Arkham House, 1976.
The full corpus of most of Lovecraft's important letters to his many correspondents. A useful supplement to these volumes is *An Index to the Selected letters of H. P. Lovecraft* by S. T. Joshi (Necronomicon Press, 1980).

7–44. Owings, Mark, and Jack L. Chalker. **The Revised H. P. Lovecraft
Bibliography.** Mirage Press, 1973.
Of all the many Lovecraft bibliographies, this is the most complete to date,
but is rather jumbled in its presentation. It covers Lovecraft's essays, verse,
fiction, collaborations, collections (including foreign language), revisions,
and mythos stories, plus less complete data on comic-book adaptations and
material about Lovecraft. This index was a revision of Jack L. Chalker's own
The New H. P. Lovecraft Bibliography (Anthem Press, 1962), which, while less
complete, is useful for its clarity of presentation.

Arthur Machen (1863–1947)
7–45. Gekle, William Francis. **Arthur Machen: Weaver of Fantasy.** Round
Table Press, 1949.
An enthusiastic study of Machen's stories, essays, and translations, with a
good bibliography. (RD)

*7–46. Goldstone, Adrian, and Wesley Sweetser. **A Bibliography of Arthur
Machen.** Univ. of Texas Press, 1965.
The definitive and complete bibliography, this supersedes *Arthur Machen: A
Bibliography* by Henry Danielson (1923), which is nevertheless important for
its introduction by Henry Savage and the notes "biographical and critical"
by Machen himself. (RD)

7-47. Machen, Arthur. **Far Off Things.** Knopf, 1922. **Things Near and Far.** Knopf, 1923. Reprinted in one volume as *The Autobiography of Arthur Machen*, Garnstone Press, 1974.

Contains a number of interesting revelations about the background circumstances of Machen's fiction, but aggravatingly glosses over many other aspects of his life and works. The account does not follow a strict chronological order, and the lack of an index limits its usefulness. Should be used in conjunction with [7-49].

7-48. Reynolds, Aidan, and William Charlton. **Arthur Machen: A Short Account of His Life and Work.** Richards Press, 1963.

A comprehensive, although short, biography. (RD)

7-49. Sweetser, Wesley D. **Arthur Machen.** Twayne, 1964.

An excellent critical-analytical study of the life and work of Machen (no. 8 in Twayne's English Authors series). The three pervading elements of Machen's works—romanticism, symbolism, and mysticism—and weird and occult are well covered. Good index, copious notes, and a checklist including his books, pamphlets, translations, and prefaces. (RD)

Jack Mann (1882–1947)

7-50. Lofts, W. O. G. **"On the Trail of the Mysterious Jack Mann."** *Mystery Newsletter* (November 1973).

The only biographical information available on the writer of fantastic adventures and mysteries.

Edgar Allan Poe (1809–1849)

7-51. Allan, Hervey. **Israfel: The Life and Times of E. A. Poe.** 2 vols. Brentano, 1927.

Once considered the best biography of Poe, but now superseded by Quinn [7-54]. Still useful for its interpretation of Poe's life and works.

7-52. Haining, Peter. **The Edgar Allan Poe Scrapbook.** New English Library, 1977.

A useful aid to any Poe collection. It includes many items associated with the writer that are not readily available elsewhere, including early reviews and essays by Poe. Profusely illustrated (designed by Stephen Knowlden), foreword by Robert Bloch.

7-53. Mankowitz, Wolf. **The Extraordinary Mr. Poe.** Wiedenfeld & Nicolson, 1978.

Although this adds nothing new to earlier biographies, it is among the best written and most enjoyable of all the books, with many illustrations. Attractively designed by Gill Mouqué.

*7–54. Quinn, Arthur Hobson. **Edgar Allan Poe: A Critical Biography.** Appleton-Century, 1941.
One of the best biographies of Poe, very thorough and extremely well researched. Excellent index and selective bibliography, illustrations of his family and homes, and reproductions of the title pages of his first editions and important letters. Twelve interesting appendixes include the Tales of the Folio Club, Poe's revision of the "Phantasy Pieces," and a possible new Poe satire. (RD)

*7–55. Robertson, John W. **Bibliography of the Writings of Edgar A. Poe** and **Commentary on the Bibliography of Edgar A. Poe.** Russian Hill Private Press, 1934. Combined under the former title, Kraus Reprint, 1969. The most thorough bibliography of Poe's published works, including (1) a chronological list of the writings of Poe; (2) publications; (3) magazines contributed to by Poe; (4) gift books and annuals contributed to by Poe. The commentary follows through Poe's writings in chronological order with observations and biographical anecdotes.

7–56. Symons, Julian. **The Tell-Tale Heart: The Life and Works of Edgar Allan Poe.** Faber & Faber, 1978.
A brief biography with no new information, but written in the usual scholarly Symons style, coupled with an analysis of Poe's writings divided into the different categories Poe adopted.

Jean Ray (1887–1964)
7–57. Van Genechten, Jan. **"Jean Ray: An Introduction of the Author and His Work to American Fandom."** *Fandom Unlimited* No. 2 (Spring 1977).
A short but valuable biography of this overlooked Belgian writer with information not available elsewhere.

Sax Rohmer (1883–1959)
7–58. Van Ash, Cay, and Elizabeth Sax Rohmer. **Master of Villainy: A Biography of Sax Rohmer.** Ed. by Robert E. Briney. Bowling Green Univ. Press, 1972.
This book was originally conceived in the mid-1950s by Rohmer himself as a collaboration with his wife. It was planned not as a formal biography, but rather as a collection of reminiscences and anecdotes. The work was later abandoned, but some years after Rohmer's death in 1959, his widow completed the manuscript with Cay Van Ash, a friend of her husband. Much of the biographical material was erroneous and the chronology hazy, however, so Robert E. Briney (a long-time collector of Rohmer's works) was called in to annotate the manuscript. The result is extremely readable, with a useful bibliography and index. (RD)

William Clark Russell (1844–1911)
7–59. Hutchison, B. **"William Clark Russell, 1844–1911."** Brighton, UK: *Book Collecting & Library Monthly* No. 25 (May 1970).
A basic bibliography of Russell's books.

Mary Shelley (1797–1851)
7–60. Dunn, Jane. **Moon in Eclipse: A Life of Mary Shelley.** Weidenfeld & Nicolson, 1978.
The most recently available biography of Mary Shelley.

*7–61. Lyles, W. H. **Mary Shelley: An Annotated Bibliography.** Garland, 1975.
The definitive Shelley bibliography, divided into three parts. Part I: works by Mary Shelley (journals and letters, novels, dramas, stories, poems, travel works, biographies, articles and reviews, edited works); Part II: works about Mary Shelley (books, periodicals, reviews, graduate research, foreign works, and as a character in works of fiction); and four appendixes covering (1) Mary Shelley's works in chronological order; (2) the legend of George of Frankenstein; (3) theatrical, film, and television versions of Frankenstein; and (4) selling prices for editions of her books. There is also a thorough index.

7–62. Small, Christopher. **Ariel like a Harpy: Shelley, Mary and "Frankenstein."** Victor Gollancz, 1972; Univ. of Pittsburgh Press, 1973, *Mary Shelley's Frankenstein: Tracing the Myth.*
One of the many recent books about Mary Shelley with an emphasis on the origins of her famous novel.

M. P. Shiel (1865–1947)
7–63. Morse, A. Reynolds, and John D. Squires. **The Works of M. P. Shiel.** 4 vols. John D. Squires, 1979–1980.
Originally intended as an update of the previous "model bibliography," *The Works of M. P. Shiel* by Morse (Fantasy Publishing, 1948), this has now become the definitive deluxe work on Shiel. Volume 1, published in 1979 under the title *The Empress of the Earth and The Purple Cloud,* is a facsimile reproduction of these two novels plus 15 short stories, each with an introduction by Morse providing background details. Volumes 2 and 3 comprise the bibliography of Shiel's work. All entries are fully annotated, and there are many photographs and facsimile reproductions. Also included is a 164-page essay by Morse, "The Quest for Redonda," which describes his expedition to Shiel's West Indian island kingdom together with autobiographical items by Shiel and much more. A projected fourth volume, *Shiel in Diverse Hands,* is a collection of essays on Shiel and his works.

Clark Ashton Smith (1893–1961)

7–64. Sidney-Fryer, Donald. **Emperor of Dreams: A Clark Ashton Smith Bibliography.** Donald M. Grant, 1978.

The definitive bibliography of Smith listing his entire output in every category, including fiction, nonfiction, poetry, letters, epigrams, reprintings, and translations, plus essays and items about Smith and his works, details of library collections, and reminiscences in the form of letters from Fritz Leiber, Ray Bradbury, August Derleth, Avram Davidson, Harlan Ellison, and others.

7–65. Smith, Clark Ashton. **The Black Book of Clark Ashton Smith.** Ed. by Donald Sidney-Fryer. Arkham House, 1980.

A transcription of the notebook kept by Smith of his stories and ideas. It also includes two memoirs of Smith by George F. Haas.

7–66. Smith, Clark Ashton. **Planets and Dimensions: Collected Essays of Clark Ashton Smith.** Ed. by Charles K. Wolfe. Mirage Press, 1973.

This volume reprints most of Smith's important nonfiction and includes essays on horror and fantasy fiction, William Hope Hodgson, and H. P. Lovecraft.

George Sterling (1869–1926)

7–67. Benediktsson, Thomas E. **George Sterling.** Twayne, 1980.

First full-scale biography of Clark Ashton Smith's mentor and stereotyped romanticist-decadent of California. Sympathetic yet balanced evaluation of Sterling's art in its proper perspective (late Victorian aestheticism)—after decades of oblivion. Several of the poems discussed in depth are supernatural. Important bibliography, including scattered articles on Sterling's life and art. A major event in current Sterling renaissance.

7–68. Johnson, Cecil. **A Bibliography of the Writings of George Sterling.** Windsor Press, 1931; Folcroft, 1969.

Important bibliography of major weird-fantasy poet ("A Wine of Wizardry" and others) and Clark Ashton Smith's mentor. Collates the first editions physically and lists their contents; also lists poems in books and in magazines; thus, an invaluable tool for collecting the scattered Sterling verses. Omits articles about Sterling and Sterling's still unearthed, pseudonymous short stories. This affectionately compiled volume is still a key to Sterling collecting and study.

Bram Stoker (1847–1912)

7–69. Farson, Daniel. **The Man Who Wrote Dracula.** Michael Joseph, 1975.

Basically a rewrite of Ludlam's book [7–70], with notes on recent developments (such as the Dracula "industry"), and some new analytical, psychological, and medical opinions added. (RD)

*7–70. Ludlam, Harry. **A Biography of Dracula: The Life Story of Bram Stoker.** Foulsham, 1962.

Pioneer biography that revived the interest in Stoker half a century after his death. Written with the assistance of Stoker's son, who died in 1961, and Hamilton Deane, the actor-manager who revived Dracula on the stage in the 1920s. Very well researched and a source used in all subsequent books and articles on Stoker and Dracula. [*Note:* Neither of these volumes contains a bibliography or notes, but a *Stoker Bibliography* by Richard Dalby is now in press.] (RD)

Montague Summers (1880–1948)

7–71. d'Arch Smith, Timothy. **A Bibliography of the Works of Montague Summers.** Nicholas Vane, 1964.

The definitive bibliography listing all of Summers's books and pamphlets, his contributions to other books and pamphlets and periodicals, plus his unpublished and projected works. There is also a chronological listing of all his work, appendixes on the Phoenix and other theatrical societies, and a useful index.

7–72. Jerome, Joseph. **Montague Summers: A Memoir.** Cecil & Amelia Woolf, 1965.

Brief but illuminating memoir, with useful bibliographical checklist (abridged from d'Arch Smith's volume [7–71]). Contains a foreword by Dame Sybil Thorndike. (RD)

7–73. Summers, Montague. **The Galanty Show.** Cecil Woolf, 1980.

Long-delayed work (originally announced for publication in 1950 by Rider, but eventually rejected by that firm). Rather than autobiography, a collection of childhood memories and dissertations on the chief interests on which Summers built his considerable literary reputation—restoration plays, Gothic and Victorian novels, ghosts, witchcraft, and demonology. The style, as with his earlier books, suffers from a tendency to extremism in praise and blame. (RD)

Horace Walpole (1717–1797)

7–74. Hazen, A. T. **A Bibliography of Horace Walpole.** Yale Univ. Press, 1948; Dawson's, 1973.

A useful guide to the works of the father of Gothic horror, especially valuable for its listing of the various editions of *The Castle of Otranto.*

Charles Williams (1886–1945)

7–75. Glenn, Lois. **Charles W. S. Williams: A Checklist.** Kent State Univ. Press, 1976.

A listing of all Williams's books and periodical appearances, plus an extensive bibliography of criticism about him.

8

Criticism, Indexes, and General Reference

Mike Ashley

The annotations in this chapter cover criticism, indexes, and general reference works in horror literature. Annotations by Richard Dalby are identified by RD in parentheses after the text.

8–1. Ashley, Mike. **Who's Who in Horror & Fantasy Fiction.** Elm Tree, 1977.
An A–Z coverage of 400 writers giving brief bio/bibliographical details. Supplemented by a chronology of seminal works and appendixes listing key stories and books, selected weird fiction anthologies, weird and horror fiction magazines, and genre awards. Contains much information not available elsewhere.

8–2. Baine, Rodney M. **Daniel Defoe and the Supernatural.** Univ. of Georgia Press, 1968.
Thorough study of Defoe's theology, its supernatural elements, and influence on his journalism and fiction. Good review of his occult works that possibly influenced Poe. Discusses Defoe's essays on apparitions (included the often anthologized "Mrs. Veal"), and various spurious occult writings mis-

attributed to Defoe. Detailed notes. Valuable study of pre-Gothic supernatural prose literature.

8-3. Barclay, Glen St. John. **Anatomy of Horror: The Masters of Occult Fiction.** Weidenfeld & Nicolson, 1978; St. Martin, 1979.
A series of unsympathetic essays studying the work of seven writers: Le Fanu, Stoker, Haggard, Lovecraft, Williams, Blatty, and Wheatley. Of little value as a reference aid, although Barclay does draw some interesting conclusions from his biased opinion that these writers all suffered from some sexual abnormalities.

8-4. Beck, Calvin. **Heroes of the Horrors.** Collier, 1976. **Scream Queens.** Collier, 1979.
Two companion volumes packed with photographs and behind-the-scenes revelations of all the famous early names in horror films, including Lon Chaney, Sr., Bela Lugosi, Boris Karloff, Peter Lorre, Vincent Price, Fay Wray, Bette Davis, and Joan Crawford.

8-5. Birkhead, Edith. **The Tale of Terror.** Constable, 1921.
Well-researched account of the growth of supernatural fiction in English literature, beginning with the vogue of the Gothic romance and tale of terror toward the close of the eighteenth century. Chapters on Horace Walpole, Ann Radcliffe, Lewis and Maturin, Beckford, Godwin, Scott, satires, later developments, and American tales of terror. Thoroughly indexed. (RD)

*8-6. Bleiler, Everett F. **The Checklist of Science-Fiction and Supernatural Fiction.** Firebell Books, 1978.
A major revision of Bleiler's original pioneer bibliography *The Checklist of Fantastic Literature* (Shasta, 1948). This work lists first editions of some 6,000 SF/supernatural books by author and title up to the original cutoff date of 1948. No attempt has been made to continue the list (now supplemented by Tuck [8-89] and Reginald (see [8-89]), but each entry is categorized by theme (such as vampires and ghosts). Of more importance in the supernatural than the science fiction field.

8-7. Briggs, Julia. **Night Visitors: The Rise and Fall of the English Ghost Story.** Faber, 1977.
The first major treatise on the English ghost story since Penzoldt [8-61]. Briggs discusses the reason for the flood of ghost stories in the 80 years from 1850 to 1930, and the influence of the times on the tales. In her opinion, Walter de la Mare was the last and greatest exponent of the ghost story—all the modern masters, such as Robert Aickman, being ignored. Stevenson, Le Fanu, Kipling, Vernon Lee, Henry James, and M. R. James are all treated in detail, and there is an epilogue on the ghosts in the poetry of Hardy, Yeats, and Eliot. (RD)

8–8. Butler, Ivan. **The Horror Film.** A. Zwemmer, 1967; 1970 as *Horror in the Cinema.*

A good, basic introduction to the horror film by an actor who has had a long association with the cinema.

*8–9. Clarens, Carlos. **An Illustrated History of the Horror Film.** Putnam, 1967; Secker & Warburg, 1968, as *Horror Movies: An Illustrated Survey.*

A thorough chronological history of the horror film. Very few of its successors have superseded it, or bettered the filmography. (RD)

*8–10. Cockcroft, T. G. L. **Index to the Weird Fiction Magazines: Index by Author.** Lower Hutt, New Zealand: Privately printed, 1964. **Index by Title,** 1962.

Covers all stories and articles in the pulp magazines *Weird Tales, Strange Tales, Strange Stories, The Thrill Book, Oriental Stories/Magic Carpet Magazine, Golden Fleece,* and the English reprint publication *Strange Tales.* Invaluable as a guide to original publication details of stories by many of today's leading names. Cockcroft has also published privately *Index to the Verse in Weird Tales* (1960).

8–11. Copper, Basil. **The Vampire in Legend, Fact and Art.** Robert Hale, 1973.

General study of the vampire in legend, literature, film, theater, and in fact. The reader must be wary of several unsubstantiated claims—for example, that Bram Stoker was "a professor of English" and "the son of a country clergyman." There is a chapter on Prest's Varney, although ten years earlier Louis James (in *Fiction For the Working Man, 1830–1850,* Oxford Univ. Press, 1963) had argued convincingly that J. M. Rymer was the true author. Index and haphazard selective bibliography. (RD)

8–12. Copper, Basil. **The Werewolf in Legend, Fact and Art.** St. Martin, 1977.

Sequel to the vampire volume, a study of the werewolf in fact and in the media. Most of the literary classics are well covered, but unfortunately the selected bibliography is again very haphazard. (RD)

8–13. Daniels, Les. **Living in Fear: A History of Horror in the Mass Media.** Scribner, 1975.

A blending of historical commentary, illustrations, and fiction. Too superficial for the devotee, but a useful introduction to the field.

8–14. Davis, Richard, ed. **The Octopus Encyclopedia of Horror.** Octopus, 1981.

A companion to this publisher's earlier successful *Encyclopedia of Science Fiction* (1978), this follows the same format of thematic articles profusely illustrated with a series of appendixes. The contributors include Michael Ashley (ghosts and the supernatural), Richard Cavendish (black arts), Basil Copper (werewolves and vampires), Richard Davis (zombies), Denis Gifford (comics), Tom Hutchinson (monsters), and Michel Parry (Frankenstein). Intended as an introductory volume, but with additional data to interest the devotee.

8-15. Day, Bradford M. **Bibliography of Adventure.** Wehman Bros., 1964.
Checklists of Talbot Mundy, Sax Rohmer, H. Rider Haggard, and Edgar Rice Burroughs. The Haggard entries are the most detailed and useful for those unable to obtain J. E. Scott's bibliography [7–23]. (RD)

8-16. Day, Bradford M. **An Index on the Weird and Fantastica in Magazines.** New York: Privately printed, 1953.
A useful guide to original publication details of stories first published in the nongenre magazines like *Argosy* and *All-Story*.

8-17. De la Ree, Gerry. **Fantasy Collector's Annual—1974** and **Fantasy Collector's Annual—1975.** De la Ree, 1974.
Both fascinating miscellanies reprinting items from de la Ree's impressive collection: 1974 *Annual* includes letters and essays on and by Lovecraft, Finlay, Blackwood, Poe, Fabian, and Cabell; 1975 *Annual* presents Quinn, Derleth, Blaine, Finlay, Fabian, and others.

8-18. Derleth, August. **Thirty Years of Arkham House, 1939–1969.** Arkham, 1970.
An essay on the history of the leading weird fiction publisher (including a defense of copyright policies) is followed by a bibliography of the first 98 Arkham House titles, 14 Mycroft & Moran, and 14 Stanton & Lee. Also included are 22 photographs of the most important members of the Arkham House clan, such as Lovecraft, Smith, Long, Bloch, Quinn, Keller, Wandrei, and Wakefield. (RD)

8-19. Derry, Charles. **Dark Dreams: The Horror Film from Psycho to Jaws.** Yoseloff, 1977.
Divided into three cycles: "The Horror of Personality" starting with *Psycho;* "The Horror of Armageddon" starting with *The Birds;* and "The Horror of the Demonic" starting with *Rosemary's Baby.* A useful coverage of the horror cinema since the 1960s. Illustrated with over 150 stills.

8-20. Drake, Douglas. **Horror!** Macmillan, 1966.
Drake's journalistic approach makes this book a refreshing read. He discusses the facts and legends behind the main horror themes and traces their interpretations in fiction and film. The themes covered are vampires, werewolves, monsters, the mummy, the walking dead, the schizophrenic, and the phantom. There are also three chapters on Poe, Lovecraft, and Machen. The book has a superficial bibliography and film list; lacks an index. (RD)

8–21. Durie, Alistair. **Weird Tales.** Jupiter, 1979.
This book lacks much textual detail, but reproduces 157 of the 279 covers of *Weird Tales* (mostly in monochrome) in chronological order. Notes to the covers give an idea of the issues' contents and an introduction gives a short history of *Weird Tales*, but far more detail will be found in Weinberg's volume [8–91].

8–22. Dutt, Sukumar. **The Supernatural in English Romantic Poetry, 1780–1830.** Univ. of Calcutta, 1938; Folcroft, 1972.
Outstanding long study, beginning with romantic precursors and covering the Scottish ballad-collectors and poets and the Gothic period, and treating the horror elements of Coleridge, Southey, Keats, Beddoes, and Hood. Harsh on Southey's orientalism—from the author's Indian perspective—and on "lurid" aspects of the genre, but enthusiastic for the best in the field. Makes many apt distinctions between strains of horror poetry, erecting a handy classification system for this complex genre and period. Solid but brief footnotes, lacking in a bibliography. Compare to Spacks [8–78].

*8–23. Ellis, Stewart Marsh. **Mainly Victorian.** Hutchinson, 1925.
Nearly 60 essays on the Victorian era and "novelists who once were famous." Subjects include Sheridan Le Fanu, Rhoda Broughton, Arthur Machen, Richard Middleton, Ann Radcliffe and her literary influence, and the ghost story and its exponents. These very readable and interesting essays originally appeared in *The Bookman, The Fortnightly Review, Chamber's Journal,* and other periodicals. (RD)

*8–24. Ellis, Stewart Marsh. **Wilkie Collins, Le Fanu, and Others.** Constable, 1931, 1951.
"Mr. Ellis may be compared to the archeologist who, by systematic excavation of the remoter corners of an important site, makes a series of illuminating discoveries," *The Observer* aptly stated. The subjects are: Wilkie Collins, Charles Allston Collins, Mortimer Collins, R. D. Blackmore, Sheridan Le Fanu, Edward Bradley and George Lawrence, Mary Ann and Thomas Hughes, James Crossley, and Mrs. J. H. Riddell. Excellent bibliographies are added to all chapters (except Wilkie Collins, who had already been covered in Michael Sadleir's *Excursions In Victorian Bibliography,* 1922). Ellis was working on a sequel volume, *Miss Braddon, Miss Mulock and Others,* when he died in 1933. (RD)

8–25. Frank, Alan. **Monsters and Vampires.** Octopus, 1976.
Useful for its coverage of early vampire films and the careers of Bela Lugosi and Christopher Lee. Illustrated with nearly 200 film stills.

8–26. Frank, Alan. **The Movie Treasury: Horror Movies.** Octopus, 1974.
A basic coverage with the emphasis on film stills. Special sections on Frankenstein and Dracula. A more thorough coverage is found in the Gifford *History* [8–31].

8–27. Frank, Frederick S. **"The Gothic Novel: A Checklist of Modern Criticism."** *Bulletin of Bibliography* 30 (April–June 1973).
A 10-page checklist.

8–28. Frank, Frederick S.; Gary W. Crawford; and Benjamin Franklin Fisher IV. **"The 1978 Bibliography of Gothic Studies."** *Gothic* 1 (December 1979).
A thorough and useful checklist.

8–29. Franzetti, Jack P. **A Study of the Preternatural Fiction of Sheridan Le Fanu and Its Impact upon the Tales of Montague Rhodes James.** St. John's University, 1956.
Interesting work on the well-known author.

8–30. Gawsworth, John (Terence Ian Fytton Armstrong). **Ten Contemporaries: Notes toward Their Definitive Bibliography.** Second Series. Joiner & Steele, 1933.
Bibliographies of, and original essays by, Dorothy M. Richardson, Frederick Carter, Liam O'Flaherty, Stella Benson, Oliver Onions, E. M. Delafield, Thomas Burke, L. A. G. Strong, John Collier, and H. E. Bates. Preface by P. H. Muir. (RD)

8–31. Gifford, Denis. **A Pictorial History of Horror Films.** Hamlyn, 1973.
The best of the illustrated film surveys, with over 350 stills covering the history of the genre. A popular volume in its eighth printing.

8–32. Glut, Donald F. **The Dracula Book.** Scarecrow, 1975.
An all-encompassing history of the vampire in legend, fact, fiction, and film; useful index.

8–33. Glut, Donald F. **The Frankenstein Legend: A Tribute to Mary Shelley and Boris Karloff.** Scarecrow, 1973.
The history of the Frankenstein monster in legend, fact, fiction, theater, cinema, and other mass media. This and *The Dracula Book* [8–32] are good for their overall coverage of a very detailed subject.

8–34. Haining, Peter. **Terror! A History of Horror Illustrations.** Souvenir, 1976.
An excellent selection of illustrations from the original Gothic novels and chapbooks, through the Victorian melodramas to the pulps, with special relevance to *Weird Tales* and more recent magazines, all brought to life by Haining's text and notes, which pack considerable information into a series of small spaces. Lacks index.

8–35. Harris, Anthony. **Witchcraft and Magic in Seventeenth Century English Drama.** Manchester Univ. Press, 1980.
One of the few books to look in detail at this neglected area of supernatural fiction, highlighting many overlooked items.

8-36. Hawkins, Jean. **"Ghost Stories and Tales of the Supernatural."** *Bulletin of Bibliography* (1909).

An excellent checklist by Jean Hawkins on the New York State Library of approximately 300 novels and anthologies in the supernatural genre. A few nonfiction titles are also included. Jean Hawkins states in her introduction: "This list was begun in a public library to supply the constant demand for ghost stories which are hard to find because they are often short stories hidden in collections. The idea was to include none in which the mystery was explained, but some of these are now placed at the end under the heading 'Humorous.' " (RD)

8-37. Hearn, Lafcadio. **Interpretations of Literature.** Dodd, Mead, 1916.

Includes a chapter on "The Value of the Supernatural in Literature," in which Hearn argues that ghost stories are necessary and that the best are dream-inspired.

8-38. Hoffman, Stuart. **An Index to Unknown and Unknown Worlds.** Sirius Press, 1955.

A 34-page index, unique in that, apart from the author and title listings, it also details the characters and locales in each story. It is marred, however, by reference to volume and issue number rather than cover date. A more recent index is by Metzger [8-53].

8-39. Howells, Coral Ann. **Love, Mystery and Misery: Feeling in Gothic Fiction.** Athlone, 1978.

A well-researched scholarly treatise exploring the emotional themes of Gothic fiction and their intended emotional response to the original works. Divided into seven chapters with special coverage of *The Mysteries of Udolpho, The Monk, The Children of the Abbey, Manfroné, Northanger Abbey, Melmoth the Wanderer,* and *Jane Eyre.* Useful index.

8-40. Jensen, Paul M. **Boris Karloff and His Films.** Yoseloff, 1975; Barnes, 1975.

The most complete book of its kind, divided into four main sections covering the years 1877-1931, 1931 (Frankenstein), 1931-1938, and 1939-1968. Also contains bibliography, filmography, and index to names and films.

8-41. Jones, Robert K. **The Shudder Pulps.** FAX Collectors' Editions, 1975.

A well-researched history of the terror magazines *Dime Mystery, Terror Tales, Horror Stories, Thrilling Mystery,* and others, with considerable background detail on the authors, editors, and publishers. Well illustrated with magazine covers and interiors; has a good index.

8–42. Jones, Robert K. **The Weird Menace.** Ed. by Camille Cazedessus, Jr. Opar Press, 1972.

A small booklet containing Jones's essay on "Popular's Weird Menace Pulps" plus an index to the magazines *Dime Mystery, Horror Stories, Sinister Stories, Startling Mystery, Terror Tales,* and *Thrilling Mystery* by author.

8–43. Joshi, S. T. **Lovecraft: Four Decades of Criticism.** Ohio Univ. Press, 1980.

Spanning nearly 40 years of criticism, this anthology embodies the wide range of opinions evoked by Lovecraft's work. Provides a fine starting point for a study of H. P. L.

8–44. Ketterer, David. **Frankenstein's Creation: The Book, the Monster, and the Human Reality.** University of Victoria, 1979.

An in-depth study of *Frankenstein* in the light of Ketterer's hypothesis that the novel was a pioneer in the literary category of "apocalyptic" fiction. A most revealing study.

8–45. Ketterer, David. **The Rationale of Deception in Poe.** Louisiana State Univ. Press, 1979.

With this and his earlier *New Worlds for Old: The Apocalyptic Imagination, Science Fiction and American Literature* (1974), the author sets out to establish his category of apocalyptic fiction in a new interpretation of Poe's work as an attempt to remove the imagination from the confines of space, time, and self.

*8–46. Lee, Walt. **Reference Guide to Fantastic Films: Science Fiction, Fantasy & Horror.** 3 vols. Chelsea-Lee Books, 1972–1974.

The definitive index to fantasy films.

8–47. Locke, George. **Ferret Fantasy's Christmas Annual for 1972** and **Ferret Fantasy's Christmas Annual for 1973.** Ferret Fantasy, 1972 and 1974.

A useful aid to any collector. The bulk of both *annuals* consists of "An Annotated Addendum to Bleiler and Day" with full bibliographical details and notes on content and theme.

8–48. Locke, George. **A Spectrum of Fantasy.** Ferret Fantasy, 1980.

The bibliography of a collection of fantastic literature built up over 30 years. It comprises more than 3,000 books of the nineteenth and twentieth centuries, and ranges across the entire spectrum of fantasy from hard-core SF to ghost stories; contains bibliographical information not found elsewhere. (RD)

8–49. Lovecraft, H. P. **Supernatural Horror in Literature.** Abramson, 1945; Dover, 1973.

Superb encapsulation, in fewer than 30,000 words, of the history of supernatural fiction from Pliny the Younger and Phlegon through Gothic romance, Poe, spectral literature on the Continent, to Machen, Blackwood, Hodgson, Dunsany, and M. R. James. First published in 1927 (in W. Paul

Cook's *The Recluse*), the revised version appeared in *The Outsider*. The 1973 Dover edition replaced the Derleth foreword with a new introduction by E. F. Bleiler, and a good index. (RD)

8–50. MacAndrew, Elizabeth. **The Gothic Tradition in Fiction.** Columbia Univ. Press, 1979.

MacAndrew's survey takes her from Horace Walpole to Iris Murdoch. She shows how twentieth-century novelists have reworked Gothic motifs, but she makes less distinction than one would expect between the way these motifs were available to novelists in different periods. There is a very detailed analysis of *The Turn of the Screw*. (RD)

8–51. McNutt, Dan J. **The Eighteenth-Century Gothic Novel: An Annotated Bibliography of Criticism and Selected Texts.** Garland, 1975.

A valuable supplement to Summers's *Gothic Bibliography* [8–84]. The first seven sections cover bibliographies and research guides, aesthetic background—painting and such, literary background, psychological background, eighteenth-century Gothic in general studies, studies devoted to eighteenth-century Gothic, and the Gothic legacy. The next six chapters detail the work of Horace Walpole, Clara Reeve, Charlotte Turner Smith, Ann Radcliffe, M. G. Lewis, and William Beckford, listing selected texts, bibliographies, full-length studies, articles, essays, introductions, notices in works, diaries, and early reviews. Also contains a foreword by Devendra Varma and Maurice Lévy.

8–52. Marshall, Gene, and Carl F. Waedt. **"An Index to the Health-Knowledge Magazines,"** *Science Fiction Collector*, 3 (1977).

An author and issue index to the Robert A. W. Lowndes's-edited reprint magazines *Magazine of Horror, Startling Mystery Stories, Famous Science Fiction, Weird Terror Tales,* and *Bizarre Fantasy Tales,* with details of original publication dates. A supplemental index by Paul C. Allen provides issue contents of companion nonfantasy magazines *World Wide Adventure* and *Thrilling Western*.

8–53. Metzger, Arthur. **An Index and Short History of Unknown.** T-K Graphics, 1976.

A title and author index to *Unknown*. It lacks an issue index, but the introduction, which serves as a short history, covers most of the contents in chronological order. There is also a brief list of important reprints. See also [8–38].

8–54. Mosig, Dirk W. **"Toward a Greater Appreciation of H. P. Lovecraft: The Analytic Approach,"** *Whispers* (July 1973) and **"Lovecraft: The Dissonance Factor in Imaginative Literature,"** *Gothic,* (June 1979).

In these essays, Mosig applies two noted psychological theories to the interpretation of Lovecraft's fiction; in the first, Carl Jung's analytic theory, in the second, Leon Festinger's cognitive dissonance theory.

8–55. Moskowitz, Sam. **Explorers of the Infinite.** World, 1963; Hyperion, 1974.

Although this series of essays is intended as a sequential history of the origins of science fiction, Moskowitz has much to say on the supernatural output of certain authors. Of special relevance are Chapters 2, The Sons of Frankenstein; 3, The Prophetic Edgar Allan Poe; 4, The Fabulous Fantast—Fitz-James O'Brien; 9, The World, the Devil, and M. P. Shiel; and 15, The Lore of H. P. Lovecraft. These essays first appeared in the fantasy magazines and a few in the series were not reprinted in book form. See especially "Shiel and Heard: The Neglected Thinkers of SF," *Fantastic* (August 1960) and "Tennessee Williams, Boy Wonder," *Satellite Science Fiction* (October 1957).

8–56. Moskowitz, Sam. **Seekers of Tomorrow.** World, 1965; Hyperion, 1974.

A companion volume to [8–55], studying the work of more recent writers of science fiction, but with chapters on Fritz Leiber, C. L. Moore, Henry Kuttner, Robert Bloch, and Ray Bradbury, of interest to the supernatural fan. Moskowitz's essays are all bio/bibliographical in nature, with no attempt at a critical analysis of the writers' works.

8–57. Naha, Ed. **Horrors: From Screen to Scream.** Avon, 1975.

An A–Z listing of 850 horror, fantasy, and science fiction films providing details of plot, director, actors, and other facts. Also, entries on most of the important actors and directors, especially from the 1930s and 1940s. Profusely illustrated and a useful basic reference.

8–58. Nethercott, Arthur H. **The Road to Tryermaine: A Study of the History, Background, and Purposes of Coleridge's "Christabel."** Univ. of Chicago Press, 1939; Russell & Russell, 1962, 1978.

A masterly literary detective tale (inspired by John Lowes's *The Road to Xanadu*), tracing sources, influences, and background of an immortal supernatural-horror poem. Coleridge's readings in the occult are revealed, and the many contemporary reactions are reviewed (often negative, especially the parodies); the poem is scrutinized line by line. Rich discussion of the vampire and lamia lore; place and person names in the poem also well researched. Grace, zeal, and a sense of humor enliven the sure scholarship brought to this enigmatic poem.

8–59. Northey, Margot. **The Haunted Wilderness: the Gothic and Grotesque in Canadian Fiction.** Univ. of Toronto Press, 1976.

Northey's survey is an enlightening investigation of Gothic fiction in a nation where the literature is usually overshadowed by its southern neighbor.

8–60. Parsons, Coleman O. **Witchcraft and Demonology in Scott's Fiction.** Oliver & Boyd, 1964.

Parsons, a lifelong contributor to our knowledge of Walter Scott, takes up an important aspect of Scott's fictional world—the use of the supernatural in poetry and prose—and relates it to the attitudes of fellow Scots and to the rich store of Scottish literature and folklore that was at his disposal. The many unearthly agents and forces described by Scott in the Waverley novels are analyzed in detail. The supernatural is also traced in Scottish narrative poetry from Barbour to Burns, and in prose fiction from Scott's contemporaries (James Hogg and John Galt) to the half-dozen leading Scottish romancers of modern times (George Macdonald, Margaret Oliphant, Robert Louis Stevenson, John Buchan, Neil Gunn, and Eric Linklater). (RD)

*8-61. Penzoldt, Peter. **The Supernatural in Fiction.** Peter Nevill, 1952; Humanities Press, 1965.
Stimulating doctoral thesis with a psychoanalytical approach, concentrating chiefly on the English short story. The first part is a general survey of the whole field, and the second concentrates mainly on the work of five authors: Le Fanu, Kipling, M. R. James, de la Mare, and Blackwood. The chapter on Blackwood (to whom the book is dedicated) is most interesting, being based on personal correspondence shortly before his death. Well researched, although the bibliography does contain a few editions that never existed (such as Stoker, *Dracula and Other Stories*, 1886). Copious notes, but no index. (RD)

8-62. Pirie, David. **A Heritage of Horror: The English Gothic Cinema, 1946–72.** Gordon Fraser, 1973.
This volume studies certain aspects (such as Dracula and Frankenstein) from the viewpoint of various directors, and also discusses in detail specific films.

8-63. Pirie, David. **The Vampire Cinema.** Hamlyn, 1977.
Of special relevance for its reproduction of many rare film stills and posters, but not as thorough as the Silver and Ursini volume [8–76].

8-64. Prawer, Siegbert S. **The "Uncanny" in Literature: An Apology for Its Investigation.** London: Westfield College, 1965.
A small booklet (28 pp.) reprinting an inaugural lecture delivered at Westfield College in London on February 2, 1965. Learned treatise by the professor of German at London University, who has turned his attention to horror films (*Caligari's Children*, Oxford Univ. Press, 1980). (RD)

8-65. Radcliffe, Elsa J. **Gothic Novels of the Twentieth Century: An Annotated Bibliography.** Scarecrow, 1979.
This volume was prepared "to make available to the reading public a fairly comprehensive bibliography and to give some indication of relative quality to help the reader and librarian select from the mind-boggling quantity." The result is a rather erratic listing, which includes many titles that are definitely not Gothic by any standards (as Anne McCaffrey's *Decision at Doona*) and excludes some that are (*Crucible of Evil* by Lyda Belknap Long). But the book is useful for the many personalized annotations that supplement most of the entries, giving both plot resume and opinion of worth. Author entries

are also annotated with brief biographical detail, mostly copied from *Contemporary Authors*. Nearly 2,000 titles listed by both author and title. The term *Gothic* is given its widest interpretation for inclusion.

8-66. Railo, Eino. **The Haunted Castle: A Study of the Elements of English Romanticism.** George Routledge, 1927; Dutton, 1927.

An excellent guide to English horror-romanticism, especially strong on the career and writings of "Monk" Lewis. The book is divided into the following sections: The Haunted Castle (Walpole, Radcliffe, and others), Matthew Gregory Lewis, Later Developments of the Picture of the Haunted Castle (Scott, Maturin, Southey, and others), The Criminal Monk, The Wandering Jew and the Problem of Never-Ending Life, The Byronic Hero, Ghosts and Demoniac Beings, Incest and Romantic Eroticism, The Young Hero and Heroine and Other Characters, Other Themes (Poe, Wilde, Mary Shelley, and others), and Suspense and Terror. There is no index or bibliography, but this is amply compensated for by the very useful copious notes that occupy the last 60 pages of the book. [Note: The original edition was published in Helsinki, 1925, as *Haamulinna, Aineistohistoriallinen tutkimus Englannin kauhuromantiikasta.*] (RD)

8-67. Rottensteiner, Franz. **The Fantasy Book: The Ghostly, the Gothic, the Magical, the Unreal.** Thames & Hudson, 1978; Macmillan, 1978.

Intended as a companion to this Austrian critic and collector's previous volume *The Science Fiction Book* (1975), this volume has a more balanced coverage of the subject matter. As Rottensteiner explains, "This book does not aspire to be a scholarly study. The aim is to provide a succinct overview of the variety of literary fantasy in all its forms," and in this he succeeds, adeptly telescoping much information into brief chapters, yet sustaining a narrative thread. The strength of the book is in its many (202) illustrations and its coverage of fantasy and the supernatural in non-English-language countries. It has its faults, such as calling H. Russell Wakefield "the last living representative of the classic ghost story writer" 14 years after Wakefield's death, but such errors are few. A good index, but the bibliography is of more use to continental European readers than to English.

*8-68. Rovin, Jeff. **The Fabulous Fantasy Films.** Yoseloff, 1977; Barnes, 1977.

One of the most complete histories of the horror/fantasy film. It covers over 600 motion pictures with nearly 400 stills, including many rare stills from *King Kong, Fantasia,* and a silent version of *Paradise Lost.*

8-69. St. Armand, Barton Levi. **H. P. Lovecraft: New England Decadent.** Silver Scarab Press, 1979.

A comparatively shorter (56 pp.) study than [8-70], examining the aesthetic influence on Lovecraft's work, with special reference to paintings.

8–70. St. Armand, Barton Levi. **The Roots of Horror in the Fiction of H. P. Lovecraft.** Dragon Press, 1977.

A long (102 pp.) psychological and symbolic study of primarily one story by Lovecraft, "The Rats in the Walls," which St. Armand interprets in terms of Jungian criteria.

8–71. Scarborough, Dorothy. **The Supernatural in Modern English Fiction.** Putnam, 1917; Humanities Press, 1965.

An excellent pioneer work in the genre, particularly strong on Bierce, Blackwood, Crawford, Dunsany, Hawthorne, Machen, Poe, and Wells, but no mention of Le Fanu, M. R. James, or the Benson brothers. Here the word *modern* covers the previous two centuries. The text is divided into: The Gothic Romance, Later Influences, Modern Ghosts, The Devil and His Allies, Supernatural Life, The Supernatural in Folk-Tales, and Supernatural Science. Excellent index, but no bibliography. While researching this book, Scarborough compiled a massive bibliography numbering over 3,000 titles, but "far too voluminous to be included here." (RD)

8–72. Schiff, Gert. **Images of Horror and Fantasy.** Abrams, 1979.

A thematic study of how artists like Dali, Goya, and Munch express human anxieties, illustrated with 119 pictures.

8–73. Sidney-Fryer, Donald. **The Last of the Great Romantic Poets.** Silver Scarab Press, 1973.

Important monograph on Clark Ashton Smith's poetry, stressing its larger romantic tradition—from Renaissance French and Spenser's *The Faerie Queen* through California romanticist (and mentor of Smith) George Sterling. Important discussion of changes and deletions that Smith made while assembling his *Selected Poems* [6–52], of which Sidney-Fryer was the textual editor after Smith's death. Interesting comparisons of Smith's poetry with Sterling's. Valuable study of a major modern weird master whose vital poetry is highly praised, but almost never examined. Written by Smith's friend and bio/bibliographer (see *Emperor of Dreams* [7–64]).

8–74. Sieger, James R. **Stories of Ghosts.** Ed. by Camille Cazedessus, Jr. Opar Press, 1973.

A booklet built around an index (by author only) to the pulp magazine *Ghost Stories* (1926–1931). Also included are an introduction by Sam Moskowitz, which details the brief life story of the magazine, and the reprint of a story by Robert E. Howard, "The Apparition in the Prize Ring," from the April 1929 issue.

8–75. Siemon, Fred. **Ghost Story Index.** Library Research Associates, 1967.

A far from exhaustive index by author and title to over 2,200 supernatural/horror stories in 190 collections and anthologies.

8-76. Silver, Alain, and James Ursini. **The Vampire Film.** Tantivy Press, 1976; Barnes, 1976.
One of the best of the thematic film surveys studying the development of the vampire in the cinema, with a good filmography and bibliography.

8-77. Slusser, George Edgar. **The Bradbury Chronicles.** Borgo Press, 1977.
Number 4 in the Milford Series of 64-page booklets on Popular Writers of Today. A particularly good analysis of Bradbury's output, with special emphasis on his early output.

8-78. Spacks, Patricia Myer. **The Insistence of Horror: Aspects of the Supernatural in Eighteenth Century Poetry.** Harvard Univ. Press, 1962.
Unique, gap-filling study of the emerging supernatural theme in graveyard verse, literary ballads, and preromantic horror poetry. Condemns the excesses of the period's supernatural poetry—that is, trite themes and diction and quotes from some of the amusing contemporary attacks. Good grasp of the larger legacy of witchcraft, alchemy, and folklore bequeathed to the often unreasonable eighteenth century. Deals with three periods, with a chapter each (1700–1740, 1741–1780, 1781–1800), and also with "personification" in two chapters (1700–1750, 1751–1800). Thorough referencing and ample bibliography—especially "theology and witchcraft" for rare sources—which could aid a later scholar to collect and annotate a large anthology of the period's horror verse.

8-79. Steinbrunner, Chris, and Otto Penzler. **Encyclopedia of Mystery and Detection.** McGraw-Hill, 1976; Routledge & Kegan Paul, 1976.
Although aimed chiefly at the crime fiction field, this A–Z volume has much to interest the horror fan. The editors explain, "We have defined mystery fiction very broadly to include the gothic romance, such as *Frankenstein* and the works of Radcliffe." There are over 600 entries with many photographs and useful checklists.

8-80. Stone, Harry. **Dickens and the Invisible World.** Macmillan, 1980.
No modern critic has insisted more forcefully on the importance of the supernatural to an understanding of Dickens's work than Harry Stone. In a series of articles stretching back to the 1960s, he has traced in Dickens's novels the significance of ogres and dwarfs, giants and Cinderellas, ghostly visitations and transformations. Most of these articles have now been gathered together, edited, and expanded to make this fascinating new volume. (RD)

8-81. Sullivan, Jack. **Elegant Nightmares: The English Ghost Story from Le Fanu to Blackwood.** Ohio Univ. Press, 1978.
Within the confines of his deliberately limited scope, Sullivan studies the development of the English ghost story in the century following the 1830s, with special emphasis on the works of Le Fanu, M. R. James, and Blackwood,

and their influences. The book has been extensively revised for paperback publication to include more recent writers such as Aickman and Campbell.

*8-82. Summers, Montague. **A Gothic Bibliography.** Fortune Press, 1940; Russell & Russell, 1964.

Another monumental opus from Summers, with much new data on the genre. As a compendium of information and as a testament to its author's wide reading, tireless industry, and genuine enthusiasm for his theme, the book is as imposing as its bulk. (The more famous names like Wilkie Collins, Le Fanu, Marryat, and Mrs. Riddell were purposely omitted as they had been amply covered before by Ellis, Sadleir, and others, to make room for lesser novelists not previously studied in detail.) (RD)

ˇ8-83. Summers, Montague. **The Gothic Quest: A History of the Gothic Novel.** Fortune Press, 1938; Russell & Russell, 1964.

Pioneer study with much on the historic Gothic and the later terror Gothic; and of a group of prominent Gothic practitioners about whom (in particular Francis Lathom) Summers discovered many interesting details not previously recorded. Dr. Andre Parreaux, authority on the Gothic novel, wrote of this book in 1960: "The amount of information offered, its general reliability, the perfect good faith of the author, and his clear sense of values (at least when not obscured by extraliterary consideration) make *The Gothic Quest* a unique and valuable book, indispensable to the student of the period, and not likely to be replaced soon." (RD)

8-84. Summers, Montague. **The Vampire: His Kith and Kin.** Kegan Paul, Trench, Trubner, 1928; Dutton, 1929.

Comprehensive study of the origins, generation, traits, and practice of vampirism. The chapter on "The Vampire in Literature" (pp. 271–340) and Bibliography is especially useful, based on Summers's own extensive collection of rare books in this genre. The second edition (New York: University Books, 1960) contains an article, "The Quest for Montague Summers," by the publisher Felix Morrow. (RD)

8-85. Summers, Montague. **The Vampire in Europe.** Kegan Paul, Trench, Trubner, 1929.

Sequel to the above volume, of interest for the evidence it contains that Summers's researches were not solely in libraries, but had included on-the-spot inquiry in Greece and other places where belief in vampirism was still common. Reports of supposedly true cases of vampirism are interspersed with pure fiction, including a few pages from *Varney the Vampire*. The second edition (1962) contains a foreword by Fr. Brocard Sewell. (RD)

8-86. Summers, Montague. **The Werewolf.** Kegan Paul, Trench, Trubner, 1933; University Books, 1966.

Detailed study of the history of the werewolf in Britain and all corners of Europe. The style is stodgier than usual, with the characteristic doses of

Greek and Latin, and even the closest Summers admirers have admitted that his English is virtually incomprehensible in places. His essay on "The Werewolf in Literature" (pp. 262–277) is much shorter than the comparable vampire piece and a few classics (such as Biss and Kerruish) are omitted, but it is still useful, and the bibliography—as one expects—is excellent. (RD)

8–87. Thompson, G. Richard, ed. **The Gothic Imagination: Essays in Dark Romanticism.** Washington State Univ. Press, 1974.
A series of essays on various aspects of Gothic fiction. Thompson has also edited *Romantic Gothic Tales, 1790–1840* (Harper, 1979), a useful introduction to the genre consisting of criticism, a selection of 15 pieces of fiction, and a good bibliography.

8–88. Truxell, Janet Camp, ed. **Rossetti's Sister Helen.** Yale Univ. Press, 1939; Kennikat Press, 1973.
Dante Gabriel Rossetti's immortal horror poem is here presented in a facsimile of its first appearance (*Dusseldorf Artists' Album,* 1854). The editor has collated the other versions of this poem and has reproduced corrected galley proofs (and one mysterious forgery!), and has traced all known changes through the final version in *Poems* (1881). Also given are fascinating alternate readings of lines. Annotations suggest sources for the poem and reveal a Pre-Raphaelite craftsman at work on this famous horror poem—anthologized, incidentally, by Derleth in *Dark of the Moon* [6–15].

*8–89. Tuck, Donald H. **The Encyclopedia of Science Fiction and Fantasy. Volume 1: Who's Who, A–L.** Advent, 1974. **Volume 2: Who's Who, M–Z.** Advent, 1978. **Volume 3** (forthcoming).
The standard reference work for the fantasy field, with exceptionally good coverage of horror/supernatural collections and anthologies detailing variant editions and listing all contents. Each entry is annotated with brief biographical information and then a listing of works. Some entries are restricted, especially in the case of novels, as this is intended as a supplement to Bleiler's *Checklist* [8–6]. The book is complete to 1968; supplements updating the work to the 1970s are in preparation. Volume 3 will cover magazines, paperbacks, pseudonyms, connected stories, publishers, and films. This book has not been superseded by Robert Reginald's *Science Fiction and Fantasy Literature: A Checklist, 1700–1974* (Gale, 1979), which is an unannotated although very thorough bibliography.

*8–90. Varma, Devendra P. **The Gothic Flame: Being a History of the Gothic Novel in England: Its Origins, Efflorescence, Disintegration, and Residuary Influences.** Arthur Barker, 1957; Russell & Russell, 1957, 1966.
Highly regarded work that supersedes and improves on earlier, similar works—for example, Birkhead [8–5] and Railo [8–66]. Chapters on the "Gothic" spirit, background (origins and cross-currents), the first Gothic tale (*Otranto*), the historical Gothic school (the heirs of *Otranto*), Mrs. Ann Rad-

cliffe and the "craft of terror," *Schauer-romantik* (or Chambers of Horror), "Gothic" distributaries (the residuary influences), and quest of the numinous (the Gothic flame). With appendixes, index, and a very useful bibliography, plus a foreword by Sir Herbert Read and an introduction by Dr. J. M. S. Tompkins. Professor Varma has also written *The Evergreen Tree of Diabolical Knowledge* (1972). (RD)

8-91. Weinberg, Robert. **The Weird Tales Story.** FAX Collector's Editions, 1977.
An enthusiastic and dedicated history of the most important of all fantasy pulp magazines. It contains much information not available elsewhere, especially in the chronological summary of the magazine's fiction (pp. 19-47), cover art (pp. 62-78), and interior art (pp. 79-111). E. Hoffman Price provides a long memoir of the pulp's most famous editor, Farnsworth Wright, and there are a dozen recollections of *Weird Tales* by such contributors as Frank Belknap Long, Greye La Spina, H. Warner Munn, Edmond Hamilton, Wallace West, Carl Jacobi, Robert Bloch, Lee Brown Coye, and Joseph Payne Brennan. There are reproductions of many illustrations and covers plus a selection of letters and comments from *The Eyrie*. Some of the items here have been reprinted from Weinberg's earlier *WT50* (1974), but this booklet also contains much by way of additional information and a selection of fiction that could have (but did not) appear in the magazine.

8-92. Weinberg, Robert, and E. P. Berglund. **Reader's Guide to the Cthulhu Mythos.** Rev. ed. Silver Scarab Press, 1973.
A comprehensive, but not necessarily definitive, checklist of stories by Lovecraft and others fitting into the Cthulhu framework. See also checklist in Carter's *Lovecraft* [7-39].

8-93. Weinberg, Robert, and Lohr McKinstry. **The Hero Pulp Index.** Rev. ed. Robert Weinberg, 1973.
A borderline but useful publication listing issues of all the hero pulp magazines, such as *Doc Savage, Operator 5,* and *The Shadow,* with details of lead novels and authors (with a guide to pen names). A separate section provides a resume of the fictional careers of all the heroes.

8-94. Willis, Donald C. **Horror and Science Fiction Films: A Checklist.** Scarecrow Press, 1972.
A useful basic filmography, but no comparison to Lee [8-46].

8-95. Wimberly, Lowry C. **Folklore in the English and Scottish Ballads.** Univ. of Chicago Press, 1928; Frederick Unger, 1959; Dover, 1965.
This long study examines in great detail the supernatural elements (horror and nonhorror) of the ballads. Chapter titles such as "The Grave or Barrow World," "The Otherworld Journey," "The Ballad Witch," and "The Ballad Ghost" suggest the depth of this book. Great empathy for the ballad writers

and the lore that inspired them, and detailed analyses of representative ballads for their supernatural elements. Careful footnotes reflect the many texts and versions; there is an extensive bibliography, and the index (by supernatural topic and subtopic) is actually entertaining.

8–96. Wolff, Robert Lee. **Strange Stories: Explorations in Victorian Fiction—the Occult and the Neurotic.** Gambit, 1971.

Wolff is reputed to be the world's foremost collector of Victorian fiction, and also one of its ablest and most lucid interpreters. The main body of the book explores the strange stories of Lord Bulwer-Lytton, the most notable practicing occultist of all Victorian writers. Wolff also analyzes the work of Laurence Oliphant and Harriet Martineau, and there are several illustrations from his unrivaled book collection. (RD)

8–97. Yardley, Edward. **The Supernatural in Romantic Fiction.** Longmans, Green, 1880.

The title promises more than it offers: a very large number of subjects discussed in a short volume (141 pp.) from the mythology, legends, and stories of many countries, including Persia, India, Turkey, France and Scandinavia. Demogorgons, devils, valkyrs, hindoo deities, migration of souls, sea phantoms, vampires, and animated corpses are a few of the themes mentioned. This volume serves as a mere taster to later, more expansive works, such as Spence's *Encyclopedia* of occultism. The books of authors still alive in 1880 are excluded. No index or bibliography. (RD)

9
Periodicals

Mike Ashley

The following list features only those magazines with emphasis on non-fiction, although a few do feature stories. All titles are current at the time of compilation, and no defunct magazines are listed. It is worth remembering, however, that many such magazines (*The Arkham Collector, Search and Research, Shadow,* and others) are fine repositories of bio/bibliographical information and should not be overlooked.

9–1. August Derleth Society Newsletter. Richard Fawcett, ed.

9–2. British Fantasy Society Bulletin. Carl Hiles, 2 John Spencer Sq., London N1 2LZ, England.

9–3. Count Dracula Society Quarterly. Newsletter of the Count Dracula Society, 334 W. 54 St., Los Angeles, CA 90037.

9–4. Dark Horizons. John Merritt, ed. 41 Debenham Rd., South Yardley, Birmingham B25 8TB, England. Official organ of the British Fantasy Society. Features both articles and fiction.

9-5. Fantasy Macabre. David Reeder, ed. 32a Lambourne Rd., Chigwell Row, Essex, England. A new magazine featuring both fiction and articles with an emphasis on artwork.

9-6. Fantasy Media. Stephen Jones, David A. Sutton, Gordon Larkin, Jon M. Harvey, eds. Subscriptions: 194 Station Rd., Kings Heath, Birmingham B14 7TE, England. News magazine covering both fiction and the cinema. Includes reviews, interviews, and occasional articles. (*Fantasy Media* suspended publication after Vol. 2, No. 3, August/September 1980. News of revival not known at time of compilation.)

*9-7. Fantasy Newsletter. Paul C. Allen, ed. Box 170A, Rochester, NY 14601. The newsletter of the fantasy field. Reliable monthly schedule since its first issue in June 1978. Recently expanded its coverage. Features news on all fantasy, SF, and horror book releases in hardcover and paperback, and all specialty books, magazines, and fanzines. Regular column on "The British Scene" by Mike Ashley and "On Fantasy" by Fritz Leiber and Karl E. Wagner alternatively. Occasional interviews and film column.

9-8. Fantasy Readers' Guide. Mike Ashley, ed. Publisher, R. Reginald, Box 2845, San Bernardino, CA 92406. An occasional bibliographical booklet. Number 1 was a complete index to the books and magazines published by John Spencer/Badger Books, including the *Supernatural Stories* series. Number 2 is devoted to Ramsey Campbell with a complete bibliography of and articles about his work plus two new stories.

9-9. Ghosts & Scholars. Rosemary Pardoe, ed. 11b Cote Lea Sq., Southgate, Runcorn, Cheshire, England. An occasional booklet of fiction and nonfiction and the work and influences of M. R. James.

*9-10. Gothic. Gary W. Crawford, ed. Gothic Press, 4998 Perkins Rd., Baton Rouge, LA 70808. A twice-yearly magazine (first issue June 1979) with scholarly treatises on various aspects of Gothic fiction and short pieces of fiction. No illustrations. Alternate issues carry a useful checklist of recent Gothic studies. Contributing editors include Benjamin Franklin Fisher IV, Frederick S. Frank, Elizabeth MacAndrew, Mark M. Hennelly, Jr., Barton Levi St. Armand, G. R. Thompson, and Devendra P. Varma.

*9-11. Locus. Charles N. Brown, ed. Box 3938, San Francisco, CA 94119. The newspaper of the science fiction field, but of interest to fantasy and horror fans. Monthly, now in its fourteenth year.

9-12. Lovecraft Studies. S. T. Joshi, ed. Publisher, Marc A. Michaud, Necronomicon Press, 101 Lockwood St., West Warwick, RI 02893. A scholarly journal devoted to the life and works of H. P. Lovecraft.

*9-13. Megavore: The Journal of Popular Fiction. J. Grant Thiessen, ed. c/o Pandora Books, Ltd., Box 86, Neche, ND 58265. Formerly *The Science-*

Fiction Collector, now combined with *Age of the Unicorn.* Bimonthly. An important magazine of bibliography, now incorporating a sizable specialist advertising section. Well illustrated.

9–14. The Mervyn Peake Review. Journal of the Mervyn Peake Society, c/o John Watney, Flat 36, 5 Elm Park Gardens, London SW10 9QQ, England. Twice yearly, spring and autumn.

9–15. Nightshade. Ken Amos, ed. Nightshade Press, 7005 Bedford Lane, Louisville, KY 40222. Biannual, first issue 1975. Features articles and reviews on most aspects of fantasy and the supernatural with special emphasis on the works of Manly Wade Wellman and Thomas Burnett Swann.

*9–16. Nyctalops. Harry Morris, ed. Silver Scarab Press, 502 Elm St., S.E.; Albuquerque, NM 87102. Devoted to the memory of Lovecraft.

9–17. Poe Studies. G. R. Thompson and Alexander Hammond, eds. Washington State Univ. Press, Pullman, WA 99164. Semiannual, first issue 1968. Devoted to the life and work of Edgar Allan Poe.

*9–18. The Romantist. John C. Moran, ed., F. Marion Crawford Memorial Society, Saracinesca House, 3610 Meadowbrook Avenue, Nashville, TN 37205. A literary annual devoted to modern romanticism (late nineteenth century onward), has featured articles not only on Crawford, but Clark Ashton Smith, Thomas Burke, John Gawsworth, and M. P. Shiel. An attractive, large-size magazine with many facsimile reproductions.

*9–19. Science Fiction Chronicle. Andrew Porter, ed. Algol Press, Box 4175, New York, NY 10017. The new newspaper of the science fiction field has more illustrations than *Locus* and more details of forthcoming book releases and especially market reports. Monthly and more regular than *Locus,* but not as wide a coverage as *Fantasy Newsletter* or *Locus.*

9–20. Wark Annual. Rosemary Pardoe, ed. 11b Cote Lea Sq., Southgate, Runcorn, Cheshire, England. A yearly summary of nonprofessional fantasy publications.

9–21. The Weird Tales Collector. Robert Weinberg, ed. 15145 Oxford Dr., Oak Forest, IL 60452. Occasional publication devoted to *Weird Tales* and the other fantasy publications. The first five issues ran an issue index to *Weird Tales.*

*9–22. Whispers. Stuart David Schiff, ed. 70 Highland Ave., Binghamton, NY 13905. The premier fantasy publication with the emphasis on fiction, but also features articles and news and reviews. The anthology series *Whispers* was derived from this magazine.

9–23. Xenophile. Nils Harden, ed. 26 Chapala #5, Santa Barbara, CA 93101. Recently resumed publication; this is the magazine for fantasy collectors, with articles and bibliographies.

10
Societies and Organizations

Mike Ashley

10-1. Academy of Science Fiction, Fantasy and Horror Films. Founded in 1972 by Dr. Donald A. Reed to present awards for merit and recognition. The Golden Scroll Award is presented at an annual ceremony in Hollywood. House Organ: *Popcorn.* Address: 334 W. 54 St., Los Angeles, CA 90037.

10-2. The August Derleth Society. Formed in 1977 by Richard Fawcett for the expansion of public appreciation of August Derleth's work in all its forms. Regular newsletter [9-1].

10-3. The Bram Stoker Society. Formed in 1980 by Leslie Shepard and John C. Leahy to promote appreciation of the work of Bram Stoker. Twice-yearly *Newsletter.* Address: 4 Nassau St., Dublin 2, Eire. (RD)

10-4. British Fantasy Society. Formed in 1971 at the suggestion of Ramsey Campbell as a forum for the study and discussion of fantasy fiction, art, and cinema. Annual convention at which is presented the British Fantasy Awards (the August Derleth Fantasy Award for Best Novel). Regular bulletin [9-2] and magazine *Dark Horizons* [9-4] plus occasional publications. Address: Rob Butterworth (Treasurer), 79 Rochdale Rd., Milnrow, Rochdale, Lancashire OL16 4DT, England.

Note: Annotations by Richard Dalby are indicated by RD in parentheses.

10–5. Count Dracula Fan Club (not same as [10–6] or [10–7]). Formed in 1978 by Dr. Jeanne Youngson as a friendly Dracula/Vampire Appreciation Society. Biannual journal. Address: Penthouse North, 29 Washington Sq. W., New York, NY 10011. (RD)

10–6. The Count Dracula Society (not same as [10–5] or [10–7]). Formed in 1962 by Dr. Donald A. Reed for the study of horror films and Gothic literature. Regular newsletter *Count Dracula Society Quarterly* [9–3]. The Ann Radcliffe Award [11–1] is presented at an annual dinner. Address: 334 W. 54 St., Los Angeles, CA 90037.

10–7. The Dracula Society (not same as [10–5] or [10–6]). Formed in 1973 for the "encouragement and enjoyment of interest in Gothic literature, plays, and films, in particular of the works of Bram Stoker, of *Dracula* and its derivatives, the literature of vampirism, lycanthropy monsters and other related themes." Newsletter: *The Dracula Journals*. Organizes meetings and trips. Presents Annual Actor of the Year Award for Best Gothic role. Address: Mr. Bruce Wightman (Chairman), 36 High St., Upper Upnor, Rochester, Kent, England.

10–8. Fantasy Association. Founded in 1973 for the serious study and exchange of ideas on fantasy literature. Journal *Fantasiae* and magazine *The Eildon Tree* (discontinued). Box 24560, Los Angeles, CA 90024.

10–9. F. Marion Crawford Memorial Society. Founded in 1975 for the appreciation of all modern romantic fiction with special reference to the life and works of F. Marion Crawford. Annual magazine *The Romantist* [9–18]. Address: Saracinesca House, 3610 Meadowbrook Ave., Nashville, TN 37205.

10–10. Gothique Film Society. Formed in 1966 for the promotion and screening of horror and fantasy films. Address: Robin James, 75 Burns Ave., Feltham, Middlesex, England.

10–11. The H. P. Lovecraft Society. Founded in 1974 by Ray Ramsey for the study and appreciation of the works of H. P. Lovecraft and his friends. Regular *Journal* of serious studies. Address: Scott Connors, 6004 Kingston Dr., Aliquippa, PA 15001.

10–12. The Mervyn Peake Society. Founded in 1975 "to promote Peake's work through the establishment of a responsible corpus of critical opinion." Regular *Newsletter* and journal *Mervyn Peake Review* [9–14]. Information: John Watney, Flat 36, 5 Elm Park Gardens, London SW10 9QQ, England.

10–13. Prisoner Appreciation Society: Six of One. Founded in 1977 by David Barrie as a forum for the promotion and discussion of ideas inspired by the television series *The Prisoner* starring Patrick McGoohan, first screened in 1967. Regular newsletter *Alert*. Annual conventions held at Port Merion, Wales, the locale of The Village. Address: Box 61, Cheltenham, Gloucestershire, England.

11
Awards

Mike Ashley

11-1. Ann Radcliffe Award. Given annually by the Count Dracula Society [10-6] for recognition of the best in television, cinema, and literature in the horror genre. Previous winners included Forrest J Ackerman (first award in 1962) and Donald A. Wollheim (1972).

11-2. August Derleth Fantasy Award (ADFA). Presented annually since 1972 by the British Fantasy Society [10-4] for best novel, short story, film, and comic. Reorganized in 1977 as the *British Fantasy Award* (BFA) with the August Derleth Fantasy Award title reserved for the novel category. The following have won the novel and short story category. (*Note:* The year cited is year of presentation of the award, not of publication of the fiction.)

1972   Novel: *The Knight of the Swords*, Michael Moorcock
1973   Novel: *The King of the Swords*, Michael Moorcock
        Story: "The Fallible Fiend," L. Sprague de Camp
1974   Novel: *Hrolf Kraki's Saga*, Poul Anderson
        Story: "The Jade Man's Eyes," Michael Moorcock
1975   Novel: *The Sword and the Stallion*, Michael Moorcock
        Story: "Sticks," Karl Edward Wagner

1976 Novel: *The Hollow Lands,* Michael Moorcock
Story: (collection) *The Second Book of Fritz Leiber*

1977 Novel: *The Dragon and the George,* Gordon R. Dickson (ADFA)
Story: "Two Suns Setting," Karl Edward Wagner (BFA)

1978 Novel: *A Spell For Chameleon,* Piers Anthony (ADFA)
Story: "In the Bag," Ramsey Campbell (BFA)

1979 Novel: (Trilogy) *The Chronicles of Thomas Covenant the Unbeliever,* Stephen R. Donaldson (AFDA)
Story: "Jeffty Is Five," Harlan Ellison

1980 Novel: *Death's Master,* Tanith Lee
Story: "The Button Moulder," Fritz Leiber

11-3. Balrog. Founded in 1979 by Jonathan Bacon for outstanding achievements in publishing, literature, and the arts in the field of fantasy. Awarded annually at the Fool-Con SF & Fantasy Convention, Overland Park, KS. Categories are for Best Novel, Short Fiction, Collection/Anthology, Poet, Artist, Amateur Publication, Professional Publication, plus an Outstanding Amateur Achievement Award (OAAA) and an Outstanding Professional Achievement Award (OPAA).

1979 Novel: *Blind Voices,* Tom Reamy
Story: "Death From Exposure," Pat Cadigan
OAAA: Paul C. Allen, *Fantasy Newsletter*
OPAA: Donald M. Grant (publisher) and J. R. R. Tolkien
Collection: *Born to Exile,* Phyllis Eisenstein
Poet: Ray Bradbury
Artist: Tim Kirk

1980 Novel: *Dragondrums,* Anne McCaffrey
Story: "The Last Defender of Camelot," Roger Zelazny
OAAA: Paul C. Allen, *Fantasy Newsletter*
OPAA: Ann McCaffrey
Collection: *Night Shift,* Stephen King
Poet: H. Warner Munn
Artist: Michael Whelan

11-4. British Fantasy Award. See August Derleth Fantasy Award [11-2].

11-5. Edgar Allan Poe Award. Despite the title, this is presented by the Mystery Writers of America and has no connection with the horror/supernatural field other than by chance.

11-6. Fritz Leiber Award. Presented annually since 1977 at the Fantasy Faire organized by William Crawford of Alhambra, CA. For recognition of services to fantasy fiction.

11–7. Gandalf: Book Length Fantasy. Initiated as a separate award in 1978 and presented annually along with the Grand Master Award [11–8]. The award was dropped from 1980.

1978   *The Silmarillion,* J. R. R. Tolkien
1979   *The White Dragon,* Anne McCaffrey

11–8. Gandalf: Grand Master of Fantasy. Founded in 1974 by Lin Carter and presented annually at the World Science Fiction Convention along with the Hugo Awards (with which it should not be confused).

1974   J. R. R. Tolkien
1975   Fritz Leiber
1976   L. Sprague de Camp
1977   Andre Norton
1978   Poul Anderson
1979   Ursula K. Le Guin
1980   Ray Bradbury

11–9. Golden Scroll. Presented annually by the Academy of Science Fiction, Fantasy and Horror Films [10–1] for excellence in various categories pertaining to cinema and television.

11–10. Howard. See *World Fantasy Awards* [11–12].

11–11. Locus. Presented annually at the "Westercon" held in Los Angeles. Initiated by Charles N. Brown, publisher of *Locus* [9–11]. Originally these awards were for science fiction, but it was decided in 1980 to include a new category for fantasy novels following the increase in their numbers and in their greater sales. Voted by readers of *Locus.*

1980   Novel: *Harpist in the Wind,* Patricia McKillip

11–12. World Fantasy Awards—Howards. Presented annually since 1975 at the World Fantasy Convention for contributions to fantasy literature. Categories are for Best Novel, Short Fiction, Collection/Anthology, and Artist; there is a Special Award and a Life Achievement Award.

1975   Novel: *The Forgotten Beasts of Eld,* Patricia McKillip
       Story: "Pages from a Young Girl's Diary," Robert Aickman
       Collection: *Worse Things Waiting,* Manly Wade Wellman
       Life Achievement: Robert Bloch
1976   Novel: *Bid Time Return,* Richard Matheson
       Story: "Belsen Express," Fritz Leiber
       Life Achievement: Fritz Leiber
1977   Novel: *Doctor Rat,* William Kotzwinkle
       Story: "There's a Long, Long Trail a'Winding," Russell Kirk
       Collection: *Frights,* ed. by Kirby McCauley
       Life Achievement: Ray Bradbury

1978 Novel: *Our Lady of Darkness,* Fritz Leiber
 Story: "The Chimney," Ramsey Campbell
 Collection: *Murgunstruum and Others,* Hugh B. Cave
 Life Achievement: Frank Belknap Long
1979 Novel: *Gloriana,* Michael Moorcock
 Story: "Naples," Avram Davidson
 Collection: *Shadows,* ed. by Charles L. Grant
 Life Achievement: Jorge Luis Borges
1980 Novel: *Watchtower,* Elizabeth A. Lynn
 Story: "The Woman Who Loved the Moon," Elizabeth A. Lynn
 and "Macintosh Willy," Ramsey Campbell
 Collection: *Amazons!* Jessica A. Salmonson
 Life Achievement: Manley Wade Wellman

12
Research Collections

Mike Ashley

Although science fiction collections available to the public have been on the increase in recent years, similar collections of horror and supernatural fiction have not. In some cases they form part of the SF collections, but the following are limited to those with a special relevance to the supernatural genre.

United States

Arizona
12–1. University of Arizona. University Library, Special Collections Dept., Tucson, AZ 85721. Over 5,100 issues of magazines, including long runs of *Astounding/Analog, Amazing Stories, Famous Fantastic Mysteries, Fantastic, Galaxy, If, F & SF, Planet Stories,* and *Weird Tales.*

California
12–2. Fantasy Foundation. Ackerman Archives, 2495 Glendower Ave., Hollywood, CA 90027. Probably the most complete collection of fantasy in the world. Built up by Forrest J Ackerman in over 50 years. Runs to over 200,000 books and magazines (complete runs of all titles), plus numerous other items of films, manuscripts, correspondence, fanzines, paintings, and film props.

12–3. San Francisco Public Library. Civic Center, San Francisco, CA 94102. Houses the McComas collection donated by J. Francis McComas (1910–78), founder–editor of *The Magazine of Fantasy & Science Fiction.* Features complete runs of 92 SF and fantasy magazines from 1926 to date (over 5,000 issues).

12–4. University of California, Los Angeles. University Research Library, Los Angeles, CA 90024. Comprises the UCLA Nitka Collection of Fantastic Fiction with over 6,500 magazines and 9,000 books. Strong in near-complete sets of *Astounding/Analog* and *Weird Tales.* Also includes manuscripts, correspondence, and interviews of Ray Bradbury, Clark Ashton Smith, Fritz Leiber, L. Sprague de Camp, Henry Kuttner, A. E. van Vogt, and Forrest J Ackerman.

12–5. University of California, Riverside. University Library, Box 5900, Riverside, CA 92507. Houses the J. Lloyd Eaton fantasy and science fiction collection. Especially strong in turn-of-the-century fantastic fiction with major collections of authors H. Rider Haggard, Edgar Rice Burroughs, David H. Keller, H. P. Lovecraft, A. Merritt, Talbot Mundy, and S. Fowler Wright. Magazine collection weak, but does include substantial runs of *Galaxy* and *Startling Stories.*

12–6. University of Southern California. University Library, University Park, Los Angeles, CA 90007. The American Literature Collection contains the complete works of Ambrose Bierce, Edgar Rice Burroughs, August Derleth, Jack London, and Ray Bradbury, with some additional items of correspondence and interviews.

Illinois
12–7. Northern Illinois University Library. Swen F. Parsons Library, College Ave. & Normal Rd., DeKalb, IL 60115. A complete collection of all U.S. SF magazines from 1926 to date. An H. P. Lovecraft collection is in the making.

12–8. Wheaton College Library. 101 E. Seminary Ave., Wheaton, IL 60187. Houses the Marion E. Wade Collection, established in 1965. Especially strong in Charles Williams (950 letters, some manuscripts, including a first-draft *Descent into Hell*), and C. S. Lewis (1,115 original letters), plus G. K. Chesterton, George Macdonald, Dorothy L. Sayers, and J. R. R. Tolkien.

Indiana
12–9. Indiana University. Lilly Library, Bloomington, IN 47401. Started in 1972 and now houses complete first editions of H. G. Wells, H. Rider Haggard, G. K. Chesterton, August Derleth, and H. P. Lovecraft, plus over 2,000 manuscript items by Derleth and papers of Anthony Boucher and Fritz Leiber. Also a run of Arkham House books.

Kansas
12-10. University of Kansas. Spencer Research Library, Lawrence, KS 66045. Houses the Stewart Fantasy Collection, including a long run of *Weird Tales*, plus books by H. P. Lovecraft, Arthur Machen, and Frank Belknap Long.

Massachusetts
12-11. MIT Science Fiction Society Library. Room W20–421, MIT Student Center, Cambridge, MA 02139. Over 30,000 items including complete or near-complete runs of all U.S./U.K. magazines, plus many books and fanzines.

New Mexico
12-12. Eastern New Mexico University. University Library, Portales, NM 88130. Extensive magazine collection including complete or near-complete runs of *Astounding/Analog, Fantastic Adventures, Future, Galaxy, If, F & SF, Marvel, Startling Stories,* and *Weird Tales,* plus nongenre pulps like *Argosy* and *Blue Book.* Also many papers, manuscripts, and letters of Jack Williamson, Edmond Hamilton, and Leigh Brackett.

12-13. University of New Mexico. Zimmerman Library, Albuquerque, NM 87106. Houses the Donald B. Day SF collection of all magazines indexed in Day's *Index to the Science Fiction Magazines 1926–50,* which includes *Unknown, Astounding,* and many more.

Ohio
12-14. Ohio State University. University Libraries, 1858 Neil Ave., Columbus, OH 43210. Near-complete collection of all SF/fantasy magazines 1926 to date.

Pennsylvania
12-15. Pennsylvania State University. Pattee Library, University Park, PA 16801. Complete files of *Famous Fantastic Mysteries* and *Unknown* plus extensive runs of various SF magazines and Arkham House books.

Rhode Island
12-16. Brown University Library. 20 Prospect St., Providence, RI 02912. Houses the H. P. Lovecraft Collection founded in 1937 by his literary executor, Robert H. Barlow. More than 5,000 manuscripts, amateur journals, letters, and other items relating to Lovecraft. Complete file of *Weird Tales,* plus runs of leading weird magazines *Nyctalops, Macabre, Whispers, Weirdbook,* and the *H. P. Lovecraft Society Journal.* Other associational items.

South Carolina
12-17. University of South Carolina. Thomas Cooper Library, Columbia, SC 29208. A complete run of Arkham House volumes, plus several Lovecraft items (near-complete run of first editions).

Texas
12–18. Texas A & M University Library. College Station, TX 77843. Formed in 1970 and now comprises over 4,000 books, 8,000 monographs, 6,000 fanzines, and 5,500 magazines, including complete runs of *Amazing Stories, Astounding/Analog, Famous Fantastic Mysteries, Fantastic Adventures, Galaxy, F & SF, Planet Stories, Startling Stories,* and near-complete *Weird Tales,* plus many other extensive runs.

Utah
12–19. Brigham Young University. Harold B. Lee Library, Provo, UT 84601. Complete run of *F & SF,* and extensive run of Arkham House books.

Wisconsin
12–20. University of Wisconsin, La Crosse. Murphy Library, 1631 Pine St., La Crosse, WI 54601. Houses Paul Skeeter's Collection of Gothic Fiction and Horror Literature with over 1,000 titles from 1764 to date. Also contains a near-complete run of Arkham House books.

Wyoming
12–21. University of Wyoming. University Library, Laramie, WY 82070. Contains correspondence, books, magazines, and fan material collected by Donald A. Wollheim, Forrest J. Ackerman, and J. Vernon Shea, plus Robert Bloch, who has bequeathed most of his effects to the Special Collection.

Canada

12–22. Queen's University. Douglas Library, Kingston, Ontario K7L 5C4, Canada. Houses Gothic Fantasy Collection established in 1968 and featuring eighteenth-, nineteenth-, and twentieth-century examples. Also includes a number of H. P. Lovecraft books.

12–23. Spaced Out Library. 40 St. George St., Toronto, Ontario M5S 2E4, Canada. The only fully public specialist SF library in the world. Established in 1970 with the donation of Judith Merril's 5,000-item collection and now houses over 17,000 books and magazines, including first-edition Arkham House books.

Australia

12–24. Queensland University. St. Lucia, Brisbane, Queensland QLD 4067, Australia. Now houses the Donald Tuck Collection of science fiction and fantasy up to 1968, "the second largest collection in Australia." Contains most of the items entered in Tuck's encyclopedia [8–89].

12–25. Sydney University. Fisher Library, Sydney, New South Wales NSW 2006, Australia. Received the Ronald E. Graham Collection bequeathed at his death. Regarded by Graham as the biggest fantasy library in the world, containing over 90,000 directly related books and magazines.

England

12–26. Science Fiction Consultants. Gerry M. Webb, 67 Shakespeare Rd., Hanwell, London W7. Largest available collection of reference and illustrative material in U.K. Complete runs of all magazines and extensive run of hardcover editions.

Switzerland

12–27. Maison D'Ailleurs. Pierre Versins, rue du Four 5, Yverdon, Switzerland. Opened April 1976 based on Versins's private collection. Over 15,000 novels and collections plus 1,000 reference works. Strength in foreign-language editions.

Core Collection Checklist

Core collection titles are listed in the same sequence as they appear in text. (Those titles are indicated in the text by an asterisk preceding the entry number.) Numbers in parentheses following titles in this checklist indicate entry numbers, which refer the reader to the proper chapters where the core collection books may be checked for full details, including annotations, variant titles, sequels, author pseudonyms, and the like.

1   The Gothic Romance: 1762–1820

Austen, Jane. *Northanger Abbey* (1–11)
Barbauld, Anne Letitia Aiken. "Sir Bertrand" (1–18)
Barrett, Eaton Stannard. *The Heroine* (1–22)
Beckford, William. *Vethek: An Arabian Tale* (1–25)
Brown, Charles Brockden. *Wieland* (1–46)
———. *Arthur Mervyn* (1–47)
———. *Ormond* (1–48)
———. *Edgar Huntly* (1–49)
Choderlos de Laclos, Pierre-Ambroise-Francois. *Les Liaisons dangereuses* (1–67)
Curties, T. J. Horsley. *The Monk of Udolpho* (1–85)
Dacre, Charlotte. *Confessions of the Nun of Saint Omer* (1–89)
———. *Zofloya* (1–90)
———. *The Libertine: A Novel* (1–91)
———. *The Passions* (1–92)
Diderot, Denis. *La Religieuse* (1–95)

501

Godwin, William. *Things as They Are* (1-128)
———. *Saint Leon: A Tale of the Sixteenth Century* (1-129)
Green, William Child. *The Abbot of Montserrat* (1-136)
Grosse, Karl. *Horrid Mysteries* (1-139)
Helme, Elizabeth. *Saint Margaret's Cave* (1-158)
Hoffmann, Ernst Theodor Amadeus. *Die Elixiere des Teufels* (1-163)
Hogg, James. *The Private Memoirs and Confessions of a Justified Sinner* (1-165)
Ireland, William Henry. *The Abbesse: A Romance* (1-177)
Irving, Washington. "The Spectre Bridegroom" (1-181)
Kahlert, Karl Friedrich. *Der Geisterbanner* (1-186)
Kelly, Isabella. *The Abbey of Saint Asaph* (1-188)
Lamb, Caroline. *Glenarvon* (1-199)
Lathom, Francis. *Midnight Bell* (1-206)
Lee, Sophia. *The Recess: A Tale of Other Times* (1-214)
Leland, Thomas. *Longsword, Earl of Salisbury* (1-216)
Lewis, Matthew G. *The Monk: A Romance* (1-218)
———. *The Castle Spectre* (1-219)
Mackenzie, Henry. *The Man of Feeling* (1-234)
Maturin, Charles Robert. *The Fatal Revenge* (1-239)
———. *Bertram* (1-242)
———. *Melmoth the Wanderer* (1-244)
———. *The Albigenses: A Romance* (1-245)
Meeke, Mary. *Count Saint Blancard* (1-248)
Moore, George. *Grasville Abbey: A Romance* (1-267)
Parsons, Eliza. *The Castle of Wolfenbach: A German Story* (1-290)
———. *The Mysterious Warning: A German Tale* (1-291)
Peacock, Thomas Love. *Headlong Hall* (1-294)
———. *Nightmare Abbey* (1-295)
Polidori, John William. *The Vampyre* (1-304)
Radcliffe, Ann. *The Castles of Athlin and Bunbaydne: A Highland Story* (1-313)
———. *A Sicilian Romance* (1-314)
———. *The Romance of the Forest, Interspersed with Some Pieces of Poetry* (1-315)
———. *The Mysteries of Udolpho* (1-316)
———. *The Italian* (1-317)
Radcliff, Mary-Anne. *Manfroné* (1-318)
Reeve, Clara. *The Old English Baron: A Gothic Story* (1-322)
Roche, Regina Maria. *The Children of the Abbey* (1-324)
———. *Clermont: A Tale* (1-325)
———. *The Nocturnal Visit: A Tale* (1-326)
Sade, Donatien-Alphonse-Francois Marquis de. *Justine* (1-331)
Schiller, Johann Friedrich von. *Der Geisterscher* (1-336)
———. *Die Räuber* (1-337)
Scott, Sir Walter. *The Bride of Lammermoor* (1-341)
Shelley, Mary Wollstonecraft Godwin. *Frankenstein* (1-348)

Shelley, Percy Bysshe. *Zastrozzi: A Romance* (1–349)

———. *Saint Irvyne* (1–350)

Sleath, Elanor. *The Orphan of the Rhine* (1–358)

Smith, Catherine. *Barozzi* (1–361)

Smith, Charlotte. *Emmeline* (1–362)

———. *The Old Manor House* (1–364)

Walpole, Horace. *The Castle of Otranto: A Story* (1–398)

———. *The Mysterious Mother.* (1–399)

Warner, Richard. *Netley Abbey: A Gothic Story* (1–401)

2 The Residual Gothic Impulse: 1824–1873

Braddon, Mary Elizabeth. *Lady Audley's Secret* (2–9)

Bronte, Charlotte. *Jane Eyre* (2–10)

Bronte, Emily. *Wuthering Heights: A Novel* (2–11)

Broughton, Rhoda. *Tales for Christmas Eve* (2–12)

Bulwer-Lytton, Edward George Earl. "The Haunters and the Haunted" (2–16)

———. "Monos and Daimonos" (2–17)

Collins, Wilkie. *After Dark* (2–22)

———. *The Moonstone* (2–24)

———. *The Woman in White* (2–26)

Crowe, Catherine. *The Night Side of Nature* (2–27)

Dalton, James. *The Gentleman in Black* (2–29)

Dickens, Charles. *Bleak House* (2–30)

———. *The Mystery of Edwin Drood* (2–34)

———. *Our Mutual Friend* (2–35)

Felix, Charles. *The Notting Hill Mystery* (2–36)

Haining, Peter. *The Penny Dreadful* (2–43)

Hawthorne, Nathaniel. "Alice Doane's Appeal" (2–45)

———. *The Scarlet Letter* (2–46)

———. *Twice-Told Tales* (2–47)

Hogg, James. *The Private Memoirs and Confessions of a Justified Sinner, Written by Himself* (2–48)

Irving, Washington. *Tales of a Traveller* (2–52)

Le Fanu, Joseph Sheridan. *Best Ghost Stories of J. Sheridan Le Fanu* (2–58)

———. *Checkmate* (2–59)

———. *Uncle Silas* (2–63)

Melville, Herman. *Moby Dick* (2–68)

Mudford, William. *The Five Nights of St. Albans* (2–71)

———. *The Iron Shroud* (2–72)

Paulding, James Kirke. *Koningsmarke, The Long Finne: A Story of the New World* (2–73)

———. *Tales of the Good Woman, by a Doubtful Gentleman* (2–74)

———. "The Vroucolacas: A Tale" (2–75)

Poe, Edgar Allen. *Collected Works of Edgar Allen Poe* (2–77)
———. *The Narrative of Arthur Gordon Pym of Nantucket* (2–78)
Prest, Thomas. *Varney, the Vampire* (2–81)
Reynolds, George William MacArthur. *Wagner, the Wehr-Wolf* (2–82)
Summers, Montague. *The Grimoire and Other Supernatural Stories* (2–93)
———. *Supernatural Omnibus* (2–94)
———. *Victorian Ghost Stories* (2–95)
Thompson, G. Richard. *Romantic Gothic Tales* (2–97)

3   Psychological, Antiquarian, and Cosmic Horror: 1872–1919

Benson, E. F. "And the Dead Spake" and *The Horror Horn* (3–13)
———. *More Spook Stories* (3–14)
———. *The Room in the Tower and Other Stories* (3–15)
———. *Spook Stories* (3–16)
———. *Visible and Invisible* (3–17)
Bierce, Ambrose. *Can Such Things Be?* (3–21)
———. *Ghost and Horror Stories of Ambrose Bierce* (3–22)
———. *In the Midst of Life* (3–23)
Blackwood, Algernon. *Ancient Sorceries and Other Tales* (3–25)
———. *Best Ghost Stories of Algernon Blackwood* (3–26)
———. *The Dance of Death and Other Tales* (3–27)
———. *Day and Night Stories* (3–28)
———. *The Doll and One Other* (3–29)
———. *The Empty House and Other Ghost Stories* (3–30)
———. *Incredible Adventures* (3–31)
———. *John Silence, Physician Extraordinary* (3–32)
———. *The Listener and Other Stories* (3–33)
———. *The Lost Valley and Other Stories* (3–34)
———. *Pan's Garden* (3–35)
———. *Shocks* (3–36)
———. *Strange Stories* (3–37)
———. *The Tales of Algernon Blackwood* (3–38)
———. *Ten Minute Stories* (3–39)
———. *Tongues of Fire and Other Sketches* (3–40)
———. *The Willows and Other Queer Tales* (3–41)
Chambers, Robert W. *The King in Yellow* (3–49)
———. *The King in Yellow and Other Horror Stories* (3–50)
———. *The Maker of Moons* (3–51)
———. *The Mystery of Choice* (3–52)
———. *The Slayer of Souls* (3–53)
———. *The Tree of Heaven* (3–54)
Conrad, Joseph. *Heart of Darkness* (3–55)

————. *The Life Work of Henri Rene Albert Guy de Maupassant* (3–167)
Onions, Oliver. *The Collected Ghost Stories of Oliver Onions* (3–187)
————. *Ghosts in Daylight* (3–188)
————. *The Painted Face* (3–189)
————. *Widdershins* (3–190)
Stevenson, Robert Louis. *Island Night's Entertainment* (3–228)
————. *The Merry Men and Other Tales and Fables* (3–229)
————. *The Strange Case of Dr. Jekyll and Mr. Hyde* (3–230)
————. *Tales and Fantasies* (3–231)
————. *Thrawn Janet: Markheim* (3–232)
Stoker, Bram. *The Bram Stoker Bedside Companion* (3–233)
————. *Dracula* (3–234)
————. *Dracula's Guest* (3–235)
Turgenev, Ivan. *Phantoms and Other Stories* (3–239)
————. *A Reckless Character and Other Stories* (3–240)
Wells, H. G. *Complete Short Stories* (3–243)
————. *The Country of the Blind and Other Stories* (3–244)
————. *The Plattner Story and Others* (3–245)
————. *The Stolen Bacillus and Other Incidents* (3–246)
————. *Thirty Strange Stories* (3–247)
————. *Twelve Stories and a Dream* (3–248)
————. *The Valley of Spiders* (3–249)
Wharton, Edith. *The Ghost Stories of Edith Wharton* (3–250)
————. *Ghosts* (3–251)
————. *Here and Beyond* (3–252)
————. *Tales of Men and Ghosts* (3–253)
————. *Xingu and Other Stories* (3–254)
Wilde, Oscar. *The Picture of Dorian Gray* (3–257)

4   The Modern Masters: 1920–1980

Aickman, Robert. *Cold Hand in Mine* (4–1)
————. *Dark Entries* (4–2)
————. *Painted Devils: Strange Stories* (4–3)
————. *Powers of Darkness* (4–4)
————. *Sub Rosa: Strange Tales* (4–5)
————. *Tales of Love and Death* (4–6)
———— and Elizabeth Jane Howard. *We Are for the Dark* (4–7)
Asquith, Cynthia. *This Mortal Coil* (4–10)
Bloch, Robert. *Cold Chills* (4–29)
————. *The Opener of the Way* (4–30)
————. *Psycho* (4–32)
————. *Such Stuff as Screams Are Made Of* (4–35)
Block, Lawrence. *Ariel* (4–37)

———. *Dagon, and Other Macabre Tales* (4–159)
———. *The Dunwich Horror, and Others* (4–160)
———. *The Outsider, and Others* (4–162)
Malden, R. H. *Nine Ghosts* (4–171)
Munby, A. N. L. *The Alabaster Hand, and Other Ghost Stories* (4–180)
Munn, H. Warner. *Tales of the Werewolf Clan: Vol. I. In the Tomb of the Bishop* (4–181)
———. *Tales of the Werewolf Clan: Vol. II. The Master Goes Home* (4–182)
———. *The Werewolf of Ponkert* (4–183)
Oates, Joyce Carol. *Night-Side* (4–184)
Quinn, Seabury. *The Phantom-Fighter* (4–191)
———. *Roads* (4–192)
Rice, Ann. *Interview with the Vampire* (4–194)
Smith, Clark Ashton. *The Abominations of Yondo* (4–200)
———. *Genius Loci, and Other Tales* (4–201)
———. *Lost Worlds* (4–202)
———. *Out of Space and Time* (4–204)
———. *Tales of Science and Sorcery* (4–205)
Stewart, Desmond. *The Vampire of Mons* (4–206)
Sturgeon, Theodore. *Some of Your Blood* (4–209)
Tryon, Thomas. *The Other* (4–211)
Walter, Elizabeth. *In the Mist, and Other Uncanny Encounters* (4–215)
Wellman, Manly Wade. *Who Fears the Devil?* (4–222)
———. *Worse Things Waiting* (4–223)
Wheatley, Dennis. *The Devil Rides Out* (4–224)
Whitehead, Henry S. *West India Lights* (4–330)

Anthologies
Aickman, Robert. *The Fontana Book of Great Ghost Stories* (4–236)
———. *The Second Fontana Book of Great Ghost Stories* (4–237)
———. *The Third Fontana Book of Great Ghost Stories* (4–238)
———. *The Fourth Fontana Book of Great Ghost Stories* (4–239)
———. *The Fifth Fontana Book of Great Ghost Stories* (4–240)
———. *The Sixth Fontana Book of Great Ghost Stories* (4–241)
———. *The Eighth Fontana Book of Great Ghost Stories* (4–242)
Asquith, Cynthia. *The Ghost Book* (4–244)
———. *The Second Ghost Book* (4–245)
———. *The Third Ghost Book* (4–246)
Campbell, Ramsey. *New Tales of the Cthulhu Mythos* (4–249)
———. *New Terrors* (4–250)
———. *New Terrors Two* (4–256)
Davis, Richard. *The Year's Best Horror Stories: I* (4–252)
———. *The Year's Best Horror Stories: II* (4–253)
———. *The Year's Best Horror Stories: III* (4–254)

Derleth, August. *Dark Mind, Dark Heart* (4–255)
———. *The Night Side* (4–257)
———. *Sleep No More* (4–260)
———. *The Sleeping and the Dead* (4–261)
———. *Tales of the Cthulhu Mythos* (4–262)
———. *Who Knocks?* (4–265)
Grant, Charles L. *Nightmares* (4–266)
———. *Shadows* (4–267)
———. *Shadows 2* (4–268)
———. *Shadows 3* (4–269)
Haining, Peter. *The Black Magic Omnibus* (4–270)
———. *The Lucifer Society: Macabre Tales by Great Modern Writers* (4–272)
———. *Weird Tales* (4–273)
Karloff, Boris. *And the Darkness Falls* (4–276)
Lamb, Hugh. *Cold Fear: New Tales of Terror* (4–277)
———. *Return from the Grave* (4–278)
———. *The Taste of Fear: Thirteen Eerie Tales* (4–279)
———. *The Thrill of Horror* (4–280)
———. *A Tide of Terror: An Anthology of Rare Horror Stories* (4–281)
———. *A Wave of Fear* (4–282)
McCauley, Kirby. *Dark Forces* (4–283)
———. *Frights: New Stories of Suspense and Supernatural Terror* (4–284)
Marguiles, Leo. *Weird Tales* (4–285)
———. *Worlds of Weird* (4–286)
Mazzeo, Henry. *Hauntings: Tales of the Supernatural* (4–287)
Page, Gerald W. *The Years' Best Horror Stories: V* (4–290)
———. *The Year's Best Horror Stories: VI* (4–291)
———. *The Year's Best Horror Stories: VII* (4–292)
Schiff, Stuart David. *Whispers* (4–294)
———. *Whispers II* (4–295)
——— and Fritz Leiber. *The World Fantasy Awards: Vol. 2* (4–296)
Thompson, Christine Campbell. *At Dead of Night* (4–297)
———. *By Daylight Only* (4–298)
———. *Grim Death* (4–299)
———. *Gruesome Cargoes* (4–300)
———. *Keep on the Light* (4–301)
———. *Nightmare by Daylight* (4–302)
———. *Not at Night* (4–303)
———. *More Not at Night* (4–304)
———. *Switch on the Night* (4–305)
———. *Terror by Night* (4–306)
———. *You'll Need a Light* (4–307)
Wagner, Karl Edward. *The Year's Best Horror Stories: VIII* (4–308)
Wilson, Gahan. *First World Fantasy Awards* (4–309)

Wise, Herbert A. and Phyllis Fraser. *Great Tales of Terror and the Supernatural* (4–310)

6   Supernatural Verse in English

Bacon, Jonathan and Steve Troyanovich. *Omniumgathum* (6–3)
Beddoes, Thomas Lovell. *The Works of Thomas Lovell Beddoes* (6–4)
Bürger, Gottfried. *The Earliest English Translations of Burger's Lenore* (6–8)
Coblentz, Stanton A. *Unseen Wings* (6–13)
Derleth, August. *Dark of the Moon* (6–15)
———. *Fire and Sleet and Candlelight* (6–16)
Hayes, Michael. *Supernatural Poetry* (6–25)
Lewis, Matthew Gregory. *Tales of Wonder* (6–32)
Lovecraft, H. P. *Collected Poems* (6–36)
Smith, Clark Ashton. *Selected Poems* (6–52)
Widdemer, Margaret. *The Haunted Hour* (6–63)

7   Biography, Autobiography, and Bibliography

Ray Bradbury
Noland, William F. *The Ray Bradbury Companion* (7–9)

Walter de la Mare
McCrosson, Doris Ross. *Walter de la Mare* (7–13)

Sir Henry Rider Haggard
Haggard, Lilias Rider. *The Cloak That I Left* (7–22)
Scott, J. E. *A Bibliography of the Works of Sir Henry Rider Haggard* (7–23)

William Hope Hodgson
Moskowitz, Sam. *Out of the Storm* (7–25)

M. R. James
Lubbock, S. G. *A Memoir of Montague Rhodes James* (7–31)

H. P. Lovecraft
de Camp, L. Sprague. *Lovecraft: A Biography* (7–41)

Arthur Machen
Goldstone, Adrian and Wesley Sweetser. *A Bibliography of Arthur Machen* (7–46)

Edgar Allan Poe
Quinn, Arthur Hobson. *Edgar Allan Poe: A Critical Biography* (7–54)
Robertson, John W. *Bibliography of the Writings of Edgar A. Poe* and *Commentary on the Bibliography of Edgar A. Poe* (7–55)

Mary Shelley
Lyles, W. H. *Mary Shelley: An Annotated Bibliography* (7–61)

Bram Stoker
Ludlam, Harry. *A Biography of Dracula: The Life Story of Bram Stoker* (7–70)

8 Criticism, Indexes, and General Reference

Bleiler, Everett F. *The Checklist of Science-Fiction and Supernatural Fiction* (8–6)
Clarens, Carlos. *An Illustrated History of the Horror Film* (8–9)
Cockcroft, T. G. L. *Index to the Weird Fiction Magazines: Index by Author* (8–10)
Ellis, Stewart Marsh. *Mainly Victorian* (8–23)
————. *Wilkie Collins, Le Fanu, and Others* (8–24)
Lee, Walt. *Reference Guide to Fantastic Films: Science Fiction, Fantasy & Horror* (8–46)
Penzoldt, Peter. *The Supernatural in Fiction* (8–61)
Rovin, Jeff. *The Fabulous Fantasy Films* (8–68)
Summers, Montague. *A Gothic Bibliography* (8–82)
————. *The Gothic Quest: A History of the Gothic Novel* (8–83)
Tuck, Donald H. *The Encyclopedia of Science Fiction and Fantasy, Vol. I.* (8–89)
Varma, Devendra P. *The Gothic Flame* (8–90)

9 Periodicals

Fantasy Newsletter (9–7)
Gothic (9–10)
Locus (9–11)
Megavore: The Journal of Popular Fiction (9–13)
Nyctalops (9–16)
The Romantist (9–18)
Science Fiction Chronicle (9–19)
Whispers (9–22)

Directory of Publishers

This directory lists most publishers, with current addresses, in the United States, Canada, and Great Britain for in-print annotated books. Publishers are alphabetized by key word (for example, Thomas Y. Crowell is listed under Crowell).

AMS Press
56 E. 13 St.
New York, NY 10003

Abrams
110 E. 59 St.
New York, NY 10022

Acrostic Press
7923 Lafon Pl.
St. Louis, MO 63130

Adams Press
30 W. Washington St.
Chicago, IL 60602

W. H. Allen & Co.
44 Hill St.
London W1X 8LB, England

American Book Co.
135 W. 50 St.
New York, NY 10020

Appleton-Century-Crofts
Englewood Cliffs, NJ 07632

Arbor House
235 E. 45 St.
New York, NY 10017

Arden Library
Mill & Main Sts.
Darby, PA 19023

Arkham House
Sauk City, WI 53583

Arno Press
330 Madison Ave.
New York, NY 10017

Arrow Books
3 Fitzroy Square
London W1P 6JD, England

Athlone Press
Atlantic Highlands, NJ 07716

Avon Books
959 Eighth Ave.
New York, NY 10019

Award Books
235 E. 45 St.
New York, NY 10017

Ballatine Books
201 E. 50 St.
New York, NY 10022

Bantam Books
666 Fifth Ave.
New York, NY 10019

A. S. Barnes
11175 Flintkote Ave.
Suite C
San Diego, CA 92121

Berkley Publishing
200 Madison Ave.
New York, NY 10016

Blackie & Son
400 Edgware Rd.
London W2 1EG, England

Bobbs-Merrill
4300 W. 62 St.
Indianapolis, IN 46468

Bodley Head
9 Bow St.
London W2CE 7AL, England

Books for Libraries
330 Madison Ave.
New York, NY 10017

Borgo Press
Box 2845
San Bernardino, CA 92406

Bowling Green University Press
Bowling Green, OH 43403

John Calder
18 Brewer St.
London W1R 4AS, England

Cambridge University Press
32 E. 57 St.
New York, NY 10022

Jonathan Cape
30 Bedford Sq.
London WC1B 3EL, England

Carcosa
Box 1064
Chapel Hill, NC 27514

Centaur Books
799 Broadway
New York, NY 10003

Chelsea-Lee Books
Box 66273
Los Angeles, CA 90066

Clarendon. *See* Oxford University
Press

College & University Press
267 Chapel St.
New Haven, CT 06513

Collier Books
366 Third Ave.
New York, NY 10022

Collins-World
2080 W. 117 St.
Cleveland, OH 44111

Columbia University Press
562 W. 113 St.
New York, NY 10025

Constable & Co.
10 Orange St.
Leicester Sq.
London WC2, England

Core Collection Books
11 Middle Neck Rd.
Great Neck, NY 11021

Corgi Books
Century House
61/63 Uxbridge Rd.
London W5 5SA, England

Coronet Books
47 Bedford Sq.
London WC1B 3DP, England

Coward, McCann & Geoghegan
200 Madison Ave.
New York, NY 10016

Thomas Y. Crowell
10 E. 53 St.
New York, NY 10022

Curtis Books
600 Third Ave.
New York, NY 10017

DAW Books
1633 Broadway
New York, NY 10019

Dawson Publishing
Box 4327
995 Sherman Ave.
Hamden, CT 06514

Delacorte Press
245 E. 47 St.
New York, NY 10017

Dell Publishing Co.
245 E. 47 St.
New York, NY 10017

J. M. Dent
26 Albemarle St.
London W1X 4QY, England

Dobson Books
80 Kensington Church St.
London W8 4BZ, England

Doubleday & Co.
245 Park Ave.
New York, NY 10017

Dover Publications
180 Varick St.
New York, NY 10014

Dragon Press
Church St.
Elizabethtown, NY 12932

E. P. Dutton
2 Park Ave.
New York, NY 10016

Elm Tree Press
Box 185
La Crosse, WI 54602

Emerson Books
Reynolds Lane
Buchanan, NY 10511

Faber & Faber
3 Queens Sq.
London WC1N 3AU, England

Fantasy Publishing
1855 W. Main St.
Alhambra, CA 91801

Fantome Press
720 N. Park Ave.
Warren, OH 44483

Farrar, Straus & Giroux
19 Union Sq. W.
New York, NY 10003

Fawcett Books
1515 Broadway
New York, NY 10036

FAX Collector's Editions
Box 851
Mercer Island, WA 98040

Ferret Fantasy
27 Beechcroft Rd.
Upper Tooting
London SW17, England

Firebell Books
Box 804
Glen Rock, NJ 07452

Fleet Press
160 Fifth Ave.
New York, NY 10010

Folcroft Library Editions
Box 182
Folcroft, PA 19032

Folio Magazine Publishing Corp.
Box 697
125 Elm St.
New Canaan, CT 06840

Folly Press
3315 N. 36 St.
Tacoma, WA 98407

Fontana Books
Bath Rd.
Harmondsworth
Middlesex UB7 ODA, England

Fraser Publishing
309 S. Willard St.
Burlington, VT 05401

Gale Research
Book Tower
Detroit, MI 48226

Gambit
27 N. Main St.
Meeting House Green
Ipswich, MA 01938

Garland Publishing
136 Madison Ave.
New York, NY 10016

Garnstone Press
Box 233
London SW3, England

Garrad Publishing
1607 N. Market St.
Champaign, IL 61820

Victor Gollancz
14 Henrietta St.
London WC2E 8QJ, England

Gordon Press
Box 459
Bowling Green Sta.
New York, NY 10004

Donald M. Grant
West Kingston, RI 02892

Greenwood Press
88 Post Rd. West
Westport, CT 06881

Grove Press
196 W. Houston St.
New York, NY 10014

Gubblecote Press. *See* Shire
Publications

Hafner Press
866 Third Ave.
New York, NY 10022

Robert Hale
Clerkenwell House
45–47 Clerkenwell Green
London EC1R OHT, England

Hamish Hamilton
90 Great Russell St.
London WC1B 3PT, England

The Hamlyn Group
Astronaut House
Hounslow Rd.
Feltham, Middlesex TW14 9AR,
England

Harper & Row
10 E. 53 St.
New York, NY 10022

Hart-Davis
Box 9, 29 Frogmore St.
St. Albans
Hertfordshire AL2 2NF, England

Harvard University Press
70 Garden St.
Cambridge, MA 02138

William Heinemann
15–16 Queen St.
London W1X 8BE, England

Hodder & Stoughton
47 Bedford Sq.
London WC1B 3DP, England

Holiday House
18 E. 56 St.
New York, NY 10022

Holt, Rinehart, Winston
383 Madison Ave.
New York, NY 10017

Houghton Mifflin
2 Park St.
Boston, MA 02107

Humanities Press
Atlantic Highlands, NY 07716

Hutchinson Publishing Group
3 Fitzroy Sq.
London W1P 6JD, England

Hyperion Press
45 Riverside Ave.
Westport, CT 06880

Marshall Jones
Francestown, NH 03043

Jove Press
200 Madison Ave.
New York, NY 10016

Jupiter Press
Box 101
Lake Bluff, IL 60044

Kennikat Press
90 S. Bayles Ave.
Port Washington, NY 11050

Kent State University Press
Kent, OH 44242

Alfred A. Knopf
201 E. 50 St.
New York, NY 10022

Kraus Reprint
Rt. 100
Millwood, NY 10546

Library Research Associates
Dunderberg Rd.
R.D. 5, Box 41
Monroe, NY 10950

Louisiana State University Press
Baton Rouge, LA 70803

Macabre House
26 Fowler St.
New Haven, CT 06515

McGraw-Hill
1221 Ave. of Americas
New York, NY 10020

Macmillian Publishing
866 Third Ave.
New York, NY 10022

Manchester University Press
156 Fifth Ave.
New York, NY 10010

F. Marion Crawford Society
3610 Meadowbrook Ave.
Nashville, TN 37205

Merrill Publishing
1300 Alum Creek Dr.
Columbus, OH 43216

Millington Books
109 Southampton Row
London WC1B 4HH, England

Minerva Books
100 Park Ave.
New York, NY 10017

Mirage Press
Box 28
Manchester, MD 21102

Modern Library
201 E. 50 St.
New York, NY 10022

William Morrow
105 Madison Ave.
New York, NY 10016

Multimedia Publishing
7 Garber Hill Rd.
Blauvelt, NY 10913

Mycroft & Moran
Sauk City, WI 53583

National Book League
7 Albemarle St.
London W1X 4BB, England

New American Library
1633 Broadway
New York, NY 10019

New English Library
Barnard's Inn, Holborn
London EC1N 2JR, England

Northwoods Press
Box 249
Stafford, VA 22554

W. W. Norton
500 Fifth Ave.
New York, NY 10036

Octopus Books
59 Grosvenor St.
London W1X 9DA, England

Odyssey Press
4300 W. 62 St.
Indianapolis, IN 46206

Ohio State University Press
2070 Niel Ave.
Columbus, OH 43210

Oliver & Boyd
Croythorn House
23 Ravelston Terrace
Edinburgh EH4, Scotland

Outre House
1622 N. St. #302
Sacramento, CA 95814

Oxford University Press
200 Madison Ave.
New York, NY 10016

Pan Books
Cavaye Pl.
London SW10 9PG, England

Panther Books
Box 9, 29 Frogmore St.
St. Albans
Hertfordshire AL2 2NF, England

Peacock Press
666 Fifth Ave.
New York, NY 10019

Penguin Books
625 Madison Ave.
New York, NY 10022

Pillar Books
757 Third Ave.
New York, NY 10017

Pinnacle Books
One Century Plaza
2029 Century Park E.
Los Angeles, CA 90067

Playboy Press
757 Third Ave.
New York, NY 10017

Popular Library
1515 Broadway
New York, NY 10036

Clarkson Potter
One Park Ave.
New York, NY 10016

Prentice-Hall, Inc.
Englewood Cliffs, NJ 07632

G. P. Putnam's
200 Madison Ave.
New York, NY 10016

Pyramid Publishers
9 Garden St.
Moonachie, NJ 07074

Random House
201 E. 50 St.
New York, NY 10022

Red Dove Press
Box 864
Madison, WI 53701

Gerry de la Ree
7 Cedarwood Lane
Saddle River, NJ 07458

Robinson Press
1137 Riverside Dr.
Fort Collins, CO 80521

Routledge & Kegan Paul
9 Park St.
Boston, MA 02108

Rupert Hart-Davis
Box 9, 29 Frogmore St.
St. Albans
Hertfordshire AL2 2NF, England

Russell & Russell
597 Fifth Ave.
New York, NY 10017

Rutgers University Press
30 College Ave.
New Brunswick, NJ 08903

St. Martin's Press
175 Fifth Ave.
New York, NY 10010

Scarecrow Press
52 Liberty St.
Metuchen, NJ 08840

Scholarly Press
19722 E. Nine Mile Rd.
Saint Clair Shores, MI 48080

Scholars' Facsimiles & Reprints
Box 344
Delmar, NY 12054

Scholars Press
101 Selem St.
Chico, CA 95926

Scolar Press
39 Great Russell St.
London WC1B 3PH, England

Charles Scribner's
597 Fifth Ave.
New York, NY 10017

Sheridan House
175 Orawaupum St.
White Plains, NY 10606

Shire Publications
Cromwell House
Church St.
Aylesbury HP 17 9AJ, England

Signet Books
135 W. 50 St.
New York, NY 10020

Silver Scarab Press
500 Wellesley S.E.
Albuquerque, NM 87106

Simon & Schuster
1230 Ave. of the Americas
New York, NY 10020

Sirius Books
Box 6294
Eureka, CA 95501

Charles Skilton Ltd.
2 & 3 Abbeymount
Edinburgh 8, Scotland

Peter Smith
6 Lexington Ave.
Magnolia, MA 01930

Souvenir Press
43 Great Russell St.
London WC1B 3 PA, England

Neville Spearman
Priory Gate
57 Friars St.
Sudbury, Suffolk, England

Spectre Press
18 Cefn Rd.
Mynachdy
Cardiff CF4 3HS, England

Sphere Books
30–32 Gray's Inn Rd.
London WC1X 8JL, England

Star Publishing Co.
505 Eighth St.
New York, NY 10018

Strange Company
Box 864
Madison, WI 53701

Stygian Island Press
7613 #A
Shawnee, KS 66214

Tandem Publishing
123 King St.
Hammersmith
London W6 9JG, England

Tantivy Press
Magdalen House
136–148 Tooley St.
London SE1 2TT, England

Taplinger Publishing
132 W. 22 St.
New York, NY 10011

Thames & Hudson
500 Fifth Ave.
New York, NY 10036

Transatlantic Arts
88 Bridge Rd.
Central Islip, NY 10036

Turnstile Press
Great Turnstile
London WC1V 75J, England

Twayne Publishers
70 Lincoln St.
Boston, MA 02111

Underwood-Miller
239 N. 4 St.
Columbia, PA 17512

Fredrick Ungar Publishing
250 Park Ave. S.
New York, NY 10003

University Books
120 Enterprise Ave.
Secaucus, NJ 07094

University of California Press
2223 Fulton St.
Berkeley, CA 94720

University of Georgia Press
Athens, GA 30601

University of Nebraska Press
901 N. 17th St.
Lincoln, NE 68588

University of Pittsburgh Press
127 N. Bellefield Ave.
Pittsburgh, PA 15260

University of Texas Press
Box 7819
University Sta.
Austin, TX 78712

University of Toronto Press
33 E. Tupper St.
Buffalo, NY 14203

University of Virginia Press
Box 3608, Univ. Sta.
Charlottesville, VA 22903

Viking Press
625 Madison Ave.
New York, NY 10022

Washington State University Press
Pullman, WA 99164

Wehman Bros.
Ridgedale Ave.
Morris County Mall
Cedar Knolls, NJ 07927

Weinberg, Robert
15145 Oxford Dr.
Oak Forest, IL 60452

Wiedenfeld & Nicolson
11 St. John's Hill
London SW11 1XA, England

World Books
1915 Las Lomas Rd, N.E.
Albuquerque, NM 87106

Yale University Press
302 Temple St.
New Haven, CT 06520

Zebra Books
21 E. 40 St.
New York, NY 10016

A. Zwemmer
24 Litchfield St.
London WC2H 9NJ, England

Author and Title Index

References in this index are to entry numbers, not page numbers. Names of authors, illustrators, and titles in the annotations are omitted. Societies and Organizations, Awards, and Research Collections (Chapters 10–12) are not included. In the case of multiple authorship, only the name of the first author is listed. Book titles appear in italics; short stories in quotation marks. Subtitles of books are generally omitted.